D1241526

General Equilibrium, Growth, and Trade

Essays in Honor of Lionel McKenzie

This is a volume in
ECONOMIC THEORY, ECONOMETRICS,
AND MATHEMATICAL ECONOMICS

A Series of Monographs and Textbooks

Consulting Editor: KARL SHELL

A complete list of titles in this series appears at the end of this volume.

General Equilibrium, Growth, and Trade
Essays in Honor of Lionel McKenzie

Edited by *JERRY R. GREEN*

DEPARTMENT OF ECONOMICS
HARVARD UNIVERSITY
CAMBRIDGE, MASSACHUSETTS

JOSÉ ALEXANDRE SCHEINKMAN

DEPARTMENT OF ECONOMICS
UNIVERSITY OF CHICAGO
CHICAGO, ILLINOIS

ACADEMIC PRESS   New York   San Francisco   London   1979
A Subsidiary of Harcourt Brace Jovanovich, Publishers

055177

ACADEMIC PRESS, INC.
111 Fifth Avenue, New York, New York 10003

HB
135
.G445
1979

United Kingdom Edition published by
ACADEMIC PRESS, INC. (LONDON) LTD.
24/28 Oval Road, London NW1 7DX

Library of Congress Cataloging in Publication Data
Main entry under title:

General equilibrium, growth, and trade.

(Economic theory, econometrics, and mathematical economics)
Includes bibliographies.
    1. Economics, Mathematical--Addresses, essays, lec-
tures. 2. Equilibrium (Economics)--Addresses, essays,
lectures. 3. Economic development--Addresses, essays,
lectures. 4. Commerce--Addresses, essays, lectures.
5. McKenzie, Lionel W. I. McKenzie, Lionel W.
II. Green, Jerry R. III. Scheinkman, Jose Alexandre.
HB135.G445   330'.01'51   79-50216
ISBN 0-12-298750-0

CONTENTS

Part 1   GENERAL EQUILIBRIUM

Continuously Dispersed Preferences, Regular Preference–Endowment Distribution, and Mean Demand Function

Employment Policies for the Multiperiod Monopolist–Monopsonist with Implications for Macroeconomic Control

A Stable Price Adjustment Process

ANJAN MUKHERJI

Price Adjustment in a Competitive Market and the Securities Exchange Specialist

JAMES BRADFIELD AND EDWARD ZABEL

An Infinite Horizon Model with Money

CHARLES WILSON

Consumption under Uncertainty

SANFORD GROSSMAN, DAVID LEVHARI, AND LEONARD J. MIRMAN

Balanced Outcome Functions Yielding Walrasian and Lindahl Allocations at Nash Equilibrium Points for Two or More Agents

LEONID HURWICZ

Stochastic Stability of Market Adjustment in Disequilibrium

W. HILDENBRAND AND R. RADNER

Identifiability of the von Neumann–Morgenstern Utility Function from Asset Demands

JERRY R. GREEN, LAWRENCE J. LAU, AND

HERAKLIS M. POLEMARCHAKIS

Part 2 GROWTH

An Integration of Stochastic Growth Theory and the Theory of Finance, Part I: The Growth Model

WILLIAM A. BROCK

Fair Division of a Random Harvest: The Finite Case

DAVID GALE AND JOEL SOBEL

Characterizing Inefficiency of Infinite-Horizon Programs in Nonsmooth Technologies

LAWRENCE M. BENVENISTE AND TAPAN MITRA

Notes on Comparative Dynamics

ALOISIO P. DE ARAUJO AND JOSÉ ALEXANDRE SCHEINKMAN

Efficient Intertemporal Allocation, Consumption-Value Maximization, and Capital-Value Transversality: A Unified View

DAVID CASS AND MUKUL MAJUMDAR

Part 3   TRADE

The Theory and Application of Trade Utility Functions

JOHN S. CHIPMAN

A Model of Trade and Unemployment

KAMRAN NOMAN AND RONALD W. JONES

Two Propositions on the Global Univalence of Systems of Cost Function

ANDREU MAS-COLELL

On The Concepts of Factor Intensities and the Relation between Commodity Prices and Factor Rewards

YASUO UEKAWA

Factor Price Equalization with More Industries Than Factors

TROUT RADER

The General Equilibrium Framework of Economic Analysis: Stocks and Flows—with Special Application to Macroeconomic Models

JOHN Z. DRABICKI AND AKIRA TAKAYAMA

LIST OF CONTRIBUTORS

Numbers in parentheses indicate the pages on which the authors' contributions begin.

ALOISIO P. DE ARAUJO* (217), Department of Economics, University of Chicago, Chicago, Illinois 60637

LAWRENCE M. BENVENISTE (199), Department of Economics, University of Rochester, Rochester, New York 14627

JOHN P. BONIN (25), Department of Economics, Wesleyan University, Middletown, Connecticut 06457

JAMES BRADFIELD (51), Department of Economics, Hamilton College, Clinton, New York 13323

WILLIAM A. BROCK (165), Department of Economics, University of Chicago, Chicago, Illinois 60637, and Department of Economics, University of Wisconsin, Madison, Wisconsin 53706

DAVID CASS (227), Division of Humanities and Social Sciences, California Institute of Technology, Pasadena, California 91106, and Department of Economics, University of Pennsylvania, Philadelphia, Pennsylvania 19174

JOHN S. CHIPMAN (277), Department of Economics, University of Minnesota, Minneapolis, Minnesota 55455

JOHN Z. DRABICKI (355), Department of Economics, University of Arizona, Tucson, Arizona 85721

*Present address: IMPA, Rio de Janeiro, Brazil.

DAVID GALE (193), Department of Mathematics, University of California, Berkeley, California 94720

JERRY R. GREEN (1, 151), Department of Economics, Harvard University, Cambridge, Massachusetts 02138

SANFORD GROSSMAN (105), Department of Economics, University of Pennsylvania, Philadelphia, Pennsylvania 19174

W. HILDENBRAND (139), Department of Economics, University of Bonn, Bonn, West Germany

LEONID HURWICZ (125), Department of Economics, University of Minnesota, Minneapolis, Minnesota 55455

RONALD W. JONES (297), Department of Economics, University of Rochester, Rochester, New York 14627

LAWRENCE J. LAU (151), Department of Economics, Stanford University, Stanford, California 94305

DAVID LEVHARI (105), Department of Economics, The Hebrew University, Jerusalem, Israel

MUKUL MAJUMDAR (227), Department of Economics, Cornell University, Ithaca, New York 14853

ANDREU MAS-COLELL (323), Department of Economics, University of California, Berkeley, California 94720

LEONARD J. MIRMAN (105), Department of Economics, University of Illinois, Urbana, Illinois 61801

TAPAN MITRA (199), Department of Economics, State University of New York, Stony Brook, New York 11790

ANJAN MUKHERJI (43), The Center for Economic Studies and Planning, Jawaharlal University, New Delhi, India

KAMRAN NOMAN (297), Department of Economics, University of Rochester, Rochester, New York 14627

HERAKLIS M. POLEMARCHAKIS (151), Department of Economics, Columbia University, New York, New York 10027

TROUT RADER (347), Department of Economics, Washington University, St. Louis, Missouri 63130

R. RADNER (139), Department of Economics, University of California, Berkeley, California 94720, and Kennedy School of Government, Harvard University, Cambridge, Massachusetts 02138

JOSÉ ALEXANDRE SCHEINKMAN (1, 217), Department of Economics, University of Chicago, Chicago, Illinois 60637

JOEL SOBEL (193), Department of Economics, University of California at San Diego, La Jolla, California 92093

AKIRA TAKAYAMA (355), Department of Economics, Krannert School of Management, Purdue University, West Lafayette, Indiana 47907, and Department of Economics, College of Liberal Arts, Texas A&M University, College Station, Texas 77843

YASUO UEKAWA (333), Department of Economics, Kobe University of Commerce, Tarumi, Kobe, Japan

CHARLES WILSON (79), Social Systems Research Institute, University of Wisconsin, Madison, Wisconsin 53706

AKIRA YAMAZAKI (13), Department of Economics, University of Illinois, Chicago, Illinois 60637

EDWARD ZABEL (51), Department of Economics, University of Rochester, Rochester, New York 14627

PREFACE

We undertook the editing of this volume in honor of Professor Lionel McKenzie, our teacher and friend, at the suggestion of William Brock, Michael Mussa, and Ronald Jones. We hope to portray his excellence as a scholar by demonstrating the depth and breadth of his influence throughout economic theory.

Professor McKenzie began teaching at the University of Rochester in the academic year of 1957–1958. He brought with him a novel and rigorous approach to economic theory which has been felt most strongly in the construction of the basic price theory sequence. This continues up to the present, even though McKenzie taught the course during only the first few years. The course blends modern analytical techniques and heavy emphasis on general equilibrium theory with a careful grounding in the classic writings of the past hundred years: Walras, Marshall, Wicksell, Hicks, and Samuelson. This approach may not seem so unusual today, but it was fresh and novel in 1957, when economic theory as we now know it was in its formative stages. In Professor McKenzie's first class one of the three students was Akira Takayama, one of the contributors to this volume and McKenzie's first graduate student at Rochester. The stream of Rochester Ph.D.s has been steady throughout the past twenty years. We are particularly pleased that many former students are among the authors of these essays in Professor McKenzie's honor.

Many individuals have helped us in organizing and refereeing the papers here collected. In particular we would like to thank Nasser Saidi, Jack Schectman, and Akira Takayama. Karl Shell urged us to submit these essays to Academic Press.

Of course, our central goal is that Professor McKenzie enjoy each of the papers in this collection. Our task is made easier in this regard because of the breadth of his knowledge and interests in economics. We all stand to gain from his comments and criticisms, which will surely be forthcoming.

General Equilibrium, Growth, and Trade

Essays in Honor of Lionel McKenzie

Introduction

JERRY R. GREEN

JOSÉ ALEXANDRE SCHEINKMAN

Lionel McKenzie's scientific research has had a lasting impact on economic theory. His insights, high standards, and vigorous scholarship form a model for his many students and colleagues.

This volume is divided into three parts, paralleling Professor McKenzie's three main areas of research: general equilibrium theory, international trade, and economic growth. The extent and depth of his influence are apparent in all of the papers collected here in his honor. In this brief introduction we merely hope to highlight the principal aspects of McKenzie's work and provide a brief guide to their impact on the literature.

McKenzie's first scientific paper, "Ideal Output and the Interdependence of Firms" (1951), addresses a most difficult problem which has not yet been resolved in full generality, although twenty-seven years have since passed. It is noteworthy not only for its depth of analysis and because it showed the courage and insight to challenge an accepted doctorine, but also because it foretold of interests that were to occupy McKenzie's attention for some time to come. When prices diverge from marginal costs because of monopolistic or other imperfections, the standard prescription to restore welfare optimality was to enforce an "equal degree of monopoly" across the sectors. This leads to the "proportionality hypothesis"—prices should exceed marginal costs by a fixed percentage. McKenzie, recognizing the roundabout nature of the productive process, proved that this corrective policy is not appropriate in general. The interindustry nature of production is a theme that runs throughout his work on general equilibrium theory and, of course, is the *raison d'etre* for the von Neumann model of production.

1

He explicitly rejected the study of first-order conditions for constrained optimality as being Utopian and therefore unlikely to be of practical value. Rather, he is concerned with methods for improving existing allocations and for evaluating changes in policy parameters [see also Lesourne (1975), Starett (1977)]. Written in 1951, before the development of modern optimal tax theory (except Ramsey), this paper was well ahead of its time and is still a benchmark from which progress can be measured.

Finally, this paper is notable for what it is not. Although analytic and rigorous it is neither heavily, nor even explicitly, mathematical. It is the last such paper McKenzie has written. Throughout the rest of his career, his writing is a masterpiece of clarity combined with mathematical rigor, sufficient to convince any skeptic of the virtues of the mathematical method.

McKenzie's paper "Demand Theory without a Utility Index" (1957) has perhaps had the widest impact among all those written before he came to Rochester. It is notable for the theoretical construct of the "minimum income function," which has come to be called the expenditure function. It is the clear precursor of duality theory, which is an indispensible ingredient in modern consumption theory, and its econometric implementation. The recoverability of utility from demand behavior had already been established at the time this paper was written. McKenzie addresses the basic concept underlying both utility and demand: the preference relation. This is important because it exposes the underlying mathematics of the theory of demand free from artificial constructs—an exercise of "Occam's razor," as McKenzie was fond of pointing out.

McKenzie's paper (1956) on the existence of an equilibrium when preferences depend on prices is noteworthy for two reasons. First, the technique used to prove existence was novel, and variants of it were adopted by many later writers. Second, the problem of price-dependent preferences became important when the intertemporal character of general equilibrium theory was developed, and a system of future price expectations was superimposed on the short-period equilibration process [see, for example, Grandmont (1974) and Green (1973)].

McKenzie then pursued the existence problem to its fundamental determinants. After the work of von Neumann, which connected the existence of a competitive equilibrium to fixed points of functions, attention centered on modeling the basic actors in the economic system realistically and on providing plausible conditions on their interrelationship so as not to lose the properties of excess demand essential to the existence argument. McKenzie shows a great sensitivity to this matter from both technical and economic standpoints in his seminal paper of 1959.

First, he introduced the concept of irreducibility of an economy—each subset of agents being able to provide something of value to every other—in order to ensure that the situation of minimum wealth would be precluded, disposing of its attendant risks of nonexistence of an equilibrium. McKenzie's condition is the most general way of avoiding this problem. The importance of the notion of irreducibility is twofold. By finding the most general set of circumstances under which his result could be derived, he has illuminated the structure of the model more clearly than if stronger sufficient conditions had been used. But, more important perhaps, irreducibility is compatible with endowments that lie on the boundary of the consumption set and with preferences that display indifference to some commodities, situations of great economic importance, especially in productive environments.

This paper also introduced the concept of irreversibility of production to avoid some problems of boundedness in the production plans of firms. McKenzie was interested in doing without the free disposability condition in order to permit zero and even negative prices in equilibrium.

Finally, this paper makes a major depature from all of previous general equilibrium theory by utilizing free entry of firms together with the necessity of entrepreneurial resources for establishing firms. These resources, like all others, are paid their competitive returns. Other versions of the Walrasian model postulate the existence of a fixed set of firms, each being owned by a preassigned set of individuals who are to share any excess of resources over costs according to a linear sharing rule. Of course, in equilibrium all firms may not be active. Nevertheless, McKenzie's modeling of the endogenous creation of firms and the payment of entrepreneurial factors represented an attempt to go one level deeper into the fundamental determinants of the allocation process.

In his paper on matrices with dominant diagonals (1960b), McKenzie lays out the mathematics central to propositions in stability analysis, the theory of linear production models, and many other areas, such as income propagation models. McKenzie establishes the properties of the eigenvalues of these matrices, as well as the properties of their inverses, the latter being crucial to any local comparative statics.

His fundamental contribution to the theory of global stability (1960a) shows the same sensitivity toward the structure of economic relationships that characterized his paper on existence. He used to remark that zero was a special number in science: Physical scientists (whose work he follows with some expertise) test the robustness of their models by perturbing the estimated variables in their systems; but they do not perturb mutual influences among physical magnitudes that are known to be unrelated on theoretical grounds. Similarly, in economics, McKenzie was unwilling to assume that all pairs of commodities were strong gross substitutes. The weak gross-substitute case, which is much harder, yielded to the use of the value of positive excess demand as a Lyapunov function.

Until the 1950s the traditional theory of international trade was typically concerned with the model of two countries trading two produced commodities. Furthermore, the analysis had been carried out largely in terms of arithmetic examples or graphical devices. These two features were so predominant in the profession at that time that deviations were, though it may sound unbelievable today, considered almost heresy. McKenzie's papers on trade theory made a gigantic step forward in breaking loose from this mold, in addition to their substantive scientific content.

The inadequacy of the classical two-country, two-commodity framework to describe a multicountry, multicommodity world had long been argued by McKenzie's teacher at Princeton, Frank D. Graham. General equilibrium repercussions in the model with two commodities can become inadequate when a third commodity is considered. McKenzie explicitly states that "the methods of the classical economists are entirely appropriate only to the analysis of trade between two countries" and that "the deficiency of the classical method . . . is their dependence on bilateral comparison" (1954a, p. 180).

McKenzie successfully reformulated Graham's discussions into a systematic theory that is characterized by rigor, generality, and a considerable amount of modern flavor. The basis of his formulation is activity analysis, which was a new theoretical apparatus that was being developed concurrently. Since activity analysis allows for any number of factors (as well as commodities), McKenzie's discussion of Graham's one-factor model can readily be extended to more general models.

The use of activity analysis in dealing with the classical theory of international trade of Ricardo, Mill, and Graham is very natural. For example, the classical theory of comparative advantage and specialization is nothing but the problem of selecting the maximum (or an efficient) world output, while activity analysis is concerned with the similar problem of selecting a productive process to achieve an efficient point. Moreover, both typically assume linear, additive, and convex technology. This ingenious observation was the basis of McKenzie (1954a), in which he obtained an important theorem within his extended "Graham's model" corresponding to a fundamental theorem in activity analysis; namely, an efficient world output is achieved if and only if there exists a price vector such that no production process can earn positive profits and all processes actually used earn zero profits. McKenzie's graphic technique in his analysis in (1954a) is based on the observation that his model shares the property of triangularity of the coefficient matrix with the transportation models of Koopmans. What underlies this technique is Dantzig's algorithm for the transportation problem [cf. McKenzie (1954a, p. 169), and Chipman (1965, p. 497)]. McKenzie, in the course of his analysis of Graham's model, came up with an interesting multiplicative formula (1954a, p. 171), which extends the Ricardian bilateral rule determining the pattern of specialization to a multicommodity, multi-country world. His proposition is stated in terms of minimizing the product of labor coefficients from the set of various "assignments" (of the production) of a particular commodity to a particular country. This rule was later obtained by Jones (1961) in a different way, via the Hawkins–Simon theorem on the Leontief matrix.

McKenzie (1954a, 1955) then showed that such a rule (which incor-porates the Ricardian rule as a special case) breaks down in the presence of trade in intermediate products or in the presence of jointly produced outputs. McKenzie offered the first systematic analysis of international trade in intermediate products. He pointed out the possibility of *reversal* in the pattern of specialization in such models, compared to the pattern dicated by the classical rule. But then he notes, "there is nothing shocking to common sense in these results. A moment's reflection will convince one that Lancashire would be unlikely to produce cotton cloth if the cotton had to be grown in England" (1954a, p. 179). The problem of intermediate products had some-how been strangely ignored in the literature, and yet it is one of considerable and growing importance.

The strong parallel between Graham's model of world trade and activity analysis led McKenzie to one of the most important contributions in modern general equilibrium theory. Namely, in (1954b) he showed the existence and uniqueness of equilibrium in the Graham model. Though the model is based on Graham's restrictive assumption on demand, the results and the basic method of proof, via the Kakutani fixed-point theorem, apply to a general competitive economy.

While the classical theory of comparative advantage is concerned with the assignment of a particular country to the specialization in production of a particular commodity, the factor price equalization theorem is concerned with the uniqueness of factor prices, given goods prices in the absence of specialization of countries, to different goods. The observation of this converse relation of the two different theories led McKenzie to his elegant formulation of the factor price equalization theorem in terms of activity analysis. This theorem states that if all goods are produced in the trading countries in question, then the factor prices must be equalized among the countries, provided that the "univalence condition" is satisfied. But if the goods are produced under a constant returns to scale technology, then the "zero profit condition" must be satisfied. Combining these observations McKenzie reformulates the factor price equalization theorem.

McKenzie's discussion here follows the general spirit of analysis prevalent throughout his work, i.e., freeing international trade theory from the mold of the 2×2 (or the $2 \times 2 \times 2$) analysis. Indeed, his analysis allows for any number of commodities, factors, and countries. Clearly, he was motivated by a fundamental work on the topic by Samuelson (1953), as well as by his earlier works on Graham's model.

In the theory of economic growth, although he worked on the problem of existence of optimal solutions, as well as the existence of prices that decentralize optimal programs, his main interest concerned the so-called turnpike conjecture of Dorfman *et al.* (1958). This conjecture originally stated that an optimal growth path would run "close to" the von Neumann path of maximal proportional growth for most of the time. Later, the name was used to refer to a whole class of convergence properties of solutions to dynamic optimization problems.

The original work in this area was done in the context of the von Neumann model. Here consumption may only appear as a necessary input to processes of production. The first contribution, that of Dorfman *et al.* (1958), dealt with the case where the objective is to maximize the distance from the origin of the terminal stocks along a prescribed ray. They proved a local turnpike theorem for a neoclassical technology with two goods. McKenzie's paper "The Dorfman–Samuelson–Solow Turnpike Theorem" (1963a) provides a proof of the original local theorem for *n* goods. In doing so, he noticed that one must go beyond the establishment of the reciprocity of the roots to ensure the local stability of the balanced growth path. An assumption must be made to guarantee that the stable manifold of the system of Euler equations has a full dimensional projection in the space of initial capital stocks.

McKenzie (1960c) and Morishima (1961) proved independently a global turnpike theorem for a model with no-joint production. His generously titled paper "The Turnpike Theorem of Morishima" (1963b) contains his version of the result.

Radner's contribution (1961) provided a global result for a model with strong convexity restrictions. McKenzie recognized early that "[T]he Radner Theorem . . . seems to offer the greatest promise of a general theory of capital accumulation in closed linear models" (1963b, p. 169). Not only was this prediction correct with respect to closed linear models, but the Radner approach turned out to be the one used to establish theorems for the multisector version of Ramsey's (1928) problem, first by McKenzie's student Hiroshi Atsumi (1965) in the context of a two-sector model, followed by Gale (1967), Tsukui (1967), and McKenzie (1968b). Later, Radner's technique was also used with success in analyzing the discounted utility case.

McKenzie's own work in extending Radner's results was initially done in the context of what he called a generalized Leontief model (McKenzie, 1963c), although as he points out, his results can be applied to a more general framework. He noticed that if one wishes to dispense with Radner's assumption that there is a unique production process that is not unprofitable at the von Neumann prices, the extension of Radner's method suffices only to show convergence to the set of processes that break even at the von Neumann prices, i.e., what he calls the "Neumann facet." Such a facet will have a dimensionality greater than one unless strong external economies are present.[1] In order to prove a stronger result, an analysis of the growth paths that stay in the facet is needed. In this paper McKenzie uses the fact that such paths must satisfy a linear difference equation, together with an assumption that rules out periodic paths to show that they must converge to the Neumann ray, which is assumed to be unique. This, combined with the convergence to the facet, establishes the turnpike result.

In "Maximal Paths in the von Neumann Model" (1967), he extends the results concerning convergence to the Neumann facet to the Kemeny *et al.* (1956) generalization of the von Neumann model. He also deals with the problem of unproducible and overproduced goods in the von Neumann equilibrium.

McKenzie's most recent contribution to the literature concerning optimality with respect to terminal conditions (1971) extended his previous results on finitely generated linear technologies to general convex technologies. Here again the most delicate point concerns convergence on the Neumann facet.

His 1968 paper in the volume honoring Hicks was the first one in which he dealt with the multisectoral version of the Ramsey model. Previous work by Atsumi (1965) and Gale (1967) had extended Radner's approach to this case. Gale's treatment consisted of defining a utility function directly on activity levels that he assumed to be strictly concave. McKenzie's approach consisted of assuming a general convex technology set of triples $(u, k', -k)$ where $u \in R$, $k' \in R^n_+$, and $k \in R^n_+$. Here k is to be interpreted as initial stocks, k' as final stocks, and u as utility levels. Using Atsumi's extension of Radner's fundamental lemma, he showed that optimal paths must approach the von Neumann facet. A difficult analysis, using the theory of pencils of matrices [cf. Gantmachter (1959)], is then made to analyze the convergence on the Neumann facet. By making special assumptions concerning the structure of the points that generate the facet, convergence to the unique von Neumann point was shown. However, he also dealt with more general cases where convergence to a larger subset of the facet is all that is established.

In "Turnpike Theorems with Technology and Welfare Function Variable" (1974) he establishes the existence of infinite optimal paths according to the overtaking criteria for a model with variable technology and utility function, using the methods developed by Brock (1970). He also proves what he calls a "straight-down-the-turnpike theorem" [cf. Winter (1967)]. Such theorem compares a finite horizon optimal path from an initial stock $\underline{k}$ to a final

---

[1] Koopman's paper (1964) contains a nice discussion of the meaning of the technology set of Radner's assumption.

stock $\bar{k}$ with the infinite horizon optimal path starting from $\underline{k}$. Finally the existence of support prices in the fashion of Weitzman (1973) is also shown.

Although local results [cf. Kurz (1968), Levhari and Leviatan (1972)] had been proved for the case of a discounted sum of utilities, there were no global results available for this case. In Scheinkman's 1973 Rochester dissertation written under McKenzie's supervision, it was established that the global turnpike result held for discount factors sufficiently near 1 (cf. Scheinkman (1976)]. In the next few years a large literature appeared dealing with the discounted utility problem. McKenzie's "Turnpike Theory" (1976) proves a theorem that, as in Brock and Scheinkman (1976), (1978), Cass and Shell (1976), and Rockafellar (1976), utilizes an assumption that compares the degree of concavity of the utility function to the discount factor. He also generalizes the method to cover the case of nonstationary utility. In his proof he dispenses with the transversality condition, assumed by Cass and Shell, on the boundedness of prices; assumed by Brock and Scheinkman, by making use of prices that support simultaneously the maximal paths and the value function. The existence of such prices is established using the method of Weitzman (1973) as generalized by McKenzie (1974).

In "A New Route to the Turnpike" (1977) McKenzie extended the work of Araujo and Scheinkman (1977), which provided a different method of proof for turnpike theorems, as well as a framework for comparative dynamics. His extension consisted of considering the case of nonstationary utility, as well as proving that convergence is exponential.

As this introduction was being written, we had access to a preliminary draft of McKenzie's chapter for the *Handbook of Mathematical Economics* [edited by Arrow and Intrilligator (1979)]. We do not hope to have surveyed the myriad facets of McKenzie's work and its influences on later developments in any detail. Rather, paralleling the style of McKenzie's own classroom lectures, we hope to emphasize only a few of the highlights in a unified way.

REFERENCES

Araujo, A., and Scheinkman, J. A. (1977). Smoothness, comparative dynamics, and the turnpike property, *Econometrica* **45**, (3), 601–620.

Arrow, K. J., and Intriligator, M. (eds.) (1979). "Handbook of Mathematical Economics." North-Holland Publ., Amsterdam.

Atsumi, H. (1965). Neoclassical growth and the efficient program of capital accumulation, *Rev. Econ. Stud.* **32**, 127–136.

Brock, W. A. (1970). On existence of weakly maximal programmes in a multi-sector economy, *Rev. Econ. Stud.* **37**, 275–280.

Brock, W. A., and Scheinkman, J. A. (1976). Global asymptotic stability of optimal control systems with applications to the theory of economic growth, *J. Econ. Theory* **12**, 164–190.

Brock, W. A., and Scheinkman, J. A. (1978). On the long-run behavior of a competitive firm, *in* "Equilibrium and disequilibrium in Economic Theory" (G. Schwödiauer, ed.). Reidel, Vienna.

Cass, D., and Shell, K. (1976). The structure and stability of competitive dynamical systems, *J. Econ. Theory* **12**, 31–70.

Chipman, J. S. (1965). A survey of the theory of international trade: Part 1, The classical theory, *Econometrica* **33**, 477–519.

Dorfman, R., Samuelson, P. A., and Solow, R. M. (1958). "Linear Programming and Economic Analysis." McGraw Hill, New York.

Gale, D. (1967). On optimal development in a multi-sector economy, *Symp. Optimal Infinite Prog., Rev. Econ. Stud.* **34**, (97), 1–18.

Gantmachter, F. R. (1959). "Applications of the Theory of Matrices." Chelsea, New York.

Grandmont, J.-M. (1974). On the short-run equilibrium in a monetary economy, *in* "Allocation Under Uncertainty, Equilibrium and Optimality" (J. Dreze, ed.). Macmillan, New York.

Green, J. (1973). Temporary general equilibrium in a sequential trading model with spot and futures transactions, *Econometrica* **41**, 1103–1123.

Jones, R. W. (1961). Comparative advantage and the theory of tariffs: A multi-country multi-commodity model, *Rev. Econ. Stud.* **28**, 161–175.

Kemeny, J. G., Morgenstern, O., and Thompson, G. L. (1965). A generalization of the von Neumann model of an expanding economy, *Econometrica* **24**, 115–135.

Koopmans, T. C. (1964). Economic growth at a maximal rate, *Q. J. Econ.* **78**, 355–394.

Kurz, M. (1968). The general instability of a class of competitive growth processes, *Rev. Econ. Stud.* **35**, 155–174.

Lesourne, J. (1975). "Cost-Benefit Analysis and Economic Theory," (transl. by A. Silvey). North-Holland Publ., Amsterdam.

Levhari, D., and Leviatan, N. (1972). On stability in the saddle point sense, *J. Econ. Theory* **4**, 88–93.

McKenzie, L. W. (1951). Ideal output and the interdependence of firms, *Econ. J.* **61**, 758–803.

McKenzie, L. W. (1954a). Specialization and efficiency in world production, *Rev. Econ. Stud.* **21**, 165–180.

McKenzie, L. W. (1954b). On equilibrium in Graham's model of world trade and other competitive systems, *Econometrica* **22**, 147–161.

McKenzie, L. W. (1955). Specialization in production and the production possibility locus. *Rev. Econ. Stud.* **23**, 56–64.

McKenzie, L. W. (1956). Competitive equilibrium with dependent consumer preferences, *Symp. Linear Programming, 2nd*, pp. 277–294. National Bureau of Standards, Washington, D.C.

McKenzie, L. W. (1957). Demand theory without a utility index, *Rev. Econ. Stud.* **24**, 185–189.

McKenzie, L. W. (1959). On the existence of general equilibrium for a competitive market, *Econometrica* **27**, 54–71.

McKenzie, L. W. (1960a). Stability of equilibrium and the value of positive excess demand, *Econometrica* **28**, 606–617.

McKenzie, L. W. (1960b). Matrices with dominant diagonals and economic theory, "Mathematical Methods in the Social Sciences, 1959" (K. J. Arrow, S. Karlin, and P. Suppes, eds.), pp. 47–62. Stanford Univ. Press, Stanford, California.

McKenzie, L. W. (1960c). Price Quality and the Turnpike theorem. Paper presented to Econometric Society.

McKenzie, L. W. (1963a). The Dorfman-Samuelson-Solow turnpike theorem, *Int. Econ. Rev.* **4**, 29–43.

McKenzie, L. W. (1963b). The turnpike theorem of Morishima, *Rev. Econ. Stud.* **30**, 169–176.

McKenzie, L. W. (1963c). Turnpike theorems for a generalized Leontief model, *Econometrica* **31**, 165–180.

McKenzie, L. W. (1967). Maximal paths in the von Neumann model, *in* "Activity Analysis in the Theory of Growth and Planning" (E. Malinvaud and M.O.L. Barach, eds.), pp. 43–63. Macmillan, London.

McKenzie, L. W. (1968a). International trade: Mathematical theory, "International Ency-clopedia of Social Sciences," pp. 96–104. Macmillan, New York.

McKenzie, L. W. (1968b). Accumulation programs of maximum utility and the von Neumann facet, *in* "Value, Capital and Growth" (J. N. Wolfe, ed.), pp. 353–383. Edinburgh Univ. Press, Edinburgh.

McKenzie, L. W. (1971). Capital accumulation optimal in the final state, *in* "Contributions to the von Neumann Growth Model," (G. Bruckmann and M. Weber, eds.). Springer-Verlag, Berlin and New York.

McKenzie, L. W. (1974). Turnpike theorems with technology and welfare function variable, *in* "Mathematical Models in Economics" (J. Los and M. W. Loś, eds.), pp. 271–287. American Elsevier, New York.

McKenzie, L. W. (1976). Turnpike Theory, *Econometrica* **44**, (5), 841–865.

McKenzie, L. W. (1977). A new route to the turnpike, "Mathematical Economics and Game Theory" (R. Henn and L. O. Moeschlin, eds.). Springer-Verlag, Berlin and New York.

Morishima, M. (1961). Prices and turnpike II: Proof of a turnpike theorem; The 'no joint production case,' *Rev. Econ. Stud.* **28**, 89–97.

Radner, R. (1961). Paths of economic growth that are optimal with regard only to final states. *Rev. Econ. Stud.* **28**. 98–104.

Ramsey, F. (1928). A mathematical theory of saving, *Econ. J.* **38**, 543–559.

Rockafellar, R. T. (1976). Saddlepoints of Hamiltonian systems in convex problems having a positive discount rate, *J. Econ. Theory* **12**, 71–113.

Samuelson, P. A. (1953). Prices of factors and goods in General equilibrium, *Rev. Econ. Stud.* **21**, 1–20.

Scheinkman, J. (1976). On optimal steady states of n-sector growth models when utility is discounted, *J. Econ. Theory* **12** 11–30.

Starett, D. (1977). Welfare Measurement for Local Public Finance, Technical Rep. no. 228. Institute for Mathematical Studies in the Social Sciences, Stanford Univ., Stanford, California.

Tsukui, J. (1967). The consumption and the output turnpike theorems in a von Neumann type of model: A finite term problem, *Symp. Opt. Infinite Programmes, Rev. Econ. Stud.* **34**, (97), 85–93.

Weitzman, M. L. (1973). Duality theory for infinite horizon convex models, *Management Sci.* **19**, 783–789.

Winter, S. (1967). The norm of a closed technology and the straight-down-the-turnpike theorem, *Rev. Econ. Stud.* **34**, 67–84.

Jerry R. Green
DEPARTMENT OF ECONOMICS
HARVARD UNIVERSITY
CAMBRIDGE, MASSACHUSETTS

José Alexandre Scheinkman
DEPARTMENT OF ECONOMICS
UNIVERSITY OF CHICAGO
CHICAGO, ILLINOIS

Part 1
GENERAL EQUILIBRIUM

Continuously Dispersed Preferences, Regular Preference–Endowment Distribution, and Mean Demand Function

AKIRA YAMAZAKI

1. INTRODUCTION

This paper is concerned with what has been called the "smoothing by aggregation" problem in a continuum of economic agents model: It studies the regularizing effects of aggregation over nonregular microrelations. Since the pioneering work of Mas-Colell [6] and Sondermann [12, 13] contributions have been made by several authors. (See for example Ichiishi [5], Mas-Colell and Neufeind [10], and Araujo and Mas-Colell [1].) I follow Mas-Colell [6] and Sondermann [12, 13] in that I am interested in finding sufficient conditions under which the aggregate (mean) behavior becomes more regular than that of individual agents. It is highly intuitive that the diversification of agents' characteristics plays the central role in this problem.

Let A be a set of parameters, $\mathscr{P}$ a set of preference relations, and $\mathscr{E}_1$ a mapping from A into $\mathscr{P}$. So far in the literature, some sort of differentiability of the mapping $\mathscr{E}_1$ has been required. And the idea of "dispersed preference distribution" has been expressed by a regularity condition on the mapping $\mathscr{E}_1$, which was called the Sondermann condition by Araujo and Mas-Colell [1], together with the "dispersion of distribution of parameters" on A. Let us call such requirements *the differentiable dispersion of preferences.*

With the positive orthant of R^l as the consumption set on which all the preference relations are defined, Sondermann [12, 13] proved that the mean demand is a continuous function if the preference distribution is differentiably dispersed. However, Araujo and Mas-Colell [1] presented an example that shows that the differentiable dispersion of preferences does not necessarily guarantee the differentiability of the mean demand. Let us quote Mas-Colell: "A *tentative* conclusion seems to be emerging from the work on smoothing by aggregation, namely that there is a substantial difference between the continuous and the smooth case. While meaningful 'dispersion of preferences' conditions are available yielding the continuity of mean excess demand, not a single (significant) one exists yielding its smoothness (C^1)" [8, p. 20].

The situation being so, a meaningful step to be taken appears to be an extension of the framework of a model in which one can obtain the continuity of the mean demand. Araujo and Mas-Colell [1, Theorem 1] made a contribution toward this direction: They proved the single-valuedness of the mean demand for economies where all the agents have the same but not necessarily convex consumption set and the same endowments, under the differentiable dispersion of preferences. Of course, this result does not go far enough. Thus, suppose that we are only interested in establishing the continuity of mean demand; then one may ask the following questions to understand the scope and the applicability of the regularizing effect of aggregation:

(i) Can we replace the "differentiable dispersion of preferences" by suitably defined "continuous dispersion of preferences"?

(ii) Can we allow consumption sets to be nonconvex and relax the requirement of identical endowments for almost all agents?

(iii) Can we allow preference relations that are not transitive? (This question was first asked Sondermann by Sonnenschein. See Sondermann [14, Discussion].)

(iv) Can we allow different consumers to have different consumption sets?

The purpose of this paper is to present an affirmative answer to the first three questions in the preceding paragraph. The first and the third questions will be answered affirmatively by the introduction of the concept of intermediate preferences, which was successfully used by Grandmont [3] for a different purpose. Our answer to the second question is affirmative if the preference–endowment distribution is "regular."

In Section 2 we present the model and give the statement of results. Their proofs are given in Section 3.

2. MODEL AND THE STATEMENT OF RESULTS

There are finitely many distinguishable commodities, the number of which is given by a positive integer l. Thus an element $x = (x^1, \ldots, x^l)$ of l-dimensional Euclidean space R^l represents a combination of commodities without any regard to the physical feasibility of its consumption and to the needs of consumers. R^l is the *commodity space* and an element x of R^l, a *commodity bundle*. The physical characteristics of commodities such as indivisibility and/or mutual exclusiveness of consumptions, as well as the feasibility of consumptions and the needs of consumers, are expressed through a subset X of R^l: A nonempty closed subset X of R^l which is bounded from below is called the *consumption set*. A *preference relation* $\succsim$ is a subset of the product of the consumption set, $X \times X$. It is complete if for any x and y in X one has $(x, y) \in \succsim$ or $(y, x) \in \succsim$. Relations $\precsim, \succ, \prec, \sim$ are induced from $\succsim$ in the familiar way. (See, for example, Debreu [2, Section 4.4].) Sometimes it is visually convenient to write $x \succsim y$ instead of $(x, y) \in \succsim$. ($y \precsim x, x \succ y, y \prec x$, and $x \sim y$ are defined similarly.) A preference relation $\succsim$ is called continuous if the induced relation $\succ$ is open relative to $X \times X$.

A pair $(\succsim, e)$ consisting of a preference relation and a commodity bundle (initial endowments) $e \in R^l$ describes a consumption characteristic of agents. (Of course, it should be understood here that all the points in R^l do not necessarily represent a physically feasible combination of commodities.)

Let $\mathscr{P}$ denote the set of all complete and continuous preference relations with the following property: For every price vector p in $R^l_{++} = \{z \in R^l \,|\, z^i > 0$ for all $i\}$, the set $D(\succsim, e, p)$ of greatest elements for $\succsim$ in the *budget set* $B(\succsim, e, p) = \{x \in X \,|\, p \cdot x \leq p \cdot e\}$ is nonempty whenever $B(\succsim, e, p)$ is not empty. It is well known that a complete and continuous preference relation $\succsim$ belongs to $\mathscr{P}$ if it is transitive or convex (in the sense that the set $\{z \in X \,|\, z \succ x\}$ is convex for every $x \in X$, as well as the set X itself). (See Sonnenschein [15] and Mas-Colell [7].) We endow the set $\mathscr{P}$ with Hausdorff's topology of closed convergence; then $\mathscr{P}$ becomes a separable metric space. (For details see Hildenbrand [4].) The space $\mathscr{P} \times R^l$ is the space of agents' (consumption) characteristics.

In the problem of smoothing by aggregation, it is essential to have a well-behaved parametrization of agents' characteristics. Let m be a positive integer. A nonempty, convex, and open subset A of R^m is a set of parameters or "names" attached to the consumption characteristics of consumers. An *economy* is then described by a pair $(\mathscr{E}, \nu)$ consisting of a (Borel) measure ν on A and a measurable mapping $\mathscr{E}: A \to \mathscr{P} \times R^l$. The interpretation is that a indicates the characteristics $\mathscr{E}(a)$ in $\mathscr{P} \times R^l$ and ν is a distribution of parameters; thus $\mathscr{E}$ and ν together give us a distribution of characteristics of agents. For each a in A write $\mathscr{E}(a) = (\mathscr{E}_1(a), \mathscr{E}_2(a))$; then the mappings $\mathscr{E}_1: A \to \mathscr{P}$ and $\mathscr{E}_2: A \to R^l$ indicate the "name" of preference relations and endowments, respectively. We often write $(\succsim_a, e_a)$ instead of $(\mathscr{E}_1(a), \mathscr{E}_2(a))$. $\mathscr{E}_1$ and $\mathscr{E}_2$ will be called the *preference assignment* and the *endowment assignment* for $(\mathscr{E}, \nu)$. When the mapping $\mathscr{E}$ is measurable, the integral of the

correspondence $D(\succsim_a, e_a, p)$ is well defined; the aggregate (mean) demand of
the economy $(\mathscr{E}, v)$ is given by the integral

$$\Phi(p) = \int_A D(\succsim_a, e_a, p)\, dv \qquad \left(= \int_A D(\mathscr{E}(a), p)\, dv \right).$$

Let us consider the problem of single-valuedness of mean demand $\Phi(p)$
first. This, as has been understood by the earlier work of Sondermann [12, 13]
and Araujo and Mas-Colell [1], crucially depends on an orderly distribution
of preference relations in terms of parameters. It is to be noted that the
dispersion of endowments does not help much at this stage. It suffices to
give a simple example: Suppose that the distribution of characteristics in
the economy $(\mathscr{E}, v)$ is such that the preference relation described in the Fig. 1
has weight one; then, even if endowments are distributed along the line

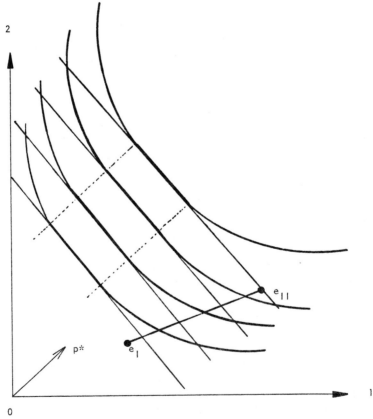

FIGURE 1

segment $[e_I, e_{II}]$ in such a manner that no single points on the line segment carries positive weight, $\Phi(p)$ is not single-valued at $p = p^*$.

We shall introduce several conditions which, when taken together, express the idea that *the distribution of preferences is continuously (and orderly) dispersed*. First, the distribution of parameters should be dispersed:

(T.1) ν is absolutely continuous with respect to l-dimensional Borel–Lebesgue measure.

Second, the naming of parameters, i.e., the assignment of parameters to preference relations, should be done in a continuous fashion:

(T.2) $\mathscr{E}_1 : A \to \mathscr{P}$ is continuous.

The dispersion of parameters (T.1) and the continuity of parameter assignment (T.2) need not imply that the distribution of preference relations is indeed dispersed: For example, let $(\mathscr{E}, \nu)$ be an economy where ν satisfies (T.1) and $\mathscr{E}_1$ is a constant map; then, $(\mathscr{E}, \nu)$ satisfies both (T.1) and (T.2), but obviously the distribution of preferences is hardly dispersed. Thus we add the following third condition:

(T.3)   For any x and y in X such that $x \neq y$, there exists a in A such that $x \nsim_a y$.

It simply says that for any two commodity bundles in the consumption set that are not identical, there is at least one agent to whom these bundles are not indifferent. It is clear that the conditions (T.1)–(T.3) still fail to guarantee the dispersion of preferences. (See also Remark 2 below.) What we need is a sort of regularity condition on the way parameters are assigned to preference relations. In order to state such a condition, let us introduce the concept of intermediate preferences as used by Grandmont [3] in a different context. A preference relation $\succsim$ is said to be *intermediate* between $\succsim_1$ and $\succsim_2$, denoted $\succsim \in [\succsim_1, \succsim_2]$, if

(i) $\succsim_1 \cap \succsim_2 \subset \succsim$;
(ii) $\succsim \subset \succsim_1 \cup \succsim_2$;
(iii) $(\sim_1 \cap \succ_2) \cup (\succ_1 \cap \sim_2) \subset \succ$.

(i) is equivalent to $\succ \subset \succ_1 \cup \succ_2$. (ii) is equivalent to $\succ_1 \cap \succ_2 \subset \succ$. (For some discussion on this concept, see Grandmont [3].)

The fourth condition, a regularity condition, which enables us to drop the requirement of differentiability of the mapping $\mathscr{E}_1$ and the Sondermann condition is the following:

(T.4)   For every a_1 and a_2 in A, one has $\succsim_a \in [\succsim_{a_1}, \succsim_{a_2}]$ whenever $a \in \,]a_1, a_2[\; (= \{ta_1 + (1 - t)a_2 | 0 < t < 1\}.)$

If an economy $(\mathscr{E}, v)$ satisfies the conditions (T.1)–(T.4), the preference distribution of $(\mathscr{E}, v)$ is said to be *continuously dispersed*.

Remark 1   The condition (T.3) appears so weak that it may be misleading to readers. I would like to point out that a factor that has made such a weak statement possible is the assumption of convexity of the set of parameters A. Indeed, it is possible to obtain the results of this paper without the convexity of the set A, in which case the condition (T.3) should be strengthened to the following:

(T.3′)   Given any x, y in X such that $x \neq y$, any a in A, and any neighborhood U of a, there exists a' in $U \cap A$ such that $x \sim_{a'} y$.

And the condition (T.4) should be modified to

(T.4′)   If U is a convex subset of A, then for every a_1 and a_2 in U, one has $\succsim_a \in [\succsim_{a_1}, \succsim_{a_2}]$ whenever $a \in \,]a_1, a_2[$.

Remark 2   Araujo and Mas-Colell [1] have given an example that shows that the condition (T.3′) is not sufficient to guarantee the single-valuedness of the mean demand. To understand the need for a regularity condition such as (T.4) [or (T.4′)], let us reproduce their example here: Let $X = [0,1]$, $A = \,]0,1[$, and $K \subset A$ be a Cantor middle-third set. For a in A, let $g(a)$ be the distance from a to K. Put $u(x, a) = xg(a)$ and $\succsim_a = \{(x, y) \in X \times X \,|\, u(x, a) \geq u(y, a)\}$. If $x \sim_a y$, then $x \sim_{a'} y$ for a' arbitrarily close to a. However, given a compact subset B of X, the set of a' for which $\succsim_{a'}$ does not have a unique greatest element is K, which may have Lebesgue measure as close to one as we wish. Of course, the trouble here is that even if (T.3′) is satisfied, all a in K have the same preference relation.

If the budget sets of agents are identical, that is, if the endowment distribution is concentrated on a point in the commodity space, the continuous dispersion of preference relations does guarantee the single-valuedness of the mean demand. In fact, we can state the following result, which is an analog of Theorem 1 in Araujo and Mas-Colell [1, p. 116] in our framework:

PROPOSITION 1   *Let $(\mathscr{E}, v)$ be an economy where the preference distribution is continuously dispersed. If B is a compact subset of the consumption set X, then it has at most one greatest element with respect to $\succsim_a$, v-a.e.*

In a very special case where endowments are concentrated on one point in the commodity space, the result implies that the mean demand set is singleton whenever it is nonempty. However, we *do need the dispersion of endowments* to obtain the upper hemicontinuity of the mean demand when the consumption set X is not necessarily a convex set. (See Mas-Colell [9] and Yamazaki [16, 17].)

In this paper I would like to strengthen the conclusion of Proposition 1 by excluding irregular "correlation" of the mappings $\mathscr{E}_1$ and $\mathscr{E}_2$. In order to be more specific, let us define first the concept of distribution of characteristics. Given an economy $(\mathscr{E}, v)$, the *preference–endowment distribution* for $(\mathscr{E}, v)$, denoted by $\mu_{\mathscr{E},v}$, is defined by $\mu_{\mathscr{E},v} = v \circ \mathscr{E}^{-1}$; i.e.,

$$\mu_{\mathscr{E},v}(G) = v(\{a \in A \,|\, \mathscr{E}(a) \in G\}) \qquad \text{for every Borel subset } G \text{ of } \mathscr{P} \times R^l.$$

The marginal distribution of $\mu_{\mathscr{E},v}$ on $\mathscr{P}$ and on R^l is denoted by $\mu_{\succsim}$ and μ_e, respectively; i.e., $\mu_{\succsim} = v \circ \mathscr{E}_1^{-1}$ and $\mu_e = v \circ \mathscr{E}_2^{-1}$. Denote the product measure of $\mu_{\succsim}$ and μ_e by $\mu_{\succsim} \times \mu_e$. *The preference–endowment distribution $\mu_{\mathscr{E},v}$ is said to be independent if $\mu_{\mathscr{E},v} = \mu_{\succsim} \times \mu_e$.* (This notion of independence of characteristics distribution in the context of the measure theoretical model of general equilibrium analysis first appeared in Hildenbrand [4, Example 2, p. 117].) Let us now introduce a concept that is much more general than that of independent preference–endowment distribution. We say that *the dependence between the preference assignment $\mathscr{E}_1$ and the endowment assignment $\mathscr{E}_2$ is regular*, or, alternatively, that *the preference–endowment distribution $\mu_{\mathscr{E},v}$ is regular if $\mu_{\mathscr{E},v}$* is absolutely continuous with respect to the measure $\mu_{\succsim} \times \mu_e$. (See Yamazaki [17].) Trivially, if $\mu_{\mathscr{E},v}$ is independent, then it is regular.

Define two subsets of $\mathscr{P} \times R^l$ by

$$C_p = \{(\succsim, e) \in \mathscr{P} \times R^l \,|\, \#D(\succsim, e, p) > 1\},$$

$$G_p = \{(\succsim, e) \in \mathscr{P} \times R^l \,|\, \text{every } x \text{ in } B(\succsim, e, p) \text{ such that } p \cdot x$$
$$= p \cdot e \text{ has local cheaper points}\}.[1]$$

One can show exactly as in Theorem 2.1 of Ichiishi [5, pp. 10–12] that $C_p \cap G_p$ is an F_σ-set. Hence, it is measurable.

We can now state the following result:

THEOREM 1 *Let $(\mathscr{E}, v)$ be an economy where the preference distribution is continuously dispersed and the preference–endowment distribution is regular. Then, for every price vector p in R^l_{++}, we have $\mu_{\mathscr{E},v}(C_p \cap G_p) = 0$.*

Theorem 1 implies that the mean demand $\Phi(p)$ is a continuous function if the consumption set X is convex, and if we have $p \cdot e_a > \inf\{p \cdot x \,|\, x \in X\}$, v-a.e., for every p in R^l_{++}. In order to establish the continuity of mean demand

---

[1] A consumption bundle x in X is said to have *local cheaper points* or *a sequence of cheaper points* if for every neighborhood U of x there exists a consumption bundle z in $U \cap X$ such that $p \cdot z < p \cdot x$. The concept of local cheaper points plays an important role in general equilibrium analysis when we allow possible nonconvexity of consumption sets. (See Yamazaki [16, 17].) The concept has been familiar to Rochester students for some time through the lecture notes on general equilibrium theory circulated by L. W. McKenzie among his students since 1962. The importance of the cheaper points concept in demand theory had already been noted in McKenzie [11, pp. 186–187].

in a general setting, we must now turn to the regularizing effect coming from dispersed endowment distribution.

   The endowment distribution for $(\mathscr{E}, v)$ is said to be weakly dispersed if for any price vector p in R^l_{++}, the resulting wealth distribution $\mu_{p,e}$ defined by

$$\mu_{p,e}(G) = v(\{a \in A \,|\, p \cdot \mathscr{E}_2(a) \in G\}) \qquad \text{for every Borel subset } G \text{ of } R,$$

does not give positive weight to any particular amount; i.e.,

$$\mu_{p,e}(\{b\}) = 0 \qquad \text{for any} \quad b \in R.$$

   From now on we assume that $e_a \in X$, v-a.e. The following result is due to Yamazaki [16, 17]:

   THEOREM 2   Let $(\mathscr{E}, v)$ be an economy where the endowment distribution is weakly dispersed. Then (1) for every p in R^l_{++} we have $\mu_{\mathscr{E}, v}(\mathscr{P} \times R^l \backslash G_p) = 0$; (2) the mean demand correspondence $\Phi: R^l_{++} \to R^l$ is upper hemicontinuous.

   As a corollary to Theorems 1 and 2 above, we obtain the main result of this paper.

   THEOREM 3   Let $(\mathscr{E}, v)$ be an economy where the preference distribution is continuously dispersed, the preference–endowment distribution is regular, and the endowment distribution is weakly dispersed. Then, the mean demand $\Phi: R^l_{++} \to R^l$ is a continuous function.

3.   PROOFS

   We first present a lemma which is a trivial consequence of Proposition in Grandmont [3, p. 322]. However, it plays an important role in our approach to the smoothing-by-aggregation problem.

   LEMMA 1   (Grandmont)   Let $(\mathscr{E}, v)$ be an economy where the preference distribution is continuously dispersed. Then, for every x and y in X such that $x \neq y$, either the following (1) or (2) holds:

   (1)   Either $x \succ_a y$ for all a, or $y \succ_a x$ for all a;
   (2)   There exist a vector q in R^m, $\|q\| = 1$, and a real number c such that for every a in A, we have $x \succ_a y$ (respectively, $x \sim_a y$, $x \prec_a y$) if and only if $q \cdot a > c$ (respectively, $q \cdot a = c$, $q \cdot a < c$).

   Proof   First, we show that the sets $\Lambda_{xy} = \{a \in A \,|\, x \succsim_a y\}$ for x and y in X are closed relative to A. Let a_n be a sequence in Λ_{xy} converging to a_0 in A. Then, by continuity of the mapping $\mathscr{E}_1: a \mapsto \succsim_a$, $\succsim_{a_n} \to \succsim_{a_0}$. It follows that $(x, y) \in \succsim_{a_0}$ since $(x, y) \in \succsim_{a_n}$ for all n. Thus $a_0 \in \Lambda_{xy}$.

   The conditions (H. 1) and (H. 2) of the proposition in Grandmont [3, p. 322] are thus satisfied, as (T. 4) holds by assumption. Hence, the conclusion of this lemma follows from (T. 3) and the conclusion of the proposition in Grandmont. Q.E.D.

Let B be a compact subset of the consumption set X. For every a in A and a subset S of R^l, put

$$d(a, S) = \{z \in S \cap B \mid z \succsim_a y \text{ for all } y \text{ in } B\}.$$

Then $d(a, B)$ is the set of all greatest elements of B with respect to $\succsim_a$, and $d(a, S) = d(a, B) \cap S$ for $S \neq B$. The symbol Δ denotes the diagonal of $X \times X$. For a vector q in R^m such that $\|q\| = 1$, and a real number c, $H(q, c)$ denotes the hyperplane $\{a \in R^m \mid q \cdot a = c\}$ in R^m. L_q denotes the set $\{\lambda q \mid \lambda \in R\}$.

LEMMA 2   *Let $(\mathscr{E}, v)$ be an economy where the preference distribution is continuously dispersed, and B a compact subset of the consumption set X. Then, given any $\bar{a} \in A$ and $(x, y) \in B \times B \backslash \Delta$, there exist an open neighborhood V of $\bar{a}$ and closed neighborhoods W_x, W_y of x and y, respectively, such that for any closed neighborhoods $W'_x \subset W_x$, $W'_y \subset W_y$ of x and y, we have*

$$v(\{a \in V \mid d(a, W'_x) \neq \varnothing \text{ and } d(a, W'_y) \neq \varnothing\}) = 0.$$

Proof   Let $\bar{a} \in A$ and $(x, y) \in B \times B \backslash \Delta$. By the continuity of preference relations and the mapping $\mathscr{E}_1 : a \mapsto \succsim_a$, the conclusion of this lemma is true if $x \sim_{\bar{a}} y$. Thus, from now on we assume that $x \sim_{\bar{a}} y$.
We first show:

(1)   The set $A_S = \{a \in A \mid d(a, S) \neq \varnothing\}$ is closed in A for any closed subset S of B.

Let $a_n \to a$ in A and $d(a_n, S) \neq \varnothing$ for all n. Write $\succsim_a = \succsim$ and $\succsim_{a_n} = \succsim_n$ for each n. It follows from the continuity of $\mathscr{E}_1$ that $\succsim_n \to \succsim$. For every n there is an x_n in S such that $x_n \succsim_n z$ for any z in B. Since the set $S \subset B$ is compact, there is a convergent subsequence of (x_n), still denoted by (x_n), such that $x_n \to x^* \in S$. We have $x^* \succsim z$ for all z in B because for each n it is true that $x_n \succsim_n z$ for all z in B. Therefore, x^* belongs to $d(a, S)$, which implies that a is in A_S. This proves (1).
It follows from (1) that the set $\{a \in V \mid d(a, W'_x) \neq \varnothing$ and $d(a, W'_y) \neq \varnothing\}$ is measurable for any open set V in A and any closed sets W'_x, W'_y in R^l.

We now claim:

(2)   There exist an open neighborhood V of $\bar{a}$ and closed neighborhoods W_x, W_y of x and y, respectively, such that for every a in V and closed neighborhoods $W'_x \subset W_x$, $W'_y \subset W_y$ of x and y, we have

$$\#\{a' \in (L_q + a) \cap V \cap A \mid d(a', W'_x) \neq \varnothing \text{ and } d(a', W'_y) \neq \varnothing\} \leqq 1.$$

Suppose that the claim is false. If we put for every $n = 1, 2, \ldots$

$$V_n = \{a \in R^m \,|\, \|\bar{a} - a\| < 1/n\},$$
$$W_{x,n} = \{z \in R^l \,|\, \|x - z\| \leq 1/n\},$$
$$W_{y,n} = \{z \in R^l \,|\, \|y - z\| \leq 1/n\},$$

then for each n there are $a_n, a'_n \in V_n \cap A$, closed neighborhoods $W'_{x,n} \subset W_{x,n}$, $W'_{y,n} \subset W_{y,n}$ of x and y, $x_n \in W'_{x,n} \cap B$, $y_n \in W'_{y,n} \cap B$, such that we have $a_n - a'_n = \lambda_n q$, $\lambda_n > 0$, $x_n \in d(a'_n, W'_{x,n})$, and $y_n \in d(a_n, W'_{y,n})$. It follows that $a_n, a'_n \to \bar{a}$, $\lambda_n \to 0$, $(x_n, y_n) \to (x, y)$, and $y_n \gtrsim_{a_n} x_n$, $x_n \gtrsim_{a'_n} y_n$ for each n. Since we have $x \sim_{\bar{a}} y$, by Lemma 1 there exists a hyperplane $H(q, c)$ in R^m such that for every a in A, $x \succ_a y$ (respectively, $x \sim_a y$, $x \prec_a y$) if and only if $q \cdot a > c$ (respectively, $q \cdot a = c$, $q \cdot a < c$). Also, for each (x_n, y_n), there is a hyperplane $H(q_n, c_n)$ such that $x_n \succ_a y_n$ (respectively, $x_n \sim_a y_n$, $x_n \prec_a y_n$) if and only if $q_n \cdot a > c_n$ (respectively, $q_n \cdot a = c_n$, $q_n \cdot a < c_n$), because $[y_n \gtrsim_{a_n} x_n$ and $x_n \gtrsim_{a'_n} y_n]$ implies that (1) of Lemma 1 cannot hold. From now on we write $\gtrsim_n, \gtrsim'_n, \gtrsim$ instead of $\gtrsim_{a_n}, \gtrsim_{a'_n}, \gtrsim_{\bar{a}}$.

We shall consider three exhaustive cases.

Case I $x_n \succ'_n y_n$ for infinitely many n.

By restricting our attention to a subsequence of (x_n, y_n), we can assume that $x_n \succ'_n y_n$ for all n.

For each n the entire line segment $[a'_n, a_n]$ cannot lie on the hyperplane $H(q_n, c_n)$. Thus the intersection of $]a'_n, a_n]$ and $H(q_n, c_n)$ must be singleton. Let it be denoted a''_n for each n. (Note that $a''_n \to \bar{a}$ as $[a'_n, a_n]$ is contained in V_n.) Put $\delta_n = \|a'_n - a''_n\|$; then $\delta_n > 0$ and $a'_n = -\delta_n q + a''_n$. Since A is open, there exists a positive number ε such that $-\varepsilon q + \bar{a} \in A$. We have $q \cdot (-\varepsilon q + \bar{a}) = -\varepsilon \|q\|^2 + c < c$.

On the other hand, $x_n \succ'_n y_n$ implies that $q_n \cdot a'_n > c_n$; i.e., $q_n \cdot (-\delta_n q + a''_n) > c_n$. It follows from $0 < \delta_n \leq \lambda_n$ and $\lambda_n \to 0$ that $\delta_n < \varepsilon$ for all $n \geq n_0$ for some positive integer n_0. Since $q_n \cdot (-\delta_n q) > 0$ (as $q_n \cdot a''_n = c_n$), we obtain that $q_n \cdot (-\varepsilon q + a''_n) > c_n$ for all $n \geq n_0$. There is a positive integer $n_1 \geq n_0$ such that for all $n \geq n_1$ we have $-\varepsilon q + a''_n \in A$ because the set A is open and $(-\varepsilon q + a''_n) \to (-\varepsilon q + \bar{a}) \in A$. Put $\gtrsim''_n = \gtrsim_{(-\varepsilon q + a''_n)}$ for each $n \geq n_1$. Then, $x_n \gtrsim''_n y_n$ for all $n \geq n_1$. By the continuity of $\mathscr{E}_1 \gtrsim''_n \to \gtrsim_{(-\varepsilon q + \bar{a})}$. Thus, $(x_n, y_n) \to (x, y)$ implies that $x \gtrsim_{(-\varepsilon q + \bar{a})} y$; that is, $q \cdot (-\varepsilon q + \bar{a}) \geq c$, a contradiction.

Case II $y_n \succ_n x_n$ for infinitely many n.

We can assume that $y_n \succ_n x_n$ for all n. There is $a''_n \in [a'_n, a_n[$ such that $y_n \sim_{a''_n} x_n$. Put $\delta_n = \|a''_n - a_n\| > 0$. By an argument similar to that in Case I, $q_n \cdot (\delta_n q + a''_n) < c_n$ leads to a contradiction, $q \cdot (\varepsilon q + \bar{a}) \leq 0$.

Case III $x_n \sim_n y_n$ and $x_n \sim'_n y_n$ for all but finitely many n, say for $n \geq n_0$.

Let Π be the perpendicular projection of R^m onto the hyperplane $H(q, c)$. For each n, put $\bar{\bar{a}}_n = \Pi(a_n) = \Pi(a'_n)$. $a_n, a'_n \in L_q + \bar{\bar{a}}_n$. For all $n \geq n_0$, $L_q + \bar{\bar{a}}_n \subset H(q_n, c_n)$, in particular $q_n \cdot \bar{\bar{a}}_n = c_n$. Note that $\bar{\bar{a}}_n \to \bar{a}$ as we have $\|\bar{\bar{a}}_n - \bar{a}\| \leq \|a_n - \bar{a}\|$ and $a_n \to \bar{a}$.

Now, there is a positive number ε such that the 2ε-ball centered at $\bar{a}$ is contained in A, in particular $\varepsilon q + \bar{a} \in A$. We have $q \cdot (\varepsilon q + \bar{a}) > c$. Now set $\bar{a}_n = \varepsilon q + \bar{\bar{a}}_n \in L_q + \bar{\bar{a}}_n$. As $\bar{\bar{a}}_n \to \bar{a}$, $\bar{a}_n \to \varepsilon q + \bar{a} \in A$, and thus there is a positive integer $n_1 \geq n_0$ such that for all $n \geq n_1$ we have $\bar{a}_n \in A$. $\bar{a}_n \in L_q + \bar{\bar{a}}_n$ implies that $x_n \sim_{\bar{a}_n} y_n$ for all $n \geq n_1$. Since $\bar{a}_n \to \varepsilon q + \bar{a}$, by the continuity of $\mathscr{E}_1$ and preference relations, $(x_n, y_n) \to (x, y)$ implies that $x \sim_{(\varepsilon q + \bar{a})} y$; i.e., $q \cdot (\varepsilon q + \bar{a}) = c$, a contradiction.

This completes the proof of (2). The conclusion of the lemma now follows from (2) and Fubini's theorem.   Q.E.D.

Proof of Proposition 1   Let K be a nonempty compact subset of A. Given (x, y) in $B \times B \backslash \Delta$, let V_a, $W_{x,a}$, $W_{y,a}$ be as in Lemma 2 for each a in K. Since K is compact, there is a nonempty finite subset F of K such that $K \subset \bigcup_{a \in F} V_a$. Put $W_x = \bigcap_{a \in F} W_{x,a}$, $W_y = \bigcap_{a \in F} W_{y,a}$, $K_{xy} = \{a \in K \mid d(a, W_x) \neq \emptyset$ and $d(a, W_y) \neq \emptyset\}$. By Lemma 2 we have $\nu(K_{xy}) = 0$. Since $B \times B \backslash \Delta$ is a Lindelöf space, there is a countable subset $\mathscr{B}$ of $B \times B \backslash \Delta$ such that $B \times B \backslash \Delta \subset \bigcup_{(x,y) \in \mathscr{B}} W_x \times W_y$. It is easy to check that the set $\{a \in K \mid \# d(a, B) > 1\}$ is contained in the set $\bigcup_{(x,y) \in \mathscr{B}} K_{xy}$. It follows that for ν-a.e. a in K, $\succsim_a$ has at most one greatest element. Since A is σ-compact, the conclusion follows.

Q.E.D.

Proof of Theorem 1   Let p be in R_{++}^l, and for each x in R^l let C_x, C_x^* be the x-section of the sets $C_p \cap G_p$ and C_p, respectively. Trivially, $C_x \subset C_x^*$. It follows from Proposition 1 that C_x^* is a $\mu_{\succsim}$-null set so that we have $\mu_{\succsim}(C_x) = 0$ for each x in R^l. Hence we obtain

$$[\mu_{\succsim} \times \mu_e](C_p \cap G_p) = \int_{R^l} \mu_{\succsim}(C_x)\, d\mu_e(x)$$

$$= 0.$$

It now follows from the regularity of the preference–endowment distribution that $\mu_{\mathscr{E},\nu}(C_p \cap G_p) = 0$.   Q.E.D.

REFERENCES

1. Araujo, A., and Mas-Colell, A., Notes on the smoothing of aggregate demand, *J. Math. Econ.* **5** (1978), 113–127.
2. Debreu, G., "Theory of Value." Wiley, New York (1959).

3. Grandmont, J.-M., Intermediate preferences and the majority rule, *Econometrica* **46** (1978), 317–330.
4. Hildenbrand, W., "Core and Equilibria of a Large Economy." Princeton Univ. Press, Princeton, New Jersey, (1974).
5. Ichiishi, T., Economies with a Mean Demand Function, Working Paper IP 199. Univ. of California, Berkeley, California (1974). (A shortened version is in *J. Math. Econ.* **3** (1976), 167–171.)
6. Mas-Colell, A., On Aggregate Demand in a Measure Space of Agents, Working Paper IP 183. Univ. of California, Berkeley, California (1973).
7. Mas-Colell, A., An equilibrium existence theorem without complete or transitive preferences, *J. Math. Econ.* **1** (1974), 237–246.
8. Mas-Colell, A., Handout for the Aggregation Workshop. Stanford Univ., Standford, California (1976).
9. Mas-Colell, A., Indivisible commodities and general equilibrium theory, *J. Econ. Theory* **16** (1977), 443–456.
10. Mas-Colell, A., and Neufeind, W., Generic properties of aggregate excess demand and an application, *Econometrica* **45** (1977), 591–599.
11. McKenzie, L. W., Demand theory without a utility index, *Rev. Econ. Stud.* **24** (1957), 185–189.
12. Sondermann, D., Smoothing demand by aggregation, *J. Math. Econ.* **2** (1975), 201–223.
13. Sondermann, D., Smoothing demand by aggregation 11, Manuscript. Univ. of Hamburg, Hamburg, Germany (1975).
14. Sondermann, D., Some results and remarks on the "smoothing by aggregation" problem, *in* "Systèmes Dynamiques et Modèles Économiques" (Colloque Internationaux du Centre National de la Recherche Scientifique No. 259), pp. 89–93, Centre National de la Recherche Scientifique, Paris, 1977.
15. Sonnenschein, H., Demand theory without transitive preferences, with applications to the theory of competitive equilibrium, *in* "Preferences, Utility, and Demand" (J. Chipman *et al.*, eds.). Harcourt, New York, 1971.
16. Yamazaki, A., An equilibrium existence theorem without convexity assumptions, *Econometrica* **46** (1978), 541–555.
17. Yamazaki, A., Regularizing Effect of Aggregation and Existence Theorems in a Large Nonconvex Economy, manuscript (1978).

DEPARTMENT OF ECONOMICS
UNIVERSITY OF ILLINOIS
CHICAGO, ILLINOIS

Employment Policies for the Multiperiod Monopolist–Monopsonist with Implications for Macroeconomic Control

JOHN P. BONIN

The theory of a multiperiod monopolist incurring nonseparable labor adjustment costs is developed when investment is irreversible. Optimal input stocks are shown to exist and be unique in any period for any finite horizon model. Optimal input policies are characterized by considering the difference between initial stocks and optimal ones in each period. The sensitivity of disequilibrium policies to parametric changes is examined. A potentially dangerous result for macroeconomic policy makers is derived under recessionary conditions. Even though the optimal labor stock is negatively related to changes in the discount rate, the optimal labor policy is positively related to such changes. Hence, in recessionary situations, decreases in the interest rate may weaken present employment demand from the multiperiod monopolist–monopsonist. This result is attributable to a horizon effect that operates only in disequilibrium situations. Under our assumptions and in contrast to other work, several well-known comparative static results are derived, and a link between the durability of capital and employment policies is demonstrated.

I. INTRODUCTION

Macroeconomic policy is intended to influence employment through its effect on aggregate demand. Labor demand is derived from product demand, so that increases in aggregate demand tend to increase employment. Also, at the high level of input aggregation considered in most macroeconomic models, complementarity between capital and labor provides a further link between employment and macroeconomic control. By decreasing a target interest rate, policy makers exert an upward pressure on demand for both

25

capital and labor. Hence, the expansion of aggregate demand coupled with declining interest rates is expected to stimulate employment demand and consequently decrease the rate of unemployment.

This scenario follows from well-known results in static equilibrium microeconomic models. However, since the macroeconomic policymaker is concerned mainly with disequilibrium situations, much attention has been paid recently to disequilibrium behavior in multiperiod models of the microeconomic production unit as a basis for understanding macroeconomic phenomena. Work on the microeconomic underpinnings of the investment accelerator was stimulated by the paper of Eisner and Strotz [1], which introduced adjustment costs to the capital input in a multiperiod theory of the firm. Nerlove [4] gives an excellent critical survey of the resulting cross-fertilization between multiperiod neoclassical theories of the firm and the empirical work on the investment accelerator.

Recent work on the Phillips curve trade-off has introduced adjustment costs to the labor input in the tradition of Holt et al. [2] to include work force smoothing in the multiperiod model of the firm. When labor adjustment costs are nonseparable, the firm is a monopsonist with respect to employment decisions (cf. Nerlove [4] or Treadway [6] for a discussion of the monopsonistic character of nonseparable adjustment costs). Our purpose is to construct a multiperiod model of a monopoly–monopsony that is sufficiently complex to allow an examination of disequilibrium employment demand. A further link between the interest rate and employment is explored through the discount rate applied by the firm to future earnings. When input planning policies are determined over a multiple-period horizon, changes in the discount rate affect the firm's rate of adjustment to long-run equilibrium input stocks. Hence, if labor cannot be adjusted costlessly, a horizon effect should be included along with the aggregate demand effect and the complementary input effect in discussions of macroeconomic control.

This paper develops the theory of a multiperiod monopolist when nonseparable adjustment costs are applied to the labor input and investment is irreversible. Any change in labor usage causes the firm to incur costs above an externally imposed wage rate; hence, labor is heuristically a quasi-fixed input. On the other hand, capital can be accumulated by buying at a fixed purchasing price but reduced only at a rate no greater than the depreciation rate. These simplifying assumptions about capital supply conditions allow employment decisions depending on the current stocks of both inputs to be highlighted. At the same time, the irreversibility of investment allows us to separate the complementary input effect from the horizon effect. Equilibrium stocks of both capital and labor are shown to be indirectly related to the interest rate, while conditions under which optimal employment policies are directly related to the interest rate are derived. Consequently, although long-run equilibrium stocks respond positively to decreases in the interest rate as predicted from complementarity, immediate employment demand may be decreased by such a policy due to the domination of the horizon effect. This suggests a trade-off between the long- and short-run effects of macroeconomic control due to changes in the rate of adjustment to equilibrium stocks.

Interestingly, we discover it is precisely in recessionary periods, when both inputs are being reduced, that the conflict between equilibrium and disequilibrium responses arises. This conflict is exposed by explicit consideration of the interaction between two-state variables in a dynamic programming context. As a by-product of this two-state-variable specification, we clarify problems involved in Treadway's inability to demonstrate several well-known comparative static results in his multiperiod case in Treadway [7]. By examining the sensitivity of our optimal policies to other external parameters, we conclude that the ambiguities found by Treadway depend on the way in which adjustment costs are specified rather than on nonseparability. Indeed, our monopolist–monopsonist reacts to parameter changes in the normal way even in disequilibrium phases.

II. THE MODEL OF THE MULTIPERIOD MONOPOLIST–MONOPSONIST

Our multiperiod monopolist–monopsonist makes input planning decisions under certainty conditions where output demand and input supply conditions are fixed over time. We assume that all output produced in a period is delivered to the market in that period; hence revenue in any period is determined by known demand conditions. Difficulties have arisen in previous work when optimal sales decisions over time are considered for a monopolist faced with uncertainty (cf. Zabel [8,9]). Therefore, we specify a deterministic model to ease the computational burden and employ Treadway's hunch "that an attack on stochastic problems will be facilitated by a thorough understanding of the deterministic case."[1]

In any period the firm is assumed to produce a single output using two inputs, the stock of capital K and the stock of labor L. Technological change is ignored, and the production function is assumed to be neoclassical. Capital may be purchased at the beginning of any period at a price k, while the per-unit maintenance cost per period of capital is given by m. The capital stock depreciates periodically according to the deterministic rate $(1 - \delta)$, where $1 > \delta > 0$. A capital purchase, assumed to be delivered immediately, is defined to be the difference between the optimal stock in a period and the

[1] Treadway [7, p. 19].

stock inherited from the previous period. If this difference is negative, no capital is purchased. The stock of capital in any period, therefore, depends on depreciation and ordering policies. The stock of labor in any period is physically unconstrained although in addition to a basic wage rate w paid by the firm for each unit of labor used, positive costs are associated with any change in the labor stock over time.

Further production and market conditions are given by the following assumptions.

(A-1) The production function $q(L, K)$ is twice differentiable. Both inputs are necessary for production, and marginal products are positive. Also, for any positive K, $\lim_{L \to 0} q_L = \infty$ and $\lim_{L \to \infty} q_L = 0$, while for any positive L, $\lim_{K \to 0} q_K = \infty$ and $\lim_{K \to \infty} q_K = 0$.

(A-2) Revenue is a strictly concave differentiable function of inputs, denoted $R[q(L, K)]$ to indicate the role of production.[2] Also, $R[0] = 0$, $R'[0] > 0$, and R' is bounded.

(A-3) The marginal revenue product of one input increases in response to an increase in the other input; i.e.,

$$R_{LK} \equiv R'q_{LK} + q_L q_K R'' > 0.$$

(A-4) A strictly convex differentiable penalty function is associated with any adjustment in the labor variable. With L_0 as the initial labor input, the specification of this cost is

$$\psi(L - L_0) > 0 \quad \text{for} \quad L \neq L_0,$$

$$\psi'(L - L_0) \gtreqless 0 \quad \text{as} \quad L \gtreqless L_0 \quad \text{and} \quad \psi''(L - L_0) > 0 \quad \text{for all} \quad L.$$

Costs to the firm associated with adjusting the labor variable are well known from empirical and theoretical work. Increases in the labor input may result in overtime rates, increased personnel costs, or search costs. Decreasing the amount of labor used is often achieved by the underutilization of a labor force. In other situations severance considerations raise the cost of labor above the basic wage rate. Reasons for including adjustment costs when varying the labor input are fully discussed in Holt et al. [2], along with some empirical justifications from the data studied. In any case such considerations cause the monopolist to view the labor market as imperfect in the short run, even if the wage rate is parametric in the long run.[3]

---

[2] For the competitive firm, $R' = p$. Then, the conditions are equivalent to strict concavity of the production function. Since an imperfect product market has been assumed, this property of production is no longer necessary as long as revenue is concave.

[3] For increases in labor, short-run supply conditions are similar to those facing a monopsonist.

The optimization problem is to maximize profits, discounted over time using a fixed factor α, for a finite number of periods. The functional equation for any period n is

$$f^n(L_0, K_0) = \max_{\substack{K \geq K_0 \\ L}} \{R[q(L, K)] - wL - mK - k \cdot (K - K_0)$$

$$- \psi(L - L_0) + \alpha f^{n-1}(L, \delta K)\}. \tag{1}[4]$$

Due to the simplifying assumptions made about the capital market, this can be rewritten as

$$f^n(L_0, K_0) = \max_{K \geq K_0} \{G^n(L_0, L, K) + kK_0\},$$

where

$$G^n(L_0, L, K) = R[q(L, K)] - wL - (m + k)K - \psi(L - L_0) + \alpha f^{n-1}(L, \delta K).$$

If $G^n(L_0, L, K)$ is strictly concave, the term within brackets above is strictly concave. Then $f^n(L_0, K_0)$ is strictly concave for any n, by a lemma reported by Iglehart [3, pp. 199–200]. To show that $G^n(L_0, L, K)$ is strictly concave, divide it into $G^1(L_0, L, K) + \alpha f^{n-1}(L, \delta K)$. $G^1(L_0, L, K)$ is strictly concave from (A-2) and (A-4). Hence, strict concavity of $G^n(L_0, L, K)$ and $f^n(L_0, K)$ can be established by mathematical induction on n and repeated application of the Iglehart lemma.

The concavity of $f^n(L_0, K_0)$ guarantees the existence, uniqueness, and continuity of a solution to the functional equation. Indeed, optimal stocks for labor and capital can be determined from solving the first-order conditions for a maximum of $G^n(L_0, L, K)$. Optimal input policies can then be determined. The proof of the existence and uniqueness of optimal input stocks and the derivation of optimal input policies follows in the next section.

III. OPTIMAL INPUT POLICIES

Optimal input stocks under various specifications for initial conditions are characterized by four functions. Simultaneous solution of certain pairs of these functions yield the optimal input stocks whose existence and uniqueness are shown.

Assumption (A-1) limits the feasible solution set of optimal stocks to the positive orthant of (L, K) space. Assumption (A-3) establishes the slope of all four functions in this space. Indeed, this assumption also allows us to

---

[4] Superscripts are used to indicate the number of periods in the optimization horizon. Also, $k \cdot (K - K_0)$ indicates multiplication through the parentheses.

determine the sign of the cross partial derivatives of the functional equation. Similar analysis could be performed if the reverse strong inequality were assumed. However, we choose to consider only the normal case here, while the substantive changes in our results if the perverse case were assumed will be taken up in the final section.

In the theorem, optimal input stocks are derived by performing the following steps sequentially. At first, optimal input stocks are calculated, ignoring initial conditions. Then, an arbitrary initial labor stock is introduced, and optimal stocks are revised. Finally, the initial capital stock is considered as a possible constraint on the achievement of optimal stocks. To aid the reader, a diagram indicating optimal stocks is given.

THEOREM   Given assumptions (A-1)–(A-4), there exist unique optimal functions $L^{n*}(L_0, K_0)$ and $K^{n*}(L_0, K_0)$ solving Eq. (1), which may be determined from four unique functions $l^n(K)$, $h^n(K)$, $x^n(L_0, K)$ and $y^n(L_0)$ for any finite horizon of n periods. Also,

$$f_{L_0}^n(L_0, K_0) = \psi'(L^{n*}(L_0, K_0) - L_0) \quad \text{and} \quad 0 < L^{n*}(L_0, K_0) < 1,$$

$$-m/(1 - \alpha\delta) \leq f_{K_0}^n(L_0, K_0) \leq k \quad \text{and} \quad f_{L_0 K_0}^n = f_{K_0 L_0}^n \geq 0.$$

Proof   The proof proceeds by mathematical induction on n. The results are established for $n = 1$. By assuming the results for $n = N - 1$, they can be shown for any N.

Now

$$f^1(L_0, K_0) = \max_{\substack{K \geq K_0 \\ L}} G^1(L_0, L, K) + kK_0$$

where

$$G^1(L_0, L, K) \equiv H^1(L, K) - \psi(L - L_0)$$

and

$$H^1(L, K) \equiv R[q(L, K)] - wL - (m + k)K.$$

We first consider the maximization of $H^1(L, K)$ with respect to L and K. Let $l^1(K)$ solve $R'q_L(l^1(K), K) - w = 0$ for any positive K. Let $h^1(K)$ solve $R'q_K(h^1(K), K) - (m + k) = 0$ for any positive K. The existence of positive $l^1(k)$ and $h^1(K)$ follows from the assumptions on limits of marginal products in (A-1). Uniqueness depends on (A-1) and (A-3).

Since $H^1(L, K)$ is strictly concave by (A-1) and (A-2), we show that the simultaneous solution of $l^1(K)$ and $h^1(k)$ yields an unique optimal labor stock for some particular unique capital stock. Differentiating the first-order conditions, we obtain,

$$h_K^{1*}(K) = \frac{-(R'q_{KK} + q_K R'')}{R'q_{KL} + q_K q_L R''} \equiv \frac{F}{-C} > 0$$

and

$$l_K^{1*}(K) = \frac{-(R'q_{LK} + q_L q_K R'')}{R'q_{LL} + q_L^2 R''} > 0.$$

Then $h_K^{1*}(K) > l_K^{1*}(K)$ by (A-2). Hence, uniqueness is assured. The existence of the simultaneous solution of $l^1(K)$ and $h^1(K)$ for some positive K follows from (A-1).

We now consider maximizing $G^1(L_0', L, K)$ for some arbitrary positive L_0'. Let $x^1(L_0', K)$ solve

$$G_L^1(L_0', L, K) = R'q_L(x^1(L_0', K), K) - w - \psi'(x^1(L_0', K) - L_0') = 0.$$

We show

$$L_0' \gtreqqless x^1(L_0', K) \gtreqqless l^1(K).$$

The equality follows from the definition of $l^1(K)$.

Now

$$G_{LL}^1(L_0', L, K) = R'q_{LL} + q_L^2 R'' - \psi'' \equiv B < 0$$

and

$$G_{LL_0}^1(L_0, L, K) = \psi'' > 0.$$

Therefore $L_0' > l^1(K)$ implies

$$G_L^1(L_0', l^1(K), K) > 0 \qquad \text{and} \qquad G_L^1(L_0', L, K) = 0 \qquad \text{for} \quad L > l^1(K).$$

By definition of $x^1(L_0', K)$, when $L_0' > l^1(K)$, $L_0' > x^1(L_0', K) > l^1(K)$. A similar argument will establish the reverse inequality.

The uniqueness of $x^1(L_0', K)$ follows from $G_{LL}^1 = B < 0$. The simultaneous solution of $x^1(L_0', K)$ and $h^1(K)$ determines the optimal stocks maximizing $G^1(L_0', L, K)$ for arbitrary L_0'. Uniqueness of this solution follows from differentiation and applying (A-2) and (A-3).

$$x_K^1(L_0', K) = \frac{-(R'q_{LK} + q_L q_K R'')}{R'q_{LL} + q_L^2 R'' - \psi''} \equiv \frac{-C}{B} > 0.$$

Comparing $x_K^1(L_0', K)$ and $h_K^1(K)$ yields

$$h_K^1(K) > x_K^1(L_0', K)$$

since $FB - C^2 < 0$ from (A-2). Existence of a solution follows from the above bounds.

Given $l^1(K)$, $h^1(K)$, and $x^1(L_0, K)$, the initial capital stock K_0 can be introduced to the maximization exercise by calculating a function depending on the specification for L_0. Let $y^1(L_0)$ solve

$$G_L^1(L_0, x^1(L_0, y^1(L_0)), y^1(L_0)) = G_K^1(L_0, x^1(L_0, y^1(L_0)), y^1(L_0)) = 0.$$

In particular, for the arbitrary L_0' chosen above, $y^1(L_0')$ is constructed by equating $h^1(y^1(L_0'))$ to $x^1(L_0', y^1(L_0'))$.

The existence of $y^1(L_0')$ for any arbitrary L_0' follows from the bound on $x^1(L_0', K)$ and the properties of $l^1(K)$ and $h^1(K)$. For any L_0, $y^1(L_0)$ is single-valued. This is ensured by $x_K^1(L_0^1, K) < h_K^1(K)$. Also $y_{L_0}^1(L_0) > 0$. This is established by differentiating the defining condition $h^1(y^1(L_0)) = x^1(L_0, y^1(L_0))$ and noting $x_K^1 = -C/B$ and $x_{L_0}^1 = -\psi''/B$. $y_{L_0}^1$ is then given by $\psi''C/FB - C^2 > 0$ from (A-2), (A-3), and (A-4).

$y^1(L_0)$ plays a dual role. For any L_0, optimal stocks are given by $y^1(L_0)$ for capital and $x^1(L_0, y^1(L_0))$ for labor. However, if K_0 exceeds $y^1(L_0)$, for the given L_0, the capital constraint is effective. The constrained optimal capital stock is then K_0 and the constrained optimal labor stock given by $x^1(L_0, K_0)$. Hence, $y^1(L_0)$ is a region dividing function for initial stocks.

The solution to $f^1(L_0, K_0)$ must be divided into two cases, depending on whether or not the initial capital stock is constraining. We have

$$L^{1*}(L_0, K_0) = \begin{cases} x^1(L_0, y^1(L_0)) & \text{in I} \\ x^1(L_0, K_0) & \text{in II}; \end{cases}$$

and

$$K^{1*}(L_0, K_0) = \begin{cases} y^1(L_0) & \text{in I,} \\ K_0 & \text{in II.} \end{cases}$$

The differentiation of optimal stocks and Eq. (1) yield the following results;

$$f_{L_0}^1 = \psi'(L^{1*}(L_0, K_0) - L_0)$$

and

$$L_{L_0}^{1*}(L_0, K_0) = \begin{cases} -\psi''F/FB - C^2 & \text{in I,} \\ -\psi''/B & \text{in II.} \end{cases}$$

By definitions of F, B, and C, $0 < L_{L_0}^{1*}(L_0, K_0) < 1$.

$$f_{K_0}^1(L_0, K_0) = \begin{cases} k & \text{in I,} \\ R'q_K - m & \text{in II.} \end{cases}$$

In II, $R'q_K - m < k$ by definition. In I, $f_{K_0}^1(L_0, K_0) = k > -m/(1 - \alpha\delta)$. The lower bound can be established in II by noticing that $\alpha < 1$. Since $f_{L_0}^1 = \psi'(L^{1*}(L_0, K_0) - L_0)$, $f_{L_0 K_0}^1 = \psi''L_{K_0}^{1*}(L_0, K_0)$. In I, $L_{K_0}^{1*} = 0$, which implies $f_{L_0 K_0}^1 = 0 = f_{K_0 L_0}^1$ in I. In II, $L_{K_0}^{1*} = -C/B$. Therefore, $f_{L_0 K_0}^1 = -\psi''C/B = CL_{L_0}^{1*}(L_0, K_0) = f_{K_0 L_0}^1$ in II. Also, $-\psi''C/B > 0$ from (A-2), (A-3), and (A-4). Hence the theorem is shown for $n = 1$.

Due to the length of the proof, we sketch the results for $n = N$, when they are assumed for $n = N - 1$. The key to proving the theorem for the N-period case lies in the results derived for the derivatives of (1).

Along with $f^1_{L_0 L_0} \leq 0$ and $f^1_{K_0 K_0} \leq 0$, which follow from concavity, $f^1_{K_0 L_0} = f^1_{L_0 K_0} \geq 0$ has been shown. Indeed $f^1_{L_0 L_0} < 0$ can be derived. With the bounds on the first-order partials, a proof of the theorem for $n = N$ can then be obtained by a straightforward application of the method used above. We sketch the procedure.

To derive optimal stocks, the functions $l^N(K)$, $h^N(K)$, and $x^N(L_0, K)$ are defined to include the effects of present policies on future conditions. In particular,

$$l^N(K) \quad \text{solves} \quad R'q_L - w + \alpha f^{N-1}_{L_0}(l^N(K), \delta K) = 0,$$

$$h^N(K) \quad \text{solves} \quad R'q_K - (m + k) + \alpha f^{N-1}_{K_0}(h^N(K), \delta K) = 0,$$

and

$$x^N(L_0, K) \quad \text{solves}$$

$$R'q_L - w - \psi'(x^N(L_0, K) - L_0) + \alpha f^{N-1}_{L_0}(x^N(L_0, K), \delta K) = 0.$$

The existence of $l^N(K)$ is shown by considering (A-1) and the bounds on $f^{N-1}_{L_0}$ from the induction hypothesis. Uniqueness follows by arguments similar to those in the one-period case, noting that $f^{N-1}_{L_0 L_0} < 0$. The existence of $h^N(K)$ follows from (A-1) and the bounds on $f^{N-1}_{K_0}$ from the induction hypothesis. Uniqueness can be established since $f^{N-1}_{K_0 L_0} \geq 0$.

The existence and uniqueness of $x^N(L_0, K)$ is established in a manner similar to that of $l^N(K)$ and the bounded property shown in the one-period case can be established.

The existence of all optimal stocks can be established by considering (A-1) and the bounds on $f^{N-1}_{L_0}$ and $f^{N-1}_{K_0}$ from the induction hypothesis.

The construction of $y^N(L_0)$ is analogous to that of $y^1(L_0)$. Properties equivalent to those of $y^1(L_0)$ can be shown.

The qualitative results reported from the differentiation in the one-period case can also be extended trivially to the N-period case.   Q.E.D.

Now that optimal input stocks have been derived in the theorem, optimal input policies can be discussed. With the aid of Fig. 1, optimal policies for capital and labor can be shown for any specification of initial conditions. Initial stocks of labor and capital in region I of Fig. 1, e.g., points B or C, require a capital order to bring the capital stock to $K^{n*}(L_0)$, the optimal level. The required labor policy is then to adjust to the optimal stock $x^n(L_0, K^{n*}(L_0))$, either by reducing or augmenting the labor input (cases B and C, respectively). Initial stocks of labor and capital in region II, e.g., points A or D, result in no capital order due to the constraining nature of

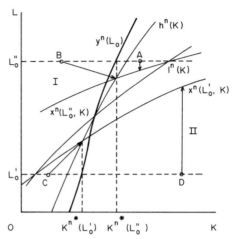

FIGURE 1   Optimal capital and labor policies for representative pairs of initial conditions.

the initial capital stock K_0. The optimal labor policy is an increase or decrease in the initial stock to the stock $x^n(L_0, K_0)$ (cases D and A, respectively). The following section discusses the manner in which optimal input policies are affected when conditions originally assumed parametric to the optimization problem change.

IV.   THE SENSITIVITY OF OPTIMAL POLICIES
   ## TO PRICE PARAMETERS

A taxonomic division into four possible situations confronting a multiperiod monopolist–monopsonist arises from the earlier characterization of

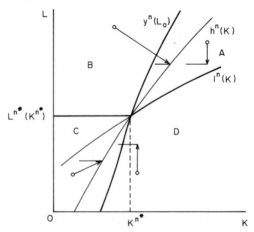

FIGURE 2   Taxonomy according to initial and optimal stocks.

optimal input policies. In Fig. 2, these cases are delineated by the heavy black dividing lines. Although not derived from technical specifications of the model, a label is attached to each case as an intuitive explanation of the taxonomy. Case A, a situation in which the optimal first period policy requires diminishing both input stocks, would describe behavior for a firm facing declining demand for its product. Hence, A is said to be a recessionary phase for the profit maximizer. On the other hand, both input stocks are initially augmented in case C describing behavior of a firm increasing output to meet growing demand for its product. Hence, C is called an expansionary situation for the monopolist. A and C refer to cases in which adjustments are required for product market equilibrium. On the other hand, B and D refer to initial situations of disequilibrium, primarily in factor markets. In case B, capital is ordered but labor decreased, suggesting an initial capital–labor stock ratio that is too low given present factor prices. In case D, capital is allowed to depreciate while the labor force is augmented, representing initially stocks that are too capital-intensive relative to the optimal choice of technique. Hence, B is referred to as an undercapitalized situation, while D is referred to as an overcapitalized one.

Arrows in Fig. 2 represent optimal policies in the first decision period and the resulting initial conditions for the subsequent period. The arrow tip on the solid line indicates a movement to optimal stocks $L^{n*}(L_0, K_0)$ and $K^{n*}(L_0, K_0)$, as previously diagrammed in Fig. 1 (this is always a point on $x^n(L_0, K)$). The end of the horizontal line represents the initial stock for the following period; i.e., $L^{n*}(L_0, K_0)$ and $\delta K^{n*}(L_0, K_0)$. In this manner, sequential consequences of optimal policies can be diagrammed.

Of particular interest are parametric changes in the discount factor α. Since the discount rate is assumed to be directly related to the interest rate, an increase in the interest rate will decrease the discount factor. The net result of combining the horizon effect with production complementarity is shown in the following proposition.

PROPOSITION 1   (Horizon Effect)

$$\frac{dL^{n*}}{d\alpha} = \frac{f_L^{n-1}}{B'} \qquad\qquad \text{when} \quad \frac{dK^{n*}}{d\alpha} = 0,$$

$$\frac{dL^{n*}}{d\alpha} = Mf_L^{n-1} + N\delta f_K^{n-1} \qquad \text{otherwise,}$$

where $M > 0$, $N > 0$, and $B' < 0$ for any L^{n*} and K^{n*}.

Proof   For any positive, finite horizon $n > 1$, optimal stocks $L^{n*}(K^{n*})$ and $K^{n*}(L_0)$ maximizing $G^n(L_0, L, K)$ for arbitrary L_0 simultaneously satisfy $R'q_K[L^{n*}(K^{n*}), K^{n*}(L_0)] - (m + k) + \alpha\delta f_K^{n-1}[L^{n*}(K^{n*}), \delta K^{n*}(L_0)] = 0$, and $R'q_L[L^{n*}(K^{n*}), K^{n*}(L_0)] - w - \psi'(L^{n*} - L_0) + \alpha f_L^{n-1}[L^{n*}(K^{n*}), \delta K^{n*}(L_0)] = 0$.

In this proposition and the ones to follow, the functional arguments of optimal stocks are omitted.

Differentiating the two first-order conditions above with respect to α and rearranging terms yields

$$
\frac{dK^{n*}}{d\alpha} = \frac{\delta f_K^{n-1} - (R''q_Kq_L + q_{KL}R' + \alpha\delta f_{KL}^{n-1})(dL^{n*}/d\alpha)}{R''q_K^2 + R'q_{KK} + \alpha\delta^2 f_{KK}^{n-1}}
$$

$$
\equiv \frac{-\delta f_K^{n-1} - C'(dL^{n*}/d\alpha)}{F'},
$$

and

$$
\frac{dL^{n*}}{d\alpha} = \frac{-f_L^{n-1} - (dK^{n*}/d\alpha)(R'q_{LK} + q_Lq_KR'' + \alpha\delta f_{LK}^{n-1})}{R'q_{LL} + q_L^2R'' - \psi'' + \alpha f_{LL}^{n-1}}
$$

$$
\equiv \frac{-f_L^{n-1} - (dK^{n*}/d\alpha)C'}{B'}.
$$

The first part of the proposition is obvious from the latter.

Continuing by substitution,

$$
\frac{dL^{n*}}{d\alpha} = \frac{-f_L^{n-1}}{B'} + \frac{\delta f_K^{n-1}C'}{B'F'} + \frac{(C')^2}{B'F'}\frac{dL^{n*}}{d\alpha}.
$$

Therefore,

$$
\frac{dL^n}{dx} = \frac{-f_L^{n-1}F'}{B'F' - (C')^2} + \frac{\delta f_K^{n-1}C'}{B'F' - (C')^2}.
$$

Let

$$
M \equiv -F'/[B'F' - (C')^2] \qquad \text{and} \qquad N \equiv C'/[B'F' - (C')^2].
$$

Now $B'F' - (C')^2 > 0$ by concavity and $B' < 0$, $C' > 0$, $F' < 0$ by assumption and the above theorem; $M > 0$ and $N > 0$ for any L^{n*} and K^{n*}. Hence,

$$
\frac{dL^{n*}}{d\alpha} = Mf_L^{n-1} + N\delta f_K^{n-1} \qquad \text{when} \qquad \frac{dK^{n*}}{d\alpha} \neq 0. \qquad \text{Q.E.D.}
$$

Intuitively, an increase in α makes the value of the functional equation more sensitive to future periods, and this changes equilibrium stocks. For $L^{n*}(K^{n*})$ and K^{n*}, it can be easily shown that $f_K^{n-1} = k$ and $f_L^{n-1} = 0$. Therefore, $dL^{n*}(K^{n*})/d\alpha > 0$ from the above equation and $dK^{n*}/d\alpha > 0$. More heuristically, since an increase in α corresponds to a decrease in the discount rate applied to future profits, the equilibrium stock of capital increases as the opportunity cost of capital falls. Production complementarity yields an increase in the equilibrium stock of labor. Consequently, equilibrium stocks respond in the normal fashion to a change in the discount rate. However, the horizon effect for disequilibrium optimal policies combines with this to make the net result indeterminate in general.

In two situations, the structure of the model is sufficient to determine the sign of $dL^{n^*}/d\alpha$. If initial stocks are in C before the parameter changes, $f_K^{n-1} = k$ and $f_L^{n-1} > 0$. Intuitively, since both labor and capital are to be increased in the second period, an extra unit of capital inherited from the first period is worth its purchase price and an extra unit of inherited labor saves the positive adjustment cost. If α increases, $L^{n^*}(K^{n^*})$ and $y^n(L_0)$ shift outward locally; hence case C still applies.[5] Therefore, $dL^{n^*}/d\alpha > 0$, since $f_L^{n-1} > 0$ and $f_K^{n-1} > 0$. This is the normal case in which optimal policies increase along with equilibrium stocks in response to a decrease in the discount rate, i.e., an increase in α.

Interestingly enough, the other situation producing determinate results shows equilibrium stocks declining, while the optimal labor policy is increasing for a firm in a recessionary phase. If $K \geq K_0$ is effective before and after a change in the parameter, $dL^{n^*}/d\alpha = -f_L^{n-1}/B'$.[6] Now, when α decreases, equilibrium stocks fall and initial stocks of capital that were constraining before the change remain so. Therefore, if case A originally describes the initial conditions of a firm, decreasing α can be shown to lead to an increase in the optimal labor stock. For case A or B, $f_L^{n-1} < 0$ and therefore, $dL^{n^*}/d\alpha < 0$, since $B' < 0$.

It is now clear that sensitivity results depend in a more or less messy way on the taxonomy. To simplify the exposition, two assumptions will be employed from here on. First, parameter changes are assumed not to affect the category into which initial stocks originally fell. Since parameter changes affect the dividing lines in Fig. 2, this means that small changes are being considered, and initial stocks are represented by points that are not too close to the dividing lines. Second, two new cases are defined, each a subset of a previous situation. A' and D' are used to denote regions in which the capital stock is severely constraining; i.e., $K^{n^*}(L_0, K_0) = K_0$, and $K^{n-1^*}(L^{n^*}, \delta K_0) = \delta K_0$. In these extreme disequilibrium situations, $f_K^{n-1} = 0$. The division into A', B, C, D' then corresponds to a division according to the sign of f_K^{n-1}. Remembering that our major interest lies in disequilibrium situations, since policies respond normally in the neighborhood of equilibrium, such a tactic seems justified. Under these two assumptions $dL^{n^*}/d\alpha$ is positive in C and D', negative in A', and indeterminate in B.

Turning to the influence of the rate of depreciation on optimal labor policies, the following proposition can be demonstrated.

---

[5] On the other hand, if α decreases, some situations originally described by case C before the change in α would now fall into some other category due to these shifts.

[6] Essentially, the change in α leaves the capital stock chosen unchanged and, therefore, affects only the optimal labor stock. Here, $B' \equiv R'q_{LL} + q_L^2 R'' - \psi'' + \alpha f_{LL}^{n-1}$.

PROPOSITION 2

$$\frac{dL^{n*}}{d\delta} = \frac{-\alpha f_{LK} K_0}{B'} \qquad\qquad when \ \frac{dK^{n*}}{d\delta} = 0,$$

$$\frac{dL^{n*}}{d\delta} = M\alpha f_{LK}^{n-1} K^{n*} + N(\alpha f_K^{n-1} + \alpha \delta f_{KK}^{n-1}) \qquad otherwise.$$

Proof Now

$$\frac{dK^{n*}}{d\delta} = \frac{-\alpha f_K^{n-1} - \alpha \delta f_{KK}^{n-1} - C'(dL^{n*}/d\delta)}{F'}$$

and

$$\frac{dL^{n*}}{d\delta} = \frac{-\alpha f_{LK}^{n-1} K^{n*} - (dK^{n*}/d\delta)C'}{B'}.$$

Observation, substitution, and rearrangement yield the result.   Q.E.D.

Increased durability of capital will be assumed to correspond to a decrease in the rate of depreciation, i.e., an increase in δ. In other words, the rate of depreciation is taken to be an economic, rather than an accounting measure. Now in B and C, $f_{LK} = 0 = f_{KK}$ and $f_K = k$. Therefore, $dL^{n*}/d\delta > 0$, when $L^{n*}(L_0, K_0)$ and $K^{n*}(L_0, K_0)$ also satisfy case B or C. On the other hand, if $K^*(L_0, K_0) = K_0$ before and after the change in δ, $dL^{n*}/d\delta = Mf_{LK}^{n-1} K_0$. If initial stocks $L^{n*}(L_0, K_0)$ and δK_0 are in D or A, $f_{LK} > 0$ and thus $dL^{n*}/d\delta > 0$. Therefore, an increase in δ, which means a decrease in the economic rate of depreciation $(1 - \delta)$, will increase the optimal labor policy in A', B, C, and D'. Hence, increased durability of capital increases employment demand unambiguously.

The sensitivity of multiperiod input policies to other factor prices can be determined similarly and is reported, without proof, in Proposition 3.

PROPOSITION 3

(a) $\quad \dfrac{dL^{n*}}{dw} = \dfrac{1}{B'} < 0 \qquad\qquad if \ \dfrac{dK^{n*}}{dw} = 0,$

$\quad \dfrac{dL^{n*}}{dw} = \dfrac{F'}{F'B' - (C')^2} < 0 \quad when \ \dfrac{dK^{n*}}{dw} = \dfrac{C'}{F'B' - (C')^2} < 0.$

(b) $\quad \dfrac{dL^{n*}}{dm} = \dfrac{-C'}{F'B' - (C')^2} < 0 \quad when \ \dfrac{dK^{n*}}{dm} = \dfrac{B'}{F'B' - (C')^2} < 0,$

$\quad \dfrac{dL^{n*}}{dm} = 0 \qquad\qquad\qquad when \ \dfrac{dK^{n*}}{dm} = 0.$

TABLE 1

*Effect on Employment Policies of
Parameter Changes*

Case[a]	$d\alpha$	$d\delta$	dm	dw
$A^{\prime b}$	<0	>0	0	<0
B^c	?	>0	<0	<0
C^d	>0	>0	<0	<0
$D^{\prime e}$	>0	>0	0	<0

[a] Taxonomy (partial).
[b] Severely recessionary phase, declining product market.
[c] Undercapitalized, technique too labor-intensive.
[d] Expansionary phase, expanding product market.
[e] Severely overcapitalized, technique too capital-intensive.

V. CONCLUSION: DISEQUILIBRIUM COMPARATIVE STATICS AND MACROECONOMIC POLICY

Table 1 records the sensitivity of disequilibrium employment policies to external parameters. A policy maker using changes in a target interest rate to achieve overall economic objectives should be particularly interested in column 1. The firm's discount factor α is assumed to be indirectly related to the external interest rate. Consequently, a horizon effect combines with revenue complementarity to generate the net effect of interest rate changes on present employment policies. Therefore, decreasing the interest rate increases the equilibrium input stocks and stimulates present demand for labor when the firm is expanding or initially overcapitalized. However, in a severe recessionary phase, a lower interest rate causes short-run contraction of labor demand. It should be noted that this is not caused by substitution of capital for labor. Equilibrium stocks of both inputs increase, but the rate of adjustment to these equilibrium values, still below initial stocks, also increases. The net result is a decrease in the demand for labor in the present period.

This perverse horizon result is important to macroeconomic policy because it suggests a trade-off between short- and long-run objectives due to factor market effects. If input planning policies are more sensitive in the short run to revisions of the discount rate than to increased availability of credit, expansionary monetary policy with a resulting decrease in interest rates will not succeed immediately in reducing unemployment. Quite the contrary, an immediate increase in unemployment would be expected to follow any decrease in the interest rate in periods of severe recession. Although the long-run effects of such a policy stimulate employment by increasing equilibrium labor stocks, present employment demand is depressed. Paradoxically, expansionary fiscal policy with a resulting increase in interest rates due to deficit financing would generate a short-run stimulus to employment demand from both an aggregate demand effect and factor market effects. Unfortunately, the increased interest rate will, *ceteris paribus*, decrease equilibrium input stocks. The conflict between disequilibrium policies and equilibrium stocks in recessionary situations provides a further reason for understanding the microeconomic basis of macroeconomics. The lesson seems to be to avoid misreading immediate results as symptoms of incorrect policy prescriptions.

Other sensitivity results generate interesting links between external conditions and employment demand. From column $d\delta$ in Table 1, any increase in the durability of technology will stimulate employment. Consequently, the rate of unemployment is always negatively related to the durability of capital for the multiperiod monopolist–monopsonist. Several comparative static results are contained in Table 1 for disequilibrium situations. The normal own price effect of wages is recorded in the final column. A symmetric cross-effect exists between the responses of employment policies to changes in the capital maintenance cost and optimal capital stocks to changes in the wage rate.[7] Therefore, normal comparative static results can be extended to the multiperiod case, even when an input is subject to nonseparable adjustment costs. Perhaps Treadway's inability to demonstrate similar results stems from his rather unnatural introduction of adjustment costs directly into the production function.[8]

Finally, we mention the sensitivity of these results to the assumption made. With the exception of the own price effect of wages, everything depends more or less crucially on the assumption of revenue complementarity between inputs. Although at this level of input aggregation, this seems to cover the more normal technical and market conditions, the alternative assumption, an inverse relationship between changes in one input and the marginal revenue product of the other input, is briefly explored. Retaining enough structure to yield a concave functional equation, the directional

[7] Rader [5] shows input gross complementarity under Hicksian normality for the static profit maximizer. To convert the multiperiod monopolist considered here to Rader's case, assume $R'' = 0$. Then, Rader's result is extendable to input stocks in the multiperiod case.

[8] In Treadway [7], one input is freely variable, while the other is subject to adjustment costs. Removing the irreversibility assumption from capital makes input policies always responsive to price changes. The comparative static results then follow directly.

results in columns 2 and 3 of Table 1 would be reversed.[9] The symmetric cross-effect between responses of optimal stocks to price changes would still hold, but with a different sign. With respect to the horizon effect, the results reported in column 1 for A' and D' would be unaffected. However, the directional result in C would become ambiguous, while that in B would be negative. Consequently, the structure developed can be used to derive results under revenue complementarity or substitutability of inputs—whichever seems more appropriate to the problem at hand.

REFERENCES

1. Eisner, R., and Strotz, R. H., Determinants of business investment, *in* "Impacts of Monetary Policy, Commission on Money and Credit." Prentice-Hall, Englewood Cliffs, New Jersey, 1963.
2. Holt, C., Modigliani, F., Muth, J., and Simon, H., "Planning Production, Inventories, and Work Force." Prentice-Hall, Englewood Cliffs, New Jersey, 1960.
3. Iglehart, D., Capital accumulation and production for the firm: Optimal dynamic policies, *Management Sci.* **12** (1965), 193–205.
4. Nerlove, M., Lags in economic behavior, *Econometrica* **40** (2) (1972), 221–253.
5. Rader, T., Normally, factor inputs are never gross substitutes, *J. Pol. Econ.* **76** (1) (1968), 38–43.
6. Treadway, A., Adjustment costs and variable inputs in the theory of the competitive firm, *J. Econ. Theory* **2** (4) (1970), 329–348.
7. Treadway, A., The globally optimal flexible accelerator, *J. Econ. Theory* **7** (1) (1974), 17–40.
8. Zabel, E., Monopoly and uncertainty, *Rev. Econ. Stud.* **37** (110) (1970), 205–221.
9. Zabel, E., Multiperiod monopoly under uncertainty, *J. Econ. Theory* **5** (3) (1973), 524–537.

I wish to express my gratitude to my dissertation adviser at the University of Rochester, Edward Zabel, for his assistance with the structure of the two-state variable dynamic programming model and his continuing help and encouragement. My colleagues, Michael Lovell, Bruce Greenwald, John Conlisk, and Thomson Whitin, have provided many helpful suggestions and ideas. Of course, all errors and omissions are my own.

DEPARTMENT OF ECONOMICS
WESLEYAN UNIVERSITY
MIDDLETOWN, CONNECTICUT

[9] These results and others to be reported here follow from an examination of the previous section. In particular, note that in the proof of Proposition 1, N is defined to depend on C'. The assumption now used reverses the sign of C' to be negative along with f_{LK}. Other signs depend on concavity and are not altered.

A Stable Price Adjustment Process

ANJAN MUKHERJI

I

The only known example of a convergent process of price adjustment under rather general conditions is due to Smale [5]; however, this process involves, at each stage, the Jacobian of the excess demand functions, and, as such, there are two problems associated with it. First of all, this type of information is very difficult to obtain, and second, it is impossible to characterize the situations when a price ought to be raised or lowered. So far as the first point is concerned, it is now known that without such information, it will not be possible to guarantee the convergence of prices, in general (Saari & Simon [4]).

The purpose of the present chapter is to present a process that does not require at each stage of adjustment the Jacobian of the excess demand functions, and yet this process generates prices that approach an equilibrium over time. Clearly, for such a process to work, the excess demand functions must be restricted in some manner. We shall construct such a process and show that the only substantial restriction pertains to the region when all nonnumeraire prices are very small. Moreover, at each stage the rate of price change involves only excess demands and prices, and so one may easily check whether the Walrasian postulate of raising the price of a good in excess demand and lowering the price of a good in excess supply is satisfied.[1]

---

[1] The most general form of price adjustment was studied by McKenzie [2]: It satisfies the Walrasian postulate exactly without introducing any other restriction. He showed that under weak gross substitutes, the process converges.

II

The economy is characterized by the following assumptions regarding excess demand functions:

(A) $E_i(\cdot)$, the excess demand function for the ith commodity, $i = 1, \ldots, n$ is a continuously differentiable function of prices $p = (p_1, \ldots, p_n)$ for all $p \in R_n^+$, the strictly positive orthant of the n-dimensional Euclidean space. In addition, $E_i(p)$ is continuous in p for all $p \geq 0$, $p \neq 0$, and

(i) $E_i(\mu p) = E_i(p)$, $p \geq 0$, $p \neq 0$, $\mu > 0$, for all i;
(ii) $\sum_{i=1}^{n} p_i E_i(p) = 0$ for all $p \geq 0$, $p \neq 0$.

(B) There is a commodity, say n, and a number M such that $\|p\| > M$ with $p_n = 1$ implies $E_n(p) > 0$. This commodity is called the numeraire.

(C) (i) $\exists \delta > 0$ such that $\sum_{j=1}^{n-1} p_j \leq \delta$ and $p_n = 1$ implies

$$E_j(p) > 0 \qquad \text{for all} \quad j$$

and

$$\sum_{j=1}^{n-1} E_j(p) > 2 \left(\sum_{j=1}^{n-1} p_j |E_n(p)| \bigg/ \sum_{j=1}^{n-1} p_j^2 \right);$$

(ii) $\exists \varepsilon > 0$ such that $p_n = 1$, $p_i \leq \varepsilon$; $\sum_{j=1}^{n-1} p_j > \delta \Rightarrow E_i(p) > 0$; and $E_i(p) > |E_n(p)|$ if $E_n(p) < 0$.
(iii) For any $j < n$, $E_j(p(j)) > 0$ where

$$p(j) = (p_1, \ldots, p_{j-1}, 0, p_{j+1}, \ldots, 1).$$

From now on, we shall consider only prices in $D = \{p/p \geq 0, p_n = 1\}$. This is possible by virtue of (Ai). (A) and (B) are standard assumptions and require little comment. (Ci) would be satisfied if $E_j(0, 0, \ldots, 0, 1) > 0$ for all all j and if $\sum_{j=1}^{n-1} p_j |E_n(p)| / \sum_{j=1}^{n-1} p_j \to 0$ as $\sum_{j=1}^{n-1} p_j \to 0$, for example. Notice that $E_n(0, 0, \ldots, 0, 1) = 0$ by virtue of (Aii); so that the above amounts to a restriction on the nature of the excess demand function for the numeraire when all prices are small. (Cii) entails that if some good has a very low price and the other goods have prices that are relatively large, then the good with the low price should be in excess demand and the magnitude of this should be larger than the fixed supply of the numeraire, say; this would ensure (Cii). (Ciii) merely guarantees that a free good is always in excess demand. We shall return to these conditions later on.

III

In the following $\sum$ indicates the sum over j from 1 to $n - 1$ unless otherwise stated. Consider

$$\dot{p}_j = E_j(p) - f(p)|E_j(p)| + p_j E_n(p) \left[1 + \sum p_j^2\right]^{-1}, \qquad j = 1, \ldots, n - 1$$

with $p_n = 1$ and $f(p) = (1 + h)/(1 + h + \sum p_j^2)$, $0 < h < \delta^2/(n - 1)$ where δ is as in (C). We shall demonstrate the validity of the following.

THEOREM There is a solution $p(t, p^0)$ to the above system for any p^0 in D. Further, if p^0 is chosen arbitrarily large in each component j, $j \neq n$, then every limit point to the solution $p(t, p^0)$ is an equilibrium for the economy.

This result will be established via a number of simple claims. Let us write the system as $\dot{p}_j = g_j(p)$. First of all,

1. There is a solution $p(t, p^0)$ to the above system for any p^0 in D.

To guarantee this, we essentially use an argument in Nikaido and Uzawa [3]. Briefly, this is as follows. First of all, since $g_j(p)$ is continuous in p for all $p \in D$, given any $p^0 \in D$, there is a solution $p(t, p^0)$ for some small time interval $[0, s]$, $s > 0$. Next, notice that $p(t, p^0) \in D$ for all $t \in [0, s]$; this follows, since $p_j = 0 \Rightarrow g_j(p) \geq 0$.[2] The fact that $p(t, p^0)$ may now be contained to $[0, +\infty]$ follows from the fact that $g_j(p)$ is bounded in D and so the argument in Nikaido and Uzawa [3, proof of Proposition 1, p. 54] applies.

Consider next, $V(p(t)) = \frac{1}{2}\sum p_j^2(t)$. Then

$$\dot{V}(t) = \sum p_j g_j(p(t))$$

$$= -E_n(p(t)) - f(p)\sum p_j|E_j(p(t))| + E_n(p(t))\frac{\sum p_j^2}{1 + \sum p_j^2}$$

$$= -E_n(p(t))\frac{1}{1 + \sum p_j^2} - f(p)\sum p_j|E_j(p(t))|. \tag{1}$$

We are now ready for

2. For any p^0 in D, $p(t, p^0)$ is bounded.

First, notice that $\sum p_j(t) > \delta$ for all t. This follows, since

$$\sum p_j(t) = \delta \Rightarrow \sum g_j(p) = (1 - f(p))\sum E_j(p) + E_n(p)\frac{\sum p_j}{1 + \sum p_j^2}$$

$$= \frac{\sum p_j^2}{1 + h + \sum p_j^2}\sum E_j(p) + E_n(p)\frac{\delta}{1 + \sum p_j^2}$$

$$> \frac{\delta}{1 + \sum p_j^2}|E_n(p)| + E_n(p)\frac{\delta}{1 + \sum p_j^2} \geq 0,$$

[2] $p_j = 0 \Rightarrow g_j(p) = (1 - f(p))E_j(p)$, where $f(p) \leq 1$ and $E_j(p) > 0$, by (Ciii). This is the counterpart of the proof of Lemma 3 in [3, p. 54]. For the proof of [3] Proposition 1, the crucial property is the boundedness of the functions $g_j(p)$; this is obtained by virtue of the continuity of the excess demand functions on the unit simplex and hence on D. See, for instance [3, Lemma 1]. For an alternative method of approach to the problem of existence of solution to the differential equation system, see footnote 4 below.

the penultimate step follows by (Ci), and since $2(1 + \sum p_j^2) > (1 + h + \sum p_j^2)$. Thus $\sum \dot{p}_j(t) = \delta \Rightarrow \sum g_j(p) > 0 \Rightarrow \sum \dot{p}_j(t) > 0 \Rightarrow \sum p_j(t) > \delta$ for all t. Further, $p_i(t) > \varepsilon$ for all i. This follows since $p_i(t) = \varepsilon$, $p_n = 1$, and $\sum p_j(t) > \delta$ (just established) $\Rightarrow E_i(p) > |E_n(p)|$ by (Cii). Without any loss of generality, we may take $\varepsilon < h/2$. Thus $\frac{1}{2} > \varepsilon/h > \varepsilon/(h + 1)$; hence

$$E_i(p) > [\varepsilon/h + \varepsilon/(h + 1)]|E_n(p)|$$
$$> p_i[1/h + 1/(1 + \sum p_j^2)]|E_n(p)|,$$

since

$$\sum p_j > \delta \Rightarrow \sum p_j^2 > \delta^2/(n - 1) \geq h.$$

Thus

$$E_i(p)\frac{h}{1 + h + \sum p_j^2} > \frac{p_i}{1 + \sum p_j^2}|E_n(p)|$$

from which it follows that $g_i(p) > 0$ or $\dot{p}_i > 0$. So along the solution path, the prices are bounded below.

Next, let $\|p(t, p^0)\| \to +\infty$. So, by (B), $E_n(p(t)) > 0$ for all $t > T$, say; from (1) it then follows that $\dot{V} < 0$ for all $t > T$, and this contradicts $\|p(t, p^0)\| \to +\infty$. This establishes the claim.

3. $\dot{V}(p(t)) = 0 \Rightarrow p(t) \in Z = \{p^*/E_j(p^*) = 0 \text{ for all } j\}$.

From (1),

$$\dot{V}(p(t)) = 0 \Leftrightarrow -E_n(p(t))(1 + \sum p_j^2)^{-1} = f(p)\sum p_j|E_j(p(t))|;$$

suppose that $E_n(p(t)) \neq 0$; then $E_n(p(t)) < 0$, and

$$\frac{\sum p_j|E_j(p(t))|}{-E_n(p(t))} = \frac{1 + h + \sum p_j^2}{(1 + h)(1 + \sum p_j^2)} < 1$$

since $h\sum p_j^2 > 0$. Hence, $\sum p_j|E_j(p(t))| < -E_n(p(t)) = \sum p_j E_j(p(t))$, a contradiction. So $\dot{V} = 0$ implies $E_n(p(t)) = 0$; hence $\sum p_j|E_j(p(t))| = 0$; also, since $p_j(t) > \varepsilon > 0$, it must be the case that $E_j(p(t)) = 0$ for all j and $p(t) \in Z$.

Proof of the Theorem Choose $p^0 \in D$ such that the components of p^0 are arbitrarily large and in particular, $\|p^0\| > M$, where M is as in B. Then $E_n(p^0) > 0$. We have shown that there is a solution $p(t, p^0)$ through p^0 and that the solution is bounded. Thus limit points exist. Let p^* be one such; i.e., there is a subsequence $p(t_s)$, $p(t_s) \to p^*$ as $s \to \infty$.

Since $E_n(p^0) > 0$, it follows that $\dot{V}(p(t)) < 0$ for t close to zero. By virtue of 3, it is true that $\dot{V}( ) < 0$ for all t, since otherwise $p(t, p^0)$ passes through an equilibrium. Thus $V(p(t, p^0))$ is monotone decreasing and hence $V(p(t, p^0))$ converges since $V(\ )$ is known to be bounded below by 2.

We assert[3] that under the present circumstances, $\dot{V}(p(t, p^0)) \to 0$ as $t \to \infty$. Since $p(t_s, p^0) \to p^*$ as $s \to \infty$ and since $\dot{V}(p(t, p^0))$ is continuous in p, $\dot{V}(p(t_s, p^0)) \to \dot{V}(p^*)$ as $s \to \infty$. But $\dot{V}(p(t, p^0)) \to 0$ as $t \to \infty$; hence $\dot{V}(p^*) = 0$. Thus from 3, $E_n(p^*) = 0$ and since $p_i(t) > \varepsilon$ for all i, $p_i^* > 0$ for all i; hence $E_j(p^*) = 0$ for all j and $p^* \in Z$. This proves the theorem.

IV

We conclude by indicating the following facts about the process discussed above:

1. It is very easy to characterize the situations when prices are raised or lowered. For example, if $E_n(p) > 0$, then the price of a good in excess demand is always raised; if $E_n(p) < 0$, then the price of a good in excess supply is always lowered. Moreover if $E_n(p) > 0$ and $E_j(p) < 0$, $\dot{p}_j < 0$ whenever

$$\frac{2(1 + h) + \sum p_j^2}{1 + h + \sum p_j^2} E_j(p) + E_n(p) \frac{\sum p_j}{1 + \sum p_j^2} < 0,$$

and this would be true for some j at least, since $\sum p_j, \dot{p}_j < 0$ when $E_n(p) > 0$. So the Walrasian postulate mentioned at the beginning is usually met. In any case, since no derivatives are involved, it is easy to identify the situations where prices are raised or lowered.

2. To implement a process such as the one discussed in the last section, we have to know δ. We intend to discuss in a later work the implications of choosing some approximate value for δ. However, for the present, note that the only restrictions are the ones where prices are small, and it is in this region that detailed information is required.

3. Although the convergence exhibited in the last section is weaker than the one in Smale [5], notice that we may get multiple limit points only in

---

[3] Under the present circumstances, $\dot{V}(t)$ cannot be bounded away from zero and so $\dot{V}(t_s) \to 0$ for some subsequence (t_s). However, if there is another limit point $-\theta < 0$, then it may be shown that

$$\ddot{V}^+(t) = \lim_{h \to 0_+} \frac{\dot{V}(t + h) - \dot{V}(t)}{h} \quad \text{or} \quad \ddot{V}^-(t) = \lim_{h \to 0_-} \frac{\dot{V}(t + h) - \dot{V}(t)}{h}$$

must become unbounded. It is tedious to check that $\ddot{V}^+(t)$ and $\ddot{V}^-(t)$ are continuous functions of p (since they involve only $\dot{p}_j$ and $\dot{E}_j$), and since $p(t)$ may be taken to lie in a compact set, it follows that $\ddot{V}^+(t)$ and $\ddot{V}^-(t)$ are bounded. Thus no other limit point $-\theta < 0$ can exist. Since $\dot{V}(t) < 0$ for all t, the assertion in the text follows.

the improbable situation of there being multiple equilibria all equidistant from the origin. This follows immediately from the method of proof involving the convergence of the function $V(\ )$.

And finally, a word about the boundary conditions:

4.   We have seen that (Ci) is satisfied if $\sum p_j \cdot E_n(p)/\sum p_j^2 \to 0$ as $\sum p_j \to 0$. In fact, so long as $\sum p_j \cdot E_n(p)/\sum p_j^2$ remains bounded as $\sum p_j \to 0$, it may be reasonable to expect that the inequality in (Ci) is true at $(0, 0, \ldots, 1)$ and hence holds for some δ small. This appears to be the only substantive restriction in the paper.[4] We like to see, next, how this compares with the boundary conditions in Smale [5]; on one point the difference is clear; we do not require the nonsingularity of the Jacobian of the excess demand functions on the boundary.

There is another problem in Smale [5], viz., the "extended boundary condition" is never made explicit. Smale introduces a boundary condition on E thus: for $p \in \partial R_{n-1}^+$ let J_p denote the set of indices for which $p_i = 0$; then the system of linear equations

$$\sum_{j=1}^{n-1} E_{kj} v_j = -E_k, \qquad k = 1, \ldots, n-1,$$

where E_{kj} are the usual partial derivatives of E_k with respect to the jth price, have an unique solution $v_1, \ldots, v_{n-1}$, and $v_i > 0$ for $i \in J_p$. But in Theorem C, Smale requires the extended boundary condition; all that we are told about this condition is contained in the following: "Now extend the boundary condition to the numeraire good or to all $l+1$ prices and commodities to obtain the extended boundary condition on ζ" [5, p. 116]. If one were to interpret this in a straightforward manner, one should insist that

$$\sum_{j=1}^{n} E_{kj} v_j = -E_k, \qquad k = 1, \ldots, n$$

---

[4] It should be pointed out at this stage that (Ciii) is, strictly speaking not essential. We could have considered the modified system

$$\dot{p}_j = \begin{cases} g_j(p) & \text{if } p_j \neq 0 \\ \max(0, g_j(p)) & \text{if } p_j = 0 \end{cases} \qquad j = 1, \ldots, n-1$$

with $p_n = 1$. For such a system, there would be a solution $p(t, p^0)$ for any $p^0 \in D$; this follows from the work of Henry [1] and since our functions g_j satisfy his conditions (viz., continuity and boundedness on D). Next, by virtue of our claim 2., since for any solution $p(t, p^0)$, $p_j(t) \geq \varepsilon$, it is clear that the above modification will never be needed. I am indebted to Jerry Green for this suggestion.

should have an unique solution $v_1, \ldots, v_n$ with $v_i > 0$ for $i \in J_p$. This, however, is *never* satisfied; this is due to the fact that the matrix $(E_{kj}), k, j = 1, \ldots, n$ is singular, by virtue of homogeneity. In these circumstances the only way to include the numeraire price and good in the boundary condition is to require that

$$\sum_{j=1}^{n-1} E_{kj} v_j = -E_k, \qquad k = 1, \ldots, n-1$$

have an unique solution $v_1, \ldots, v_{n-1}$ with $v_i > 0$ for $i \in J_p$ for any collection of $n - 1$ goods and prices. Of course, the heuristic explanation in Smale [5], shows that our (C), and the boundary condition used by Smale are similar in that the intuitive appeal for both lies on common ground, viz., that goods with small prices have large excess demands. We make this explicit through alternative channels. Finally, it should be pointed out that these restrictions should be carefully employed; consider the claim. "If ξ satisfies G.S., then $D\xi(p)$ is non-singular for all price systems p" [5, p. 116, last paragraph]. This is then taken to be true on the boundary and is shown to lead to Theorem E [5, p. 117]. However, there is a problem in that G.S. cannot be extended to the boundary. For, consider $p(i) = (p_1, \ldots, p_{i-1}, 0, p_{i+1}, \ldots, p_n)$. Then $E_i(p(i)) = E_i(2p(i))$ by homogeneity, whereas $E_i(p(i)) < E_i(2(p(i)))$ by G.S., and usually the former property of excess demand functions is taken to be the more basic one. So the nonsingularity of $D\xi(p)$ on the boundary does not seem to be guaranteed by invoking G.S. Although this a minor point, it is worth noting precisely because it uncovers the problems that one faces when prices go to zero.

REFERENCES

1. Henry, C., Differential equations with discontinuous right-hand side, *J. Econ. Theory* **4** (1972), 545–551.
2. McKenzie, L. W. Stability of equilibrium and the value of positive excess demand, *Econometrica* **28** (1960), 606–617.
3. Nikaido, H. and Uzawa, H. Stability and non-negativity in a Walrasian tatonnement Process, *Int. Econ. Rev.*, **1** (1960), 50–59.
4. Saari, D. G. and Simon, C. P. Effective Price Mechanisms, Discussion Paper No. 259. Centre for Mathematical Studies in Economics and Management Science, Northwestern Univ. (1976).
5. Smale, S., A convergent process of price adjustment and global Newton methods, *J. Math. Econ.* **3** (1976), 107–120.

I am deeply indebted to Avner Shaked, Jerry Green, Hugo Sonnenschein and Carl Simon for comments, criticisms, and very helpful suggestions. An earlier version was presented to the

Mathematical Economics Seminar at Cambridge University and comments and suggestions from Douglas Gale and Oliver Hart are gratefully acknowledged.

CENTER FOR ECONOMIC STUDIES AND PLANNING
JAWAHARLAL NEHRU UNIVERSITY
NEW DELHI, INDIA

Price Adjustment in a Competitive Market and the Securities Exchange Specialist

JAMES BRADFIELD

EDWARD ZABEL

I. INTRODUCTION

It is a commonplace that the theory of pure competition is incomplete. Essentially, since each trader in the economy is a price-taker, the theory cannot explain the determination of prices, except by appeal to devices exogenous to the theory, e.g., tâtonnement processes or, to use more colorful terminology, the invisible hand. Kenneth Arrow, for example, has argued, "Each individual participant in the economy is supposed to take prices as given and determine his choices as to purchases and sales accordingly; there is no one left over whose job it is to make a decision on price" [1, p. 143]. Numerous other economists have voiced similar complaints. Surprisingly, only a few theorists have risen to the challenge of completing the theory of pure competition, and no satisfactory resolution has emerged.[1]

The modest objective in this paper is to study the behavior of a price-maker in a competitive market as a preliminary step to a more complete

---

[1] However, this problem and related questions are now attracting considerable attention. Survey articles by McCall [14], Rothschild [17], and Lippman and McCall [12] discuss numerous recent studies. Other relevant work is developed in papers by Fisher [7, 8], Obst [15, 16], Barro [2], and Hurwicz *et al.* [9].

analysis of pure competition. Moreover, the focus of the paper is quite different from the standard approach to a study of competitive markets. In the standard approach the determination of competitive equilibrium prices is emphasized. Stability of the system is studied by invoking the invisible hand, i.e., by examining properties of some ad hoc price adjustment process in which, with some exceptions, trading is not allowed until equilibrium is achieved. While the undefined agency that adjusts prices may be confounded by properties of demand and supply relationships, its single-minded objective is the attainment of a predetermined equilibrium: It dutifully increases price when excess demand is positive and reduces price when excess demand is negative.[2]

The emphasis here is the study of a trading process in which transactions may occur each period of some horizon. All participants, including a price-maker, are interested in their own gains, and exchanges are made whenever the announced price is mutually acceptable to two or more individuals. No one has a motivation to establish a competitive equilibrium. In particular, while the price-maker is required to take a "position" in the market, he is not obligated to balance the price-takers' demands and supplies. Consequently, no one attempts to steer the system in any direction, except indirectly as adjustments are made in the pursuit of individual gains. While we may choose to equate equilibrium with underlying stationary characteristics of the system, an important distinction is that a definition of equilibrium is irrelevant to a study of the trading process. Moreover, since the objective is to examine the period-by-period operation of the system, no sharp distinction between equilibrium analysis and stability analysis is needed.

To lend support to our approach to price-making in pure competition, we offer a description and analysis of a real-world market with features approximating the economist's notion of a competitive process. Specifically, we turn to a discussion of price formation on an organized security exchange, using the specialist system to facilitate trading. The *specialist* is a price-maker

---

[2] Naturally, the absence of an explicit price-maker is most apparent in stability analysis. In his discussion of the "Law of Supply and Demand," Kenneth Arrow offers the following comment, "It asserts that price rises when demand exceeds supply and falls in the contrary case . . . however, the Law is not on the same logical level as the hypotheses underlying equation 1 (the demand and supply functions). It is not explained whose decision it is to change prices in accordance with equation 3 (the Law of Supply and Demand)," [1, p. 43]. Tjalling Koopmans's remark is also relevant; "If, . . . the net rate of increase in price is assumed to be proportional to the excess of demand over supply, whose behavior is thereby expressed? And how is that behavior motivated? And is the alternative hypothesis, that the rate of increase in supply is proportional to excess of demand price over supply price any more plausible, or any better traceable to behavior motivation?" [10, p. 179].

in a particular security who has exclusive knowledge of a collection of offers to buy or sell, which arrive randomly throughout the day. He is required to maintain "a fair and orderly market" in that security by trading for his own account. In the next section we provide a brief description of activities in such a securities market. In Section III we construct a model of the specialist's activities that lends some insight into the trading process and price formation. Section IV derives stationary properties of the probability distribution of prices in the market and the probability distribution of the specialist's inventory holdings of the security. Section V briefly introduces an extension of the model. Section VI is a concluding section which discusses further extensions of the research. An appendix provides various proofs.

II. THE TRADING PROCESS

An organized security exchange (stock market) is often cited as an example of a real-world purely competitive market. With some reservations, important requirements of a competitive market are satisfied. Shares of a particular security are obviously homogeneous, a large number of small traders submit offers to buy or sell, and at any moment within the trading day transactions occur at single prices announced for purchases and sales (the bid and the ask). A major reservation concerns block trading of mutual funds and other large investors. The fixed number of shares outstanding in any security creates possibilities of "corners" or "takeovers," and "insider information" may disrupt trading. Moreover, controversy exists about the "monopoly" power of the specialist (we comment on this charge later in the paper). On balance, the degree of departure from pure competition is unclear, but, in any event, we plan to focus attention on the competitive features of the trading process.

Trading on the exchange is governed by offers, or tenders, submitted by investors through brokers.[3] The most popular tender is a *market order*, an offer to buy or sell a specified quantity of shares at the best price available when the order reaches the trading floor. A market order must be executed immediately, which is made possible by the existence of other market orders, trading by the specialist, and *limit orders*. A limit order is an offer to buy some amount of shares at a price no more than (or sell at a price no less than) a specified limit price. For example, a limit buy order for 100 shares

---

[3] This brief description of trading activities on organized security exchanges has been derived from several sources. Detailed expositions are provided in a Securities and Exchange Commission report [18], Leffler and Farwell [11], and West and Tinic [22]. The study by Baumol [3] emphasizes the specialists' role as price-makers.

at 48 is an offer to buy 100 shares for no more than $48 per share. Each security has a single specialist assigned to it.[4] At each moment the specialist holds a collection of unexecuted limit orders, called the book. Once the market is open to trading, the minimum limit sell price must exceed the maximum limit buy price; otherwise some limit orders could be "crossed" with others and thus removed from the book.

The mechanism that generates actual transactions and prices involves a "double auction" procedure, which is guided by the specialist. A trading day consists of a sequence of double auctions. Each auction is begun by the specialist who quotes two prices: a bid and an ask. The bid is the maximum price at which some trader is now standing ready to buy shares. On the other side of the market, the ask is the minimum price at which some trader is ready to sell shares. The specialist has considerable freedom in establishing a double quotation. He may simply quote the maximum limit buy price and the minimum limit sell price directly from his book. He may also quote the quantities available from the book at these prices. Alternatively, the specialist may choose to "narrow the spread" on the book by offering to trade for his own account. In effect, the specialist is adding limit buy and sell orders of his own to those already on the book.

Trading may occur at prices other than the bid and ask. A broker at the trading post with a market order may attempt to arrange an exchange within the bid and the ask among other available traders. These traders may raise and lower the bid and the ask until an agreement is reached, thus participating in the "double auction." However, in this process the broker with a market order runs the risk of "missing the market." If the broker fails to conclude an exchange before the specialist changes the bid and the ask to his disadvantage, and if the customer can prove that his broker delayed unnecessarily in executing the order, the broker may be required to guarantee the missed price to the customer. Indeed, the need to process other market orders at other trading posts will also inhibit long delays by the broker before he submits the order to the specialist for execution.

The outline of the trading process sketched above does not sufficiently emphasize the key role of the specialist in the formation of prices. He has a variety of opportunities and responsibilities as a price-maker. Exchange rules require the specialist to maintain "a fair and orderly market." Since no exact definition exists of what constitutes a fair and orderly market, the specialist enjoys considerable freedom in calling prices. The rules do require

---

[4] Some specialist firms make markets for more than one security. A few securities are traded by more than one specialist unit, but these specialists share the same trading post rather than being competitive. Recently, however, the practice of registering more than one competing specialist for a given group of securities has been instituted on a limited scale (Wall Street Journal [20]).

him to participate in trading to achieve this goal, but apart from restrictions prohibiting the specialist from ignoring the priority of orders left in his keeping in order to trade for his own account, and some reference to imprecise criteria to evaluate his activities (which we discuss later), he may select the bid and the ask with impunity. As noted earlier, he may narrow the spread on the book by quoting for his own account a bid and an ask that lie within the maximum limit buy price and the minimum limit sell price. Or he may choose to narrow the spread by taking a single position, quoting, say, a bid for his own account which is just below the minimum limit sell price on the book. In that case the book and the specialist each determine one side of the market.

A particularly powerful move the specialist can make is "reaching across the market." Here the specialist trades for his own account directly with the book in a volume sufficient to satisfy all the limit orders on the book at prices above or below some particular price. For example, if the maximum limit buy price is, say, 50, and the minimum limit sell price is 51, he may eliminate the entire tier of sell orders at 51 by purchasing the shares for his own account, thereby raising the minimum limit sell price without affecting the maximum limit buy price. The specialist is then likely to narrow this spread with new quotes for his own account, but the point is that he is not restricted to narrowing the spread, or making a market, within the confines of the book. He may shift the book.

Another powerful role played by the specialist is in opening the day's trading in his security. While trading is prohibited prior to the opening bell, investors may nevertheless submit orders before the opening quotations. The specialist's day begins with an accumulation of orders that have collected since closing on the previous day. These will include unexecuted limit orders, new limit orders, and market orders requiring immediate execution. Rather than have a press of brokers, all scurrying to execute market orders at the opening, these market orders are submitted to the specialist who arbitrates a single opening price. The market is thus opened not with bid and ask quotes but with the announcement of a "transaction"—so many shares at a specific price. All accumulated market orders must be executed at this price. Moreover, all eligible limit orders on the book must be satisfied at the same price. Thus the act of opening the market clears the book of any overlap among limit buy and sell orders. While the specialist is free to choose any opening price, he is obligated to absorb any excess demand at that price by trading for his own account.

Earlier, we made reference to criteria sometimes invoked by Exchange officials or others in evaluating the specialist's performance in conducting a fair and orderly market. However, it should be emphasized that these criteria do not constitute hard and fast rules of performance. First is the maintenance of narrow spreads. Obviously, brokers favor narrow spreads to reduce the cost of trading to their customers. Second is a property called depth. A bid of 50 is said to have depth if there are enough limit buy orders at 50 so that a considerable volume of market sell orders may enter the market and be executed without driving the price below 50. Similarly one could speak of "depth at the ask." To provide depth, Exchange officials encourage specialists to trade for their own accounts. Thus, if the specialist quotes a bid from the book at a price that has very few limit buy orders, he should be prepared to support that bid by trading for his own account. Equally, if the quoted bid is for his own account initially, he must support that bid in some depth. For the market order investor this has the advantage that he can be reasonably confident that his order will be executed near the last price that appeared on the tape prior to his order.

It is also important for the specialist to be able to change the quotes at which he stands ready to provide depth, which leads to the third property: continuity. The idea here is that the specialist should not permit the price to change by large jumps between subsequent transactions. In a declining market, for example, he should buy for his own account at each step on the way down so that even in the event of voluminous sell orders the price falls "continuously" rather than by sizable increments. A fourth property by which specialists might be judged is the range within which the price fluctuates. Some specialists have testified that they consider their opening price successful if during the day the price does not depart too far from the level at which it opened.

The literature suggests that narrow spreads and depth are the constraints that have most force. The burden of maintaining continuity in price is difficult to enforce and is relieved to some extent by the occasional practice of a halt in trading. The property of range of price is not emphasized and in practice does not appear to have much weight. Generally, despite the fact that narrow spreads and depth tend to be genuine constraints, Exchange officials take a very expansive view of what is necessary to maintain a fair and orderly market.

In brief, the system appears to operate in the following fashion. Market and limit orders arrive randomly throughout the day, joining a queue for execution. The specialist has the responsibility of calling the bid and the ask, which he may adjust periodically during trading hours. Most trades occur at the bid and the ask, but some brokers may negotiate exchanges within the spread. The specialist has an obligation to support the bid and the ask prices by trading for his own account to satisfy excess demand. His duty here as the trader of last resort is essential to the immediate execution of market orders. While market orders are only revealed during the course of trading, the specialist does have exclusive knowledge of the accumulation of limit orders, the book. Various rules exist to constrain his activities, some emphasized more than others, but enforcement tends to be lax, allowing the specialist considerable freedom in calling prices.

In this process the specialist clearly provides a valuable service. His announcement and support of prices enables traders, who so desire, to obtain immediate execution of orders. In providing this service he bears the cost of waiting (holding charges on his inventory of securities and the risk of capital losses). Part of his reward derives from the spread, the returns he earns by arranging purchases at the bid and sales at the ask. He also shares brokerage commissions. A less obvious source of revenue is the increased opportunity of capital gains open to him by the informational advantage available in his exclusive knowledge of the book.[5]

Perhaps rightly, charges of monopoly have centered on the service the specialist provides in arranging immediate exchanges and in the reward he receives in the bid–ask markup.[6] While it is clear that some competitive pressures exist to limit the size of the spread chosen by the specialist, their combined force is not well known. Brokers at the trading post do attempt to arrange exchanges inside the bid and the ask, some trading occurs privately and at other exchanges, like securities offer opportunities for substitute trades, and other market trading procedures are now available or in the planning stages, particularly for block trading.

With some qualification, the specialist's monopoly power does appear to reside in whatever freedom he has in establishing the spread between the bid and the ask. He does not command the favored position of the traditional monopolist or monopsonist in that he has no direct control over either demand or supply of securities. As he accommodates the flow of orders originating with customers, he influences demand and supply only indirectly as he announces prices and arranges trades. Qualification arises on two counts. He does acquire shares of the security, and his accumulation may become sizable. Moreover, his exclusive knowledge of the book gives him unique opportunities to exploit market conditions and predict future orders. With these reservations in mind, it would seem that the specialist more closely resembles the retailer with few competitors than the traditional monopolist or monopsonist.

[5] Demsetz has described the service provided by the specialist as follows: "Predictable immediacy is a rarity in human actions, and to approximate it requires that costs be borne by persons who specialize in standing ready and waiting to trade with the incoming orders of those who demand immediate servicing of orders. The ask-bid spread is the markup that is paid for predictable immediacy of exchange in organized markets; in other markets, it is the inventory markup of retailer or wholesaler" [6, pp. 35–36].

[6] West and Tinic [22, Chap. 6] provide a lucid discussion and evaluation of the specialist's advantage in choosing the bid–ask spread.

As we noted earlier, in constructing a model we plan to emphasize the competitive features of the system with regard to the generation of orders by customers. In fact, the system appears to work best under essentially competitive conditions—a large number of small traders submitting a steady stream of offers throughout the day.[7] Since the specialist is obligated to absorb excess demand, he must depend on the flow of buy and sell orders to offset his position in securities. While he may encourage trading by adjusting price, he may not actively solicit orders if volume is low. When the security is inactive, it becomes difficult for the specialist to adjust his inventory of shares, and the cost of waiting, which he bears, tends to become large (along with reductions in revenue). Specialists have testified that they are reluctant to take positions in inactive stocks. Similarly, the cost of waiting also tends to become large, relative to revenues, when volume is sufficient, but the size distribution of orders has a large variance, which is one consequence of block trading by large investors.[8]

III. THE SPECIALIST'S ACTIVITIES
AND SECURITY PRICES

Some earlier efforts have been made to simulate selected features of trading on a securities exchange. However, these simulations do not attempt to provide any explanation of price adjustment by a price-maker. Stigler [19] introduces a limit order model in which single offers to buy or sell a unit of shares at specified prices are generated randomly. Offers are accumulated and a transaction occurs at the bid whenever a bid exceeds an ask; otherwise no exchange occurs. This process generates a sequence of transaction prices that vary around an average price. Stigler makes no mention of a broker in this process, but clearly some agent is needed to collect information and execute transactions. West [21] extends Stigler's model to include market orders and an explicit agent, the specialist. The specialist announces bid and ask prices and guarantees trades in the absence of offsetting limit orders within the spread. This model again generates a sequence of transaction prices, but the bid and the ask and price adjustments are chosen arbitrarily. A recent paper by Logue [13] does present a careful

---

[7] Exchange rules provide some presumption of competitive conditions. Firms eligible for listing on an exchange must have a minimum number of outstanding shares (1,000,000 on the New York Stock Exchange) and a minimum number of shareholders (2000 on the New York Stock Exchange). However, no limitation on the size distribution of shareholding is imposed.

[8] On the other side of the coin, it would seem to be a costly and/or perilous venture for customers to submit market orders in inactive securities or ones subject to block trading. The spread tends to vary inversely with volume of trading, and sizable buy or sell orders could lead to large, sudden changes in prices (or halts in trading).

discussion of gains the specialist earns as a price-maker, in contrast to the usual emphasis on the bid–ask spread, but he does not provide any explicit rationale for a price policy.

The emphasis here is the specialist's choice of a price policy in a competitive process. We assume that the specialist chooses prices sequentially to maximize expected profits over some horizon, under the constraint of absorbing excess demand by trading for his own account. In this initial effort we consider a simplified process that we believe illustrates essential features of price-making in a competitive market and also enables us to obtain explicit properties of long-run price variability. A particular simplification is that we do not attempt to explain the spread here. To do so adequately, we believe, would require some explicit consideration of competitive forces limiting the spread. Thus we assume that the specialist chooses single prices rather than separate bid and ask prices. This procedure does not neglect the spread entirely, since it is easy to show that the choice of single prices is qualitatively equivalent to the choice of bid and ask prices with a fixed spread. We explain this claim in more detail in the next section.

Throughout the paper we assume that limit and market orders are represented by independent, stationary random processes with properties analogous to riskless excess demand functions. We also make the extreme assumption that these processes are known to the specialist.[9] This assumption does allow us to capture the current advantage the specialist gains by exclusive knowledge of the book but not the edge he has in learning about any unknown properties of random processes generating orders. Moreover, we assume that these random processes are not affected by any efforts to second guess the specialist's price policy, which seems reasonable to us. First, vital information is not available to traders: the book and the specialist's own position in a security.[10] Second, attempts by the small trader to predict the specialist's behavior would appear to be very costly (in terms of collecting and processing information), relative to possible gains.[11]

As noted earlier, the specialist has several sources of revenue: possible capital gains, the return on the bid–ask spread, and commissions shared with brokers. We explicitly take into account the capital gains he may earn on his inventory of securities. Again, as we explain later, we also implicitly

[9] Alternately, we could suppose that the specialist forms subjective estimates of these random processes and does not revise his estimates. The interpretation of the text is preferable later in making comparisons with an alternative pricing mechanism.

[10] The announcement of transactions gives the total number of shares traded, not the separate dealings of the specialist and customers. Thus, information about the specialist's holding of a security is not generally available.

[11] Even for the large investor, it is not clear that attempts to second guess the specialist would be profitable in the absence of information about the book and the specialist's inventory of the security.

account for the return on a fixed bid–ask spread (which could include an allowance for fixed commissions). As we also noted, the specialist has one important variable cost: charges associated with management of his portfolio of securities. Since all traders, including the specialist, settle accounts at the end of the day, the relevant inventory of a security is the "overnight position." A trader whose sales exceed his ownership of shares borrows stock certificates to settle his account, carrying a negative or "short" position. A trader who owns shares at the end of the day has a positive or "long" overnight position. Either position imposes costs on the specialist, including explicit costs of financing and implicit costs of any imbalances in his portfolio of various securities caused by his obligation to satisfy excess demand.[12]

Inventory costs clearly provide some incentive for the specialist to duplicate the activities of the auctioneer in a tâtonnement process. For example, an observation of large negative excess demand today, which increases inventory, lends some encouragement to the specialist to reduce future prices. Nevertheless, the association of price decreases with current negative excess demand is tenuous. Negative excess demand combined with an extreme short position inherited from the past may signal future price increases rather than the reverse. The accumulation of past excess demands, the specialist's position, is obviously more relevant in forecasting prices than a current observation. Similarly, the specialist's efforts to earn capital gains by exploiting the book and his inventory of securities may also induce price movements that are opposite to those indicated by the sign of current excess demand.

With this background, we specify the model in detail. The horizon consists of an infinite number of *trading days* with each day divided into a finite number N of *trading periods* (double auctions). The specialist opens each period by announcing a price. He must then absorb whatever excess demand exists among the limit orders currently on the book and the market orders that arrive during the period. Thus the specialist guarantees a specific price for a discrete time interval. Adjustments in the book that occur during the period are not considered for execution until the beginning of next period. Accordingly, the book is revised only once per period. Market orders that arrive during the period are executed immediately. Hence no unexecuted market orders remain at the close of the period.

Market orders and limit orders are represented by excess demand functions, which are linear, additive random processes. Given p as the price announced by the specialist, market orders arriving during a period satisfy the excess demand function $M(p) + \xi$, where $M(p)$ is linear with negative

---

[12] West and Tinic [22, Chap. 6] discuss inventory costs of the specialist's position in some detail and suggest that marginal inventory costs are increasing for both long and short positions.

slope and ξ is a random disturbance with a zero mean and finite variance. Similarly, the set of limit orders on the book at the beginning of any future period satisfies the excess demand function $L(p) + \beta$, where $L(p)$ and β have analogous properties. These random processes are stationary, and the disturbances are independently distributed over time and of each other. As we observe later in this section, we could allow interdependence between the disturbance terms without changing the qualitative form of price behavior.

In this framework the specialist observes outcomes of the random variables β and ξ once each period. The book is observed at the beginning of a period prior to the announcement of a price, and if b is the current observation of β, the book is expressed by the excess demand function $L(p) + b$. The observation b will serve as the variable describing the state of the book. The outcome of ξ, the random component of market orders, is learned only after a price is chosen. Combining market and limit orders, the total expected excess demand is then given by

$$M(p) + L(p) = Ap + a \tag{1}$$

where $A < 0$ and $a > 0$ are constants.

As mentioned earlier, West and Tinic [22] suggest that marginal inventory cost is increasing for both long and short overnight positions. To preserve the simplicity of the model and yet to incorporate increasing marginal cost, we represent inventory charges by the quadratic function

$$S(z) = \tfrac{1}{2}cz^2 \tag{2}$$

where $c > 0$ is constant and z is the number of shares in the overnight position. Naturally, the function $S(z)$ does not fully express the structure of overnight costs. In particular, overnight costs will depend on the closing price of the security, as well as on the quantity of shares.

We adopt one other simplifying assumption. We suppose that prices are unrestricted. The gain here is that first-order optimality conditions are now always expressed by interior equalities. We should emphasize that the usefulness of other simplifications hinges on ignoring the nonnegativity of prices. We have experimented with models including nonnegative prices, more general random processes generating orders, and more general inventory cost functions. But it is then much more difficult to obtain explicit properties of the long-run distribution of prices. We shall report on these results elsewhere.

The specialist's problem of choosing prices sequentially to maximize expected trading profits may now be described by a set of N stochastic functional equations. Each member of the set expresses the problem of choosing a price at the beginning of a trading period and takes into account the entire future. Since inventory costs are charged only at the end of a day, each functional equation will depend on the time of the day, the current inventory of shares of the security, and the state of the book. Accordingly, define $F_i(x, b)$ as the maximum expected return over an infinite horizon when i periods remain in the current day, x gives the inventory of shares, and b specifies the state of the book. To express overnight inventory costs, only the equation for the final trading period of the day (period 1) explicitly accounts for inventory charges. Thus, we obtain the set of equations

$$F_i(x, b) = \max_p \left\{ p(Ap + a + b) + \iint F_{i-1}(x - Ap - a - b - \xi, \beta) \, d\Phi(\xi) \, d\Psi(\beta) \right\},$$

$$1 < i \leqq N,$$

(3)

$$F_1(x, b) = \max_p \left\{ p(Ap + a + b) - \tfrac{1}{2}c \int [x - Ap - a - b - \xi]^2 \, d\Phi(\xi) \right.$$

$$\left. + \alpha \iint F_N(x - Ap - a - b - \xi, \beta) \, d\Phi(\xi) \, d\Psi(\beta) \right\}.^{13}$$

The first term on the right in each equation is the expected value of revenue in the current period if the specialist announces price p and absorbs excess demand from both limit and market orders. Since only the excess demand among limit orders is known when a decision is made, the remaining random variable ξ vanishes on taking the expectation. The revenue term may be positive or negative depending on the price chosen by the specialist. It will be negative, for example, if the specialist plans to buy for his account by announcing a price sufficiently high relative to b. The distribution functions for the random variables are given by $\Phi(\xi)$ and $\Psi(\beta)$. The random variable, $x - Ap - a - b - \xi$, gives the next period's inventory of shares, and β updates the state of the book for next period. If the next period occurs on the following day, the expected overnight inventory costs are subtracted, and the expected maximum return for future periods and days is discounted by the discount factor $0 < \alpha < 1$.

Solutions to the set of equations in (3) are given in the appendix. The strategy of the proof is the following. We first prove that functions $F_i(x, b)$ which satisfy (3) are second-degree polynomials in the variables $(a + b)$ and x. The functions have the general form

$$F_i(x, b) = \gamma_i(a + b)^2 + \pi_i(a + b)x + \tfrac{1}{2}\delta_i x^2 + \eta_i(a + b) + \theta_i x + \rho_i \quad (4)$$

---

[13] An earlier, finite horizon version of this model was developed by Bradfield [4, 5]. In addition to providing a solution for the infinite horizon model here, we also obtain explicit properties of the long-run distribution of price and develop some preliminary results about the influence of the spread on price variability. More emphasis is also placed here on the specialist's role as a price-maker in a competitive market and on the evolution of an equilibrium price and a price distribution as consequences of the specialist's efforts to maximize his own gains.

where the constants are real, finite numbers. The functions in (4) must then satisfy constraints imposed by cost and revenue parameters of the problem. For example, the key constants δ_i must satisfy the conditions

$$\frac{\delta_1}{2} = \frac{(\alpha\delta_N - c)}{2 + A(\alpha\delta_N - c)}, \qquad \frac{\delta_i}{2} = \frac{\delta_{i-1}}{2 + A\delta_{i-1}}, \qquad 1 < i \leq N. \tag{5}$$

Successive substitutions in (5) then give

$$\frac{\delta_i}{2} = \frac{(\alpha\delta_N - c)}{2 + iA(\alpha\delta_N - c)}, \qquad 1 \leq i \leq N. \tag{6}$$

When $i = N$, (6) provides a quadratic equation for obtaining δ_N. The two solutions for δ_N are real, with one value being negative and the other positive. We prove that only the negative root is relevant for the specialist's problem. All other constants are easily obtained in terms of δ_N and given parameters.

Optimal prices $p_i^*(x, b)$ may be derived, initially, by substituting (4) into (3) and performing the maximization operations, which yield

$$p_1^*(x, b) = \frac{(\alpha\delta_N - c)x - [1 + A(\alpha\delta_N - c)][(a + b)/A] + \alpha(a\pi_N + \theta_N)}{2 + A(\alpha\delta_N - c)}$$

$$\tag{7}$$

$$p_i^*(x, b) = \frac{\delta_{i-1}x - [1 + A\delta_{i-1}][(a + b)/A] + (a\pi_{i-1} + \theta_{i-1})}{2 + A\delta_{i-1}}, \qquad 1 < i \leq N.$$

Now using (6) and values for $(a\pi_i + \theta_i)$ computed in the appendix, we obtain finally

$$p_i^*(x, b) = \frac{p^0[1 + iAT] - [2 + (i + 1)AT](b/2A) + Tx + \alpha H}{2 + iAT},$$

$$1 \leq i \leq N, \tag{8}$$

where $T = (\alpha\delta_N - c)$, $H = (a\pi_N + \theta_N)$, and $p^0 = -a/A$. From (1) it is seen that p^0 is the price at which expected excess demand is zero.

In any trading period, since $T < 0$ and $A < 0$, optimal price varies directly with b and inversely with x. Thus, increases in inventory x have an opposite effective on price, which represents the specialist's attempt to increase excess demand to offset changes in his inventory. However, the specialist's desire to adjust inventory may be reinforced or counterbalanced by his incentive to exploit current speculative opportunities available in the book. For example, the combination of increases in both inventory x and b (an increase in excess demand for limit orders) have offsetting effects on price. The outcome depends on the relative magnitude of changes, but, from (8), it also depends on the time of the day. As the day progresses, the price becomes more sensitive to changes in either b or x, since the positive coefficient of b increases as i becomes smaller, as does the absolute value of the negative coefficient of x.

In understanding the specialist's behavior, it is more useful to focus directly on his efforts to adjust inventory rather than on price. Since the specialist guarantees an announced price by absorbing excess demand, the choice of a price also implies a decision about next period's expected inventory, $y = x - (Ap + a + b)$. The optimal expected inventory at the start of the next period (period $i - 1$) is then given by

$$y_i^*(x, b) = x - [Ap_i^*(x, b) + a + b], \tag{9}$$

or, using (8),

$$y_i^*(x, b) = \frac{[2 + (i - 1)AT]x - a - [2 + (i - 1)AT]\frac{1}{2}b - \alpha AH}{2 + iAT}. \tag{10}$$

We next identify a target level of inventory x^*, which hereafter we call the *equilibrium inventory*. We justify calling x^* the equilibrium inventory in two ways. First, in this section we show that, in the absence of speculative opportunities provided by the book, the specialist always adjusts expected inventory in the direction of x^*. Second, in the next section we show that, taking speculative opportunities into account, the long-run average level of inventory is x^*. In other words, x^* is the expected value of the stationary probability distribution of the specialist's inventory.

Equilibrium inventory satisfies the condition

$$y_i^*(x^*, 0) = x^*, \qquad 1 \leq i \leq N. \tag{11}$$

It is that level of inventory in the current period that equals next period's optimal expected inventory, in the event $b = 0$. From (10) we obtain

$$x^* = \frac{-[(a/A) + \alpha H]}{T} = \frac{p^0 - \alpha H}{T}. \tag{12}$$

Substituting (12) into (10) gives:

$$y_i^*(x, b) = x - \frac{[2 + (i - 1)AT]\frac{1}{2}b + AT(x - x^*)}{2 + iAT}. \tag{13}$$

From (13) it is easily seen that $y_i^*(x, 0)$ is a convex combination of x and x^*. Thus, $x > y_i^*(x, 0) > x^*$ if $x > x^*$ and $x < y_i^*(x, 0) < x^*$ if $x < x^*$. Consequently, optimal expected inventory $y_i^*(x, 0)$ always adjusts in the direction of equilibrium inventory. The adjustment depends on the time of day. To examine this relationship, we consider the rate of adjustment $(x - y_i^*(x, 0))/(x - x^*)$. From (13) it follows that the rate of adjustment becomes larger in later periods. In other words, the specialist is less willing to take speculative positions in shares as the day progresses and the time to incur overnight inventory charges draws closer.

The inventory changes resulting from the book are also apparent in (13). Speculative opportunities represented by b may reinforce or counteract movements toward equilibrium, so that, on balance, $y_i^*(x, b)$ may overshoot or move away from equilibrium inventory. For example, suppose that $b > 0$, which creates an opportunity to sell, and also that $(x - x^*) > 0$. Since $(x - x^*) > 0$, the specialist has an incentive to sell in the current period in order to adjust x toward x^*. A positive b leads him to plan even larger current sales, since the book is strong. If b is sufficiently large relative to $(x - x^*)$, expected inventory will adjust beyond equilibrium inventory. In this case the book has shifted so far to the right that the specialist will plan to sell more than $(x - x^*)$ in the current period. In general, the effect of b on the adjustment in inventory also depends on the period of the day. Here we consider the ratio $(x^* - y_i^*(x^*, b))/b$, which measures the expected rate of adjustment away from equilibrium resulting from opportunities in the book, given that current inventory is at the equilibrium level. From (13) this ratio diminishes over the day. An analogous result holds if we compute the ratio $(x^* - y_i^*(x, b))/b$, keeping inventory x fixed. Thus, the closer is the end of the day and its overnight charges, the smaller is the amount by which the specialist will adjust inventory to exploit the book, and the more willing he becomes to change his position in the direction of the equilibrium level.

Since expected inventory and price are equivalent variables, an equilibrium inventory implies an *equilibrium price*. Substituting (12) into (8) yields

$$p_i^*(x, b) = p^0 - \frac{[2 + (i + 1)AT](b/2A) - T(x - x^*)}{2 + iAT}. \tag{14}$$

Then $p_i^*(x^*, 0) = p^0$ defines the equilibrium price, which is the price at which expected excess demand equals zero. That is, to satisfy the equation for equilibrium inventory, $y_i^*(x^*, 0) = x^*$, implies choosing a price such that expected inventory does not change. Similarly, to adjust expected inventory implies adjusting price around the equilibrium level p^0. Variations in price, as in inventory, reflect the desire to exploit the book, as well as the attempt to adjust price toward the equilibrium level, with the magnitude of changes depending on the time of the day.

In this section we have focused attention on the specialist's attempt to adjust his position in shares of the security. Price is the instrument he uses to induce desired changes. In the next section we shift attention to observed market prices and derive properties of long-run price variability. Though the specialist's position is not observed by traders, and it is not of direct interest in that section, we also obtain properties of long-run inventory variability as an aid in the study of price behavior. Before turning to this task, however, we briefly justify an earlier claim. We stated that we could allow interdependence between the disturbance terms without changing the qualitative form of behavior. Suppose (ξ, β) are jointly distributed random variables with $\bar{\xi}_b$ as the conditional expectation $E[\xi/b]$. In (3) the first terms on the right now become the conditional expected revenue $p(Ap + a + b + \bar{\xi}_b)$. The solution functions $F_i(x, b)$ retain the general form given in (4). In fact, the constraints on constants in (4) are unchanged, with the exception that the constants ρ_i now take into account additional variance and covariance terms. Consequently, (13) and (14) describe behavior if b is replaced by the sum $(b + \bar{\xi}_b)$. Supposing sign $\bar{\xi}_b$ equals sign b, efforts to exploit the book now lead to greater variations in price and inventory.

IV. PRICE VARIABILITY

In the discussion of long-run price behavior, it is convenient to date all variables explicitly as to trading periods and trading days. As in the previous section, $i = N, \ldots, 1$ refers to trading periods, and now we let $t = 1, 2, \ldots$ designate trading days. It is also helpful to obtain results about inventories before turning to prices. Relating inventories to the random variables (ξ, β), we obtain

$$x_{it} = y_{i+1,t} - \xi_{i+1,t}, \quad y_{i+1,t} = x_{i+1,t} - (Ap_{i+1,t} + a + \beta_{i+1,t}), \quad 1 \leq i < N; \tag{15}$$

$$x_{Nt} = y_{1,t-1} - \xi_{1,t-1}, \quad y_{1,t-1} = x_{1,t-1} - (Ap_{1,t-1} + a + \beta_{1,t-1}).$$

On collecting terms, (13) and (15) give

$$x_{it} = \frac{[2 + iAT]}{[2 + (i+1)AT]} x_{i+1,t} - \frac{[\frac{1}{2}(2 + iAT)\beta_{i+1,t} - ATx^*]}{2 + (i+1)AT} - \xi_{i+1,t},$$
$$1 \leq i < N; \tag{16}$$

$$x_{Nt} = \frac{2}{[2 + AT]} x_{1,t-1} - \frac{[\beta_{1,t-1} - ATx^*]}{2 + AT} - \xi_{1,t-1}.$$

If we iterate indefinitely over previous periods and days in the equation above for x_{Nt}, the term involving inventory x goes to zero with the result:

$$x_{Nt} = -\sum_{j=1}^{\infty} d^{j-1} \sum_{i=1}^{N} \left(\frac{2}{2+(i-1)AT}\right)\left[\frac{\frac{1}{2}(2+(i-1)AT)\beta_{i,t-j} - ATx^*}{2 + iAT} + \xi_{i,t-j}\right] \tag{17}$$

where $d = 2/(2 + NAT)$. Since $1/(1 - d) = (2 + NAT)/NAT$ and

$$\sum_{i=1}^{N} \left(\frac{2}{2 + (i-1)AT}\right)\left(\frac{1}{2 + iAT}\right) = \frac{N}{2 + NAT} \tag{18}$$

(which is proved by induction), the terms involving x^* sum to x^*, and on combining terms, we derive

$$x_{Nt} - x^* = -\sum_{j=1}^{\infty} d^{j-1} \sum_{i=1}^{N} \left[\frac{\beta_{i,t-j}}{2+iAT} + \left(\frac{2}{2+(i-1)AT} \right) \xi_{i,t-j} \right]. \quad (19)$$

It now easily follows that $E[x_{Nt} - x^*] = 0$ and for $i = N$, we have verified that the average level of inventory is x^*. Returning to (16), iteration over trading periods verifies that x^* is the average level of inventory in any trading period. For example, from (16) and $E[x_{Nt}] = x^*$:

$$E[x_{N-1,t}] = \frac{[2+(N-1)AT]}{[2+NAT]} x^* + \frac{ATx^*}{[2+NAT]} = x^*. \quad (20)$$

From (16) and (19) and the stationarity and independence of (ξ, β), it is clear that the random variable x_{it} does not depend on t. Thus, x_{it} is independently and identically distributed over time and hereafter we omit the subscript t. For the same reasons we also omit the subscript t on prices p_{it}. From (19) and $1/(1 - d^2) = [2 + NAT]^2/NAT[4 + NAT]$, we now obtain

$$\text{var}[x_N] = \frac{[2+NAT]^2}{NAT(4+NAT)} \left(\sum \frac{1}{(2+iAT)^2} \right) \sigma_\beta^2$$

$$+ \frac{[2+NAT]^2}{NAT(4+NAT)} \left(\sum \left(\frac{2}{2+(i-1)AT} \right) \right)^2 \sigma_\xi^2 \quad (21)$$

where σ_β^2 and σ_ξ^2 are the variances of the random variables (ξ, β). The first equations in (16) also provide the result:

$$\text{var}[x_i] = \frac{[2+iAT]^2}{[2+(i+1)AT]^2} \text{var}[x_{i+1}] + \frac{[2+iAT]^2}{4[2+(i+1)AT]^2} \sigma_\beta^2 + \sigma_\xi^2,$$

$$1 \leqq i < N. \quad (22)$$

With these preliminary outcomes available, we turn to price variation. From (14) we derive

$$p_i - p^0 = \frac{(2A)^{-1}[2+(i+1)AT]\beta_i - T(x_i - x^*)}{2+iAT}. \quad (23)$$

It follows at once from (23) and $E[x_i - x^*] = 0$ that $E[p_i - p^0] = 0$, which justifies a claim that p^0 is the average price in any period. In considering variations in price around p^0, it is useful first to examine (23) in some detail. For example, suppose $(x_i - x^*)$ is fixed in amount across periods. It is then seen from (23) that for any β_i the variation in price $(p_i - p^0)$ becomes greater the later the period of the day. Similarly, if β_i is fixed throughout the day, then for any x_i the variation in price again becomes greater as the day progresses. These characteristics suggest that the variance of price increases with the period of the trading day. We verify this suggestion next by proving that $\text{var}[p_{i-1}] > \text{var}[p_i]$.

From (23),

$$\text{var}[p_i] = \frac{[2+(i+1)AT]^2}{4[2+iAT]^2}\frac{\sigma_\beta^2}{A^2} + \frac{T^2}{[2+iAT]^2}\text{var}[x_i]. \tag{24}$$

In forming the difference $\text{var}[p_{i-1}] - \text{var}[p_i]$, terms involving inventory variances vanish if we make an appropriate substitution. That is, in applying (24) to obtain $\text{var}[p_{i-1}]$, we may use (22) to make a substitution for $\text{var}[x_{i-1}]$, which leads to cancellation of terms involving $\text{var}[x_i]$. Thus, after collecting terms,

$$\text{var}[p_{i-1}] - \text{var}[p_i] = \left\{\frac{[2+iAT]^2}{4[2+(i-1)AT]^2} - \frac{[2+(i+1)AT]^2}{4[2+iAT]^2} + \frac{(AT)^2}{4[2+iAT]^2}\right\}$$

$$\times \frac{\sigma_\beta^2}{A^2} + \frac{(AT)^2}{[2+(i-1)AT]^2}\frac{\sigma_\xi^2}{A^2}. \tag{25}$$

To prove $\text{var}[p_{i-1}] - \text{var}[p_i] > 0$, it suffices to show that the coefficient of σ_β^2/A^2 is positive, which is easily verified. Consequently, the variance of price increases throughout the day.

A similar result does not apply to inventory variances. The reason is found in the discussion of (13), which gives an expression for $y_i^*(x, b)$. As noted there, changes in expected inventory with respect to $(x - x^*)$ are magnified throughout the day, whereas they are diminished with respect to b. The difference $\text{var}[x_{i-1}] - \text{var}[x_i]$ thus depends on a balance of opposite forces. We have obtained some results here using numerical calculations. For all $N \geq 2$, $\text{var}[x_{N-1}] > \text{var}[x_N]$. All other comparisons depend on N and other parameters. For example, for a fixed set of parameter values, we have shown $\text{var}[x_{N-2}] > \text{var}[x_{N-1}]$ if $N = 4$, but $\text{var}[x_{N-2}] < [x_{N-1}]$ if $N = 3$. The general pattern appears to be the following: $\text{var}[x_{i-1}] > \text{var}[x_i]$ holds in earlier periods of the day with a reversal of the inequality occurring in later periods of the day.

To derive individual price variances in terms of parameters, we combine (21), (22), (24), and (25) to obtain

$$\text{var}[p_i] = \left\{\frac{AT}{N[4+NAT]}\sum_{j=1}^{N}\left(\frac{1}{2+jAT}\right)^2 + \frac{(AT)^2}{4}\sum_{j=i+1}^{N}\left(\frac{1}{2+jAT}\right)^2\right.$$

$$+ \frac{[2+(i+1)AT]^2}{4[2+iAT]^2}\right\}\frac{\sigma_\beta^2}{A^2} + \left\{\frac{AT}{N[4+NAT]}\sum_{j=1}^{N}\left(\frac{2}{2+(j-1)AT}\right)^2\right.$$

$$+ (AT)^2\sum_{j=i}^{N-1}\left(\frac{1}{2+jAT}\right)^2\right\}\frac{\sigma_\xi^2}{A^2}, \tag{26}$$

where the summations involving i vanish in the event $i = N$. To lend some meaning to (26), other than observations about dependence of variances on parameters, it is useful to compare the specialist system with pricing in an alternative scheme we call the *clerk system*. Under the clerk system, an agent would announce prices, but he would be neutral in that he would not trade for his own account. Each period, after market orders have arrived, the agent would execute orders at a price determined by crossing the excess demand among market orders against limit orders already on the book. In other words, he would announce a market clearing price. This system requires that the agent know the realized excess demand function each period.[14] If e is the current realization of ξ, under the clerk system price p_c would satisfy the equation $Ap_c + a + b + e = 0$ with expectation $E[p_c] = p^0$ and variance

$$\text{var}[p_c] = (\sigma_\beta^2/A^2) + (\sigma_\xi^2/A^2). \tag{27}$$

The comparison of price variability under the two systems depends on the values of the bracketed variance coefficients in (26). For the first trading period both coefficients are less than 1 [which follows from the inequalities $\sum(1/(2 + jAT))^2 \leq N/(2 + AT)^2$ and $\sum(2/(2 + (j - 1)AT))^2 \leq N$] so that

$$\text{var}[p_c] > \text{var}[p_N]. \tag{28}$$

At the beginning of the day when the specialist is more willing to take positions away from equilibrium inventory, he is induced to reduce price variability. In all other periods comparisons depend on parameter values. When $N = 2$, for example, our numerical computations show that $\text{var}[p_c] > \text{var}[p_1]$ for small values of AT. However, the inequality is reversed when AT becomes sufficiently large. Since AT is increasing in $|A|$, c, and α, the reason for this behavior is apparent. With large values of c, for instance, inventory costs become large and the specialist becomes more anxious to maintain inventory near the equilibrium level, which increases price variability. With an increase in $|A|$, $\text{var}[p_c]$ and $\text{var}[p_1]$ both decrease, but $\text{var}[p_c]$ decreases at a greater rate than $\text{var}[p_1]$. On balance, which system leads to greater price variability is unclear.

---

[14] It is questionable whether the clerk system would be feasible in practice. It requires the accumulation and rapid processing of large amounts of information. The costs may well exceed those of the specialist system, which does not require the specialist to have detailed knowledge of the excess demand function. Moreover, the clerk system obligates traders to reveal their overall trading strategies to brokers. Many may be reluctant to do so. In recent papers Obst [15, 16] explores some of the features of the clerk system.

V.   A DIGRESSION ON THE BID–ASK SPREAD

Here we justify the claim that the choice of single prices is qualitatively equivalent to the choice of bid and ask prices with a fixed spread. In particular, taking revenue on the spread into account, we demonstrate that the variance of prices and the equilibrium inventory are unchanged when the spread is fixed. Naturally, the equilibrium price will change since a fixed spread is analogous to the imposition of a fixed tax per share on both buyers and sellers.

To economize on notation and to shorten the exposition, we ignore limit orders and suppose that each trading day has a single trading period. As the exposition progresses, it is easy to see that the argument remains valid even in a model with both market and limit orders and more than one trading period. If we let $2t$ dollars represent the spread, p_a the ask and p_b the bid, then $p_a = p + t$ and $p_b = p - t$ where p is the average of the bid and ask prices. Thus, since t is fixed, we may construct the model as one in which the average price p is the choice variable. Market order demand satisfies the demand function $A_d p_a + a_d + \xi_d$ where $a_d > 0$, $A_d < 0$, and ξ_d is a random disturbance with zero mean and finite variance. Similarly, market order supply is described by the function $A_s p_b + a_s + \xi_s$ with $A_s > 0$ and ξ_s as the analogous random variable. In terms of the previous model, $a = (a_d - a_s)$, $A = (A_d - A_s)$, and $\xi = \xi_d - \xi_s$. While we do not impose any sign restriction on a_s, we do assume $(a_d - a_s) > 0$, which is consistent with an earlier assumption about the excess demand function.

Taking the return on the spread into account, the single-period expected revenue is given by $p_a(A_d p_a + a_d) - p_b(A_s p_b + a_s)$. If we now define $A_T = (A_d + A_s)$, $a_T = (a_d + a_s)$, $\hat{a} = a + 2t A_T$, and $\bar{a} = t(a_T + tA)$, we then obtain:

$$p_a(A_d p_a + a_d) - p_b(A_s p_b + a_s) = p(Ap + \hat{a}) + \bar{a}. \tag{29}$$

Moreover, in this notation expected excess demand equals $Ap + a + tA_T$ which means that next period's inventory is given by $x - Ap - a - tA_T - \xi$. Finally, if we define $F(x)$ as the maximum expected return over an infinite horizon, the model becomes

$$F(x) = \max_p \left\{ p(Ap + \hat{a}) + \bar{a} - \tfrac{1}{2}c \int [x - Ap - a - tA_T - \xi]^2 \, d\Phi(\xi) \right.$$

$$\left. + \alpha \int F(x - Ap - a - tA_T - \xi) \, d\Phi(\xi) \right\}, \tag{30}$$

where $\Phi(\xi)$ is obtained as the convolution of the random variables (ξ_d, ξ_s). The proof in the appendix, which guarantees that (4) satisfies (3), also proves that the function $F(x) = \pi x + \delta/2 \cdot x^2 + \rho$ satisfies (30). Following the procedure of the last section, we obtain as the optimal price

$$p^*(x) = \frac{(\alpha\delta - c)x - [1 + A(\alpha\delta - c)](a/A) + \alpha\pi}{2 + A(\alpha\delta - c)} - t\frac{A_T}{A}. \tag{31}$$

Equilibrium inventory x^* then satisfies $Tx^* = -(a/A + \alpha\pi)$ where $T = (\alpha\delta - c)$ and equilibrium price $p_m^0 = p^*(x^*)$ satisfies the condition $Ap_m^0 + a + tA_T = 0$ or $p_m^0 = -[a + tA_T]/A$. Substitution into (31) then yields:

$$p^*(x) = p_m^0 + (T(x - x^*)/(2 + AT)). \tag{32}$$

If we now compare results here with the earlier outcomes in circumstances when $N = 1$ and $b = 0$, it is easy to show that the T's are the same in both cases and that $\pi = H$. Thus, the equilibrium inventories are identical. Moreover, while the equilibrium prices differ by the amount $(-tA_T/A)$, a comparison of (7) and (14) with (31) and (32) indicates that the prices in the bid–ask model are translates of the prices in the earlier model by that amount, and thus that the variances of prices are identical. Analogous outcomes apply to the ask $p_a^*(x) = p^*(x) + t$ and the bid $p_b^*(x) = p^*(x) - t$.

VI. CONCLUSIONS

In any market one or more participants provide a service by announcing prices at which exchanges may occur. The obligations of price-makers in guaranteeing prices, however, may vary widely among markets, and, in general, it seems plausible that long-run characteristics of market behavior would depend on who sets prices and on the price-makers' responsibilities. In studying a market, or system of markets, it would thus seem desirable that price-makers and their responsibilities be clearly identified.

The specialist system in an organized security exchange provides an opportunity to explore these ideas. The specialist calls prices with an obligation of satisfying excess demand by trading for his own account. He arranges immediate exchanges by bearing the cost of waiting. Like any other participant in the market, he attempts to maximize his gains by making appropriate decisions. Our objective in studying this market is to gain some insight into characteristics of the trading system. Specifically, we derived properties of the stationary probability distribution of prices. The mean of the stationary distribution is the price equating expected excess demand to zero. We offered justification for calling this price the equilibrium price. However, our study suggests that the dispersion of the price distribution is also important in describing behavior in a securities market and that the dispersion is not invariant to the trading environment.

For example, the variance of price depends not only on characteristics of the excess demand function but also on elements of the trading environment:

the specialist's exclusive knowledge of the book and his obligation to satisfy excess demand. The importance of the trading environment is again illustrated in the comparison of the specialist and the clerk systems. There it was seen that both systems provide the same equilibrium prices but different price variances. Any attempt to evaluate the two systems would seem to require comparison of entire distributions of price rather than only values of some single parameter such as the mean price. Moreover, though we did not emphasize this point, since we did not develop any measure of the cost of the clerk system, in any evaluation the relative costs of operating the systems as reflected, for example, in the bid–ask spread would also be important.

Our study represents a beginning only. We focused on the specialist and represented the activities of other traders by an excess demand function or by supply and demand functions. We made a number of simple assumptions to enable us to derive explicit results. In a more general setting there is some question whether a number of our explicit outcomes would be verified, but we believe the general nature of the argument is valid: Stationary distributions of prices, if they exist, would have characteristics that are sensitive to features of the trading environment.

Our study of price adjustment in a competitive market is incomplete in another sense. Trading on a securities exchange is a special case of a competitive market. The exchange of ownership shares, rather than commodities, facilitates the specialist's obligation to satisfy excess demand. Even if he lacks an inventory of shares at the moment, he may yet satisfy positive excess demand by borrowing shares or going short. Offers by traders to buy or sell shares thus tend to be realized independently of the specialist's current inventory of shares (except, of course, in extreme situations). In a market where commodities are exchanged, the environment becomes more complex. The price-makers' opportunities to borrow commodities or produce on demand may be limited. Traders who demand the commodity may find that their plans are thwarted by shortages. In these circumstances traders, as well as price-makers, may hold commodity inventories to offset possible market disappointments. Perhaps needless to emphasize, the analysis of a market trading process then becomes more difficult. We plan to extend research in this direction also, and some preliminary results have been obtained elsewhere by Zabel [23, 24].

APPENDIX.   VERIFICATION OF OPTIMAL BEHAVIOR

To shorten the exposition, we provide a detailed analysis only of the case $N = 2$. An analogous argument provides solutions when N is any given finite integer.

The relevant functional equations are

$$F_2(x,b) = \max_p \left\{ p(Ap + a + b) + \iint F_1(x - Ap - a - b - \xi, \beta) \, d\Phi(\xi) \, d\Psi(\beta) \right\},$$

$$F_1(x,b) = \max_p \left\{ p(Ap + a + b) - \tfrac{1}{2}c \int [x - Ap - a - b - \xi]^2 \, d\Phi(\xi) \right. \qquad \text{(A1)}$$

$$\left. + \alpha \iint F_2(x - Ap - a - b - \xi, \beta) \, d\Phi(\xi) \, d\Psi(\beta) \right\}.$$

The hypothesis is:

$$\begin{aligned} F_2(x,b) &= \gamma_2(a + b)^2 + \pi_2(a + b)x + \tfrac{1}{2}\delta_2 x^2 + \eta_2(a + b) + \theta_2 x + \rho_2, \\ F_1(x,b) &= \gamma_1(a + b)^2 + \pi_1(a + b)x + \tfrac{1}{2}\delta_1 x^2 + \eta_1(a + b) + \theta_1 x + \rho_1, \end{aligned} \qquad \text{(A2)}$$

where the constants are real finite numbers. If we now set $y = x - Ap - a - b$ and substitute the first equation of (A2) into the second equation of (A1), we obtain

$$F_1(x,b) = \max_p \left\{ p(Ap + a + b) - \tfrac{1}{2}c \int (y - \xi)^2 \, d\Phi(\xi) \right.$$

$$+ \alpha \iint [\gamma_2(a + \beta)^2 + \pi_2(a + \beta)(y - \xi) + \tfrac{1}{2}\delta_2(y - \xi)^2$$

$$\left. + \eta_2(a + \beta) + \theta_2(y - \xi) + \rho_2] \, d\Phi(\xi) \, d\Psi(\beta) \right\}. \qquad \text{(A3)}$$

Using the independence of the random variables $E[\xi] = E[\beta] = 0$ and integrating,

$$F_1(x,b) = \max_p \{ p(Ap + a + b) + \tfrac{1}{2}(\alpha\delta_2 - c)y^2 + \alpha z_2 y + D_2 \}, \qquad \text{(A4)}$$

where

$$\begin{aligned} z_2 &= a\pi_2 + \theta_2 \\ D_2 &= \tfrac{1}{2}(\alpha\delta_2 - c)\sigma_\xi^2 + \alpha[\gamma_2(a^2 + \sigma_\beta^2) + a\eta_2 + \rho_2]. \end{aligned} \qquad \text{(A5)}$$

It is now more convenient to choose y as the decision variable which gives

$$F_1(x,b) = \max_y \left\{ \frac{(x - y)^2 - (a + b)(x - y)}{A} + \frac{(\alpha\delta_2 - c)}{2} y^2 + a z_2 y + D_2 \right\}. \qquad \text{(A6)}$$

Next we let $G_1(y, x, b)$ represent the maximand of (A6) and assume $[2 + A(\alpha\delta_2 - c)] > 0$, which we justify later. With this assumption it is easily seen that the second partial derivative $D_{yy}G_1 < 0$ and that the first partial derivative D_yG_1 is negative for large y and positive for small y. Thus the y which maximizes $G_1(y, x, b)$ satisfies the first-order condition $D_yG_1 = 0$. Solving the first-order condition for the optimizing expected inventory $y_1^*(x, b)$ yields

$$y_1^*(x, b) = (2x - (a + b) - \alpha Az_2)/(2 + A(\alpha\delta_2 - c)). \tag{A7}$$

Substituting (A7) into (A6) we obtain

$$F_1(x, b) = \frac{1}{2A[2 + A(\alpha\delta_2 - c)]}(a + b)^2 - \frac{(\alpha\delta_2 - c)}{2 + A(\alpha\delta_2 - c)}(a + b)x$$

$$+ \frac{(\alpha\delta_2 - c)}{2 + A(\alpha\delta_2 - c)}x^2 - \frac{\alpha z_2}{2 + A(\alpha\delta_2 - c)}(a + b)$$

$$+ \frac{2\alpha z_2}{2 + A(\alpha\delta_2 - c)}x - \frac{A(\alpha z_2)^2}{2[2 + A(\alpha\delta_2 - c)]} + D_2. \tag{A8}$$

Thus, $F_1(x, b)$ in (A2) and in (A8) have the same form.

Next, after substituting the second equation of (A2) into the first equation of (A1), we derive similar outcomes, given the assumption $(2 + A\delta_1) > 0$ which, again, we justify later. The optimizing expected inventory $y_2^*(x, b)$ satisfies

$$y_2^*(x, b) = (2x - (a + b) - Az_1)/(2 + A\delta_1) \tag{A9}$$

and

$$F_2(x, b) = -\frac{1}{2A[2 + A\delta_1]}(a + b)^2 - \frac{\delta_1}{2 + A\delta_1}(a + b)x + \frac{\delta_1}{2 + A\delta_1}x^2$$

$$- \frac{z_1}{2 + A\delta_1}(a + b) + \frac{2z_1}{2 + A\delta_1}x - \frac{Az_1^2}{2[2 + A\delta_1]} + D_1, \tag{A10}$$

where

$$z_1 = a\pi_1 + \theta_1, \qquad D_1 = \tfrac{1}{2}\delta_1\sigma_\xi^2 + \gamma_1(a^2 + \sigma_\beta^2) + a\eta_1 + \rho_1. \tag{A11}$$

Again, $F_2(x, b)$ in (A2) and (A11) have the same form.

Now, if $F_2(x, b)$ and $F_1(x, b)$ in (A2) are to satisfy the equations in (A1), the parameters in these functions must equal the corresponding parameters specified by (A8) and (A10). In particular, the following conditions must be satisfied:

$$\tfrac{1}{2}\delta_1 = (\alpha\delta_2 - c)/(2 + A(\alpha\delta_2 - c)), \qquad \tfrac{1}{2}\delta_2 = \delta_1/(2 + A\delta_1). \tag{A12}$$

Using the first equation in (A12) to eliminate δ_1 in the second equation, we obtain

$$\tfrac{1}{2}\delta_2 = (\alpha\delta_2 - c)/(2 + 2A(\alpha\delta_2 - c)), \tag{A13}$$

which provides a quadratic equation in δ_2. The two solutions for δ_2 are real, with one value being negative and the other positive. If δ_2 is negative, the conditions $[2 + A(\alpha\delta_2 - c)] > 0$ and $(2 + A\delta_1) > 0$ are obviously satisfied. In fact, if δ_2 is positive, a detailed analysis of the solutions of the quadratic equation indicate that the two conditions are satisfied even in this case. Thus, at the moment we have no reason to reject either solution. We raise this issue again later.

On comparing the equations in (A2), (A8), and (A10), it is also easy to see that all other unknown parameters may be expressed in terms of δ_2 and given parameters. Thus, we shall not provide the explicit solutions except that we need to relate z_1 and z_2 in order to transform (A7) and (A9) into relationships involving common terms. Let $T = (\alpha\delta_2 - c)$. Then, it is possible to show that $cz_2 = a\delta_2 T$ and $cz_1[2 + AT] = \alpha cz_2 + aT^2$. Moreover, from (A12) and (A13), $[2 + A\delta_1] = 2[2 + 2AT]/[2 + AT]$. If we now let $z_2 = H$, we may use the above expressions to obtain:

$$y_1^*(x, b) = \frac{2x - (a + b) - \alpha AH}{2 + AT},$$

$$y_2^*(x, b) = \frac{[2 + AT]x - a - [2 + AT]\frac{1}{2}b - \alpha AH}{2 + 2AT}.$$

(A14)

From (A14), $y = x - Ap - a - b$ and $p^0 = -a/A$, we finally derive that optimal prices satisfy

$$p_1^*(x, b) = \frac{p^0[1 + AT] - [2 + 2AT](b/2A) + Tx + \alpha H}{2 + AT},$$

$$p_2^*(x, b) = \frac{p^0[1 + 2AT] - [2 + 3AT](b/2A) + Tx + \alpha H}{2 + 2AT}.$$

(A15)

To show that δ_2 must be negative, we consider a sequence of problems in which the number of trading days is finite. If n is any positive integer, then using an inductive procedure we can show that $F_{1n}(x, b)$ and $F_{2n}(x, b)$, the maximum expected returns with n days remaining in the horizon, are functions of the form specified by (A2) in which the unknown constants have n as an additional subscript. Moreover, the constants δ_{1n} and δ_{2n} are negative. Thus, the returns $F_{1n}(x, b)$ and $F_{2n}(x, b)$ are concave in x. It can also be shown that the sequences $\{F_{1n}(x, b)\}$ and $\{F_{2n}(x, b)\}$ converge uniformly to the functions in (A2) when the constants satisfy the constraints specified by (A8) and (A10). Now, since the limit functions $F_1(x, b)$ and $F_2(x, b)$ must be concave in x, the constants must also satisfy the additional constraints that $\delta_1 < 0$ and $\delta_2 < 0$. As we have shown, the limit functions satisfy the infinite horizon functional equations.

It is now apparent, as we claimed, that an analogous argument provides extensions to situations where N is any finite integer and thus that this argument justifies the development in Section III.

REFERENCES

1. Arrow, K. J., Toward a theory of price adjustment, *in* "The Allocation of Economic Resources" (M. Abramovitz, ed.), Stanford Univ. Press, Stanford, California (1959).
2. Barro, R. J., A theory of monopolistic price adjustment, *Rev. Econ. Stud.* **39** (1), No. 117 (1972), 17–26.
3. Baumol, W. J., "The Stock Market and Economic Efficiency," Millan Lectures, No. Six. Fordham Univ. Press, New York, 1965.
4. Bradfield, J., A Dynamic Programming Model of the Stock Market Specialist. Unpublished Ph.D. Dissertation, Univ. of Rochester (1973).
5. Bradfield, J., A formal dynamic model of market-making, *J. Financial Quant. Anal.* **14** (1) (1979).
6. Demsetz, H., The cost of transacting, *Q. J. Econ.* **82**, No. 1 (1968), 33–53.
7. Fisher, F. M., Quasi-competitive price adjustment by individual firms, *J. Econ. Theory* **2**, No. 1 (1970), 195–206.
8. Fisher, F. M., On price adjustment without an auctioneer, *Rev. Econ. Stud.* **39** (1), No. 117 (1972), 1–16.
9. Hurwicz, L., Radner, R., and Reiter, S., A stochastic decentralized resource allocation process: Part I, *Econometrica* **43**, No. 2 (1975), 187–221.
10. Koopmans, T. C., "Three Essays on the State of Economic Science." McGraw-Hill, New York, 1957.
11. Leffler, G. L., and Farwell, L. C., "The Stock Market," 3rd ed. Ronald Press, New York, 1963.
12. Lippman, S. A., and McCall, J. J., The economics of job search: A survey, *Econ. Inquiry* **15**, No. 2 (1976), 155–189.
13. Logue, D. E., Market-making and the assessment of market efficiency, *J. Finance* **30**, No. 1 (1975), 115–123.
14. McCall, J. J., Probabilistic microeconomics, *Bell J. Econ. Management Sci.* **2**, No. 2 (1971), 403–433.
15. Obst, N. P., Stability in periodic markets, *Am. Econ. Rev.* **61**, No. 4 (1971), 638–648.
16. Obst, N. P., On organized markets under uncertainty, *Western Econ. J.* **10**, No. 2 (1972), 182–192.
17. Rothschild, M., Models of market organization with imperfect information: A survey, *J. Political Econ.* **81**, No. 6 (1973), 1283–1308.
18. Securities and Exchange Commission, Report of the Special Study of the Securities Markets of the Securities and Exchange Commission, Part 2, 89th Congress, 1st Session, House Document No. 95, Part 2, pp. 57–171. U.S. Goverment Printing Office, Washington, D.C., 1963.
19. Stigler, G. J., Public regulation of the securities markets, *J. Business*, **37**, No. 2 (1964), 117–133.
20. Wall Street Journal, p. 2, Friday, July 30, 1976.
21. West, R. R., Simulating securities markets operations: Some examples, observations and comments, *J. Financial Quant. Anal.* **5**, No. 1 (1970), 115–137.
22. West, R. R., and Tinic, S. M., "The Economics of the Stock Market." Praeger Publ., New York, 1971.

23. Zabel, E., Competitive Firm Behavior Under Risk in Disequilibrium Trading. Discussion Paper, Univ. of Rochester, Rochester, New York (October 1976).
24. Zabel, E., Consumer behavior under risk in disequilibrium trading, *Int. Econ. Rev.* **18**, No. 2 (1977), 323–343.

James Bradfield
DEPARTMENT OF ECONOMICS
HAMILTON COLLEGE
CLINTON, NEW YORK

Edward Zabel
DEPARTMENT OF ECONOMICS
UNIVERSITY OF ROCHESTER
ROCHESTER, NEW YORK

An Infinite Horizon Model with Money

CHARLES WILSON

In [7] I have analyzed a simple perfect foresight model with a transactions demand for money for the case where the horizon is finite. This paper extends the analysis to the infinite horizon. The model consists of a number of identical individuals who supply labor in each period and consume a single consumption good composed of the labor of other individuals. There is no capital or storable commodities. All markets are competitive, but any transaction must use fiat money. In each period goods can be purchased only with money accumulated before the market is open. Consequently, the budget constraint of the individual must be supplemented by a liquidity constraint of the form suggested by Clower [5]. Borrowing and lending is permitted through the sale and purchase of one-period bonds whose returns are also denominated in units of money.

The model is designed to focus on the role of government policy in determining the nature of the equilibrium. Therefore, in order to provide a framework for examining as large a class of issues as possible, I permit not only government transfers (or taxes) but also open market operations (i.e., government borrowing and lending). Through these instruments, the supply of money in each period is determined.

Because there are two instruments of government policy, however, a distinction may be drawn between the supply of money and the level of private wealth in any period. Consequently, it is necessary that the budget constraint of the individual be specified with some care. In this model I require only that some subsequence of private wealth levels be bounded below. Subject to this constraint, the problem of the consumer is to choose a

79

sequence of labor and consumption that maximizes the discounted sum of utility. The problem is slightly complicated, however, because I want to permit the possibility that the utility function is bounded neither above nor below. Consequently, it may be the case that the discounted sum of utilities is not always well defined. In this case the individual will choose a consumption sequence that is maximal in the sense of Brock [2]. In the following section I provide a set of conditions that are necessary and sufficient for a sequence of consumption and labor to be maximal. For any stream of transfer payments, prices, and interest rates, it is shown that the maximal sequence is unique.

Equilibrium is defined as a sequence of prices, interest rates, and consumption for which the supply and demand for goods and bonds are equal to zero in each period. The characterization of maximal sequences is then combined with the conditions for an equilibrium to provide a characterization of the equilibrium sequences in terms of a second-order difference equation in real and nominal money balances and a set of transversality conditions on the sequence of government transfer payments and borrowing. I then turn my attention to a number of general issues, with particular reference to a comparison of the properties of the infinite horizon model with those that obtain when the horizon is finite.

The key to analyzing the models is to recognize that besides affecting the relative price of future versus present consumption, the money rate of interest acts as a tax on consumption. Since income earned from selling labor today cannot be spent on consumption until tomorrow, an increase in current consumption must be financed by borrowing at the market rate of interest. In order to repay the loan, therefore, the current supply of labor must be increased in proportion to the change in consumption times the interest factor. This observation leads to the immediate implication that Pareto optimality can be attained only if the money rate of interest is zero in each period.

Except for a few examples, the question of the existence of an equilibrium for a given sequence of government policies is generally ignored in this paper. I do show, however, that subject to some restrictions on its rate of growth, any sequence of real balances can be generated as an equilibrium by an appropriate choice of government policies. In fact, there is a simple characterization of those policies that are equivalent. In general, any change in government policy will leave the equilibrium unchanged as long as the supply of money in each period is unaffected and the resulting sequence of private wealth does not diverge so sharply from the original sequence that the equilibrium consumption level is no longer maximal. These restrictions are not terribly severe. They allow for a large class of actions in the bond market to be offset by appropriate adjustments in the tax policy, and vice versa.

Those policies that generate Pareto optimal equilibria have a particularly simple characterization. Subject to a lower bound on the growth rate of money, a Pareto optimal equilibrium exists if and only if the sum of government transfers goes to zero. This proves to be a much weaker condition than requiring the supply of money to decline at the time rate of preference. Furthermore, unless government policy is restricted solely to open market operations, the same government policies are generally consistent with other inefficient equilibria as well.

The final section examines in more detail the nature of the equilibrium when only transfer payments are used. Here the results differ quite sharply from those obtained in the finite horizon model. For a given stock of money, the character and size of the class of equilibria are quite sensitive to the properties of the utility function. For a large class of utility functions, the equilibrium is unique; for another class, a one-parameter family of cycling equilibrium exists; for yet another class, hyperinflation equilibria may appear.

A final word on the purpose of this paper. As in [9], my emphasis is on the general structure of model. Obvious comparative dynamic exercises have been postponed for another paper. I am more concerned here with a complete presentation of those results that are a consequence of the equilibrium conditions and the budget constraints. Results that depend on the particular structure of the utility function are presented primarily to indicate the various possibilities for the nature of the equilibrium. Throughout the paper I have gone to some effort to indicate the role of the various assumptions in obtaining each result.

THE INDIVIDUAL AGENTS

The economy consists of a number of identical individuals who consume a single consumption good c_t and supply labor services l_t in each period t from 0 to infinity. Neither labor nor consumption goods are storable.

Let $\Omega = \{(c, l) : c > 0, \ l > 0\}$, let $u(c, l)$ be the one-period utility function over consumption and labor, and let $\delta > 0$ be the time rate of preference. Assume

(A1) $u : \Omega \to R$ is continuously differentiable and strictly concave with $u_c > 0$ and $u_l < 0$.[1]

---

[1] Note that the utility function is only defined on the interior of the positive orthant. Thus we will automatically be restricting our consideration to interior solutions. Since my concern is only with characterizing equilibrium consumption sequences, the assumption does not impose any essential restrictions. We could permit an upper bound on the supply of labor; the only complication is that some of the conditions that follow must be modified to allow for boundary solutions. It is important that we do not require the utility function to be defined on the boundary of the positive quadrant, however, because some of the utility functions I want to consider are not bounded below as $c \to 0$.

The benefit of any sequence (c_t, l_t) up to time T is given by the sum of the discounted utility from 0 to T. I assume the individual will choose a consumption sequence for which the total utility up to period T is higher by a positive amount than that of any other permissible sequence for an infinite number of periods T. Brock [2] calls such sequences *maximal*.

(D1)   A sequence (c_t^0, l_t^0) is *(weakly) maximal* with respect to a set of sequences $C \subset \Omega$ if $(c_t^0, l_t^0) \in C$ and there is no other sequence $(c_t, l_t) \in C$ such that

$$\liminf_{T \to \infty} \sum_{t=0}^{T} [u(c_t, l_t) - u(c_t^0, l_t^0)]\delta^t \geqq (>) \, 0.^2$$

At the outset of each period, the individual is awarded a transfer payment of X_t units of money (a tax if X_t is negative). He may also choose to borrow or lend money by selling one-period bonds for money at interest rate i_t. If he was a borrower or lender from the previous period, these accounts are also settled at this time. The net result is to leave the individual holding M_t units of money and bonds equal in value to A_t units of money.

Once these transactions are concluded, the market for current goods and services opens (there is no market for future delivery of goods and services). In order to concentrate on the relation among the price level, the interest rate, and the money supply, I will assume that for any given individual, one unit of consumption is equal to one unit of any *other* individual's labor. From the perspective of any individual consumer, therefore, all labor can be partitioned into two types: his own, which he supplies, and that of other consumers, which he consumes. If all markets are competitive, this will imply that the equilibrium prices of labor and consumption goods in each period are identical. Therefore the market for labor services is identical with the market for goods. Let P_t refer to the money price of labor in time t.

The critical assumption of the model is that any transactions for goods and services requires money. An individual wishing to purchase c_t units of consumption must supply $P_t c_t$ units of money. Conversely, an individual supplying l_t units of labor will receive $P_t l_t$ units of money. Since these transactions occur simultaneously, however, money received for current labor services cannot be used to finance current consumptions. Therefore, the value of current consumption $P_t c_t$ cannot exceed the money holdings at the

---

[2] If u is bounded and $\delta < 1$, then $\lim_{T \to \infty} \sum_{t=0}^{T} u(c_t, l_t)\delta^t = \sum_{t=0}^{\infty} u(c_t, l_t)\delta^t$ is always well defined. In this case (c_t^0, l_t^0) is maximal with respect to C if and only if $\sum_{t=0}^{\infty} u(c_t^0, l_t^0) > \sum_{t=0}^{\infty} u(c_t, l_t)$ for all other $(c_t, l_t) \in C$.

I could have used a stronger concept of optimality to determine the individual's consumption choice—$\liminf_{T \to \infty} \sum_{t=0}^{T} [u(c_t^0, l_t^0) - u(c_t, l_t)]\delta^t \geqq 0$. However, the results that follow would require much stronger assumptions than those used in this paper.

beginning of the trading period, M_t. The net transfer of money to the next period resulting from trade is then $P_t(l_t - c_t)$.

In order to give the consumer a well-defined problem, an additional "solvency" constraint is required. Some kind of lower bound is needed on the level of debt an individual may maintain over time. There are several possible candidates. However, in order to include in my analysis government policies, which generate wildly fluctuating income streams, I want this bound to be as loose as possible. Therefore, I will require only the individual's level of wealth, measured in terms of current consumption, to rise periodically above some lower bound. Formally, this means that some subsequence of wealth levels must be bounded away from $-\infty$. Consequently, as long as the real rate of interest is positive, the individual cannot increase current consumption by engaging in a "Ponzi" game.[3] It is important to specify the constraint in real rather than nominal terms, however, in order to account for changes in the price level over time.

The formal problem of the consumer is then to choose a sequence (c_t, l_t, M_t, A_t)[4,5] that is maximal with respect to

$$P_t c_t \leqq M_t, \qquad\qquad t = 0, 1, 2, \ldots, \quad (1)$$

$$M_{t+1} + A_{t+1} = M_t + P_t(l_t - c_t) + I_t A_t + X_{t+1}, \qquad t = 0, 1, 2, \ldots, \quad (2)$$

$$M_0 + A_0 = X_0, \qquad\qquad (3)$$

$$\limsup_{t \to \infty} (M_t + A_t)/P_t > -\infty, \qquad\qquad (4)$$

where $I_t = 1 + i_t$ is the interest factor at time t. Relation (1) is the liquidity constraint. The value of purchase at time t cannot exceed the money available for spending at time t. Equation (2) is the single-period budget constraint. It states that money balances at the start of trading in period $t + 1$ must equal the money balances in period t plus the net proceeds from buying and selling labor services in period t minus net lending in period $t + 1$ plus the return to lending in period t plus transfer payments (or minus taxes) in period $t + 1$. Relation (3) states that wealth in period 0 is equal to the transfer payments in that period. Relation (4) is the transversality condition discussed above.

---

[3] Note that this constraint is weaker than an alternative constraint that the sequence of wealth levels be *uniformly* bounded below. It is not obvious, *a priori*, which is the better constraint. I can construct examples where a stationary consumption stream is maximal for the first constraint and not the second and, by adjusting the income stream, make it maximal for the second and not the first. In cases where the income stream is relatively well behaved, however, both generate the same maximal sequence.

[4] (c_t, l_t, M_t, A_t) refers to the sequence $(c_t, l_t, M_t, A_t)_{t=0}^{\infty}$.

[5] Although I am treating c_t, l_t, A_t, and M_t as choice variables, any sequence of three of these variables implies the fourth through relations (1)–(3). Therefore, I will typically describe the individual's optimal program by a sequence of (c_t, l_t, A_t) or (c_t, l_t, M_t).

Some subsequence of real wealth must be bounded away from $-\infty$. Note, however, that the constraint is on *total* wealth only. Net borrowing may be unbounded if offset by an accumulation of real balances.

Because individuals are permitted to borrow and lend at a single rate of interest in each period, constraints (1)–(4) can be reduced to a single budget constraint on the sequence (c_t, l_t). Let $R_t = 1/\prod_{s=0}^{t-1} I_s$ be the discounted value of money in period t evaluated at time 0. Multiplying the constraints in (2) by R_{t+1}, summing from 0 to T, and canceling redundant terms yields, on substituting Eq. (3) for $M_0 + A_0$,

$$\sum_{t=0}^{T} R_{t+1}[P_t(l_t - c_t) - i_t M_t + X_{t+1}] + X_0 = R_{T+1}(M_{T+1} + A_{T+1}). \quad (5)$$

All that remains to be determined is the value of M_t. Following the argument in Wilson [9], I can show that a maximal sequence exists only if $i_t \geq 0$ for $t = 0, \ldots, T$. Otherwise, obvious arbitrage opportunities permit the individual to increase consumption in any period without bound. In addition, if $i_t > 0$, the individual will never have an incentive to hold money in excess of the amount required to finance current consumption, since bonds earn a higher rate of return. Therefore, any sequence (M_t) that is consistent with a maximal sequence (c_t, l_t) must satisfy the condition

$$i_t(M_t - P_t c_t) = 0. \quad (6)$$

Substituting (6) into (5) and using condition (4) then reduces the problem to

$$\limsup_{T \to \infty} \frac{1}{P_{T+1} R_{T+1}} \sum_{t=0}^{T} R_{t+1}[P_t(l_t - I_t c_t) + X_{t+1}] + X_0 \geq -\infty. \quad (7)$$

Subject to the condition that $I_t \geq 1$, a sequence (c_t, l_t) satisfies (7) if and only if there is a sequence (A_t, M_t) such that (c_t, l_t, A_t, M_t) satisfies (1)–(4).

It will be convenient for future reference to rewrite (7) using first-period consumption as numeraire. Let $x_t = (P_0/P_t)X_t$ and $a_t = (P_0/P_t)A_t$, and let $Q_t = (P_t/P_0)R_t$ be the discounted value of consumption in period t in terms of consumption at period 0. Then relation (7) can be written:

$$\limsup_{T \to \infty} \frac{1}{Q_{T+1}} \sum_{t=0}^{T} Q_t\left(\frac{l_t}{I_t} + x_t - c_t\right) + x_{T+1} > -\infty. \quad (8)$$

The effect of the liquidity constraint is revealed clearly in condition (8). It acts as a tax on consumption proportional to the rate of interest i_t. If the individual wishes to increase consumption by one unit in period t, he must borrow P_t units of money. In order to keep his wealth intact in the following period, however, he must supply I_t units of labor. Therefore, rather than equating the marginal rate of substitution of consumption for labor to the relative price (in this case 1), the individual will instead equate it to the relative price *times* interest factor at time t. It is immediate, therefore, that in order for a monetary economy to allocate resources efficiently, the money rate of interest must be zero in all periods.

A CHARACTERIZATION OF MAXIMAL SEQUENCES

We turn our attention now to finding a simple characterization of those consumption sequences that are maximal with respect to the budget constraint (8). In addressing this issue it will be useful to consider first the solution of the problem with a more familiar budget constraint. The characterization of a solution for constraint (8) is then related to the solution for the second problem.

In the previous section, I noted that the existence of a maximal sequence requires that the interest rate be nonnegative in each period. An examination of relation (8) reveals an additional restriction on the sequence of prices and interest rates that must be satisfied if a maximal sequence is to exist.

LEMMA 1 Suppose (c_t^0, l_t^0) is maximal with respect to constraint (8). Then, for any subsequence (T^s),

$$\liminf_{T^s \to \infty} \frac{1}{Q_{T^s}} \sum_{t=0}^{T^s-1} Q_t \left(\frac{l_t^0}{I_t} + x_t - c_t^0 \right) + x_{T^s} > -\infty \quad \text{implies} \quad \lim_{T^s \to \infty} Q_{T^s} = 0.$$

Proof Suppose not. Then there is a subsequence of (T^s) which we may take to be (T^s) such that $Q_{T^s} > \varepsilon > 0$ for all $s > 0$. Define (c_t', l_t') to equal (c_t^0, l_t^0) except for $c_0' = c_0^0 + \varepsilon_1$. Then for any $\varepsilon_1 > 0$, there is an $\varepsilon_2 > 0$ such that

$$\liminf_{T^s \to \infty} \frac{1}{Q_{T^s}} \sum_{t=0}^{T^s-1} Q_t \left(\frac{l_t'}{I_t} + x_t - c_t' \right) + x_{T^s} > -\infty$$

and

$$\sum_{t=0}^{T} [u(c_t', l_t') - u(c_t^0, l_t^0)]\delta^t > \varepsilon_2, \quad \text{for all} \quad T \geq 0.$$

Therefore

(c_t^0, l_t^0) is not maximal with respect to (8).   Q.E.D.

An immediate implication of Lemma 1 is that the existence of a maximal sequence requires $Q_{t_s} \to 0$ for some subsequence (t_s). Roughly, this says that in order for a sequence to be maximal, the money rate of interest must, on average, exceed the rate of inflation. The reason is obvious. If the money rate of interest is less than or equal to the rate of inflation, an individual may borrow for consumption today, and by simply rolling over the loan plus interest payments in each future period, he may maintain his debt, measured in terms of current consumption at a level that does not increase over time.

Now consider a second problem. Suppose we substitute for (4) the condition

$$\limsup_{T \to \infty} Q_T(a_T + m_T) \geq 0. \tag{4a}$$

Relation (4a) replaces the restriction on the sequence of real wealth levels with a restriction on the sequence of wealth levels discounted back to time 0. Following the same procedure used to reduce constraints (1)–(4) to relation (8), we may reduce constraints (1)–(4a) to the following constraint on the discounted sum of consumption:

$$\limsup_{T \to \infty} \sum_{t=0}^{T} Q_t\left(\frac{l_t}{I_t} + x_t - c_t\right) + Q_{T+1}x_{T+1} \geq 0. \tag{8a}$$

I have not seriously examined the question of what conditions on the utility function and the sequence (P_t, I_t, X_t) are necessary and/or sufficient for the existence of a maximal sequence with respect to (8a). For my purposes, however, the results stated in the next theorem will suffice.

Following the analysis of Wilson [9], we may show that the first-order conditions for a maximal sequence require

$$u_c^t + I_t u_l^t = 0,^6 \qquad\qquad t = 0, 1, 2, \ldots, \tag{9}$$

$$\delta u_c^t = \frac{Q_t}{Q_{t-1}} u_c^{t-1} = \frac{P_t}{I_{t-1}P_{t-1}} u_c^{t-1}, \qquad t = 1, 2, 3, \ldots . \tag{10}$$

Equation (9) reflects the static distortion in the marginal rate of substitution between labor and consumption induced by a positive interest factor. Equation (10) states that the marginal rate of substitution of period t consumption for period $t - 1$ consumption must equal one plus the real rate of interest. These conditions become sufficient if, in addition, the budget constraint (8a) is satisfied with equality.

THEOREM 1   A sequence (c_t, l_t) is maximal with respect to constraint (8a) if and only if (9) and (10) are satisfied for $t = 0, 1, 2, \ldots$, and (8a) is satisfied with equality. This sequence is unique.

Proof   The necessity of these conditions follows immediately from (A1). Next consider sufficiency. Suppose (c_t^0, l_t^0) satisfies (9) and (10) and (8a) with equality, and let (c_t, l_t) be some other sequence that also satisfies (8a). Suppose (c_t, l_t) does not satisfy (9) and (10) for all t. Then for some $T' > 0$ and $\varepsilon, \varepsilon_1 > 0$,

---

^{6} $u_x^t = u_x(c_t, l_t)$ for $x = c, l$.

there is another sequence (c_t', l_t') such that

$$\sum_{t=0}^{T'} Q_t\left[\left(\frac{l_t'}{I_t} - c_t'\right) - \left(\frac{l_t}{I_t} - c_t\right)\right] > \varepsilon$$

and

$$\sum_{t=0}^{T'} [u(c_t', l_t') - u(c_t, l_t)]\delta^t > \varepsilon_1.$$

Since (c_t, l_t) satisfies (8a) and (c_t^0, l_t^0) satisfies (8a) with equality, there is a subsequence (T^s) such that

$$\sum_{t=0}^{T^s} Q_t\left[\left(\frac{l_t^0}{I_t} - c_t^0\right) - \left(\frac{l_t}{I_t} - c_t\right)\right] < \varepsilon \qquad \text{for all} \quad s \geqq 0.$$

Now define a new sequence $(c_t'', l_t'') = (c_t', l_t')$ for $t \leqq T'$ and $(c_t'', l_t'') = (c_t, l_t)$ for $t > T'$. Then by construction,

$$\sum_{t=0}^{T^s} Q_t\left[\left(\frac{l_t''}{I_t} - c_t''\right) - \left(\frac{l_t^0}{I_t} - c_t^0\right)\right] > 0 \qquad \text{for all} \quad T^s > T'.$$

Since (c_t^0, l_t^0) satisfies (9) and (10), it then follows that

$$\sum_{t=0}^{T^s} [u(c_t^0, l_t^0) - u(c_t'', l_t'')]\delta^t > 0 \qquad \text{for each} \quad T^s > 0.$$

Therefore,

$$\sum_{t=0}^{T^s} [u(c_t^0, l_t^0) - u(c_t, l_t)]\delta^t$$

$$= \sum_{t=0}^{T^s} [u(c_t^0, l_t^0) - u(c_t'', l_t'')]\delta^t + \sum_{t=0}^{T^s} [u(c_t'', l_t'') - u(c_t, l_t)]\delta^t$$

$$> \sum_{t=0}^{T'} [u(c_t', l_t') - u(c_t, l_t)]\delta^t > \varepsilon_1 \qquad \text{for all} \quad T^s > T'.$$

Now suppose (c_t, l_t) satisfies (9) and (10) for all t. Given any $T > 0$, there is a compact rectangle $G \subset \Omega$ containing the vectors (c_t^0, l_t^0) and (c_t, l_t) in its interior for all $t \leqq T$. For each $t \leqq T$, let $\bar{E}_t = \{E: c - l/I_t \leqq E$ for some $(c, l) \in G\}$. For any $E \in \bar{E}_t$, define $V_t(E) = \max u(c, l)$ subject to $c - l/I_t \leqq E$, and let $\hat{c}_t(E)$ and $\hat{l}_t(E)$ be the corresponding values c and l. Then V_t is strictly concave. (To see this, consider any distinct pair, E_1, E_2. Note that $\hat{c}_t(E) - \hat{l}_t(E)/I_t = E$ implies $[\lambda\hat{c}_t(E_1) + (1 - \lambda)\hat{c}_t(E_2)] - [\lambda\hat{l}_t(E_1) + (1 - \lambda)\hat{l}_t(E_2)]/I_t = \lambda E_1 + (1 - \lambda)E_2$. Therefore, for $0 < \lambda < 1$, $V_t(\lambda E_1 + (1 - \lambda)E_2) \geqq U(\lambda\hat{c}_t(E_1) + (1 - \lambda)\hat{c}_t(E_2), \lambda\hat{l}_t(E_1) + (1 - \lambda)\hat{l}_t(E_2)) > \lambda U(\hat{c}_t(E_1), \hat{l}_t(E_1)) + (1 - \lambda)U(\hat{c}_t(E_2), \hat{l}_t(E_2)) = \lambda V_t(E_1) + (1 - \lambda)V_t(E_2)$.) Furthermore, when $(\hat{c}_t(E), \hat{l}_t(E))$ lies in the interior of G, then $u_c(\hat{c}_t(E), \hat{l}_t(E)) + I_t u_l(\hat{c}_t(E), \hat{l}_t(E)) = 0$ and $V_t'(E) = u_c(\hat{c}_t(E), \hat{l}_t(E))$. Therefore, defining $E_t = c_t - l_t/I_t$, we have $c_t = \hat{c}_t(E_t)$, $l_t = \hat{l}_t(E_t)$, and $V_t'(E_t) = u_c(c_t, l_t)$. Likewise, for $E_t^0 = c_t^0 - l_t^0/I_t$. Equation (10) then implies $\delta^t V_t'(E_t) = Q_t V_t'(E_0)$ for all $t \leq T$. Likewise for sequence (E_t^0). Since $V_t(E)$ is strictly concave, $V_t'(E)$ is invertible and monotonic. Therefore, $E_0^0 \leq (\geq) E_0$ if and only if $E_t^0 \leq (\geq) E_t$ for all $t \leq T$.

(a) Suppose $E_0^0 = E_0$. Then $(c_t^0, l_t^0) = (c_t, l_t)$ for all $t \leq T$. Since T was chosen arbitrarily, this implies $(c_t^0, l_t^0) = (c_t, l_t)$ for all $t > 0$.

(b) Suppose $E_0 < E_0^0$. Then $E_t < E_t^0$ for all $t > 0$ and there is an $\varepsilon > 0$ such that $\sum_{t=0}^{T} [u(c_t^0, l_t^0) - u(c_t, l_t)]\delta^t > \varepsilon$, where ε can be chosen independently of T.

(c) Suppose $E_0^0 < E_0$. Then $E_t^0 < E_t$ for all $t < T$, and therefore there is an $\varepsilon > 0$ such that for any $T > 0$, $\sum_{t=0}^{T} Q_t(E_t - E_t^0) > \varepsilon$. But by assumption,

$$\limsup_{T \to \infty} \sum_{t=0}^{T} Q_t(x_t - E_t^0) + Q_{T+1} x_{T+1} = 0.$$

Therefore

$$\limsup_{T \to \infty} \sum_{t=0}^{T} Q_t(x_t + l_t/I_t - c_t) + Q_{T+1} x_{T+1}$$
$$= \limsup_{T \to \infty} \sum_{t=0}^{T} Q_t(x_t - E_t) + Q_{T+1} x_{T+1} < -\varepsilon.$$

So (c_t, l_t) does not satisfy (8a). This establishes that (c_t^0, l_t^0) is maximal. Interchanging (c_t, l_t) and (c_t^0, l_t^0) in the last argument establishes uniqueness.[7]
Q.E.D.

Return now to the problem of characterizing those sequences that are maximal with respect to the original constraint (8). Subject to the conditions of Lemma 1, a sequence (c_t^0, l_t^0) that satisfies condition (8) is maximal with respect to (8) if and only if it is maximal with respect to (8a). To prove this, I will need the following result, the proof of which is very similar to that of Theorem 2 and is omitted.

LEMMA 2 A sequence (c_t^0, l_t^0) is maximal with respect to (8) [or (8a)] if and only if it is weakly maximal with respect to 8 [or 8(a)].[8]

Lemma 2 is essentially a consequence of the strict concavity of u. We may now state:

[7] Uniqueness could be proved directly if (4a) were replaced with $\liminf_{T \to \infty} Q_T(a_T + m_T) \geq 0$. In this case, the constraint set is convex and uniqueness follows directly from the concavity of u.
[8] See (D1) for the difference between maximality and weak maximality.

THEOREM 2   A sequence (c_t^0, l_t^0) satisfying (8) is maximal with respect to (8) if and only if (a) it is maximal with respect to (8a); and (b) it satisfies the conditions of Lemma 1.

Proof   The necessity of (b) is Lemma 1. To prove that (a) is necessary, assume (c_t^0, l_t^0) is maximal with respect to (8) but not with respect to (8a). Then by Lemma 1, there is a subsequence (T^s), such that $(Q_{T^s}) \to 0$ and

$$\limsup_{T^s \to \infty} \frac{1}{Q_{T^s}} \sum_{t=0}^{T^s-1} Q_t \left(\frac{l_t^0}{I_t} + x_t - c_t^0 \right) + x_{T^s} > -\infty.$$

Therefore,

$$\limsup_{T^s \to \infty} \sum_{t=0}^{T^s-1} Q_t \left(\frac{l_t^0}{I_t} + x_t - c_t^0 \right) + Q_{T^s} x_{T^s} \geqq 0$$

which means that (c_t^0, l_t^0) satisfies (8a). Therefore, by Lemma 2 there is an $\varepsilon > 0$ and a sequence (c_t, l_t) that also satisfies (8a) for which

$$\liminf_{T \to \infty} \sum_{t=0}^{T} [u(c_t, l_t) - u(c_t^0, l_t^0)] \delta^t > \varepsilon.$$

Define (c_t', l_t') to equal (c_t, l_t) except $l_0' = l_0 + \varepsilon_1$. Then for $\varepsilon_1 > 0$ sufficiently small, $\sum_{t=0}^{T} [u(c_t', l_t') - u(c_t^0, l_t^0)] \delta^t > \varepsilon/2$ for all T sufficiently large and (8a) is satisfied with strict inequality. Therefore (c_t', l_t') satisfies (8), which contradicts the maximality of (c_t^0, l_t^0).

To establish sufficiency, suppose that (c_t^0, l_t^0) satisfies conditions (a) and (b), and suppose there is a sequence (c_t, l_t) also satisfying (8) such that

$$\liminf_{T \to \infty} \sum_{t=0}^{T} [u(c_t, l_t) - u(c_t^0, l_t^0)] \delta^t \geqq 0.$$

Now consider a subsequence (T^s) such that for all

$$\frac{1}{Q_{T^s}} \sum_{t=0}^{T^s-1} Q_t \left(\frac{l_t}{I_t} + x_t - c_t \right) + x_{T^s} > -K \qquad \text{for some} \quad K > 0.$$

Then since (c_t^0, l_t^0) satisfies (9) and (10), it follows that

$$\frac{1}{Q_{T^s}} \sum_{t=0}^{T^s-1} Q_t \left(\frac{l_t^0}{I_t} + x_t - c_t^0 \right) + x_{T^s} > -K \qquad \text{for all} \quad T^s$$

sufficiently large. Therefore condition (b) implies $\lim_{T^s \to \infty} Q_{T^s} = 0$, and hence

$$\limsup_{T^s \to \infty} \sum_{t=0}^{T^s-1} Q_t \left(\frac{l_t}{I_t} + x_t - c_t \right) + Q_{T^s} x_{T^s} \geqq 0.$$

Therefore (c_t, l_t) satisfies (8a), which contradicts (a).   Q.E.D.

Theorems 1 and 2 suggest a procedure for finding the maximal sequence with respect to constraint (8). First, find those sequences which satisfy (9) and (10). From the proof of Theorem 1, we know this will be a one-parameter family. Next check to see if for any of these sequences, (8a) is satisfied with equality. If not, then Theorem 1 implies that there is no sequence that is maximal with respect to (8). If there is a maximal sequence with respect to (8a), check to see if it satisfies constraint (8). If, in addition, the conditions of Lemma 1 are satisfied, then Theorem 2 implies that the sequence will be maximal with respect to (8) as well.[9]

One might argue that in those cases where no sequence is maximal with respect to (8), constraint (8a) is the appropriate restriction anyway. The gain from using the weaker restriction (8a) is that it may generate equilibria in some cases where (8) does not. If, for instance, government lending is going to infinity at less than a geometric rate, but the money supply is being held constant, equilibrium may require a sequence of individual debt that violates (4) but not (4a). For the remainder of the paper, however, I will assume that relation (4) is the appropriate constraint.

EQUILIBRIUM

Government policy in this model is limited to two kinds of actions. In each period, it may make money transfers (or tax) and it may buy or sell bonds. I assume that each individual correctly anticipates the sequence of transfer payments he will receive and the sequence of prices and interest rates he will face in all periods. The economy is then in equilibrium when the sequence of prices and interest rates have adjusted so that both the market for goods and services and the bond market clear in each period. Let (X_t) be the sequence of government transfers and (B_T) be the sequence of government purchases of bonds. Then equilibrium may be defined as

(D2)   Given $(B_t, X_t), (P_t, I_t, c_t)$ is an *equilibrium* if

$$l_t = c_t, \qquad t = 0, 1, 2, \ldots, \tag{11}$$

$$A_t = B_t, \qquad t = 0, 1, 2, \ldots \tag{12}$$

implies (c_t, l_t, A_t) is maximal with respect to constraints (1)–(4).

---

[9] An examination of the proof of Theorem 1 actually reveals a more direct procedure. Consider all those sequences that satisfy (9) and (10). They may be ordered by the value of $E_0 = I_0 c_0 - l_0$. If there is a largest E_0 such that constraint (8) is satisfied and the conditions of Lemma 1 are satisfied for the corresponding sequence (c_t, l_t), then (c_t, l_t) is maximal with respect to (8). Otherwise no maximal sequence exists.

When analyzing the model, it will be convenient to focus on the money market rather than the bond market. Although the supply of money $\bar{M}_t$ is not a direct policy instrument, it may nevertheless be determined by government policy, directly, through the choice of (B_t, X_t) and indirectly through the consequent effect on the sequence of interest rates. At time t, after the financial transactions have been concluded, the supply of money $\bar{M}_t$ is equal to

$$\bar{M}_t = \bar{M}_{t-1} - B_t + I_{t-1}B_{t-1} + X_t. \tag{13}$$

Summing (13) from 0 to t then gives the supply of money at t as a function of only transfers and government borrowing:

$$\bar{M}_t = -B_t + X_t + \sum_{s=0}^{t-1} (X_s + i_s B_s). \tag{14}$$

At time t, the supply of money equals the sum of government transfers plus interest payments up to time t minus government debt at time t. It may be readily verified by summing over Eq. (2) and using (11) and (12) that in equilibrium the demand for money M_t equals the supply $\bar{M}_t$.

A Characterization of the Equilibrium Sequences

By combining the conditions that characterize maximal sequences with the definition of equilibrium, it is possible to provide a simple characterization of the equilibrium sequences. Following the procedure adopted in [7] for the finite horizon model, I will show that the set of equilibria correspond to the set of solutions of a second-order difference equation. The distinction between the infinite horizon and the finite horizon models lies in the form of the transversality conditions. In addition to the requirements of Lemma 1, any equilibrium sequence must satisfy two transversality conditions that correspond to budget constraints (8) and (8a).

Assumption (A1) requires that $c_t > 0$ for each $t \geq 0$. Therefore, it follows immediately from the liquidity constraint (1) that in equilibrium the supply of money must be positive in each period. From Eq. (13) this imposes the following restrictions on the sequence of transfers, government debt, and interest rates:

$$M_T = \bar{M}_T = X_T - B_T + \sum_{t=0}^{T-1} (X_t + i_t B_t) > 0, \qquad T = 1, 2, 3, \ldots . \tag{15}$$

The solvency condition (4) also implies another constraint. In equilibrium,

$$\limsup_{T \to \infty} \frac{M_T + B_T}{P_T} = \limsup_{T \to \infty} \frac{1}{P_T} \left[X_T + \sum_{t=0}^{T-1} (X_t + i_t B_t) \right] > -\infty. \tag{16}$$

In order for an equilibrium to exist, however, Theorems 1 and 2 imply that (4a) must be satisfied with equality. In nominal terms using condition (12):

$$\limsup_{T \to \infty} R_T(B_T + M_T) = \limsup_{T \to \infty} R_T \left[X_T + \sum_{t=0}^{T-1} (X_t + i_t B_t) \right] = 0. \quad (16a)$$

The conditions of Lemma 1 can also be translated in terms of the sequences of (B_t, X_t) and (I_t) to yield

$$\liminf_{s \to \infty} \frac{1}{P_{T^s}} \left[X_{T^s} + \sum_{t=0}^{T^s} (X_t + i_t B_t) \right] > -\infty \quad \text{implies} \quad \lim_{s \to \infty} P_{T^s} R_{T^s} = 0.$$

$$(17)$$

Relations (16), (16a), and (17) provide the transversality conditions. They are essentially a consequence of summing over the budget constraints of all individuals and using the conditions for an equilibrium. If lim sup were replaced by lim inf, they would still be necessary for the existence of an equilibrium even if we were to consider an economy with many goods and heterogeneous preferences.

The construction of the difference equation that will generate the equilibrium sequences requires one additional result. We need to be able to determine the level of consumption from the level of real balances. Define $m_t = M_t/P_t$. From relation (1) we know that $c_t \leq m_t$ and from Eq. (6) we know that the relation must hold with equality whenever $i_t > 0$. This information is sufficient to yield the necessary result. Assume

(A2)   There is a c^* such that $u_c(c^*, c^*) + u_l(c^*, c^*) = 0$.[10]

Since u is quasi-concave, this point is unique. From (9) we know that the individual always equates the marginal rate of substitution of c for l to the interest factor I_t. Therefore, if the interest rate is zero, the equilibrium consumption level must be c^*. On the other hand, if the interest rate is positive, then a higher marginal rate of substitution requires that the corresponding consumption level must be less than c^*.[11] Therefore, if $m_t < c^*$, then (1) implies $c_t < c^*$, and hence the interest rate i_t must be positive. Therefore, $c_t = m_t$. If $m_t \geq c^*$, then i_t must be zero, and hence $c_t = c^*$; otherwise, Eq. (6) is violated. This establishes

LEMMA 3   If (c_t, m_t) is consistent with equilibrium, $m_t \leq c^*$ implies $c_t = m_t$ and $m_t \geq c_t$ implies $c_t = c^*$.

---

[10] The assumption is relatively weak. It is necessary for the existence of a Pareto optimal equilibrium.

[11] If $-l$ is a normal good, then the equilibrium level of c_t will be a decreasing function of I_t.

Now consider Eq. (10). Substituting in Eq. (9) and using the definition of m_t yields

$$m_t u_c^t = (-M_t/\delta M_{t-1})m_{t-1}u_l^{t-1}. \tag{18}$$

Given a sequence (M_t) and a sequence (m_t) satisfying Eq. (18), we can determine (P_t) and use Lemma 3 and Eq. (9) and (11) to determine (I_t) and (c_t). If this sequence satisfies (13) and the transversality conditions (16), (16a), and (17), then it is an equilibrium. In fact, one may readily verify that these conditions are equivalent to the conditions used to define an equilibrium. Therefore we may state

THEOREM 3   Given (B_t, X_t), (P_t, I_t, c_t) is an equilibrium if and only if (a) relations (16), (16a), and (17) are satisfied, and (b) given (9), (11), and the conditions of Lemma 3, the corresponding sequences (M_t) and (m_t) satisfy (15) and (18).

Equation (18) is illustrated in Fig. 1. The curve in the southwest quadrant represents the relation between m_{t-1} and $m_{t-1}u_l^{t-1}$. For $m_{t-1} < c^*$, Lemma 3 implies $c_{t-1} = l_{t-1} = m_{t-1}$. Therefore, over this range the curve may be interpreted as describing $mu_l(m, m)$ as a function of m. Without additional assumptions on u, such as separability, the curve need not be monotonic;

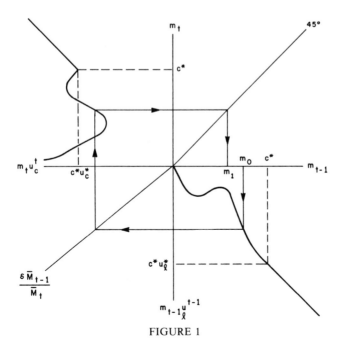

FIGURE 1

however, if $u_l(m, m)$ is bounded below as m goes to zero, the curve will start on the origin. At $m_{t-1} = c^*$, the curve continues as a ray from the origin with slope $u_l(c^*, c^*)$. Along this segment u_l^t is held constant at $u_l(c^*, c^*)$ and only m_{t-1} increases.

In the northwest quadrant is the curve representing the relation between m_t and $m_t u_c^t$. For $m < c^*$, the curve is a graph of $mu_c(m, m)$ as a function of m. It may be either positively or negatively sloped and may even by bounded away from zero if u is unbounded below.[12] At $m_t = c^*$, the curve continues as a ray from the origin with slope $-1/u_c(c^*, c^*)$. Again, this reflects the indeterminancy in m_t when $c_t = c^*$; u_c^t is held constant at $u_c(c^*, c^*)$, but m_t may take on any value greater than c^*.

A 45-deg line in the northeast quadrant translates m_t into m_{t-1}, and in the southwest quadrant is a graph of Eq. (18). Since $m_{t-1} u_l^{t-1}$ is measured on the vertical axis and $m_t u_c^t$ is measured on the horizontal axis, this curve must be a straight line through the origin with slope $\delta \bar{M}_{t-1}/\bar{M}_t$. Starting with any m_{t-1} and moving clockwise around the graph yields those values of m_t that are consistent with Eq. (18). As is apparent from Fig. 1, there may be several such values or none at all. Translating these values to the horizontal axis then permits us to determine m_{t+1}, etc.

If $M_t/\bar{M}_{t-1}$ changes with t, then the slope of the line must be adjusted for each t accordingly. However, it is always the case that $\bar{M}_t$ and $\bar{M}_{t-1}$ can be determined independently of m_t. If we know $\bar{M}_{t-1}$ and m_{t-1}, then we may use Lemma 3 and Eq. (9) to determine i_{t-1} and (13) to determine $\bar{M}_t$. If government borrowing is identically zero, then the sequence $(\bar{M}_t)$ is independent of the sequence of interest rates. In this case, Eq. (18) becomes a first-order difference equation in m_t. In any case, $\bar{M}_0$ is fixed by Eq. (14).

Many of the results in the following sections depend only on the transversality conditions, particularly (16a). These results hold for models much more general than the one being analyzed here. Some of the results, however, do require more structure, particularly when I discuss the question of the uniqueness of equilibrium at the end of the paper. For this issue Eq. (18) will be exploited to explicitly characterize different equilibrium sequences.

THE EXISTENCE OF EQUILIBRIUM AND EQUIVALENT GOVERNMENT POLICIES

An obvious question to consider at this point are the conditions on the sequence (B_t, X_t) which are necessary for an equilibrium to exist. As with the finite horizon model in Wilson [7], I have not found a satisfactory answer to this question. In general, it appears to depend in a complicated way on the

---

[12] If $u(c, l)$ is log linear in c, then $m_t u_c^t$ will be constant at $c^* u_c(c^*, c^*)$.

properties of the utility function. However, we can establish a general theorem if the question is turned around: Under what conditions is a sequence (P_t, I_t, c_t) an equilibrium for some sequence (B_t, X_t)? I will also address a second question. Roughly, how large is the class of sequences that generate the same equilibrium?

For all of the results obtained in the earlier sections, no restrictions have been necessary on the value of the discount factor δ, other than it be positive. This is because we were concerned only with characterizing an equilibrium, not with establishing its existence. Most of the results in the remainder of the paper will require the following assumption:

(A3) $0 < \delta < 1$.

In investigating the finite horizon model, I showed that for any sequence of real balances, there is a sequence (B_t, X_t) that generates that sequence in equilibrium. In fact, the sequence can be chosen so that $B_t = 0$ for each t. In the infinite horizon model, this statement must be qualified. The theorem remains valid only if we put some bounds on the sequence of real balances that depend on the time rate of preference δ and the marginal utility of consumption.

THEOREM 4 For any $P_0^* > 0$ and $(m_t) \in R_+^\infty$, there is a sequence (B_t, X_t) with $B_t = 0$ for all $t \geq 0$ for which a corresponding equilibrium sequence (P_t, I_t, c_t) generates (m_t) and satisfies $P_0 = P_0^*$ if and only if (a) $\lim_{t \to \infty} \delta^t m_t = 0$, and (b) $\lim_{t \to \infty} \delta^t u_c(c_t, c_t) = 0$.

Proof Since from Lemma 3 and Eq. (11), m_t determines u_c^t and u_i^t, we may use Eq. (18) to determine the sequence (M_t/M_{t-1}), which is consistent with (m_t) in equilibrium. Since $M_0 = m_0 P_0^*$, this determines the sequence (M_t), which in turn determines the sequence (P_t). The sequence (I_t) is determined directly from (m_t) and Eq. (9). Since $B_t = 0$ for all $t \geq 0$, Eq. (13) requires $X_0 = M_0$ and $X_t = M_t - M_{t-1}$ for $t > 0$. This establishes that (m_t) satisfies (18) for sequence (X_t, B_t).

Turning to the transversality conditions, (15) implies $\sum_{t=0}^T X_t > 0$ for all $T \geq 0$; so (16) is satisfied. It also implies that (17) is satisfied if and only if $\lim_{t \to \infty} P_t R_t = 0$. From Eq. (10) we have $\delta^t u_c^t = P_t R_t (u_c^0/P_0)$ or $\delta^t m_t u_c^t = R_t M_t (m_0 u_c^0/M_0)$ for all $t > 0$. Therefore $\lim_{t \to \infty} P_t R_t = 0$ if and only if $\lim_{t \to \infty} \delta^t u_c^t = 0$. Finally Eq. (16a) is satisfied if and only if $R_T \sum_{t=0}^T X_t = R_T M_T \to 0$ as $T \to \infty$. Since $\delta^t u_c^t \to 0$ as $t \to \infty$, this condition will be satisfied if and only if $\lim_{t \to \infty} m_t \delta^t = 0$. Q.E.D.

Condition (b) on the sequence (u_c^t) is essentially a restriction on how quickly the sequence of real balances can approach zero. It is required to ensure that the rate of inflation does not consistently exceed the nominal rate of interest. This condition must be satisfied for at least some subsequence t^s even if the government is permitted to enter the bond market.[13]

Condition (a) on the $(m_t,)$ sequence can be removed, however, if we permit the government to adjust its borrowing and lending appropriately. The problem is to guarantee that the sequence of the values of private wealth, measured in terms of current consumption, is bounded near zero. This can be accomplished if the government uses open market operations to adjust the money supply and transfer payments to offset interest payments, keeping private wealth equal to zero in each period.[14]

THEOREM 5   For any $P_0^* > 0$ and any $(m_t) \, \varepsilon \, R_+^\infty$, there is a sequence (B_t, X_t) for which a corresponding equilibrium sequence (P_t, I_t, c_t) generates (m_t) and satisfies $P_0 = P_0^*$ if and only if condition (b) of Theorem 4 is satisfied for some subsequence (T^s).

Proof   The proof is identical to that of Theorem 4 up to the point where the sequence (I_t) and (M_t) is determined. Let $X_0 = 0$, $X_t = -i_{t-1}B_{t-1}$ for $t \in (T^s)$, and $X_t = -i_{t-1}B_{t-1} - tP_t$ for $t \notin (T^s)$. Then define $B_0 = M_0$, and $B_t = -M_t + M_{t-1} + i_{t-1}B_{t-1} + X_t$ for all $t > 0$. Then (15) is satisfied, and $X_T + \sum_{t=0}^{T-1}(X_t + i_t B_t) = 0$ for $T \in (T^s)$ and $X_T + \sum_{t=0}^{T-1}(X_t + i_t B_t) = -TP_T$ for $T \notin (T^s)$; so (16) and (16a) are satisfied. Following the proof of Theorem 4, condition (b) implies that (17) is satisfied as well.   Q.E.D.

The proof of Theorem 5 suggests that it may be possible to construct a large class of (B_t, X_t) sequences all of which generate the same equilibrium sequence. This in fact the case.

THEOREM 6   An equilibrium sequence (P_t, I_t, c_t) generated by (B_t, X_t) can be generated by any (B_t', X_t') for which (a) $X_0' - B_0' = X_0 - B_0$ and and $X_t' - B_t' + I_{t-1}B_{t-1}' = X_t - B_t + I_{t-1}B_{t-1}$ for $t > 0$, and (b) (16), (16a), and (17) are satisfied. Condition (b) implies

$$\limsup_{T \to \infty} \sum_{t=0}^{T} R_t(X_t - X_t') \geqq 0 \geqq \liminf_{T \to \infty} \sum_{t=0}^{T} R_t(X_t - X_t').$$

Proof   By construction (B_t', X_t') generates the same (M_t) sequence as (B_t, X_t), given sequence (I_t), and hence the same (m_t) sequence given sequence (P_t). Therefore (13) is satisfied. Since (16), (16a), and (17) are satisfied by assumption, the theorem is proved.

---

[13] If the consumer's solvency constraint (4) were replaced by (4a), the restriction would not be necessary at all.

[14] If the model contained capital goods, then private wealth would equal the value of capital goods in each period.

The last statement of the theorem follows upon substituting (11) and (12) into (5) to obtain

$$\sum_{t=0}^{T} R_{t+1}(X_{t+1} - i_t M_t) + X_0 = R_{T+1}(M_{T+1} + B_{T+1}).$$

Therefore (16a) implies

$$\limsup_{T \to \infty} \sum_{t=0}^{T} R_{t+1}(X_{t+1} - i_t M_t) + X_0 = 0.$$

Since (B_t, X_t) and (B_t', X_t') generate the same (M_t) sequence for interest rate sequence (I_t), the statement is proved.   Q.E.D.

Condition (a) of Theorem 6 is necessary and sufficient condition that (B_t', X_t') generate the same sequence $(\bar{M}_t)$ as did (B_t, X_t) given the interest rate sequence (I_t). However, this is not a sufficient condition for the original (P_t, I_t, c_t) sequence to remain an equilibrium. In order to ensure that the equilibrium (c_t, l_t) sequence remains maximal, (X_t) must be chosen so that the solvency conditions of Theorems 1 and 2 and Lemma 1 are still satisfied. This is essentially the role of condition (b). Nevertheless, the class of equivalent government policies is quite large. For any sequence (B_t') there is a sequence (X_t') that satisfies condition (a); similarly, for any sequence (X_t'), a sequence (B_t') can be found that satisfies (a). Furthermore, as long as the value of the discounted sum of transfer payments remains unchanged, the transversality condition (b) will continue to be satisfied. This corresponds to the result obtained for the finite horizon.

Pareto Optimal Equilibria

We turn our attention now to characterizing those government policies that generate Pareto optimal equilibria. Here Pareto optimality is defined without reference to the transactions constraint (1). This section contains two important results. First, Pareto optimality implies a zero rate of interest in each period. Second, a Pareto optimal equilibrium can exist only if the lim sup of the sum of transfer payments in *nominal* terms equals zero.

(D3)   A sequence (c_t, l_t) is Pareto optimal if (c_t, l_t) is maximal with respect to all sequences satisfying (11), $c_t = l_t$ for $t \geq 0$.

It is not difficult to verify that $c_t = l_t = c^*$ for all t is the only Pareto optimal sequence. Furthermore, the fact that u is differentiable implies that, in equilibrium, this sequence is maximal with respect to (8) if and only if

$I_t = 1$ for all t. Inspection of Eq. (10) then reveals that the sequence of prices must satisfy $P_t = \delta P_{t-1}$ for all $t > 0$. Therefore we may state

THEOREM 7   If (P_t, I_t, c_t) is an equilibrium, the corresponding consumption sequence (c_t, c_t) is Pareto optimal if and only if $P_t = \delta^t P_0$, $I_t = 1$, and $c_t = c^*$ for $t = 0, 1, 2, \ldots$.

As in the finite horizon model, the class of Pareto optimal equilibria is a one-parameter family indexed by the initial price P_0. Consumption is constant at c^* and the price level falls at a constant rate δ. In more general models, such stationarity is not necessary. What is required is that the real variables of the system must correspond to a competitive equilibrium and the sequences of prices correspond to the associated sequence competitive prices. The restriction on the sequence of interest rates, however, is quite general. Otherwise, the economy will behave as if there is a tax on consumption.

Theorem 8 characterizes those sequences (B_t, X_t) that generate Pareto optimal equilibria.

THEOREM 8 (B_t, X_t) generates a one-parameter family of Pareto optimal equilibria if and only if (a) there is a $K > 0$ such that $-B_T + \sum_{t=0}^{T} X_t > K^T$ for $T = 0, 1, 2, \ldots$, and (b) $\lim \sup_{T \to \infty} \sum_{t=0}^{T} X_t = 0$ and $\lim \sup_{T \to \infty} \delta^{-T} \sum_{t=0}^{T} X_t > -\infty$.

Proof   Since Theorem 7 requires $I_t = 1$ for all t, (15) implies $\bar{M}_t = B_T + \sum_{t=0}^{T} X_t$. Since $P_t = \delta^t P_0$ and $c_t = c^*$ for all t, constraint (1) requires that $P_0 \delta^t c^* < B_T + \sum_{t=0}^{T} X_t$ for some $P_0 > 0$. This establishes the necessity of (a). The necessity of (b) is implied directly from (16) and (16a).

Sufficiency is established by noting that setting $P_0 \leqq K/c^*$ and setting $I_t = 1$ for all t generates an (m_t) sequence that satisfies (18) and a (P_t) sequence for which $P_t = \delta^t P_0$ for all t. Since $R_t = 1$ for all t, (17) is satisfied, as is (16) and (16a). Therefore, the conditions of Theorem 1 are satisfied.   Q.E.D.

Theorem 8 has a number of implications that are of interest. First, if government borrowing is identically zero in each period, equilibrium can be Pareto optimal only if the nominal value of the sum of government transfers converges to zero. In the absence of government borrowing, the sum of transfers equals the supply of money in each period. This means that the nominal supply of money converges to zero. However, this does not imply that the level of real balances is necessarily constant or even bounded above. Any growth factor of the money supply that is between δ and 1 is consistent with an efficient equilibrium. If the supply of money grows at rate σ where $\delta < \sigma < 1$, the level of real balances may grow to infinity at rate σ/δ, while the price level decays at rate δ. Thus, in this model, there is an interval of optimal growth rates of the money supply, only one of which equals the time rate of preference as argued by Friedman [6].[15]

This result is a consequence of the factor that when the interest rate is zero, the economy is in a liquidity trap. Given that his real balances are sufficiently large to satisfy constraint (1), the individual is indifferent between holding money or bonds. Therefore, the individual is willing to hold any level of real balances that do not grow so large that consumption can be increased and the solvency constraint satisfied without a corresponding increase in the supply of labor. But as long as the nominal supply of money is being taxed away to zero, this cannot happen. Any small increase in consumption without a corresponding increase in the supply of labor must eventually result in a level of nominal wealth bounded below zero. But since the price level is also converging to zero, this implies that the value of private wealth measured in real terms falls without bound.

Theorem 8 also has some important implications when government policy is restricted solely to open market operations ($X_t = 0$ for all t). In this case condition (b) is automatically satisfied. Therefore, a Pareto optimal equilibrium exists if and only if the government is a net lender in each period and lending does not decrease at a rate less than δ.

In fact, when government transfers are identically zero in each period, any equilibrium must be Pareto optimal. Upon substituting (11) and (12) into (5) and setting $(X_t) = 0$, it follows that if $M_t > 0$ for all t, (16a) can only be satisfied if $i_t = 0$ for all t. Therefore we may state

THEOREM 9 If $X_t = 0$ for $t = 0, 1, 2, \ldots$, then an equilibrium exists if and only if there is a $K > 0$ such that $-B_t > K\delta^t$ for $t = 0, 1, 2, \ldots$. In this case, all equilibria are Pareto optimal.

I strongly suspect that many of the results of this section depend critically on the assumption that the *individual* plans for an infinite horizon. It would be interesting to investigate how the class of Pareto optimal policies change when we consider an overlapping generations model. I suspect that at least some of the indeterminancy in the price level would be removed.

Equilibrium with No Government Borrowing

In this section, I examine in more detail the nature of the equilibrium when government policy is restricted solely to transfer payments. This will require that we exploit in more detail the special structure of the model captured in Eq. (18).

[15] This result could also be obtained in models where money enters the utility function, as in Brock [4], if the marginal utility of real balances is zero above some finite level. We should not expect to obtain this result, however, in models with finite-lived overlapping generations.

One of the more striking results of the finite horizon model is that when the government does not borrow or lend, if one equilibrium exists, then a one-parameter family of equilibria exist, an interval of which is Pareto optimal, another interval of which is not. Furthermore, it was shown that depending on the properties of the utility function, it is sometimes possible to construct equilibria as inefficient as we desire. This result is essentially a consequence of the fact that in the finite horizon model the demand for money can equal the supply in each period only if the sum of the transfer payments across all periods is equal to zero. Thus, the conditions necessary for the existence of any equilibrium are also sufficient for the existence of Pareto optimal equilibria. When the horizon becomes infinite, however, this is no longer true. It is possible for the sum of transfers to be bounded away from zero and still generate an equilibrium. In fact, the equilibrium may be unique.

Consider an example where $X_0 = \bar{M}_0 > 0$ and $X_t = 0$ for all $t > 0$. Suppose that utility is separable in c and l so that $u(c, l) = v(c) + w(l)$, and assume that $cv'(c)$ is increasing in c. Also assume that there is a $\hat{c}$ such that $v'(\hat{c}) + (1/\delta)w'(\hat{c}) = 0$. Then since $\bar{M}_t = X_0$ for all $t \geq 0$, it is not difficult to verify that $(m_t = \hat{c})$ satisfies Eq. (18). Also, since $P_t = X_0/c^*$ and Eq. (9) implies $I_t = 1/\delta$ for all t, transversality conditions (16), (16a), and (17) are also satisfied. Therefore $(P_t = X_0/\hat{c}, I_t = 1/\delta, c_t = \hat{c})_{t=0}^{\infty}$ is an equilibrium.

The equilibrium is illustrated in Fig. 2. Because $M_t = M_0$ for all t, the $\delta \bar{M}_{t-1}/\bar{M}_t$ line has slope δ. Therefore, starting at $m_0 = \hat{c}$ and moving clockwise around the graph generates m_1, also equal to $\hat{c}$.

We may also investigate whether or not other equilibria exist as well. Since u is separable and strictly concave, the slope of a ray from the origin to the $m_t u_c^t$ curve must be strictly increasing in m_t from 0 to c^*. For $m_t \geq c^*$, it stays constant—similarly for the $m_{t-1} u_l^{t-1}$ curve. This implies that any path starting from any point different from $\hat{c}$ will diverge.

Suppose the initial price P_0' were less than $X_0/\hat{c}$. Then the initial real balances would be higher than $\hat{c}$, and the resulting sequence (m_t') would eventually rise above c^* growing by a factor of $1/\delta$ in each period. The consumption level would eventually stay constant at c^* and the interest factor at $I_t = 1$. Such a sequence, however, violates transversality condition (16a). Since the interest rate is zero for all but a finite number of periods, (R_t) is bounded away from zero, and consequently (16a) reduces to $\limsup_{T \to \infty} X_0 = 0$. A contradiction. Therefore, the initial price of any equilibrium sequence must be less than or equal to $X_0/\hat{c}$.[16]

---

[16] If $v'(c)$ is bounded above and $w'(c)$ is bounded below zero, then for δ sufficiently small, there may be no $\hat{c}$ such that $v'(\hat{c}) + (1/\delta)\omega'(\hat{v}) = 0$. In this case any (m_t) sequence must diverge to $+\infty$, and consequently there is no equilibrium. Any interest rate high enough to be consistent with equilibrium distorts the marginal rate of substitution between consumption and labor to the point where only autarchy is possible.

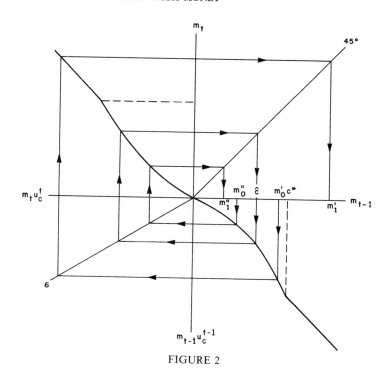

FIGURE 2

Next consider the case where the initial P_0'' is greater than $X_0/\hat{c}$, resulting in an initial level of real balances $m_0'' < \hat{c}$. As is apparent from Fig. 2, in this case an equilibrium can only exist if $\lim_{c \to 0} cv'(c) = 0$. If this condition is satisfied, then (m_t'') converges to zero, (P_t'') goes to infinity, and (I_t'') is bounded above 1. Therefore (R_t'') also converges to zero, from which it follows immediately that condition (16a) will be satisfied as well as (16). Whether or not (17) is satisfied, however, depends on the properties of v.

From Eq. (10), we may show

$$\delta^t v'(m_t) = P_t R_t [v'(m_0)/P_0]. \tag{10'}$$

If $\lim_{c \to 0} v'(c) < \infty$, then it follows immediately from (10') that $\lim_{t \to \infty} P_t R_t = 0$, satisfying (17). In this case any $P_0 \leqq X_0/\hat{c}$ generates an equilibrium.

Suppose, however, that $-cv''(c)/v'(c) > K > 0$ for all c near 0. Then one may show that for $c < \hat{c}$ there is a $\gamma > 0$ such that $\delta v'(c/\gamma) > v'(c)$.[17] From Eq. (18), we have $m_t/m_{t-1} = 1/\delta[-w'(m_{t-1})/v'(m_t)]$. Since $w'(l)$ is bounded below for l near 0, and $v'(c) \to \infty$ as $c \to 0$, $m_t \to 0$ implies $m_t/m_{t-1} \to 0$. Therefore, for t sufficiently large, $\delta v'(m_t) > v'(m_{t-1})$. Equation (10') then

[17] $v'(c/2) - v'(c) = -\int_{c/2}^{c} v''(x)\,dx > \int_{c/2}^{c} K[v'(x)/x]\,dx > K[v'(c)/c]c/2 = (K/2)v'(c)$. Therefore $v'(c/2') > [(2 + K)/2]^t v'(c)$.

implies that $P_t R_t$ must be bounded away from zero. In this case, therefore, the equilibrium is unique. If the initial price were less than $X_0/\hat{c}$, then the result would be a hyperinflation in which the price level grows faster than the rate of interest. Consequently, consumers would be able to borrow today to increase consumption without increasing their supply of labor.

Even if we are able to rule out the possibility of hyperinflation equilibria, however, it is not necessarily the case that the equilibrium is unique or even locally unique. If $cv'(c)$ is a decreasing function of c, there may be a one-parameter family of equilibria that cycle. Consider a utility function of the form $u(c, l) = -\theta^{-1}(c^{-\theta} + l^{\theta})$ for $\theta > 1$, the properties of which are illustrated in Fig. 3. Assuming again that $\bar{M}_t = X_0$ for all t, define $\hat{c} = \delta^{1/2\theta}$. The reader may verify that setting $m_0 = \hat{c}$ generates a stationary equilibrium. Now suppose we choose $m_0 > \hat{c}$ but less than $c^* = 1$. Then Eq. (18) implies $m_0 = \delta^{1/\theta}/m_1$ and $m_1 = \delta^{1/\theta}/m_2$, which in turn implies $m_0 = m_2$. In this case, therefore, the equilibrium displays a two-period cycle as illustrated in Fig. 3. Real balances alternately rise and fall at the same time that prices and interest rates alternately fall and then rise.

Essentially the same analysis could be applied to any sequence of transfers that generates a constant positive growth rate of the money supply. Generally, the higher the growth rate of money, the lower will be the stationary state level of real balances and the higher will be the interest rate.

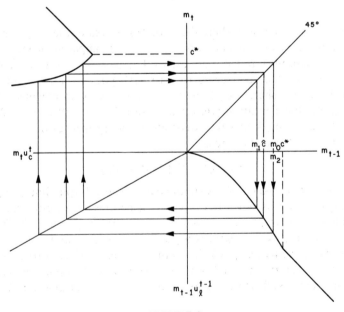

FIGURE 3

If the growth rate of money is negative, however, those sequences of real balances generated by an initial $m_0 > \hat{c}$ will satisfy all of the transversality conditions. In this case, the sum of transfer approaches zero as $T \to \infty$, so it is not necessary that the discount factor R_t go to zero. This result is consistent with the result obtained earlier that such sequences may generate Pareto optimal equilibria. What we have demonstrated here is that a one-parameter family of inefficient equilibria is generally possible as well. Only in the case where the growth factor of the money supply exactly equals δ may we expect all equilibria to be Pareto optimal.

CONCLUSION

The primary motivation of this paper has been twofold: first, to demonstrate how the finite horizon model developed in Wilson [7] can be extended to the infinite horizon; second, to investigate which of those properties of the finite horizon model can also be obtained when the horizon is infinite. Ultimately, any differences between the two models stem from the differences in the form of the budget constraint. The same difference equation characterizes the solution, and the same conditions for efficiency are obtained. Because, the horizon is infinite, however, the solvency constraint may be relaxed so that private wealth need never exactly equal zero. This relaxes the restrictions on the sequence of transfer payments and interest rates which must be satisfied in equilibrium.

The differences between the two models are most striking when we examine the case where government debt is always zero. In the finite horizon the sum of transfer payments must equal zero, and the set of equilibria is a one-parameter family of equilibria, some of which are Pareto optimal and some of which are not. In the infinite horizon, transfer payments need not sum to zero if the discount factor goes to zero.As a consequence, equilibria need no longer be efficient and may even be unique.

Although most of the paper has been concerned with developing the general properties of the model, the analysis in the last section also illustrates that comparative dynamic exercises are quite tractable. The model may therefore be considered as an alternative to models where real balances enter as a direct argument in the utility function. Not only may such issues as the optimal growth rate of the money supply or the effect of anticipated changes in monetary policy be reexamined (see e.g., Brock [3, 4]), but because government debt has also been incorporated into the model, we may compare the impact of open market operations versus government transfers as instruments for controlling the supply of money. Nor do we need to restrict consideration to fixed sequences of government debt and taxes. Following Black [1], we might also consider government policies in which the level of government borrowing or transfer payments are functions of current market variables.

Space does not permit an adequate discussion of possible extensions of the model to incorporate capital or overlapping generations. Some extensions are treated briefly in Wilson [7]. I will mention only that even the most modest extensions appear to complicate considerably a detailed description of equilibria in the model. The simplest overlapping generations model I can construct converts the problem from a first-order difference equation to a second-order difference equation. Adding capital and eliminating labor make it a third-order difference equation. Perhaps the model can still yield some useful insights in these cases, but I expect the analysis must be relatively more complicated.

REFERENCES

1. Black, F., The uniqueness of the price level in monetary growth models, *J. Econ. Theory* **7** (1974), 53–65.
2. Brock, W. A., On the existence of weakly maximal programmes in a multi-sector economy, *Rev. Econ. Stud.* **37** (1970), 275–280.
3. Brock, W. A., Money and growth: The case of long run perfect foresight, *Int. Econ. Rev.* **15** (1974), 750–777.
4. Brock, W. A., A simple perfect foresight monetary model, *J. Monetary Econ.* **1** (1975), 133–150.
5. Clower, R. W., A reconsideration of the microfoundations of money, *Western Econ. J.* **6** (1967), 1–9.
6. Friedman, M., "The Optimum Quantity of Money and Other Essays." (Adeline, Chicago, Illinois, 1969.
7. Wilson, C., A Perfect Foresight Model with a Transactions Demand for Money. SSRI Discussion Paper 7808, Univ. of Wisconsin, (June 1978).

The research reported in this paper was supported by NSF Grant SOC-77-08568. I want to thank William Brock and José Scheinkman for uncovering several mistakes in an earlier draft. They refuse to take responsibility for any remaining errors.

SOCIAL SYSTEMS RESEARCH INSTITUTE
UNIVERSITY OF WISCONSIN
MADISON, WISCONSIN

Consumption under Uncertainty

SANFORD GROSSMAN

DAVID LEVHARI

LEONARD J. MIRMAN

The effects of uncertainty on optimal decisions constitutes an increasingly important area of economic research. The problem of choosing an optimal policy in the context of a dynamic model and the effects of that policy on the accumulation of capital have received much attention lately. This paper is intended mainly to put some of the results in a convenient and integrated context through the use of dynamic programming techniques. In particular we deal with a model of consumer choice in which the consumer's wealth is derived from earned income, as well as from the return on investments (or savings). In this paper a sequence of optimal policies is studied as the horizon is increased. In Section I no borrowing is allowed. Under this assumption it is shown that consumption for each value of initial capital decreases as the horizon gets longer. Moreover it is also shown that if the random income stream is replaced by its mean, consumption decreases under the assumption that the marginal utility of consumption is convex [7, 11]. This analysis is carried out with an explicit treatment of the effects of constraints, e.g., no borrowing. In particular we study the effect of possible boundary solutions on the optimal policies, e.g., zero consumption or the consumption of the entire stock. The importance of these results can be seen from the work of Schechtman [9, 10] and Yaari [12]. In particular it is implicit in this paper that Yaari's result is applicable only to the special case of no discounting and unit rate of return. Our results also emphasize the effect of boundaries or borrowing constraints on the optimal policies. These considerations are also studied by Schechtman.

The next section analyzes the problem when borrowing is allowed. The assumption that all borrowing must eventually be paid back is made. This assumption is similar to the assumptions made by Hakansson [1] and also used by Miller [4, 5]. Under this assumption the consumer may not borrow more than the present discounted value of his entire *sure* earnings. If there is no sure income, or if any nonzero income may occur with positive probability, then this assumption allows no borrowing. Under these assumptions on borrowing, the consumer tends to smooth out the stream of consumption, as is the case in the Schechtman–Yaari analysis when there are no borrowing restrictions. However, again, existence of discounting and of a rate of return that is different from one, as well as limits on borrowing and consumption, implies that complete smoothing is not an optimal policy. An appendix showing that with a linear technology the "value" function of dynamic programming inherits the sign of the utility function completes the paper. See [2, 3, 6, 8] for the analysis of related problems.

I

Consider an individual consumer who must decide, at each period of time, how much to consume and how much to invest. Investment opportunities are represented by a single rate of return r, which is assumed to be fixed over time. Moreover in each period the consumer is assumed to receive an exogenous income which may be stochastic. It is further assumed that when incomes are stochastic, their values are drawn from the same distribution in each time period, i.e., they are i.i.d. random variables. Decisions are made so as to maximize the discounted sum of utilities over time. It is assumed initially that the consumer can lend at the rate r, but cannot borrow.

For this analysis we shall study optimal finite horizon decisions and the behavior of these decisions as the horizon tends to infinity. The existence of optimal policies, as well as all transversality conditions, is assumed, so that the limit of optimal policies is optimal. In particular we shall study the relationship between optimal decisions under uncertainty and their counterparts under certainty with the random variable replaced by its mean.[1]

Let $u(c)$ be the utility of consumption. Suppose that $u'(0) = +\infty$, $u' > 0$, $u'' < 0$. Let the discount factor be $0 < \delta < 1$. The objective function for a

---

[1] A more general comparison is implied by the analysis. This will be pointed out below.

T-period horizon problem is given by

$$E \sum_{t=0}^{T} \delta^t u(c_t), \tag{1-1}$$

where E is the expectation operator, subject to,

$$x_t^T = r(x_{t-1}^T - c_{t-1}^T + y_t), \qquad t = 1, \ldots, T - 1,$$

$$x_0^t = x, \qquad \text{given} \quad x_T^T = 0.$$

Here r is one plus the rate of return and y_t is the value of the random income at time t. Let $Ey = \bar{y}$. The optimal values of consumption and wealth at period t are c_t^T, x_t^T, respectively. Suppose further that $u''' > 0$. Using this formulation a dynamic programming argument may be employed. Let

$$W_T(x) = \max_{\{c_0^T, \ldots, c_T^T\}} E \sum_{t=0}^{T} \delta^t u(c_t^T), \tag{1-2}$$

in which case

$$W_T(x) = \max_{0 \le c \le x} \{u(c) + \delta E W_{T-1}[r(x - c + y)]\}. \tag{1-3}$$

For our purposes it is necessary to find c_0^T, $T = 1, \ldots$, and then take limits (if they exist) of these policies as $T \to \infty$. Note also that $u''' > 0$ implies that $W_T''' > 0$ for all T. This is shown in the appendix.

In the certainty case, i.e., $y \equiv \bar{y}$, we find that

$$V_T(x) = \max_{\{c_0^T, \ldots, c_T^T\}} \sum_{t=0}^{T} \delta^t u(c_t^T) \tag{1-4}$$

and

$$V_T(x) = \max_{0 \le c \le x} \{u(c) + \delta V_{T-1}[r(x - c + \bar{y})]\}. \tag{1-5}$$

In order to generate a sequence of optimal policies, consider a one-period horizon problem under certainty. Let

$$V_1(x) = \max_{0 \le c \le x} \{u(c) + \delta u[r(x - c + \bar{y})]\}. \tag{1-6}$$

The first-order conditions yield solutions that are either boundary or interior; note that $c = 0$ is not possible since $u'(0) = \infty$. The boundary solution is $c = x$ and satisfies the condition,

$$u'(c) - \delta r u'[r(x - c + \bar{y})]\big|_{c=x} \ge 0. \tag{1-7}$$

The interior solution is $c < x$ and satisfies

$$u'(c) = \delta r u'[r(x - c + \bar{y})].\tag{1-8}$$

First consider the boundary solution from inequality (1-7),

$$u'(x) \geq \delta r u'(r\bar{y}).\tag{1-9}$$

This solution is valid when $x \leq \bar{x}_c^1$, where $\bar{x}_c^1$ is defined by the equation

$$u'(\bar{x}_c^1) = \delta r u'(r\bar{y}).\tag{1-10}$$

Note that if $\delta r \leq 1$, $r\bar{y} \leq \bar{x}_c^1$ and $r\bar{y} > \bar{x}_c^1$ whenever $\delta r > 1$. Hence for $x \leq \bar{x}_c^1$, $c = x$ and from Eq. (1-6)

$$V_1(x) = u(x) + \delta u(r\bar{y}).\tag{1-11}$$

Hence

$$V'_1(x) = u'(x);\tag{1-12}$$

also

$$V''_1(x) = u''(x)\tag{1-13}$$

and

$$V'''_1(x) = u'''(x), \quad \text{for} \quad x \leq \bar{x}_c^1.\tag{1-14}$$

Consider again Eq. (1-8), which is necessary for an interior solution. Let $c = g_c^1(x)$ be the optimal consumption policy for a one-period horizon under certainty. In this case, i.e., for $x \geq \bar{x}_c^1$,

$$V_1(x) = u[g_c^1(x)] + \delta u[r(x - g_c^1(x) + \bar{y})].^2\tag{1-15}$$

Hence

$$V'_1(x) = \delta r u'[r(x - g_c^1(x) + \bar{y})] = u'[g_c^1(x)].^3\tag{1-16}$$

Next consider the case of uncertainty, again looking at a one-period horizon. Let

$$W_1(x) = \max_{0 \leq c \leq x} \{u(c) + \delta E u[r(x - c + y)]\}.\tag{1-17}$$

Again, since $u'(0) = +\infty$, only two cases need be considered. First the boundary solution, when $c = x$, satisfies the inequality

$$u'(c) - \delta r E u'[r(x - c + y)]|_{c=x} \geq 0,\tag{1-18}$$

---

[2] Note that at $\bar{x}_c^1$, V_1 as defined by (1-11) and (1-15) are equal.
[3] Note also that $V'_1(x)$ is differentiable at $x = \bar{x}_c^1$.

i.e., when

$$u'(x) \geq \delta r E u'(ry). \tag{1-19}$$

Then a boundary solution is valid for all $x \leq \bar{x}_u^1$, where $\bar{x}_u^1$ is defined by the equation

$$u'(\bar{x}_u^1) = \delta r E u'(ry). \tag{1-20}$$

Note that since $u''' > 0,$[4]

$$u'(\bar{x}_c^1) = \delta r u'(r\bar{y}) < \delta r E u'(ry) = u'(\bar{x}_u^1). \tag{1-21}$$

Hence it follows that

$$\bar{x}_c^1 > \bar{x}_u^1. \tag{1-22}$$

Also note that for a boundary solution, i.e., for $x < \bar{x}_u^1$,

$$W_1(x) = u(x) + \delta E u(ry). \tag{1-23}$$

From which it follows that

$$W_1'(x) = u'(x), \tag{1-24}$$

$$W_1''(x) = u''(x), \tag{1-25}$$

and

$$W_1'''(x) = u'''(x). \tag{1-26}$$

Consider the case of an interior solution. The first-order conditions are given by

$$u'(c) = \delta r E u'[r(x - c + y)]. \tag{1-27}$$

Let $c = g_u^1(x)$ be the optimal policy function for a one-period interior solution under uncertainty. Then

$$W_1(x) = u[g_u^1(x)] + \delta E u[r(x - g_u^1(x) + y)]. \tag{1-28}$$

---

[4] If comparisons were made between the effect of two random variables rather than a random variable and its mean, this step would read

$$\delta r E u'(r\bar{y}) < \delta r E u'(ry) \tag{1-21'}$$

where $\bar{y}$ is a random variable that is assumed to be less risky than the random variable y. Here $\bar{y}$ is less than y if for all concave functions

$$\int g(z) \, d\bar{F}(z) > \int g(z) \, dF(z).$$

Here $\bar{F}$ and F are the distribution functions for $\bar{y}$ and y, respectively. Since $u''' > 0$, $-u'$ is concave. Hence (1-21') follows.

Hence, for $x > \bar{x}_u^1$,

$$W_1'(x) = \delta r E u'[r(x - g_u^1(x) + y)] = u'[g_u^1(x)].^5 \qquad (1\text{-}29)$$

From (1-27) and the definition of $g_u^1(x)$, it follows, using Jensen's inequality with $u''' > 0$, that

$$0 \le u'[g_u^1(x)] - \delta r u'\{r[x - g_u^1(x) + \bar{y}]\}. \qquad (1\text{-}30)$$

Thus from the concavity of u and Eq. (1-16),

$$g_c^1(x) > g_u^1(x). \qquad (1\text{-}31)$$

The one-period optimal consumption function for both certainty and uncertainty is depicted in Figure 1.1. Hence it follows that

$$u'[g_c^1(x)] = V_1'(x) < W_1'(x) = u'[g_u^1(x)]. \qquad (1\text{-}32)$$

Next we shall consider the general case. Suppose that

$$V_{n-1}(x) = u(x) + \delta V_{n-2}(r\bar{y}), \qquad \text{if } x \le \bar{x}_c^{n-1}, \qquad (1\text{-}33)$$

and

$$V_{n-1}(x) = u[g_c^{n-1}(x)] + \delta V_{n-2}\{r[x - g_c^{n-1}(x) + y]\} \qquad \text{for } x \ge \bar{x}_c^{n-1}.$$

$$(1\text{-}34)$$

Thus,

$$V_{n-1}'(x) = u'(x), \qquad x \le \bar{x}_c^{n-1}, \qquad (1\text{-}35)$$

$$V_{n-1}'(x) = u'[g_c^{n-1}(x)], \qquad x \ge \bar{x}_c^{n-1}. \qquad (1\text{-}36)$$

---

[5] It is also easy to show that $\bar{x}_u^1 > \bar{x}_u^2$. Let $W_2(x) = \max\{u(c) + \delta E W_1[r(x - c + y)]\}$. Then $\bar{x}_u^2$ is defined by the equation,

$$u'(c) - \delta r E W_1'[r(\bar{x}_u^2 - c + y)]\big|_{c=\bar{x}_u^2} = 0;$$

i.e.,

$$u'(\bar{x}_u^2) = \delta r \int_{ry > x_u^1} u'(ry) + \int_{ry < x_u^1} u'[g_u^2(ry)]$$

$$> \delta r E u'(ry) = u'(\bar{x}_u^1).$$

A similar proof shows that $x_c^1 > x_c^2$. Moreover letting

$$W_2(x) = \max_c \{u(c) + \delta E W_1[r(x - c + y)]\},$$

the first-order conditions imply that

$$u'[g_u^2(x)] = \delta r E W_1'\{r[x - g_u^2(x) + y]\} = \delta r E u'(g_u'\{r[x - g_u^2(x) + y]\})$$

$$> \delta r E u'\{r[x - g_u^2(x) + y]\}.$$

It follows that $g_u^2(x) \le g_u^1(x)$ for all x. Similarly $g_c^2(x) \le g_c^1(x)$ for all x.

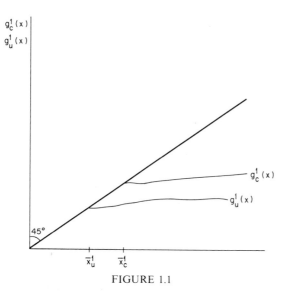

FIGURE 1.1

Notice that $V_{n-1}(x)$ is differentiable at $\bar{x}_c^{n-1}$, where $g_c^{n-1}(x) = x$. Also suppose that

$$W_{n-1}(x) = u(x) + \delta EW_{n-2}(ry), \qquad \text{if} \quad x \le \bar{x}_u^{n-1}, \qquad (1\text{-}37)$$

and

$$W_{n-1}(x) = u[g_u^{n-1}(x)] + \delta W_{n-2}\{r[x - g_u^{n-1}(x) + y]\} \qquad \text{for} \quad x \ge \bar{x}_u^{n-1}. \qquad (1\text{-}38)$$

Again

$$W'_{n-1}(x) = u'(x), \qquad x \le \bar{x}_u^{n-1}, \qquad (1\text{-}39)$$

and

$$W'_{n-1}(x) = u'[g_u^{n-1}(x)], \qquad x \ge \bar{x}_u^{n-1}, \qquad (1\text{-}40)$$

with $W_{n-1}(x)$ differentiable at $x = \bar{x}_u^{n-1}$. Finally suppose that $g_u^{n-1}(x) \le g_u^{n-2}(x)$ and $g_c^{n-1}(x) \le g_c^{n-2}(x)$ for all x. Suppose moreover that (1-32) holds for $n-1$ periods; i.e., $V'_{n-1}(x) < W'_{n-1}(x)$ for all x. It will then be shown that $g_u^n(x) < g_c^n(x)$, that $\bar{x}_c^n > \bar{x}_u^n$, and that $V'_n(x) < W'_n(x)$ for all x.

Again, let us begin by studying the case of certainty. Consider the functional equation

$$V_n(x) = \max_{0 \le c \le x} \{u(c) + \delta V_{n-1}[r(x - c + \bar{y})]\}. \qquad (1\text{-}41)$$

The boundary solution that satisfies the condition

$$u'(c) - \delta r V'_{n-1}[r(x - c + \bar{y})]|_{c=x} \geq 0 \qquad (1\text{-}42)$$

is valid for all $x \leq \bar{x}_c^n$. Here $\bar{x}_c^n$ is defined by the equation

$$u'(\bar{x}_c^n) = \delta r V'_{n-1}(r\bar{y}). \qquad (1\text{-}43)$$

It is easy to see that if $\delta r \leq 1$, $\bar{x}_c^1 = \bar{x}_c^2 = \cdots = \bar{x}_c^n$, since from Eq. (1-10) for $\delta r \leq 1$, $r\bar{y} \leq \bar{x}_c^1$. Hence $V'_1(r\bar{y}) = u'(r\bar{y})$, and from (1-43) for $n = 2$, $u'(\bar{x}_c^2) = \delta r V'_1(r\bar{y}) = \delta r u'(r\bar{y}) = u'(\bar{x}_c^1)$. In general, when $\delta r \leq 1$, $r\bar{y} \leq \bar{x}_c^{n-1}$, $V'_{n-1}(r\bar{y}) = u'(r\bar{y})$, and thus $\bar{x}_c^n = \cdots = \bar{x}_c^1$. On the other hand if $\delta r > 1$, $\bar{x}_c^n < \bar{x}_c^{n-1} < \cdots < \bar{x}_c^1$. If $\delta r > 1$, from Eq. (1-10), $r\bar{y} > \bar{x}_c^1$. Hence $V'_1(r\bar{y}) = u'[g_c^1(r\bar{y})] > u'(r\bar{y})$. Thus $u'(\bar{x}_c^2) = \delta r V'_1(r\bar{y}) > \delta r u'(r\bar{y}) = u'(\bar{x}_c^1)$. Hence $\bar{x}_c^2 < \bar{x}_c^1$. Similarly $r\bar{y} > \bar{x}_c^{n-1}$, and $\bar{x}_c^n < \cdots < \bar{x}_c^1$. Note also that, for a boundary solution

$$V_n(x) = u(x) + \delta V_{n-1}(r\bar{y}), \qquad (1\text{-}44)$$

$$V'_n(x) = u'(x). \qquad (1\text{-}45)$$

Next let us turn to an interior solution; the necessary condition is

$$u'(c) = \delta r V'_{n-1}[r(x - c + \bar{y})]. \qquad (1\text{-}46)$$

Again letting $c = g_c^n(x)$ be the optimal consumption function for an n-period horizon under certainty,

$$V_n(x) = u[g_c^n(x)] + \delta V_{n-1}\{r[x - g_c^n(x) + \bar{y}]\}, \qquad (1\text{-}47)$$

in which case

$$V'_n(x) = \delta r V'_{n-1}\{r[x - g_c^n(x) + \bar{y}]\} = u'[g_c^n(x)]. \qquad (1\text{-}48)$$

The n-period horizon uncertainty problem is next. Here

$$W_n(x) = \max_{0 \leq c \leq x} \{u(c) + \delta E W_{n-1}[r(x - c + y)]\}. \qquad (1\text{-}49)$$

Again starting with the conditions for a boundary solution,

$$u'(c) - \delta r E W'_{n-1}[r(x - c - y)]|_{c=x} \geq 0. \qquad (1\text{-}50)$$

Hence the boundary solution is valid for all x such that

$$u'(x) \geq \delta r E W'_{n-1}(ry).$$

Let $\bar{x}_u^n$ be defined by the equation

$$u'(\bar{x}_u^n) = \delta r E W'_{n-1}(ry)$$

$$= \delta r \int_{ry \leq \bar{x}_u^{n-1}} u'(ry) + \delta r \int_{ry \geq \bar{x}_u^{n-1}} u'[g_u^{n-1}(ry)]. \qquad (1\text{-}51)$$

However assume that $\bar{x}_u^{n-2} > \bar{x}_u^{n-1}$, as an induction hypothesis; then since $g_u^{n-1}(ry) < ry$,

$$\delta r \int_{ry \le \bar{x}_u^{n-1}} u'(ry) + \delta r \int_{ry \ge \bar{x}_u^{n-1}} u'[g_u^{n-1}(ry)]$$

$$\ge \delta r \int_{ry \le \bar{x}_u^{n-2}} u'(ry) + \delta r \int_{ry \ge \bar{x}_u^{n-2}} u'[g_u^{n-1}(ry)] \qquad (1\text{-}52)$$

Moreover since $g_u^{n-2}(x) > g_u^{n-1}(x)$,

$$\int_{ry \ge \bar{x}_u^{n-1}} u'[g_u^{n-1}(ry)] > \int_{ry \ge \bar{x}_u^{n-1}} u'[g_u^{n-2}(ry)]. \qquad (1\text{-}53)$$

In which case

$$u'(\bar{x}_u^n) > \delta r \int_{ry \le \bar{x}_u^{n-2}} u'(ry) + \delta r \int_{ry \ge \bar{x}_u^{n-2}} u'[g_u^{n-2}(ry)] = u'(\bar{x}_u^{n-1}); \qquad (1\text{-}54)$$

i.e., if $\bar{x}_u^{n-2} > \bar{x}_u^{n-1}$, then

$$\bar{x}_u^{n-1} > \bar{x}_u^n. \qquad (1\text{-}55)$$

Hence by induction

$$\bar{x}_u^1 > \bar{x}_u^2 > \cdots > \bar{x}_u^n, \qquad \text{for all} \quad n. \qquad (1\text{-}56)$$

Now consider the conditions for an interior solution,

$$W_n(x) = u[g_u^n(x)] + \delta E W_{n-1}\{r[x - g_u^n(x) + y]\} \qquad (1\text{-}57)$$

and

$$W_n'(x) = \delta r E W_{n-1}'\{r[x - g_u^n(x) + y]\} = u'[g_u^n(x)]. \qquad (1\text{-}58)$$

From the first-order condition,

$$u'(c) = \delta r E W_{n-1}'[r(x - c + y)]$$

$$= \delta r \left\{ \int_{r(x-c+y) \le \bar{x}_u^{n-1}} W_{n-1}'[r(x - c + y)] \right.$$

$$\left. + \int_{r(x-c+y) \ge \bar{x}_u^{n-1}} W_{n-1}'[r(x - c + y)] \right\}. \qquad (1\text{-}59)$$

Here, for corner solutions,

$$\int_{r(x-c+y) \le \bar{x}_u^{n-1}} W_{n-1}'[r(x - c + y)] = \int_{r(x-c+y) \le \bar{x}_u^{n-1}} u'[r(x - c + y)], \qquad (1\text{-}60)$$

and for interior solutions,

$$\int_{r(x-c+y) \ge \bar{x}_u^{n-1}} W_{n-1}'[r(x - c + y)] = \int_{r(x-c+y) \ge \bar{x}_u^{n-1}} u'\{g_u^{n-1}[r(x - c + y)]\}. \qquad (1\text{-}61)$$

Hence using (1-59) replacing $g_u^{n-1}(x)$ by x in (1-61) yields

$$u'(c) = \delta r \int W'_{n-1}[r(x - c + y)] \geq \delta r \int u'[r(x - c + y)]. \quad (1\text{-}62)$$

Thus $g_u^n(x) \leq \tilde{g}_u^n(x)$, where $c = g_u^n(x)$ satisfies Eq. (1-58) and $\tilde{g}_u^n(x)$ is defined by the equation

$$u'[\tilde{g}_u^n(x)] = \delta r \int W'_{n-1}\{r[x - \tilde{g}_u^n(x) + y]\}$$
$$> \delta r W'_{n-1}\{r[x - \tilde{g}_u^n(x) + \bar{y}]\}. \quad (1\text{-}63)$$

The last inequality is by Jensen's inequality and the fact that W'_{n-1} is convex, which is shown in the appendix. Hence under the assumption that $V'_{n-1}(x) < W'_{n-1}(x)$ for all x,

$$0 = u'[g_c^n(x)] - \delta r V'_{n-1}\{r[x - g_c^n(x) + \bar{y}]\}$$
$$> u'[g_c^n(x)] - \delta r W'_{n-1}\{r[x - g_c^n(x) + \bar{y}]\}. \quad (1\text{-}64)$$

By concavity of u and W_{n-1}, it follows that

$$g_c^n(x) > \tilde{g}_u^n(x). \quad (1\text{-}65)$$

Moreover, since $\tilde{g}_u^n(x) \geq g_u^n(x)$,

$$g_c^n(x) > g_u^n(x). \quad (1\text{-}66)$$

Hence from (1-48) and (1-58)

$$W'_n(x) = u'[g_u^n(x)] > u'[g_c^n(x)] = V'_n(x). \quad (1\text{-}67)$$

Thus

$$W'_n(x) > V'_n(x). \quad (1\text{-}68)$$

Hence the following theorem has been proved by induction.

THEOREM Under the assumptions of the model with $u''' > 0$, for each n,

$$W'_n(x) > V'_n(x) \qquad \text{for all} \quad x. \quad (1\text{-}69)$$

Also

$$g_c^n(x) > g_u^n(x) \qquad \text{for all} \quad x \geq \bar{x}_c^n, \quad (1\text{-}70)$$

Moreover

$$\bar{x}_u^n < \bar{x}_c^n. \quad (1\text{-}71)$$

The next question is what happens to $g_c^n(x)$ and $g_u^n(x)$ as $n \to \infty$? Also the same question applies to $\bar{x}_u^n$ and $\bar{x}_c^n$. The key to the convergence of these functions is contained in Lemma 2.10 of Schechtman [9], which is reproduced in the notation of this paper.

LEMMA   The sequence $V'_n(x)$ and $W'_n(x)$ converges uniformly in any finite and closed interval to a continuous nonincreasing function $V'(x)$ and $W'(x)$, respectively. Here $\lim_{n\to\infty} V_n(x) = V(x)$, and $\lim_{n\to\infty} W_n(x) = W(x)$.

Proof   (*Schechtman*)   Since $g_c^{n-1}(x) \geq g_c^n(x)$ for all x, with $g_c(x) = x$ for a boundary solution, then

$$V'_n(x) = u'[g_c^{n-1}(x)] \leq u'[g_c^n(x)] = V'_{n+1}(x); \qquad (1\text{-}72)$$

similarly for $W'_n(x)$.

Moreover $W'_n(x)$ and $V'_n(x)$ are well defined for all x, with $W'_n(0) = V'_n(0) = +\infty$. Hence pointwise convergence of $W'_n(x)$ and $V'_n(x)$ is assured. The remainder of the argument is exactly the same as in Schechtman since the fact that $\delta = r = 1$ is never used there.

Let

$$V'(x) = \lim_{n\to\infty} V'_n(x) \qquad (1\text{-}73)$$

and

$$W'(x) = \lim_{n\to\infty} W'_n(x). \qquad (1\text{-}74)$$

Moreover let

$$\bar{x}_u = \lim_{n\to\infty} \bar{x}_u^n \qquad (1\text{-}75)$$

and

$$\bar{x}_c = \lim_{n\to\infty} \bar{x}_c^n. \qquad (1\text{-}76)$$

Then for $x \leq \bar{x}_u$

$$W'(x) = u'(x), \qquad (1\text{-}77)$$

and for $x > \bar{x}_u$

$$W'(x) = u'[g_u(x)], \qquad (1\text{-}78)$$

where $g_u(x) = \lim_{n\to\infty} g_u^n(x)$. Similarly for certainty, i.e., when $x \leq \bar{x}_c$,

$$V'(x) = u'(x), \qquad (1\text{-}79)$$

and when $x > \bar{x}_c$,

$$V'(x) = u'[g_c(x)], \qquad (1\text{-}80)$$

where $g_c(x) = \lim_{n \to \infty} g_c^n(x)$. In general, the limits of the necessary conditions for an optimum are

$$u'[g_c(x)] \geq r\delta V'\{r[x - g_c(x) + \bar{y}]\} \tag{1-81}$$

with equality for $x \geq \bar{x}_c$ and

$$u'[g_u(x)] \geq r\delta EW'\{r[x - g_u(x) + y]\} \tag{1-82}$$

with equality for $x \geq \bar{x}_u$. Finally note that

$$W_n'(x) \geq V_n'(x) \qquad \text{for all} \quad x. \tag{1-83}$$

Hence

$$W'(x) \geq V'(x) \qquad \text{for all} \quad x. \tag{1-84}$$

Also $\bar{x}_u^n < \bar{x}_c^n$; again in the case $u''' > 0$,

$$\bar{x}_u \leq \bar{x}_c. \tag{1-85}$$

Hence for $x \leq \bar{x}_u$, $g_u(x) = g_c(x) = x$. If $\bar{x}_c > \bar{x}_u$, then for $\bar{x}_u < x < \bar{x}_c$

$$g_u(x) < x = g_c(x). \tag{1-86}$$

For $x > \bar{x}_c$, $g_u(x) < g_c(x)$, since if $g_u(x) = g_c(x)$,

$$u'(g_c) = r\delta V'[r(x - g_c + \bar{y})] \tag{1-87}$$

and

$$u'(g_u) = r\delta EW'[r(x - g_u + y)]. \tag{1-88}$$

However since W' is strictly convex as shown in the appendix,

$$V'[r(x - g_c + \bar{y})] = EW'[r(x - g_u + y)] > W'[r(x - g_u + \bar{y})]$$
$$> W'[r(x - g_c + \bar{y})] \tag{1-89}$$

since $g_c(x) = g_u(x)$. However this contradicts (1-84). Hence $g_u(x) < g_c(x)$. Moreover the opposite in equality occurs if $u''' < 0$. In fact the only time when $g_c(x) = g_u(x)$ is if $x = g_c(x)$ and $g_u(x) = x$.

II

In this section we shall consider the optimal consumption–savings problem under uncertainty but without the very strong assumption that there can be no borrowing. However, in order to allow borrowing, it is necessary to impose restrictions on the amount of borrowing; otherwise it would be possible to have unbounded debts, as in the Yaari model. Two different assumptions will be made, the first more stringent than the second. First, properties of finite horizon policies will be studied paying careful attention to boundary solutions. Then the limiting policy will be discussed. Again under appropriate assumptions, these limit policies will also be optimal policies. This question will not be discussed.

Let the income at time t be given by y_t. The sequence $\{y_t\}$ is a sequence of independent, identically distributed random variables. The first assumption about the limit on borrowing is that the debt must be paid back with probability 1. This will be called the Hakanson–Miller borrowing limit. Let $y_t = y + R_t$ where $\Pr\{R_t \le 0\} = 0$. Let $h(R)$ be the density function of the random variable R. Hence y is the sure part of the random income, i.e., $y_t \ge y$ always. It will be assumed that $Eu(R) < \infty$, $u'(0) = +\infty$, and $Eu'(R) < \infty$. Hence under this assumption $c_t > 0$. Moreover $r > 1$ is assumed. Let

$$D_i = y\left(1 + \frac{1}{r} + \cdots + \frac{1}{r^{i-1}}\right). \tag{2-1}$$

Consider first a two-period horizon problem. Note that with initial stock x the debt limit is $x + y$, where y is the minimum income received in the next period. In the next period the consumer receives interest on his savings (which may be negative) plus a draw from the random income $y + R_1$. In this case the objective function is

$$V_1(x) = \max_{0 \le c \le x + D_1 = x + y} \{u(c) + \delta Eu[r(x - c + y) + R]\}, \tag{2-2}$$

for $x > -D_1$; if not $c = 0$ [since $u'(0) = +\infty$, only $x > -D_1$ need be considered]. For a boundary solution to occur, it is necessary that

$$u'(c) - \delta r Eu'[r(x - c + y) + R]|_{c = x + y} \ge 0;$$

that is,

$$u'(x + y) \ge \delta r Eu'(R).$$

This is valid for all $x \le \bar{x}_1$, where $\bar{x}_1$ is defined by

$$u'(\bar{x}_1 + y) = E\delta r u'(R). \tag{2-3}$$

Whenever $x \le \bar{x}_1$,

$$V_1(x) = u(x + y) + \delta Eu(R);$$

hence for $x \le \bar{x}_1$,

$$V_1'(x) = u'(x + y). \tag{2-4}$$

For an interior solution it is necessary that

$$u'(c) = \delta r Eu'[r(x - c + y) + R]. \tag{2-5}$$

Let $g_1(x) = c$; then

$$u'[g_1(x)] = V'_1(x). \tag{2-6}$$

The one-period consumption function is depicted in Fig. 2.1. Note that it is possible for the capital stock to be less than zero (but greater than $-y$, or else zero consumption is the only possibility). If $x < 0$, previous borrowing must be repaid. Note also that if $x < 0$, it is necessary for the consumer to continue to borrow in order to consume.

Next consider the two-period horizon problem,

$$V_2(x) = \max_{0 \le c \le x + D_2} \left\{ u(c) + \delta \int_{r(x-c+y)+R \le \bar{x}_1} V_1[r(x - c + y) + R]h(R)\,dR + \delta \right.$$
$$\left. \times \int_{r(x-c+y)+R \ge \bar{x}_1} V_1[r(x - c + y) + R]h(R)\,dR \right\}. \tag{2-7}$$

For a boundary solution one obtains

$$u'(c) - \delta r \left[\int_{r(x-c+y)+R \le \bar{x}_1} V'_1[r(x - c + y) + R]h(R)\,dR + \delta \right.$$
$$\left. \times \int_{r(x-c+y)+R \ge \bar{x}_1} V'_1[r(x - c + y) + R]h(R)\,dR \right] \Bigg|_{c = x + D_2} \ge 0, \tag{2-8}$$

which yields,

$$u'(x + D_2) \ge \delta r \int_{R-y \le \bar{x}_1} u'(R)h(R)\,dR + \delta r \int_{R-y \ge \bar{x}_1} u'[g_1(R - y)]h(R)\,dR. \tag{2-9}$$

The first expression on the right-hand side comes from (2-4), while the second expression comes from (2-6). Note that as with $\bar{x}_1$, $\bar{x}_2$ can be defined from (2-9) when equality holds. Moreover since $g_1(R - y) \le R$ for each R,

$$u'[g_1(R - y)] \ge u'(R).$$

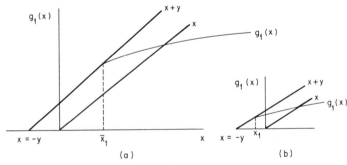

FIGURE 2.1

Hence

$$u'(x + D_2) = u'\left(x + \frac{r+1}{r}y\right) \geq \delta r \int u'(R)h(R)\,dR,$$

in which case

$$u'(\bar{x}_2 + D_2) \geq \delta r \int u'(R)h(R)\,dR = u'(\bar{x}_1 + y).$$

Thus

$$\bar{x}_2 + y + (1/r)y \leq \bar{x}_1 + y,$$

or

$$\bar{x}_2 + (y/r) \leq \bar{x}_1, \qquad (2\text{-}10)$$

which implies that

$$\bar{x}_2 < \bar{x}_1. \qquad (2\text{-}11)$$

Finally

$$V_2'(x) = u'\{x + [(1 + r)/r]y\}, \qquad \text{for} \quad x \leq \bar{x}_2. \qquad (2\text{-}12)$$

An interior solution is derived from the functional equation:

$$u'(c) = \int_{r(x-c+y)+R \leq \bar{x}_1} V_1'[r(x - c + y) + R]h(R)\,dR$$

$$+ \int_{r(x-c+y)+R \geq \bar{x}_1} V_1'[r(x - c + y) + R]h(R)\,dR, \qquad (2\text{-}13)$$

or

$$u'(c) = \int_{r(x-c+y)+R \leq \bar{x}_1} u'[r(x - c + y) + y + R]h(R)\,dR$$

$$+ \int_{r(x-c+y)+R \geq \bar{x}_1} V_1'[r(x - c + y) + R]h(R)\,dR.$$

Hence there is a $g_2(x)$ such that

$$V_2'(x) = u'[g_2(x)].$$

The solution is depicted in Fig. 2.2.

The interesting point is that the result that present consumption decreases as the horizon increases is no longer valid when borrowing is allowed. This can be seen using a Cobb–Douglass utility function, with $\delta = r = 1$, even in the certain case, i.e., with y constant. This is so since it is possible, with borrowing, to smooth out the stream of consumption, much in the same way Yaari's result is due to the ability of the consumer to smooth out the stream of consumption even though the stream of income can vary stochastically.

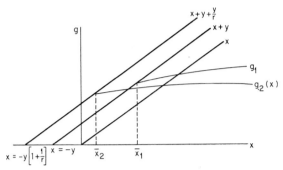

FIGURE 2.2

However the assumption that $\delta = r = 1$ in Yaari's model also plays a crucial role, since time preference and the rate of return has an effect on the time profile of consumption. In sum, borrowing will help smooth out consumption, but present capital or wealth also affects consumption, since the rate of return and time preference makes the value of present and future consumption different. In general, i.e., for an infinite horizon problem, the consumption function $g(x)$, under this borrowing assumption, is depicted in Figs. 2.3a and b and is given by the functional equation.

$$u'(c) = \int_{r(x-c+y)+R \leq \bar{x}} u'\{r(x-c+y) + R + [y/(1-r)]\}h(R)\,dR$$

$$+ \int_{r(x-c+y)+R \geq \bar{x}} V'[r(x-c+y) + R]h(R)\,dR,$$

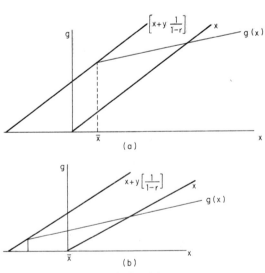

FIGURE 2.3

where $\bar{x}$ is defined by the equation

$$u'\left(\bar{x} + \frac{y}{1-r}\right) = \delta r \int_{R-y \leq \bar{x}} u'(R)h(R)\,dR + \delta r \int_{R-y \geq \bar{x}} u'g(R-y)h(R)\,dR.$$

Note that these conditions are not very simple statements, since, in general, the functions $V(x)$ and $g(x)$ will be quite complicated.

Next consider the borrowing limit to be the *expected* lifetime income. Hence, on average, consumers will end up in debt. In this case define

$$D_i = Ey\left(1 + \frac{1}{r} + \cdots + \frac{1}{r^{i-1}}\right).$$

The difficulty with this borrowing constraint, or any borrowing constraint in which there is the possibility of bankruptcy, is that the assumption $u'(0) = +\infty$ implies that no policy that allows bankruptcy can be chosen. Hence it must be the case that $u'(0) < \infty$. The analysis for this problem is similar to the problem discussed above, except that now $c = 0$ is possible. Figures 2.4a and b depict examples of the type of infinite horizon policies that are possible.

APPENDIX

Consider the conditions:

$$V_1'(x) = u'[g_1(x)] \tag{A1}$$

and

$$u'[g_1(x)] = r\delta u'\{r[x - g_1(x) + y]\}. \tag{A2}$$

Let $x = \lambda x_1 + (1 - \lambda)x_2$, and $g_1(x_1) \neq g_1(x_2)$; then if

$$g_1[\lambda x_1 + (1 - \lambda)x_2] \geq \lambda g_1(x_1) + (1 - \lambda)g_1(x_2), \tag{A3}$$

it follows that

$$u'\{g_1[\lambda x_1 + (1 - \lambda)x_2]\} \leq u'[\lambda g_1(x_1) + (1 - \lambda)g_1(x_2)]$$
$$< \lambda u'[g_1(x_1)] + (1 - \lambda)u'[g_1(x_2)]$$

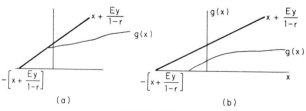

(a)   (b)

FIGURE 2.4

by the convexity of u'. Hence if (A3) holds, (A1) implies that

$$V'_1[\lambda x_1 + (1 - \lambda)x_2] < \lambda V'_1(x_1) + (1 - \lambda)V'_1(x_2). \tag{A4}$$

On the other hand suppose that

$$g_1[\lambda x_1 + (1 - \lambda)x_2] < \lambda g_1(x_1) + (1 - \lambda)g_1(x_2).$$

Then

$$\lambda x_1 + (1 - \lambda)x_2 - g_1[\lambda x_1 + (1 - \lambda)x_2]$$
$$> \lambda x_1 + (1 - \lambda)x_2 - \lambda g_1(x_1) - (1 - \lambda)g_1(x_2).$$

Hence

$$r\delta u'(r\{\lambda x_1 + (1 - \lambda)x_2 - g_1[\lambda x_1 + (1 - \lambda)x_2] + y\})$$
$$< r\delta u'(r\{\lambda[x_1 - g_1(x_1)] + (1 - \lambda)[x_2 - g_1(x_2)] + y\})$$
$$= r\delta u'\{\lambda r[x_1 - g_1(x_1) + y] + (1 - \lambda)r[x_2 - g_1(x_2) + y]\}$$
$$< r\delta\lambda u'\{r[x_1 - g_1(x_1) + y]\} + \delta r(1 - \lambda)u'\{r[x_2 - g_1(x_2) + y]\}.$$

Hence

$$V'_1[\lambda x_1 + (1 - \lambda)x_2] = u'\{g_1[\lambda x_1 + (1 - \lambda)x_2]\}$$
$$< \lambda u'[g_1(x_1)] + (1 - \lambda)u'[g_2(x_2)]$$
$$= \lambda V'_1(x_1) + (1 - \lambda)V'_2(x_2).$$

In either case $V'_1(\lambda x_1 + (1 - \lambda)x_2) < \lambda V'_1(x_1) + (1 - \lambda)V'(x_2)$. Hence the convexity of u' implies the convexity of V'_1. Moreover a similar argument applies to the function $W'_1(x)$ in the uncertainty case.

Also the general case is similar. Suppose that $V'_{n-1}(x)$ is convex. Then the following equations must be satisfied:

$$V'_n(x) = u'[g_n(x)], \tag{A5}$$

and

$$u'[g_n(x)] = r\delta V'_{n-1}\{r[x - g_n(x) + y]\}. \tag{A6}$$

Hence since u' and V'_{n-1} are convex, it follows that $V'_n(x)$ is convex by exactly the same argument as above.

Finally it can also be shown, using a similar argument, that the limit function $V'(x)$ is also strictly convex. The function $V(x)$ satisfies the first-order conditions and the envelope property; namely,

$$u'[g(x)] = r\delta V'\{r[x - g(x) + y]\}. \tag{A7}$$

Here $g(x)$ is the limit optimal policy, and

$$u'[g(x)] = V'(x). \tag{A8}$$

Let $x = \lambda x_1 + (1 - \lambda)x_2$; then if

$$\lambda g(x_1) + (1 - \lambda)g(x_2) < g[\lambda x_1 + (1 - \lambda)x_2],$$

the convexity of u' and (A8) guarantee that

$$V'[\lambda x_1 + (1 - \lambda)x_2] < \lambda V'(x_1) + (1 - \lambda)V'(x_2).$$

If

$$\lambda g(x_1) + (1 - \lambda)g(x_2) > g[\lambda x_1 + (1 - \lambda)x_2],$$

then the limit of convex functions is convex, so $V'(x)$ is convex and

$$
\begin{aligned}
u'\{g[\lambda x_1 + (1-\lambda)x_2]\} &= r\delta V'(r\{\lambda x_1 + (1-\lambda)x_2 - g[\lambda x_1 + (1-\lambda)x_2] + y\}) \\
&< r\delta V'(\lambda\{r[x_1 - g(x_1) + y]\} + (1-\lambda)\{r[x_2 - g(x_2) + y]\}) \\
&\leq \lambda r\,\delta V'(r[x_1 - g(x_1) + y]) \\
&\quad + (1-\lambda)r\,\delta V'(r[x_2 - g(x_2) + y]) \\
&= \lambda u'[g(x_1)] + (1-\lambda)g(x_2).
\end{aligned}
$$

Thus

$$V'[\lambda x_1 + (1 - \lambda)x_2] < \lambda V'(x_1) + (1 - \lambda)V'(x_2).$$

Hence V' is strictly convex.

REFERENCES

1. Hakansson, N., Optimal investment and consumption strategies under risk for a class of utility functions, *Econometrica* **38** (1970), 587–607.
2. Levhari, D., Mirman, L. J., and Zilcha, I., Capital accumulation under uncertainty. 1977. Unpublished Mimeo.
3. McCabe, J. L., and Sibley, D. S., Optimal foreign debt accumulation with export revenue uncertainty, *Int. Econ. Rev.* **17** (1976), 675–86.
4. Miller, B. L., Optimal consumption with a stochastic income stream, *Econometrica* **42** (1974), 253–266.
5. Miller, B., The effect on optimal consumption of increased uncertainty in labor income in the multiperiod case, *J. Econ. Theory* **13** (1976), 154–167.
6. Mirman, L. J., and Postlewaite, A., On the finiteness of some infinite horizon problems. 1977. Unpublished Mimeo.
7. Neave, E. H., Multiperiod consumption investment decisions and risk preferences, *J. Econ. Theory* **3**, No. 1 (1971), 40–60.
8. Phelps, E., The accumulation of risky capital: A sequential utility analysis, *Econometrica* **30** (1962), 729–743.
9. Schechtman, J., An income fluctuation problem, *J. Econ. Theory* **11** (1975), 218–41.
10. Schechtman, J., and Escudero, V. L. S., Some results on an income fluctuation problem, *J. Econ. Theory* **16**, No. 2 (1977), 151–66.
11. Sibley, D., Permanent and transitory income effects in a model of optimal consumption and wage income uncertainty, *J. Econ. Theory* **11** (1975), 68–82.

12. Yaari, M. E., A law of large numbers in the theory of consumer's choice under uncertainty, *J. Econ. Theory* **12** (1976), 202–217.

Research support from the NSF under Grants SOC 75-05317 and SOC 76-18771 is gratefully acknowledged.

Sanford Grossman   *David Levhari*   *Leonard J. Mirman*
DEPARTMENT OF ECONOMICS   DEPARTMENT OF ECONOMICS   DEPARTMENT OF ECONOMICS
UNIVERSITY OF PENNSYLVANIA   THE HEBREW UNIVERSITY   UNIVERSITY OF ILLINOIS
PHILADELPHIA, PENNSYLVANIA   JERUSALEM, ISRAEL   URBANA, ILLINOIS

Balanced Outcome Functions Yielding Walrasian and Lindahl Allocations at Nash Equilibrium Points for Two or More Agents

LEONID HURWICZ

In a note, Schmeidler (1976) constructed a balanced[1] outcome function having the property of yielding, for every "classical" pure exchange private goods (Edgeworth Box) economy with at least three agents (or with one agent), equality of the Nash and Walrasian allocation sets. Later, Hurwicz (1976) constructed a balanced outcome function yielding the same equality as well as another balanced outcome function yielding, for economies with one private and one public good, the equality of Nash and Lindahl allocation sets—in both cases for economies with three or more agents. The Hurwicz outcome functions are smooth, in fact polynomial; Schmeidler's are discontinuous. Neither uses an auctioneer (fictitious extra player). Neither guarantees individual feasibility away from equilibrium, but the balance identities are satisfied away from as well as at equilibrium.

The case of two agents ($n = 2$), excluded by both types of balanced[2] outcome rules, was naturally puzzling, even if not of overwhelming importance.

---

[1] I.e., such that the balance equations ($\sum_i z^i = 0$ for pure exchange and $y = \sum_i t^i$ for public goods economies) hold not only at, but also away from, equilibrium.

[2] It was shown in Hurwicz (1976) that if the balance property (away from equilibrium) is not required, then there exist outcome functions yielding the Nash–Walras and Nash–Lindahl equivalence for $n \geq 2$. The same is true if an auctioneer is introduced.

Hurwicz found that, for the Edgeworth Box economies, the identity of Nash and Walras sets cannot be achieved by smooth outcome functions satisfying certain solvability conditions. This suggested that if it is at all possible to handle the $n = 2$ case, the Schmeidler (discontinuous) type functions are more likely to work. Such, in fact, turned out to be the case. Indeed, by a modification of the Schmeidler rule for the T_0 ("loners") sets of agents, while retaining Schmeidler's other rules, we obtain a mechanism that works for economies with two or more agents (Section 1).

Furthermore, the device we used for Edgeworth Box economies suggested a similar approach for public goods economies. Here again (Section 2) we obtain a balanced (but discontinuous) outcome function yielding the equality of Nash and Lindahl allocations for two or more agents.

1. THE NASH–WALRAS EQUIVALENCE FOR TWO OR MORE AGENTS

1.1. The Case of Two Agents ($n = 2$)

We start with this subcase because it clarifies the basic idea of this outcome function.

We assume a pure exchange economy with strictly positive initial endowments w^i and preferences that are strictly increasing in all goods and strictly quasi-concave. (These assumptions can be relaxed to a considerable extent.) There are l goods. A net trade (increment) in the commodity space is denoted by z. The first component of z is denoted by x, the other $l - 1$ component vector by y. We find it convenient to make x numéraire (with price $= 1$).

The ith agent's strategy vector is the message pair $m_i = (p_i, y_i)$ where p_i and y_i are both $(l - 1)$-dimensional vectors representing, respectively, i's proposed price of y and net trade increment of y for himself. We write $m = (m_1, m_2)$. p_i is required to be positive in all components. Agent i's complete net trade proposal is $z_i = (x_i, y_i)$, with $x_i = -p_i y_i$; i.e., it satisfies the budget equation. (We often omit dots in writing inner products.)

The crucial distinction is whether the two price proposals are identical. When they are ($p_1 = p_2$), Schmeidler's rationing rules apply, so that:

For $p_1 = p_2 = p$ (say), the net trade increments are given by

$$Y^1(m) = (y_1 - y_2)/2, \qquad Y^2(m) = (y_2 - y_1)/2,$$
$$X^1(m) = -p \cdot (y_1 - y_2)/2 = -p \cdot Y^1(m), \qquad (0.1)$$
$$X^2(m) = -p \cdot (y_2 - y_1)/2 = -p \cdot Y^2(m).$$

The departure from Schmeidler's rules comes when the two price proposals differ ($p_1 \neq p_2$). The outcome function is so designed that at least one agent has an incentive to depart from the price he has proposed and to accept the price proposed by the other. (In fact, for $n = 2$ both will have this incentive.[3] However, when $n = 3$, we do not claim that every agent has such an incentive but only that at least one of them does.) Explicitly, the rule is:

For $p_1 \neq p_2$, the net trade increments are given by

$$Y^1(m) = (p_1 - p_2)/2, \qquad Y^2(m) = (p_2 - p_1)/2,$$
$$X^1(m) = [(p_1 + p_2)/2][(p_2 - p_1)/2] = -P \cdot Y^1(m), \qquad (0.2)$$
$$X^2(m) = [(p_1 + p_2)/2][(p_1 - p_2)/2] = -P \cdot Y^2(m),$$

where $P = (p_1 + p_2)/2$ is the average of the two prices. We note that the outcome function so defined is balanced and symmetric with respect to agents.

For an economy e, we shall denote by $W(e)$ the set of its Walrasian allocations. Denoting the outcome function by h, we denote by $v_h(e)$ the set

---

[3] For $n = 2$, $l = 2$, the situation is illustrated in Fig. 1. The diagram shows a part of the Edgeworth Box, with origin 0 at the point of initial endowment, so that the coordinates of a point represent net trades. The two price lines represent the case $p_1 > p_2$. (In the diagram, $p_1 = 5$, $p_2 = 3$, $P = 4$.) Then formula (0.2) would mandate the allocation $A = (-4, 1)$. But if agent 1 switches to $p'_1 = p_2$, then formula (0.1) would enable him to obtain a point such as $B \geq A$—which is preferable to A because of the assumed strict monotonicity of preferences. Similarly, agent 2 would find it preferable to use $p'_2 = p_1$, since this would enable him to go to $C \leq A$.

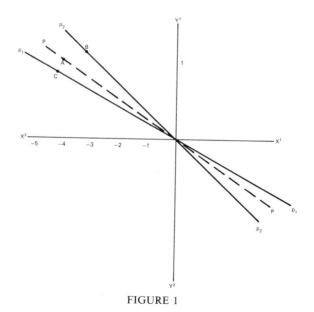

FIGURE 1

of Nash equilibrium strategy pairs $m = (m_1, m_2)$ for e, and by $N_h(e)$ the set of its Nash allocations. [z is a Nash allocation in e for h if and only if $z = h(m)$ for some m in $v_h(e)$.]

PROPOSITION 1.1(2)   For every e, if $z^* \in W(e)$, then $z^* \in N_h(e)$. (The economy is assumed "classical," and h is the above outcome function.)

Proof   Let $((1, p^*), z^*)$ be a Walrasian equilibrium for e, with $z^* = (z^{*1}, z^{*2})$ allocation and $(1, p^*)$ price vector. By the definition of Walrasian equilibrium, we have

$$x^{*i} + p^* y^{*i} = 0 \qquad (i = 1, 2), \qquad \text{where} \quad z^{*i} = (x^{*i}, y^{*i}), \tag{1}$$

$$z^{*1} + z^{*2} = 0, \tag{2}$$

$$x^i + p^* y^i < 0 \text{ implies } z^i \ominus_i z^{*i} \qquad (i = 1, 2), \qquad \text{where} \quad z^i = (x^i, y^i). \tag{3}$$

The last implication follows from the assumptions made on the preferences. [Inequalities in circles denote preferences; the latter are understood in the extended sense of Hurwicz (1976), i.e., valid for individually infeasible trades.]

We shall show that $\bar{m} = (\bar{m}_1, \bar{m}_2)$, $\bar{m}_i = (\bar{p}_i, \bar{y}_i)$ given by (4) below is the required Nash equilibrium strategy pair. The formula defining it is

$$\begin{aligned} \bar{p}_i &= p^* \qquad (i = 1, 2) \\ \bar{y}_1 &= 2y^{*1}, \qquad \bar{y}_2 = 0. \end{aligned} \tag{4}$$

We shall now show that

$$\bar{m} \in v_h(e) \tag{5}$$

and

$$z^* = h(\bar{m}). \tag{6}$$

(i)   Since $\bar{p}_1 = \bar{p}_2$, we have by (0.1)

$$Y^1(\bar{m}) = (\bar{y}_1 - \bar{y}_2)/2 = 2y^{*1}/2 = y^{*1},$$

and analogously

$$Y^2(\bar{m}) = -y^{*1} = y^{*2}.$$

In turn,

$$X^1(\bar{m}) = -p^* \cdot Y^1(\bar{m}) = -p^* \cdot y^{*1} = x^{*1},$$

and

$$X^2(\bar{m}) = -X^1(\bar{m}) = -x^{*1} = x^{*2}.$$

Hence (6) holds. [The equalities between the *-entities follow from (1) above.]

(ii) To prove (5), we show that no agent has a strategy option more advantageous than $\bar{m}_i$, given that the other agent retains his strategy $\bar{m}_j$, $j \neq i$. To simplify notation we consider agent 1; the argument for agent 2 is obtained by the interchange of indices 1, 2.

Suppose agent 1 uses a strategy $m_1 = (p_1, y_1) \neq (\bar{p}_1, \bar{y}_1) = \bar{m}_1$. Consider first the case where $p_1 = \bar{p}_1 = \bar{p}_2 = p^*$. Writing

$$Z^1(m) = (X^1(m), Y^1(m)),$$

we have, by (0.1)

$$(1, p^*) \cdot Z^1(m_1, \bar{m}_2) = 0,$$

and, since (by the Walrasian property) z^{*1} maximizes satisfaction subject to $(1, p^*) \cdot Z^1 = 0$, it follows that

$$Z^1(m_1, \bar{m}_2) \leqslant_1 z^{*1} = Z^1(\bar{m}_1, \bar{m}_2) = h^1(\bar{m}) \qquad \text{whenever} \quad p_1 = \bar{p}_2. \quad (7.1)$$

Hence no strategy change leaving the price component the same would raise 1's level of satisfaction. It remains to consider strategy changes modifying the price proposal.

Let, therefore, the alternative strategy considered be $m_1 = (p_1, y_1)$ with $p_1 \neq \bar{p}_2 = p^*$. In this situation the outcome is determined by formulas (0.2), so that

$$Y^1(m_1, \bar{m}_2) = (p_1 - \bar{p}_2)/2,$$

and

$$X^1(m_1, \bar{m}_2) = [(p_1 + \bar{p}_2)/2] \cdot [(\bar{p}_2 - p_1)/2].$$

We shall now calculate the value of the bundle $Z^1(m_1, \bar{m}_2)$ at the price $\bar{p}_2$ and show that this value is negative. We have

$$(1, \bar{p}_2) \cdot ([(p_1 + \bar{p}_2)/2] \cdot [(\bar{p}_2 - p_1)/2], (p_1 - \bar{p}_2)/2)$$
$$= [(p_1 + \bar{p}_2)/2] \cdot [(\bar{p}_2 - p_1)/2] + \bar{p}_2(p_1 - \bar{p}_2)/2$$
$$= [(\bar{p}_2 - p_1)/2] \cdot [(p_1 + \bar{p}_2)/2 - \bar{p}_2]$$
$$= [(\bar{p}_2 - p_1)/2] \cdot [(p_1 - \bar{p}_2)/2] = -(p_1 - \bar{p}_2) \cdot (p_1 - \bar{p}_2) < 0$$

since, by hypothesis, in this case $p_1 \neq \bar{p}_2$.

But here $\bar{p}_2$ is the Walrasian p^*; therefore, by (3), we have

$$Z^1(m_1, \bar{m}_2) \leqslant_1 z^{*1} = Z^1(\bar{m}_1, \bar{m}_2) = h^1(\bar{m}) \qquad \text{whenever} \quad p_1 \neq \bar{p}_2. \quad (7.2)$$

Thus (7.1) and (7.2) together show that agent 1 cannot benefit by departing from the $\bar{m}_1$ strategy given that agent 2 retains $\bar{m}_2$. Similarly, agent 2 cannot benefit by departing from $\bar{m}_2$ strategy given that agent 1 retains $\bar{m}_1$. Hence $\bar{m}$ is a Nash equilibrium and (5) has been established. This completes the proof of Proposition 1.1(2).

PROPOSITION 1.2(2)   For every e, if $\bar{z} \in N_h(e)$, then $\bar{z} \in W(e)$.

Proof   We shall show that given $\bar{m} \in v_h(e)$ such that $\bar{z} = h(\bar{m})$ there exists p^* such that $((1, p^*), \bar{z})$ is a Walrasian equilibrium for e.

As above, we write $\bar{m} = (\bar{m}_1, \bar{m}_2)$, $\bar{m}_i = (\bar{p}_i, \bar{y}_i)$, $i = 1, 2$. We first show that

$$\bar{m} \in v_h(e) \qquad \text{implies} \qquad \bar{p}_1 = \bar{p}_2. \tag{8}$$

Suppose (8) false. Then, for some e satisfying our assumptions and some $\bar{m} \in v_h(e)$, we have

$$\bar{p}_1 \neq \bar{p}_2,$$

and, by (0.2),

$$\bar{z}^1 = ([(\bar{p}_1 + \bar{p}_2)/2] \cdot [(\bar{p}_2 - \bar{p}_1)/2], (\bar{p}_1 - \bar{p}_2)/2). \tag{9}$$

But we shall see that agent 1 has available a strategy different from $\bar{m}_1$ yielding a higher level of satisfaction given that agent 2 retains $\bar{m}_2$. This will contradict the hypothesis that $\bar{m} \in v_h(e)$ and so prove (8).

Now the alternative superior strategy $m' = (p'_1, y'_1)$ available to agent 1 is obtained as follows. First, $p'_1 = \bar{p}_2$. I.e., agent 1 switches to 2's price proposal, thus qualifying for outcomes specified by formulae (0.1) rather than (0.2). Second he chooses y'_1 so that the resulting allocation $\bar{z}^1 = (\tilde{x}^1, \tilde{y}^1)$ as given by (0.1) maximizes agent 1's satisfaction subject to the budget $x^1 + \bar{p}_2 \cdot y^2 = 0$. (Agent 1 will obtain the desired allocation $\bar{z}^1$ by choosing $p'_1 = \bar{p}_2$ and $y'_1 = 2\tilde{y}^1 + \bar{y}_2$.)

We shall now show that

$$\tilde{z}^1 \bigotimes_1 \bar{z}^1, \tag{10}$$

which will complete the proof of (8). To establish (10), we evaluate the two bundles $\tilde{z}^1$ and $\bar{z}^1$ at the price $\bar{p}_2$. By construction, we have

$$(1, \bar{p}_2) \cdot \tilde{z}^1 = 0, \tag{11}$$

since $\tilde{z}^1$ is 1's satisfaction maximizer subject to $(1, \bar{p}_2) \cdot z^1 = 0$.

On the other hand, by calculations like those above, we find that

$$(1, \bar{p}_2) \cdot \bar{z}^1 = -(\bar{p}_2 - \bar{p}_1) \cdot (\bar{p}_2 - \bar{p}_1)/4 < 0, \tag{12}$$

since, by hypothesis, $\bar{p}_1 \neq \bar{p}_2$.

Clearly, by the revealed preference principle, relations (11) and (12) imply (10). (Actually, strict monotonicity of preferences seems enough here.) Hence (8) follows.

Since, by hypothesis, $\bar{m} \in v_h(e)$, it follows from (8) that $\bar{p}_1 = \bar{p}_2 = \bar{p}$ (say). As seen in the proof of (8), for each agent i, every point of the budget set $\{z^i : (1, \bar{p}) \cdot z^i = 0\}$ is accessible through a suitable choice of y_i. Therefore, by definition of Nash equilibrium, $\bar{z}^i$ maximizes i's satisfaction over this budget set for $i = 1, 2$. Furthermore, since the outcome function h is balanced by construction, we have $\bar{z}^1 + \bar{z}^2 = 0$. Hence $((1, \bar{p}), \bar{z})$ is a Walras equilibrium. This completes the proof of Proposition 1.2(2).

1.2. The case of $n \geq 2$ agents

As mentioned in the introduction, our outcome function here is a modification of that due to Schmeidler (1976); the modification pertains to rules governing the members of the set T_0 of "loners." Another difference is that we only permit strictly positive price vectors. (This could also be relaxed.)

The ith strategy is of the form $m_i = (p_i, y_i)$ with both components of dimension $l - 1$. The set of agents is denoted by $N = \{1, \ldots, n\}$, with $n \geq 2$. Given an n-tuple $(m_i)_{i \in N}$ of strategies, the set N is partitioned in such a manner that (1) if agent i has proposed a price p_i that has not been proposed by anyone else, then i belongs to the subset T_0 of N, and only such "loners" belong to T_0; (2) if a price q has been proposed by two or more members of N, then all those proposing q belong to the subset $T(q)$ of N. Let $q^1, \ldots, q^k$ be the complete list of distinct price vectors such that, for each $r \in \{1, \ldots, k\}$, q^r has been proposed by two or more agents. If there are none, then $N = T_0$. Otherwise we write $T(q^r) = T_r, r \in \{1, \ldots, k\}$. Thus a set $T_r, r \geq 1$, consists of all those agents who have proposed the price vector q_r and must have at least two members. T_0, on the other hand, may be empty or have any number of members, not excluding n. The set N is thus partitioned into $T_0, T_1, \ldots, T_k$ with some of these possibly empty.

The outcome rule is defined as follows. If $T_0 \neq N$ and agent i belongs to the subset $T_r, r \in \{1, \ldots, k\}$, then

$$Y^i(m) = y_i - \left(\sum_{j \in T_r} y_j \right) \Big/ \# T_r$$

(0.1)

$$X^i(m) = -q^r \cdot Y^i(m).$$

(This is precisely Schmeidler's rule.)

If T_0 is nonempty and i belongs to T_0 (which means that the price p_i he has proposed has not been proposed by anyone else), then

$$Y^i(m) = p_i - P$$
$$X^i(m) = -P \cdot Y^i(m) = -P \cdot (p_i - P)$$

(0.2)

where

$$P = \left(\sum_{j \in T_0} p_j \right) \Big/ \# T_0.$$

(This rule is different from Schmeidler's rule for T_0.)

It will be noted that the outcome function is balanced, and indeed balanced within each set of the partition. Thus for $r \in \{1, \ldots, k\}$, we have

$$\sum_{i \in T_r} Y^i(m) = \sum_{i \in T_r} y_i - (\#T_r)\left(\sum_{j \in T_r} y_j\right)\bigg/\#T_r = 0 \qquad \text{for all} \quad m,$$

and

$$\sum_{i \in T_r} X^i(m) = -q^r \cdot \sum_{i \in T_r} Y^i(m) = 0 \qquad \text{for all} \quad m.$$

Similarly for the "loners" set we have

$$\sum_{i \in T_0} Y^i(m) = \sum_{i \in T_0} p_i - (\#T_0)P = 0 \qquad \text{for all} \quad m,$$

and

$$\sum_{i \in T_0} X^i(m) = -P \cdot \sum_{i \in T_0} Y^i(m) = 0 \quad \text{for all} \quad m.$$

In what follows we shall be using the following

LEMMA   If the set T_0 is nonempty and if, for agent i belonging to T_0, $p_i \neq P$, then there is an agent $j \neq i$ also in T_0 such that

$$(p_j - P) \cdot (p_i - P) < 0. \tag{1}$$

Proof   When $\#T_0 = 1$, the hypothesis $p_i \neq P$ cannot be satisfied; hence the assertion of the lemma is vacuously true. Hence let $\#T_0 \geqq 2$ and suppose that for some i in T_0 and all $j \neq i$ the inequality (1) is false. Then

$$(p_j - P) \cdot (p_i - P) \geqq 0 \qquad \text{for all} \quad j \text{ in } T_0\backslash\{i\}.$$

Summing over j we get

$$\sum_{j \in T_0\backslash\{i\}} (p_j - P) \cdot (p_i - P) \geqq 0.$$

Writing $n_0 = \#T_0$, we then have

$$\left(\sum_{j \in T_0\backslash\{i\}} p_j - (n_0 - 1)P\right) \cdot (p_i - P) \geqq 0.$$

But

$$\sum_{j \in T_0\backslash\{i\}} p_j = \sum_{k \in T_0} p_k - p_i = n_0 P - p_i.$$

Hence the preceding inequality becomes

$$(n_0 P - p_i - (n_0 - 1)P) \cdot (p_i - P) \geqq 0.$$

After simplification this becomes

$$(P - p_i) \cdot (p_i - P) \geq 0,$$

i.e.,

$$(p_i - P) \cdot (p_i - P) \leq 0,$$

which contradicts the hypothesis $p_i \neq P$.   Q.E.D.

We now state and prove the general versions (for $n \geq 2$) of the two propositions established in Section 1.1 for $n = 2$.

PROPOSITION 1.1   For every e, if $z^* \in W(e)$ then $z^* \in N_h(e)$. [The economy is assumed "classical" and the outcome function is defined by Eqs. (0.1)–(0.2) in Section 1.2.]

Proof   Let $((1, p^*), z^*)$ be a Walrasian equilibrium, with $z^* = (z^{*i})_{i \in N}$, $z^{*i} = (x^{*i}, y^{*i})$. As before, we construct a Nash equilibrium n-tuple $\bar{m}$ given by

$$\bar{p}_i = p^* \qquad \text{(for all i in N)},$$

$$\bar{y}_j = y^{*j} + \sum_{k=1}^{n-1} y^{*k}, \tag{1}$$

$$\bar{y}_n = 0.$$

It is easily seen that

$$z^* = h(\bar{m}) \tag{2}$$

since here T_0 is empty and formulas (0.1) together with (1) imply (2). It remains to be shown that $\bar{m}$ is a Nash equilibrium, i.e., that no agent can derive a benefit from abandoning $\bar{m}$. Clearly there can be no advantage in changing y_i while leaving $p_i = \bar{p}_i$, the argument being precisely the same as for $n = 2$.

Suppose, therefore, that agent i departs from $\bar{p}_i$. If $n \geq 3$, agent i then constitutes a 1-element T_0 set and, by (0.2), his allocation is 0. But since 0 was already available to him previously, this cannot be an improvement for agent i. Hence it remains to consider the case $n = 2$. But this has already been disposed of in Section 1.1, since the outcome functions given by Eqs. (0.1)–(0.2) of Section 1.1 are those obtained from (0.1)–(0.2) of the present section by setting $n = 2$. This completes the proof of Proposition 1.1.

PROPOSITION 1.2   For every e, if $\bar{z} \in N_h(e)$, then $\bar{z} \in W(e)$.

Proof   The argument parallels that of Schmeidler, but with an important exception: it need not be true that T_0 is empty at a Nash equilibrium. Instead, we show that the set T_0 has at most one member. For suppose that $\#T_0 \geq 2$. Then, since by construction the $\bar{p}_i$ for i in T_0 are all distinct, there is at least one i such that $p_i \neq P$ where P denotes the average of the p_k for k in T_0. Hence, by the lemma established at the beginning of this section, there is an agent j in T_0 such that i would benefit from switching from $\bar{p}_i$ to $\bar{p}_j$. Hence at a Nash equilibrium $\#T_0 \leq 1$.

It follows that $T_0 \neq N$ and $k \geq 1$. Now any agent, whether he belongs to $T_0, T_1, \ldots$, or T_k can join one of the sets $T_1, \ldots, T_r$. By joining T_r $(r \geq 1)$, as shown by Schmeidler, he can obtain the net trade maximizing his satisfaction subject to the budget with price vector q^r. Hence for every agent i in N and for every r in $\{1, \ldots, k\}$, the Nash allocation $\bar{z}^i$ maximizes i's satisfaction subject to the budget $(1, q^r) \cdot z^i = 0$, since, if this were false for some (i, r), the agent i could remedy it by joining T_r. Hence $\bar{z} = (\bar{z}^i)_{i \in N}$ is a Walrasian allocation for every price vector $(1, q^r)$, $r \in \{1, \ldots, k\}$. This completes the proof.

2. THE NASH–LINDAHL EQUIVALENCE FOR TWO OR MORE AGENTS

We confine ourselves to economies with two goods, the private good being denoted by x, the public one by y. Preferences are assumed strictly monotone in both goods. The ith agent's strategy is $m_i = (p_i, y_i)$ where p_i is a positive real and y_i any real. The interpretation is that y_i is i's proposed *increment* in the provision of the public good and p_i the proposed share of cost to be borne by i. (By requiring that the p_i be positive rather than non-negative we implicitly rule out economies in which there are Lindahl solutions of the "corner" type.)

The outcome function is defined as follows (with all summations over $N = \{1, \ldots, n\}$ unless otherwise indicated)

$$Y(m) = \sum y_i/n$$
$$X^i(m) = -Y(m)p_i \qquad \text{if } \sum p_i = 1 \qquad (0.1)$$

and

$$Y(m) = \sum p_j - 1$$
$$X^i(m) = -(p_i/\textstyle\sum p_j)Y(m) \qquad \text{if } \sum p_i \neq 1. \qquad (0.2)$$

The balance condition is

$$Y(m) + \sum X^i(m) = 0 \qquad \text{for all} \quad m,$$

and it is easily verified both for (0.1) and (0.2).

PROPOSITION 2.1   Every Lindahl allocation is a Nash allocation.

Proof   Let $[(x^{*i}, r^{*i})_{i \in N}, y^*]$ be a Lindahl equilibrium, with $x^{*i} + r^{*i} y^* = 0$, $\sum r^{*i} = 1$, for all $i \in N$. We shall then show that the following $\bar{m}$ is a Nash equilibrium and yields the given Lindahl allocation: $\bar{m} = (\bar{m}_1, \bar{m}_2, \ldots, \bar{m}_n)$, $\bar{m}_i = (\bar{p}_i, \bar{y}_i)$, with

$$\begin{aligned} \bar{p}_i &= r^{*i} \qquad \text{for all} \quad i \in N, \\ \bar{y}_i &= y^*. \end{aligned} \tag{1}$$

First, since $r^{*i} = 1$, (1) implies that (0.1) is applicable. It immediately follows that

$$Y(\bar{m}) = y^*,$$

and, since $x^{*i} + r^{*i} y^* = 0$ for all $i \in N$,

$$X^i(\bar{m}) = x^{*i} \qquad \text{for all} \quad i \in N.$$

Hence $\bar{m}$ does yield the given Lindahl allocation. It must still be shown that $\bar{m}$ is a Nash equilibrium for the outcome function specified by (0.1)–(0.2).

First, by the definition of Lindahl equilibrium, (x^{*i}, y^*) maximizes i's satisfaction subject to the budget condition $x^i + r^{*i} y^i = 0$, with r^{*i} fixed. Hence no agent can benefit by changing his y_i while leaving $p_i = \bar{p}_i$ unchanged. For in such a case, with (0.1) being the applicable outcome formula, he cannot get off this budget equation.

It remains to be seen whether any agent i could benefit by choosing some $p_i \neq \bar{p}_i$ while all other agents retain their strategies $\bar{m}_j$, $j \in N \backslash \{i\}$. Now this strategy change makes (0.2) the applicable outcome formula. Hence the new ith allocation is

$$\tilde{Y} = \sum q_j - 1, \qquad \tilde{X}^i = - \tilde{Y} q_i / \sum q_j$$

where we write

$$q_i = p_i \qquad \text{and} \qquad q_j = \bar{p}_j \qquad \text{for all} \quad j \in N \backslash \{i\},$$

so that

$$\sum q_j \neq 1.$$

We shall now show that agent i cannot prefer $(\tilde{X}^i, \tilde{Y})$, which he gets by changing strategy to p_i, to the original allocation (x^{*i}, y^*). This follows from the fact that the value of the new allocation $\tilde{Z}^1$ calculated at the original "Lindahl price" $\bar{p}_i$ is lower than the value of the original allocation z^{*i} calculated at $\bar{p}_i$.

Since the value of z^{*i} at $\bar{p}_i = r^{*i}$ is zero by the Lindahl budget condition, it remains to show that the value v_i of Z^i at $\bar{p}_i$ is negative. We have (since

$\sum \bar{p}_j = 1)$

$$
\begin{aligned}
v_i = (1, \bar{p}_i)(\tilde{X}^i, \tilde{Y}) &= \left(1, 1 - \sum_{k \ne i} \bar{p}_k\right)(\tilde{X}^i, \tilde{Y}) \\
&= \tilde{X}^i + \tilde{Y} - \tilde{Y} \sum_{k \ne i} q_k = - \tilde{Y} q_i / \sum q_j + \tilde{Y} - \tilde{Y}(\sum q_j - q_i) \\
&= \tilde{Y}[-q_i/\sum q_j + 1 - \sum q_j + q_i] \\
&= (\tilde{Y}/\sum q_j)[-q_i + \sum q_j - (\sum q_j)^2 + q_i \sum q_j] \\
&= (\tilde{Y}/\sum q_j)[q_i(\sum q_j - 1) - q_j(\sum q_j - 1)] \\
&= (\tilde{Y}/\sum q_j)(\sum q_j - 1)(q_i - \sum q_j) = [(\sum q_j - 1)/\sum q_j](\sum q_j - 1)(q_i - \sum q_j) \\
&= -(\sum q_j - 1)^2(\sum q_j - q_i)/\sum q_j < 0,
\end{aligned}
$$

since, by hypothesis, $\sum q_j \ne 1$ and all q_j are positive.
This completes the proof of Proposition 2.1.

PROPOSITION 2.2   Every Nash allocation is a Lindahl allocation.

Proof   Let $\bar{m}$ be a Nash equilibrium for the outcome function h defined by (0.1)–(0.2), with $\bar{m} = (\bar{m}_i)_{i \in N}$, $\bar{m}_i = (\bar{p}_i, \bar{y}_i)$. We first note that

$$\sum \bar{p}_k = 1. \tag{2}$$

This is seen as follows. On the one hand, suppose that (2) holds so that (0.1) is applicable. Then the value of $Z^i(\bar{m})$ at $\bar{p}_i$ equals zero for every $i \in N$. On the other hand, suppose that (2) is false. Then (0.2) is applicable. By reasoning completely analogous to that used in the proof of the preceding proposition, it can be shown that in that case the value at p_i of the ith allocation, say $\tilde{z}^i$, is negative. But under the (0.1) regime the ith agent can obtain any allocation compatible with the budget constraint $(1, \bar{p}_i) \cdot z^i = 0$, and in view of the definition of Nash equilibrium, he will choose the $Z^i(\bar{m})$ maximizing his satisfaction subject to this budget. It follows that $Z^i(\bar{m})$ is preferred by i to $\tilde{z}^i$. Hence (2) must hold.

Now given (2), the relations (0.1) which ensue, and the fact that $Z^i(\bar{m})$ maximizes every agent's satisfaction subject to the Lindahl budget constraint $(1, \bar{p}_i) \cdot z^i = 0$, we see that $[(X^i(\bar{m}), \bar{p}_i)_{i \in N}, Y(\bar{m})]$ is a Lindahl equilibrium. This completes the proof of Proposition 2.2.

REFERENCES

Hurwicz, L. (1976). Outcome functions yielding Walrasian and Lindahl allocations at Nash equilibrium points, Mimeographed Handout for Presentation at a Stanford Seminar, Nov. 21, 1976. (An earlier version circulated for Econ. 208, Berkeley. A modified version to appear in the *Review of Economic Studies*.)

Schmeidler, D. (1976). A remark on a game theoretic interpretation of Walras equilibria, November (or earlier) 1976 Mimegraphed Report. (An earlier version was circulated at a Minneapolis seminar, March, 1976.)

Research supported by National Science Foundation Grant No. SOC 76-14786.

DEPARTMENT OF ECONOMICS
UNIVERSITY OF MINNESOTA
MINNEAPOLIS, MINNESOTA

Stochastic Stability of Market Adjustment in Disequilibrium

W. HILDENBRAND

R. RADNER

1. INTRODUCTION

In a system of markets in which prices, demands, and supplies are re-peatedly subject to random disturbances, one cannot typically expect excess demands to be exactly zero at all times. Strictly speaking, such a system of markets might be said to be always in disequilibrium. On the other hand, one would want to distinguish situations in which prices and quantities fluctuated in some "steady" manner around long-run averages from situations in which prices or quantities, or both, fluctuated with greater and greater variance or increased without bound. To describe the first situation, it is natural to use the concept of a *stationary stochastic process*, which is the generalization to the case of uncertainty of the concept of a deterministic equilibrium. However, it is important to emphasize that the stationarity of a stochastic process does not rule out fluctuations of varying period and amplitude.

In a large number of markets, inventories and back-orders serve as buffers against random variations in supply and demand. We use the term *stock* to denote the level of an inventory (positive stock) or back-orders (negative stock). The levels and movements of stocks provide important signals about past and current excess demands, and these signals in turn influence the movements of prices. On the other hand, prices are influenced by signals other than stocks, and themselves serve as signals that influence supplies and demands, and thus also the stocks. In this paper we study conditions under which the stochastic process of interdependent prices and stocks converges to a stationary process; i.e., we study conditions sufficient for *stochastic stability.*

Our assumptions about price and stock adjustment are similar in spirit to the diagonal dominance assumption used by Lionel McKenzie to study the stability of a tâtonnement adjustment process in the deterministic case. (See [1, 5].) Our assumptions are not directly comparable with diagonal dominance, however, because of the difference in the model.[1] Our assumptions about adjustment can be paraphrased as follows: For every commodity when its stock is sufficiently high (low), its own money price will fall (rise) *on the average*, and when its price is sufficiently high (low), its stock will rise (fall) on the average.

We also make use of two other assumptions: (B) The (one-period) increments of prices and stocks are uniformly bounded, and (M) the stochastic process of prices and stocks is Markovian, with stationary transition probabilities and a discrete state space. With these assumptions we can show that the Markov process converges to a stationary process, which, as we have noted, is the stochastic analog of an "equilibrium". Our assumptions do not preclude a multiplicity of equilibria, but they do ensure that there are only finitely many of them. In general, from any starting state there will be a probability distribution on the set of ultimate equilibria, i.e., on the set of alternate stationary processes to which the process may converge.

Even without the Markovian assumption (M) we can prove a stabilitylike result: There is a bounded set D such that from every initial state, every trajectory (almost surely) enters D, and the expected time to the first entry is finite.

Our results can be compared with those of Green and Majumdar [4]. Green and Majumdar consider a tâtonnement-type Markovian adjustment process in which the state variables are the prices and excess demands (stocks are not explicitly represented in the system). They give sufficient conditions for the process to be ergodic, i.e., to converge to a unique stationary process. However, the stationary process (equilibrium) may have the property that the mean excess demand is different from zero. This contrasts with the situation in our model in which the stationarity of stocks implies that the mean excess demand (flow) is zero (unless, of course, there is asymmetric attrition of inventories and back-orders).

---

[1] In addition to being deterministic, the model used by McKenzie (and others in that literature) differs from ours in that the state variables are prices and *excess demands*, rather than prices and stocks. For a general discussion of such tâtonnement models see, e.g., [2, Chaps. 11, and 12].

2. THE STOCHASTIC STABILITY THEOREM

We consider a system of H interrelated markets, operating at dates $t = 0, 1, \ldots,$ *ad infinitum*. At each date t, the state of market h is characterized by the price p_t^h of commodity h and the stock (inventory) v_t^h of that commodity. We shall assume that $p_t^h \in R_+$ and $v_t^h \in R$. Negative stocks are interpreted as accepted but unfilled orders. Let

$$p_t = (p_t^1, \ldots, p_t^H) \quad \text{and} \quad v_t = (v_t^1, \ldots, v_t^H)$$

denote the H − tuples of prices and stocks, respectively, at date t. The *state* s_t of the economy at date t is characterized by the pair $s_t = (p_t, v_t)$.

We make four assumptions about the *process* (s_t), which are listed below. The first is that (s_t) is a *stochastic process*. In the second part of the theorem we strengthen this assumption by assuming that the stochastic process (s_t) is *Markovian* with stationary transition probabilities and discrete state space. The second assumption (B) is technical, but essential; it requires the increments in the variables p_t^h, v_t^h to be uniformly bounded. The third and fourth assumptions (PA and SA) concern price and stock adjustment, respectively. These last two assumptions can be paraphrased as follows: For every commodity when *its* stock is sufficiently high (low), its own price will fall (rise) *on the average*, and when its price is sufficiently high (low), its stock will rise (fall) *on the average*.

We now give the precise statements of these four assumptions.

(S) *The process* (p_t, v_t) *is a stochastic process defined on some probability space* $(\Omega, \mathscr{F}, P)$.

Let $\mathscr{F}_t$ denote the sub-σ-field of $\mathscr{F}$ generated by partial histories of the process up through date t; i.e., $\mathscr{F}_t$ is the smallest sub-σ-field of $\mathscr{F}$ such that the random variables $s_1, \ldots, s_t$ are measurable. All statements about random variables defined on $(\Omega, \mathscr{F}, P)$ are to be understood as holding P-almost surely.

(B) *The coordinates of* p_t *and* v_t *have uniformly bounded increments. This bound will be denoted by* γ; i.e., *for every* h *and* t, $|p_{t+1}^h - p_t^h| \leq \gamma$ *and* $|v_{t+1}^h - v_t^h| \leq \gamma$.

(PA) *For every commodity* h *there exist numbers* $v^{*h} > 0, \alpha^{*h} > 0, v_*^h \leq 0,$ *and* $\alpha_*^h > 0$ *such that*

1. $E(p_{t+1}^h | \mathscr{F}_t) \leq max\{0, p_t^h - \alpha^{*h}\}$ *on* $\{v_t^h \geq v^{*h}\}$,
2. $E(p_{t+1}^h | \mathscr{F}_t) \geq p_t^h + \alpha_*^h$ *on* $\{v_t^h \leq v_*^h\}$.

(SA) *For every commodity* h *there are positive numbers* $p^{*h}, \beta^{*h}, p_*^h, \beta_*^h$ *with* $p_*^h < p^{*h}$ *such that*

1. $E(v_{t+1}^h | \mathscr{F}_t) \geq v_t^h + \beta^{*h}$ *on* $\{p_t^h \geq p^{*h}\}$,
2. $E(v_{t+1}^h | \mathscr{F}_t) \leq max(0, v_t^h - \beta_*^h)$ *on* $\{p_t^h \leq p_*^h\}$.

THEOREM   *Assumptions (S), (B), (PA) and (SA) imply that there exists a bounded set $D \subset R_+^H \times R^H$ of states of the stochastic process (p_t, v_t) such that P-almost every trajectory intersects D, and the expected time for the first intersection is finite; i.e.,*

$$E(T) < \infty, \quad \text{where} \quad T(\omega) = \inf\{t \,|\, (p_t(\omega), v_t(\omega)) \in D\}.$$

Furthermore, if the stochastic process (p_t, v_t) is Markovian with stationary transition probabilities and discrete state space, then there is a partition of the state space into finitely many positive recurrent classes and a set of transient states that contains no closed set.

We would like to mention that the first part of the theorem can be strengthened. Using a result of Föllmer [3], who generalized and strengthened considerably an argument that we used in an earlier version of this paper,[2] one can assert that the set D is positive recurrent in the sense that every trajectory spends a positive fraction of time in D; i.e., there exists a number $c > 0$ such that

$$\liminf_t (1/t) \sum_{k=0}^{t-1} 1_D \circ s_k \geq c, \quad \text{P-a.s.}$$

(For any subset A of a set B, the symbol 1_A denotes the function that is 1 on A and 0 otherwise, i.e., the "indicator function" for the set A.) For a proof of this stronger result we refer to Föllmer [3].

Proof of the Theorem

The complex part of the proof consists in showing that there exists a positive function L (Liapunov) defined on the state space S of the process (s_t) such that for $d \geq 0$ the set $\{s \in S \,|\, L(s) \leq d\}$ is bounded, and that the stochastic process $(L \circ s_t)$ has the following "conditional strict supermartingale" property: (SSM) *There exist $\varepsilon > 0$ and $d > 0$ such that*

$$E(L \circ s_{t+1}) \,|\, \mathscr{F}_t) \leq L \circ s_t - \varepsilon \quad on \quad \{L \circ s_t \geq d\}.$$

In the first part of the proof we show that the existence of a function L with the above properties implies the theorem.[3] In the second part we construct the function L.

I. Lemma 1 proves the first assertion of the theorem.

---

[2] Presented at the Third World Congress of the Econometric Society, Toronto, 1975.

[3] In this part of the proof we use several suggestions of Föllmer, which are gratefully acknowledged. Our proof in an earlier version of this paper was less elementary.

LEMMA 1   *Given a probability space* $(\Omega, \mathscr{F}, P)$, *an increasing sequence* $(\mathscr{F}_t)$ *of sub-σ-fields of* $\mathscr{F}$, *and a sequence* (x_t) *of positive random variables such that* x_t *is* $\mathscr{F}_t$*-measurable and* $E(x_0) < \infty$, *assume that there exist* $\varepsilon > 0$ *and* $d > 0$ *such that*

$$E(x_t - x_{t+1} | \mathscr{F}_n) \geq \varepsilon \qquad on \quad \{\omega | x_t(\omega) \geq d\}.$$

Let $T(\omega) = \inf\{t | x_t(\omega) \leq d\}$. *Then* $E(T) < \infty$. *Hence, in particular,* $T(\omega) < \infty$, *P-a.s.*

Proof   For every integer N let $T_N(\omega) = \min\{T(\omega), N\}$, and let x_{T_N} be the random variable defined by $x_{T_N}(\omega) = x_t(\omega)$, when $t = T_N(\omega)$. Then

$$E(x_0 - x_{T_N}) = E\left(\sum_{t=0}^{N} (x_t - x_{t+1}) \cdot 1_{\{T_N > t\}} \right)$$

$$= \sum_{t=0}^{N} E[E(x_t - x_{t+1}) \cdot 1_{\{T_N > T\}} | \mathscr{F}_t]$$

$$= \sum_{t=0}^{N} E[E(x_t - x_{t+1} | \mathscr{F}_t) \cdot 1_{\{T_N > t\}}],$$

since $1_{\{T_N > t\}}$ is $\mathscr{F}_t$-measurable. By the above assumption (SSM) we obtain

$$E[E(x_t - x_{t+1} | \mathscr{F}_t) \cdot 1_{\{T_N > t\}}] \geq \varepsilon \cdot P\{T_N > t\}.$$

Hence

$$E(x_0) \geq E(x_0 - x_{T_N}) \geq \varepsilon \cdot E(T_N) \qquad for\ all \quad N.$$

By the monotone convergence theorem this implies $E(x_0) \geq \varepsilon E(T)$. Hence $E(T) < \infty$, since $E(x_0) < \infty$.   Q.E.D.

We shall now assume that (s_t) is a Markov process with stationary transition probabilities and *discrete* state space S (i.e., S is a countable subset of $R_+^H \times R^H$ such that every bounded set is finite). Then every state in S is either recurrent or transient according to the classification of states for Markov processes. We shall show that

(1)   *every recurrent state of* (s_t) *is positive recurrent.*

Let the state s be recurrent. Then its communicating class is closed; hence, by the first part of the theorem, the class intersects the set D. Since recurrence is a class property, we can assume without loss of generality that $s \in D$.

Let $R(\omega) = \inf\{t \geq 1 | s_t(\omega) = s\}$. We have to show that the expected time to return to s is finite; i.e., $E_s(R) < \infty$.

We now consider the Markov process "on" the finite set D. This process is formally defined as follows: Let d_t denote the successive times the process

(s_t) spends in D; thus, at time $d_t(\omega)$ the trajectory $s_t(\omega)$ is for the tth time in D. The process (s_t^D) "on" D is defined by $s_t^D = s_{d_t}$. The state s, being recurrent for the process (s_t), is also recurrent for the process on D. Since this process is a finite Markov chain it follows that s is positive recurrent for the process on D; i.e.,

$$E_s(R^D) < \infty, \qquad \text{where} \quad R^D = \inf\{t \geq 1 \,|\, s_t^D = s\}.$$

Let r_t denote the waiting time from d_{t-1} until the next return to D; i.e., $r_t = d_t - d_{t-1}$, or equivalently,

$$r_t(\omega) = \inf\{t' \geq 1 \,|\, s_n(\omega) \in D, n = t' + d_t(\omega)\}.$$

With this notation we obtain

$$R = r_1 + \cdots + r_{R^D}.$$

$$E_s(R) = E_s\left[\sum_{t=1}^{\infty} r_t \cdot 1_{\{R^D \geq t\}}\right] = \sum_{t=1}^{\infty} E_s[E_s(r_t \cdot 1_{\{R^D \geq t\}} | \mathscr{F}_{d_t})]$$

$$= \sum_{t=1}^{\infty} E_s[E_s(r_t | \mathscr{F}_{d_t}) \cdot 1_{\{R^D \geq t\}}].$$

Now, $E_s(r_t | \mathscr{F}_{d_{t-1}}) = E_s d_{t-1}$ (return time to D). Hence we obtain from the first part of the theorem that $E_s(r_t | \mathscr{F}_{d_{t-1}})$ is bounded. Since D is finite, we obtain that there exists a bound b such that

$$E_s(r_t | \mathscr{F}_{d_{t-1}}) \leq b \qquad \text{for all} \quad t.$$

Hence it follows that $E_s(R) \leq b \cdot E_s(R^D) < \infty$.

Let C be a closed set of states. By the first part of the theorem and the strong Markov property, every sample path in C intersects D infinitely often. Hence $C \cap D$ must contain a recurrent state. This proves

(2) *there are recurrent, and hence by* (1) *positive recurrent, classes; since D is finite, there are at most finitely many recurrent classes;*

(3) *there is no closed set of transient states; hence every transient state is inessential.*

II. *Existence of a Liapunov function L.* First we make some notational simplifications. Define

$$p^* = \max_h p^{*h}, \qquad p_* = \min_h p_*^h,$$

$$\beta = \min_h \min\{\beta^{*h}, \beta_*^h\},$$

$$v^* = \max_h v^{*h}, \qquad v_* = \min_h v_*^h$$

$$\alpha = \min_h \min\{\alpha^{*h}, \alpha_*^h\}.$$

Assumptions (PA) and (SA) are now satisfied with p^{*h}, p_*^h, v^{*h}, v_*^h replaced by p^*, p_*, v^*, v_*, respectively, with β^{*h} and β_*^h replaced by β, and with α^{*h} and α_*^h replaced by α. Note that α, β, and p_* are positive. We may assume that $p^* > p_*$, $v^* > v_*$, $\alpha < p_*$, and $\beta < v^*$.

From now on we fix a commodity, say h, and consider the stochastic process (p_t^h, v_t^h) on the state space $S_h = R_+ \times R$. We prove the following lemma:

LEMMA 2   *There is a function L^h of S_h into R that has the following properties: there are numbers $d^h > 0$ and $\varepsilon^h > 0$ such that*

(i)   *the set $\{(p, v) \in S_h \,|\, L^h \circ (p, v) \le d^h\}$ is bounded;*
(ii) $E(L^h \circ (p_{t+1}^h, v_{t+1}^h) \,|\, \mathscr{F}_t) \le L^h \circ (p_t^h, v_t^h) - \varepsilon^h$,
   on $\{L^h \circ (p_t^h, v_t^h) \ge d^h\}$.

Proof   To simplify the notation, we suppress the index h. The function $L(p, v)$ shall be of the form

$$\max_{0 \le m \le M} K_m(p, v),$$

where the functions K_m (to be specified later) are of the form:

if $0 \le m \le N$,

$$K_m(p, v) = a_m p - v + c_m, \qquad a_0 < a_1 < \cdots < a_{N-1} < 0, \qquad \text{and} \qquad a_N > 0;$$

if $N \le m \le M$,

$$K_m(p, v) = a_N p + b_m v + c_m,$$

$$-1 = b_N < b_{N+1} < \cdots < b_{M-1} < 0, \qquad \text{and} \qquad b_M > 0.$$

We shall show that the function L will have the required property provided the numbers N and M and the coefficients a_m, b_m, and c_m are suitably chosen. Figure 1 illustrates two level curves of the function L. With the notation used in Fig. 1 we have

$$K_m(p^* + \gamma(1 + 2m), v) = K_{m+1}(p^* + \gamma(1 + 2m), v), \qquad 0 \le m < N;$$

(4)   *hence* $c_{m+1} - c_m = -(a_{m+1} - a_m)(p^* + \gamma(1 + 2m))$ *and*

$$K_m(p, v^* + \gamma(1 + 2(m - N))) = K_{m+1}(p, v^* + \gamma(1 + 2(m - N))), \qquad N \le m < M;$$

hence $c_{m+1} - c_m = -(b_{m+1} - b_m)(v^* + \gamma(1 + 2(m - N)))$.

We now determine the integer N and the slope of the level curve $K_m =$ constant, i.e., a_m for $m \le N$.

(a_0):   Let a_0 be such that $\varepsilon_0 =_{Df} -a_0 \alpha - \gamma > 0$; hence $a_0 < 0$.
(a_N):   Let $\bar{a} > 0$, but such that $\bar{\varepsilon} =_{Df} \beta - \bar{a}\gamma > 0$.

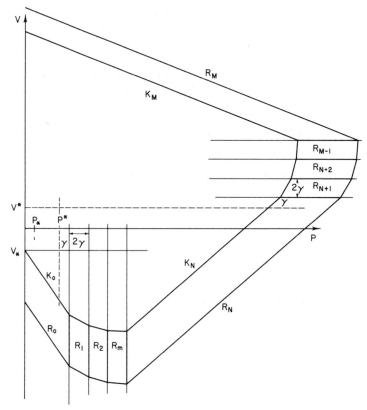

FIGURE 1

(N)   The integer N is then determined by

$$\frac{\bar{a} - a_0}{N} < \frac{1}{\gamma} \min\{\varepsilon_0, \bar{\varepsilon}\}.$$

Now we define

(a_m): $a_1 = a_0 + \Delta$, $a_m = a_0 + m\Delta$, $a_N = \bar{a}$, where $\Delta = (\bar{a} - a_0)/N$.

Let $\varepsilon =_{Df} -\Delta\gamma + \min\{\varepsilon_0, \bar{\varepsilon}\}$; hence $0 < \varepsilon < \min\{\varepsilon_0, \bar{\varepsilon}\}$. We now prove the strict supermartingale property for $L(s_t)$ on $\bigcup_{m=0}^{N} R_m$; i.e.,

(SSM) $E(L(p_{t+1}, v_{t+1}) | \mathscr{F}_t) \le L(p_t, v_t) - \varepsilon$ on $(p_t, v_t) \in \bigcup_{m=0}^{N} R_m$,   where the regions R_m are defined as in Fig. 1.

   1.   Let $R_0^- = \{(p, v) \in R_0 | p \le p^*\}$. On $\{s_t \in R_0^-\}$ then follows

$$E(L(p_{t+1}, v_{t+1}) | \mathscr{F}_t) = E(K_0(p_{t+1}, v_{t+1}) | \mathscr{F}_t)$$
$$= a_0 E(p_{t+1} | \mathscr{F}_t) - E(v_{t+1} | \mathscr{F}_t) + c_0.$$

By assumption (PA2), $E(p_{t+1}|\mathscr{F}_t) \geq p_t + \alpha$ and by assumption (B), $v_{t+1} \geq v_t - \gamma$. Hence, on $\{s_t \in R_0^-\}$,

$$E(L(s_{t+1}|\mathscr{F}_t) \leq a_0 p_t + a_0\alpha - v_t + \gamma + c_0 = K_0 \circ (p_t, v_t) + a_0\alpha + \gamma$$
$$\leq L \circ (p_t, v_t) - \varepsilon_0 \leq L \circ s_t - \varepsilon.$$

2. Let $R_m^+ = \{(p,v) \in R_m | (p-\gamma, v) \in R_m, \ 0 \leq m < N$. On $\{s_t \in R_m^+\}$ it follows

$$E(L \circ s_{t+1}|\mathscr{F}_t) = E(\max\{K_m \circ s_{t+1}, \ K_{m+1} \circ s_{t+1}\}|\mathscr{F}_t)$$
$$= E(K_m \circ s_{t+1}|\mathscr{F}_t) + \int_{R_{m+1}} [K_{m+1}(s) - K_m(s)] \hat{P}(ds|\mathscr{F}_t),$$

where $\hat{P}(s|\mathscr{F}_t)$ is a regular conditional distribution for s_{t+1} given $\mathscr{F}_t$. By definition of K_m we obtain from (4)

$$K_{m+1}(s) - K_m(s) = (a_{m+1} - a_m)p + (c_{m+1} - c_m)$$
$$= (a_{m+1} - a_m)(p - (p^* + \gamma(1 + 2m))).$$

Hence

$$\int_{R_{m+1}} [K_{m+1}(s) - K_m(s)] \hat{P}(ds|\mathscr{F}_t) \leq \Delta \cdot \gamma.$$

By assumptions (PA2), (SA1), and (B) for $0 \leq m < N$, we obtain on $\{s_t \in R_m^+\}$,

$$E(K_m \circ s_{t+1}|\mathscr{F}_t) \leq a_m E(p_{t+1}|\mathscr{F}_t) - E(v_{t+1}|\mathscr{F}_t) + c_m \leq K_m \circ s_t + \alpha a_m - \beta.$$

Hence, since $a_m < a_N$ and $\alpha < \gamma$,

$$E(L \circ s_{t+1}|\mathscr{F}_t) \leq L \circ s_t + \alpha a_m - \beta + \Delta\gamma \leq L \circ s_t + \gamma a_N - \beta$$
$$\leq L \circ s_t - \varepsilon \qquad \text{on} \quad \{s_t \in R_m^+\}.$$

3. Let $R_m^- = \{(p,v) \in R_m | (p+\gamma, v) \in R_m\}, \ 1 \leq m \leq N$. The proof is similar to the previous case. On $\{s_t \in R_m^-\}$ it follows that

$$E(L \circ s_{t+1}|\mathscr{F}) = E(K_m \circ s_{t+1}|\mathscr{F}_t) + \int_{R_{m-1}} [K_{m-1}(s) - K_m(s)] \hat{P}(ds|\mathscr{F}_t)$$
$$\leq (K_m \circ s_t + \alpha a_m - \beta) + \Delta\gamma$$
$$\leq L \circ s_t - \varepsilon.$$

4. Let $R_N^+ = \{(p,v) \in R_N | (p-\gamma, v) \in R_N\}$. On $\{s_t \in R_N^+\}$ we obtain by assumptions (SA1) and (B) and property (a_N),

$$E(L \circ s_{t+1}|\mathscr{F}_t) = E(K_N \circ s_{t+1}|\mathscr{F}_t) \leq K_N \circ s_t + a_N\gamma - \beta$$
$$\leq L \circ s_t - \varepsilon.$$

This completes the proof of property (SSM) on $\{s_t \in \bigcup_{m=0}^N R_m\}$.

We shall not give the details for the functions $K_m, m > N$. The arguments are similar. One has to increase the coefficient b_m slowly enough (recall $b_N = -1$) until it becomes positive but not greater than $(\alpha/\gamma) \cdot a_N$. We just define the last function K_M. The slow turning around from K_N to K_M is done analogously as from K_0 to K_N.

Let $\bar{b} > 0$ such that $\bar{b} < (\alpha/\gamma)a_N$. Consider the function $K_M(p, v) = a_N p + \bar{b}v + \bar{c}$. On $\{s_t \in R_M$ and $p_t \geq p_*\}$ we obtain from assumption (PA1) (note that $\alpha < p_*$) and (B) that

$$E(K_M \circ s_{t+1}|s_t) = a_N E(p_{t+1}|s_t) + \bar{b}E(v_{t+1}|s_t) + \bar{c}$$
$$\leq K_M \circ s_t - a_N\alpha + \bar{b}\gamma = K_M \circ s_t - \varepsilon_2$$

with $\varepsilon_2 = a_N\alpha - \bar{b}\gamma > 0$.

On $\{s_t \in R_M$ and $p_t < p_*\}$ we obtain from assumption (SA2) that

$$E(K_M \circ s_{t+1}|s_t) \leq a_N p_t + \bar{b}(v_t - \beta) + \bar{c} = K_M \circ s_t - \bar{b}\beta.$$

In summary, we showed that there is $\varepsilon > 0$ such that

$$E(L \circ s_t|\mathcal{F}_t) \leq L \circ s_t - \varepsilon \qquad \text{on} \quad s_t \in \bigcup_{m=0}^{M} R_m, \quad \text{P-a.s.}$$

The shape of the level curves of L clearly shows that the set $\{s \in S | L(s) \leq d\}$ is bounded. This proves Lemma 2.

The function L is now defined by

$$L(s^1, \ldots, s^H) = \sum_{h=1}^{H} (L^h(s^h))^2.$$

It remains to verify that the stochastic process $L \circ s_t$ has the "conditional strict supermartingale" property. For every stochastic process $(L^h \circ s_t^h)$, $h = 1, \ldots, H$, there are, by Lemma 2, numbers $d^h > 0$ and $\varepsilon^h > 0$ such that properties (i) and (ii) of Lemma 2 hold. Let $\delta = \max_h d^h$ and $\bar{\varepsilon} = \min_h \varepsilon^h$.

LEMMA 3 *For every $0 < \varepsilon \leq \bar{\varepsilon}$ there is $d > 0$ such that*

$$E(L \circ s_{t+1}|\mathcal{F}) \leq L \circ s_t - \varepsilon \qquad on \quad L \circ s_t \geq d.$$

Proof To simplify the notation, $l_t^h = L^h(s_t)$. Since

$$E((l_{t+1}^h)^2|\mathcal{F}_t) = E(l_{t+1}^h|\mathcal{F}_t)^2 + \text{var}(l_{t+1}^h|\mathcal{F}_t),$$

we obtain from Lemma 2 that

$$E((l_{t+1}^h)^2|\mathcal{F}_t) \leq (l_t^h - \varepsilon)^2 + \lambda^2 \qquad \text{on} \quad \{l_t^h > \delta\},$$

where λ denotes a uniform bound on the increments of the processes $L^h \circ s_t^h$, which exists according to assumption (B). If $l_t^h \leq \delta$, then, clearly, $l_{t+1}^h \leq \delta + \lambda$. Hence

$$E(L \circ s_{t+1}|\mathcal{F}_t) = \sum_{h=1}^{H} E((l_{t+1}^h)^2|\mathcal{F}_t)$$
$$\leq \sum_{\{h|l_t^h > \delta\}} [(l_t^h - \varepsilon)^2 + \lambda^2] + \sum_{\{h|l_t^h \leq \delta\}} (\delta + \lambda)^2$$
$$\leq L \circ s_t - \sum_{\{h|l_t^h > \delta\}} 2\varepsilon l_t^h + H(\varepsilon^2 + \lambda^2 + \delta^2 + 2\delta\lambda).$$

The third term is a given number and the second term can be made as negative as we want. Indeed, $L(s_t) \geq d$ implies for at least one h that $l_t^h > \sqrt{d}/H$. Hence, given the numbers $0 < \varepsilon \leq \bar{\varepsilon}$, λ, and δ, there is a number d such that

$$E(L \circ s_{t+1} \mid \mathscr{F}_t) \leq L \circ s_t - \varepsilon \quad \text{on} \quad L \circ s_t \geq d. \quad \text{Q.E.D.}$$

Remark As the proof for the existence of the function L^h shows, the assumpions (PA) and (SA) can be slightly weakened.

(PA) 1. $E(p_{t+1}^h \mid \mathscr{F}_t) \leq p_t^h - \alpha^*$ *on* $\{v_t^h \geq v^* \text{ and } p_t^h \geq p_*^h\}$
        $\leq p_t^h$ *on* $\{v_t^h \geq v^*\}$;

    2. $E(p_{t+1}^h \mid \mathscr{F}_t) \geq p_t^h + \alpha_*$ *on* $\{v_t^h \leq v_* \text{ and } p_t^h \leq p^*\}$
        $\geq p_t^h$ *on* $\{v_t^h \leq v_*\}$.

(SA) 1. $E(v_{t+1}^h \mid \mathscr{F}_t) \geq v_t^h + \beta^*$ *on* $\{p_t^h \geq p^* \text{ and } v_t^h \leq v^*\}$
        $\geq v_t^h$ *on* $\{p_t^h \geq p^*\}$;

    2. $E(v_{t+1}^h \mid \mathscr{F}_t) \geq v_t^h - \beta_*$ *on* $\{p_t^h \leq p_* \text{ and } v_t^h \geq v^*\}$
        $\geq v_t^h$ *on* $\{p_t^h \leq p_*\}$.

REFERENCES

1. Arrow, K. J., Block, H. D., and Hurwicz, L., "On the stability of the competitive equilibrium II," *Econometrica* **27** (1959), 82–109.
2. Arrow, K. J., and Hahn, F. H., "General Competitive Analysis." Holden-Day, San Francisco (1971).
3. Föllmer, H., A principle for Liapunov semimartingales, *Proc. Symp. Pure Math.* **31** Am. Math. Soc., (1977).
4. Green, J., and Majumdar, M., The nature of stochastic equilibrium, *Econometrica*, **43** (1975), 647–660.
5. McKenzie, L., Matrices with dominant diagonal and economic theory, *in* "Mathematical Methods in the Social Sciences" (K. J. Arrow, S. Karlin, and P. Suppes eds.), Chap. 4, pp. 47–62. Stanford University Press, Stanford, Calif. (1969).

We gratefully acknowledge the support of the National Science Foundation, Grant SOC76-14768, and the Deutsche Forschungsgemeinschaft, Sonderforschungsbereich 21. A preliminary version of this paper was presented at the Summer Workshop of the IMSSS, Stanford University, 1975.

W. Hildenbrand
DEPARTMENT OF ECONOMICS
WASHINGTON UNIVERSITY
ST. LOUIS, MISSOURI

R. Radner
DEPARTMENT OF ECONOMICS
UNIVERSITY OF CALIFORNIA
BERKELEY, CALIFORNIA

KENNEDY SCHOOL OF GOVERNMENT
HARVARD UNIVERSITY
CAMBRIDGE, MASSACHUSETTS

Identifiability of the von Neumann–Morgenstern Utility Function from Asset Demands

JERRY R. GREEN

LAWRENCE J. LAU

HERAKLIS M. POLEMARCHAKIS

If the demand for risky assets is determined by the maximization of an analytic von Neumann–Morgenstern utility function, and if these demands are known as a function of the assets' prices, then this utility function can be constructed without ambiguity.

1

The theory of revealed preference posed the question of the properties that, if satisfied by a correspondence, allow it to be characterized as the demand correspondence derived from the maximization of a monotone, quasi-concave utility function subject to a budget constraint. A converse to this question can be phrased as follows: Consider a demand correspondence and suppose that it is indeed derived from utility maximization subject to a budget constraint. Does the demand correspondence contain sufficient information to identify the particular utility function (or preferences) in the family of quasi-concave, monotone utility functions (or convex, monotone complete, preference preorders) from which it has been derived? In the case of maximization of an ordinal utility function the answer is clear: If nominal prices and income vary independently, the range of the demand correspondence can be assumed to contain an open subset of the consumption set.

The utility function over this range can be identified up to a monotone transformation, given some very mild regularity conditions on demand behavior [see Mas-Colell (1977)].

The question of identifiability acquires additional complexity in the case of assets demanded by an investor who maximizes a von Neumann–Morgenstern utility function. As the prices of assets vary, and, as is likely to be the case in a framework of incomplete markets, the number of states of nature exceeds the number of assets, only a lower dimensional subspace of the space of state-dependent values of terminal wealth is attainable. No direct observations can be made on preferences for state-contingent wealth patterns outside this subspace. The standard argument for identifiability thus fails. On the other hand, the utility function can be assumed to have the special additively separable form implied by the axioms of expected utility theory. It is the purpose of this paper to demonstrate that knowledge of the asset demands is sufficient to identify the von Neumann–Morgenstern utility function, provided the latter can be assumed to be independent of the state of nature and analytic over the nonnegative real line.

The problem of identifiability of the utility function is of empirical as well as theoretical interest. From a theoretical point of view, identifiability is necessary if the theory of choice under uncertainty is to possess explanatory power. From an empirical viewpoint, changes in the tax structure, introduction of new assets, and the acquisition of previously unavailable information are instances of changes in the economic environment faced by economic agents. Knowledge of the agent's von Neumann–Morgenstern utility function is necessary if, for example, we want to evaluate the impact of these changes on his market behavior or on his welfare. By virtue of the main result of this paper, these effects can be ascertained by observations related to one system of asset returns and need not be reassessed after the environment has been altered.

2

We consider an investor who must divide his initial wealth among m assets. The quantity of his asset holdings is denoted $x = (x_1, \ldots, x_m)$. Each asset j has a random gross return $\mathbf{r}_j$. The collection of random variables[1] $\mathbf{r} = (\mathbf{r}_1, \ldots, \mathbf{r}_m)$ describes their joint distribution, and hence the distribution of the value of any portfolio $\mathbf{r} \cdot x$.

We assume that $\mathbf{r}$ satisfies:

r(i) $\mathbf{r}$ is nonnegative with probability 1;

---

[1] These are understood to be defined on an underlying measure space, which need not be mentioned explicitly.

r(ii)   for each j, $\mathbf{r}_j$ is not zero with probability 1;

r(iii)   for each j, $\mathbf{r}_j$ cannot be written as a linear combination of $\{\mathbf{r}_k\}_{k \neq j}$, with probability 1;

r(iv)   for each j, and each postive integer l, $E\mathbf{r}_j^l < \infty$.

By virtue of r(i), r(ii), and r(iv) we can choose the units of measurement of each asset so that

$$E\mathbf{r}_j = 1 \qquad \text{for each} \quad j. \tag{1}$$

Condition r(i) is not objectionable because the $\mathbf{r}_j$ represents gross returns.[2] Conditions r(ii) and r(iii) are technical in nature and are designed to rule out redundancies and assets that will never be purchased in positive quantity.[3] Condition r(iv) is of some importance and is surely not innocuous in practice. It is assured in any model with a finite set of states (i.e., where $\mathbf{r}$ can take only finitely many values).

The investor is assumed to be a von Neumann–Morgenstern utility maximizer. He is assumed to know the distribution of $\mathbf{r}$ and to have a von Neumann–Morgenstern utility function u. We assume that u satisfies

u(i) u is defined over the domain of all nonnegative real numbers;

u(ii) u is increasing;

u(iii) u is concave;

u(iv) u is analytic.[4]

For example, the function $u(w) = -e^{-\rho w}, \rho > 0, w \geq 0$, satisfies u(i)–u(iv). Among these conditions, only the first and the last require comment.

The fact that u is defined at zero rules out such functions as the logarithm which are unbounded. These can perhaps be ruled out on other grounds.[5] Analyticity is a much stronger condition, which cannot be justified behaviorally, except that an arbitrary function can always be approximated

---

[2] In the absence of limited liability corporations, some $\mathbf{r}_j$ might be negative with positive probability. If these could be bounded below; our problem would be essentially unchanged, although some modifications would have to be made in the treatment of the domain of von Neumann–Morgenstern utility.

[3] In a general equilibrium model the price of such an asset is sure to be zero; so if present, it can be deleted *ab initio* without loss of generality.

[4] To define $u^{(l)}(0)$, we extend u to an open set containing the nonnegative real line and use the derivative of this extension at zero.

[5] Menger (1934) was perhaps the first to note that bounded utility is required if expected utility is to order all distributions of returns in a consistent fashion. Arrow (1971), Ryan (1974), Arrow (1974), and Fishburn (1976) have explored the relationship between the class of distributions to be ordered and the restrictions that can be placed on the von Neumann–Morgenstern utility function. The interested reader might consult Aumann (1977) and Shapley (1977a,b) for discussions, in a closely related vein, of the St. Petersburg paradox.

pointwise by an analytic function.[6] It implies, of course, that derivatives of all orders exist. In particular, it implies that $u'(0)$ exists and is finite, a fact that will be used heavily in the proof of our main theorem. [For example $u(w) = (1/\alpha)w^{\alpha}$, $\alpha < 1$, would fail to satisfy this property.]

The investor chooses $x \in X$ facing prices $p = (p_1, \ldots, p_m)$ where $X = \{x | \mathbf{r} \cdot x \geqq 0$ with probability $1\}$. Without loss of generality we can take his initial level of wealth to be unity. Thus his problem is

$$\max_{x \in X} Eu(\mathbf{r} \cdot x)$$

$$\text{subject to} \quad p \cdot x \leqq 1. \tag{2}$$

PROPOSITION 1   The objective function $Eu(\mathbf{r} \cdot x)$ is concave in x and is defined over a domain that includes all nonnegative $x \in \mathbb{R}^m$.

Proof Concavity follows directly. The domain of the expected utility X includes all x for which $\mathbf{r} \cdot x$ is within the domain of definition of u with probability 1. Assumptions r(i) and u(i) guarantee this whenever $x \in \mathbb{R}^m$ is nonnegative. ∎

PROPOSITION 2 $dEu(\mathbf{r} \cdot x)/dx_j$ exists and is given by

$$Er_j u'(\mathbf{r} \cdot x) \quad \text{for all} \quad x \in X.$$

Proof Let $h^j = (0, \ldots, h, \ldots, 0)$ where the h is in the jth place. By definition,

$$\frac{dEu(\mathbf{r} \cdot x)}{dx_j} = \lim_{h \to \infty} \frac{Eu(\mathbf{r} \cdot x + h^j) - Eu(\mathbf{r} \cdot x)}{h}.$$

We now show that this limit exists for any $x \in X$ and for any sequence $\langle h_k^j \rangle$ with $\lim_k h_k^j = 0$. Consider the sequence of functions

$$f_k(\mathbf{r}) = \frac{u(\mathbf{r} \cdot x + h_k^j) - u(\mathbf{r} \cdot x)}{h_k}.$$

Monotonicity of u and nonnegativity of r imply that $f_k(\mathbf{r}) \geqq 0$. Concavity of u implies that $f_k(\mathbf{r}) \leqq r_j u'(0)$, which is finite by analyticity of u. $Er_j u'(0)$ is

---

[6] There are several open questions concerning the approximation problem. Let u be a smooth, concave, increasing utility generating demands $\xi(p)$. If u is approximated by a sequence of concave analytic utility functions, does the corresponding sequence of demands converge to $\xi(p)$ in an appropriate sense? Furthermore if the demands are observed with error and are perceived to be $\hat{\xi}(p)$, can the utility generating $\hat{\xi}(p)$ be used as an approximation to u? This last question is made more complicated by the observation that even if $\hat{\xi}(p)$ satisfies revealed preference conditions, it may not be generated by any von Neumann–Morgenstern utility at all. Indeed the precise necessary and sufficient conditions on demands to ensure compatibility with the axioms of expected utility theory are unknown to us at present.

finite by virtue of r(iv). Since u is differentiable for all values of its argument,

$$f_k(\mathbf{r}) \to \mathbf{r}_j u'(\mathbf{r} \cdot x)$$

for all $\mathbf{r} = 0$. Therefore the sequence $f_k(\mathbf{r})$ satisfies the hypotheses of the Lebesque dominated convergence theorem. Hence,

$$\mathbf{Er}_j u'(\mathbf{r} \cdot x) = \lim_k \frac{Eu(\mathbf{r} \cdot x + h_k^j) - Eu(\mathbf{r} \cdot x)}{h_k}$$

$$= \frac{dEu(\mathbf{r} \cdot x)}{dx_j}. \quad \blacksquare$$

Let us write the vector of marginal rates of substitution of assets $j = 1, \ldots, m$ for asset k by

$$s_{jk}(x) = \frac{dEu(\mathbf{r} \cdot x)/dx_j}{dEu(\mathbf{r} \cdot x)/dx_k},$$

which is well defined by Proposition 2.

PROPOSITION 3   For all $x \in \mathbb{R}^m_+$, $s_{jk}(x)$ is a nonzero real number for all pairs j, k.

Proof Differentiability, monotonicity, and concavity of u imply that $u'(\cdot)$ is bounded. Finiteness of mean returns $[r(\text{iv})]$ implies that

$$0 < \mathbf{Er}_j u'(\mathbf{r} \cdot x) < \infty$$

for each j. $\blacksquare$

For each $p \in \mathbb{R}^m_+ \backslash \{0\}$, the investor tries to solve (2). At some prices the maximum may fail to exist.[7]

PROPOSITION 4
(i)   For each $x \in \mathbb{R}^m_+ \backslash \{0\}$ there exists $p \in \mathbb{R}^m_+ \backslash \{0\}$ such that x solves (2) at prices p.
(ii)   For each $x \in \mathbb{R}^m_+ \backslash \{0\}$ there is a unique $p \in \mathbb{R}^m_+ \backslash \{0\}$ so that x is demanded at p.

Proof
(i)   follows by choosing $p \in \mathbb{R}^m$ for each $x \in \mathbb{R}^m$, so that $(p_2, \ldots, p_m)$ is proportional to $(s_{21}, \ldots, s_{m1})$ and so that $p \cdot x = 1$. (Note $x = 0$ is not observed at any finite price system.)

[7] For example, if for two assets j and k, $(r_j/p_j) > (r_k/p_k)$ with probability 1, then a sure profit can be gained by buying j and selling k short. Thus no maximum can be found unless further restrictions are placed on x, such as a prohibition of short sales.

(ii)   follows from the differentiability of u, and the fact that x has at least one positive element. ∎

Let the demand correspondence be denoted by $\xi: P \to R^m$ where P is the set of prices for which a solution to (2) exists.

The correspondence ξ is observable. We want to be able to deduce from ξ the individual's von Neumann–Morgenstern utility function, of course up to a positive linear transformation. In addition to ξ we assume a knowledge of the distribution of $\mathbf{r}$. Given $\mathbf{r}$ and ξ, a quantity is called *observable* if it can be deduced without ambiguity.

PROPOSITION 5   The marginal rates of substitution $s_{jk}(x)$ are observable for any pair of assets j, k and any $x \in \mathbb{R}^m_+ \{0\}$.

Proof   By Proposition 4, there is a unique p such that $x \in \xi(p)$. The s_{jk} can be computed as ratios of the components of this p. ∎

PROPOSITION 6 $s_{jk}(0) = 1$ for all j, k, independent of u.

Proof

$$\frac{(d/dx_j)Eu(\mathbf{r} \cdot x)}{(d/dx_k)Eu(\mathbf{r} \cdot x)} = \frac{Er_j u'(\mathbf{r} \cdot x)}{Er_k u'(\mathbf{r} \cdot x)}$$

and by Proposition 2, at $x = 0$ we have

$$s_{jk}(0) = Er_j/Er_k = 1$$

by virtue of our normalization (1). ∎

Thus the functions $s_{jk}(\cdot)$ are observable throughout $\mathbb{R}^m_+$. If their derivatives exist, these quantities are also observable because they are defined by the functions $s_{jk}(\cdot)$ themselves.

PROPOSITION 7   The derivatives of $s_{jk}(\cdot)$ at $x = 0$ of all orders exist and are observable.

Proof   Consider the first expression

$$\frac{Er_k u'(\mathbf{r} \cdot x)Er_j r_i u''(\mathbf{r} \cdot x) - Er_j u'(\mathbf{r} \cdot x) \cdot Er_k r_i u''(\mathbf{r} \cdot x)}{(Er_k u'(\mathbf{r} \cdot x))^2}, \tag{3}$$

which, if well defined, would be the value of $ds_{jk}(x)/dx_i$. At $x = 0$ we have

$$\frac{ds_{jk}(0)}{dx_i} = \frac{u'(0)u''(0)(Er_k Er_j r_i - Er_j Er_k r_i)}{(u'(0))^2(Er_k)^2}$$

$$= \frac{u''(0)}{u'(0)} (Er_j r_i - Er_k r_i).$$

In order for this to be well defined, it is required that the two expectations in the last expression exist. Note that, by Hölder's inequality[8]

$$(Er_j r_i)^2 \leq (Er_j^2)(Er_i^2),$$

which is finite by virtue of r(iv).

Higher order derivatives follow by successive differentiation of (3) and repeated application of Hölder's inequality. ∎

We now come to our main result: the uniqueness of the von Neumann–Morgenstern utility explaining the demand ξ, within the class of all analytic utility functions.

THEOREM   Let v be analytic and generate the demand correspondence ξ. Then $v \equiv u$, up to a positive linear transformation.

Proof   Without loss of generality we can suppose $u(0) = v(0) = 0$ and $u'(0) = v'(0) = 1$. We will show how to construct the higher derivatives of v at zero recursively, thus defining v uniquely within the class of analytic functions. That $v \equiv u$ follows directly.

If v generates ξ, the marginal rates of substitution implied by r must be the same as those that are observable through knowing ξ, by Proposition 5. Moreover, the derivatives of the marginal rates of substitution under v must be the same as those observable at zero through knowing ξ, by Propositions 6 and 7.

Proposition 7 holds for any j, k, and any higher derivative of $s_{jk}(x)$ at $x = 0$. We need only two assets and a particular sequence of derivatives. Let us consider assets 1 and 2 and the derivatives

$$\frac{d}{dx_1} s_{21}(0), \frac{d^2}{dx_1^2} s_{21}(0), \ldots, \frac{d^l}{dx_1^l} s_{21}(0), \ldots$$

and

$$\frac{d}{dx_2} s_{12}(0), \frac{d^2}{dx_2} s_{12}(0), \ldots, \frac{d^l}{dx_2^l} s_{12}(0), \ldots$$

all of which are observable by virtue of Proposition 7.

---

[8] Hölder's inequality states that if z_1 and z_2 are nonnegative random variables, and if $(1/p) + (1/q) = 1$, then

$$Ez_1 z_2 \leq (Ez_1^p)^{1/p}(Ez_2^q)^{1/q}$$

with equality holding if and only if $z_1 = cz_2$ for some c, with probability 1. [See, e.g., Royden (1963), pp. 95 and 202).]

If v explains the same demands as u, then

$$\left(\frac{d}{dx_1} Ev(\mathbf{r} \cdot x)\right) \cdot s_{21}(x) = \left(\frac{d}{dx_2} Ev(\mathbf{r} \cdot x)\right) \tag{4}$$

holds as an identity in x. Let us identify successive derivatives of each side in x_1, at $x = 0$. Differentiating (4) we have

$$s_{21}(x)E\mathbf{r}_1^2 v''(\mathbf{r} \cdot x) + E\mathbf{r}_2\mathbf{r}_1 v''(\mathbf{r} \cdot x)$$

$$= -\left(\frac{d}{dx_1} s_{21}(x)\right)(E\mathbf{r}_1 v'(\mathbf{r} \cdot x)).$$

Substituting $x = 0$ we have

$$v''(0)(E\mathbf{r}_1^2 - E\mathbf{r}_2\mathbf{r}_1) = -\frac{d}{dx_1} s_{21}(0).$$

Since the right-hand side is observable, a unique value of $v''(0)$ compatible with the demand function ξ exists provided

$$E\mathbf{r}_1^2 - E\mathbf{r}_2\mathbf{r}_1 \neq 0. \tag{5}$$

Similarly, by reversing the roles of commodities 1 and 2 we can conclude that

$$E\mathbf{r}_2^2 - E\mathbf{r}_2\mathbf{r}_1 \neq 0 \tag{6}$$

would be sufficient to recover $v''(0)$ uniquely.

Assume that (5) and (6) were both false. Multiplying equals by equals we would have

$$(E\mathbf{r}_2\mathbf{r}_1)^2 = (E\mathbf{r}_2^2)(E\mathbf{r}_1^2). \tag{7}$$

From Hölder's inequality we know that (7) can occur only if $r_2 = cr_1$ with probability 1 for some constant c. This would clearly violate r(iii). Therefore either (5) or (6) must hold, and $v''(0)$ is uniquely recoverable.

Differentiating (4) again in x_1 we find

$$s_{21}(x)E\mathbf{r}_1^3 v'''(\mathbf{r} \cdot x) + E\mathbf{r}_2\mathbf{r}_1^2 v'''(\mathbf{r} \cdot x)$$

$$= \left(\frac{-d}{dx_1} s_{21}(x)\right)(2E\mathbf{r}_1^2 v''(\mathbf{r} \cdot x)) - \left(\frac{d^2}{dx_1^2} s_{21}(x)\right)E\mathbf{r}_1 v'(\mathbf{r} \cdot x).$$

Evaluating at $x = 0$, we have

$$v'''(0)\{E\mathbf{r}_1^3 - E\mathbf{r}_2\mathbf{r}_1^2\} = \frac{-d}{dx_1} s_{21}(0)(E\mathbf{r}_1^2)(\mathbf{r}''(0)) - \frac{d^2}{dx_1^2} s_{21}(0).$$

Again the right-hand side is known, either by direct observation or by deduction at the previous stage. Therefore $v'''(0)$ will be uniquely recoverable whenever

$$Er_1^3 - Er_2r_1^2 \neq 0.$$

Similarly, to recover the lth derivative $v^l(0)$ for any $l \geq 3$ by this method, we must have either

$$Er_1^l - Er_2r_1^{l-1} \neq 0 \tag{8}$$

or

$$Er_2^l - Er_1r_2^{l-1} \neq 0. \tag{9}$$

Suppose both of these fail; then,

$$(Er_1r_2^{l-1})(Er_2r_1^{l-1}) = (Er_2^l)(Er_1^l). \tag{10}$$

By Hölder's inequality

$$Er_1r_2^{l-1} \leq (Er_1^l)^{1/l}(Er_2^l)^{l-1/l} \tag{11}$$

and

$$Er_2r_1^{l-1} \leq (Er_1^l)^{l-1/l}(Er_2^l)^{1/l} \tag{12}$$

with equality in both relations if and only if $r_1 = cr_2^{l-1}$ and $r_2 = dr_1^{l-1}$, with probability 1, for two constants c and d. Therefore, since all the terms in (10)–(12) are nonnegative,

$$(Er_1r_2^{l-1})(Er_2r_1^{l-1}) < (Er_2^l)(Er_1^l) \tag{13}$$

unless $r_1 = cr_2^{l-1}$ and $r_2 = dr_1^{l-1}$ with probability 1. From the latter we would have $r_1 = d^{-1/l-1}r_2^{1/l-1}$ with probability 1. Combining this with the former,

$$1 = cd^{1/l-1}r_2^{(l-1)} - (1/l - 1)$$

with probability 1. Since $l \geq 3$, this implies that r_2 is a constant, almost surely. Reversing the roles of assets 1 and 2 in this argument, we would have that r_1 is a constant almost surely, and hence that there are two safe assets—which would violate r(iii). Therefore (13) holds and at least one of (8) and (9) is true, so that $v^l(0)$ is uniquely determined given $v^{(l-l')}(0)$ for $l' = 1, \ldots, l$. Since $v \equiv u$ clearly suffices, this uniqueness argument completes the proof. ∎

3

We have shown in our main theorem that it is possible to identify uniquely the von Neumann–Morgenstern utility function from an asset demand correspondence defined for all $p \in \mathbb{R}_+^m \setminus \{0\}$ provided that the joint distribution of gross returns is known and satisfies certain conditions and provided that the utility function is analytic and concave on the nonnegative real line. From the structure of our proof, it is clear that if the utility function is state dependent, then there is in general no possibility of unique identification of each of the state-dependent utility functions.

There are a number of open questions concerning the possible relaxation of the assumptions of the main theorem that remain to be investigated.

First, it is of interest to examine the case in which the asset demand correspondence is defined only on a bounded subset of $\mathbb{R}^m_+ + \{0\}$. The implication of this restriction on the domain of the asset demand correspondence is that the range of the asset demand correspondence can no longer be assumed to include all of $\mathbb{R}^m_+ + \{0\}$. In particular, the origin may be disjoint from the range of the asset demand correspondence. Our proof, which is based on an analytic expansion of the utility function at the origin, will no longer apply.

Second, it is of interest to examine the case in which the joint distribution of the returns is unknown. The question is whether one can determine the joint distribution of returns and the von Neumann–Morgenstern utility function uniquely from an asset demand correspondence. The finiteness of the states of nature may make a difference in this regard.

Third, it is of interest to examine the case in which the utility function is not analytic on the nonnegative real line. There are at least two possible directions of relaxation. First, one may assume that the utility function is analytic only over the positive real line, thus admitting the case in which marginal utility is unbounded at the origin. Second, one may investigate the possibility of approximation of an arbitrary concave function defined on the nonnegative real line by a concave and analytic function. The sense in which this approximation is taken will be related to the sense in which the demand correspondence can be approximated by one derived from an analytic utility function.[9]

Resolution of each of the three open questions will enhance the usefulness of our main result derived here.

REFERENCES

Arrow, K. J. (1971). "Essays in the Theory of Risk Bearing." North-Holland Publishing, Amsterdam.
Arrow, K. J. (1974). The use of unbounded utility functions in expected utility maximization: Response, *Q. J. Econ.* **88**, 136–138.

[9] There exists an increasing concave function that is analytic everywhere except at zero; for example,

$$\alpha e^{-1/w} - e^{-\rho w}, \quad w \geqq 0, \quad \alpha, \rho > 0, \quad \text{and} \quad \alpha \text{ sufficiently small.}$$

For this utility function the method of recovering if used in our proof above would not work—it would recover only the $e^{-\rho w}$ part. But since these preferences do not coincide, the identity of the marginal rates of substitution does not hold globally. Whether analyticity can be dropped if concavity is maintained remains therefore an open question.

Aumann, R. J. (1977). The St. Petersburg paradox: A discussion of some recent comments, *J. Econ. Theory* **14**, 443–445.

Fishburn, P. (1976). Unbounded utility functions in expected utility theory, *Q. J. Econ.* **90**, 163–168.

Mas-Colell, A. (1977). The recoverability of consumers' preferences from market demand behavior, *Econometrica* **45**, 1409–1430.

Menger, K. (1934). The role of uncertainty in economics, *in* "Essays in Mathematical Economics in Honor of Oskar Morgenstern," (Martin Shubik, ed.), pp. 211–231. Princeton University Press, Princeton, N.J., translated by Wolfgang Schoellkopf from the *Zeitschrift fur National Okonomie*, *5*, pp. 349–485.

Royden, H. L. (1963). "Real Analysis." Macmillan, New York.

Ryan, T. M. (1974). The use of unbounded utility functions in expected utility Maximization: Comment, *Q. J. Econ.* **88**, 133–135.

Shapley, L. S. (1977a). The St. Petersburg paradox—Acon game? *J. Econ. Theory* **14**, 439–442.

Shapley, L. S. (1977b). Lotteries and menus: A comment on unbounded utilities, *J. Econ. Theory* **14**, 446–453.

This research was supported by Grants APR 77-06999 to Harvard University, SOC 78-06162 to the National Bureau of Economic Research, and SOC 77-11105 to the Institute for Mathematical Studies in the Social Sciences, Stanford University, from the National Science Foundation. We would like to thank A. Mas-Colell, A. McLennan, J. Pratt, and H. Sonnenschein for helpful discussion and correspondence.

Jerry R. Green
HARVARD UNIVERSITY
CAMBRIDGE, MASSACHUSETTS

Heraklis M. Polemarchakis
COLUMBIA UNIVERSITY
NEW YORK, NEW YORK

Lawrence J, Lau
STANFORD UNIVERSITY
STANFORD, CALIFORNIA
and
HARVARD UNIVERSITY
CAMBRIDGE, MASSACHUSETTS

Part 2
GROWTH

An Integration of Stochastic Growth Theory and the Theory of Finance, Part I: The Growth Model

WILLIAM A. BROCK

1. INTRODUCTION

This paper develops "the growth theoretic part" of an intertemporal general equilibrium theory of capital asset pricing, which is an attempt to put together ideas from the modern finance literature and the literature on stochastic growth models. In this way we will obtain a theory that is capable of addressing itself to such general equilibrium questions as (1) "What is the impact of an increase in the corporate income tax on the relative prices of risky stocks? "(2)" What is the impact of an increase in progressivity of the personal income tax on the relative price structure of risky assets?"

The main intent of this paper is to show that the type of growth theory that Lionel McKenzie has been a major figure in developing is a useful tool in applied areas such as finance. The finance side of the theory presented here derives part of its inspiration from Merton [18]. However Merton's intertemporal capital asset pricing model (ICAPM) is not a general equilibrium theory in the sense of Arrow–Debreu; i.e., the *technological* sources of uncertainty are not related to the equilibrium prices of the risky assets in Merton [18]. A discussion of the limitations of Merton's ICAPM when it is viewed as an Arrow–Debreu model is contained in Hellwig [12]. We build a general equilibrium model here and preserve the empirical tractability of Merton's formulation.

Basically what is done here is to modify the stochastic growth model of Brock–Mirman [8] in order to put a nontrivial investment decision into the asset pricing model of Lucas [14]. This is done in such a way to preserve the empirical tractibility of the Merton formulation and at the same time determine endogenously the risk prices derived by Ross [22] in his arbitrage theory of capital asset pricing. Ross's price of systematic risk k at date t, denoted by λ_{kt} (which is induced by the kth source of systematic risk $\tilde{\delta}_{kt}$), is determined by the covariance of the marginal utility of consumption with $\tilde{\delta}_{kt}$. In this way Ross's λ_{kt} are determined by the interaction of sources of production uncertainty and the demand for risky assets.

The work of Cox *et al.* [10] is closely related to this work, except that they assume constant returns in production. The work of Magill [15] is also related to ours, except that Magill does not introduce a separate market for claims to pure profits.

The paper proceeds as follows. Section 1 contains the introduction. Section 2 presents an N-process version of the 1-process stochastic growth model of Brock–Mirman [8]. The N-process growth model will form the basis for the quantity side of the asset-pricing model developed in Brock [5a].

In Section 2 it is proved that optimum paths generated in the N-process model are described by time-independent continuous optimum policy functions a la Bellman. A functional equation is developed that determines the state valuation function using methods that are standard in the stochastic growth literature. It is also proved that for any initial state the optimum stochastic process of investment converges in distribution to a limit distribution independent of the initial state.

The Brock paper [5a] converts the growth model of Section 2 into an asset-pricing model by introducing competitive rental markets for the capital goods and introducing a market for claims to the pure rents generated by the ith firm $i = 1, 2, \ldots, N$. Each of the N processes is identified with one "firm." Firms pay out rentals to consumers. The residual is pure rent. Paper claims to the pure rent generated by each firm i and a market for these claims are introduced along the line of Lucas [14].

Equilibrium is defined using the concept of rational expectations as in Lucas [14]; i.e., both sides of the economy possess subjective distributions on pure rents, capital rental rates, and share prices. Both sides draw up demand and supply schedules conditioned on their subjective distributions. Market clearing introduces an objective distribution on pure rents, capital rental rates, and share prices. A rational expectations equilibrium (REE) is defined by the requirement that the objective distribution equal the subjective distribution at each date.

In Brock [5a] it is shown using recent results of Benveniste–Scheinkman [1] that the quantity side of an REE is identical to the quantity side of the

N-process growth model developed in Section 2. The key idea used is the Benveniste–Scheinkman [1] result that the standard transversality condition at infinity is *necessary*, as well as sufficient, for an infinite horizon concave programming problem.

The financial side of the economy is now easy to develop. A unique asset-pricing function for stock i of the form $P_i(y)$ is shown to exist by use of a contraction mapping argument along the line of Lucas [14].

My paper [5a] uses a special case of the growth model studied here to develop an intertemporal general equilibrium theory that determines the risk prices of Ross [22] endogenously.

It is also shown that the price of an equity share of company i at date t is the expected discounted present value of risk-adjusted profits discounted at the risk-free rate. Here risk-adjusted profits are defined by taking the expected profit of firm i and subtracting from it the Ross price of systematic risk k times the standard deviation of firm i's profits with respect to systematic risk k summed over all k. This shows that the Sharpe–Lintner formula of finance can be derived from a stochastic growth model.

The convergence result in Section 2 allows stationary time series methods based on the mean ergodic theorem to be used to estimate the risk prices of Ross, provided that the economy is in stochastic steady state.

In Brock [5a] an explicit example of the N-process model is solved for the optimum in closed form. The asset-pricing function $P_i(y)$ turns out to be linear in output y for this case. The risk prices of Ross can also be calculated in closed form for the example.

Finally the Appendix develops technical results that are needed but are somewhat tangential to the main issue addressed in each section.

NOTATION   Equations are numbered consecutively within each section. Thus, for example, Eq. 2 in Section 2 is written "(2.2)." Assumptions, theorems, lemmas, and remarks are numbered consecutively within each section. For example, Assumption 2 in Section 2 will be written "Assumption 2.2."

The convention is the same in the appendix except that "A" appears to separate entities in the appendix from those in the main text. For example, Assumption 2 in the Appendix to Section 2 will be written "Assumption A2.2."

2. THE OPTIMAL GROWTH MODEL

Since the model to be given below is studied in detail in Brock [5a,b] we shall be brief where possible.

The model is given by

$$\text{maximize} \quad E_1 \sum_{t=1}^{\infty} \beta^{t-1} u(c_t), \tag{2.1}$$

$$\text{s.t.} \quad c_{t+1} + x_{t+1} - x_t = \sum_{i=1}^{N} [g_i(x_{it}, r_t) - \delta_i x_{it}], \tag{2.2}$$

$$x_t = \sum_{i=1}^{N} x_{it}, \quad x_{it} \geq 0, \quad i = 1, 2, \ldots, N, \quad t = 1, 2, \ldots, \tag{2.3}$$

$$c_t \geq 0, \quad t = 1, 2, \ldots, \tag{2.4}$$

$$x_1, x_{i1}, \quad i = 1, 2, \ldots, N, r_1, \tag{2.5}$$

historically given, where E_1, β, u, c_t, x_t, g_i, x_{it}, r_t, δ_i denote mathematical expectation conditioned at time 1, discount factor on future utility, utility function of consumption, consumption at date t, capital stock at date t, production function of process i, capital allocated to process i at date t, random shock which is common to *all* processes i, and depreciation rate for capital installed in process i, respectively.

The space of $\{c_t\}_{t=1}^{\infty}$, $\{x_t\}_{t=1}^{\infty}$ over which the maximum is being taken in (2.1) needs to be specified. Obviously decisions at date t should be based only upon information at date t. In order to make the choice space precise, some formalism is needed. We borrow (copy) from Brock–Majumdar [7] at this point.

The *environment* will be represented by a sequence $\{r_t\}_{t=1}^{\infty}$ of real vector-valued random variables, which will be assumed to be independently and identically distributed. The common distribution of r_t is given by a measure $\mu: \mathscr{B}(R^m) \to [0, 1]$ where $\mathscr{B}(R^m)$ is the Borel σ-field of R^m. In view of a well-known one-to-one correspondence (see, e.g., Loève [13, pp. 230–231]), we can adequately represent the environment as a measure space $(\Omega, \mathscr{F}, \nu)$ where Ω is the set of all sequences of real m vectors, $\mathscr{F}$ is the σ-field generated by cylinder sets of the form $\prod_{t=1}^{\infty} A_t$ where

$$A_t \in \mathscr{B}(R^m), \quad t = 1, 2, \ldots, \quad \text{and} \quad A_t = R^m$$

for all but a finite number of values of t. Also ν (the stochastic law of the environment) is simply the product probability induced by μ (given the assumption of independence).

The random variables r_t may be viewed as the tth coordinate function on Ω; i.e., for any $\omega = \{\omega_t\}_{t=1}^{\infty} \in \Omega$, $r_t(\omega)$ is defined by

$$r_t(\omega) = \omega_t.$$

We shall refer to ω as a possible state of the environment (or an environment sequence) and to ω_t as the environment at date t. In what follows, $\mathscr{F}_t$

is the σ-field guaranteed by partial histories up to period t [i.e., the smallest σ-field generated by cylinder sets of the form $\prod_{\tau=1}^{\infty} A_{\tau}$ where A_{τ} is in $\mathscr{B}(R^m)$ for all t, and $A_{\tau} = R^m$ for all $\tau > t$]. The σ-field $\mathscr{F}_t$ contains all of the information about the environment that is available at date t.

In order to express precisely the fact that decisions c_t, x_t only depend on information that is available at the time the decisions are made, we simply require that c_t, x_t be measurable with respect to $\mathscr{F}_t$.

Formally the maximization in (2.1) is taken over all stochastic processes $\{c_t\}_{t=1}^{\infty}$, $\{x_t\}_{t=1}^{\infty}$ that satisfy (2.2)–(2.5) and such that for each $t = 1, 2, \ldots$, c_t, x_t are measurable $\mathscr{F}_t$. Call such processes "admissible."

Existence of an optimum $\{c_t\}_{t=1}^{\infty}$, $\{x_t\}_{t=1}^{\infty}$ may be established by imposing an appropriate topology $\mathscr{T}$ on the space of admissible processes such that the objective (2.1) is continuous in this topology and the space of admissible processes is $\mathscr{T}$-compact. While it is beyond the scope of this article to discuss existence, presumably a proof can be constructed along the lines of Bewley [2].

The notation almost makes the working of the model self-explanatory. There are N different processes. At date t it is decided how much to consume and how much to hold in the form of capital. It is assumed that capital goods can be costlessly transformed into consumption goods on a one-for-one basis. After it is decided how much capital to hold, it is then decided how to allocate the capital across the N processes. After the allocation is decided, nature reveals the value of r_t, and $g_i(x_{it}, r_t)$ units of new production are available from process i at the end of period t. But $\delta_i x_{it}$ units of capital have evaporated at the end of t. Thus net new produce is $g_i(x_{it}, r_t) - \delta_i x_{it}$ from process i. The total produce available to be divided into consumption and capital stock at date $t + 1$ is given by

$$\sum_{i=1}^{N} [g_i(x_{it}, r_t) - \delta_i x_{it}] + x_t = \sum_{i=1}^{N} [g_i(x_{it}, r_t) + (1 - \delta_i)x_{it}]$$

$$\equiv \sum_{i=1}^{N} f_i(x_{it}, r_t) \equiv y_{t+1}, \qquad (2.6)$$

where

$$f_i(x_{it}, r_t) \equiv g_i(x_{it}, r_t) + (1 - \delta_i)x_{it} \qquad (2.7)$$

denotes the total amount of produce emerging from process i at the end of period t. The produce y_{t+1} is divided into consumption and capital stock at the beginning of data $t + 1$, and so on it goes.

Note that we are assuming that it is costless to install capital into each process i and costless to allocate capital across processes at the beginning of each date t.

The objective of the optimizer is to maximize the expected value of the discounted sum of utilities over all consumption paths and capital allocations that satisfy (2.2)–(2.5).

In order to obtain sharp results, we will place restrictive assumptions on this problem. We collect the basic working assumptions into one place

ASSUMPTION 2.1   The functions $u(\cdot)$, $f_i(\cdot)$ are all concave, increasing, and are twice continuously differentiable.

ASSUMPTION 2.2   The stochastic process $\{r_t\}_{t=1}^{\infty}$ is independently and identically distributed. Each $r_t \colon (\Omega, \mathscr{B}, \mu) \to R^m$ where $(\Omega, \mathscr{B}, \mu)$ is a probability space. Here Ω is the space of elementary events, $\mathscr{B}$ is the σ-field of measurable sets w.r.t. μ, and μ is a probability measure defined on subsets $B \subseteq \Omega$, $B \in \mathscr{B}$. Furthermore, the range of r_t, $r_t(\Omega)$ is *compact*.

ASSUMPTION 2.3   For each $\{x_{i1}\}_{i=1}^{N}$, r_1 the problem (1) *has* a unique optimal solution (unique up to a set of realizations of $\{r_t\}$ of measure zero).

Notice that Assumption 2.3 is implied by Assumption 1 and *strict* concavity of u, $\{f_i\}_{i=1}^{N}$. Rather than try to find the weakest possible assumptions sufficient for uniqueness of solutions to (2.1), it seemed simpler to reveal the role of uniqueness in what follows by simply *assuming* it. Furthermore, since we are not interested in the study of existence of optimal solutions in this article, we have simply assumed that also.

Since the case $N = 1$ of the above model has been dealt with by Brock and Mirman [8, 9] and Mirman–Zilcha [19–21], we shall be brief where possible.

By Assumption 2.3 we see that to each output level y_t, optimum c_t, x_t, x_{it}, given y_t, may be written

$$c_t = g(y_t), \qquad x_t = h(y_t), \qquad x_{it} = h_i(y_t). \tag{2.8}$$

The optimum policy functions $g(\cdot)$, $h(\cdot)$, $h_i(\cdot)$ do not depend on t because the problem given by (2.1)–(2.5) is time stationary.

Another useful optimum policy function may be obtained. Given x_t, r_t, Assumption 2.3 implies that the optimal allocation $\{x_{it}\}_{i=1}^{N}$ and next period's optimal capital stock x_{t+1} is unique. Furthermore, these may be written in the form

$$x_{it} = a_i(x_t, r_{t-1}), \tag{2.9}$$

$$x_{t+1} = H(x_t, r_t). \tag{2.10}$$

Equations (2.9) and (2.10) contain r_{t-1} and r_t, respectively, because the allocation decision is made after r_{t-1} is known, but before r_t is revealed;

but the capital–consumption decision is made after y_{t+1} is revealed, i.e., after r_t is known.

Equation (2.10) looks very much like the optimal stochastic process studied by Brock–Mirman and Mirman–Zilcha. It was shown in Brock and Mirman [8, 9] for the case $N = 1$ that the stochastic difference equation (2.10) converges in distribution to a unique limit distribution independent of initial conditions. We show in Brock [5b] that the same result may be obtained for our N-process model by following the argument of Mirman–Zilcha. We collect some facts here that are established in Brock [5b].

RESULT 2.1 (Assume Assumption 2.1.) Let $U(y_1)$ denote the maximum value of the objective in (2.1), given initial resource stock y_1. Then $U(y_1)$ is concave, nondecreasing in y_1, and for each $y_1 > 0$, the derivative $U'(y_1)$ exists and is nonincreasing in y_1.

Proof Mirman–Zilcha [21] prove that

(a) $$U'(y_1) = u'(g(y_1)), \quad \text{for} \quad y_1 > 0$$

for the case $N = 1$. The same argument may be used here. The details are left to the reader.

Remark 2.1 Equation (a) shows that $g(y_1)$ is nondecreasing since $u''(c) < 0$ and $U'(y)$ is nonincreasing in y due to the concavity of $U(\cdot)$.

RESULT 2.2 (Assume Assumption 2.1.) Also assume that units of utility may be chosen[1] so that $u(c) \geq 0$, for all c. Furthermore, assume that along optima

$$E_1 \beta^{t-1} U(y_t) \to 0, \quad \text{as} \quad t \to \infty.$$

Then if $\{c_t\}_{t=1}^\infty, \{x_t\}_{t=1}^\infty, \{x_{it}\}_{i=1}^N, t = 1, 2, \ldots$ is optimal, the following conditions must be satisfied: For each i, t

$$u'(c_t) \geq \beta E_t\{u'(c_{t+1}) f'_i(x_{it}, r_t)\}, \tag{2.10a}$$

$$u'(c_t)x_{it} = \beta E_t\{u'(c_{t+1}) f'_i(x_{it}, r_t)x_{it}\}, \tag{2.10b}$$

and

$$\lim_{t \to \infty} E_1\{\beta^{t-1} u'(c_t)x_t\} = 0. \tag{2.10c}$$

Proof The proof of (2.10a,b) is an obvious application of calculus to (2.1) with due respect to the constraints $c_t \geq 0$, $x_t \geq 0$. An argument analogous to

---

[1] It is important to recognize that this assumption rules out cases such as $u(c) = \log c$. Such cases can be handled individually however.

that of Benveniste–Scheinkman [1] establishes (2.10c). By concavity of f_i, $i = 1, 2, \ldots, N$, $U(\cdot)$, and by Result 2.1 we have for any constant γ, $0 < \gamma < 1$,

$$E_1 \beta^{t-1} \left\{ U\left[\sum_{i=1}^{N} f_i(x_{i,t-1}, r_{t-1}) \right] - U\left[\sum_{i=1}^{N} f_i(\gamma x_{i,t-1}, r_{t-1}) \right] \right\}$$

$$\geqq E_1 \beta^{t-1} U'(y_t) \left[\sum_{i=1}^{N} f'_i(x_{i,t-1}, r_{t-1})(1 - \gamma) x_{i,t-1} \right]$$

$$= (1 - \gamma) E_1 \beta^{t-1} u'(c_t) \left[\sum_{i=1}^{N} f'_i(x_{i,t-1}, r_{t-1})(x_{i,t-1}) \right]. \qquad (2.10d)$$

But since U is nondecreasing in y_t, $u(c) \geqq 0$, and each f_i is increasing in x_i, the left-hand side of (2.10d) is bounded above by

$$E_1 \beta^{t-1} U(y_t),$$

which goes to zero as $t \to \infty$. Since $u' \geqq 0$, $y_t \geqq 0$, the right-hand side of (2.10d) must go to zero as well. Here $y_t \geqq 0$ because each $f_i \geqq 0$ [cf. (2.6)]. But by (2.10b)

$$E_1 \beta^{t-1} u'(c_t) \left[\sum_{i}^{N} f'_i(x_{i,t-1}, r_{t-1})(x_{i,t-1}) \right]$$

$$= E_1 \beta^{t-2} \left(\sum_{i}^{N} u'(c_{t-1}) x_{i,t-1} \right)$$

$$= E_1 \beta^{t-2} u'(c_{t-1}) x_{t-1} \to 0, \qquad t \to \infty$$

as was to be shown.

LEMMA 2.1   The function $h(y)$ is continuous in y, increasing in y, and 0 when $y = 0$.

Proof   Precise conditions for the validity of Lemma 2.1 and a proof will be found in the appendix.

Now by Assumption 2.3 and (2.8)–(2.10) it follows that y_{t+1} may be written

$$y_{t+1} = F(x_t, r_t). \qquad (2.11)$$

Following Mirman and Zilcha [21], define

$$\underline{F}(x) \equiv \min_{r \in R} F(x, r), \qquad \bar{F}(x) \equiv \max_{r \in R} F(x, r) \qquad (2.12)$$

where R is the range of the random variable

$$r : (\Omega, \mathscr{B}, \mu) \to R^m,$$

which is compact by Assumption 2.2. The following lemma shows that $\underline{F}$, $\bar{F}$ are well defined.

LEMMA 2.2   The function $F(x, r)$ is continuous in r.

Proof   See Appendix for the hypotheses and a proof.

Let x, $\bar{x}$ be *any* two fixed points of the functions

$$\underline{H}(x) \equiv h(\underline{F}(x)), \qquad \bar{H}(x) \equiv h(\bar{F}(x)), \tag{2.13}$$

respectively. Then

LEMMA 2.3   Any two fixed points of the pair of functions defined in (2.13) must satisfy

$$\underline{x} \leqq \bar{x}. \tag{2.14}$$

We may apply arguments similar to Brock–Mirman [8] and prove

THEOREM 2.1   There is a distribution function $F(x)$ of the optimum aggregate capital stock x such that

$$F_t(x) \to F(x)$$

uniformly for all x. Furthermore $F(x)$ does not depend on the initial conditions (x_1, r_1). Here

$$F_t(x) \equiv \Pr\{x_t \leqq x\}. \tag{2.15}$$

Theorem 2.1 shows that the distribution of optimum aggregate capital stock at date t, $F_t(x)$, converges pointwise to a limit distribution $F(x)$.

Theorem 2.1 is important because we will use the optimal growth model to construct equilibrium asset prices and risk prices. Since these prices will be time-stationary functions of x_t and since x_t converges in distribution to F, we will be able to use the mean ergodic theorem and stationary time series methods to make statistical inferences about these prices on the basis of time series observations. More will be said about this later.

The Price of Systematic Risk

Steve Ross in [22] produced a theory of capital asset pricing that showed that the assumption that all systematic risk-free portfolios earn the risk-free rate of return plus the assumption that asset returns are generated by a K-factor model lead to the existence of "prices" $\lambda_0, \lambda_1, \lambda_2, \ldots, \lambda_K$ on mean returns and on each of the K factors. These prices satisfied the property that expected returns $E\widetilde{\mathscr{Z}}_i \equiv a_i$ on each asset i was a linear function of the standard deviation of the returns on asset i with respect to each factor k; i.e.,

$$a_i = \lambda_0 + \sum_{k=1}^{K} \lambda_k b_{ki}, \qquad i = 1, 2, \ldots, N, \tag{2.16}$$

where the original model of asset returns is given by

$$\tilde{\mathscr{T}}_i = a_i + \sum_{k=1}^{K} b_{ki} \tilde{\delta}_k + \tilde{\varepsilon}_i, \qquad i = 1, 2, \ldots, N. \tag{2.17}$$

Here $\tilde{\mathscr{T}}_i$ denotes random *ex ante* anticipated returns from holding the asset one unit of time, $\tilde{\delta}_k$ is systematic risk emanating from factor k, $\tilde{\varepsilon}_i$ is unsystematic risk specific to asset i, and a_i, b_{ki} are constants. Assume that the means of $\tilde{\delta}_k, \tilde{\varepsilon}_i$ are zero for each k, i, that $\tilde{\varepsilon}_1, \ldots, \tilde{\varepsilon}_N$ are independent, and that $\tilde{\delta}_k, \tilde{\varepsilon}_i$ are uncorrelated random variables with finite variances for each k, i.

Ross proved that $\lambda_0, \lambda_1, \ldots, \lambda_K$ exist that satisfy (2.16) by forming portfolios $\eta \in R^N$ such that

$$\sum_{i=1}^{N} \eta_i = 0, \tag{2.18}$$

and constructing the η_i such that the coefficients of each $\tilde{\delta}_k$ in the portfolio returns

$$\sum_{i=1}^{N} \eta_i \tilde{\mathscr{T}}_i = \sum_{i=1}^{N} \eta_i \left[a_i + \sum_{k=1}^{K} b_{ki} \tilde{\delta}_k + \tilde{\varepsilon}_i \right]$$
$$= \sum_{i=1}^{N} \eta_i a_i + \sum_{k=1}^{K} \left(\sum_{i=1}^{N} b_{ki} \eta_i \right) \tilde{\delta}_k + \sum_{i=1}^{N} \eta_i \tilde{\varepsilon}_i \tag{2.19}$$

are zero, and requiring that

$$\sum_{i=1}^{N} \eta_i a_i = 0 \tag{2.20}$$

for all such systematic risk-free zero-wealth portfolios.

Here (2.18) corresponds to the zero-wealth condition. The condition

$$0 = \sum_{i=1}^{N} b_{ki} \eta_i, \qquad k = 1, 2, \ldots, K \tag{2.21}$$

corresponds to the systematic risk-free condition. Actually Ross did not require that (2.20) hold for *all* zero-wealth systematic risk-free portfolios, but only for those that are "well diversified" in the sense that the η_i are of comparable size, so that he could use the assumption of independence of

$\tilde{\varepsilon}_1, \ldots, \tilde{\varepsilon}_N$ to argue that the random variable

$$\sum_{i=1}^{N} \eta_i \tilde{\varepsilon}_i$$

was "small" and hence bears a small price in a world of investors who would pay a positive price only for the avoidance of risks that could *not* be diversified away.

Out of this type of argument Ross argues that the condition, for all $\eta \in R^N$,

$$\sum_{i=1}^{N} \eta_i = 0, \quad \sum_{i=1}^{N} \eta_i b_{ki} = 0, \quad k = 1, 2, \ldots, K \qquad (2.22a)$$

implies that in *equilibrium*

$$\sum_{i=1}^{N} \eta_i a_i = 0 \qquad (2.22b)$$

should hold. All that (2.22) says is that zero-wealth, zero systematic risk portfolios should earn a zero mean rate of return. Condition (2.22) is economically compelling because in its absence rather obvious arbitrage opportunities appear to exist.

Whatever the case, (2.22) implies there exists $\lambda_0, \lambda_1, \lambda_2, \ldots, \lambda_K$ such that (2.16) holds and the proof is just simple linear algebra. Notice that Ross made no assumptions about mean variance investor utility functions or normal distributions of asset returns common to the usual Sharpe–Lintner type of asset-pricing theories, which are standard in the finance literature.

However Ross's model, like the standard capital asset-pricing models in finance, does not link the asset returns to underlying sources of uncertainty. Our growth model is in Brock [5a] as a module in the construction of an intertemporal general equilibrium asset-pricing model, where relationships of the form (2.17) are determined within the model, and hence the $\lambda_0, \lambda_1, \ldots, \lambda_K$ are determined within the model as well. Such a model of asset price determination preserves the beauty and empirical tractability of the Ross–Sharpe–Lintner formulation but at the same time gives us a context where we can ask such general equilibrium questions as, "What is the impact of an increase of the progressivity of the income tax on the demand for and supply of risky assets and the $\lambda_0, \lambda_1, \ldots, \lambda_K$?"

Let us get on with relating the growth model to (2.16). For simplicity assume all processes i are active; i.e., (2.10a) holds with equality. We record (2.10a) here for convenience:

$$u'(c_t) = \beta E_t\{u'(c_{t+1})f'_i(x_{it}, r_t)\}. \qquad (2.23)$$

Now (2.17) is a special hypothesis about asset returns. What kind of hypothesis about "technological" uncertainty corresponds to (2.17)? Well, as an example, put for each $i = 1, 2, \ldots, N$

$$f_i(x_{it}, r_t) \equiv (A_{it}^0 + A_{it}^1 \tilde{\delta}_{1t} + A_{it}^2 \tilde{\delta}_{2t} + \cdots + A_{it}^K \tilde{\delta}_{Kt}) f_i(x_{it})$$
$$\equiv r_{it} f_i(x_{it}), \tag{2.24}$$

where

$$A_{it}^k \equiv A_i^k$$

are constants and

$$\{\tilde{\delta}_{kt}\}_{t=1}^{\infty}$$

are independent and identically distributed random variables for each k and for each k, t the mean of $\tilde{\delta}_{kt}$ is zero, the variance is finite, and δ_{st} is independent of $\tilde{\delta}_{kt}$ for each s, k, t. Furthermore assume that $f(\cdot)$ is concave, increasing, and twice differentiable, that $f'(0) = +\infty$, $f'(\infty) = 0$, and that there is a bound ε_0 such that

$$r_{it} > \varepsilon_0 > 0$$

with probability 1 for all t_i. These assumptions are stronger than necessary, but will enable us to avoid concern with technical tangentialities. Define, for all t

$$\tilde{\delta}_{0t} \equiv 1,$$

so that we may sum from $k = 0$ to K in (2.25) below.
  Insert (2.24) into (2.23) to get for all t, k, i

$$u'(c_t) = \beta E_t \left\{ u'(c_{t+1}) \left(\sum_{k=0}^{K} A_{it}^k \tilde{\delta}_{kt} \right) f_i'(x_{it}) \right\}$$
$$= \sum_{k=0}^{K} ([A_{it}^k f_i'(x_{it})] E_t \{ \beta u'(c_{t+1}) \tilde{\delta}_{kt} \}). \tag{2.25}$$

Now set (2.25) aside for a moment and look at the marginal benefit of saving one unit of capital and assigning it to process i at the beginning of period t. At the end of period t, r_t is revealed and extra produce

$$\mathscr{Z}_{it} \equiv A_{it}^0 f_i'(x_{it}) + \sum_{k=1}^{K} A_{it}^k f_i'(x_{it}) \tilde{\delta}_{kt}, \tag{2.26}$$

emerges. Putting

$$a_i \equiv A_{it}^0 f_i'(x_{it}), \qquad b_{ki} \equiv A_{it}^k f_i'(x_{it}), \qquad \tilde{\delta}_{kt} = \tilde{\delta}_k, \tag{2.27}$$

Eq. (2.26) is identical with Ross's (2.17) with $\tilde{\varepsilon}_i \equiv 0$. We proceed now to generate the analog to (2.16) in our model. Turn back to (2.25). Rewrite (2.25) using (2.27); thus

$$u'(c_t) = \sum_{k=1}^{K} b_{ki} E_t\{\beta u'(c_{t+1})\tilde{\delta}_{kt}\} + a_i E_t\{\beta u'(c_{t+1})\}. \tag{2.28}$$

Hence

$$a_i = \frac{u'(c_t)}{\beta E_t\{u'(c_{t+1})\}} - \sum_{k=1}^{K} b_{ki}\left(\frac{E_t\{u'(c_{t+1})\tilde{\delta}_{kt}\}}{E_t\{u'(c_{t+1})\}}\right) \tag{2.29}$$

so that $\lambda_0, \lambda_1, \ldots, \lambda_K$ defined by

$$\lambda_0 \equiv u'(c_t)/\beta E_t\{u'(c_{t+1})\}, \qquad \lambda_k \equiv -E_t\{u'(c_{t+1})\tilde{\delta}_{kt}\}/E_t\{u'(c_{t+1})\} \tag{2.30}$$

yields

$$a_i = \lambda_0 + \sum_{k=1}^{K} b_{ki}\lambda_k. \tag{2.31}$$

Here t subscripts are dropped to ease typing.

These results are extremely suggestive and show that the model studied in this section may be quite rich in economic content. Although the model is a normative model, in Brock [5a] we turn it into an equilibrium asset-pricing model so that the λ_k becomes equilibrium risk prices. Let us explore the economic meanings of (2.30) in some detail.

Suppose that $K = 1$ and that there is a risk-free asset N in the sense that

$$b_{N1} \equiv A_{Nt}^1 f'(x_{Nt}) = 0, \tag{2.32}$$

i.e.,

$$A_{Nt}^1 = 0. \tag{2.33}$$

Then by (2.33)

$$a_N = \lambda_0, \qquad a_i = a_N + b_{1i}\lambda_1, \tag{2.34}$$

so that for all $i, j \neq N$

$$(a_i - a_N)/b_{1i} = (a_j - a_N)/b_{1j}. \tag{2.35}$$

The second part of Eq. (2.34) corresponds to the security market line, which says that expected return and risk are linearly related in a one-factor model. Equation (2.35) corresponds to the usual Sharpe–Lintner Mossin capital asset-pricing model result that in equilibrium the "excess return" per unit of risk must be equated across all assets.

The economic interpretation of λ_0 given in (2.30) is well known and needs no explanation here. Look at the formula for λ_k. The covariance of the marginal utility of consumption at time $t + 1$ with the zero-mean finite variance shock $\tilde{\delta}_{kt}$ appears in the numerator. Since output increases when $\tilde{\delta}_{kt}$ increases, and since

$$c_{t+1} = g(y_{t+1})$$

does not decrease when y_{t+1} increases, this covariance is therefore likely to be negative, so that the sign of λ_k is positive. We will look into the determinants of the magnitudes of $\lambda_0, \lambda_1, \ldots, \lambda_K$ in more detail later. Let us show how our model may be helpful in the empirical problem in estimating the $\lambda_0, \lambda_1, \ldots, \lambda_K$ from time series data.

First how is one to close Ross's model (2.17) since the $\tilde{\mathscr{X}}_i$ are *subjective*? The most natural way to close the model in markets as well organized as U.S. securities markets would seem to be rational expectations: The subjective distribution of $\tilde{\mathscr{X}}_i$ is equal to the actual or objective distribution of $\tilde{\mathscr{X}}_i$. We show in Brock [5a] that the asset-pricing model under rational expectations that is developed in Brock [5a] generates the same solution for the "real side" $\{x_t, c_t, x_{1t}, \ldots, x_{Nt}\}_{t=1}^{\infty}$ as the normative model discussed above. Hence the convergence theorem implies that $\{x_t, c_t, x_{1t}, x_{2t}, \ldots, x_{Nt}\}_{t=1}^{\infty}$ converges to a stationary stochastic process.

Thus the mean ergodic theorem, which says very loosely that the *time* average of any function G of a stationary stochastic process equals the *average* of G over the stationary distribution of that process, allows us to apply time series methods developed for stationary stochastic processes to estimate $\lambda_0, \lambda_1, \ldots, \lambda_K$. As is well known, *time* series data are useful for the estimation of $\lambda_0, \lambda_1, \ldots, \lambda_K$.

However Black [3] points out that in the real world the underlying uncertainty may not be time stationary—in particular, the variance of returns could be highly variable. Our model could be easily generalized to allow finite-order Markov processes $\{\tilde{\delta}_{kt}\}_{t=1}^{\infty}$ with time-dependent transition probabilities. Furthermore, time-dependent utility may be introduced. The only thing lost would be the stochastic turnpike theorem. But even here it may be possible to produce stochastic analogs of the time-dependent turnpike theorems of McKenzie [16]. Hence we may still be able to obtain useful econometric restrictions on the $\lambda_0, \lambda_1, \ldots, \lambda_K$. Furthermore, it may be possible to usefully transform the variables so that the underlying stochastic processes of technology and utility become time stationary. This is, at the least, highly speculative.

The reader is referred to Brock [5a] for a more complete discussion of the applications of the kind of growth theory developed in this paper to finance. It would be interesting to develop an N-process form of Bourgignon–Merton's [4, 17] continuous-time one-sector growth model in order to generate a continuous-time analog of the theory presented here.

APPENDIX. SECTION 2

Consider the Bellman equation

$$U(y_1) = \max\{u(y_1 - x_1) + \beta E_1 U(y_2)\}$$
$$= \max\left\{u(y_1 - x_1) + \beta E_1 U\left[\sum_{j=1}^{N} f_j(x_{j1}, r_1)\right]\right\}, \quad (A2.1)$$

where the maximum is taken over all nonnegative x_{i1} such that

$$\sum_{i=1}^{N} x_{i1} = x_1$$

and all nonnegative x_1. The maximum is achieved because U, u, $\{f_j\}$ are all continuous. The set of maxima is convex because U, u, $\{f_j\}$ are all concave. Equation (A2.1) may be rewritten thus:

$$U(y_1) = \max_{x_1 \geq 0}\left\{u(y_1 - x_1) + \max_{\substack{\eta_1 \geq 0, \ldots, \eta_N \geq 0 \\ \Sigma_j \eta_j = 1}} \beta E_1 U\left[\sum_{j=1}^{N} f_j(\eta_j x_1, r_1)\right]\right\} \quad (A2.2)$$

by putting

$$\eta_j \equiv x_{j1}/x_1.$$

Hence to each $x_1 > 0$ there is a unique solution $\eta_j(x_1)$ to (A2.2). Notice that $\{\eta_j(x_1)\}_{j=1}^{N}$ solves

$$\text{maximize} \quad E_1 U\left[\sum_{j=1}^{N} f_j(\eta_j x_1, r_1)\right] \quad (A2.3)$$

subject to

$$\eta_1 \geq 0, \ldots, \eta_N \geq 0, \quad \sum_{j=1}^{N} \eta_j = 1, \quad (A2.4)$$

so that each $\eta_j(x_1)$ only depends on x_1 and not on y_1. The solution is unique because U is strictly concave by virtue of the strict concavity of u, $\{f_j\}$. It is also easy to see that using the continuity of U and the uniqueness of the maximum, each $\eta_j(x_1)$ is continuous in x_1 for $x_1 > 0$.

Since $\eta_j(x_t)$ depends only on x_t, we may write (2.9) as

$$x_{it} = a_i(x_t, r_{t-1}) = \eta_j(x_t)x_t \equiv a_i(x_t), \qquad (A2.5)$$

where $a_i(\cdot)$ is continuous in x_t. Furthermore, we may use the monotony, continuity, and strict concavity of U and (A2.1) to show that optimum x_1 can be written in the time-independent form

$$x_1 = h(y_1), \qquad (A2.6)$$

where h is continuous in y_1 and $h(0) = 0$.

We will finish the proof of Lemma 2.1 if we can demonstrate that $h(y_1)$ is increasing in y_1. This property will be demonstrated by using the first-order necessary conditions

$$U'(y_1)x_{i1} = u'[g(y_1)]x_{i1} = \beta E_1\{u'(c_2)f_i'(x_{i1}, r_1)\}x_{i1}$$
$$= \beta E_1\left\{U'\left[\sum_{j=1}^{N} f_j(x_{j1}, r_1)\right]f_i'(x_{i1}, r_1)\right\}x_{i1}. \qquad (A2.7)$$

First we need

RESULT A2.1   Let $G(X)$ be a continuously differentiable function of the n vector X. Then $G(X)$ is concave on R^n if for all $X, \bar{X} \in R^n$, we have

$$G(X) - G(\bar{X}) \leq \sum_{i=1}^{n} G_{x_i}(\bar{X})(X_i - \bar{X}_i). \qquad (A28)$$

Proof   see [11, p. 84].

Now put $X = (x_{11}, x_{21}, \ldots, x_{N1})$ and

$$G(X, r_1) \equiv U\left[\sum_{j=1}^{N} f_j(x_{j1}, r_1)\right]. \qquad (A2.9)$$

In (A2.7) let y_1 change to $y_1 + \Delta y_1, \Delta y_1 > 0$. Then x_{i1} changes to $x_{i1} + \Delta x_{i1}$ and

$$U'(y_1 + \Delta y_1)\Delta x_{i1} = \beta E_1\{G_{x_i}(X + \Delta X, r_1)\}\Delta x_{i1}, \qquad (A2.10)$$

$$U'(y_1)\Delta x_{i1} = \beta E_1\{G_{x_i}(X, r_1)\}\Delta x_{i1}. \qquad (A2.11)$$

Equations (A2.10) and (A2.11) follow directly from (A2.7) for processes i such that

$$x_{i1}(y_1) > 0, \qquad x_{i1}(y_1 + \Delta y_1) > 0.$$

Assuming for the moment that (A2.10) and (A2.11) hold for *all* processes i subtract (A2.11) from (A2.10) to get

$$
\begin{aligned}
\Delta U' \Delta x_{i1} &\equiv [U'(y_1 + \Delta y_1) - U'(y_1)]\Delta x_{i1} \\
&= \beta E_1 \{ G_{x_i}(X + \Delta X, r_1) - G_{x_i}(X, r_1)\}\Delta x_{i1} \\
&\equiv \beta E_1 \{\Delta G_{x_i}\Delta x_{i1}\}.
\end{aligned}
\tag{A2.12}
$$

Sum (A2.12) over i to get

$$
\begin{aligned}
& [U'(y_1 + \Delta y_1) - U'(y_1)]\Delta x_1 \\
&= \beta E_1 \left\{ \sum_i \left[G_{x_i}(X + \Delta X, r_1) - G_{x_i}(X, r_1) \right]\Delta x_{i1} \right\}.
\end{aligned}
\tag{A2.13}
$$

CLAIM   The right-hand side of (A2.13) is nonpositive.

Proof of Claim   Let $G(X)$ be any concave function of X; then by (A2.8)

$$
\begin{aligned}
G(X + \Delta X) - G(X) &\leqq \sum_{i=1}^{n} G_{x_i}(X)(x_i + \Delta x_i - x_i) \\
&= \sum_{i=1}^{n} G_{x_i}(X)(\Delta x_i),
\end{aligned}
\tag{A2.14}
$$

$$
G(X) - G(X + \Delta X) \leqq \sum_{i=1}^{n} G_{x_i}(X + \Delta X)(-\Delta x_i).
\tag{A2.15}
$$

Add (A2.14) and (A2.15) to obtain

$$
0 \leqq \sum_{i=1}^{n} [G_{x_i}(X) - G_{x_i}(X + \Delta X)](\Delta x_i).
\tag{A2.16}
$$

This ends the proof of the claim.

Hence putting $X \equiv (x_{11}, \ldots, x_{N1})$, we must have

$$
\begin{aligned}
& [U'(y_1 + \Delta y_1) - U'(y_1)]\Delta x_1 \\
&\leqq \beta E_1 \{ \sum_{i=1}^{n} [G_{x_i}(X + \Delta X, r_1) - G_{x_i}(X, r_1)](\Delta x_{i1}) \} \leqq 0.
\end{aligned}
\tag{A2.17}
$$

Note that by strict concavity of $G(X, r_1)$ in X the rightmost inequality in (A2.17) is strict if $(\Delta x_{11}, \Delta x_{21}, \ldots, \Delta x_{N1} \neq 0$.

Now if

$$U'(y_1 + \Delta y_1) - U'(y_1) < 0, \qquad (A2.18)$$

we are done; i.e., $\Delta x_1 \geqq 0$. If $U'(y_1 + \Delta y_1) = U'(y_1)$, then $U(y)$ is affine on the closed interval $[y_1, y_1 + \Delta y_1]$ and hence is not strictly concave. But this contradicts the strict concavity of U. Thus Lemma 2.1 is established, provided that (A2.12) is established. It is enough to show that the right-hand side of (A2.12) is greater than or equal to the left-hand side. If process i is active at y_1 but not at $y_1 + \Delta y_1$, then (A2.11) holds and $\Delta x_{i1} = x_{i1}(y_1 + \Delta y_1) - x_{i1} < 0$, so that

$$U'(y_1 + \Delta y_1) = u'[g(y_1 + \Delta y_1)] \geqq \beta E_j\{G_{x_i}(X + \Delta X, r_1)\}.$$

Hence

$$U'(y_1 + \Delta y_1)\Delta x_{i1} \leqq \beta E_1\{G_{x_i}(X + \Delta X, r_1)\}\Delta x_{i1} \qquad (A2.19)$$

for such processes i. Hence

$$\Delta U'\Delta x_{i1} \leqq \beta E_1\{\Delta G_{x_i}\Delta x_{i1}\}.$$

If process i is inactive at y_1 and active at $y_1 + \Delta y_1$, then $x_{i1} = 0$, $x_{i1} + \Delta x_{i1} > 0$; then (A2.10) holds with equality and

$$U'(y_1)\Delta x_{i1} \geqq \beta E_1\{Gx_i(X, r_1)\}\Delta x_{i1},$$

so that

$$\Delta U'\Delta x_{i1} \leqq \beta E_1\{\Delta G_{x_i}\Delta x_{i1}\} \qquad (A2.20)$$

for this case also.

Finally if process i is inactive at y_1 and inactive at $y_1 + \Delta y_1$, then $\Delta x_{i1} = 0$ and (A2.20) holds trivially. Thus in all cases (A2.20) holds, so that by summing over i we get

$$\Delta U'\Delta x_1 \leqq \beta E_1\left\{\sum_{i=1}^{N} \Delta G_{x_i}\Delta x_{i1}\right\} \leqq 0. \qquad (A2.21)$$

This established Lemma 2.1. We summarized the above discussion into a formal statement below.

LEMMA 2.1   Assume that $u'(c) > 0$, $u'(c) < 0$, $u'(0) = +\infty$. Furthermore assume that $f_j(0, r) = 0$, $f'_j(x, r) > 0$, $f''_j(x, r) \leqq 0$ for all values of r. Also suppose that there is a set of r values with positive probability such that f_j is strictly concave in x. Then the function $h(y)$ is continuous in y, increasing in y, and 0 when y is 0.

Remark   The hypotheses of Lemma 2.1 imply that U is strictly concave in y. Suppose not. Then there is y_1, y'_1, $y_1 \neq y'_1$, $0 < \alpha < 1$, such that

$U[\alpha y_1 + (1 - \alpha)y_1'] = \alpha U(y_1) + (1 - \alpha)U(y_1')$. Let $\{x_{it}\}$, $\{x_{it}'\}$ be optimizers from y_1, y_1', respectively. Then $\{\bar{x}_{it}\} \equiv \{\alpha x_{it} + (1 - \alpha)x_{it}'\}$ is feasible from $\alpha y_1 + (1 - \alpha)y_1' \equiv \bar{y}_1$. Also

$$U(\bar{y}_1) \geq u(\bar{y}_1 - \bar{x}_1) + \beta E_1 u\left(\sum_{j=1}^{N} f_j(\bar{x}_{j1}, r_1) - \bar{x}_2 \right)$$

$$+ \beta^2 E_1 u\left(\sum_{j=1}^{N} f_j(\bar{x}_{j2}, r_2) - \bar{x}_3 \right) + \cdots$$

$$> \alpha\left[u(y_1 - x_1) + \beta E_1 u\left(\sum_{j=1}^{N} f_j(x_{j1}, r_1) - x_2 \right) + \cdots \right]$$

$$+ (1 - \alpha)\left[u(y_1' - x_1') + \beta E_1 u\left(\sum_{j=1}^{N} f_j(x_{ji}', r_1) - x_2' \right) + \cdots \right]$$

$$= \alpha U(y_1) + (1 - \alpha)U(y_1'). \tag{A2.22}$$

The second strict inequality follows from $u'(c) > 0$ and the assumed strict concavity of each $f_j(x, r_1)$ in x for a set of r_1 of positive measure, provided that $\{x_{it}\} \neq \{x_{it}'\}$ a.e.

It is easy to see that $\{x_{it}\} \neq \{x_{it}'\}$ a.e.: Suppose

$$\{x_{it}\} = \{x_{it}'\} \quad \text{a.e.} \quad \text{for all} \quad i, t.$$

Then from (A2.7)

$$u'(c_1)x_{i1} = \beta E_1\{u'(c_2)f_i'(x_{i1}, r_1)x_{i1}\} \tag{A2.23}$$

$$u'(c_1')x_{i1}' = u'(c_1')x_{i1} = \beta E_1\{u'(c_2')f_i'(x_{i1}', r_1)x_{i1}'\}$$

$$= \beta E_1\{u'(c_2)f_i'(x_{i1}, r_1)x_{i1}\}. \tag{A2.24}$$

Here $c_2 = c_2'$ from the hypothesis $x_{it} = x_{it}'$ a.e., for all i, t. Since at least one $x_{i1} > 0$, we must have

$$u'(c_1) = u'(c_1'). \tag{A2.25}$$

But $u''(c) < 0$ and (A2.25) imply

$$c_1 = c_1',$$

a contradiction to $y_1 \neq y_1'$. This establishes the remark.

LEMMA 2.2 Assume the hypotheses of Lemma 2.1 and suppose that each $f_i(x, r)$ is continuous in r for each x. Then $F(x, r)$ is continuous in r.

Proof This is easy because

$$y_{t+1} \equiv \sum_j f_j(x_{jt}, r_t) = \sum_j f_j(\eta_j(x_t)x_t, r_t) \equiv F(x_t, r_t).$$

Since $\eta_j(x_t)$ is continuous in $x_t > 0$ and each $f_j(x, r)$ is continuous in r, we have $F(x, r)$ continuous in x and r. This ends the proof of Lemma 2.2.

In order to establish Theorem 2.1 we need to find conditions on u, f_i such that the process (2.10) converges in distribution. The optimum stochastic process is recorded here for convenience.

$$x_{t+1} = H(x_t, r_t), \qquad (A2.26)$$

where x_1, r_1 are historically given. By definition of $h(\cdot)$, $H(\cdot, \cdot)$ and $\{\eta_j(\cdot)\}$, we have

$$x_{t+1} = h\left(\sum_{j=1}^{N} f_j(x_{jt}, r_t)\right) = h\left(\sum_{j=1}^{N} f_j(\eta_j(x_t)x_t, r_t)\right) \equiv H(x_t, r_t). \quad (A2.27)$$

If we can show for all $r \in R$ there exists $\underline{x}(r)$ such that if $0 < \underline{x}_1 < x(r)$, then

$$x_2 \equiv H(x_1, r) > x_1, \qquad (A2.28)$$

and if we can show that H is increasing in x_1 for each value $r \in R$, then since we have already shown (Lemma 2.3) that fixed points of (2.13) satisfy (2.14), the argument of Brock–Mirman [8, Section 4] may be directly adapted to show that $\{x_t\}_{t=1}^{\infty}$ converges in distribution. To do this, we need

ASSUMPTION A2.1   Consider the problem: Given $a \geq 0$, $b(r) \geq 0$, for all $r \in R$, solve the problem

$$\text{maximize} \quad Eu\left(\sum_{j=1}^{N} f_j(a_j, r) - b(r)\right) \qquad (A2.29)$$

$$\text{s.t.} \quad \sum_{j=1}^{N} a_j \leq a, \quad a_j > 0, \quad j = 1, 2, \ldots, N, \quad a \geq 0.$$

Assume for all $r \in R$, except for a set of μ measure zero, that

$$\sum_{j=1}^{N} f_j(a_j(a)a, r) \equiv L(a, r, b(\cdot))$$

increases in a. Here $a_j(a)$ denotes the optimum fraction of a in the jth activity.

Remark   Assumption A2.1 is strong, but the reader can easily show that in the deterministic case ($r = \bar{r}$ with probability 1) $f'_j(a_j, \bar{r}) > 0$ for all j implies $L(a, \bar{r}, b(\cdot))$ increases in a. If u is linear, $\int f'_j(a_j, r)\mu(dr) > 0$ for all j implies $L(a, r, b(\cdot))$ is increasing in a. Also the example with log utility, multiplicative uncertainty, and Cobb–Douglas technology presented in Brock [5a] satisfies Assumption A2.1. Let us turn to establishing (A2.28).

In order to find sufficient conditions for (A2.28), it is helpful to develop the problem (A2.29) with $b(\cdot) \equiv 0$.
Let x_0, r_0 be given. Consider the problem

$$\text{maximize} \quad u\left(\sum_{j=1}^{N} f_j(x_{j0}, r_0) - x_1\right) + \beta E u\left(\sum_{j=1}^{N} f_j(x_{j1}, r_1)\right) \quad \text{(A2.30)}$$

$$\text{s.t.} \quad \sum_{j=1}^{N} x_{j1} = x_1, \quad x_{j1} \geqq 0, \quad j = 1, 2, \ldots, N, \quad x_1 \geqq 0. \quad \text{(A2.31)}$$

Let

$$x_1^*(x_{10}, x_{20}, \ldots, x_{N0}, r_0) \equiv M(x_{10}, \ldots, x_{N0}, r_0) \quad \text{(A2.32)}$$

solve (A2.30). Suppose that

$$x_{j0} \geqq 0, \quad j = 1, 2, \ldots, N, \quad \sum_{j=1}^{N} x_{j0} = x_0, \quad x_0 \geqq 0. \quad \text{(A2.33)}$$

ASSUMPTION A2.2   For each $r_0 \in R$ there is $\varepsilon_0 > 0$ such that for all $\{x_{j0}\}_{j=1}^{N}, x_0$ satisfying (A2.33) and

$$x_0 < \varepsilon_0,$$

we have

$$x_1^*(x_{10}, \ldots, x_{N0}, r_0) > x_0.$$

ASSUMPTION A2.3   Let $b(\cdot)$ be a nonnegative random variable. Let $\bar{x}_1, \bar{x}_1^*$ solve, respectively,

$$\text{maximize} \quad u(y_1 - x_1) + E u\left(\sum_{j=1}^{N} f_j(x_{j1}, r_1) - b(r_1)\right) \quad \text{(A2.34)}$$

$$\text{s.t.} \quad x_1 \geqq 0, \quad \sum_{j=1}^{N} x_{j1} \leqq x_1, \quad x_{j1} \geqq 0, \quad j = 1, 2, \ldots, N.$$

$$\text{maximize} \quad u(y_1 - x_1) + \beta E u\left(\sum_{j=1}^{N} f_j(x_{j1}, r_1)\right) \quad \text{(A2.35)}$$

$$\text{s.t.} \quad x_1 \geqq 0, \quad \sum_{j=1}^{N} x_{j1} \leqq x_1, \quad x_{j1} \geqq 0, \quad j = 1, 2, \ldots, N.$$

Then for any $y_1 \geqq 0$ we have

$$\bar{x}_1 \geqq x_1^*. \quad \text{(A2.36)}$$

Let us clarify the meaning of (A2.36) below. Suppose that (A2.36) did *not* hold. Then $\bar{x}_1 < x_1^*, \bar{c}_1 > c_1^*, u'(\bar{c}_1) < u'(c_1^*)$. Therefore for all processes i that are active at both $\bar{x}_1$, $\bar{x}_1^*$ or for processes i that are not active at $\bar{x}_1$ but are active at x_1^*, we must have

$$E\{u'(\bar{c}_2)f_i'(\bar{x}_{i1}, r_1)\} < E\{u'(c_2^*)f_i'(x_{i1}^*, r_1)\}. \qquad (A2.37)$$

Call such processes i "order preserving."

If it were the case that $\bar{x}_{i1} \leq x_{i1}^*$ for an order-preserving process i, then

$$f_i'(\bar{x}_{i1}, r_1) \geq f_i'(x_{i1}^-, r_1). \qquad (A2.38)$$

Inequalities (A2.37) and (A2.38) imply there is a set X such that $\mu(X) > 0$ such that

$$u'(\bar{c}_2) < u'(c_2^*) \qquad \text{on} \quad X.$$

Hence on X

$$\bar{c}_2 > c_2^*.$$

But

$$\bar{c}_2 \equiv \sum_{j=1}^N f_{j1}(\bar{x}_{j1}, r_1) - b_2(r_1) \leq \sum_{j=1}^N f_{j1}(\bar{x}_{j1}, r_1),$$

$$\bar{c}_2 > c_2^* \equiv \sum_{j=1}^N f_{j1}(x_{j1}^*, r_1) \qquad (A2.39)$$

imply

$$\sum_{j=1}^N f_{j1}(\bar{x}_{j1}, r_1) > \sum_{j=1}^N f_{j1}(x_{j1}^*, r_1),$$

which is quite unlikely when $\bar{x}_1 < x_1^*$ and $b(\cdot) \geq 0$. Hence Assumption A2.3 is a natural assumption to make.

It is clear that there *is* an order-preserving process; otherwise, for all i

$$\bar{x}_{i1} \geq x_{i1}^*.$$

But then

$$\bar{x}_1 \geq x_1^*,$$

which contradicts

$$\bar{x}_1 < x_1^*.$$

THEOREM A2.1   Assume Assumptions A2.1–A2.3. Then consider the problem

$$\text{maximize} \quad \left\{ u(y_1 - x_1) + \beta Eu\left(\sum_{j=1}^{N} f_j(x_{j1}, r_1) - x_2 \right) + \cdots \right\} \quad (A2.40)$$

$$\text{s.t.} \quad x_t \geq 0, \quad \sum_{j=1}^{N} x_{jt} \leq x_t, \quad x_{jt} \geq 0, \quad j = 1, 2, \ldots, N, \quad t = 1, 2, \ldots .$$

Then the optimal solution may be written in the form

$$x_{t+1} = H(x_t, r_t), \qquad H(0, r_t) = 0 \qquad (A2.41a)$$

for some $H(\cdot, \cdot)$ that are increasing in x_t for each $r_t \in \mathcal{R}$. Also for each $r_t \in \mathcal{R}$, except for a set of μ measure zero, there is $\varepsilon_0(r_t) > 0$ such that

$$x_t < \varepsilon_0(r_t) \qquad \text{implies} \qquad H(x_t, r_t) > x_t. \qquad (A2.41b)$$

Proof   From the form of (A2.40) it is clear that for any given x_t, the path $x_{t+1}, x_{t+2}, \ldots$ must solve

$$\text{maximize} \quad \left\{ Eu\left(\sum_{j=1}^{N} f_j(x_{jt}, r_t) - x_{t+1} \right) + \cdots \right\} \qquad (A2.42)$$

$$\text{s.t.} \quad x_s \geq 0, \quad \sum_{j=1}^{N} x_{js} \leq x_s, \quad x_{js} \geq 0, \quad j = 1, 2, \ldots, N, \quad s = t, \quad t + 1, \ldots$$

Since problem (A2.42) is time stationary and the solution $x_{t+1}, x_{t+2}, \ldots$ is unique given x_t, it is clear that there is $H(\cdot, \cdot)$ satisfying (A2.41a).

Assumption A2.1 with $b(r)$ replaced by $x_{t+1}(r_t)$ implies that $H(x_t, r_t)$ is increasing in x_t for each r_t.

Assumptions A2.3 and A2.2 with $b(r_1)$ replaced by $x_{t+1}(r_t)$ give (A2.41b). This ends the proof.

Assumptions A2.1–A2.3 are *very* strong. We hope to improve matters in future work.

Turn now to the proof of Lemma 2.3.

Proof of Lemma 2.3   The first-order necessary conditions (2.10a,b) must hold along any optimum. We shall use (2.10a,b) to show

$$\underline{x}_i \leq \bar{x}_i, \qquad i = 1, 2, \ldots, N, \qquad (A2.43)$$

where

$$\underline{x} = \sum_{i=1}^{N} \underline{x}_i, \qquad \bar{x} = \sum_{i=1}^{N} \bar{x}_i \qquad (A2.44)$$

and $\underline{x}_i$ and $\bar{x}_i$ are the optimum allocation of $\underline{x}$ and $\bar{x}$, respectively, to process i.

Look at the necessary condition (2.10a) for the case of active processes, i.e., the case where equality holds:

$$u'(c_t) = \beta E_t\{u'(c_{t+1})f'_i(x_{it}, r_t)\}. \tag{A2.45}$$

Now using (2.11), (A2.45) may be rewritten as

$$u'[g(F(x_{t-1}, r_{t-1}))] = \beta E_t\{u'[g(F(x_t, r_t))]f'_i(x_{it}, r_t)\}. \tag{A2.46}$$

Consider first the fixed point $\underline{x}$:

$$\underline{x} = \underline{H}(\underline{x}) \equiv h(\underline{F}(x)) \equiv h\left(\min_{r \in R} F(\underline{x}, r)\right) \equiv h(F(\underline{x}, \underline{r})) \tag{A2.47}$$

where $\underline{r}$ is an element of R that attains the minimum of $F(\underline{x}, r)$ over $r \in R$. A minimizer exists since $F(x, r)$ is continuous in r for each x and R is compact.

In (A2.46) put $x_{t-1} = \underline{x}, r_{t-1} = \underline{r}$, and use

$$x_t = H(x_{t-1}, r_{t-1}) = H(\underline{x}, \underline{r}) \equiv h(F(\underline{x}, \underline{r})) \equiv h\left(\min F(\underline{x}, \underline{r})\right) = \underline{x}, \tag{A2.48}$$

$$x_{it} = x_i, \tag{A2.49}$$

to get

$$u'[g(F(\underline{x}, r))] = \beta E_t\{u'[g(F(\underline{x}, r_t))]f'_i(\underline{x}_i, r_t)\}. \tag{A2.50}$$

Since $g(\cdot)$ is nondecreasing and continuous,

$$g(F(\underline{x}, r_t)) \geq g\left(\min_{r \in R} F(\underline{x}, r)\right) = g(F(\underline{x}, \underline{r})). \tag{A2.51}$$

Thus since u is concave, u' is nonincreasing; hence

$$u'[g(F(\underline{x}, r_t)] \leq u'[g(F(\underline{x}, \underline{r}))]. \tag{A2.52}$$

It follows that

$$u'[g(F(\underline{x}, \underline{r}))] \leq \beta u'[g(F(\underline{x}, \underline{r}))]E_t\{f'_i(\underline{x}_i, r_t)\}. \tag{A2.53}$$

Since $u'(c) > 0$ for $c \geq 0$, (A2.53) yields

$$1 \leq \beta E\{f'_i(\underline{x}_i, r)\}, \qquad i \quad \text{active at} \quad \underline{x}. \tag{A2.54}$$

Put (A2.54) aside for the moment and turn to the set of processes at date t where (2.10a) holds with *strict* inequality. In this case $x_{it} = 0$ so that $\underline{x}_i \leq \bar{x}_i$ automatically. Turn now to the analogous inequality to (A2.54) for $\bar{x}_i$.

For active processes, follow exactly the same steps (A2.48)–(A2.53) as used to get (A2.54) to get (A2.55) below:

$$1 \geq \beta E\{f'_i(\bar{x}_i, r)\}, \qquad i \text{ active at } \bar{x}. \tag{A2.55}$$

Now let

$$A(x,r), \qquad A^c(x,r)$$

denote the set of processes where (2.10a) holds with equality and strict inequality, respectively, when

$$x_{t-1} = x, \qquad r_{t-1} = r.$$

To date we have shown

$$i \in A(\underline{x},\underline{r}) \qquad \text{implies} \quad 1 \leqq \beta E\{f_i'(\underline{x}_i,r)\}, \qquad \text{(A2.56)}$$

$$i \in A(\bar{x},\bar{r}) \qquad \text{implies} \quad 1 \geqq \beta\{f_i'(\bar{x}_i,r)\}, \qquad \text{(A2.57)}$$

$$i \in A^c(\underline{x},\underline{r}) \qquad \text{implies} \quad \underline{x}_i = 0, \qquad\qquad \text{(A2.58)}$$

and

$$i \in A^c(\bar{x},\bar{r}) \qquad \text{implies} \quad \bar{x}_i = 0. \qquad\qquad \text{(A2.59)}$$

Notice that (A2.56) and (A2.57) imply for $i \in A(\underline{x},\underline{r}) \cap A(\bar{x},\bar{r})$

$$E\{f_i'(\underline{x}_i,r)\} \geqq E\{f_i'(\bar{x}_i,r)\}. \qquad \text{(A2.60)}$$

Hence $f_i''(x,r) < 0$ for all (x,r) implies

$$\underline{x}_i \leqq \bar{x}_i, \qquad i \in A(\underline{x},\underline{r}) \cap A(\bar{x},\bar{r}). \qquad \text{(A2.61)}$$

In order to establish $\underline{x}_i \leqq \bar{x}_i$ for *all* i, the only possibility left to consider is $i \in A(\underline{x},\underline{r}) \cap A^c(\bar{x},\bar{r})$. This implies

$$\underline{x}_i \geqq 0, \qquad \bar{x}_i = 0. \qquad \text{(A2.62)}$$

If $\underline{x}_i = 0$, we are done. Suppose $\underline{x}_i > 0$. By definition of $i \in A^c(\bar{x},\bar{r})$ it is the case that (2.10a) holds with strict inequality at $(x_{t-1},r_{t-1}) = (\bar{x},\bar{r})$. Now (A2.54) holds for $i \in A(\underline{x},\underline{r})$. For $i \in A^c(\bar{x},\bar{r})$ we have

$$u'[g(F(\bar{x},\bar{r}))] > \beta E_t\{u'[g(F(\bar{x},r))]f_i'(\bar{x},r)\}. \qquad \text{(A2.63)}$$

But

$$g(F(\bar{x},r)) \leqq g(\max_r F(\bar{x},r)) = g(F(\bar{x},\bar{r})) \qquad \text{(A2.64)}$$

so that

$$u'[g(F(\bar{x},r))] \geqq u'[g(F(\bar{x},\bar{r}))]. \qquad \text{(A2.65)}$$

Therefore from (A2.63) and (A2.65) we get

$$1 > \beta E_t\{f_i'(\bar{x}_i,r)\}. \qquad \text{(A2.66)}$$

Now (A2.54) and (A2.66) give

$$\bar{x}_i > \underline{x}_i;$$ (A2.67)

so the case of (A2.62) cannot arise.
Hence we have established that in *all* cases

$$\underline{x}_i \leqq \bar{x}_i.$$

Therefore

$$\underline{x} \leqq \bar{x}.$$

This ends the proof of Lemma 2.3.

THEOREM A2.2   Assume the hypotheses of Theorem A2.1. Then the sequence of distribution functions defined by

$$F_{x_{t+1}}(x) \equiv \Pr\{x_{t+1} < x\} \equiv \Pr\{H(x_t, r_t) < x\}$$
$$= \int \Pr\{x_t < q(x, r_t)\} \mu(dr_t)$$
$$\equiv \int F_{x_t}[q(x, r)] \mu(dr)$$ (A2.68)

converges to a unique limit distribution function $F(x)$. Furthermore $F(\cdot)$ is independent of initial conditions.

Proof   Since it was established in Section 2 that the process

$$x_{t+1} = H(x_t, r_t)$$

has only one stable interval, the argument of Brock–Mirman [8, Section 4] may be applied. This ends the proof.

Remark   The Mirman–Zilcha[20] caveat on the proof technique of Brock–Mirman is not relevant here because we have established (A2.41b). The Mirman–Zilcha caveat refers to Lemma 3.1 of Brock–Mirman[8] where property (A2.41b) is established for all points of $R \equiv [\alpha, \beta]$ except α. Brock–Mirman did not establish that $H(x, \alpha)$ satisfied (A2.41b). We have provided hypotheses sufficient for (A2.41b) in this paper. It is worth remarking that Assumptions A2.1 and A2.2 are not nearly so strong in the Brock–Mirman one-sector one-process case.

REFERENCES

1. Benveniste, L. M., and Scheinkman, J. A. Duality Theory for Dynamic Optimization Models of Economics: The Continuous Time Case. Univ. of Chicago, Chicago, Illinois, Revised (August 1977).
2. Bewley, T., Existence of equilibria in economies with infinitely many commodities, *J. Econ. Theory*, **4**, No. 3 (1972), 514–540.

3. Black, F., Studies of stock price volatility changes, *Proc. Meetings Am. Statist. Assoc.* (1976).
4. Bourgignon, F., A particular class of continuous-time stochastic growth models, *J. Econ. Theory* **9** (1974), 141–158.
5a. Brock, W. A., An Integration of Stochastic Growth Theory and the Theory of Finance. Univ. of Chicago, Chicago, Illinois (February 9, 1978).
5b. Brock, W. A., Asset Prices in a Production Economy. Univ. of Chicago, Chicago, Illinois (April 1978).
6. Brock, W. A., and Magill, M. J. P., Dynamics under uncertainty, *Econometrica* (1979) (forthcoming).
7. Brock, W. A., and Majumdar, M., Global asymptotic stability results for multi-sector models of optimal growth under uncertainty when future utilities are discounted, revised May 1977, *J. Econ. Theory* **18**, No. 2 (1978), 225–243.
8. Brock, W. A., and Mirman, L., Optimal economic growth and uncertainty: The discounted case, *J. Econ. Theory* **4**, No. 3 (1972), 479–513.
9. Brock, W. A., and Mirman, L., Optimal economic growth and uncertainty: The no discounting case, *Int. Econ. Rev.* **14**, No. 3 (1973), 560–573.
10. Cox, J., Ingersoll, J., and Ross, S., Notes on A Theory of the Term Structure of Interest Rates. Stanford Univ., Univ. of Chicago, and Yale Univ. (undated).
11. Hadley, G., "Nonlinear and Dynamic Programming." Addison-Wesley, Reading, Massachusetts, 1964.
12. Hellwig, M., A Note on the Intertemporal Capital Asset Pricing Model. Princeton Univ., Department of Economics (undated).
13. Loève, M., "Probability Theory." Van Nostrand-Reinhold, Princeton, New Jersey, 1963.
14. Lucas, R. E., Jr., Asset Prices in An Exchange Economy. Univ. of Chicago, Chicago, Illinois, August 1975, *Econometrica* **46**, No. 6 (1978), 1429–1446.
15. Magill, M. J. P., Equilibrium and Investment Under Uncertainty. The Center for Mathematical Studies in Economics and Management Science, Northwestern Univ. (April 1978).
16. McKenzie, L., Turnpike theory, *Econometrica* **44** (1976), 841–865.
17. Merton, R., An asymptotic theory of growth under uncertainty, *Rev. Econ. Stud.* **42** (3), No. 131 (1979), 373–393.
18. Merton, R., An intertemporal capital asset pricing model, *Econometrica* **41**, No. 5 (1973), 867–887.
19. Mirman, L., and Zilcha, I., Characterizing optimal policies in a one-sector model of economic growth under uncertainty, *J. Econ. Theory* **14**, No. 2 (1977), 389–401.
20. Mirman, L., and Zilcha, I., Unbounded shadow prices for optimal stochastic growth models, *Int. Econ. Rev.* **17**, No. 1 (1976), 121–132.
21. Mirman, L., and Zilcha, I., On optimal growth under uncertainty, *J. Econ. Theory* **2**, No. 3 (1975).
22. Ross, S., The arbitrage theory of capital asset pricing, *J. Econ. Theory* **13**, No. 8 (1976), 341–359.

This research was partially supported financially by NSF Grant SOC 74-19692 to the University of Chicago. Part of this paper was written while I was at the Australian National University, Summer 1977. The stimulating research environment at the Australian National University was very helpful. Some of this work was done at the University of Wisconsin, Madison, Wisconsin, Fall 1977, which provided me an excellent academic environment. This work has been presented at the Australian Graduate School of Management; The University of Texas Business School at Austin; The University of Houston, Dept. of Economics; The University of Wisconsin, Madison workshop of Economic Theory; and the Graduate School of Industrial

Administration, Carnegie-Mellon University. I would like to thank R. Lucas, S. Magee, M. Magill, M. Miller, J. Scheinkman, R. Kihlstrom, L. Mirman, and M. Rothschild for helpful comments. Most of all, I wish to thank F. R. Chang for a careful reading of this paper and for finding errors.

None of the above are responsible for any errors or shortcomings of this paper.

DEPARTMENT OF ECONOMICS
UNIVERSITY OF CHICAGO
CHICAGO, ILLINOIS

DEPARTMENT OF ECONOMICS
UNIVERSITY OF WISCONSIN
MADISON, WISCONSIN

Fair Division of a Random Harvest: The Finite Case

DAVID GALE

JOEL SOBEL

A resource such as an orchard is owned jointly by m agents, the ith agent's *share* of the resource being θ_i. The yield of the resource (the *harvest*) and the utilities of each agent are functions of the state of nature. A *fair distribution scheme* is one that is (1) (Pareto) optimal and that (2) gives each agent an expected consumption proportional to his share of the resource. We show that with the usual concavity assumptions on utilities, there always exists one and only one fair distribution scheme. The proof is achieved by constructing a suitable social welfare function which is maximized at the desired distribution scheme.

1. INTRODUCTION

A number of agents who may be thought of as individuals, companies, or countries are joint owners of some productive resource such as an orchard or an ocean. The yield of this resource is a random variable depending on the state of nature. Thus the size of an apple harvest may depend on the amount of rainfall, temperature fluctuations, etc., or the catch of tuna may vary with prevailing winds and currents. Each agent A_i is assumed to have his own utility function, which may also depend on the state of nature. Thus, one's appetite for apples may be different in a dry hot summer from what it is in a cold wet one. The agents wish to arrive at some sort of a *distribution scheme*, that is, an arrangement for dividing up the harvest in each possible state of nature. Now there is one property that any such scheme ought to have, namely, it should be (Pareto) optimal, meaning that no other scheme should provide a higher *expected utility* to all of the agents. While this seems a fairly obvious requirement, it should be pointed out that it sharply limits the set of acceptable schemes. For example, the simpleminded arrangement in which each of m agents receives one-mth of the harvest regardless of the state of nature will in general be nonoptimal. In the very simplest case of two agents and two states of nature, if the agents are not identical, it will almost always be the case that both will prefer to have one agent get more than half the harvest in one state if the other gets more than half in the other, as opposed to a fifty-fifty split in both. There are, nevertheless, an infinity of possible optimal distribution schemes, but some of these are clearly "unfair," e.g., always giving the entire harvest to the first agent. To arrive at a notion of fairness, we will suppose there is given a set of positive numbers $\theta_1, \ldots, \theta_m$, which sum to 1, where θ_i is A_i's *share* of the resource. Thus, if the agents own equal shares, then $\theta_i = 1/m$ for all i. If the agents are thought of as countries, then θ_i might be proportional to the population of the ith country. If the agents are firms, the θ_i might reflect the amount each firm has invested in developing the resource. Given the shares θ_i, there is now a rather natural way to define fairness. Let $h(s)$ be the size of the harvest in state s and let $\bar{h}$ be the expected value of $h(s)$. Let $c_i(s)$ be the amount consumed by A_i in state s under some distribution scheme. We call this distribution scheme *fair* if $\bar{c}_i = \theta_i \bar{h}$ where $\bar{c}_i$ is the expected consumption of A_i under this scheme. Such a criterion would seem reasonable to an outsider who knew nothing of the utility function of the agents, or, to put it the other way, any scheme that violated this condition would appear to give some agents more or less than their share. For further discussion of this notion of fairness, see the final section.

In the present paper we consider only the case in which there are only a finite number of states of nature. A subsequent paper will take up the case where s beongs to a general probability space. For the finite case our result can be stated concisely as follows: *If all utility functions are strictly concave and increasing, then there exists exactly one distribution scheme which is both optimal and fair.* The proof is achieved by exhibiting a particular social welfare function ρ defined over the set of all fair distribution schemes. This function, being strictly concave, has a unique maximum. Our proof then consists in showing that a fair scheme is optimal if and only if it maximizes ρ. The argument consists of repeated application (4 times) of the Kuhn–Tucker theorem.

Since the social welfare function ρ is the center piece of our exposition, we will define it here for the reader to contemplate. Let $u_{ij}(c)$ be the utility of c units of consumption to A_i in state s_j, and define

$$\rho_{ij}(c) = \int_1^c \log u_{ij}'(x)\, dx. \tag{1}$$

Let $C = (c_{ij})$ be the $m \times n$ matrix corresponding to a fair distribution scheme where c_{ij} denotes the amount consumed by A_i in s_j. Then

$$\rho(C) = \sum_{i,j} \rho_{ij}(c_{ij}). \tag{2}$$

We would welcome any suggestions as to the economic interpretation of this rather curious function.

2. PRELIMINARY SIMPLIFICATIONS

Let p_j denote the probability that state s_j occurs and let h_j be the size of the harvest in this case. A fair distribution is then an $m \times n$ matrix $C = (c_{ij})$ such that

$$\sum_i c_{ij} = h_j \quad \text{for all} \quad j, \tag{3}$$

$$\sum_j p_i c_{ij} = q_i \quad \text{for all} \quad i, \tag{4}$$

where $q_i = \theta_i \sum_j p_j h_j$.

It is convenient to reduce our problem to the special case where all the p_j are equal. For this purpose introduce new variables $x_{ij} = p_j c_{ij}$ and let $k_j = p_j h_j$. Then (3) is equivalent to

$$\sum_i x_{ij} = k_j, \tag{3'}$$

and (4) is equivalent to

$$\sum_j x_{ij} = q_i. \tag{4'}$$

Note that from our definition $\sum_j k_j = \sum_i q_i$.

Finally define functions v_{ij} by

$$v_{ij}(x) = p_j u_{ij}(x/p_j). \tag{5}$$

Then the expected utility of A_i under the distribution C is

$$\sum_j p_j u_{ij}(c_{ij}) = \sum_j p_j u_{ij}(x_{ij}/p_j) = \sum_j v_{ij}(x_{ij}).$$

We denote this last sum by $v_i(X)$ where X is the $m \times n$ matrix of x_{ij}'s.

Note that the functions v_{ij} inherit the relevant properties of the u_{ij}, i.e., concavity differentiality, etc.

We will call a distribution matrix X feasible if it satisfies (3') and *fair* if it satisfies (4'). A feasible X is called *optimal* if there is no other feasible X' such that $v_i(X') \geq v_i(X)$ for all i with strict inequality for at least one i. Our result now becomes the following

THEOREM 1   If the functions v_{ij} are differentiable, concave, and increasing, then there exists a unique distribution matrix that is both fair and optimal.

3. THE KUHN–TUCKER THEOREM

We present a version of the Kuhn–Tucker theorem needed for the present application.

Let f be a strictly concave differentiable function from R^n_+ into $\bar{R}$, the reals including $\pm\infty$. Let A be an $m \times n$ matrix and b an m vector, and define K by

$$K = \{x \mid Ax = b, x \in R^n_+\}.$$

Denote by f_j the partial derivative of f with respect to x_j and denote by a_j the jth column of A.

THEOREM (*Kuhn–Tucker*) If K contains a strictly positive vector, then $\bar{x}$ maximizes f in K if and only if there exists an m vector u such that

$$
\begin{aligned}
f_j(\bar{x}) - ua_j &\leq 0 \quad && \text{for all} \quad j\\
&= 0 \quad && \text{if} \quad \bar{x}_j > 0.
\end{aligned}
$$

For a proof see, for example, [1].

4. PROOF OF THE MAIN THEOREM

As in the introduction define functions ρ_{ij} by the rule

$$\rho_{ij}(x) = \int_1^x \log v'_{ij}(t)\, dt \quad \text{for} \quad x \geq 0.$$

Since we allow the possibility that $\lim_{x\to 0} v_{ij}(x) = \infty$, it is possible also that the $\rho_{ij}(x)$ decrease to $-\infty$ as x approaches 0, in which case we define $\rho_{ij}(0) = -\infty$.

LEMMA The functions ρ_{ij} are differentiable and concave.

Proof Since v'_{ij} is positive and continuous, ρ_{ij} exists and its derivative is $\log v'_{ij}$, which is decreasing because v'_{ij} is decreasing and log is increasing; so ρ_{ij} is strictly concave. ∎

Our main result follows from

THEOREM 2 The distribution matrix X is fair and optimal if and only if it maximizes $\rho(X) = \sum_{i,j} \rho_{ij}(x_{ij})$ among all nonnegative matrices satisfying (3′) and (4′).

This theorem implies our result for since ρ is strictly concave and the set of solutions of (3′) and (4′) is compact, ρ attains a maximum at only one point.

Proof Let $\bar{X} = (\bar{x}_{ij})$ maximize ρ. Note that the positive matrix $X = (q_i k_j / \sum_i q_i)$ gives a positive solution of (3') and (4'); so the hypotheses of our Kuhn–Tucker theorem are satisfied. Therefore there exist numbers λ_i and μ_j such that

$$\log v'_{ij}(\bar{x}_{ij}) - \lambda_i \leq \mu_j \qquad \text{for all} \quad i, j$$
$$= \mu_j \qquad \text{if} \quad \bar{x}_{ij} > 0. \tag{6}$$

Letting $\alpha_i = e^{-\lambda_i}$, $\beta_j = e^{\mu_j}$, this gives

$$\alpha_i v_{ij}(\bar{x}_{ij}) \leq \beta_j \qquad \text{for all} \quad i, j$$
$$= \beta_j \qquad \text{if} \quad \bar{x}_{ij} > 0. \tag{7}$$

Applying (7) for a fixed j and using Kuhn–Tucker in the other direction, we see that $(\bar{x}_j)$ maximizes $\sum_i \alpha_i v_{ij}(x_{ij})$ subject to (3') where $\bar{x}_j = (x_{1j}, \ldots, x_{mj})$. Thus if X is any distribution matrix satisfying (3'), then

$$\sum_i \alpha_i v_{ij}(\bar{x}_{ij}) \geq \sum_i \alpha_i v_{ij}(x_{ij}). \tag{8}$$

Recall that by definition $v_i(X) = \sum_j v_{ij}(x_{ij})$. Then summing (8) on j gives

$$\sum_i \alpha_i v_i(\bar{X}) \geq \sum_i \alpha_i v_i(X), \tag{9}$$

and since $\alpha_i > 0$ for all i, we cannot have $v_i(X) \geq v_i(\bar{X})$ for all i and $v_i(X) > v_i(\bar{X})$ for some i, so $\bar{X}$ is optimal.

Conversely suppose $\bar{X}$ is fair and optimal. Let U be the set of all points $u \in R^m$ such that there exists a feasible X with $v_i(X) \leq u_i$ for all i. From the concavity of the v_i, the set U is convex and $(v_1(\bar{X}), \ldots, v_m(\bar{X}))$ is an efficient point of U since $\bar{X}$ is optimal so there exist nonnegative numbers α_i such that $\bar{X}$ maximizes

$$\sum_i \alpha_i v_i(X) = \sum_i \alpha_i \sum_j v_{ij}(x_{ij}) = \sum_j \sum_i \alpha_i v_{ij}(x_{ij});$$

so for each j

$$\bar{x}_j \quad \text{maximizes} \quad \sum_i \alpha_i v_{ij}(x_{ij}) \quad \text{subject to} \quad \sum x_{ij} = k_j. \tag{10}$$

The above means that $\alpha_1 > 0$ for all i, for, say, $\alpha_1 = 0$. Then since $q_1 > 0$, we must have $x_{1j} > 0$ for some j, say, $j = 1$; but since v_{11} is increasing, it is clear that to maximize $\sum \alpha_i v_{i1}(x_{i1})$, one would set $x_{11} = 0$, a contradiction. Applying Kuhn–Tucker to (10) for each j gives the existence of numbers β_j such that

$$\alpha_i v'_{ij}(\bar{x}_{ij}) \leq \beta_j$$
$$= \beta_j \qquad \text{if} \quad \bar{x}_{ij} > 0,$$

which is exactly (7), and since $\alpha_i > 0$ and $v'_{ij} > 0$, we have $\beta_j > 0$. Setting $\lambda_i = -\log \alpha_i$ and $\mu_j = \log \beta_j$, we get again (6), and applying Kuhn–Tucker backward once more we see that $\bar{X}$ maximizes ρ. ∎

REFERENCE

1. Luenberger, D. G., "Introduction to Linear and Nonlinear Programming." Addison–Wesley, Reading, Massachusetts, 1965.

This research has been partially supported by the Office of Naval Research under Contract N00014-76-C-0134 and the National Science Foundation under Grant MCS74-21222 A02 with the University of California. Reproduction in whole or in part is permitted for any purpose of the United States Government.

David Gale   *Joel Sobel*
DEPARTMENT OF MATHEMATICS   DEPARTMENT OF ECONOMICS
UNIVERSITY OF CALIFORNIA   UNIVERSITY OF CALIFORNIA
BERKELEY, CALIFORNIA   AT SAN DIEGO,
                                            LA JOLLA, CALIFORNIA

Characterizing Inefficiency of Infinite-Horizon Programs in Nonsmooth Technologies

LAWRENCE M. BENVENISTE

TAPAN MITRA

1. INTRODUCTION

An important problem in the theory of allocation of resources over an infinite time horizon is to find easily applicable criteria that can characterize the set of efficient (alternatively, inefficient) programs.

Restricting our attention to the standard aggregative model of economic growth, we find that there are two categories of results relating to this problem in the existing literature. One category of results relates to some partial characterizations of inefficiency under fairly general conditions on the technology (specifically, the production function f satisfies $f(0) = 0$; f is increasing; f is concave; f is continuous). On the necessity side, we have the well-known result of Malinvaud [5] that for an inefficient program the value of input is bounded away from zero. On the sufficiency side, we know that if the sequence of the value of consumption is summable, and the value of input is bounded away from zero, then the program is inefficient. These, and other related results, are discussed[1] in Section 3.

---

[1] Throughout the paper results (or minor variants of these) that are available in the existing literature are stated without proofs. In each case appropriate references where the interested reader can find complete proofs, are cited.

It is quite clear that these necessity and sufficiency results are weak in content, since the class of interesting programs that can lie "in between" is rather large. However, for special technologies, which ensure that for every efficient program the sequence of the value of consumption is summable, these results provide a complete characterization of inefficiency.[2]

A second category of results relate to complete characterizations of inefficiency under fairly restrictive conditions on the technology (specifically, the curvature of the production function has to satisfy some uniformity requirements). These include the result of Cass [3] that an interior program is inefficient if and only if the sequence of the reciprocals of prices is summable. This result and its extensions by Benveniste and Gale [2] and Mitra [6] are surveyed in Section 4.

The restrictive assumptions under which these results are obtained mean that under more general circumstances they become inapplicable. More precisely, as two examples by Cass [3] demonstrate, the necessity results break down when the production function is "flat" for some range (without being flat for all ranges); and when the production function has a "kink," then the sufficiency result does not obtain.

It seems sensible, then, in view of the shortcomings of these two categories of theorems, to try to steer an intermediate course. That is, one might choose an important class of technologies and try to solve the problem stated in the first paragraph for these technologies only, but under fairly general assumptions in all other respects. This is precisely what we attempt in Section 5. We focus our attention there on "golden-rule technologies" (that is, those which admit of a golden-rule program) since this is certainly the most important and widely accepted set of technologies. It is, of course, clear that the results we expect to obtain now will be stronger than the first category of results and weaker than the second.

On the necessity side, we find that if a program is inefficient, then (a) there is a sequence of periods for which the input level of this program exceeds the golden-rule input level, and (b) the sum of the value of the difference of the input level of this program from the golden-rule input level, for the sequence of periods referred to in (a), is divergent (Theorem 5.1). The sufficiency result may be stated as follows. First, we define a variable z_t to represent the difference of the program's input level at time t from the golden-rule input level, if the former exceeds the latter; otherwise, it simply represents the

---

[2] It has been shown in Mitra [7] that under (A.1)–(A.3) and (A.4*), every efficient program has its sequence of the value of consumption summable if and only if (A.5) is satisfied. Since (A.5) excludes many interesting technologies (for example, the "golden-rule technologies" discussed in Section 5), the scope of the general necessity and sufficiency results, in providing complete characterizations of inefficiency, is clearly limited.

program's input level at time t. Then we define an "approximate price sequence," which can be made as close as we like to the usual (competitive) price sequence. If the value of z_t at such a price sequence is bounded away from zero, the program is inefficient.[3]

In providing these results in terms of the (appropriate value of the) difference of the program's input level from the golden-rule input level, we are following the lead of the famous Phelps–Koopmans theorem. In fact, a corollary of the sufficiency theorem is a simple proof of this well-known result. But there is other evidence that convinces us that these characterizations are useful. Specifically, we examine the two examples of Cass [3], referred to earlier, where (1) the results of Section 3 do not yield enough information to characterize the given programs, and (2) the results of Section 4 cannot be applied, since the assumptions under which they are proved are not satisfied. We find that our results characterize the programs in these examples very easily.

In Section 6 we look at a special case of a golden-rule technology, namely, one that is piecewise linear. This is of interest, since we are confronted with "flats" and a "kink" in the technology simultaneously, in the simplest way. The intuition gained from studying this case might provide characterizations in general "open" polyhedral models, which are scarce in the literature. Utilizing the simple structure of this technology, we are able to strengthen considerably the results of Section 5 (cf. Theorems 6.1, 6.2). The conditions of the two theorems are seen to be fairly close, but not equivalent, and this is precisely demonstrated by two examples of programs that lie "in between."

2. THE MODEL

Consider a one-good economy with a technology given by a function f from R^+ to itself. The production possibilities consist of inputs x and outputs $y = f(x)$ for $x \geq 0$.

The following assumptions on f will be used:

(A.1) $f(0) = 0$.

(A.2) f is strictly increasing for $x \geq 0$.

(A.3) f is concave for $x \geq 0$.

(A.4) f is continuous for $x \geq 0$.

---

[3] For a precise definition of two types of "approximate price sequences," see (3.8) and (5.4). For an accurate statement of the sufficiency theorem discussed here, see Theorem 5.2.

Under our assumptions, for every $x > 0$, there exists a left-hand derivative of f, denoted by $h(x)$. Also, for every $x \geq 0$, there exists a right-hand derivative of f, denoted by $g(x)$. By (A.2), $h(x) > 0$ for $x > 0$, and $g(x) > 0$ for $x \geq 0$. [$g(0)$ can, of course, be infinite.]

The initial input **x** is considered to be historically given, and positive. A *feasible production program* is a sequence $(x, y) = (x_t, y_{t+1})$ satisfying

$$x_0 = \mathbf{x}, \qquad x_t \leq y_t \quad \text{for} \quad t \geq 1, \qquad f(x_t) = y_{t+1} \quad \text{for} \quad t \geq 0 \qquad (2.1)$$

The *consumption program* $c = (c_t)$ generated by (x, y) is defined by

$$c_t = y_t - x_t (\geq 0) \qquad \text{for} \quad t \geq 1. \qquad (2.2)$$

(x, y, c) is called a *feasible program*, it being understood that (x, y) is a production program, and c is the corresponding consumption program.

A feasible program (x', y', c') *dominates* a feasible program (x, y, c) if $c'_t \geq c_t$ for all $t \geq 1$, and $c'_t > c_t$ for some t. A feasible program (x, y, c) is *inefficient* if there is a feasible program that dominates it. A feasible program is *efficient* if it is not inefficient.

We will associate with a feasible program (x, y, c) a *price sequence* $p = (p_t)$, given by[4]

$$p_0 = 1, \qquad p_{t+1} h(x_t) = p_t \quad \text{for} \quad t \geq 0 \qquad (2.3)$$

At these prices the feasible program (x, y, c) maximizes *intertemporal profits* at each date:

$$p_{t+1} f(x_t) - p_t x_t \geq p_{t+1} f(x) - p_t x, \qquad x \geq 0, \, t \geq 0 \qquad (2.4)$$

The *value of input* sequence $v = (v_t)$ associated with a feasible program (x, y, c) is given by

$$v_t = p_t x_t \qquad \text{for} \quad t \geq 0 \qquad (2.5)$$

A feasible program (x, y, c) is called *interior* if $\inf_{t \geq 0} x_t > 0$.

3. SOME GENERAL CHARACTERIZATION RESULTS

If we restrict ourselves to the minimal set of assumptions (A.1)–(A.4), what conditions can tell us whether a feasible program is inefficient or not?

---

[4] If $x_t = 0$ for some t, then we define p_{t+1} by the equation $p_{t+1} g(x_t) = p_t$, provided $g(0)$ is finite. If $g(0)$ is infinite, we follow the convention that $p_s = 0$ for $s > t$. It should be noted that given (A.1), feasible programs for which $x_t = 0$ for some finite t are not of much interest to us, since they terminate at a finite time period. This is why these details are not included in definition (2.3).

This section is devoted to answering this question. A series of interconnected results, which represent either necessary or sufficient conditions of inefficiency, are presented below. The usefulness of these general results is demonstrated by applications to special cases, where stronger assumptions than (A.1)–(A.4) are used.

We start with the following characterization result due to Cass [3].

LEMMA 3.1 (Cass) *Under (A.1) and (A.2), a feasible program (x, y, c) is inefficient iff there is a sequence (e_t) and $1 \leq t < \infty$, such that*

$$0 < e_t < x_t \qquad \text{for} \quad t \geq t \qquad (3.1)$$

$$e_{t+1} = f(x_t) - f(x_t - e_t) \qquad \text{for} \quad t \geq t \qquad (3.2)$$

Lemma 3.1 represents a complete characterization of inefficiency. However, it is clearly difficult to apply this result directly to test the inefficiency of a given feasible program, as, in a sense, it is a "redefinition" of the concept of inefficiency. Its merit lies in providing the basis from which useful characterizations may be obtained. For example, the well-known necessity theorem of inefficiency, stated below, is a direct consequence of it.

THEOREM 3.1 (Malinvaud) *Under (A.1)–(A.4), if a feasible program (x, y, c) is inefficient, then*

$$\inf_{t \geq 0} p_t x_t > 0 \qquad (3.3)$$

This theorem yields the following useful corollary:

COROLLARY 3.1 *Under (A.1)–(A.4), if a feasible program (x, y, c) satisfies*

$$\infty > \sum_{t=1}^{\infty} p_t c_t \geq \sum_{t=1}^{\infty} p_t c_t' \qquad (3.4)$$

for every feasible program (x', y', c') then it violates (3.3) and is efficient.

Turning next to sufficient conditions of inefficiency, the following theorem seems to be the most general available result.

THEOREM 3.2 (Mitra) *Under (A.1)–(A.4), if a feasible program (x, y, c) satisfies*

$$p_t x_t > 0 \qquad \text{for} \quad t \geq 0 \qquad (3.5)$$

and

$$\sum_{t=1}^{\infty} (p_t c_t / p_t y_t) < \infty \qquad (3.6)$$

then it is inefficient.

This result was established in [6] under (A.1)–(A.3) and the following additional assumption:

(A.4*) f is differentiable for $x \geq 0$.

The reader can check that the proof goes through when (A.4*) is replaced by (A.4). A useful corollary of this Theorem is

COROLLARY 3.2   *Under (A.1)–(A.4), if an efficient program satisfies*

$$\sum_{t=1}^{\infty} p_t c_t < \infty \tag{3.7}$$

then it violates (3.3) and satisfies (3.4) for every feasible program (x', y', c').

These general results can be used to obtain complete characterizations of inefficiency in special cases where additional useful properties of f are known. For example, suppose (A.1)–(A.3) and (A.4*) are satisfied. In addition, suppose the following assumption holds:

(A.5) f satisfies one of the following three conditions:

(i) $\inf_{x \geq 0} f'(x) > 1$.
(ii) $\sup_{x \geq 0} f'(x) < 1$.
(iii) $\sup_{x \geq 0} f'(x) = 1 = f'(\underline{x})$ for some $\underline{x} > 0$.

It was shown in [7] that under (A.1)–(A.3), (A.4*), and (A.5), every efficient program (x, y, c) satisfies (3.7). Hence, using Theorem 3.1 and Corollary 3.2, we have the following complete characterization:

THEOREM 3.3   *Under (A.1)–(A.3), (A.4*), and (A.5), a feasible program (x, y, c) is inefficient if and only if it satisfies (3.3).*

Particular cases of this theorem have been obtained by McFadden [4] and Benveniste [1]. In [4] the production function f is assumed to be linear; i.e., $f(x) = dx$, where $d > 0$, so that (A.1)–(A.3), (A.4*), and (A.5) are clearly satisfied. In [1] f is assumed to satisfy (A.1)–(A.3), (A.4*), and (A.5)(i).

The general necessity result (Theorem 3.1) and the general sufficiency result (Theorem 3.2) are clearly wide apart in their contents. That is, under (A.1)–(A.4), there are many feasible programs that satisfy (3.3) and are efficient, or that are inefficient and violate (3.6). Furthermore, they are not exactly "comparable," in the sense that the two statements do not yield a clear idea of the type of programs that lie "in between." Thus it seems worthwhile to have a statement of a sufficiency theorem of inefficiency, which can be directly compared and contrasted with (3.3). For this purpose the notion of an "approximate price sequence" is useful.

Given any θ, such that $0 < \theta < 1$, an *approximate price sequence of type I*, $q(\theta) = (q_t(\theta))$, is defined by[5]

$$q_0(\theta) = 1, \qquad q_{t+1}(\theta)h(x_t - \theta x_t) = q_t(\theta) \qquad \text{for} \quad t \geq 0 \qquad (3.8)$$

Notice that as $\theta \to 0$, $q_t(\theta) \to p_t$ for $t \geq 0$. We now have the following sufficiency result.

THEOREM 3.4   *Under* $(A.1)$–$(A.4)$, *if a feasible program* (x, y, c) *satisfies*

$$\inf_{t \geq 0} q_t(\theta)x_t > 0 \qquad (3.9)$$

for some $0 < \theta < 1$, *then it is inefficient.*

Proof   Suppose (x, y, c) satisfies (3.9) for some $0 < \theta < 1$. Then, there is $\hat{e} > 0$, such that $q_t(\theta)x_t \geq \hat{e}$ for $t \geq 0$. Suppose e is a number satisfying $0 < q_t(\theta)e < \theta\hat{e} \leq \theta q_t(\theta)x_t$. Then e' is well defined by $e' = f(x_t) - f(x_t - e)$, and, furthermore, e' satisfies the condition $0 < q_{t+1}(\theta)e' < \theta\hat{e} \leq \theta q_{t+1}(\theta)x_{t+1}$. To check this, note first that since $0 < e < \theta x_t, e' > 0$ by (A.2). Also,

$$\begin{aligned} q_{t+1}(\theta)e' &= q_{t+1}(\theta)[f(x_t) - e)] \\ &\leq q_{t+1}(\theta)h(x_t - e)e \leq q_{t+1}(\theta)h(x_t - \theta x_t)e \\ &= q_t(\theta)e < \theta\hat{e} \leq \theta q_{t+1}(\theta)x_{t+1}. \end{aligned}$$

Thus, if we define $e_0 = \frac{1}{2}\theta\hat{e}$, then e_{t+1}, for $t \geq 0$, is well defined by $e_{t+1} = f(x_t) - f(x_t - e_t)$. Furthermore, for $t \geq 0$, $0 < e_t < x_t$. Hence, by Lemma 3.1 (x, y, c) is inefficient. ∎

For a trivial application of Theorem 3.4, consider the case where f is linear; i.e., $f(x) = dx$ where $d > 0$. Then, if a feasible program (x, y, c) satisfies (3.3), it satisfies (3.9) for *every* $0 < \theta < 1$. Hence, it is inefficient by Theorem 3.4. Thus by Theorem 3.1 we obtain a complete characterization of inefficiency in terms of condition (3.3).

A nontrivial application of the Theorem is that it enables us to obtain the result proved in Benveniste [1]. Suppose (A.1)–(A.3), (A.4*), and (A.5)(i) are satisfied. Then, following [1], it can be shown that given any feasible program (x, y, c), we have $\sup_{t \geq 0} p_t x_t < \infty$. Suppose, now, that a feasible program satisfies (3.3); then, using the arguments in [1] again, it can be shown that there is $N < \infty$ and $n > 1$, such that $x_{t+N} \geq nx_t$ for $t \geq 0$. Hence, choosing $(1 - \theta) = (1/n)$, we have $x_{t+N}(1 - \theta) \geq x_t$ for $t \geq 0$, or $f'(x_{t+N} - \theta x_{t+N}) \leq f'(x_t)$ for $t \geq 0$. This means that for $T \geq N$, $q_T(\theta) \geq q_N(\theta)p_T$. Since (x, y, c) satisfies (3.3), it must satisfy (3.9) as well. Hence, by Theorem 3.4, it is

---

[5] The qualifications made in footnote 4 also apply to the price sequence $(q_t(\theta))$. The definition of such a price sequence is motivated by the technique of proof employed to obtain a complete characterization result in [1].

inefficient. Thus, by Theorem 3.1 we obtain a complete characterization of inefficiency in terms of condition (3.3).

4. COMPLETE CHARACTERIZATIONS IN SMOOTH TECHNOLOGIES

If we assume (A.1)–(A.3) and (A.4*), and, furthermore, impose additional conditions on the production f to ensure that its "curvature" behaves uniformly (these are called "smoothness conditions"), then we can obtain complete characterizations of inefficiency. Furthermore, such characterizations have the advantage that they are in terms of "observable magnitudes," i.e., those that can be calculated along a feasible program without knowing the function f itself.

Notice that it is really not important for the production function actually to have "curvature," but that the curvature should satisfy certain uniformity requirements. Thus, if f has positive "curvature" in some range, it should in all ranges. Similarly, if it has zero curvature in some range (that is, it is flat), then it should be flat everywhere (that is, be a linear production function).

The most important of the complete characterizations is the one presented by Cass [3] (1) because his result relates to an important class of production functions, and (2) because his technique of proof can be used to obtain general results, as the extensions by Benveniste and Gale [2] and Mitra [6] amply demonstrate.

Cass assumes that f satisfies, in addition to (A.1) and (A.2),

(C.1) f is twice continuously differentiable for $x \geq 0$.

(C.2) f is strictly concave, with $f'' < 0$ for $x \geq 0$.

(C.3) f satisfies the endpoint conditions: $0 \leq f'(\infty) < 1 < f'(\underline{x}) < \infty$ for some $\underline{x} > 0$.

His result can be stated as follows:

THEOREM 4.1   (Cass)   *Under (A.1), (A.2), and (C.1)–(C.3), an interior program (x, y, c) is inefficient if and only if*

$$\sum_{t=0}^{\infty} (1/p_t) < \infty \tag{4.1}$$

In extending this result to a wider class of production functions, as well as a wider class of feasible programs, Benveniste and Gale [2] assume:

(B.1) f is twice differentiable for $x \geq 0$.

(B.2)   There are positive numbers, E, E', Q, Q', such that

$$E \leq [f'(x)x/f(x)] \leq E', \qquad Q \leq [-f''(x)x^2/f(x)] \leq Q' \qquad \text{for} \quad x \geq 0$$

THEOREM 4.2 (Benveniste–Gale) *Under (B.1) and (B.2), a feasible program* (x, y, c) *is inefficient if and only if*

$$\sum_{t=0}^{\infty} (1/p_t x_t) < \infty \tag{4.2}$$

It should be noted that while there is considerable overlap between the functions treated by Cass and by Benveniste and Gale, there are clearly cases in which the result of Cass applies, but not that of Benveniste and Gale, and vice versa. Also, the characterizations obtained in Theorems 4.1 and 4.2 seem to be qualitatively different from the result obtained in Theorem 3.3. It therefore seems desirable to obtain a theorem that unifies these results, and this is accomplished in [6].

In order to state this result, we assume (A.1)–(A.3) and (A.4*), and define the share of primary factor in output as

$$W(x) = 1 - [f'(x)x/f(x)] \quad \text{for} \quad x > 0; \qquad W(x) = 0 \quad \text{for} \quad x = 0 \tag{4.3}$$

and consider the following smoothness condition on the feasible program (x, y, c):

CONDITION S For some $0 < m \le M < \infty$ and $0 < \theta < 1$,

$$meW(x_t)/x_t \le \{[f(x_t) - f(x_t - e)]/ef'(x_t)\} - 1$$
$$\le MeW(x_t)/x_t \quad \text{for} \quad 0 < e < \theta x_t, \quad t \ge 0$$

THEOREM 4.3 (Mitra) *Under (A.1)–(A.3) and (A.4*), a feasible program* (x, y, c) *satisfying Condition S is inefficient if and only if it satisfies (3.3) and*

$$\sum_{s=0}^{\infty} [W(x_s)/p_s x_s] < \infty \tag{4.4}$$

It should be noted that the results of Cass, Benveniste–Gale, McFadden, and Benveniste (which have been discussed above) can be obtained as corollaries of Theorem 4.3. Furthermore, Theorem 4.3 also provides a complete characterization for certain production functions that satisfy (A.1)–(A.3), (A.4*), and the assumption

(A.6) $f'(x) > 1$ for $x \ge 0$, and $\inf_{x \ge 0} f'(x) = 1$.

The criteria proposed in the earlier theorems cannot provide a complete characterization of inefficiency for such production functions. For detailed analysis of these results, the reader is referred to [6].

5. PARTIAL CHARACTERIZATIONS IN GOLDEN-RULE TECHNOLOGIES

Suppose the production function f does not satisfy the differentiability assumption (A.4*) and the uniformity requirements on its curvature, discussed in Section 4; then the complete characterization results break down, as the examples in Cass [3, pp. 221–222], and Mitra [6, Section 5] demonstrate. So without these smoothness conditions, can we do any better than the rather weak partial characterizations of Section 3? As a matter of fact, we can, if we restrict ourselves to "golden-rule technologies"—and these are certainly the most important class of technologies one would like to discuss, in any case.

Consider, then, that f satisfies (A.1)–(A.4), and the following additional assumption:

(A.7) There is $\bar{x} < \infty$, such that $f(\bar{x}) = \bar{x}$; for $0 < x < \bar{x}$, $x < f(x) < \bar{x}$; for $x > \bar{x}$, $x > f(x) > \bar{x}$.

When (A.7) holds, we call $\bar{x}$ the maximum sustainable input level. Let $C = [c \in R : c = f(x) - x, \text{ where } 0 \le x \le \bar{x}]$. Then $C \subset R^+$, C is nonempty, closed, and bounded. Hence there is $c^* \in C$ such that $c^* \ge c$ for all $c \in C$. By (A.7), $c^* > 0$. Consider, next, the set $X = [x \in R^+ : f(x) - x = c^*]$. X is nonempty by the way c^* was defined. Also, X is closed and bounded. Hence there is $x^* \in X$, such that $x^* \le x$ for all $x \in X$. We call x^* the golden-rule input level and c^* the golden-rule consumption level. Since under (A.1)–(A.4) and (A.7) we can ensure the existence of a golden-rule input level, we refer to production functions satisfying (A.1)–(A.4) and (A.7) as "golden-rule technologies." Notice that the way x^*, c^*, were defined ensure that $g(x^*) \le 1$, and given any $e > 0$, $g(x^* - e) > 1$. Also, (A.7) ensures that $h(\bar{x}) < 1$.

Given any feasible program (x, y, c), the assumptions (A.1)–(A.4) and (A.7) ensure that x_t, y_{t+1}, $c_{t+1} \le \max(\mathbf{x}, \bar{x})$ for $t \ge 0$. We associate with each feasible program (x, y, c) a sequence $z = (z_t)$, defined for $t \ge 0$ by

$$z_t = (x_t - x^*) \quad \text{if} \quad x_t > x^*, \qquad z_t = x_t \quad \text{if} \quad x_t \le x^* \qquad (5.1)$$

We can now proceed to strengthen the partial characterizations obtained in Section 3. The main point to be noted about these stronger characterizations is that they are in terms of the value of the difference of the input level of the given feasible program from the golden-rule input level. In this respect, we are of course following the lead of the famous Phelps–Koopmans theorem. In fact, we shall see that a corollary of our sufficiency condition of inefficiency is this well-known theorem. On the necessity side, we make use of the simple observation that the *existence* of a golden-rule input level ensures that there is *some* curvature of the production function near the golden-rule input level, and apply methods similar to those used when such curvature is assumed to be present to begin with—for example, in the work of Cass [3]. We start with the necessity theorem of inefficiency.

THEOREM 5.1   *Under* $(A.1)$–$(A.4)$ *and* $(A.7)$, *if a feasible program* (x, y, c) *is inefficient, then*

(i)   *condition* (3.3) *is satisfied;*

(ii)   *the periods* t_j *for which* $x_{t_j} > x^*$ *are infinite in number;*

(iii)
$$\sum_{j=0}^{J} p_{t_j}(x_{t_j} - x^*) \to \infty \quad as \quad J \to \infty. \tag{5.2}$$

Proof   If (x, y, c) is inefficient, then (i) follows from Theorem 3.1. To prove (ii) and (iii), we note that by Lemma 3.1, there is a sequence (e_t) and $1 \le \tau < \infty$, such that (3.1) and (3.2) are satisfied.

Suppose, contrary to (ii), there is $\tau \le T < \infty$, such that $x_t \le x^*$ for $t \ge T$. Then using (3.1), we have for $t \ge T$, $e_{t+1} = [f(x_t) - f(x_t - e_t)] \ge h(x_t)e_t \ge e_t$. Hence $e_t \ge e_T > 0$ for $t \ge T$. Now clearly, $\{[f(x^*) - f(x^* - e_T)]/e_T\} = k > 1$. Otherwise, if $[f(x^*) - f(x^* - e_T)] \le e_T$, then $[f(x^*) - x^*] \le [f(x^* - e_T) - (x^* - e_T)]$, which contradicts the definition of the golden-rule input level. Hence for $t \ge T$,

$$
\begin{aligned}
e_{t+1} &= \{[f(x_t) - f(x_t - e_t)]/e_t\}e_t \\
&\ge \{[f(x^*) - f(x^* - e_t)]/e_t\}e_t \\
&\ge \{[f(x^*) - f(x^* - e_T)]/e_T\}e_t \\
&= ke_t,
\end{aligned}
$$

since $e_t \ge e_T$ and $x_t \le x^*$ for $t \ge T$. Thus $e_t \to \infty$ as $t \to \infty$, which contradicts (3.2), since $0 < e_t < x_t \le \max(\mathbf{x}, \bar{x})$. Hence (ii) must hold.

Suppose, contrary to (iii), that (5.2) is violated. By (3.1), we have $e_{t+1} = f(x_t) - f(x_t - e_t) \ge h(x_t)e_t$, so that $p_{t+1}e_{t+1} \ge p_t e_t$ for $t \ge \tau$. This means that for $t \ge \tau$, $p_t e_t \ge p_\tau e_\tau = b > 0$. Since (5.2) is violated, there is $T \ge \tau$, such that for $t_j \ge T$, we have $p_{t_j}(x_{t_j} - x^*) \le \frac{1}{2}b$. Hence for $t_j \ge T$,

$$
\begin{aligned}
e_{t_j+1} &= f(x_{t_j}) - f(x_{t_j} - e_{t_j}) \\
&\ge f(x^*) - f(x_{t_j} - e_{t_j}) \\
&= f(x^*) - f[x^* + (x_{t_j} - x^*) - e_{t_j}] \\
&\ge h(x^*)[e_{t_j} - (x_{t_j} - x^*)] \\
&\ge e_{t_j}[1 - \{p_{t_j}(x_{t_j} - x^*)/p_{t_j}e_{t_j}\}] \\
&\ge e_{t_j}[1 - \{p_{t_j}(x_{t_j} - x^*)/b\}].
\end{aligned}
$$

For $t \geq T$ and $t \neq t_j$, we have $e_{t+1} = f(x_t) - f(x_t - e_t) \geq h(x_t)e_t \geq e_t$, since $x_t \leq x^*$. Hence for $t \geq 0$,

$$e_{t+T+1} \geq e_T \prod_{T \leq t_j \leq t+T} [1 - \{p_{t_j}(x_{t_j} - x^*)/b\}] \tag{5.3}$$

Since (5.2) is violated, (5.3) implies that there is $\hat{b} > 0$, such that $e_t \geq \hat{b}$ for $t \geq \tau$. Notice also that since, for $t \geq \tau$, $p_t e_t \geq b$, so $p_t x_t \geq b$. Hence, using the fact that $x_t \leq \max(\mathbf{x}, \bar{x})$, we have $\inf_{t \geq 0} p_t > 0$. This, in turn, implies that since $p_{t_j}(x_{t_j} - x^*) \to 0$ as $j \to \infty$, so $(x_{t_j} - x^*) \to 0$ as $j \to \infty$.

We observe that $\{[f(x^*) - f(x^* - \frac{1}{2}\hat{b})]/(\frac{1}{2}\hat{b})\} = \hat{k} > 1$. Otherwise, if $f(x^*) - f(x^* - \frac{1}{2}\hat{b}) \leq \frac{1}{2}\hat{b}$, then $f(x^*) - x^* \leq f(x^* - \frac{1}{2}\hat{b}) - (x^* - \frac{1}{2}\hat{b})$, which violates the definition of the golden-rule input. Choose θ such that $\frac{1}{2} < \theta < 1$ and $k' = \hat{k}\theta > 1$. Finally, choose $N \geq T$, such that for $t_j \geq N$, $(x_{t_j} - x^*) \leq \hat{b}(1 - \theta)$. Then, for $t_j \geq N$, we have

$$
\begin{aligned}
e_{t_j+1} &= f(x_{t_j}) - f(x_{t_j} - e_{t_j}) \\
&\geq f(x^*) - f[x^* + (x_{t_j} - x^*) - e_{t_j}] \\
&\geq f(x^*) - f[x^* + e_{t_j}(1 - \theta) - e_{t_j}] \\
&= f(x^*) - f(x^* - \theta e_{t_j}) \\
&= \{[f(x^*) - f(x^* - \theta e_{t_j})]/\theta e_{t_j}\}\theta e_{t_j} \\
&\geq \{[f(x^*) - f(x^* - \theta\hat{b})]/\theta\hat{b}\}\theta e_{t_j} \\
&\geq \{[f(x^*) - f(x^* - \frac{1}{2}\hat{b})]/(\frac{1}{2}\hat{b})\}\theta e_{t_j} \\
&\geq \hat{k}\theta e_{t_j} = k'e_{t_j}.
\end{aligned}
$$

For $t \geq N$ and $t \neq t_j$, we have already noted that $e_{t+1} \geq e_t$. Hence, using the fact that $k' > 1$ and the result of (ii), we have $e_t \to \infty$ as $t \to \infty$, which contradicts (3.2), since $0 < e_t < x_t \leq \max(\mathbf{x}, \bar{x})$. Hence (iii) must hold. ∎

It was indicated earlier that a reason for obtaining the necessity result of Theorem 5.1 was that the characterization of Theorem 3.1 was too weak, while the characterizations of Section 4 were obtained under too strong a set of assumptions. The example of Cass [3, p. 221] illustrates this point very well, for there Theorem 3.1 does not yield enough useful information to judge the given feasible program to be efficient, while Theorems 4.1–4.3 give the wrong answer if they are used, since the assumptions under which they are proved no longer hold. Thus, a test of the usefulness of Theorem 5.1 is surely its capability of characterizing the feasible program of this example.

Following Cass, suppose f has a kink at x^*, such that $h(x^*) > 1 > g(x^*)$, and for $x \neq x^*$, f is differentiable. Also, f satisfies (A.1)–(A.4) and (A.7). Consider the feasible program (x, y, c) from $\mathbf{x} > x^*$, defined by $(x_{t+1} - x^*) =$

$\theta f'(x_t)(x_t - x^*)$ for $t \geq 0$, with $0 < \theta < 1$. Then, $x_t > x^*$, and

$$p_{t+1}(x_{t+1} - x^*) = \theta p_t(x_t - x^*)$$

for $t \geq 0$. Hence, $p_t(x_t - x^*) = \theta^t(x - x^*)$ for $t \geq 0$, so that (5.2) is violated. Thus, by Theorem 5.1, (x, y, c) is efficient. Notice that since (3.3) is satisfied, so Theorem 3.1 is not able to characterize (x, y, c) as efficient. Also, (4.1), (4.2), and (4.4) are all satisfied, even though (x, y, c) is efficient.

We turn our attention, now, to the sufficiency theorem. For this purpose, as for Theorem 3.4, the notion of an "approximate price sequence" is useful. Given any θ, such that $0 < \theta < 1$, define an *approximate price sequence of type II*, $r(\theta) = (r_t(\theta))$, by[6]

$$r_0(\theta) = 1, \qquad r_{t+1}(\theta)h(x_t - \theta z_t) = r_t(\theta) \qquad \text{for} \quad t \geq 0 \qquad (5.4)$$

THEOREM 5.2   *Under $(A.1)$–$(A.4)$ and $(A.7)$, if a feasible program (x, y, c) satisfies*

$$\inf_{t \geq 0} r_t(\theta)z_t > 0 \qquad (5.5)$$

for some $0 < \theta < 1$, then it is inefficient.

Proof   Suppose (x, y, c) satisfies (5.5) for some $0 < \theta < 1$. Then, there is $\hat{e} > 0$, such that $r_t(\theta)z_t \geq \hat{e}$ for $t \geq 0$. Suppose e is a number satisfying $0 < r_t(\theta)e < \theta\hat{e} \leq \theta r_t(\theta)z_t$. Then, e' is well defined by $e' = f(x_t) - f(x_t - e)$, and, furthermore, e' satisfies the condition $0 < r_{t+1}(\theta)e' < \theta\hat{e} \leq \theta r_{t+1}(\theta)z_{t+1}$. To check this, note first that since $0 < e < \theta z_t$, so by (A.2), $e' > 0$. Also,

$$r_{t+1}(\theta)e' = r_{t+1}(\theta)[f(x_t) - f(x_t - e)]$$
$$\leq r_{t+1}(\theta)h(x_t - e)e \leq r_{t+1}(\theta)h(x_t - \theta z_t)e$$
$$= r_t(\theta)e < \theta\hat{e} \leq \theta r_{t+1}(\theta)z_{t+1}.$$

Thus, if we define $e_0 = \frac{1}{2}\theta\hat{e}$, then e_{t+1}, for $t \geq 0$, is well defined by $e_{t+1} = f(x_t) - f(x_t - e_t)$. Also, $0 < e_t < z_t \leq x_t$ for $t \geq 0$. Hence by Lemma 3.1, (x, y, c) is inefficient. ∎

It should be noted that when (3.9) is not satisfied, (5.5) may still be satisfied, and vice versa. Hence Theorem 5.2 is more useful in certain circumstances than Theorem 3.4. For example, suppose $f(x) = 2x^{1/2}$ for $x \geq 0$. Then, $x^* = 1$ and $\bar{x} = 4$. Consider the feasible program (x, y, c) from $[2(11/10)^4 - 1]$, given by $x_t = \{2[(t + 11)/(t + 10)]^4 - 1\}$ for $t \geq 0$. Choosing $\theta = \frac{1}{2}$, we note that $r_t(\theta) = [(t + 10)/10]^2$ for $t \geq 0$, and $z_t \geq [1/(t + 10)]$ for $t \geq 0$; so (5.5)

---

[6] The comments of footnote 4 apply to this price sequence as well.

is satisfied, and (x, y, c) is inefficient. However, since $x_t \to x^* = 1$ as $t \to \infty$, so given any θ, such that $0 < \theta < 1$, $q_t(\theta) \to 0$ as $t \to \infty$, violating (3.9).[7]

Another test of the usefulness of Theorem 5.2 is its capability of characterizing the program in the example of Cass [3, p. 222], where, once again, the results of Section 4 are inapplicable, since the assumptions under which they are established are violated. Consider, following Cass, that f satisfies (A.1)–(A.3), (A.4*), and (A.7), and has a flat for some range of $x \geq x^*$. More precisely, $f'(x) > 1$ for $0 \leq x < x^*$, $f'(x) = 1$ for $x^* \leq x \leq \bar{\bar{x}} < \bar{x}$, and $f'(x) < 1$ for $x > \bar{\bar{x}}$. The feasible program (x, y, c) given by $x_t = \mathbf{x}$, with $x^* < \mathbf{x} \leq \bar{\bar{x}}$, clearly satisfies (5.5) for any θ, such that $0 < \theta < 1$, and is, therefore, inefficient by Theorem 5.2. Notice, however, that the conditions (4.1), (4.2), and (4.4) are all violated by this program.

As a final test, we show that the Phelps–Koopmans theorem can be obtained as a corollary of Theorem 5.2. It should be noted that this result is proved in Phelps [8] and Cass [3] under stronger sets of assumptions than (A.1)–(A.4) and (A.7).

COROLLARY 5.1   (Phelps–Koopmans)   *Under (A.1)–(A.4) and (A.7), if a feasible program (x, y, c) satisfies*

$$\liminf_{t \to \infty} x_t > x^* \qquad (5.6)$$

then it is inefficient.

Proof   If (x, y, c) satisfies (5.6), then there is $e > 0$, and $0 \leq t' < \infty$ such that $(x_t - x^*) \geq e$ for $t \geq t'$. Then, for any θ, such that $0 < \theta < 1$, we have $h(x_t - \theta z_t) = h[x_t(1 - \theta) + \theta x^*] \leq g(x^*) \leq 1$ for $t \geq t'$, since $x_t > x^*$ for $t \geq t'$. Hence $r_t(\theta) \geq r_{t'}(\theta)$ for $t \geq t'$, so that (5.5) is satisfied. Hence, by Theorem 5.2, (x, y, c) is inefficient.   ∎

6.   A SPECIAL CASE OF FLATS AND KINKS

A case of interest among golden-rule technologies is a production function that is piecewise linear. In such a case the golden-rule input level occurs at a kink between two linear sections (alternatively, at a "switching point" between two techniques of production). Viewed as a special case of the production functions discussed in previous sections, it is of interest because here we have, simultaneously, the problem of the "flats" and that of the "kink." Viewed as a particular case of an "open" von Neumann model (where primary factors, exogenously supplied, limit production), it is of interest

---

[7] For an example of a case where Theorem 3.4 is more useful than Theorem 5.2, see Example 6.2 below.

since characterizations of inefficiency in open polyhdral models are relatively scarce in the literature.

We will consider the simplest case of piecewise linear technologies.[8] Specifically, we will assume that f satisfies.

(A.8) $f(x) = \min(ax, dx + n)$ for $x \geq 0$, where $a > 1$, $0 < d < 1$, $n > 0$.

Under (A.8), the golden-rule input level $x^* = [n/(a - d)]$, and the maximum sustainable input level $\bar{x} = [n/(1 - d)]$.

If we define a capital-input-coefficients matrix $A = [n/(a - d), n/(1 - d)]$, a labor-coefficients matrix $L = [1, 1]$, and a capital-output-coefficients matrix $B = [an/(a - d), n/(1 - d)]$, and if the amount of labor exogenously supplied is stationary and normalized to unity, then the technological possibilities are given by the set

$$\mathcal{T} = [(x, y) \in R_+^2 : Az \leq x, Lz \leq 1, Bz \geq y, \text{ for some } z \in R_+^2].$$

This is easily recognized as a simple open von Neumann model. The technological possibilities given by $\mathcal{T}$ coincide exactly with those specified by (A.8).

The necessity result of Theorem 5.1 [specifically, condition (iii)] can be strengthened under this simple structure, mainly because the curvature near the golden-rule input level can be more easily exploited.

THEOREM 6.1   *Under (A.8), if a feasible program (x, y, c) is inefficient, then*

(i)   *condition (3.3) is satisfied;*

(ii)   *the periods t_j, for which $x_{t_j} > x^*$, are infinite in number;*

(iii)
$$\limsup_{j \to \infty} p_{t_j}(x_{t_j} - x^*) > 0 \tag{6.1}$$

Proof   Since (A.8) implies that (A.1)–(A.4) and (A.7) are satisfied, so (i) and (ii) follow from Theorem 5.1.

To prove (iii), suppose, on the contrary, that (6.1) is violated. Note that if (x, y, c) is inefficient, then there is a sequence (e_t) and $1 \leq \tau < \infty$, such that (3.1) and (3.2) are satisfied. Then $e_{t+1} = f(x_t) - f(x_t - e_t) \geq h(x_t)e_t$, so that $p_{t+1}e_{t+1} \geq p_t e_t$ for $t \geq \tau$. Hence $p_t e_t \geq p_\tau e_\tau = b > 0$ for $t \geq \tau$. Since (6.1) is

---

[8] It is possible to generalize from the simple case, involving two flat sections and a kink at the golden-rule input level, to any (finite) number of flat sections. The results become somewhat more complicated to state and are, therefore, omitted. It should be mentioned, in this connection, that since any smooth technology can be accurately approximated by piecewise linear technologies, it is of interest to know whether characterizations of inefficiency in the latter "approach" those in the former (in some appropriate sense) as individual flat sections become small, but the number of flats become infinitely large.

is violated, there is $T \geq \tau$, such that for $t_j \geq T$, we have $p_{t_j}(x_{t_j} - x^*) \leq \frac{1}{2}[(a-1)/(a-d)]p_{t_j}e_{t_j}$. Now, since $x_{t_j} > x^*$, so $f(x_{t_j}) = dx_{t_j} + n$; also, $[(x_{t_j} - x^*)/e_{t_j}] \leq \frac{1}{2}[(a-1)/(a-d)] < 1$; so $(x_{t_j} - e_{t_j}) < x^*$ and $f(x_{t_j} - e_{t_j}) = a(x_{t_j} - e_{t_j})$. Hence, for $t_j \geq T$,

$$
\begin{aligned}
e_{t_j+1} &= \{[f(x_{t_j}) - f(x_{t_j} - e_{t_j})]/e_{t_j}\}e_{t_j} \\
&= \{[f(x_{t_j}) - f(x^*) + f(x^*) - f(x_{t_j} - e_{t_j})]/e_{t_j}\}e_{t_j} \\
&= \{[d(x_{t_j} - x^*) + a(x^* - x_{t_j} + e_{t_j})]/e_{t_j}\}e_{t_j} \\
&= \{a - [(a-d)(x_{t_j} - x^*)/e_{t_j}]\}e_{t_j} \\
&\geq [a - \tfrac{1}{2}(a-1)]e_{t_j} = \tfrac{1}{2}(a+1)e_{t_j}
\end{aligned}
$$

since $(x_{t_j} - x^*) \leq \frac{1}{2}[(a-1)/(a-d)]e_{t_j}$. Also, for $t \geq T$, $t \neq t_j$, $e_{t+1} = f(x_t) - f(x_t - e_t) \geq h(x_t)e_t = ae_t$. Hence, for all $t \geq T$, $e_{t+1} \geq \frac{1}{2}(a+1)e_t$, which implies that $e_t \to \infty$ as $t \to \infty$. This contradicts (3.2), since $0 < e_t < x_t \leq \max(\mathbf{x}, \bar{x})$. ∎

The usefulness of Theorem 5.2 is demonstrated, once again, as we can obtain from it a sufficiency theorem in terms of conditions that are "fairly close" to those proved in the necessity theorem above.

THEOREM 6.2   *Under* $(A.8)$, *if for a feasible program* (x, y, c)

(i)   *condition* (3.3) *is satisfied,*
(ii)   *the periods* t_j, *for which* $x_{t_j} > x^*$, *are infinite in number, and*

(iii) $\liminf\limits_{j \to \infty} p_{t_j}(x_{t_j} - x^*) > 0$ (6.2)

then (x, y, c) *is inefficient.*

Proof   By (i)–(iii), there is $e > 0$, such that $p_t x_t \geq e$ for $t \geq 0$, and $p_{t_j}(x_{t_j} - x^*) \geq e$ for $j \geq 0$. Thus, for any θ, such that $0 < \theta < 1$, we have $h(x_t - \theta z_t) = h(x_t)$ for $t \geq 0$. Hence, for $t \geq 0$, $r_t(\theta)z_t = p_t z_t \geq e$, so that (5.5) is satisfied. Hence, by Theorem 5.2, (x, y, c) is inefficient. ∎

The conditions in Theorems 6.1 and 6.2 are not equivalent.[9] To clarify the difference, we will exhibit programs that lie "in between." First, we give an example of an efficient program that satisfies the necessary conditions of inefficiency of Theorem 6.1. Then we give an example of an inefficient

---

[9] It is possible to obtain some stronger necessary conditions and weaker sufficiency conditions than those stated in Theorems 6.1 and 6.2, respectively. These are still not equivalent sets of conditions, and they add significantly to the complexity of the results; so we chose to omit them.

program, that does not satisfy the sufficient conditions of inefficiency of Theorem 6.2.

EXAMPLE 6.1   Let $a = 6, d = (1/3), n = (17/3)$. Then $x^* = 1, \bar{x} = (17/2)$. Consider the feasible program (x, y, c) from $\mathbf{x} = 2$, defined by $x_t = 2$ for t odd (called t_i) and by $x_t = 1 + (\frac{1}{4})^t$ for t even (called t_j). Hence $x_t > x^*$ for $t \geq 0$, so that $p_t = 3^t$ for $t \geq 0$. Thus conditions (i) and (ii) of Theorem 6.1 are satisfied. Also, $p_{t_i}(x_{t_i} - x^*) \to \infty$ as $t_i \to \infty$; so condition (iii) of Theorem 6.1 is also satisfied. However, (x, y, c) is efficient. To verify this, suppose it were not. Then, there is a sequence (e_t) and $1 \leq \tau < \infty$, such that (3.1) and (3.2) hold. Since $p_{t_j} z_{t_j} \to 0$ as $t_j \to \infty$, so by applying an argument identical to that in Theorem 6.1, there is T, such that for $t_j \geq T$, $z_{t_j} \leq \frac{1}{2}[(a - 1)/(a - d)]e_{t_j}$ and $e_{t_j+1} \geq \frac{1}{2}(a + 1)e_{t_j} = (\frac{7}{2})e_{t_j}$. For $t_i \geq 0$, we have $e_{t_i+1} \geq (\frac{1}{3})e_{t_i}$. Hence $e_t \to \infty$ as $t \to \infty$, which contradicts (3.2), since $0 < e_t < x_t \leq \max(\mathbf{x}, \bar{x})$.

EXAMPLE 6.2   Let $a = 3, d = (\frac{1}{4}), n = (\frac{8}{3})$. Then $x^* = 1, \bar{x} = 4$. Consider the feasible program (x, y, c) from $\mathbf{x} = 2$, defined by $x_t = 2$ for t odd (called t_i) and by $x_t = 1 + (\frac{1}{4})^t$ for t even (called t_j). Then $x_t > x^*$ for $t \geq 0$, so that $p_t = 3^t$ for $t \geq 0$. Thus conditions (i) and (ii) of Theorem 6.2 are satisfied. Also, $p_{t_j}(x_{t_j} - x^*) \to 0$ as $t_j \to \infty$; so condition (iii) of Theorem 6.2 is not satisfied. However the program is inefficient. To check this, let $\theta = (\frac{3}{4})$, and notice that $h(x_0 - \theta x_0) = (\frac{1}{3})$, $h(x_t - \theta x_t) = (\frac{1}{3})$ for t odd, and $h(x_t - \theta x_t) = 3$ for t even. Hence (3.9) is satisfied, so that by Theorem 3.4, (x, y, c) is inefficient. Incidentally, this example also illustrates the fact that Theorem 3.4 may be applicable in some cases where Theorem 5.2 is not applicable.

REFERENCES

1. Benveniste, L. M., Two notes on the Malinvaud condition for efficiency of infinite horizon programs, *J. Econ. Theory* **12** (1976), 338–346.
2. Benveniste, L. M., and Gale, D., An extension of Cass' Characterisation of infinite efficient production programs, *J. Econ. Theory* **10** (1975), 229–238.
3. Cass, D., On capital overaccumulation in the aggregative neoclassical model of economic growth: A complete characterisation, *J. Econ. Theory* **4** (1972), 200–223.
4. McFadden, D., The evaluation of development programs, *Rev. Econ. Stud.* **34** (1967), 25–50.
5. Malinvaud, E., Capital accumulation and efficient allocation of resources, *Econometrica* **21** (1953), 233–268.
6. Mitra, T., Identifying inefficiency in smooth aggregative models of economic growth: A unifying criterion, *J. Math. Econ.* (1979) (forthcoming).
7. Mitra, T., On the Value-Maximising Property of Infinite Horizon Efficient Programs, *International Economic Review* (1979).
8. Phelps, E. S., Second essay on the golden rule of accumulation, *Am. Econ. Rev.* **55** (1965), 793–814.

This research was inspired by comments received from David Cass, Lionel McKenzie, and José Scheinkman, on an earlier paper of one of the authors, when it was presented at the MSSB Conference held at the Dartmouth College Conference Center in May 1977. In preparing the present version, we have benefited from conversations with Mukul Majumdar and Ronald Jones.

Lawrence M. Benveniste   *Tapan Mitra*
DEPARTMENT OF ECONOMICS   DEPARTMENT OF ECONOMICS
UNIVERSITY OF ROCHESTER   STATE UNIVERSITY OF NEW YORK
ROCHESTER, NEW YORK   AT STONY BROOK
                                  STONY BROOK, NEW YORK

Notes on Comparative Dynamics

ALOISIO P. DE ARAUJO

JOSÉ ALEXANDRE SCHEINKMAN

1. INTRODUCTION

In our previous paper [1] we set up the problem of comparing solutions to dynamic optimization problems in a framework similar to the comparative statics exercises in economics. We also showed how this problem was related to the so-called turnpike property. We did not, however, develop any "comparative dynamics" results. These notes go part way toward filling this gap. In the next section, for the sake of completeness, we redevelop the model used in Araujo and Scheinkman [1]. In Section 3 we prove a rather general "negative-definiteness" property of "stable" models. In Section 4 we use a sharper version of the dominant diagonal assumption used in Araujo and Scheinkman [1] to produce more precise comparative dynamics results. That such results were to be expected was obvious from the previous literature on dominant diagonal matrices, to which Lionel McKenzie made a fundamental contribution [7]. We then apply the results to an adjustment cost model due to Lucas [6] and are able to sign the changes in capital stocks caused by changes in certain basic parameters as the cost of investment goods and output price. In Section 5 we make an additional remark exploring an assumption on the matrix of second derivatives of V, used previously by Brock and Scheinkman to prove "turnpike"-type results (see Brock and Scheinkman [3]).

Results concerning comparison of solutions in economics tends to be rather restrictive. Ours are not less so. It should be pointed out, however, that our objective here is merely to present some theorems which may be

217

derived within this framework, without any attempt to be complete. Thus, we hope that others will be able to choose their own assumptions to derive similar results. In particular, we restrict ourselves to fixed discount factor models even though the results in Araujo and Scheinkman [1] have been generalized to the nonstationary case by McKenzie [8]. This latter case is especially interesting for economic problems, since it permits the study of parameter changes that affect the "utility function" for only a few periods as, for instance, a temporary investment tax credit would. It should be also noted that there are, of course, many other ways to obtain comparative dynamics results,[1] as well as stronger theorems concerning the behavior of stationary solutions (as in Brock [2]).

2. THE MODEL

We consider a class of discrete time maximization models of the type

$$P(k_0, \delta, \alpha) = \max_{\{k_t\}} \sum_{t=0}^{\infty} \delta^t V(k_t, k_{t+1}, \alpha),$$

subject to k_0 given

$$(k_t, k_{t+1}) \in A$$

where

$$V: A \times \mathscr{A} \to R, \qquad A \subset R_+^{2n}.$$

---

[1] For instance, from the Bellman equation if the value function W is C^2,

$$W(\hat{k}_0) = \max_{k_1} [V(\hat{k}_0, k_1) + \delta W(k_1)]$$

and hence

$$\frac{\partial V}{\partial k_1}(\hat{k}_0, k_1) + \frac{\delta \partial W}{\partial k_1}(\hat{k}_1) = 0.$$

If V is strongly concave (and hence W is concave) and C^2, we may conclude from the implicit function theorem that

$$\frac{\partial \hat{k}_1}{\partial \hat{k}_0} = -\left[\frac{\partial^2 V}{\partial k_1^2}(\hat{k}_0, k_1) + \frac{\partial^2 W}{\partial k_1^2}(\hat{k}_1)\right]^{-1} \frac{\partial^2 V(\hat{k}_0, k_1)}{\partial k_0 \, \partial k_1}.$$

Thus,

$$[\partial^2 V(\hat{k}_0, \hat{k}_1)/\partial \hat{k}_0 \, \partial \hat{k}_1]^T (\partial \hat{k}_1/\partial \hat{k}_0)$$

is semipositive definite. Obviously for a fixed V this establishes restrictions on the "policy function."

Here A is a convex bounded set with nonempty interior $\mathring{A}$, and $\mathscr{A} \subset R^s$ (the set of possible parameter values) is assumed to be open.

For each fixed *parameter value* $\alpha \in a$, $P(k_0, \delta, \alpha)$ is a rather general optimization problem.

Let $V_\alpha: A \to R$ denote function given by $V_\alpha(x, y) = V(x, y, \alpha)$. We will now state some needed assumptions.

ASSUMPTION 2.1 V is C^2 (i.e, at least twice continuously differentiable) on $A \times \mathscr{A}$. For each $\alpha \in \mathscr{A}$, V_α is strictly concave and $D^2 V_\alpha$ is negative definite in $\mathring{A}$.

Under Assumption 2.1 for each $\alpha \in \mathscr{A}$, the solution to $P(k_0, \delta, \alpha)$, if it exists, is unique. From now on we will denote by $k(k_0, \delta, \alpha)$ such an optimal solution, if it exists. We will need the following definitions:

DEFINITION 2.1 l_∞^n is the space of all sequences $k = (k_t)_{t=1}^\infty$ with $k_t \in R^n$, with finite "sup norm" $\|k\| = \sup_{t=1,2,\dots} |k_t|$, where $|k_t|$ denotes any of the equivalent norms of R^n.

DEFINITION 2.2 A path $\{k_t\}_{t=0}^\infty$ is feasible if $(k_t, k_{t+1}) \in A$ for all $t = 0, 1, 2, \dots$. We will denote by τ the set of all feasible paths. Since A is bounded, $\tau \subset l_\infty^n$.

DEFINITION 2.3 A point $(k_0, k) \in \tau$ is called a regular path if $(k_0, k) \in \mathring{\tau}$. In other words, a path is regular if it is feasible, and there exists $\varepsilon > 0$ such that $\inf_{t=0,1,2,\dots} d_H[(k_t, k_{t+1}), \partial A] > \varepsilon$ where d_H denotes the Haussdorff distance (i.e., if $x \in R^p$, $U \subset R^p$, $d_H(x, U) = \inf\{|x - y|, y \in U\}$), and ∂A is the boundary of A.)

In order to simplify the notation, we will denote by V_1 the vector of partial derivatives of V with respect to the first n coordinates of R^{2n}, and by V_2 the vector of partial derivatives of V with respect to the last n coordinates of R^{2n}. We will denote by V_{ij}, $i = 1, 2; j = 1, 2$, the matrices of partial derivatives of V_i, $i = 1, 2$.

Let us define the map

$$\xi: \mathring{\tau} \times (0, 1) \times \mathscr{A} \to l_\infty^n$$

by

$$[\xi(k_0, k, \delta, \alpha)]_t = V_2(k_{t-1}, k_t, \alpha) + \delta V_1(k_t, k_{t+1}, \alpha).$$

Note that for fixed (δ, α), ξ maps a regular path into the left-hand side of the familiar Euler difference equation system.

In Araujo and Scheinkman [1] we showed that a regular path solves $P(k_\alpha, \delta, \alpha)$ if and only if[2]

$$\xi(k_0, k, \delta, \alpha) = 0. \tag{2.1}$$

Equation (2.1), except for the fact that it involves an infinite number of variables, is just like any of the familiar first-order equilibrium conditions in economics. As in the static literature, one may use the implicit function theorem (cf. Cartan [5] for a version that is appropriate for our purposes), together with negative definiteness, diagonal dominance, and/or sign restrictions on elements of the appropriate matrix, to derive results concerning comparison of solutions. In Araujo and Scheinkman [1] we showed that if Assumption 2.1 above holds, ξ is a continuously differentiable function.[3] Hence if $\beta = (\delta, \alpha)$ and at $(\overline{k}_0, \overline{\beta})$, $D\xi_k(\overline{k}_0, k(\overline{k}_0, \overline{\beta}), \overline{\beta})$ is a linear isomorphism (i.e., a one-to-one and onto continuous linear map), there exists open sets $W \subset R^n \times (0, 1) \times \mathscr{A}$ with $(\overline{k}_0, \overline{\beta}) \in W$ and $U \subset \mathring{t} \times (0, 1) \times \mathscr{A}$ such that if $(k_0, \beta) \in W$ there exists unique $\psi(k_0, \beta) \in l_\infty^n$ such that

$$(k_0, \psi(k_0, \beta), \beta) \in U \text{ and } \xi(k_0, \psi(k_0, \beta), \beta) = 0.$$

Furthermore ψ is a C^1 function and for $(k_0, \beta) \in W$

$$D_\beta\psi(k_0, \beta) = -[D_k\xi(k_0, \psi(k_0, \beta), \beta)]^{-1} \cdot D_\beta\xi(k_0, \psi(k_0, \beta), \beta), \tag{2.2}$$

and a similar formula holds for $D_{k_0}\psi(k_0, \beta)$.

Since $\psi(k_0, \beta)$ is a regular path that solves (2.1), we have by the observation made above that $\psi(k_0, \beta) = k(k_0, \beta)$. Hence (2.2) may be used to sign first-order changes in the entire optimal path when a parameter is changed provided, we may sign the elements of $[D_k\xi]^{-1}$.

In [1] we also showed that the existence of an inverse for $D_k\xi$ "is equivalent to" the turnpike property.[4] Hence in general this inverse may not exist. We also proposed dominant diagonal conditions that imply the existence of the inverse.

---

[2] The proof in Araujo and Scheinkman [1] requires the boundedness of feasible paths, which was not assumed explicitly there. For this reason we assume here that A is bounded. Alternatively, of course, we may assume that there exists M such that if

$$|x| > M \quad \text{then} \quad |y| < |x| \quad \text{for all } y \quad \text{such that} \quad (x, y) \in A.$$

[3] In Araujo and Scheinkman [1] we did not consider V as a function of α. However with the obvious changes the proof goes through.

[4] More precisely we showed that the existence of the inverse implies "Liapunov" stability of the optimal paths. In particular if a locally asymptotically stable stationary state exists, then global asymptotic stability must hold. Conversely, if the turnpike property holds and the linearization around the stationary state is stable, then the inverse exists.

In the next section we explore the implications of the existence of $[D_k\xi]^{-1}$, and in Sections 4 and 5 the implications of particular assumptions that imply the existence of the inverse.

3. A GENERAL RESULT

We start by proving a result that holds whenever $[D_k\xi]^{-1}$ exists.

THEOREM 3.1   For the model of Section 2, if $[D_k\xi(k_0, k(k_0, \beta), \beta)]$ is a linear isomorphism, then if λ is a one-dimensional parameter of $P(k_0, \beta)$,

$$\infty > \sum_{t=1}^{\infty} \delta^t [D_\lambda k(k_0, \beta)]_t [D_\lambda \xi(k_0, k(k_0, \beta), \beta)]_t \geqq 0.$$

Proof   From (2.2) we may write, omitting the arguments where clarity is not lost, $D_\lambda k = -(D_k\xi)^{-1} D_\lambda \xi$. Hence $D_k\xi \cdot D_\lambda k = -D_\lambda \xi$. Therefore

$$\sum_{t=1}^{\infty} \delta^t D_\lambda k_t \cdot (D_k\xi \cdot D_\lambda k)_t = -\sum_{t=1}^{\infty} \delta^t D_\lambda k_t (D_\lambda \xi)_t, \tag{3.1}$$

where those sums converge since $\delta < 1$ and all derivatives belong to l^n_∞.

Let $V_{ij}(t) = V_{ij}(k_{t-1}, k_t)$. Then the left-hand side of (3.1) may be expressed as

$$\delta D_\lambda k_1 [V_{22}(1) + \delta V_{11}(2)] D_\lambda k_1 + \delta^2 D_\lambda k_1 V_{12}(2) D_\lambda k_2 + \delta^2 D_\lambda k_2 V_{21}(2) D_\lambda k_1$$
$$+ \delta^2 D_\lambda k_2 [V_{22}(2) + \delta V_{11}(3)] D_\lambda k_2 + \delta^3 D_\lambda k_2 V_{12}(3) D_\lambda k_3 + \cdots$$
$$= \delta D_\lambda k_1 V_{22}(1) D_\lambda k_1 + \sum_{t=2}^{\infty} \delta^t [D_\lambda k_{t-1}, D_\lambda k_t] \begin{bmatrix} V_{11}(t) & V_{12}(t) \\ V_{21}(t) & V_{22}(t) \end{bmatrix} \begin{bmatrix} D_\lambda k_{t-1} \\ D_\lambda k_t \end{bmatrix} \leqq 0$$

by the negative definiteness of $D^2 V$.   Q.E.D.

Theorem 3.1 may be compared with results on the question of Burmeister–Turnovsky "paradoxical" optimal stationary states (cf. Burmeister and Turnovsky [4]). A stationary state is called "nonparadoxical" if

$$D_\delta k^*(\delta) \cdot V_1(k^*(\delta), k^*(\delta)) \geqq 0 \tag{3.2}$$

where $k^*(\delta)$ denotes the optimal stationary state associated with the discount factor δ. Equation (3.2) then states that the value of the change in the steady-state capital stock corresponding to an increase in the discount factor is positive. If the model is strongly globally asymptotically stable,[5] it follows

---

[5] That is, it is globally asymptotically stable, and the linearization around the stationary state is stable.

from the results in Araujo and Scheinkman [1] that $D_k\xi$ is a linear isomorphism. Also $D_\delta\xi = V_1$. Hence

$$\sum_{t=1}^{\infty} \delta^t D_\delta k_t \cdot V_1(t) \geqq 0.$$

If $k_0 = k^*(\bar\delta)$, then we may conclude from the theorem that

$$\sum_{t=1}^{\infty} \delta^t D_\delta k_t \cdot V_1(k^*(\bar\delta), k^*(\bar\delta)) \geqq 0; \tag{3.3}$$

i.e., the discounted value of the capital stock is increased when the discount factor is increased. Even if we had assumed that the model is C' stable, i.e.,

$$\lim_{t \to \infty} D_\delta k_t = D_\delta k^*(\bar\delta),$$

the Burmeister–Turnovsky quantity would appear in (3.3) but multiplied by δ^t for t very large. This explains why a steady state may be Burmeister–Turnovsky paradoxical in stable systems, while (3.3) always holds.

4. A RESULT INVOLVING DIAGONAL DOMINANCE

In the general equilibrium theory the dominant diagonal assumption was frequently used to allow one to "sign" the impact of a change of a parameter in the solution (see, e.g., McKenzie [7]). In this section we show how the dominant diagonal, coupled with restriction on the sign of elements of the matrix $D_k\xi$, can give us comparative dynamics information. We start with a definition taken from Araujo and Scheinkman [1].

DEFINITION 4.1   Let A be an infinite matrix written as a collection of $m \times m$ blocks $A_{ij}, i = 1, 2, \ldots ; j = 1, 2, \ldots$, with $\sup_i \sum_j |A_{ij}|_1 < \infty$. A has dominant diagonal by blocks if

(a) $\sup|A_{ii}^{-1}|_1 < \infty$,

(b) $\sup_i \sum_{j \neq i} |A_{ii}^{-1} A_{ij}|_1 < 1$,

where for any $m \times m$ matrix B, $|B|_1 = \sup_{|x| = 1, x \in R^m} |Bx|$ and $|\ |$ is any norm in R^m.

Remark   In [1] we proved that if A has dominant diagonal by blocks, A^{-1} exists.

The following lemma is analogous to a well-known result on square matrices (see, e.g., McKenzie [7]). Here we write $A \geqq 0 \ (\leqq)$ for a matrix A if each entry of A is $\geqq 0 \ (\leqq 0)$.

LEMMA 4.1   Let A be an infinite matrix written as a collection of $m \times m$ blocks A_{ij}, $i = 1, 2, \ldots$, with $\sup_i \sum |A_{ij}|_1 < \infty$. If A has dominant diagonal by blocks with $A_{ii}^{-1} \leq 0$ and $A_{ij} \geq 0$ for $j \neq i$, then $A^{-1} \leq 0$.

Proof   Let Γ be an infinite matrix of $m \times m$ blocks with $\Gamma_{ii} = A_{ii}^{-1}$ and $\Gamma_{ij} = 0$ for $i \neq j$. Then as is shown in Araujo and Scheinkman [1], we may write $(\Gamma A)^{-1} = \sum_{n=1}^{\infty} (I - \Gamma A)^n$. Since $A_{ii}^{-1} \leq 0$ and $(\Gamma A)_{ii} = I$, we must have $(I - \Gamma A) \geq 0$. Hence $(\Gamma A)^{-1} \geq 0$. Since $A^{-1} = (\Gamma A)^{-1}\Gamma$ and $\Gamma \leq 0$, we have $A^{-1} \leq 0$.   Q.E.D.

Lemma 4.1 may be applied to an adjustment cost model that is essentially as in Lucas [6]. A firm produces an output that is sold at a price p^0. It uses n capital goods that are denoted $k^1 \cdots k^n$. Capital good i costs p^i per unit and depreciates at constant rate η^i, and the firm also faces costs of adjustment g^i, which is a function of $k_{t+1}^i - k_t^i$, $i = 1, \ldots, n$. Formally the firm's profit at time t is given by

$$\pi(k_t, k_{t+1}) = p^0 f(k_t) - \sum_{i=1}^{n} g^i(k_{t+1}^i - k_t^i) - \sum_{i=1}^{n} p^i(k_{t+1}^i - k_t^i + \eta^i k_t^i).$$

If the firm may borrow and lend at rate r and if $\delta = 1/1 + r$, the firm's objective is max $\sum_{t=0}^{\infty} \delta^t \pi(k_t, k_{t+1})$, subject to k_0 given. We will assume that f is C^2 strongly concave (*i.e.*, $D^2 f$ *exists and is continuous and negative definite*) and that $(D^2 f)_{ij} \geq 0$ for $i \neq j$, and that each g^i is C^2 strongly convex. Also we will restrict the parameter $\alpha = (p^0, p^1, \ldots, p^n, \eta^1, \ldots, \eta^n)$ to an open bounded set $\mathscr{A} \subset R_+^{2n+1}$, k_0 to an open bounded set G of R_+^n, and δ to an open subset Δ of $(0, 1)$. The Euler equation associated with such problems is

$$-Dg^i(k_t^i - k_{t-1}^i) - p^i + \delta[p^0 D^i f(k_t) + Dg^i(k_{t+1} - k_t) - p^i(\eta^i - 1)] = 0, \quad (4.1)$$

and the comparative dynamics matrix T may be written as a collection of $n \times n$ blocks T with

$$T_{l,s} = 0 \quad \text{if} \quad s \notin \{l - 1, l, l + 1\},$$
$$(T_{l,l-1})_{ij} = 0 \quad \text{if} \quad i \neq j, \quad (T_{l,l-1})_{ii} = D^2 g^i(k_l^i - k_{l-1}^i),$$
$$(T_{l,l})_{ii} = -D^2 g^i(k_l^i - k_{l-1}^i) + \delta[p^0(D^2 f(k_l))_{ii} - D^2 g^i(k_{l+1}^i - k_l^i)],$$
$$(T_{l,l})_{ij} = \delta p^0(D^2 f(k_l))_{ij},$$
$$(T_{l,l+1})_{ij} = 0 \quad \text{if} \quad i \neq j, \quad (T_{l,l+1})_{ii} = \delta D^2 g^i(k_{l+1}^i - k_l^i).$$

In other words, T may be written as

$T_{l,s} = 0 \qquad \text{if} \quad s \notin \{l - 1, l, l + 1\},$

$T_{l,l-1} = \Omega(l), \qquad \text{where} \quad \Omega \quad \text{is a diagonal matrix with positive diagonal},$

$T_{l,l} = -\Omega(l) + \delta p^0 D^2 f(k_l) - \delta\Omega(l + 1),$

$T_{l,l+1} = \delta\Omega(l + 1).$

We will assume

ASSUMPTION 4.1   There exists compact set $K \subset R_+^n$ such that for all parameter values $\alpha \in \mathscr{A}$, $k_0 \in G$, and $\delta \in \Delta$, an optimal solution to the firm's problem exists and is entirely contained in K.

Under Assumption 4.1 we may prove

PROPOSITION 4.1   For the model described above and under Assumption 4.1, $T^{-1} \leq 0$.

Proof   We first show that there exists an infinite matrix S with $S_{ij} = 0$ for $j \neq i$, $S_{ii} > 0$ with $\sup_i |S_{ii}| < \infty$ and $\sup_i |S_{ii}^{-1}| < \infty$ such that TS has dominant diagonal. Indeed, write $N(l) = \delta p^0 D^2 f(k_l)$. Then $N(l)$ is negative definite with nonnegative off-diagonal elements. Hence it follows (cf. McKenzie [7, Theorems 2′ and 4]) that $N^{-1}(l) \leq 0$. Let e denote the vector $(1, 1, \ldots, 1)$, and let $d(l) = -N^{-1}(l)e$. Hence $\sum_{j=1}^n N_{ij}(l)d^j(l) = -1$, and in fact since $d^i(l) = \sum_{j=1}^n [-N^{-1}(l)]_{ij}$ and each element in the sum is ≥ 0 and not all are zero, $d(l) > 0$. Since $N_{ij}(l) \geq 0$ for $i \neq j$ and $N_{ii}(l) < 0$, if $M(l)$ is the matrix such that $M_{ij}(l) = 0$ for $i \neq j$, $M_{ii}(l) = d^i(l)$, we have that $N(l)M(l)$ has dominant diagonal. Let $S(l)$ be an infinite matrix whose diagonal blocks are given by $M(l)$ and off-diagonal blocks are zero. Then since $D^2 f(k_l)$ is a continuous function of k_l and $k_l \in K$,

$$0 < \inf -N^{-1}(l)e \leq d(l) \leq \sup -N^{-1}(l)e < \infty.$$

Furthermore, TS has obviously dominant diagonal. The proof of the proposition now follows, for since TS has dominant diagonal and satisfies the assumptions of Lemma 4.1, $(TS)^{-1} = S^{-1}T^{-1} \leq 0$. Since $S \geq 0$, $T^{-1} \leq 0$.
                                                                    Q.E.D.

From (2.2) and (4.1) we can see, for instance, that

$$D_{p^i}k_t = -T^{-1}y,$$

where y is an infinite sequence of n vectors, each of which is the vector $(0, \ldots, -1 + \delta - \delta\eta^i, 0, \ldots, 0)$. Hence $D_{p^i}k_t \leq 0$; i.e., demand for all inputs in all periods either falls or stays constant if the price of some input goes up. Similarly we have

$$D_{p^0}k_t = -T^{-1}x$$

where $x_t = \delta D f(k_t)$, which it is natural to assume ≥ 0. Thus a permanent increase in output price cannot produce a decrease in the quantity held of any type of stock in any period.

The above example illustrates that as in the static case, the dominant diagonal assumption, coupled with assumptions on the sign of "off-diagonal" terms, is a device to yield results that are "natural" if one does not consider complicated second-round effects.

5. A FURTHER REMARK

In [3] Brock and Scheinkman used the assumption that the matrix

$$Q = \begin{bmatrix} \bar{\delta}V_{11} & \bar{\delta}V_{12} \\ V_{21} & V_{22} \end{bmatrix}$$

is quasi-negative definite along any optimal path to prove convergence of optimal solutions to a stationary state. In [1] we observed that under such assumption if we call T the restriction of $D_k\xi$ to l_2^n (the space of all sequences of elements z_t in $R^n \{z_t\}_{t=1}^\infty$ with finite norm $\|z\|_2 = (\sum_{t=1}^\infty |z_t|^2)^{1/2}$ where $|\ |$ denotes any norm in R^n), then T maps l_2^n onto l_2^n is invertible and negative definite; i.e., given any $z \in l_2^n$, $\sum_{t=1}^\infty z_t(Tz_t) \leqq 0$. Hence if λ is a parameter such that $D_\lambda\xi \in l_2^n$, then we may conclude that $\sum_{t=1}^\infty D_\lambda k_t(D_\lambda\xi)_t \geqq 0$.

This result is not so useful for fixed rate of discount models as the one stated in Section 2 above, since unless $\lambda = k_0^i$ for some $i = 1, \ldots, n$, $D_\lambda\xi \notin l_2^n$. The results of [1], however, as we mentioned above, has been extended for nonstationary models by McKenzie [8]. Thus one may consider, for example, parameters that affect the "utility function" only for a few periods, and hence for t large enough, $(D_\lambda\xi)_t = 0$ and obviously $D_\lambda\xi \in l_2^n$.

REFERENCES

1. Araujo, A., and Scheinkman, J. A., Smoothness, comparative dynamics, and the turnpike property, *Econometrica* **45**, No. 3 (1977), 601–620.
2. Brock, W. A., Some Applications of Recent Results on the Asymptotic Stability of Optimal Control to the Problem of Comparing Long-Run Equilibria. Cornell Univ. Working Paper (August 1976).
3. Brock, W. A., and Scheinkman, J. A., On the long run behavior of a competitive firm, 1974 *Vienna Conf. Vol. Equilibrium Disequilibrium Econ. Theory, 1974* (G. Schwödiauer, ed.). Reidel, Dordrecht, 1977.
4. Burmeister, E., and Turnovsky, S. J., Capital deepening response in an economy with heterogeneous capital goods, *Am. Econ. Rev.* **62** (1972), 842–853.
5. Cartan, H., "Calcul Différentiel." Hermann, Paris, 1967.
6. Lucas, R. E., Optimal investment policy and the flexible accelerator, *Int. Econ. Rev.* **8** (1967), 78–85.
7. McKenzie, L. W., Matrices with dominant diagonal and economic theory, *in* "Mathematical Methods in the Social Sciences" (K. Arrow, S. Karlin, and P. Suppes. eds.), Stanford Univ. Press, Stanford, California, 1959.

8. McKenzie, L. W., A new route to the turnpike, *in* "Mathematical Economics and Game Theory" (R. Henn and L. O. Moeschlin, eds.). Springer Verlag, Berlin and New York, 1977.

This chapter was very much influenced by Lionel McKenzie. In particular, the results in Section 4 were inspired by McKenzie's paper "Matrices with Dominant Diagonal and Economic Theory." More directly we were helped by his detailed comments on a previous draft of this paper, as well as on our earlier paper [1]. We also benefited in preparing this final version from reading a preliminary draft of a chapter he was writing for Arrow and Intrilligator's *Handbook of Mathematical Economics.*"

This research was supported by NSF Grant SOC 74-19692 to the University of Chicago.

DEPARTMENT OF ECONOMICS
UNIVERSITY OF CHICAGO
CHICAGO, ILLINOIS

Efficient Intertemporal Allocation, Consumption-Value Maximization, and Capital-Value Transversality: A Unified View*

DAVID CASS

MUKUL MAJUMDAR

I. INTRODUCTION AND SUMMARY

In recent years, based on Malinvaud's seminal work [15], there have been a number of important contributions [1-3, 5, 12, 14, 16, 18-20] toward resolving the following fundamental question: What observable properties characterize[1] some (all) competitive price system(s) associated with an efficient growth path? The natural focus in efforts to answer this question has been on the dynamical behavior of capital value—"natural" in the sense that Malinvaud's theorem establishes that under very general conditions efficient growth is tantamount to the existence of an associated competitive price

---

* This paper is dedicated, with respect, affection, and admiration, to Professor Lionel McKenzie on the occasion of his 60th birthday. Lionel's varied and myriad contributions, in print and otherwise, have all been to the profession's great "value-gain."

[1] In every analysis that aims to characterize efficient allocation as competitive allocation (given generalized diminishing returns), a slight gap appears between the statements of necessary and sufficient conditions, a gap occasioned by the fact that every price need not be positive. For this reason, here and in the balance of the paper we use "characterize" to mean "are necessary and also sufficient provided appropriate prices are positive." Also, partly for this reason, in characterizing efficient (or optimal) growth paths, we concentrate on establishing necessity of various valuation properties. (A more compelling reason for our emphasis is that establishing sufficiency of these same properties is usually a routine matter; see footnote 9 below.)

system with the special property that in every period capital value is minimized among all potential growth paths yielding the same stream of consumption goods thereafter. In other words, dealing with the question eventually reduces to looking for a more concrete version of Malinvaud's capital-value minimization condition.

Roughly speaking, reported results have come from two distinct approaches: first, from searching for particular productivity and substitution properties of technology, which necessarily require asymptotically insignificant capital value or *capital-value transversality* (a label suggested by the common reference to the "transversality condition," especially in optimal growth theory) [1, 12, 14, 18, 20], and second, from searching for weaker regularities in the asymptotic behavior of capital value, which necessarily emerge given particular productivity and substitution properties of technology [1–3, 5, 19]. The first approach is undoubtedly more appealing intuitively, since—at least when there are no primary factors—capital-value transversality is essentially equivalent to *consumption-value maximization*, i.e., the property that among all feasible growth paths, and at its associated consumption goods prices, an efficient growth path maximizes the total value of the whole stream of consumption goods. Unfortunately, this approach encounters great difficulty from the mere presence of primary factors[2] (and the second approach from the mere presence of polyhedral-like technology). Nonetheless, it is basically the approach we adopt here. Thus, one of our purposes in this paper is to present general conditions on static productivity characteristics and substitution possibilities that verify the property of consumption-value maximization and, incidentally, capital-value transversality as well (in Section V and Appendixes A and B).

A closely related result appears in recent contributions concerning the problem of how to characterize optimal growth paths [22–24, 27, 33]: Suppose that we are given some nonnegative, nontrivial values for the whole stream of consumption goods.[3] If at these given consumption goods values,

---

[2] We therefore intentionally defer our discussion of the problems attendant on primary factors until later in the paper (in Sections VII and VIII). It is worth mentioning now, however, that one promising possibility for surmounting these problems is to give explicit consideration to the limitational role of exhaustible resources. Besides displaying our own efforts in this direction (at the end of Appendix A), we strongly recommend looking at the interesting and original work of Mitra [18].

[3] It is noteworthy that, generally speaking, in this context the units for measuring consumption goods are interpreted in welfare or utility terms. Such interpretation is immaterial to our analysis, provided that the static technology available for producing utility and investment goods from capital stocks and primary factors exhibits generalized diminishing returns. However, such interpretation does mean that some care must be taken with the parallel interpretation of the competitive price system associated with an optimal growth path, since, again generally speaking, it could not be used for the purposes of decentralization.

a particular feasible growth path yields maximum total value among all feasible growth paths, i.e., is an optimal growth path, then it has an associated competitive price system with the special properties that (i) consumption goods prices are the same as the given values, and (ii) capital-value transversality obtains. In short, the proposition is simply that consumption-value maximization (at given consumption goods values) implies capital-value transversality (at associated capital goods prices). Another of our purposes in this paper is to present a simpler proof for this proposition (Section VI).

Perhaps our principal purpose, however, is to display the common structure underlying both consumption-value maximization in efficient growth theory and capital-value transversality in optimal growth theory. The mathematical technique we use to establish this connection is application of variants of the basic support theorem implicitly developed in the Majumdar–Mitra–McFadden proof of consumption-value maximization for the closed, multisector model of growth [14] (see also its precursors [13, 16]), and this unifying methodology is presented first (in Section II). (The reader who is primarily interested in our economic applications can skim or skip this section, which is unavoidably technical though quite straightforward.) Then, after describing our general growth model (in Section III), we turn to characterizing efficient and optimal growth paths (in Sections IV–VI) and to elaborating the complications arising from the presence of primary factors (in Sections VII and VIII). In the course of accomplishing our avowed purposes, we also develop two subsidiary results of interest in their own right: First, we present an alternative argument leading to Malinvaud's theorem, one that has the additional virtue of introducing a broader sense in which efficient growth paths yield value maximization and hence also capital-value minimization and consumption-value maximization (in Section IV). (See too the various arguments in [12, 28, 30].) Second, we present a general theorem establishing the existence of special competitive price systems associated with feasible growth paths which are optimal in various weaker senses than that of simple consumption-value maximization (at given consumption goods values; in Section VIII). (See too the related theorems in [9, 17, 25, 26, 29].)

II. FUNDAMENTAL SUPPORT PROPERTIES

We use $x = (x_0, x_1, \ldots)$ and $\pi = (\pi_0, \pi_1, \ldots)$ to denote sequences (later on x will be interpreted as quantities, π as prices), l_1 to denote the space of all summable sequences with sum norm $\|x\|_1 = \sum_{t=0}^{\infty} |x_t|$, l_0 the subspace of all finitely many nonzero-element sequences with sum norm $\|x\|_0 = \|x\|_1$, and l_∞ to denote the space of all bounded sequences with sup norm $\|x\|_\infty = \sup_t |x_t|$. Also, $\pi \cdot x$ means $\sum_{t=0}^{\infty} \pi_t x_t$, $x' \geqq x''$ means $x_t' \geqq x_t''$ for every t, $x' \geq x''$ means $x_t' \geqq x_t''$ for every t and $x_t' > x_t''$ for some t, and $x' > x''$ means $x_t' > x_t''$ for every t.

SUPPORT THEOREM FOR l_1 (Majumdar–Mitra–McFadden)   Suppose $X \subset l_1$ is closed, convex, freely disposable (i.e., if $x \in X$, $x' \in l_1$ and $x' \leq x$, then $x' \in X$) and uniformly "productive" (i.e., there exists $\delta > 0$ such that for every $t \geq 0$ there exists $x^t \in X$ such that $x_s^t \geq \delta$ for $s = t$ and $x_s^t \geq 0$ for $s \neq t$). If x^* is a boundary point of X (i.e., $x^* \in X$, but $x^* \notin$ interior X), then there exists $\pi \in l_\infty$ such that $\pi \geq 0$ and

$$\pi \cdot x^* \geq \pi \cdot x \qquad \text{for every} \quad x \in X. \tag{1}$$

Proof   Our argument is virtually identical to the original argument in [14], but since that argument is imbedded in a fairly long, model-oriented proof, we detail it here for convenience' sake. We will use two basic results from analysis:

1. (Separation of convex sets by a continuous linear functional)   If C^1 and C^2 are nonempty, convex subsets of a topological (e.g., normed) linear space S, interior $C^1 \neq \emptyset$, and interior $C^1 \cap C^2 = \emptyset$, then there exists a nontrivial, continuous linear functional f on S such that

$$f(c^2) \geq f(c^1) \qquad \text{for every} \quad c^1 \in C^1, \quad c^2 \in C^2.$$

2. (Representation of continuous linear functionals on l_1)   If f is a continuous linear functional on l_1, then there exists $\pi \in l_\infty$ such that

$$f(x) = \pi \cdot x \qquad \text{for every} \quad x \in l_1.$$

(See, for example, [10], especially Section 14 and exercises.)

Given these results, the idea of the proof is quite simple: Verify the hypotheses of the separation theorem when $S = l_1$, $C^1 = X$ and $C^2 = \{x^*\}$, and then apply the representation theorem.

Two of the hypotheses required for applying the separation theorem are easily verified (since X is assumed a nonempty, convex subset of l_1, and x^* a boundary point of X). The remaining hypothesis — that interior $X \neq \emptyset$ — requires a little more work. What we need to show is that for some $x' \in X$ there exists $\varepsilon > 0$ such that if $x \in l_1$ and $\|x - x'\|_1 < \varepsilon$, then $x \in X$. In fact, we show that $x' = 0$ will do: By free disposal and uniform "productivity" $0 \in X$. Now pick $0 < \varepsilon \leq \delta$ and suppose, without loss of generality, $x_0 \neq 0$ and $\|x - 0\|_1 = \|x\|_1 = \alpha < \varepsilon$. Then (again by free disposal and uniform "productivity"), for every $t \geq 0$ such that $x_t \geq 0$ (resp. < 0) there exists $x^t \in X$ such that $x_s^t = \alpha$ (resp. $-\alpha$) for $s = t$ and $x_s^t = 0$ for $s \neq t$. Let $\lambda_s^t = |x_s| / \sum_{u=0}^t |x_u|$ for $0 \leq s \leq t$, so that $\lambda_s^t \geq 0$ and $\sum_{s=0}^t \lambda_s^t = 1$, and let $z^t = \sum_{s=0}^t \lambda_s^t x^s$ for $t \geq 0$, so that

$$z^t = \left(\alpha \bigg/ \sum_{u=0}^t |x_u| \right) \quad (x_0, x_1, \ldots, x_t, 0, \ldots).$$

Then (by convexity) $z^t \in X$ while (by closedness) if $\lim_{t \to \infty} z^t = x$, then $x \in X$. But

$$
\left\| z^t - x \right\|_1 = \sum_{s=0}^{\infty} \left| z_s^t - x_s \right|
$$

$$
= \sum_{s=0}^{t} \left| \left(\alpha \Big/ \sum_{u=0}^{t} |x_u| \right) x_s - x_s \right| + \sum_{s=t+1}^{\infty} |x_s|
$$

$$
= \left(\alpha \Big/ \sum_{u=0}^{t} |x_u| - 1 \right) \sum_{s=0}^{t} |x_s| + \sum_{s=t+1}^{\infty} |x_s|
$$

$$
= \left(\sum_{s=0}^{\infty} |x_s| - \sum_{s=0}^{t} |x_s| \right) + \sum_{s=t+1}^{\infty} |x_s|
$$

$$
= 2 \sum_{s=t+1}^{\infty} |x_s|,
$$

that is, $\lim_{t \to \infty} z^t = x$. Now applying the separation theorem, we know that there exists a nontrivial, continuous linear functional f on l_1 such that $f(x^*) \geq f(x)$ for every $x \in X$. But applying the representation theorem, we know that there exists $\pi \in l_\infty$ such that $f(x) = \pi \cdot x$ for every $x \in l_1$. Since f is nontrivial, $\pi \neq 0$, while since X is freely disposable, $\pi \geq 0$. Hence, $\pi \geq 0$, and the proof is complete. ■

The key to the foregoing argument is the fact that the maintained assumptions on X are strong enough to guarantee that X has an interior point. Clearly weaker assumptions (for example, simply that X has an interior— which obviously does not require that X be closed) will suffice for this purpose. For the particular capital-theoretic applications we are concerned with, such weaker assumptions are hard to verify in terms of the underlying economic model. Moreover, the various technological conditions we will use to substantiate the maintained assumptions are fairly conventional (or, at least, easily interpretable). However, if—as in several of our applications—X lies in the subspace l_0, then it is possible both to dispense with closedness and to weaken uniform "productivity."

SUPPORT THEOREM FOR l_0 Suppose $X \subset l_0$ is convex, freely disposable and "productive" (i.e., for every $t \geq 0$ there exists $x^t \in X$ such that $x_s^t > 0$ for $s = t$ and $x_s^t \geq 0$ for $s \neq t$). If $x^* \in X$ but x^* is not on internal point of X (e.g., x^* is a maximal point of X), then there exists π (simply some sequence of real numbers) such that $\pi \geq 0$ and (1) obtains.

Proof   This argument differs from the previous one only in that it concerns internal points rather than interior points, and thus linear functionals rather than continuous linear functionals. Once again it is founded on two basic results from analysis:

1. (Separation of convex sets by a linear functional.) If C^1 and C^2 are nonempty, convex subsets of a topological linear space S, $\{x : x$ is an internal point of $C^1\} \neq \emptyset$ and $\{x : x$ is an internal point of $C^1\} \cap C^2 = \emptyset$, then there exists a nontrivial linear functional f on S such that

$$f(c^2) \geq f(c^1) \qquad \text{for every} \quad c^1 \in C^1, \quad c^2 \in C^2.$$

2. (Representation of linear functionals on l_0.) If f is a linear functional on l_0, then there exists π such that

$$f(x) = \pi \cdot x \qquad \text{for every} \quad x \in l_0.$$

(Again refer to [10], especially Section 14 and exercises, noting that Kelley–Namioka use different terminology regarding internal points.)

From here the logic of the argument proceeds exactly as before, except that in this case we need only employ finite convex combinations to establish that 0 is an internal point of X, i.e., that $0 \in X$ and if $x \in l_0$, then there exists $\alpha > 0$ such that $\lambda \alpha x \in X$ for $0 \leq \lambda < 1$. The details of this construction are as follows: By free disposal and "productivity", $0 \in X$. Now suppose $x = 0$ but $\max\{t : t \geq 0$ and $x_t \neq 0\} = \bar{t} < \infty$. Then (again by free disposal and "productivity"), there exists $\alpha > 0$ such that for every $0 \leq t \leq \bar{t}$ such that $x_t \geq 0$ (resp. < 0), there exists $x^t \in X$ such that $x_s^t = \alpha\|x\|_0$ (resp. $-\alpha\|x\|_0$) for $s = t$ and $x_s^t = 0$ for $s \neq t$. Let $\lambda_t = |x_t|/\|x\|_0$ for $0 \leq t \leq \bar{t}$, so that $\lambda_t \geq 0$, and $\sum_{t=0}^{\bar{t}} \lambda_t = 1$, and $z = \sum_{t=0}^{\bar{t}} \lambda_t x^t$, so that

$$z = \alpha(x_0, x_1, \ldots, x_t, 0, \ldots) = \alpha x.$$

Then (by convexity) $\alpha x \in X$, so that (also by convexity) $(1 - \lambda)0 + \lambda \alpha x = \lambda \alpha x \in X$ for $0 \leq \lambda < 1$. ∎

Finally, for most of our applications of these two support theorems it is important to know that the assumption of uniform "productivity" [resp. "productivity"] can be replaced by the following pair of assumptions: Possibility of no production (i.e., $0 \in X$) and uniform productivity (resp. productivity) (i.e., there exist $\delta > 0$ and $t^\delta < \infty$ such that for every $t > t^\delta$ there exists $x^t \in X$ such that $x_s^t \geq -\delta$ for $0 \leq s \leq t^\delta$, $x_s^t \geq \delta$ [resp. $x_s^t > 0$] for $s = t$ and $x_s^t \geq 0$ for $t^\delta < s \neq t$). This follows from the easily verified fact that, if X satisfies these as well as the remaining maintained assumptions of the support theorems, then

$$X^\delta = X + (\overbrace{\delta, \delta, \ldots, \delta}^{t^\delta}, 0, \ldots)$$

satisfies the full set of maintained assumptions, including uniform "productivity" (resp. "productivity").

III. GENERAL GROWTH MODEL

Feasible real allocations or *growth paths* in the economy are described by

$$\begin{cases} (c_t, z_t, k_t) \in T \\ k_0 = \bar{k} > 0 \end{cases} \quad \text{and} \quad k_{t+1} = z_t \quad \text{for} \quad t \geqq 0, \tag{2}$$

where $c = (c_1, c_2, \ldots, c_m)$ is an m-vector of consumption goods output, $z = (z_1, z_2, \ldots, z_n)$ is an n-vector of ("gross") capital goods, or better, investment goods output, $k = (k_1, k_2, \ldots, k_n)$ is an n-vector of capital stock inputs, $T = \{(c, z, k)\}$ is the static technology available for producing outputs from capital stock inputs,[4] t is an index representing discrete production periods (so that 0 is the initial period), and $\bar{k} = (\bar{k}_1, \bar{k}_2, \ldots, \bar{k}_n)$ is an n-vector of initial capital stocks. (The assumption that initial capital stocks are positive $\bar{k} > 0$ enters the analysis in a nontrivial way.)

Regarding the technology, we will always assume that T is a nonnegative, closed set exhibiting

T1 GENERALIZED DIMINISHING RETURNS T is convex.

T2 FREE DISPOSAL If $(c, z, k) \in T$, $0 \leqq (c', z') \leqq (c, z)$, and $k' \geqq k$, then $(c', z', k') \in T$,

T3 CONSTANT RETURNS TO SCALE T is a cone.[5]

---

[4] With minor modification, several of the results elaborated in the sequel will also carry over to a model in which the commodities and techniques available change over time (in a foreseeable manner). We have chosen not to generalize our model to encompass this sort of nonstationarity in order to avoid cluttering up the presentation.

[5] This last maintained assumption is in fact quite restrictive. Later on we effectively remove the force of this restriction by explicitly introducing (short-lived) nonproduced inputs or primary factors (e.g., labor) into the model. Note that (potentially long-lived) nonproduced inputs, both exhaustible resources (e.g., coal) and inexhaustible resources (e.g., land), are already implicitly incorporated into the model: A capital stock, say that of type 1, is an *exhaustible resource* when $(c, z, k) \in T$ implies both $z_1 \leqq k_1$ and $(c, (z_1', z_2, \ldots, z_n), (k_1', k_2, \ldots, k_n)) \in T$ for $z_1' \geqq 0$ and $k_1' - z_1' = k_1 - z_1$, while it is an *inexhaustible resource* when $(c, z, k) \in T$ implies both $z_1 \leqq k_1$ and $(c, (z_1', z_2, \ldots, z_n), k) \in T$ for $z_1' = k_1$. As mentioned earlier, we will have a good deal more to say about the implications of the presence of exhaustible resources that are also limitational (in Appendix A).

The whole of our analysis depends critically on how productive inputs are (and also, to a lesser extent, on how substitutable outputs are). For the time being we only postulate the following productivity characteristics:

T4 NECESSITY OF CAPITAL STOCKS   If $(c, z, k) \in T$ and $k = 0$, then $(c, z) = 0$.

T5 PRODUCTIVITY OF CAPITAL STOCKS   If $(c, z, k) \in T$ and $k' > k$, then there exists $(c', z') > (c, z)$ such that $(c', z', k') \in T$.

T4 is one representation of the idea of scarcity, T5 of the idea of (the productivity of) roundaboutness. Note, in particular, that T5 implies that positive outputs can be produced from positive capital stocks. Later on we systematically enlarge on this fairly unrestrictive specification.

Corresponding to (2), the "feasible" value inputations or *price systems* in the economy are described by

$$\begin{cases} (p_t, q_t, r_t) \in M & \text{and} \quad r_t = q_{t-1} \quad \text{for} \quad t \geq 0, \\ q_{-1} \geq 0 \end{cases} \tag{3}$$

where $p = (p_1, p_2, \ldots, p_m)$ is an m-vector of consumption goods prices, $q = (q_1, q_2, \ldots, q_n)$ is an n-vector of investment goods prices, $r = (r_1, r_2, \ldots, r_n)$ is an n-vector of ("gross") capital stock rents, and $M = \{(p, q, r) : (p, q) \geq 0$ and $p \cdot c + q \cdot z - r \cdot k \leq 0$ for every $(c, z, k) \in T\}$ is the nonnegative subset of the dual cone to T. Equations (3) describe, among others, all the price systems that might be observed in a perfect foresight competitive equilibrium for the economy and simply represent a convenient way of summarizing the possibilities for price systems [in exactly the same manner that (2) simply represents a convenient way of summarizing the possibilities for growth paths].[6] We will refer to a particular feasible growth path [i.e., a particular solution to (2) denoted, say, by asterisks] as being *competitive* or having an *associated competitive price system*, if there is some nontrivial "feasible" price system [i.e., some nontrivial solution to (3)] at which the given feasible growth path yields maximum profit of zero among all potential input–output combinations in each period:

$$p_t \cdot c + q_t \cdot z - q_{t-1} \cdot k \leq p_t \cdot c_t^* + q_t \cdot z_t^* - q_{t-1} \cdot k_t^* = 0$$

for every $(c, z, k) \in T$ and $t \geq 0$. \hfill (4)

---

[6] For a more complete discussion of the properties (and virtues) of this sort of representation, see Cass and Shell [7]. There is no loss of generality (and some gain in interpretability) in assuming nonnegative output prices. This assertion follows from the observation that, in light of T2, having more investment goods—and hence capital stocks—in the present never reduces consumption goods possibilities for the future. (The fact that investment goods prices are non-negative $q \geq 0$, however, enters the analysis in a nontrivial way.)

Of course, only some feasible growth paths are competitive, and only some competitive growth paths are efficient (or optimal), which is the underlying *raison d'être* for this paper.

Before proceeding with the analysis, we emphasize two implications of (4) that we will use repeatedly: Consider a particular competitive growth path (denoted again by asterisks). Since if $k_0 = \bar{k}$ and $k_{t+1} = z_t$ for $t \geq 0$, then

$$\sum_{t=0}^{\ell} p_t \cdot c_t = \sum_{t=0}^{\ell} (p_t \cdot c_t + q_t \cdot (z_t - k_{t+1}))$$

$$= \sum_{t=0}^{\ell} (p_t \cdot c_t + q_t \cdot z_t - q_{t-1} \cdot k_t) + q_{-1} \cdot \bar{k} - q_\ell \cdot k_{\ell+1} \quad \text{for} \quad \ell \geq 0,$$

it follows from (4) that

$$\sum_{t=0}^{\ell} p_t \cdot c_t \leq \sum_{t=0}^{\ell} p_t \cdot c_t + q_\ell \cdot k_{\ell+1} \leq q_{-1} \cdot \bar{k} \quad \text{for} \quad \ell \geq 0 \qquad (5)$$

for every feasible growth path (2), while

$$\sum_{t=0}^{\ell} p_t \cdot c_t^* \leq \sum_{t=0}^{\ell} p_t \cdot c_t^* + q_\ell \cdot k_{\ell+1}^* = q_{-1} \cdot \bar{k} \quad \text{for} \quad \ell \geq 0. \qquad (6)$$

Among other things, (5) tells us immediately that consumption value is uniformly bounded

$$\sum_{t=0}^{\infty} p_t \cdot c_t \leq q_{-1} \cdot \bar{k}$$

for every feasible growth path (2), so that (5) and (6) together tell us immediately that capital-value transversality implies consumption-value maximization

$$\lim_{t \to \infty} q_t \cdot k_{t+1}^* = 0 \Rightarrow \infty > \sum_{t=0}^{\infty} p_t \cdot c_t^* \geq \sum_{t=0}^{\infty} p_t \cdot c_t$$

for every feasible growth path (2). (The converse to this latter proposition will be established in Section VI.)

IV. CHARACTERIZATION OF EFFICIENCY

A particular feasible growth path (denoted once again by asterisks) is *efficient* if there is no other feasible growth path that dominates it in terms of the whole stream of consumption goods, i.e., if there is no other solution to (2) such that

$$(c_0, c_1, \ldots) \geq (c_0^*, c_1^*, \ldots). \tag{7}$$

This concept lies at the very core of (neoclassical) economics, since efficient growth paths constitute the subset of feasible growth paths that are indisputably "desirable" or "good."

In order to characterize such paths, we now interpret the quantity sequence x as

$$\overset{(\bar{k} - k_0) - (\bar{k} - k_0^*)}{\parallel} \qquad\qquad \overset{(z_t - k_{t+1}) - (z_t^* - k_{t+1}^*)}{\parallel}$$
$$x = (\overbrace{\bar{k} - k_0}, c_0 - c_0^*, z_0 - k_1, \ldots, c_t - c_t^*, \overbrace{z_t - k_{t+1}}, \ldots), \tag{8}$$

the price sequence π as

$$\pi = (q_{-1}, p_0, q_0, \ldots, p_t, q_t, \ldots), \tag{9}$$

and the set X as

$$X = \{x : x \in l_1, c_t \leq c_t' \text{ and } (c_t', z_t, k_t) \in T \text{ for } t \geq 0\}. \tag{10}$$

That is, x is taken to be the sequence of net final outputs (i.e., outputs today in excess of inputs tomorrow) over and above those generated by a particular efficient growth path, π the corresponding sequence of value imputations, and X the set of all summable x that could be produced given unlimited free disposal of consumption goods and unlimited costless availability of capital stocks. [It is basically the latter sort of flexibility that finally gives economic content to our various applications of the support theorems; a particular growth path used to generate a particular sequence of net final outputs need only be feasible in the special sense defined by (10) and not in the usual sense defined earlier by (2).]

Given these interpretations, it is relatively straightforward to verify that $X \subset l_1$ is closed,[7] convex, and freely disposable by virtue of our maintained assumptions on T (exclusive of T5). Furthermore, the quantity sequence generated by the efficient growth path itself,

$$x^* = (\bar{k} - k_0^*, c_0^* - c_0^*, z_0^* - k_1^*, \ldots, c_t^* - c_t^*, z_t^* - k_{t+1}^*, \ldots) = 0,$$

---

[7] In fact, because T is closed and satisfies T4, X is closed in the topology of pointwise convergence (from an argument similar to that found in McFadden [17, p. 45]). Though Malinvaud's original derivation required neither closedness nor any such intrinsic notion of scarcity, the loss in generality sustained from these additional assumptions seems more than compensated for by the gain in applicability of our basic separation technique. Moreover—looking ahead to the following discussion of the productivity properties of X when defined as in (10)—it can easily be shown that Malinvaud's theorem itself follows simply by further restricting X to lie in l_0, and then appealing to the support theorem for l_0.

must be a boundary point of X: Obviously, x^* is in X. Suppose it were an interior point as well. Then (appealing to the way points in X are defined) it would be possible to increase an arbitrarily chosen consumption good output (for example, $c_{10} - c_{10}^* > 0$), while at the same time maintaining every other consumption good output ($c_{i0} - c_{i0}^* = 0$ for $i \neq 1$ and $c_t - c_t^* = 0$ for $t \neq 0$), as well as feasibility ($\bar{k} - k_0 = 0$, $z_t - k_{t+1} = 0$, and $(c_t, z_t, k_t) \in T$ for $t \geq 0$). But such a possibility contradicts the fact that we began by postulating an efficient growth path.

From these considerations (together with the final comment at the end of Section II), it follows that if we could only verify that X is uniformly productive, then we could simply apply the support theorem for l_1 to derive a price characterization for all efficient growth paths. This is indeed the strategy we follow in the subsequent section (but for a simplification in the interpretation of the quantity sequence x). However, this line of attack requires more structure on T then we have thus far imposed (see for example T6 and T7 below). Here we proceed instead by noticing that although X is not necessarily *uniformly* productive, by virtue of T5 it is certainly productive in the following sense: There exists $(x_0', x_1', \ldots, x_{n-1}') < 0$ such that for every $t \geq n$ there exists $x^t \in X$ such that $x_s^t \geq x_s'$ for $0 \leq s < n$, $x_s^t > 0$ for $s = t$, and $x_s^t \geq 0$ for $n \leq s \neq t$. This seemingly complicated statement is nothing more than a formalization of the fact that T5 implies that if there were larger initial capital stocks available, then it would be feasible to produce no smaller net final outputs in every subsequent period, and actually larger net final outputs in any given subsequent period. In particular, the quantity sequences x^t for $t \geq n$ can be generated by a growth path that utilizes given additional initial capital stocks (so that $x_{j-1}' = \bar{k}_j - k_{j0} < 0$ for $1 \leq j \leq n$) to produce more investment goods output during periods 0 through $s - 1$, or more capital stock inputs for periods 0 through s, and more of both consumption goods output and investment goods output during period s [so that $n + (n + m)s < t \leq n + (n + m)(s + 1)$].

The observation that X is productive immediately suggests the following trick to render it uniformly so: Choose new units for measuring net final outputs or quantities, say v_t for $t \geq 0$, in such a manner that for some $\delta > 0$ and $t^\delta = n - 1$, $v_t x_t' \geq -\delta$ for $0 \leq t \leq t^\delta$ and $v_t x_t^t \geq \delta$ for $t > t^\delta$.[8] Clearly, such a maneuver enables us to apply the conclusion of the support theorem

---

[8] After changing units, of course, the sequences x and π would have to be appropriately reinterpreted: $x_0 = v_0(\bar{k}_1 - k_{10}), \ldots$ and $\pi_0 = q_{1-1}/v_0, \ldots$. Notice that, given $t^v < \infty$, we can always choose the new units for measuring net final outputs or quantities so that $v_t = 1$ for $0 \leq t \leq t^v$. This is a reflection of the fact that it is only the asymptotic behavior of feasible growth paths that creates fundamental difficulties in characterizing efficiency.

for l_1 (1), and thereby [referring to the interpretations (8)–(10)] to establish a fundamental proposition[9]:

Price Characterization of Efficient Growth Paths

If a feasible growth path is efficient, then there exist positive units for measuring outputs $(v_{-1}, u_0, v_0, \ldots, u_t, v_t, \ldots) > 0$ and nonnegative, nontrivial prices for evaluating outputs $(q_{-1}, p_0, q_0, \ldots, p_t, q_t, \ldots) \geq 0$ such that

$$0 \geq q_{-1} \cdot (\bar{k} - k_0) + \sum_{t=0}^{\infty} (p_t \cdot (c_t - c_t^*) + q_t \cdot (z_t - k_{t+1})) \tag{11}$$

for every growth path $(c_t, z_t, k_t) \in T$ for $t \geq 0$ such that

$$\sum_{j=1}^{n} v_{j,-1} |\bar{k} - k_{j0}| + \sum_{t=0}^{\infty} \left(\sum_{i=1}^{m} u_{it} |c_{it} - c_{it}^*| + \sum_{j=1}^{n} v_{jt} |z_{jt} - k_{jt+1}| \right) < \infty.$$

The converse obtains provided that consumption goods prices are positive $p_t > 0$ for $t \geq 0$.

In this form, our price characterization is neither very transparent nor very usable. Three immediate corollaries go part way toward remedying these defects.

Value Characterizations of Efficient Growth Paths

If a feasible growth path is efficient, then it has an associated competitive price system (4) at which

1. *Restricted Value Maximization*   Net final output value is maximized:

$$\infty > \sum_{t=0}^{\infty} p_t \cdot c_t^* - q_{-1} \cdot \bar{k} \geq \sum_{t=0}^{\infty} p_t \cdot c_t - q_{-1} \cdot k; \tag{12}$$

---

[9] The converse assertion or sufficiency follows directly upon specializing (11) to encompass only feasible growth paths

$$0 \geq \sum_{t=0}^{\infty} p_t \cdot (c_t - c_t^*) \tag{*}$$

for every feasible growth path (2) such that

$$\sum_{t=0}^{\infty} \sum_{i=1}^{m} u_{it} |c_{it} - c_{it}^*| < \infty,$$

since (*) is inconsistent with (7) when $p_t > 0$ for $t \geq 0$. For the corollaries to this proposition, as well as subsequent characterizations, proof of sufficiency is only slightly less direct—involving reference to (5) and (6) [or, when there are primary factors, (5') and (6')] in order to establish an analog of (*), since each of these characterizations is couched in terms of an associated competitive price system. Because these arguments are essentially similar and straightforward, we will omit them.

2. *Restricted Capital-Value Minimization*   Capital value is minimized:

$$\infty > \sum_{t=0}^{\infty} p_t \cdot c_t \geqq (>) \sum_{t=0}^{\infty} p_t \cdot c_t^* \Rightarrow q_{-1} \cdot \bar{k} \leqq (<) q_{-1} \cdot k; \qquad (13)$$

3. *Restricted Consumption-Value Maximization*   Consumption value is maximized:

$$k \leqq \bar{k} \Rightarrow (q_{-1} \cdot k \leqq q_{-1} \cdot \bar{k} \Rightarrow) \infty > \sum_{t=0}^{\infty} p_t \cdot c_t^* \geqq \sum_{t=0}^{\infty} p_t \cdot c_t, \qquad (14)$$

among all growth paths that (i) are feasible from nonnegative capital stocks or satisfy (2) with $\bar{k} = k \geqq 0$ and (ii) yield sufficiently small deviations in the whole stream of consumption goods or satisfy

$$\sum_{t=0}^{\infty} \sum_{i=1}^{m} u_{it} |c_{it} - c_{it}^*| < \infty$$

for some (fixed) positive units for measuring consumption goods $u_{it} > 0$ for

$$1 \leqq i \leqq m, \qquad t \geqq 0.$$

In each case (1–3) the converse obtains provided that consumption goods prices are positive $p_t > 0$ for $t \geqq 0$.

Proof   Equation (4) follows from (11) with $(c_s, z_s, k_s) = (c, z, k) \in T$ for $s = t$ and $(c_s, z_s, k_s) = (c_s^*, z_s^*, k_s^*)$ for $s \neq t$. Then, in view of (5), (12)–(14) follow from (11) when comparison is further limited to growth paths that are feasible from nonnegative capital stocks $k \geqq 0$. ∎

"Restricted" here refers to the fact that among growth paths that are feasible from nonnegative capital stocks, we have further confined comparisons to just those that yield sufficiently small deviations in the whole stream of consumption goods. Notice, on the other hand, that we could have expanded such restricted comparisons to the class of growth paths that are identical up to period t, $(c_s, z_s, k_s) = (c_s^*, z_s^*, k_s^*)$ for $0 \leqq s < t$, and then are feasible from nonnegative capital stocks in period t, $k_t = k \geqq 0$, and $(c_s, z_s, k_s) \in T$ and $k_{s+1} = z_s$ for $s \geqq t$, for arbitrary distinguished period $t \geqq 0$. (This expansion would permit a more general interpretation of capital goods prices, as detailed by one of us elsewhere [6]).

Regarding the various value characterizations themselves: Restricted value maximization is the closest analog of the standard characterization of efficient allocation in a static (or equivalently, dynamic but finite) economy, a parallel also elaborated at length in [6]. Restricted capital-value minimization is essentially a stronger version of Malinvaud's theorem, since (in light of the comments above) our condition involves a broader class of comparisons than does his (though at the cost mentioned in footnote 7). Finally, restricted consumption-value maximization basically speaks for itself. One of our prime goals is to sharpen this particular implication of (11).

Specifically, one can ask whether there are circumstances under which consumption-value maximization obtains without any restriction except feasibility. Alternatively, one can ask whether there are circumstances under which some more qualified notion of optimality obtains without any restriction except feasibility (as is the case, for example, in the one-good model analyzed by Cass and Yaari [8]). It is to the former question we now turn; we will also respond, somewhat indirectly, to the latter question later on (in Sections VII and VIII, and at the end of Appendix B).

Before addressing this question, however, we emphasize at this point that each of our subsequent arguments amounts to a variant of the argument presented in this section: Namely, in each specific case, we interpret x, π, X, and x^* in such a way that direct application of a support theorem plus judicious choice of comparison sequences lead to the desired conclusion.

V. EFFICIENCY AND CONSUMPTION-VALUE MAXIMIZATION

The argument in the preceding section underlines the basic difficulty involved in using the support theorem for l_1 as a tool for characterizing efficient growth paths: The requirements of summability (i.e., $X \subset l_1$) and interiority (i.e., interior $X \neq \varnothing$) generally reflect conflicting aspects of the productive capacities of the underlying technology. Thus, a particular growth model in which feasible growth paths necessarily yield a summable stream of consumption goods will typically be incapable of providing consumption goods at a uniform rate in any given future period, and vice versa. This trade-off is most clearly illustrated by the fact that for the general growth model we are considering, by choosing units for measuring consumption goods outputs that embody a sufficiently high rate of discount, we can guarantee summable consumption possibilities, while by choosing units that embody a sufficiently low rate, we can guarantee uniform consumption possibilities, but usually not both.

There is one class of growth models, however, in which these conflicting aspects just balance each other. This class consists of the growth models where technology exhibits the following, additional productivity characteristics:

T6 IMPOSSIBILITY OF STORAGE WITH SUSTENANCE   There exist $p > 0$ and $q \geqq 0$ such that

$$p \cdot c + q \cdot z - q \cdot k \leqq 0 \qquad \text{for every} \quad (c, z, k) \in T.$$

T7 POSSIBILITY OF STORAGE AND REGENERATION   There exist $0 \leq \hat{k} \leqq \overline{k}$ and $\overline{z} > 0$ such that both $(0, \hat{k}, \hat{k}) \in T$ and $(0, \hat{z}, \hat{k}) \in T$.

T7 is more or less self-explanatory. It simply states that the economy is capable of replicating some capital stocks from which it is also capable of producing positive investment goods output—or together with T5, positive outputs (of both consumption and investment goods) within at most two periods. T7 would be true, for instance, if the economy were capable of replicating positive capital stocks, i.e., if there exists $0 < \hat{k} \leq \bar{k}$ such that $(0, \hat{k}, \hat{k}) \in T$ (taking $\hat{k} = \hat{z} = \hat{k}$ in T7).

T6, however, requires a bit more elaboration. Its label was chosen because it implies (and is implied by) the productivity limitation that the (closure of the) set of timeless potential net outputs

$$N = \{(c, y): y = z - k \text{ and } (c, z, k) \in T\} \tag{15}$$

does not contain any (c', y') such that both $c' \geq 0$ and $y' \geq 0$. In other words, roughly speaking, T6 amounts to the assumption that the economy is not capable of replicating some capital stocks while simultaneously producing some consumption goods output. In Appendix A we establish this equivalency and present two alternative conditions on technology—one involving substitution properties of outputs, the other productivity properties of exhaustible resource inputs—which entail T6 (and which are more interpretable, if more restrictive).

In any case, for the class of growth models where the technology satisfies these two assumptions (as well as our other maintained assumptions), we have a slightly generalized version of what might (from our present perspective) be viewed as the central result in [14]:

CONSUMPTION-VALUE MAXIMIZATION   Suppose T satisfies T6 and T7. If a feasible growth path is efficient, then it has an associated competitive price system (4) at which consumption value is maximized

$$\infty > \sum_{t=0}^{\infty} p_t \cdot c_t^* \geq \sum_{t=0}^{\infty} p_t \cdot c_t, \tag{16}$$

among all feasible growth paths (2). The converse obtains provided consumption goods prices are positive $p_t > 0$ for $t \geq 0$.

Proof   We now interpret the quantity sequence x as simply net final outputs

$$x = (\bar{k} - k_0, c_0, z_0 - k_1, \dots, c_t, z_t - k_{t+1}, \dots), \tag{17}$$

but the price sequence π and set X as before in (9) and (10), respectively. The crucial steps in the proof are first (summability) establishing that by virtue of T6,

$$\sum_{t=0}^{\infty} \sum_{i=1}^{m} c_{it} < \infty \tag{18}$$

for every solution to (2), so that the set X contains every sequence of net final outputs that is generated by a feasible growth path, and second (interiority) establishing that by virtue of T7, the set X is uniformly "productive." The remainder of the argument then simply consists in applying and interpreting the support theorem for l_1.

To see that (18) follows from T6, we use the stationary feasible price system (p, q) to evaluate the whole stream of consumption goods produced along an arbitrary feasible growth path:

$$\sum_{t=0}^{\ell} \sum_{i=1}^{m} \left(\left(\min_{i'} \{p_{i'}\} \right) c_{it} \right) \leq \sum_{t=0}^{\ell} p \cdot c_t = \sum_{t=0}^{\ell} (p \cdot c_t + q \cdot (z_t - k_{t+1}))$$

$$= \sum_{t=0}^{\ell} (p \cdot c_t + q \cdot z_t - q \cdot k_t) + q \cdot \bar{k} - q \cdot k_{\ell+1}$$

$$\leq q \cdot \bar{k} \quad \text{for} \quad \ell \geq 0.$$

An immediate consequence of this value-bound is

$$\sum_{t=0}^{\ell} \sum_{i=1}^{m} c_{it} \leq q \cdot \bar{k} \Big/ \min_{i} \{p_i\} < \infty \quad \text{for} \quad \ell \geq 0,$$

and hence (18).

To see that uniform "productivity" follows from T7 (given our maintained assumptions about initial capital stocks and technology), note first that T5 implies that (i) there exists $(\bar{c}', \bar{z}') > 0$ such that $(\bar{c}', \bar{z}', \bar{k}) \in T$ and (ii) there exists $(\hat{c}', \hat{z}') > 0$ such that $(\hat{c}', \hat{z}', \hat{z}) \in T$. Hence, the following quantity sequences $x \in X$ are generated by the corresponding growth paths $(c_s, z_s, k_s) \in T$ for $s \geq 0$:

$$x = (\bar{k}, 0, \ldots) \quad \text{when} \quad (c_s, z_s, k_s) = 0 \quad \text{for } s \geq 0$$

$$= (0, \bar{c}', \bar{z}', 0, \ldots) \quad = \begin{cases} (\bar{c}', \bar{z}', \bar{k}) & \text{for } s = 0 \\ 0 & \text{for } s \geq 1 \end{cases}$$

$$= (k - \hat{k}, 0, 0, \hat{c}', \hat{z}', 0, \ldots) \quad = \begin{cases} (0, \hat{z}, \hat{k}) & \text{for } s = 0 \\ (\hat{c}', \hat{z}', \hat{z}) & \text{for } s = 1 \\ 0 & \text{for } s \geq 2 \end{cases}$$

$$= (k - \hat{k}, 0, \ldots, 0, \hat{c}', \hat{z}', 0, \ldots) \quad = \begin{cases} (0, \hat{k}, \hat{k}) & \text{for } 0 \leq s \leq t-2 \\ (0, \hat{z}, \hat{k}) & \text{for } s = t-1 \\ (\hat{c}', \hat{z}', \hat{z}) & \text{for } s = t \\ 0 & \text{for } s \geq t+1 \end{cases}$$

for $t \geqq 2$. By letting

$$\delta = \min \left\{ \min_j \bar{k}_j, \min_i \bar{c}_i', \min_j \bar{z}_j', \min_i \hat{c}_i', \min_j \hat{z}_j' \right\},$$

we see that these in turn provide the requisite quantity sequences $x^t \in X$ for $t \geqq 0$.

As in the last section, it is again relatively straightforward to establish that $X \subset l_1$ is closed, convex, and freely disposable. Moreover, again letting the quantity sequence x^* be generated by the efficient growth path under scrutiny, x^* is still a boundary point of X. Hence, the desired conclusion follows directly upon application of the support theorem for l_1, since (1) implies (4) when $(c_s, z_s, k_s) = (c, z, k) \in T$ for $s = t$ and $(c_s, z_s, k_s) = (c_s^*, z_s^*, k_s^*)$ for $s \neq t$, and (16) when $k_0 = \bar{k}$, and $(c_t, z_t, k_t) \in T$ and $k_{t+1} = z_t$ for $t \geqq 0$. ∎

It is worth emphasizing here, although we establish a stronger result in the next section, that capital-value transversality also follows from the argument just given. That is, by taking the quantity sequence $x \in X$ generated by the trivial growth path $(c_t, z_t, k_t) = 0 \in T$ for $t \geqq 0$, (1) yields

$$\sum_{t=0}^{\infty} p_t \cdot c_t^* \geqq q_{-1} \cdot \bar{k}.$$

Putting this inequality together with (6), we see immediately that it must be true that

$$\lim_{t \to \infty} q_t \cdot k_{t+1}^* = 0. \tag{19}$$

It is also important to be aware of what the consumption-value maximization theorem does *not* claim: Namely, the theorem only asserts that *some* associated competitive price system exhibits the property of consumption-value maximization. And it is easy to construct examples where a particular efficient growth path also has an associated competitive price system that does not exhibit this property. The extended example presented in Appendix B is designed in part to illustrate this point. (For a more detailed elaboration in the context of closed multisector models, see the examples and results in [20].) That extended example also illustrates another obvious but important point, that without T6 (or, more generally, without summability in "natural" units of measurement), an efficient growth path may or may not have an associated competitive price system exhibiting consumption-value maximization (even though in our general model consumption-value is necessarily bounded).

VI. OPTIMALITY (OR CONSUMPTION-VALUE MAXIMIZATION) AND CAPITAL-VALUE TRANSVERSALITY

Given nonnegative, nontrivial values for consumption goods,

$$(\bar{p}_0, \bar{p}_1, \ldots) \geq 0, \tag{20}$$

a particular feasible growth path (denoted once more by asterisks) is *optimal* if

$$\infty > \sum_{t=0}^{\infty} \bar{p}_t \cdot c_t^* \geq \sum_{t=0}^{\infty} \bar{p}_t \cdot c_t \tag{21}$$

for every feasible growth path (2). In the literature on optimal growth theory, it is usually assumed that consumption goods output consists of a single quantity (i.e., that $m = 1$), which is measured in welfare or utility terms (refer again to footnote 3), and that consumption good values are constant-rate discount factors (i.e., that $\bar{p}_t = (1 + \rho)^{-t}$ for $t \geq 0$ with $\rho \geq 0$). Neither specialization is fundamental to the price characterization of optimal growth paths (though both have been central to the detailed description of their evolution).

In this section we use the support theorem for l_0 to develop a short, simple proof of the following important proposition:

CAPITAL-VALUE TRANSVERSALITY (Peleg and Weitzman) If a particular feasible growth path is optimal, then it has an associated competitive price system (4) such that

$$p_t = \bar{p}_t \qquad \text{for} \quad t \geq 0 \tag{22}$$

and

$$\lim_{t \to \infty} q_t \cdot k_{t+1}^* = 0. \tag{19}$$

The converse obtains without qualification.

Proof For the purposes of this argument, we interpret the quantity sequence x as net final outputs of welfare and investment goods

$$x = \left(\sum_{t=0}^{\infty} \bar{p}_t \cdot c_t, \bar{k} - k_0, z_0 - k_1, \ldots, z_t - k_{t+1}, \ldots \right), \tag{23}$$

the corresponding price sequence π as

$$\pi = (u, q_{-1}, q_0, \ldots, q_t, \ldots), \tag{24}$$

and the set X as

$$X = \left\{ x : x \in l_1, x_0 \leqq \sum_{t=0}^{\infty} \bar{p}_t \cdot c_t' \text{ and } (c_t', z_t, k_t) \in T \text{ for } t \geqq 0 \right\}. \quad (25)$$

It is easily checked that the quantity sequence

$$x^* = \left(\sum_{t=0}^{\infty} \bar{p}_t \cdot c_t^*, \bar{k} - k_0^*, z_0^* - k_1^*, \ldots, z_t^* - k_{t+1}^*, \ldots \right) \quad (26)$$

$$= \left(\sum_{t=0}^{\infty} \bar{p}_t \cdot c_t^*, 0, 0, \ldots \right)$$

generated by the optimal growth path is not an internal point of X, since otherwise there would be some quantity sequence $x' \in X$ such that $x_0' > x_0^*$ and $x_t' = 0$ for $t > 0$ corresponding to a feasible growth path yielding higher welfare. Also, the set X contains every quantity sequence generated by a feasible growth path, since then $0 \leqq x \leqq x^*$. Finally, it is quite straightforward to verify that $X \subset l_0$ is convex, freely disposable and "productive".[10] Hence, now utilizing the support theorem for l_0 to derive (1), we can infer

1. Nontrivial welfare value, i.e., $u > 0$ or, without loss of generality, $u = 1$: Suppose otherwise, that is, $u = 0$. Then $\pi \cdot x^* = 0$, while—since $\pi_t > 0$ and $x^t \in X$ for some $t \geqq 0$—$\pi \cdot x > 0$ for some $x \in X$, contradicting (1).

2. Intertemporal welfare-profit maximization, i.e., (4) and (22): For the quantity sequences generated by the growth paths $(c_s, z_s, k_s) = (c, z, k) \in T$ for $s = t$ and $(c_s, z_s, k_s) = (c_s^*, z_s^*, k_s^*)$ for $s \neq t$, (1) yields

$$\bar{p}_t \cdot c + q_t \cdot z - q_{t-1} \cdot k_t \leqq \bar{p}_t \cdot c_t^* + q_t \cdot z_t^* - q_{t-1} \cdot k_t^* = 0$$

for every $(c, z, k) \in T$ and $t \geqq 0$;

in light of 1 above.

3. Capital-value transversality, i.e., (19): The argument is identical to that presented toward the end of the last section, in light of 2 above. ∎

There is an interesting, if hardly surprising corollary to the capital-value transversality theorem.

DUALITY   If there exists an optimal solution to the problem

$$\text{maximize} \sum_{t=0}^{\infty} \bar{p}_t \cdot c_t \quad \text{subject to} \quad (2), \quad (27)$$

[10] The last claim is based on two implications of the maintained assumptions $\bar{k} > 0$ and T5, first (by virtue of the hypothesis $(\bar{p}_0, \bar{p}_1, \ldots) \geq 0$), that $x^0 = x^*$ works, and second, that the economy is capable of producing positive investment goods output in any given period, i.e., that x^t for $1 \leqq t \leqq n$ can be generated by the trivial growth path, while x^t for $t \geqq n + 1$ can be generated by a growth path involving only pure capital accumulation up through period t.

then there exists an optimal solution to the problem

$$\text{minimize} \quad q_{-1} \cdot \bar{k} \quad \text{subject to (3) and } p_t = \bar{p}_t \quad \text{for} \quad t \geq 0, \quad (28)$$

and their optimal values are equal.

Proof On the one hand, we see from (5) that feasible solutions to (27) and (28) must satisfy

$$\sum_{t=0}^{\infty} \bar{p}_t \cdot c_t \leq q_{-1} \cdot \bar{k}.$$

On the other hand, appealing to the theorem just proved, we see from (6) that there is a feasible solution to (28) [namely, that associated with the optimal solution to (27)] that satisfies

$$\sum_{t=0}^{\infty} \bar{p}_t \cdot c_t^* = q_{-1} \cdot \bar{k}.$$

But this is then an optimal solution to (28) exhibiting the asserted duality property. ∎

We note in passing that many of the recent results concerning global stability of optimal growth paths have their ultimate basis in the capital-value transversality theorem (in particular, see [7] and related contributions to the same symposium).

VII. COMPLICATIONS FROM PRIMARY FACTORS

The general growth model introduced in Section III has one very unrealistic feature; it implicitly rules out the existence of primary factors. In this section we repair this defect, and in doing so establish that all but one of the foregoing results remain virtually unaffected.

Suppose now that the feasible growth paths in the economy are described by

$$\begin{cases} (c_t, z_t, k_t, l_t) \in T', \quad k_{t+1} = z_t \quad \text{and} \quad l_t = \bar{l}_t = \bar{l} > 0 \quad \text{for} \quad t \geq 0, \\ k_0 = \bar{k} > 0 \end{cases} \quad (2')$$

where $l = (l_1, l_2, \ldots, l_h)$ is an h-vector of primary factor inputs, $\bar{l}$ is an h-vector of their exogenous supply, and $T' = \{(c, z, k, l)\}$ is the static technology available for producing outputs from capital stock and primary factor inputs. In fact, there is no real loss of generality in assuming that $h = 1$ and that $T = 1$, which we henceforth will.[11] Furthermore, we will assume that T' is again a nonnegative, closed set exhibiting properties analogous to T1–T5:

T'1 T' is convex;

T'2   If $(c, z, k, l) \in T'$, $0 \leq (c', z') \leq (c, z)$, and $(k', l') \geq (k, l)$, then $(c', z', k', l') \in T'$,

T'3 T' is a cone,

T'4   If $(c, z, k, l) \in T'$ and $(k, l) = 0$, then $(c, z) = 0$

T'5   If $(c, z, k, l) \in T', l > 0$, and $k' > k$, then there exists $(c', z') > (c, z)$ such that $(c', z', k', l) \in T'$.

Notice that now T'3 is completely innocuous, since feasible growth paths only involve the projection of a particular cross section of T' (namely, the convex set $\{(c, z, k) : (c, z, k, l) \in T')\}$), and any such convex set can be viewed as the projection of a particular cross section of a convex cone in 1 higher dimension. It is also worth mentioning that T'5 is equivalent—given our other maintained assumptions (especially T'1–T'3)—to a seemingly alternative productivity characteristic quite commonly encountered in the capital theory literature since Malinvaud's corrigendum [15]:

T'5'   NONTIGHTNESS IN CAPITAL STOCKS   If $(c, z, k, l) \in T'$ and $l > 0$, then there exists $(c'', z'') > (c, z)$, $k'' \geq 0$, and $0 \leq l'' < l$ such that $(c'', z'', k'', l'') \in T'$.[12]

(See, for example, the analysis centered around this and other productivity and substitution properties in Kurz [11].)

On the price side of the economy, the description of "feasible" price

---

[11] The former assertion follows from the observation that the structure of the set $\{(c, z, k): (c, z, k, \overline{l}) \in T'\}$ contains all the information we need to know about the structure of T' itself, and that this set can be equally well viewed as the projection of a cross section from 1 higher dimension as from h higher dimensions. (See also the comment concerning T'3 below.) The latter assertion follows from the observation that setting $\overline{l} = 1$ amounts to defining the unit for measuring the primary factor.

[12] To go from T'5 to T'5' take

$$(c'', z'', k'', l'') = \alpha(c', z', k', l) \quad \text{for some} \quad 0 < \alpha < 1 \quad \text{such that} \quad \alpha(c', z') > (c, z),$$

and from T'5' to T'5

$$(c', z') = (1 - \beta)(c, z) + \beta(c'', z'') \quad \text{for some} \quad 0 < \beta < 1 \quad \text{such that} \quad (1 - \beta)k + \beta k'' \leq k'$$

[and hence $(1 - \beta)l + \beta l'' < l$].

systems corresponding to (2') is

$$\begin{cases} (p_t, q_t, r_t, w_t) \in M' & \text{and} \quad r_t = q_{t-1} \quad \text{for} \quad t \geq 0, \\ q_{-1} \geq 0 \end{cases} \tag{3'}$$

where w is a scalar, say, wage and

$$M' = \{(p, q, r, w) : (p, q) \geq 0 \text{ and } p \cdot c + q \cdot z - r \cdot k - w \cdot l \leq 0$$
$$\text{for every } (c, z, k, l) \in T'\}$$

is the nonnegative subset of the dual cone to T'. Hence, an associated competitive price system is now defined as a nontrivial solution to (3') such that

$$p_t \cdot c + q_t \cdot z - q_{t-1} \cdot k - w_t \cdot l \leq p_t \cdot c_t^* + q_t \cdot z_t^* - q_{t-1} \cdot k_t^* - w_t = 0 \tag{4'}$$

for every $(c, z, k, l) \in T'$ and $t \geq 0$.

Given this amendment to our general growth model, by and large the only modifications needed in order to validate our previous analysis involve accounting for wage payments to the primary factor. Two such modifications are essential:

1. In the first place, in order for the conclusion of the support theorems (1) to yield competitive price systems (4'), in each previous application we must reinterpret the quantity sequence x to include net final outputs of primary factors $1 - l_t$ for $t \geq 0$, and the price sequence π to include a corresponding wage imputation w_t for $t \geq 0$.[13] Thus, for example, in the argument establishing consumption-value maximization the quantity sequence (17) becomes

$$x = (\bar{k} - k_0, c_0, z_0 - k_1, 1 - l_0, \ldots, c_t, z_t - k_{t+1}, 1 - l_t, \ldots), \tag{17'}$$

while the price sequence (9) becomes

$$\pi = (q_{-1}, p_0, q_0, w_0, \ldots, p_t, q_t, w_t, \ldots). \tag{9'}$$

and the set (10) becomes

$$x = \{x : x \in l_1, c_t \leq c_t', \quad \text{and} \quad (c_t', z_t, k_t, l_t) \in T' \quad \text{for} \quad t \geq 0\}. \tag{10'}$$

2. In the second place, in calculating bounds for consumption value, we must include an imputation to the stream of primary factors $\bar{l}_t = 1$ for $t \geq 0$, as well as initial capital stocks $\bar{k}$. Thus, for example, the upper bounds (5) and (6) become, respectively,

$$\sum_{t=0}^{\ell} p_t \cdot c_t \leq \sum_{t=0}^{\ell} p_t \cdot c_t + q_\ell \cdot k_{\ell+1} \leq q_{-1} \cdot \bar{k} + \sum_{t=0}^{\ell} w_t \quad \text{for} \quad \ell \geq 0 \tag{5'}$$

---

[13] An alternative method of achieving the same result is simply to reinterpret the technology $T = \{(c, z, k) : (c, z, k, 1) \in T'\}$ and define the imputation $w_t = p_t \cdot c_t^* - q_t \cdot z_t^* - q_{t-1} \cdot k_t^*$. Then (4') follows from the left-hand inequality in (4)—which is demonstrable without reference to T3—by virtue of T'2 and T'3. However, while this maneuver does reflect the intrinsic economics of residual payment to a fixed factor, unlike the argument sketched in the text, it does not yield any additional information about value maximization (see the following discussion).

for every feasible growth path (2′) and

$$\sum_{t=0}^{\ell} p_t \cdot c_t^* \leq \sum_{t=0}^{\ell} p_t \cdot c_t^* + q_\ell \cdot k_{\ell+1}^* = q_{-1} \cdot \bar{k} + \sum_{t=0}^{\ell} w_t \qquad \text{for} \quad \ell \geq 0.^{14} \quad (6')$$

The fact that, in general, we cannot rule out an unbounded imputation

$$q_{-1} \cdot \bar{k} + \sum_{t=0}^{\infty} w_t = q_{-1} \cdot \bar{k} + \lim_{\ell \to \infty} \sum_{t=0}^{\ell} w_t = \infty$$

has several important consequences, both analytical and conceptual:

(a)   The corollaries to the price characterization theorem [itself modified to include a term $\sum_{t=0}^{\infty} w_t (1 - l_t)$ on the right-hand side of (11) and a term $\sum_{t=0}^{\infty} |1 - l_t|$ on the left-hand side of the inequality restricting comparison paths] must be restated in terms of deviations in consumption value $\sum_{t=0}^{\infty} p_t \cdot (c_t - c_t^*) (= 0$ when $c_t = c_t^*$ for $t \geq 0$), rather than in terms of simple consumption value $\sum_{t=0}^{\infty} p_t \cdot c_t (= \sum_{t=0}^{\infty} p_t \cdot c_t^*$ when $c_t = c_t^*$ for $t \geq 0$).

(b)   The argument at the end of Section V establishing capital-value transversality must be altered to accommodate the fact that with the reinterpretation (17′), the trivial growth path $(c_t, z_t, k_t, l_t) = 0 \in T'$ for $t \geq 0$ no longer generates a quantity sequence in X (since, by definition, the totality of primary factors is unbounded). This is easily accomplished once we observe that the "almost" trivial growth paths $(c_t, z_t, k_t, l_t) = 0 \in T'$ for $0 \leq t \leq \ell$ and $(c_t, z_t, k_t, l_t) = (0, 0, 0, 1) \in T'$ for $\ell < t$, for $\ell \geq 0$, do generate quantity sequences in X. Hence, for these growth paths, (1) yields

$$\infty > \sum_{t=0}^{\infty} p_t \cdot c_t^* \geq q_{-1} \cdot \bar{k} + \sum_{t=0}^{\ell} w_t \qquad \text{for} \quad \ell \geq 0$$

or

$$\infty > \sum_{t=0}^{\infty} p_t \cdot c_t^* \geq q_{-1}\bar{k} + \sum_{t=0}^{\infty} w_t.$$

In conjunction with (6′), this inequality immediately entails capital-value transversality (19).

(c)   The suitability of consumption-value maximization (at given consumption goods values) as the fundamental notion of optimality must be

---

14 Similarly, in the duality corollary to the capital-value transversality theorem, the dual problem (28) becomes

$$\text{minimize} \quad q_{-1} \cdot \bar{k} + \sum_{t=0}^{\infty} w_t \quad \text{subject to (3′) and} \quad p_t = \bar{p}_t \qquad \text{for} \quad t \geq 0. \qquad (28')$$

reappraised, since it may simply be overly restrictive (as it is, for instance, in the canonical one-good model, where the golden rule path does not yield maximum consumption value at *any* given consumption goods values).[15] Anything like a complete resolution of this issue is way beyond the scope of our paper—if not beyond the limit of our ability. However, we will briefly discuss one directly pertinent aspect—the variety of similar but broader alternatives and their respective price characterizations—in the following section.

There is a second point in the foregoing analysis at which the introduction of primary factors raises a serious substantive issue. This is in Section V, where we employed T6 to guarantee summability of the whole stream of consumption goods. While it is true that an appropriate analog

T′6   There exist $p > 0$ and $q \geqq 0$ such that

$$p \cdot c + q \cdot z - q \cdot k \leqq 0 \qquad \text{for every} \quad (c, z, k, l) \in T'$$

also implies

$$\sum_{t=0}^{\infty} \sum_{i=1}^{m} c_{it} < \infty \tag{18'}$$

for every solution to (2′), this sort of productivity characteristic may now appear—at least to one steeped in the tradition of neoclassical growth theory—to be quite restrictive. In particular, since T′6 is easily shown to be equivalent to condition A1 in Appendix A,[16] it automatically excludes the

---

[15] Here, of course, we are implicitly accepting the common convention that a maximum must be finite. This makes good sense in this instance, since otherwise consumption-value maximization may be essentially vacuous (as it is, for instance, again in the canonical one-good model, with any given consumption goods values such that $\inf_{s \geqq 0} \bar{p}_{t_s} > 0$ for some subsequence of periods $\{t_s\}$).

The example in Appendix B shows that even without primary factors, the notion of consumption-value maximization may be too limiting. Indeed, generally speaking, in order that the problem (27), or better yet, the problem

$$\text{maximize} \sum_{t=0}^{\infty} \bar{p}_t \cdot c_t \quad \text{subject to (2′)} \tag{27'}$$

have a solution, the permissible choice of consumption goods values (20) will typically exclude perfectly acceptable growth paths (i.e., some efficient growth paths) from serious consideration. (In this sense, the class of growth models considered in Section V appears to be quite special.)

[16] Obviously, after N is redefined to be compatible with T'

$$N = \{(c, y) : y = z - k \text{ and } (c, z, k, l) \in T' \text{ for some } l \geqq 0\}. \tag{15'}$$

Then the proof of this equivalency is identical to that of Lemma 1A (Appendix A) but for the substitution of (c^s, z^s, k^s, l^s) for (c^s, z^s, k^s), (c, z, k, l) for (c, z, k), and T' for T.

possibility of nontrivial (modified) golden rule paths. But while this may be analytically inconvenient, it is surely not intuitively implausible; the mere availability of primary factors may just not be enough to offset the scarcity of essential exhaustible resources. One precise formulation of this latter intuition is outlined in the last comment in Appendix A.

VIII. ALTERNATIVE NOTIONS OF OPTIMALITY

In order to circumvent the limitations of consumption-value maximization as a procedure for choosing a "best" efficient growth path, a number of related but weaker criteria have been proposed in the literature [4, 8, 9, 17, 29, 32]. For our purposes here it is useful to incorporate these in a more systematic listing of candidates, all of which involve evaluating the whole stream of consumption goods at given values (20). In rank order of decreasing strength (i.e., so each entails its successor), one could reasonably judge a particular feasible growth path (denoted, for the last time, by asterisks) to be "optimal" according to whether it exhibits

1. *Consumption-value maximization* $\infty > \sum_{t=0}^{\infty} \bar{p}_t \cdot c_t^* \geq \sum_{t=0}^{\infty} \bar{p}_t \cdot c_t$ for every feasible growth path (2'); or

2. *Deviations in consumption-value maximization (or "best" deviations in consumption value)* $0 \geq \lim_{\ell \to \infty} \sum_{t=0}^{\ell} \bar{p}_t \cdot (c_t - c_t^*)$ for every feasible growth path (2'); or

3. *"Better" deviations in consumption value* $0 \geq \limsup_{\ell \to \infty} \sum_{t=0}^{\ell} \bar{p}_t \cdot (c_t - c_t^*)$ for every feasible growth path (2'); or

4. *"Good" deviations in consumption value* $0 \geq \liminf_{\ell \to \infty} \sum_{t=0}^{\ell} \bar{p}_t \cdot (c_t - c_t^*)$ for every feasible growth path (2'); or

5. *Restricted deviations in consumption-value maximization* $0 \geq \sum_{t=0}^{\infty} \bar{p}_t \cdot (c_t - c_t^*)$ for every feasible growth path (2') such that $\sum_{t=0}^{\infty} \sum_{i=1}^{m} u_{it} |c_{it} - c_{it}^*| < \infty$; or (only when $\sum_{t=0}^{\infty} \bar{p}_t \cdot c_t^* < \infty$)

6. *Restricted consumption-value maximization* $\infty > \sum_{t=0}^{\infty} \bar{p}_t \cdot c_t^* \geq \sum_{t=0}^{\infty} \bar{p}_t \cdot c_t$ for every feasible growth path (2') such that $\sum_{t=0}^{\infty} \sum_{i=1}^{m} u_{it} |c_{it} - c_{it}^*| < \infty$,

where, in 5 and 6, $u_{it} \geq \bar{p}_{it}$ for $1 \leq i \leq m$, $t \geq 0$ are some (fixed) positive units for measuring consumption goods outputs. Since we know that efficient growth paths are "optimal" in the sense of 5 with primary factors (or in the sense of 6 without, both at associated consumption goods prices), it is quite natural to focus on this criterion in generalizing the capital-value transversality theorem of Section VI; similar results can be obtained in exactly the same manner for the criteria 2 and 4, but not for 3 (since the lim sup operation does not preserve convexity).

Before we can derive a specific price characterization, however, we will require one additional assumption concerning the possibility of substituting investment goods output for consumption goods output:

T'8 ACCUMULATION FROM FOREGONE CONSUMPTION If $(c, z, k, l) \in T'$ and $0 \leq c' \leq c$, then there exists $z' > z$ such that $(c', z', k, l) \in T'$.[17]

Thus armed—and fortified by preceding applications of the support theorems—it is almost routine to establish the following general result:

PRICE CHARACTERIZATION OF "OPTIMAL" GROWTH PATHS Suppose T' satisfies T'8. If a particular feasible growth path is "optimal" in the sense of 5, then it has an associated competitive price system (4') such that

$$p_t = \bar{p}_t \quad \text{for} \quad t \geq 0 \tag{22}$$

and

$$0 \geq \sum_{t=0}^{\infty} \bar{p}_t \cdot (c_t - c_t^*) - q_{-1} \cdot (k - \bar{k}) \tag{29}$$

for every growth path that (i) is feasible from nonnegative capital stocks, or satisfies (2') with $\bar{k} = k \geq 0$, and (ii) yields sufficiently small deviations in consumption, or satisfies

$$\sum_{t=0}^{\infty} \sum_{i=1}^{m} u_{it} |c_{it} - c_{it}^*| < \infty.$$

The converse obtains without qualification.

Remark Property (29) is only one way of expressing the fact that the associated capital goods prices reflect their marginal "welfare" value. A more complete catalog, along with a more leisurely discussion, can be found in [6].

Proof We will only sketch the essential similarities and differences between this and previous arguments. Here the quantity sequence x is

---

[17] The specific counterexample detailed at the end of Appendix B clearly shows that for the purpose of characterizing weaker notions of optimality than consumption-value maximization, something like this substitution condition cannot be dispensed with. Presently the assumptions $\bar{k} > 0$, $\bar{l}_t = 1$ for $t \geq 0$, T'5, and T'8 play (and previously, in Section VI, the assumptions $\bar{k} > 0$ and T5 played) precisely the same role as does Slater's condition (or, more generally, some version of "constraint qualification") in ordinary concave programming.

interpreted as net final outputs of "welfare," investment goods, and primary factors,

$$x = \left(\sum_{t=0}^{\infty} \bar{p}_t \cdot (c_t - c_t^*), \bar{k} - k_0, z_0 - k_1, 1 - l_0, \ldots, z_t - k_{t+1}, 1 - l_t, \ldots \right), \tag{30}$$

the corresponding price sequence π as

$$\pi = (u, q_{-1}, q_0, w_0, \ldots, q_t, w_t, \ldots), \tag{31}$$

and the set X as further constrained by the restriction on permissible deviations in consumption,

$$X = \left\{ x : x \in l_0, x_0 \leq \sum_{t=0}^{\infty} \bar{p}_t \cdot (c_t' - c_t^*), \right.$$

$$\left. \sum_{t=0}^{\infty} \sum_{i=1}^{m} u_{it} |c_{it}' - c_{it}^*| < \infty \text{ and } (c_t', z_t, k_t, l_t) \in T' \text{ for } t \geq 0 \right\}. \tag{32}$$

As with the proof of capital-value transversality, it is quite easily seen that $x^* = 0$ is not an internal point of X, and that $X \subset l_0$ is convex, freely disposable but now—rather than "productive"—productive, in the following sense: There exists $x_0' \leq 0$ such that for every $t > 0$ there exists $x^t \in X$ such that $x_0^t \geq x_0'$, $x_s^t > 0$ for $s = t$ and $x_s^t \geq 0$ for $0 < s \neq t$.[18] Thus, we can once more utilize the support theorem for l_0 to deduce (1). Then, the same reasoning employed in Section VI yields, without loss of generality, $u = 1$, as well as (4) and (22). Finally, (29) simply follows by specializing (1) to comparisons with quantity sequences generated by growth paths satisfying the requisite restrictions. ∎

Our interest in investigating this kind of characterization was greatly inspired by the careful and comprehensive work of Peleg [26] and Peleg and Zilcha [29] relating to the open, multisector model. It would be nice, if possible, to elaborate the connection between the seemingly different productivity and substitution properties underlying their and our quite similar results.

[18] Because of T′5 (given $\bar{k} > 0$ and $\bar{l}_t = 1$ for $t \geq 0$) and (20) we know that $c_t^* \geq 0$ for some $t \geq 0$. Suppose that $c_s^* = 0$ for $0 \leq s < t^* < \infty$ and $c_{t^*}^* \geq 0$. Appealing to T′8, pick $0 \leq c' \leq c_{t^*}^*$ and $z' > z_{t^*}^*$ such that $(c', z', k_{t^*}^*, 1) \in T'$. Then the growth path $(c_s, z_s, k_s, l_s) = \alpha(c_{t^*}^*, z_{t^*}^*, k_{t^*}^*, l_s^*) + (1 - \alpha)(0, 0, 0, 1)$ for $0 \leq s < t^*$, $(c_s, z_s, k_s, l_s) = \alpha(c', z', k_{t^*}^*, 1) + (1 - \alpha)(0, 0, 0, 1)$ for $s = t^*$, $(c_s, z_s, k_s, l_s) = (c_{t^*}^*, z_{t^*}^*, \alpha z', 1)$ for $s = t^* + 1$, and $(c_s, z_s, k_s, l_s) = (c_s^*, z_s^*, k_s^*, l_s^*)$ for $s > t^* + 1$ is feasible from initial capital stocks $0 \leq \alpha k_0^* < \bar{k}$ provided only that $0 < \alpha < 1$ and $\alpha z' \geq z_{t^*}^*$. Now appealing to T′5, these "surplus" initial capital stocks $\bar{k} - \alpha k_0^* > 0$ can be used to generate growth paths that yield excess investment goods output $z_t - k_{t+1} > 0$ or excess primary factor input $1 - l_t > 0$ in any given period t. These paths, in turn, generate the requisite quantity sequences x^t for $t > 0$.

APPENDIX A

In this appendix we establish equivalence between T6 and the productivity condition, defining $\bar{N} = $ closure of N [see Eq. (15)],

A1   There is no $(c, y) \in \bar{N}$ such that $c \geq 0$ and $y \geq 0$,

and sufficiency for T6 of either the substitution condition,

A2   UNIFORM SUBSTITUTION BETWEEN OUTPUT OF EACH CONSUMPTION GOOD AND OUTPUT OF ALL INVESTMENT GOODS   For every $1 \leq i \leq m$ and $\varepsilon_i > 0$ there is a $\delta_i > 0$ such that if $(c, z, k) \in T$ and $c_i \geq \varepsilon_i$, then $(c', z', k) \in T$ for $c' = c - (0, \ldots, \varepsilon_i, \ldots, 0)$ and $z' = z + \delta_i(1, 1, \ldots, 1)$,

or the productivity condition, assuming that capital stock of type 1 is an exhaustible resource (see footnote 5),

A3   STRICT DETERIORATION OF CAPITAL STOCKS WITHOUT EXHAUSTIBLE RESOURCES   If $(c, z, k) \in T$, $z_1 = k_1 = 0$ and $(c, z, k) \neq 0$, then $z_j < k_j$ for some $2 \leq j \leq n$.

LEMMA 1A   T6 obtains if and only if A1 does.

Proof   Necessity: Given T6, suppose that A1 were false, i.e., that there is $(c', y') \in \bar{N}$ such that $c' \geq 0$ and $y' \geq 0$. Then (i) there is a sequence $\{(c^s, y^s)\}$ such that $(c^s, y^s) \in N$ and $\lim_{s \to \infty}(c^s, y^s) = (c', y')$ with a corresponding sequence $\{(c^s, z^s, k^s)\}$ such that $(c^s, z^s, k^s) \in T$ and $y^s = z^s - k^s$, while (ii) $p \cdot c' + q \cdot y' \geq p \cdot c' > 0$. Hence, for sufficiently large s,

$$(c^s, z^s, k^s) \in T \qquad \text{but} \qquad p \cdot c^s + q \cdot z^s - q \cdot k^s = p \cdot c^s + q \cdot y^s > 0,$$

contradicting T6.

Sufficiency: We will use the easily verified fact that given our maintained assumptions on T, $\bar{N}$ is a closed, convex cone exhibiting free disposal in y (i.e., if $(c, y) \in \bar{N}$ and $y' \leq y$, then $(c, y') \in \bar{N}$).

Given A1, let $0 \leq n' \leq n$ be such that if $1 \leq j' \leq n'$ ($n' + 1 \leq j' \leq n$), then there is no (some) $(c, y) \in \bar{N}$ such that $c = 0$ and $y_j > 0$ for $j = j'$, $y_j = 0$ for $j \neq j'$. Partitioning $y = (y^1, y^2)$ accordingly, consider the set

$$U = \{(c, y^1):(c, y) \in \bar{N} \text{ and } y^2 = 0\}.$$

Since $\bar{N}$ is a closed, convex cone, so is U. Moreover, the hypothesis A1 together with the choice of n' imply that there is no $(c, y^1) \in U$ such that $(c, y^1) \geq 0$. Hence, appealing to a duality result characterizing 0 as a maximal point of a closed, convex cone (see Nikaido [21, pp. 35–36]), we know that there exists $(p, q^1) > 0$ such that

$$(p, q^1) \cdot (c, y^1) \leq 0 \qquad \text{for every} \quad (c, y^1) \in U. \tag{A1}$$

Now consider the set

$$V = \{(x, y^2): x \leqq (p, q^1) \cdot (c, y^1) \text{ and } (c, y) \in \bar{N}\}.$$

Since $\bar{N}$ is a convex cone exhibiting free disposal in y, V is a convex cone exhibiting free disposal (i.e., if $(x, y^2) \in V$ and $(x', y^{2\prime}) \leqq (x, y^2)$, then $(x', y^{2\prime}) \in V$). Moreover, in light of (A1), 0 must be a boundary point of V. Hence, using a standard support theorem (see again, for instance, Nikaido [21, p. 35]), we know that there exists $(\lambda, q^2) \geq 0$ such that

$$\lambda \cdot x + q^2 \cdot y^2 \leqq 0 \qquad \text{for every} \quad (x, y^2) \in V$$

or

$$\lambda(p, q^1) \cdot (c, y^1) + q^2 \cdot y^2 \leqq 0 \qquad \text{for every} \quad (c, y) \in \bar{N}. \tag{A2}$$

But without loss of generality $\lambda = 1$, since if $\lambda = 0$, then $q^2 \geq 0$ and, again by the choice of n', there is some $(0, (0, y^2)) \in \bar{N}$ such that $q^2 \cdot y^2 > 0$, contradicting (A2). Hence, we have established that there exist $p > 0$ and $q = (q^1, q^2) \geq 0$ such that

$$p \cdot c + q \cdot y \leqq 0 \qquad \text{for every} \quad (c, y) \in \bar{N},$$

which implies the desired conclusion

$$p \cdot c + q \cdot z - q \cdot k \leqq 0 \qquad \text{for every} \quad (c, z, k) \in T$$

(since $N \subset \bar{N}$). ∎

It is worth mentioning explicitly that T5 requires that $q \geq 0$ in T6 (so that, for example, our use of T6 in the text makes sense).

LEMMA 2A   If A2 obtains, then so does T6.

Proof   For this argument we require the result that the units for measuring investment goods output can be specified, consistent with our maintained assumptions together with T7, so that the following productivity limitation is satisfied:

A4   IMPOSSIBILITY OF SUSTAINED CAPITAL ACCUMULATION   There is no $(c, y) \in \bar{N}$ such that $c \geqq 0$ and $y > 0$.

Since this result is established in exactly the same fashion as the well-known result that the von Neumann growth rate in the closed, multisector model[19] can be specified equal to zero (see, in particular, the discussion and references in [14]), we omit the details of its proof.

What we will show explicitly, then, is that A2 and A4 imply A1 or, by virtue of Lemma 1A, T6: Given A2 and A4, suppose that A1 were false, i.e.,

---

[19] The closed, multisector model is the specialization of our general model in which $m = n$ and $T = \{(c, z, y): c + z = y, (c, z) \geqq 0 \text{ and } (y, k) \in S\}$, where $S = \{(y, k)\}$ is the static technology for producing (undifferentiated) outputs from capital stock inputs.

that there is some $(c', y') \in \bar{N}$ such that $c' \geq 0$ and $y' \geqq 0$ (for definiteness assume $c'_i > 0$ for $i = i'$, $c'_i \geqq 0$ for $i \neq i'$), and hence, that there is a sequence $\{(c^s, y^s)\}$ such that $(c^s, y^s) \in N$ and $\lim_{s \to \infty} (c^s, y^s) = (c', y')$ with a corresponding sequence $\{(c^s, z^s, k^s)\}$ such that $(c^s, z^s, k^s) \in T$ and $y^s = z^s - k^s$. Then, there must be some $\varepsilon_{i'} > 0$ such that, for sufficiently large s, $c^s_{i'} \geqq \varepsilon_{i'}$, and hence, by virtue of A2, some $\delta_{i'} > 0$ such that, again for sufficiently large s, $(c^{s'}, z^{s'}, k^s) \in T$ or $(c^{s'}, y^{s'}) \in N$ for

$$c^{s'} = c^s - (0, \ldots, \varepsilon_{i'}, \ldots, 0), \qquad z^{s'} = z^s + \delta_{i'}(1, 1, \ldots, 1),$$

and

$$y^{s'} = y^s + \delta_{i'}(1, 1, \ldots, 1).$$

But this means that $\lim_{s \to \infty} (c^{s'}, y^{s'}) = (c' - (0, \ldots, \varepsilon_{i'}, \ldots, 0), \; y' + \delta_{i'}(1, 1, \ldots, 1)) \in \bar{N}$, contradicting A4. ∎

LEMMA 3A   If A3 obtains, then so does T6.

Proof   What we will show here is that when capital stock of type 1 is an exhaustible resource, A3 implies A1, and hence T6: Given A3, once again suppose that A1 were false, i.e., that ... (as in the preceding proof).... Because capital stock of type 1 is an exhaustible resource, we can also suppose that $z^s_1 = 0$ and $y^s_1 = -k^s_1$ or $\lim_{s \to \infty} z^s_1 = \lim_{s \to \infty} k^s_1 = 0$ (since $\lim_{s \to \infty} (z^s_1 - k^s_1) = \lim_{s \to \infty} y^s_1 = y'_1 \geqq 0$). Now consider the sequence $\{x^s\}$ such that

$$x^s = (c^s, z^s, k^s) / \|(c^s, z^s, k^s)\| \in T$$

(since T is homogeneous). By the Bolzano–Weierstrass theorem this sequence must have an accumulation point, say, $x = (c, z, k)$. But then $(c, z, k) \in T$ (since T is closed), $z_1 = k_1 = 0$ (since $\lim_{s \to \infty} z^s_1 = \lim_{s \to \infty} k^s_1 = 0$ but $\lim_{s \to \infty} c^s = c' \geq 0$), and $(c, z, k) \geq 0$ (since $\|x^s\| = 1$), but $z_j \geqq k_j$ for all $2 \leqq j \leqq n$ (since $\lim_{s \to \infty} (z^s_j - k^s_j) = \lim_{s \to \infty} y^s_j = y'_j \geqq 0$), contradicting A3. ∎

Several comments are pertinent to the foregoing results:

1. If T is polyhedral, then N is polyhedral, and $\bar{N} = N$ (see, for instance, Rockafellar [31, pp. 171 and 175]). In this case (or, more generally, whenever $\bar{N} = N$), because we need only consider single points in N and T rather than sequences of points in N and T, Lemma 1A immediately reveals that T6 is necessary as well as sufficient for summability. Moreover, for the same reason, Lemmas 2A and 3A remain true with some weakening of A2 and A3, respectively. In particular, we can relax the uniformity requirement in A2 [to read "For every $1 \leq i \leq m$ and $\varepsilon_i > 0$ if $(c, z, k) \in T$ and $c_i \geqq \varepsilon_i$, then there is a $\delta_i > 0$ such that $(c', z', k) \in T$....," so that δ_i can depend on (c, z, k) rather than just c_i] and the strictness requirement in A3 [to read

"... then $c = 0$ or $z_j < k_j$ for some $2 \leq j \leq n$," so that $(0, k, k) \in T$ such that $k_j > 0$ for some $2 \leq j \leq n$ is permitted; see comment 4 below].

2. We can directly generalize A3 and Lemma 3A when capital stocks of type $1, 2, \ldots, n' \leq n$ are exhaustible resources (by simply replacing z_1, k_1, and 2 with $z^1 = (z_1, z_2, \ldots, z_{n'})$, $k^1 = (k_1, k_2, \ldots, k_{n'})$, and $n' + 1$, respectively). This sort of productivity condition seems to us a very natural way of modeling the most pessimistic (as well as most unimaginative) "limits of growth" prospect.

3. Neither A2 nor A3 is necessary for T6. This will be demonstrated shortly, in terms of the example we examine in the following appendix.

4. There are alternative substitution conditions that entail T6 when T7 is strengthened to

T7′ POSSIBILITY OF STORAGE WITHOUT SUSTENANCE There exists $0 < \hat{k} \leq \bar{k}$ such that $(0, \hat{k}, \hat{k}) \in T$.

For discussion and analysis of some such conditions in the context of the closed multisector model we once more refer the interested reader to [14]. Note, however, that while A3 is consistent with T7, it is not consistent with T7′.

5. When there are primary factors in the economy, analogs of neither A2 nor A3 are sufficient for T′6. However, if in addition to

A′3 If $(c, z, k, l) \in T'$, $z_1 = k_1 = 0$, and $k \neq 0$, then $z_j < k_j$ for some $2 \leq j \leq n$,

we have (some version of)

A′5 LIMITED PRODUCTIVITY OF PRIMARY FACTORS If $(c, z, k, l) \in T'$ and $l' \geq \|k\|$, then $(c, z, k, l') \in T'$,

then minor changes in the argument establishing Lemma 3A yield

LEMMA 3′A If A′3 and A′5 obtain, then so does T′6.

Proof What we will show is that, when capital stock of type 1 is an exhaustible resource, A′3 and A′5 imply A1 and hence T′6: Given A′3 and A′5, suppose that A1 were false, i.e., ... (as in the proof of Lemma 3A but with (c^s, z^s, k^s, l^s) and T' substituted for (c^s, z^s, k^s) and T, respectively) .... As before we can also suppose that $\lim_{s \to \infty} z_1^s = \lim_{s \to \infty} k_1^s = 0$, while here A′5 enables us to suppose that $l^s = \|k^s\|$. Now consider

$$x^s = (c^s, z^s, k^s, l^s)/\|(c^s, z^s, k^s, l^s)\| \in T' \qquad \text{for} \quad s \geq 0$$

with accumulation point $x = (c, z, k, l)$. Then it must be true that $(c, z, k, l) \in T'$, $z_1 = k_1 = 0$, and $k \neq 0$ (since $\|x\| = 1$, while if $k = 0$, then by virtue of A′5 $l = 0$, then by virtue of T′4 $(c, z) = 0$), but $z_j \geq k_j$ for all $2 \leq j \leq n$, contradicting A′3. ∎

Note finally that A′3 and A′5 are consistent with the analog of T7:

T′7 There exist $0 \leq \hat{k} \leq \bar{k}$ and $\hat{z} > 0$ such that both $(0, \hat{k}, \hat{k}, 1) \in T'$ and $(0, \hat{z}, \hat{k}, 1) \in T'$.

APPENDIX B

In this appendix we elaborate an extended example of our general model, one in which there are only two types of both consumption goods and capital stocks. Capital stock of type 1 is an exhaustible resource, while capital stock of type 2 serves as both an inventory of consumption goods and—in a process using up the exhaustible resource as raw material—an originator of consumption goods. Besides generally illustrating the consumption-value maximization theorem of Section V, the example specifically demonstrates that

1. neither A2 nor A3 is necessary for T6;
2. the question of whether T6 is necessary for summability [i.e., $\sum_{t=0}^{\infty} \sum_{i=1}^{m} c_{it} < \infty$ for every solution to (2)] is both open and subtle;
3. in fact, summability is not necessary for consumption-value maximization; and
4. even with summability, there may be some associated competitive price system that does not exhibit consumption-value maximization, while without summability, there may be no associated competitive price system that exhibits consumption-value maximization.

1. *Example*

$m = n = 2$

$$T = \{(c, z, k) : c_1 \leqq h(k_1 - z_1, k_2), z_1 \leqq k_1, c_2 + z_2 \leqq k_2, \text{ and } (c, z, k) \geqq 0\}$$

where $h(x_1, x_2)$ for $(x_1, x_2) \geqq 0$ is differentiable, nonnegative [strictly positive for $(x_1, x_2) > 0$], increasing [strictly increasing for $(x_1, x_2) > 0$], concave, and linear homogeneous and satisfies $h(0, x_2) = h(x_1, 0) = 0$, and

Case 1 $\lim_{x_1 \to 0^+} h_1(x_1, x_2) < \infty$ for $x_2 \geqq 0$, e.g., $h(x_1, x_2) = (1 - e^{-(x_1/x_2)})x_2$

or

Case 2a $\lim_{x_1 \to 0^+} h_1(x_1, x_2) = \infty$ for $x_2 > 0$ and for every $0 < x'_1 < \infty$, $x'_2 > 0$ there is some $0 < \alpha < 1$ such that

$$\frac{h_1(x_1, x_2)x_1}{h(x_1, x_2)} \geqq \alpha \qquad \text{for} \quad 0 \leqq x_1 \leqq x'_1, \quad x_2 \geqq x'_2$$

e.g., $h(x_1, x_2) = x_1^\alpha x_2^{1-\alpha}$ with $0 < \alpha < 1$ or

Case 2b $\lim_{x_1 \to 0^+} h_1(x_1, x_2) = \infty$ for $x_2 > 0$ and for some $0 < x_1' < \infty$, $x_2' > 0$ there is no $0 < \alpha < 1$ such that

$$\frac{h_1(x_1, x_2) x_1}{h(x_1, x_2)} \geq \alpha \quad \text{for} \quad 0 \leq x_1 \leq x_1', \quad x_2 \geq x_2'$$

e.g.,

$$h(x_1, x_2) = \begin{cases} (-\log(x_1/x_2))^{-\beta} x_2 & \text{for} \quad 0 \leq x_1/x_2 \leq e^{-\beta-1} \\ \tilde{h}(x_1/x_2) x_2 & \text{otherwise} \end{cases}$$

with $\beta > 0$, $\tilde{h}(x)$ for $x \geq e^{-\beta-1}$ any differentiable, strictly increasing, and concave function such that $\tilde{h}(e^{-\beta-1}) = (\beta + 1)^{-\beta}$ and $\tilde{h}'(e^{-\beta-1}) = (\beta + 1)^{-\beta-1} \beta e^{\beta+1}$.

One can easily verify that this particular technology satisfies all of our maintained assumptions. It also satisfies the strong version of T7 mentioned at the end of the preceding appendix, T7'. (Indeed, it is obvious that the largest possible growth rate of both capital stocks—achieved only when there is no consumption goods output—is zero.) Notice finally that this technology does not satisfy either A2 (since, for example, consumption good of type 2 cannot be converted into investment good of type 1) or A3 (since capital stock of type 2 can be costlessly stored); shortly we will show that it satisfies T6 only in Case 1.

2. Results

The example was chosen in large part because it permits direct characterization of efficiency. This in turn permits full concentration on the property of consumption-value maximization.

(a) *Efficient growth paths* A feasible growth path is efficient if and only if *outputs are not obviously wasted*, i.e., consumption goods outputs are never freely disposed, $c_{1t} = h(k_{1t} - z_{1t}, k_{2t})$ and $c_{2t} = k_{2t} - z_{2t}$ for $t \geq 0$, and *capital stocks are not superfluously maintained*, i.e., resources are eventually exhausted, $\lim_{t \to \infty} k_{1t} = 0$, while (i) if resources are exhausted in finite time, then inventories are eventually depleted, and if there is a $\bar{t}_1 < \infty$ such that $k_{1t} > 0$ for $0 \leq t \leq \bar{t}_1$ and $k_{1t} = 0$ for $\bar{t}_1 < t$, then $\lim_{t \to \infty} k_{2t} = 0$; (ii) if inventories are depleted in finite time, then resources are exhausted by the same time, and if there is a $\bar{t}_2 < \infty$ such that $k_{2t} > 0$ for $0 \leq t \leq \bar{t}_2$ and $k_{2t} = 0$ for $\bar{t}_2 < t$, then $k_{1t} = 0$ for $\bar{t}_2 < t$ (or, alternatively, if $k_{1t} > 0$, then $k_{2t} > 0$ for $t \geq 0$).

Proof For simplicity, here we will denote the given path without super-script, and various comparison paths with prime superscript.

Necessity: (i) No obvious waste: Suppose otherwise, i.e., $c_{1t} < h(k_{1t} - z_{1t}, k_{2t})$ or $c_{2t} < k_{2t} - z_{2t}$ for some t. Then, $c'_{1t} = h(k_{1t} - z_{1t}, k_{2t}) > c_{1t}$ or $c'_{2t} = k_{2t} - z_{2t} > c_{2t}$ is feasible, *ceteris paribus*, contradicting the hypothesis.

(ii) No superfluous maintenance: Note first that, since $0 \leq k_{t+1} \leq k_t$ for $t \geq 0$, we know $\lim_{t \to \infty} k_t = k_\infty \geq 0$. Then, on the one hand, suppose $\lim_{t \to \infty} k_{1t} = k_{1\infty} > 0$. It follows that $c'_{10} = h(k_{10} - z_{10} + k_{1\infty}, k_{20}) > c_{10}$, $k'_{1t} = k_{1t} - k_{1\infty} \geq 0$ for $t > 0$ is feasible, *ceteris paribus*, contradicting the hypothesis. On the other hand, suppose first that $k_{1t} > 0$ for $0 \leq t \leq \bar{t}_1 < \infty$, $k_{1t} = 0$ for $\bar{t}_1 < t$, and $\lim_{t \to \infty} k_{2t} = k_{2\infty} > 0$. Then $c'_{2\bar{t}_1} = k_{2\bar{t}_1} - z_{2\bar{t}_1} + k_{2\infty} > c_{2\bar{t}_1}$, $k'_{2t} = k_{2t} - k_{2\infty} \geq 0$ for $\bar{t}_1 < t$ is feasible, *ceteris paribus*, again contradicting the hypothesis. Now, suppose second that $k_{2t} > 0$ for $0 \leq t \leq \bar{t}_2 < \infty$, $k_{2t} = 0$ for $\bar{t}_2 < t$, and $k_{1\bar{t}_2+1} > 0$. Then [since $c_{1t} = h(k_{1t} - z_{1t}, 0) = 0$ for $\bar{t}_2 < t$] $c'_{10} = h(k_{10} - z_{10} + k_{1\bar{t}_2+1}, k_{20}) > c_{10}$, $k'_{1t} = 0$ for $\bar{t}_2 < t$ is feasible, *ceteris paribus*, also contradicting the hypothesis.

Sufficiency: We begin by noting that when there is no obvious waste, feasible capital stocks obey the dynamical equations

$$k_{1t+1} = k_{10} + \sum_{s=0}^{t} (k_{1s+1} - k_{1s}) = \bar{k}_1 - \sum_{s=0}^{t} (k_{1s} - z_{1s}) \quad \text{for} \quad t \geq 0 \quad \text{(B1)}$$

and

$$k_{2t+1} = k_{20} + \sum_{s=0}^{t} (k_{2s+1} - k_{2s}) = \bar{k}_2 - \sum_{s=0}^{t} (k_{2s} - z_{2s})$$

$$= \bar{k}_2 - \sum_{s=0}^{t} c_{2s} \quad \text{for} \quad t \geq 0. \quad \text{(B2)}$$

We then proceed by considering a number of mutually exclusive and completely exhaustive subcases. For each subcase the logic of the argument is the same; namely, we show that the supposition of a dominating [refer to Eq. (7)] feasible growth path leads to a contradiction:

(i) Suppose first that $k_{1t} > 0$ for $t \geq 0$ and $\lim_{t \to \infty} k_{1t} = 0$. (a) If $c'_t \geq c_t$ for $t \geq 0$ and there is some $t_2 < \infty$ such that $c'_{2t_2} > c_{2t_2}$, then from (B2)

$$k'_{2t+1} = \bar{k}_2 - \sum_{s=0}^{t} c'_{2s} = \bar{k}_2 - \sum_{s=0}^{t} c_{2s} - \sum_{s=0}^{t} (c'_{2s} - c_{2s})$$

$$\leq \begin{cases} k_{2t+1} & \text{for} \quad 0 \leq t < t_2, \\ k_{2t+1} - (c'_{2t_2} - c_{2t_2}) < k_{2t+1} & \text{for} \quad t_2 \leq t. \end{cases}$$

But by the last stated hypothesis of the proposition, we know that $k_{2t} > 0$ for $t \geq 0$. Hence $c_{1t} > 0$ for some $t > t_2$, or without loss of generality $c_{1t_2+1} > 0$ or

$$k'_{1t} - z'_{1t} \begin{Bmatrix} \geq \\ > \end{Bmatrix} k_{1t} - z_{1t} \quad \text{as} \quad t \begin{Bmatrix} \neq \\ = \end{Bmatrix} t_2 + 1$$

[since

$$c'_{1t} = h(k'_{1t} - z'_{1t}, k'_{2t}) \begin{Bmatrix} \geq \\ > \end{Bmatrix} h(k_{1t} - z_{1t}, k_{2t}) = c_{1t} \quad \text{as} \quad t \begin{Bmatrix} \neq \\ = \end{Bmatrix} t_2 + 1$$

and h is increasing in x] or from (B1)

$$k'_{1t+1} = \bar{k}_1 - \sum_{s=0}^{t} (k'_{1s} - z'_{1s})$$

$$= \bar{k}_1 - \sum_{s=0}^{t} (k_{1s} - z_{1s}) - \sum_{s=0}^{t} [(k'_{1s} - z'_{1s}) - (k_{1s} - z_{1s})]$$

$$\begin{aligned} \leq \\ = \end{aligned} \begin{cases} k_{1t+1} & \text{for } 0 \leq t \leq t_2 \\ k_{1t+1} - [(k'_{1t_2+1} - z'_{1t_2+1}) - (k_{1t_2+1} - z_{1t_2+1})] & \text{for } t_2 < t \end{cases}$$

or

$$\lim_{t \to \infty} k'_{1t} \leq -[(k'_{1t_2+1} - z'_{1t_2+1}) - (k_{1t_2+1} - z_{1t_2+1})] < 0,$$

which is infeasible. (b) If (ruling out the subcase already considered) $c'_{1t} \geq c_{1t}$ and $c'_{2t} = c_{2t}$ for $t \geq 0$ and there is some $t_1 < \infty$ such that $c'_{1t_1} > c_{1t_1}$, then now from B(2)

$$k'_{2t+1} = \bar{k}_2 - \sum_{s=0}^{t} c'_{2s} = \bar{k}_2 - \sum_{s=0}^{t} c_{2s} = k_{2t+1} \quad \text{for } t \geq 0$$

or

$$k'_{1t} - z'_{1t} \begin{Bmatrix} \geq \\ > \end{Bmatrix} k_{1t} - z_{1t} \quad \text{as} \quad t \begin{Bmatrix} \neq \\ = \end{Bmatrix} t_1$$

[since here

$$c'_{1t} = h(k'_{1t} - z'_{1t}, k'_{2t}) \begin{Bmatrix} \geq \\ > \end{Bmatrix} h(k_{1t} - z_{1t}, k_{2t}) = c_{1t} \quad \text{as} \quad t \begin{Bmatrix} \neq \\ = \end{Bmatrix} t_1$$

and h is increasing in x] or again from B(1)

$$k'_{1t+1} = \overline{k}_1 - \sum_{s=0}^{t} (k'_{1s} - z'_{1s})$$

$$= \overline{k}_1 - \sum_{s=0}^{t} (k_{1s} - z_{1s}) - \sum_{s=0}^{t} [(k'_{1s} - z'_{1s}) - (k_{1s} - z_{1s})]$$

$$\leqq \begin{cases} k_{1t+1} & \text{for } 0 \leqq t < t_1 \\ k_{1t+1} - [(k'_{1t_1} - z'_{1t_1}) - (k_{1t_1} - z_{1t_1})] & \text{for } t_1 \leqq t \end{cases}$$

or

$$\lim_{t \to \infty} k'_{1t} \leqq -[(k'_{1t_1} - z'_{1t_1}) - (k_{1t_1} - z_{1t_1})] < 0,$$

which is also infeasible.

(ii) Suppose second that $k_{1t} > 0$ for $0 \leqq t \leqq \overline{t}_1 < \infty$, $k_{1t} = 0$ for $\overline{t}_1 < t$ and $\lim_{t \to \infty} k_{2t} = 0$. (a) If $c'_t \geqq c_t$ for $t \geqq 0$ and there is some $t_2 < \infty$ such that $c'_{2t_2} > c_{2t_2}$, then (here and after deleting obvious repetitions of parts of the preceding argument)

$$k'_{2t+1} = \cdots \leqq \begin{cases} k_{2t+1} & \text{for } 0 \leqq t < t_2 \\ k_{2t+1} - (c'_{2t_2} - c_{2t_2}) & \text{for } t_2 \leqq t \end{cases}$$

or

$$\lim_{t \to \infty} k'_{2t} \leqq -(c'_{2t_2} - c_{2t_2}) < 0,$$

which is infeasible. (b) If (ruling out the subcase already considered) $c'_{1t} \geqq c_{1t}$ and $c'_{2t} = c_{2t}$ for $t \geqq 0$ and there is some $t_1 < \infty$ such that $c'_{1t_1} > c_{1t_1}$, then from B(2) $k'_{2t+1} = k_{2t+1}$ for $t \geqq 0$ or

$$k'_{1t} - z'_{1t} \begin{Bmatrix} \geqq \\ > \end{Bmatrix} k_{1t} - z_{1t} \quad \text{as} \quad t \begin{Bmatrix} \neq \\ = \end{Bmatrix} t_1$$

or from B(1)

$$k'_{1t+1} = \cdots \leqq \begin{cases} k_{1t+1} & \text{for } 0 \leqq t < t_1 \\ k_{1t+1} - [(k'_{1t_1} - z'_{1t_1}) - (k_{1t_1} - z_{1t_1})] & \text{for } t_1 \leqq t \end{cases}$$

or

$$k'_{1t+1} \leqq -[(k'_{1t_1} - z'_{1t_1}) - (k_{1t_1} - z_{1t_1})] < 0 \quad \text{for } \max\{\overline{t}_1, t_1\} \leqq t,$$

which is, once again, infeasible. ∎

(b) *Conditions for summability* Though in all three cases actual capital accumulation is infeasible, and only eventual resource exhaustion is efficient, in Case 1 condition T6 obtains, so that

$$\sum_{t=0}^{\infty} (c_{1t} + c_{2t}) \leqq b(\overline{k}) < \infty \tag{B3}$$

for every solution to (2), while in Case 2 (i.e., both Cases 2a and 2b) condition T6 does not obtain; in fact

$$\sum_{t=0}^{\infty} (c_{1t} + c_{2t}) = \infty \tag{B4}$$

for some solution to (2).

Proof   Case 1:   All that needs establishing is that there is some $p > 0$ and $q \geq 0$ such that

$$p \cdot c + q \cdot z - q \cdot k \leq 0 \qquad \text{for every} \quad (c, z, k) \in T.$$

But any stationary feasible price system of the form

$$p_1 = 1, \qquad 0 < h_1(0, 1) \leq q_1 < \infty, \qquad \text{and} \qquad p_2 = q_2 > 0 \tag{B5}$$

will do, since if (p, q) satisfies (B5) and $(c, z, k) \in T$, then (using various properties of h)

$$p \cdot c + q \cdot z - q \cdot k$$

$$\leq h(k_1 - z_1, k_2) - q_1(k_1 - z_1) - q_2(k_2 - z_2 - c_2)$$

$$= \begin{cases} -q_1(k_1 - z_1) - q_2(k_2 - c_2 - z_2) \leq 0 & \text{when} \quad k_2 = 0. \\ [h((k_1 - z_1)/k_2, 1) - q_2((k_1 - z_1)/k_2)]k_2 - q_2(k_2 - z_2 - c_2) \end{cases}$$

$$\leq (h_1(0, 1) - q_1)(k_1 - z_1) - q_2(k_2 - c_2 - z_2) \leq 0 \qquad \text{when} \quad k_2 > 0.$$

From the argument detailed earlier in Section V, we can even calculate a minimum value for the bound in (B3):

$$b(\overline{k}) = h_1(0, 1)\overline{k}_1 + \overline{k}_2 = \min_{0 \leq q_2 \leq 1} (h_1(0, 1)/q_2)\overline{k}_1 + \overline{k}_2$$

$$\leq (h_1(0.1)\overline{k}_1 + q_2\overline{k}_2)/\min\{1, q_2\} \leq q \cdot \overline{k}/\min\{p_1, p_2\}.$$

It is worth emphasizing once more that in this case the technology satisfies T6 without satisfying either A2 ore A3.

Case 2:   All that needs establishing is (B4) [since we demonstrated earlier that T6 implies (B3), or equivalently, that (B4) implies the denial of T6]. The argument involves constructing a feasible growth path that yields

$$\sum_{t=0}^{\infty} (c_{1t} + c_{2t}) = \sum_{t=0}^{\infty} c_{1t} = \infty. \tag{B6}$$

In particular, consider the efficient growth path with capital stocks described by

$$k_{1t} = \overline{k}_1 - \sum_{s=0}^{t-1} \varepsilon_s \qquad \text{and} \qquad k_{2t} = \overline{k}_2 \qquad \text{for} \quad t \geq 0,$$

where $\varepsilon_t = k_{1t} - z_{1t} > 0$ for $t \geqq 0$ with $\sum_{t=0}^{\infty} \varepsilon_s = \bar{k}_1$ is chosen as follows: Pick constants $0 < \alpha < 1$ and $\beta > 0$ and let the subsequence of periods $\{t_s\}$ be such that

$$t_0 = 0$$

and

$$t_{s+1} = \min\left\{t : t > t_s \text{ and } h_1\left(\frac{(1-\alpha)\bar{k}_1\alpha^s}{t - t_s}, \bar{k}_2\right)(1-\alpha)\bar{k}_1\alpha^s \geqq \beta\right\} \quad \text{for} \quad s \geqq 0.$$

[The last is legitimate since Case 2 is characterized by the property that $\lim_{x_1 \to 0^+} h(x_1, \bar{k}_2) = \infty$ for $\bar{k}_2 > 0$.] Finally, define

$$\varepsilon_t = \frac{(1-\alpha)\bar{k}_1\alpha^s}{t_{s+1} - t_s} > 0 \quad \text{for} \quad t_s \leqq t < t_{s+1}, \quad s \geqq 0,$$

which entails

$$0 < \sum_{t=0}^{\ell} \varepsilon_t < \sum_{t=0}^{\infty} \varepsilon_t = \sum_{s=0}^{\infty} \sum_{u=t_s}^{t_{s+1}-1} \frac{(1-\alpha)\bar{k}_1\alpha^s}{t_{s+1} - t_s}$$

$$= (1-\alpha)\bar{k}_1 \sum_{s=0}^{\infty} \alpha^s = \bar{k}_1 \quad \text{for} \quad \ell \geqq 0.$$

Along this particular efficient growth path consumption goods are produced at the rates

$$c_{1t} = h(\varepsilon_t, \bar{k}_2) \geqq h_1(\varepsilon_t, \bar{k}_2)\varepsilon_t \quad \text{and} \quad c_{2t} = 0 \quad \text{for} \quad t \geqq 0$$

[since $0 = h(0, \bar{k}_2) \leqq h(\varepsilon, \bar{k}_2) + h_1(\varepsilon, \bar{k}_2)(0 - \varepsilon)$ or $h(\varepsilon, \bar{k}_2) \geqq h_1(\varepsilon, \bar{k}_2)\varepsilon$ for $\varepsilon > 0$ by concavity of h]. Hence, it follows that

$$\sum_{t=0}^{t_{\sigma+1}-1} (c_{1t} + c_{2t}) = \sum_{t=0}^{t_{\sigma+1}-1} c_{1t} \geqq \sum_{t=0}^{t_{\sigma+1}-1} h_1(\varepsilon_t, \bar{k}_2)\varepsilon_t = \sum_{s=0}^{\sigma} \sum_{u=t_s}^{t_{s+1}-1} h_1(\varepsilon_{t_s}, \bar{k}_2)\varepsilon_{t_s}$$

$$= \sum_{s=0}^{\sigma} \sum_{u=t_s}^{t_{s+1}-1} h_1\left(\frac{(1-\alpha)\bar{k}_1\alpha^s}{t_{s+1} - t_s}, \bar{k}_2\right)\left(\frac{(1-\alpha)\bar{k}_1\alpha^s}{t_{s+1} - t_s}\right)$$

$$= \sum_{s=0}^{\sigma} h_1\left(\frac{(1-\alpha)\bar{k}_1\alpha^s}{t_{s+1} - t_s}, \bar{k}_2\right) \sum_{u=t_s}^{t_{s+1}-1} \frac{(1-\alpha)\bar{k}_1\alpha^s}{t_{s+1} - t_s}$$

$$= \sum_{s=0}^{\sigma} h_1\left(\frac{(1-\alpha)\bar{k}_1\alpha^s}{t_{s+1} - t_s}, \bar{k}_2\right)(1-\alpha)\bar{k}_1\alpha^s$$

$$\geqq \sum_{s=0}^{\sigma} \beta = (\sigma + 1)\beta \quad \text{for} \quad \sigma \geqq 0,$$

from which we immediately deduce (B6). ∎

We should mention explicitly that the foregoing analysis has shown that, in this example anyway, T6 is necessary as well as sufficient for summability. We have also observed the same result in other easily calculable examples, for all of which $\bar{N} \neq N$ (see comment 1 at the end of Appendix A). Whether this is just a peculiarity of relatively simple specializations of our general model remains to be seen.

(c) *Consumption-value maximization* (For simplicity, here too we will denote a given efficient growth path without superscript and various comparison growth paths with prime superscript.) Given an efficient growth path, in *Cases 1 and 2a* (i) there is some associated competitive price system such that

$$\lim_{t \to \infty} q_t \cdot k_{t+1} = 0, \tag{B7}$$

and hence (referring to the discussion at the end of Section III)

$$\infty > \sum_{t=0}^{\infty} p_t \cdot c_t \geqq \sum_{t=0}^{\infty} p_t \cdot c_t' \tag{B8}$$

for every (primed) solution to (2), but (ii) there may also be some associated competitive price system such that neither statement is true, while in *Case 2b* there may simply be no associated competitive price system such that either statement is true.

Proof   We begin by noting that the "pure inventory" competitive price system

$$p_{1t} = q_{1t-1} = 0 \quad \text{and} \quad p_{2t} \begin{Bmatrix} \leqq \\ = \end{Bmatrix} q_{2t-1} = 1 \quad \text{as} \quad c_{2t} \begin{Bmatrix} = \\ > \end{Bmatrix} 0 \quad \text{for} \quad t \geqq 0 \tag{B9}$$

is associated with every efficient growth path, since if prices satisfy (B9) and quantities satisfy

$$c_{2t} = k_{2t} - z_{2t} \quad \text{and} \quad (c_{2t}, z_{2t}, k_{2t}) \geqq 0 \quad \text{for} \quad t \geqq 0,$$

then

$$
\begin{aligned}
p_t \cdot c + q_t \cdot z - q_{t-1} \cdot k &= p_{2t}c_2 + q_{2t}z_2 - q_{2t-1}k_2 \\
&\leqq p_{2t}c_{2t} + q_{2t}z_{2t} - q_{2t-1}k_{2t} \\
&= p_t \cdot c_t + q_t \cdot z_t - q_{t-1} \cdot k_t = 0
\end{aligned}
$$

for every $(c, z, k) \in T$ and $t \geqq 0$.

Moreover, with such a competitive price system, if, in addition, $p_{20} = 1$ (e.g., $c_{20} > 0$) while $\lim_{t \to \infty} k_{2t} = k_{2\infty} > 0$ (which we already know from Subsection B.2(a) is compatible with efficiency provided $k_{1t} > 0$ for $t \geqq 0$), then

$$\infty > \sum_{t=0}^{\infty} p_t \cdot c_t' = c_{20}' = \bar{k}_2 > \bar{k}_2 - k_{2\infty} = \sum_{t=0}^{\infty} c_{2t} = \sum_{t=0}^{\infty} p_t \cdot c_t$$

for the alternative feasible growth path defined by

$$c'_{10} = h(\overline{k}_1, \overline{k}_2), \qquad c'_{20} = \overline{k}_2,$$

and

$$c'_{1t} = c'_{2t} = k'_{1t} = k'_{2t} = 0 \qquad \text{for} \quad t > 0.$$

This is consistent with (though not entailed by) a second observation about the conjunction of (B9) with an efficient growth path such that $\lim_{t \to \infty} k_{2t} = k_{2\infty} > 0$, namely, that

$$\lim_{t \to \infty} q_t \cdot k_{t+1} = \lim_{t \to \infty} k_{2t+1} = k_{2\infty} > 0.$$

That is, in both Cases 1 and 2 of the example, the competitive price system described by (B9) may exhibit neither capital-value transversality (B7) nor consumption-value maximization (B8).

In order to establish the rest of the proposition, we utilize the fact that every competitive price system associated with a particular efficient growth path yields (c_t, z_t, k_t) as an optimal solution to the concave programming problem

$$\text{maximize} \quad p_{1t}h(k_1 - z_1, k_2) + p_{2t}(k_2 - z_2) + q_{1t}z_1$$
$$+ q_{2t}z_2 - q_{1t-1}k_1 - q_{2t-1}k_2 \qquad \text{for} \quad t \geq 0$$

$$\text{subject to} \quad z_1 \leq k_1 \quad (\text{with dual variable} \quad \lambda_{1t} \geq 0) \qquad (\text{B10})$$
$$z_2 \leq k_2 \quad (\text{with dual variable} \quad \lambda_{2t} \geq 0)$$

and   nonnegativity

or satisfies that Kuhn-Tucker conditions for $t \geq 0$[20]

$$z_{1t} \leq k_{1t}, \qquad \text{equality if} \quad \lambda_{1t} > 0,$$
$$z_{2t} \leq k_{2t}, \qquad \text{equality if} \quad \lambda_{2t} > 0,$$
$$-p_{1t}h_1(k_{1t} - z_{1t}, k_{2t}) + q_{1t} \leq \lambda_{1t}, \qquad \text{equality if} \quad z_{1t} > 0,$$
$$-p_{2t} + q_{2t} \leq \lambda_{2t}, \qquad \text{equality if} \quad z_{2t} > 0, \qquad (\text{B11})$$
$$p_{1t}h_1(k_{1t} - z_{1t}, k_{2t}) - q_{1t-1} \leq -\lambda_{1t}, \qquad \text{equality if} \quad k_{1t} > 0,$$
$$p_{1t}h_2(k_{1t} - z_{1t}, k_{2t}) + p_{2t} - q_{2t-1} \leq -\lambda_{2t}, \qquad \text{equality if} \quad k_{2t} > 0.$$

---

[20] (B10) obviously satisfies Slater's condition [since $(z, k) = (0, 0, 1, 1)$ is a feasible solution]. Thus, the conditions (B11) are both necessary and sufficient. It almost goes without saying that in Case 2 these particular Kuhn–Tucker conditions only make sense provided that

$$p_{1t} = p_{1t}h_1(k_{1t} - z_{1t}, k_{2t}) = p_{1t}h_2(k_{1t} - z_{1t}, k_{2t}) = 0$$

whenever $c_{1t} = h(k_{1t} - z_{1t}, k_{2t}) = 0$ and hence $k_{1t} - z_{1t} = 0$.

It is convenient to analyze the solutions to (B11) by distinguishing two possibilities, depending on whether $\lim_{t\to\infty} k_{2t} = 0$ or $\lim_{t\to\infty} k_{2t} = k_{2\infty} > 0$:

(i) Suppose that $\lim_{t\to\infty} k_{2t} = 0$. In this case, we need only notice that the Kuhn–Tucker conditions (B11) entail the inequalities

$$-p_{1t}h_1 + q_{1t} \leq -p_{1t}h_1 + q_{1t-1} \qquad \text{or} \qquad q_{1t} \leq q_{1t-1} \leq \cdots \leq q_{1,-1} < \infty$$

and

$$-p_{2t} + q_{2t} \leq -p_{1t}h_2 - p_{2t} + q_{2t-1} \leq -p_{2t} + q_{2t-1}$$

or

$$q_{2t} \leq q_{2t-1} \leq \cdots \leq q_{2,-1} < \infty \qquad \text{for} \quad t \geq 0.$$

Hence, every competitive price system associated with a particular efficient growth path of this sort satisfies

$$q_t \cdot k_{t+1} \leq q_{-1} \cdot k_{t+1} \qquad \text{for} \quad t \geq 0,$$

and therefore

$$\lim_{t\to\infty} q_t \cdot k_{t+1} \leq \lim_{t\to\infty} q_{-1} \cdot k_{t+1} = q_{-1} \cdot \lim_{t\to\infty} k_{t+1} = 0$$

(since by hypothesis $\lim_{t\to\infty} k_{1t} = 0$ while by supposition $\lim_{t\to\infty} k_{2t} = 0$).

(ii) Suppose that $\lim_{t\to\infty} k_{2t} = k_{2\infty} > 0$. In this case, we already know from Subsection B.2(a) that though $\lim_{t\to\infty} k_{1t} = 0$, $k_{1t} > 0$ for $t \geq 0$. Using this fact in combination with the Kuhn–Tucker conditions, we will show the following: It is always possible to find some competitive price system associated with a particular efficient growth path of this sort that (a) differs from (B9) and (b) also satisfies $\lim_{t\to\infty} q_{2t} = 0$ if and only if we have Case 1 or Case 2a of the example. Since the second of the listed properties entails capital-value transversality,

$$\lim_{t\to\infty} q_t \cdot k_{t+1} = \lim_{t\to\infty} (q_{1,-1}k_{1t+1} + q_{2t}k_{2t+1})$$

$$= q_{1,-1}\left(\lim_{t\to\infty} k_{1t+1}\right) + \left(\lim_{t\to\infty} q_{2t}\right)\left(\lim_{t\to\infty} k_{2t+1}\right) = 0,$$

together with the preceding result, this establishes that it is in these cases, and only in these cases, that an efficient growth path necessarily exhibits consumption-value maximization [at some, but referring to the earlier discussion concerning (B9), perhaps not all associated competitive price systems].

The argument proceeds by closely examining the structure of the solutions to (B11) in light of the supposition that $k_t > 0$ for $t \geq 0$: Since generally we know that

$$z_{it} \left\{ \begin{matrix} < \\ = \end{matrix} \right\} k_{it} \qquad \text{as} \qquad c_{it} \left\{ \begin{matrix} > \\ = \end{matrix} \right\} 0 \qquad \text{for} \quad i = 1, 2, \quad t \geq 0,$$

while specifically we have $k_{it+1} = z_{it} > 0$ $(k_{i0} = \bar{k}_i > 0)$ for $i = 1, 2, t \geq 0$, after some straightforward logical simplification, the Kuhn–Tucker conditions for $t \geq 0$ reduce to

$$
\begin{aligned}
p_{1t} h_1(k_{1t} - z_{1t}, k_{2t}) &\leq q_{1t}, && \text{equality if} \quad c_{1t} > 0, \\
p_{2t} &\leq q_{2t}, && \text{equality if} \quad c_{2t} > 0. \\
q_{1t} &= q_{1,-1}, \\
q_{2t} &= q_{2t-1} - p_{1t} h_2(k_{1t} - z_{1t}, k_{2t}).
\end{aligned}
\tag{B12}
$$

(B12) tells us immediately that if $q_{1,-1} = 0$, then $q_{1t} = p_{1t} = p_{1t} h_1 = p_{1t} h_2 = 0$, and hence $q_{2t} = q_{2,-1} > 0$ for $t \geq 0$. Thus, a necessary (and, it turns out, also sufficient) condition for finding some competitive price system that differs from (B9) and also satisfies $\lim_{t \to \infty} q_{2t} = 0$ is finding one with $q_{1,-1} = 1$ (for simplicity, now letting initial capital of type 1 be the numéraire).

In order to establish that only Cases 1 and 2a of the example are consistent with this requirement, suppose that $q_{1,-1} = 1$ and consider the last equation in (B12)

$$
\begin{aligned}
q_{2t} &= q_{2t-1} - p_{1t} h_2(k_{1t} - z_{1t}, k_{2t}) \\
&= q_{2t-1} - p_{1t}(h(k_{1t} - z_{1t}, k_{2t}) \\
&\quad - h_1(k_{1t} - z_{1t}, k_{2t})(k_{1t} - z_{1t})) && \text{for} \quad t \geq 0
\end{aligned}
\tag{B13}
$$

(since h is linear homogeneous). If $c_{1t} = 0$, then

$$q_{2t} = q_{2t-1}$$

(since $h = 0$ only if $p_{1t} h_1 = 0$). If $c_{1t} > 0$, then

$$q_{2t} = q_{2t-1} - p_{1t} h_1(k_{1t} - z_{1t}, k_{2t}) \left(\frac{h(k_{1t} - z_{1t}, k_{2t})}{h_1(k_{1t} - z_{1t}, k_{2t})} - (k_{1t} - z_{1t}) \right)$$

[since $h > 0$ only if $(k_{1t} - z_{1t}, k_{2t}) > 0$ only if $h_1 > 0$]

$$= q_{2t-1} - \left(\frac{h(k_{1t} - z_{1t}, k_{2t})}{h_1(k_{1t} - z_{1t}, k_{2t})(k_{1t} - z_{1t})} - 1 \right)(k_{1t} - z_{1t})$$

[since, from the first inequality in (B12), if $c_{1t} > 0$, then $p_{1t}h_1 = q_{1t} = q_{1,-1} = 1$]. Hence, defining

$$\alpha_t = \begin{cases} 1 & \text{for } c_{1t} = 0 \text{ for } t \geq 0, \\[2mm] \dfrac{h_1(k_{1t} - z_{1t}, k_{2t})(k_{1t} - z_{1t})}{h(k_{1t} - z_{1t}, k_{2t})} & \text{for } c_{1t} > 0, \end{cases}$$

(B13) can be rewritten compactly as

$$q_{2t} = q_{2,-1} - \sum_{s=0}^{t} \left(\frac{1}{\alpha_s} - 1 \right)(k_{1s} - z_{1s}) \qquad \text{for } t \geq 0. \tag{B14}$$

In Case 2b, by employing a construction similar to that utilized in establishing the second part of the proposition in Subsection B.2(b) above, we can find an efficient growth path such that

$$\sum_{s=0}^{\infty} \left(\frac{1}{\alpha_s} - 1 \right)(k_{1s} - z_{1s}) = \infty.^{21}$$

Thus, for such an efficient growth path, if $q_{1,-1} = 1$, then $\lim_{t \to \infty} q_{2t} = -\infty$, which is "infeasible"; Case 2b of the example may in fact require a "pure inventory" competitive price system.

In Cases 1 and 2a, on the other hand, by picking $0 < \alpha < 1$ such that

$$\frac{h_1(x_1, x_2)x_1}{h(x_1, x_2)} \geq \alpha \qquad \text{for } 0 \leq x_1 \leq \bar{k}_1, \quad x_2 \geq k_{2\infty},$$

---

[21] Specifically, referring to the earlier construction, now let the subsequence of periods $\{t_s\}$ be such that

$$t_0 = 0$$

and

$$t_{s+1} = \min \left\{ t : t > t_s \text{ and } \left[h\left(\frac{(1-\alpha)\bar{k}_1 \alpha^s}{t - t_s}, \bar{k}_2 \right) h_1\left(\frac{(1-\alpha)\bar{k}_1 \alpha^s}{t - t_s}, \bar{k}_2 \right)^{-1} \right. \right.$$
$$\left. \left. \times \left(\frac{(1-\alpha)\bar{k}_1 \alpha^s}{t - t_s} \right)^{-1} - 1 \right](1-\alpha)\bar{k}_1 \alpha^s \geq \beta \right\} \qquad \text{for } s \geq 0$$

(which is legitimate since Case 2b is easily shown to be characterized by the property that

$$\lim_{x_1 \to 0^+} \frac{h_1(x_1, \bar{k}_2)x_1}{h(x_1, \bar{k}_2)} = 0 \qquad \text{for } \bar{k}_2 > 0).$$

Then, the rest of the argument is virtually unchanged from before, since it simply involves calculating the lower bound

$$\sum_{t=0}^{t_{\sigma+1}-1} \left(\frac{1}{\alpha_t} - 1 \right)(k_{1t} - z_{1t}) = \cdots \geq \beta(\sigma + 1) \qquad \text{for } \sigma \geq 0.$$

we see that

$$0 \leqq \sum_{s=0}^{t} \left(\frac{1}{\alpha_s} - 1\right)(k_{1s} - z_{1s}) \leqq \sum_{s=0}^{t} \left(\frac{1}{\alpha} - 1\right)(k_{1s} - z_{1s})$$

$$\leqq \left(\frac{1}{\alpha} - 1\right) \sum_{s=0}^{t} (k_{1s} - k_{1s+1})$$

$$= \left(\frac{1}{\alpha} - 1\right)(\bar{k}_1 - k_{1t+1}) \leqq \left(\frac{1}{\alpha} - 1\right)\bar{k}_1 \quad \text{for} \quad t \geqq 0.$$

Hence, for every efficient growth such that $\lim_{t \to \infty} k_{2t} = k_{2\infty} > 0$, we can find an associated competitive price system with $q_{1,-1} = 1$. Moreover, by picking

$$q_{2,-1} = \sum_{s=0}^{\infty} \left(\frac{1}{\alpha_s} - 1\right)(k_{1s} - z_{1s}) < \infty,$$

so that

$$q_{2t} = \sum_{s=0}^{\infty} \left(\frac{1}{\alpha_s} - 1\right)(k_{1s} - z_{1s}) - \sum_{s=0}^{t} \left(\frac{1}{\alpha_s} - 1\right)(k_{1s} - z_{1s})$$

$$= \sum_{s=t+1}^{\infty} \left(\frac{1}{\alpha_s} - 1\right)(k_{1s} - z_{1s}),$$

we can also ensure that this competitive price system satisfies the requisite condition $\lim_{t \to \infty} q_{2t} = 0$. ∎

(d) *Another anomalous feature of Case 2b* Consider the particular efficient growth path sketched in footnote 21. If we pick consumption goods values

$$\bar{p}_t = (h_1(k_{1t} - z_{1t}, \bar{k}_2)^{-1}, \quad 0 \quad \text{for} \quad t \geqq 0, \tag{B15}$$

then this path is "optimal" in the sense of 3 in the text

$$\theta \geqq \limsup_{t=\infty} \sum_{t=0}^{\ell} \bar{p}_t \cdot (c'_t - c_t) \tag{B16}$$

for every (primed) solution to (2), even though it has no associated competitive price system (4) such that $p_t = \bar{p}_t$ for $t \geqq 0$.

Proof Since we have already established the latter part of the assertion, all we need establish is (B16). But this follows directly from the fact that an arbitrary feasible growth path satisfies (by monotonicity of h)

$$c'_{1t} = h(k'_{1t} - z'_{1t}, k'_{2t}) \leqq h(k'_{1t} - z'_{1t}, \bar{k}_2)$$

or (by differentiability and concavity of h)

$$c'_{1t} - c_{1t} \leqq h(k'_{1t} - z'_{1t}, \bar{k}_2) - h(k_{1t} - z_{1t}, \bar{k}_2)$$
$$\leqq h_1(k_{1t} - z_{1t}, \bar{k}_2)[(k'_{1t} - z'_{1t}) - (k_{1t} - z_{1t})]$$

or [by reference to (B15)]

$$\bar{p}_t \cdot (c'_t - c_t) = \bar{p}_{1t}(c'_{1t} - c_{1t}) \leqq (k'_{1t} - z'_{1t}) - (k_{1t} - z_{1t})$$
$$= (k'_{1t} - k'_{1t+1}) - (k_{1t} - k_{1t+1})$$

or

$$\sum_{t=0}^{\ell} \bar{p}_t \cdot (c'_t - c_t) \leqq \sum_{t=0}^{\ell} [(k'_{1t} - k'_{1t+1}) - (k_{1t} - k_{1t+1})]$$
$$= k_{1\ell+1} - k'_{1\ell+1} \quad \text{for} \quad \ell \geqq 0.$$

But the last inequality entails that

$$\limsup_{\ell \to \infty} \sum_{t=0}^{\ell} \bar{p}_t \cdot (c'_t - c_t) \leqq \limsup_{\ell \to \infty} (k_{1\ell+1} - k'_{1\ell+1})$$
$$= \lim_{\ell \to \infty} (k_{1\ell+1} - k'_{1\ell+1}) = -k'_{1\infty} \leqq 0. \quad \blacksquare$$

REFERENCES

1. Benveniste, L. M., A complete characterization of efficiency for a general capital accumulation model, *J. Econ. Theory* **12**, 325–337 (1976).
2. Benveniste, L. M., Two notes on the Malinvaud condition for efficiency of infinite horizon programs, *J. Econ. Theory* **12**, 338–346 (1976).
3. Benveniste, L. M., and Gale, D., An extension of Cass' characterization of infinite efficient programs, *J. Econ. Theory* **10**, 229–238 (1975).
4. Brock, W. R., On existence of weakly maximal programmes in a multisector economy, *Rev. Econ. Stud.* **37**, 275–280 (1970).
5. Cass, D., On capital overaccumulation in the aggregate neoclassical model of economic growth: A complete characterization, *J. Econ. Theory* **4**, 224–240 (1972).
6. Cass, D., The law of demand for capital, *J. Pol. Econ.* (forthcoming).
7. Cass, D., and Shell, K., The structure and stability of competitive dynamical systems, *J. Econ. Theory Symp.* **12**, 31–70 (1976).
8. Cass, D., and Yaari, M. E., Present values playing the role of efficiency prices in the one-good growth model, *Rev. Econ. Stud.* **38**, 331–339 (1971).
9. Gale, D., On optimal development in a multi-sector economy. *Rev. Econ. Stud.* **34**, 1–18 (1967).
10. Kelley, J. L., and Namioka, I., "Linear Topological Spaces." Van Nostrand–Reinhold, Princeton, New Jersey, 1963.
11. Kurz, M., Tightness and substitution in the theory of capital, *J. Econ. Theory* **1**, 244–272 (1969).
12. Kurz, M., and Starrett, D. A., On the efficiency of competitive programmes in an infinite horizon model, *Rev. Econ. Stud.* **37**, 571–584 (1970).

13. Majumdar, M., Efficient programs in infinite dimensional spaces: A complete characterization, *J. Econ. Theory* 7, 355–369 (1974).
14. Majumdar, M., Mitra, T., and McFadden, D., On efficiency and Pareto optimality of competitive programs in closed multisector models, *J. Econ. Theory* 13, 26–46 (1976).
15. Malinvaud, E., Capital accumulation and efficient allocation of resources, *Econometrica* 21, 233–268 (1953); A corrigendum, *Econometrica* 30, 570–573 (1962).
16. McFadden, D., The evaluation of development programmes, *Rev. Econ. Stud.* 34, 25–50 (1967).
17. McKenzie, L. W., Turnpike theory, *Econometrica* 44, 841–865 (1976).
18. Mitra, T., Efficient growth with exhaustible resources in a neoclassical model, *J. Econ. Theory* 17, 114–129 (1978).
19. Mitra, T., Identifying inefficiency in smooth aggregative models, *J. Math. Econ.* (forthcoming).
20. Mitra, T., and Majumdar, M., A note on the role of the transversality condition in signalling capital overaccumulation, *J. Econ. Theory* 13, 47–57 (1976).
21. Nikaido, H., "Convex Structures and Economic Theory." Academic Press, New York, 1968.
22. Peleg, B., Efficiency prices for optimal consumption plans, *J. Math. Anal. Appl.* 29, 83–90 (1970).
23. Peleg, B., Efficiency prices for optimal consumption plans III, *J. Math. Anal. Appl.* 32, 630–638 (1970).
24. Peleg, B., Efficiency prices for optimal consumption plans II, *Israel J. Math.* 9, 222–234 (1971).
25. Peleg, B., Efficiency prices for optimal consumption plans IV, *Siam J. Control* 10, 414–433 (1972).
26. Peleg, B., On competitive prices for optimal consumption plans, *Siam J. Appl. Math.* 26, 239–253 (1974).
27. Peleg, B., and Ryder, H. E. Jr., On optimal consumption plans in a multi-sector economy, *Rev. Econ. Stud.* 39, 159–169 (1972).
28. Peleg, B., and Yaari, M. E., Efficiency prices in an infinite-dimensional space, *J. Econ. Theory* 2, 41–85 (1970).
29. Peleg, B., and Zilcha, I., On competitive prices for optimal consumption plans II, *Siam J. Appl. Math.* 32, 627–630 (1977).
30. Radner, R., Efficiency prices for infinite horizon production programmes, *Rev. Econ. Stud.* 34, 51–66 (1967).
31. Rockafellar, R. T., "Convex Analysis." Princeton Univ. Press, Princeton, New Jersey, 1970.
32. von Weizsäcker, C. C., Existence of optimal programs of accumulation for an infinite time horizon, *Rev. Econ. Stud.* 32, 85–104 (1965).
33. Weitzman, M. L., Duality theory for infinite horizon convex models, *Management Sci.* 19, 783–789 (1973).

The paper was completed during Cass' tenure as a Sherman Fairchild Distinguished Scholar at Caltech. Also, both of us received grants from the NSF during the course of the research reported on. We are grateful to both institutions for their support and encouragement.

Our ideas themselves have benefitted from comments by and conversations with many of our colleague theorists, but particularly the participants—including Lionel himself—in the MSSB seminars on dynamical systems in economics. We would especially like to thank Tapan Mitra, who was, perhaps not coincidentally, Lionel's student. His collaboration with each of us has resulted in deeper understanding of the basic issues raised in the paper (to say nothing of his specific contribution to the insights underlying the extended example worked out at the very end of the paper).

David Cass
DIVISION OF HUMANITIES
  AND SOCIAL SCIENCES
CALIFORNIA INSTITUTE OF TECHNOLOGY
PASADENA, CALIFORNIA

DEPARTMENT OF ECONOMICS
UNIVERSITY OF PENNSYLVANIA
PHILADELPHIA, PENNSYLVANIA

Mukul Majumdar
DEPARTMENT OF ECONOMICS
CORNELL UNIVERSITY
ITHACA, NEW YORK

Part 3
TRADE

The Theory and Application of Trade Utility Functions

JOHN S. CHIPMAN

1. INTRODUCTION

The idea of defining preferences over a set of trades, induced by preferences over a set of consumption bundles, has proved very useful in international trade theory. Edgeworth [11, p. 21] defined preferences over trades in the pure exchange model and subsequently in international trade [12, p. 38]. The first systematic construction was that of Meade [26], who employed ingenious geometric methods. A subsequent, but independent, treatment (without reference to international trade) was introduced by Rader [28]. Likewise, in a development of Leontief's [21] model of international trade, in which each country is assumed to have aggregable preferences, Nikaido [27] showed how one could reduce a model of international trade with production formally to an exchange model.

In the present paper I shall study formally the properties of "trade utility functions" and their derived "trade demand correspondences" strictly within the framework of the model analyzed by Leontief [21] and Meade [26], in which the underlying preferences in each country are aggregable, defined over the set of goods and services consumed and traded, and in particular are independent of factor supplies (that is, of leisure and occupational choice[1]).

---

[1] The assumption of indifference to occupational choice is not quite as stringent as might first appear, since if there is complete aversion on the part of a group of workers to all but one class of occupations, they can be defined (following Haberler [14]) as a "specific factor."

It will thus be assumed that there is a (convex) production possibility set defined on the space of commodity bundles entering individuals' (and the group's) preferences.

The assumption of aggregable preferences is, of course, highly restrictive. It has nevertheless been very popular and persistent in the literature on international trade, where the emphasis has been on adherence to simple assumptions and structures that can yield unambiguous (and empirically refutable) results, rather than on complete generality.[2] An example of aggregable preferences is found in the Mill–Graham postulate of expenditure proportionality employed in the Graham–McKenzie model of world trade [22].[3]

The key to the analytical techniques used to derive the main results is to be found in the dual relationship between utility maximization and expenditure minimization first investigated by Arrow [2] and developed by Debreu [10] (see also Koopmans [20]) in the context of welfare economics, and in the underlying concept of a minimum-income function pioneered by McKenzie [25] in consumer theory.

2. DEFINITIONS AND PRELIMINARY RESULTS

I shall start with a general formulation in which a *utility function* U is defined over a *consumption set* $\mathscr{X}$, which is a subset of n-dimensional Euclidean space. In the case of consumption of vectors x of final products, I shall at the end of this section restrict $\mathscr{X}$ to being the nonnegative orthant E_+^n of n-dimensional space. However, I shall be primarily interested in defining a "trade utility function" $\hat{U}$ over the set of *trades* z (vectors of net imports, i.e., imports less exports), which can have positive or negative components. It will therefore be necessary to deal with a more general type of consumption set—to be called the *trade set* $\mathscr{Z}$—which need not be restricted to being the nonnegative orthant. I shall therefore start with a more general interpretation in which $\mathscr{X}$ denotes an abstract consumption set over which preferences are defined.

---

[2] Individual preferences can be aggregated if they are homothetic and if, in addition, either they are identical or the distribution of income is constant (cf. Chipman [7]). The latter result can be obtained if it is assumed that all individuals share equiproportionately in the ownership of resources (including their own efficiency labor), provided there are no government transfers. An alternative assumption permitting preferences to be aggregated is that the government continually redistributes incomes in response to price changes in such a way as to maximize a Bergson–Samuelson social welfare function (cf. Samuelson [32], Chipman and Moore [9]).

[3] Expenditure proportionality is generated by a Millian or "Cobb–Douglas" utility function (cf. Chipman [4, Part 1], and (53) below).

Let the consumption set $\mathscr{X}$ be a subset of the n-dimensional Euclidean space E^n which is (i) closed, (ii) convex, and (iii) bounded from below (cf. Debreu [10, pp. 52–53]). The third condition means that there is a vector $-\bar{y}$ such that $-\bar{y} \leq x$ for all $x \in \mathscr{X}$. Let $U: \mathscr{X} \to E^1$ be a continuous real-valued function defined on $\mathscr{X}$ and satisfying the property of *local nonsaturation*; i.e., for any $x \in \mathscr{X}$ and any neighborhood $N(x)$ of x (relative to $\mathscr{X}$), there is an $x' \in N(x)$ such that $U(x') > U(x)$ (cf. Koopmans [20, p. 47]).

Let p denote the n-tuple of prices and let I denote income (a real number, possibly negative[4]). Let $\Omega(\mathscr{X})$ denote the set of all pairs (p, I) such that the *budget set*

$$B(p, I) = \{x \in \mathscr{X} : p \cdot x \leq I\} \tag{1}$$

is nonempty, and let $U(\mathscr{X})$ be the set of real numbers u for which $U(x) = u$ for some $x \in \mathscr{X}$. We define the *upper contour set* for $u \in U(\mathscr{X})$ by

$$\mathscr{X}(u) = \{x \in \mathscr{X} : U(x) \geq u\}. \tag{2}$$

The following three propositions are well known and are included so as to permit a self-contained presentation with uniform notation.

PROPOSITION 1   Let $(p^0, I^0) \in \Omega(\mathscr{X})$. If U is locally nonsaturating over $\mathscr{X}$ and if x^0 maximizes $U(x)$ over $B(p^0, I^0)$, then $p^0 \cdot x^0 = I^0$.

Proof   Denote by int $B(p^0, I^0) = \{x \in \mathscr{X} : p^0 \cdot x < I^0\}$ the interior of $B(p^0, I^0)$ *relative to* $\mathscr{X}$. It is open relative to $\mathscr{X}$; hence for each $x \in$ int $B(p^0, I^0)$ there is a neighborhood $N(x) \subseteq$ int $B(p^0, I^0)$ of x such that $U(x') > U(x)$ for some $x' \in N(x)$. Consequently, $U(x)$ has no maximum on int $B(p^0, I^0)$. Since x^0 maximizes $U(x)$ on $B(p^0, I^0)$ by hypothesis, it follows that $p^0 \cdot x^0 = I^0$.   ∎

The following propositions provide conditions for which, respectively, utility maximization implies expenditure minimization and expenditure minimization implies utility maximization (cf. Arrow [2], Debreu [10, pp. 68–71]).

PROPOSITION 2   Let x^0 maximize $U(x)$ over $B(p^0, I^0)$, where $(p^0, I^0) \in \Omega(\mathscr{X})$, and define $u^0 = U(x^0)$. Let U be locally nonsaturating on $\mathscr{X}$. Then x^0 minimizes $p^0 \cdot x$ over $\mathscr{X}(u^0)$.

Proof   If the conclusion does not hold, then there exists an $x^1 \in \mathscr{X}(u^0)$ such that $p^0 \cdot x^1 < p^0 \cdot x^0$. By local nonsaturation (and Proposition 1), $p^0 \cdot x^0 = I^0$; also by local nonsaturation, there exists an x sufficiently close

---

[4] Below, I will be identified with D, the deficit in the balance of payments on current account, which could be positive (a deficit) or negative (a surplus).

to x^1 such that $p^0 \cdot x < I^0$ and $U(x) > U(x^1) \geqq U(x^0)$. This contradicts the assumption that x^0 maximizes $U(x)$ over $B(p^0, I^0)$. ∎

PROPOSITION 3   Let x^0 minimize $p^0 \cdot x$ over $\mathscr{X}(u^0)$, where $u^0 \in U(\mathscr{X})$. Define $I^0 = p^0 \cdot x^0$, and let $I^0 > \inf_{x \in \mathscr{X}} p^0 \cdot x$. Then x^0 maximizes $U(x)$ over $B(p^0, I^0)$.

Proof   Since $I^0 > \inf_{x \in \mathscr{X}} p^0 \cdot x$, there exists an $x^1 \in \mathscr{X}$ such that $p^0 \cdot x^1 < I^0$. Now for any $x \in \mathscr{X}$ such that $p^0 \cdot x < I^0$, we have $U(x^0) > U(x)$, since if $U(x) \geqq U(x^0) \geqq u^0$, then x^0 would not minimize $p^0 \cdot x$ over $\mathscr{X}(u^0)$. Thus, $U(x^0) > U(x)$ for all $x \in \mathscr{X}$ such that $p^0 \cdot x < I^0$. Now let $x^2 \in \mathscr{X}$ satisfy $p^0 \cdot x^2 = I^0$. Since $\mathscr{X}$ is convex, for any t in the interval $0 \leqq t < 1$, we have $x^{t+1} = (1 - t)x^1 + tx^2 \in \mathscr{X}$. Clearly, $p^0 \cdot x^{t+1} < I^0$; hence by the above argument $U(x^0) > U(x^{t+1})$. Since t can be made arbitrarily close to 1, this shows that x^2 belongs to the closure of the set $\{x \in \mathscr{X} : U(x) < U(x^0)\}$; i.e., x^2 is a member of the set $\{x \in \mathscr{X} : U(x) \leqq U(x^0)\}$, since U is continuous. This shows that $U(x^0) \geqq U(x^2)$ for all $x^2 \in \mathscr{X}$ such that $p^0 \cdot x^2 = I^0$, and hence $U(x^0) \geqq U(x)$ for all $x \in B(p^0, I^0)$. ∎

Let $\mathscr{Y} \subseteq E_+^n$ be the *production possibility set*, assumed to be closed, convex, and bounded from above (i.e., such that $y \leqq \bar{y}$ for all $y \in \mathscr{Y}$ and some $\bar{y}$), and to contain the origin. We shall now (and for the remainder of the paper) assume that $\mathscr{X} = E_+^n$; i.e., the consumption set is the nonnegative orthant. We define the *trade set* $\mathscr{Z}$ by

$$\mathscr{Z} = \mathscr{X} - \mathscr{Y} = \{z = x - y : x \in \mathscr{X}, y \in \mathscr{Y}\}. \tag{3}$$

Since $\mathscr{X}$ and $-\mathscr{Y}$ are convex, so is $\mathscr{Z}$ (see Fig. 1[5]). Since $\mathscr{X}$ is closed and $\mathscr{Y}$ is closed and bounded, $\mathscr{Z}$ is closed (cf. Debreu [10, pp. 22–23]). Further, since $y \leqq \bar{y}$ for all $y \in \mathscr{Y}$, and $x \geqq 0$ for all $x \in \mathscr{X}$, it follows that $z = x - y \geqq -\bar{y}$ for all $z \in \mathscr{Z}$; i.e., $\mathscr{Z}$ is bounded below by $-\bar{y}$. Thus, $\mathscr{Z}$ has all the desired properties of a consumption set.

For any $z \in \mathscr{Z}$ the set $z + \mathscr{Y}$ (the so-called "production block" with origin at z—see Meade [26]) certainly intersects $\mathscr{X}$, for given $\bar{z} = \bar{x} - \bar{y} \in \mathscr{Z}$, the set $\bar{z} + \mathscr{Y}$ contains the point $\bar{z} + \bar{y} = \bar{x} \geqq 0$. We may therefore define the set-valued function, or correspondence,

$$\Gamma(z) = \{x \in \mathscr{X} : x \in z + \mathscr{Y}\} = (z + \mathscr{Y}) \cap \mathscr{X}, \tag{4}$$

which assigns a nonempty "consumption possibility" set to each trade vector $z \in \mathscr{Z}$ (see Fig. 2).

---

[5] Figure 1a depicts the usual Meadian "production block" and Fig. 1b a production-possibility set $\mathscr{Y}$ allowing for importation of intermediate inputs (cf. Chipman [4, Part 2, p. 687; Part 1, p. 510; Part 3, pp. 44, 47]). Analysis of trade in intermediate products was introduced into international theory by McKenzie [23].

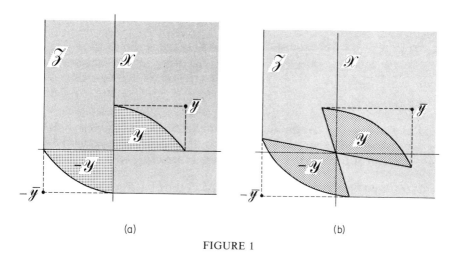

(a)   (b)

FIGURE 1

PROPOSITION 4 Γ is a continuous mapping from $\mathscr{Z}$ into $\mathscr{X}$ in terms of the relative topologies of $\mathscr{Z}$ and $\mathscr{X}$.

Proof $\Gamma(z)$ is nonempty and compact for each z, and it may be verified that for any set $\mathcal{O} \subseteq \mathscr{X}$ that is open in the relative topology of $\mathscr{X}$, the sets

$$\Gamma^{+}(\mathcal{O}) = \{z \in \mathscr{Z} : \Gamma(z) \subseteq \mathcal{O}\} \qquad \text{and} \qquad \Gamma^{-}(\mathcal{O}) = \{z \in \mathscr{Z} : \Gamma(z) \cap \mathcal{O} \neq \varnothing\}$$

are open in the relative topology of $\mathscr{Z}$. It follows (cf. Berge [3, pp. 109–10]) that Γ is upper semicontinuous and lower semicontinuous, respectively, hence continuous. ∎

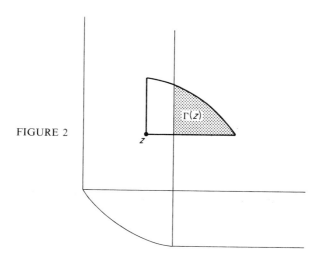

FIGURE 2

3. THE TRADE UTILITY FUNCTION

We now define the *trade utility function* $\hat{U}: \mathscr{Z} \to E^1$ by

$$\hat{U}(z) = \max_{x-z \in \mathscr{Y}} U(x) = \max_{x \in \Gamma(z)} U(x). \tag{5}$$

PROPOSITION 5 $\hat{U}$ is continuous.

Proof Since U is continuous by assumption, and since $\Gamma(z)$ is nonempty for all $z \in \mathscr{Z}$ and Γ is continuous by Proposition 4, the result is an immediate consequence of Berge's maximum theorem [3, p. 116]. ∎

PROPOSITION 6 $\hat{U}$ is locally nonsaturating on $\mathscr{Z}$.

Proof Let $z^0 \in \mathscr{Z}$ be given, and let x^0 and $y^0 = x^0 - z^0$ be such that $\hat{U}(z^0) = U(x^0)$. Let $N(z^0) \subseteq \mathscr{Z}$ be a given neighborhood of z^0, and define $N(x^0) = y^0 + N(z^0) \subseteq \mathscr{X}$. Since U is locally nonsaturating (by hypothesis), there exists $x^1 \in N(x^0)$ such that $U(x^1) > U(x^0)$. Define $z^1 = x^1 - y^0$; then $z^1 \in N(z^0)$ and

$$\hat{U}(z^1) = \max_{x \in \Gamma(z^1)} U(x) \geqq U(y^0 + z^1) = U(x^1) > U(x^0) = \hat{U}(z^0). \quad \blacksquare$$

Letting $\hat{U}(\mathscr{Z})$ denote the set of real numbers u for which $\hat{U}(z) = u$ for some $z \in \mathscr{Z}$, we define for any $u \in \hat{U}(\mathscr{Z})$ the upper contour set

$$\mathscr{Z}(u) = \{z \in \mathscr{Z} : \hat{U}(z) \geqq u\}. \tag{6}$$

PROPOSITION 7   We have

$$\hat{U}(\mathscr{Z}) \subseteq U(\mathscr{X}), \tag{7}$$

and for all $u \in \hat{U}(\mathscr{Z})$

$$\mathscr{Z}(u) = \mathscr{X}(u) - \mathscr{Y}. \tag{8}$$

Proof Let $u^0 \in \hat{U}(\mathscr{Z})$; then $\hat{U}(z^0) = u^0$ for some $z^0 \in \mathscr{Z}$. Let x^0 maximize $U(x)$ over $\Gamma(z^0)$; then $U(x^0) = \hat{U}(z^0) = u^0$. This shows that $u^0 \in U(\mathscr{X})$, establishing (7).

Now, $z^1 \in \mathscr{Z}(u^0)$ if and only if

$$\hat{U}(z^1) = \max_{x \in \Gamma(z^1)} U(x) \geqq u^0.$$

Let x^1 maximize $U(x)$ over $\Gamma(z^1) = (z^1 + \mathscr{Y}) \cap \mathscr{X}$; then $x^1 = z^1 + y^1$ for some $y^1 \in \mathscr{Y}$, and $U(x^1) = \hat{U}(z^1) \geqq u^0$; hence $x^1 \in \mathscr{X}(u^0)$. Thus,

$$z^1 = x^1 - y^1 \in \mathscr{X}(u^0) - \mathscr{Y}.$$

This shows that $\mathscr{Z}(u^0) \subseteq \mathscr{X}(u^0) - \mathscr{Y}$. Conversely, let $z^1 \in \mathscr{X}(u^0) - \mathscr{Y}$; then $z^1 = x^1 - y^1$ where $y^1 \in \mathscr{Y}$ and $U(x^1) = U(z^1 + y^1) \geqq u^0$; hence certainly

$$\max_{x \in (z + \mathscr{Y}) \cap \mathscr{X}} U(x) = \hat{U}(z^1) \geqq u^0,$$

showing that $z^1 \in \mathscr{Z}(u^0)$. ∎

PROPOSITION 8   If x^0 maximizes $U(x)$ on $(z^0 + \mathscr{Y}) \cap \mathscr{X}$, then z^0 minimizes $\hat{U}(z)$ on $x^0 - \mathscr{Y}$.

Proof   Define $u^0 = \hat{U}(z^0)$. The hypothesis then states that $U(x^0) = u^0$. From Proposition 7, formula (8), it then follows that

$$x^0 - \mathscr{Y} \subseteq \mathscr{Z}(u^0).$$

This states that for all $z \in x^0 - \mathscr{Y}$, $\hat{U}(z) \geqq u^0 = \hat{U}(z^0)$, which was to be proved. ∎

Proposition 8 is illustrated in Fig. 3; a geometric construction of this kind was introduced by Kenen [17].

We shall now establish the converse of Proposition 8, which requires, however, the additional assumption of quasi-concavity. $U : \mathscr{X} \to E^1$ is called *quasi-concave* on $\mathscr{X}$ if $\mathscr{X}(u)$ is convex for all $u \in U(\mathscr{X})$. It is immediate from Proposition 7 that if U is quasi-concave on $\mathscr{X}$ then $\hat{U}$ is quasi-concave on $\mathscr{Z}$, since $\mathscr{Y}$ (and hence $-\mathscr{Y}$) is convex. Since U and $\hat{U}$ are continuous, when U is quasi-concave the sets $\mathscr{X}(u)$ and $\mathscr{Z}(u)$ are closed and convex; hence by a well-known theorem (cf. Berge [3, p. 166]) they are equal to the intersections of their supporting half-spaces

$$\{x \in E^n : p \cdot x \geqq M(p, u)\}, \qquad \{z \in E^n : p \cdot z \geqq \hat{M}(p, u)\}$$

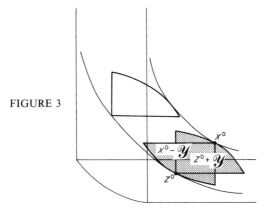

FIGURE 3

where the "minimum-income functions" M and $\hat{M}$ are defined by[6]

$$M(p,u) = \inf_{x \in \mathscr{X}(u)} p \cdot x, \qquad \hat{M}(p,u) = \inf_{z \in \mathscr{Z}(u)} p \cdot z, \tag{10}$$

respectively, where the price vectors $p \neq 0$ belong to certain sets $\mathscr{P}(u)$. (When U is monotone increasing, $p \geq 0$.) We also define the maximum-value-of-output function[7]

$$\Pi(p) = \max_{y \in \mathscr{Y}} p \cdot y. \tag{11}$$

Using (8) and the well-known properties of maxima of linear functions over sums of sets (cf. Koopmans [20, p. 12]), we find immediately that

$$\hat{M}(p,u) = M(p,u) - \Pi(p) \tag{12}$$

for all p, u in the domain of definition of these functions.

PROPOSITION 9   Let U be quasi-concave on $\mathscr{X}$. If z^0 minimizes $\hat{U}(z)$ on $x^0 - \mathscr{Y}$, then x^0 maximizes $U(x)$ on $(z^0 + \mathscr{Y}) \cap \mathscr{X}$, and $U(x^0) = \hat{U}(z^0)$.

Proof   Let z^0 minimize $\hat{U}(z)$ on $x^0 - \mathscr{Y}$, and denote $u^0 = \hat{U}(z^0)$. Since $\mathscr{Z}(u^0)$ is closed and convex, there exists a $p^0 \neq 0$ such that $p^0 \cdot z \geq p^0 \cdot z^0$ for all $z \in \mathscr{Z}(u^0)$; hence from (10) and (12) we have

$$p^0 \cdot z^0 = \hat{M}(p^0, u^0) = M(p^0, u^0) - \Pi(p^0). \tag{13}$$

Since z^0 minimizes $\hat{U}(z)$ on $x^0 - \mathscr{Y}$, (9) holds; and since z^0 is on the boundary of $\mathscr{Z}(u^0)$, and $x^0 - \mathscr{Y}$ is closed, it must also be on the boundary of $x^0 - \mathscr{Y}$. Consequently, z^0 also minimizes $p^0 \cdot z$ on $x^0 - \mathscr{Y}$; hence

$$p^0 \cdot z^0 = \min_{z \in x^0 - \mathscr{Y}} p^0 \cdot z = p^0 \cdot x^0 - \max_{y \in \mathscr{Y}} p^0 \cdot y = p^0 \cdot x^0 - \Pi(p^0), \tag{14}$$

and $z^0 = x^0 - y^0$ where y^0 maximizes $p^0 \cdot y$ on $\mathscr{Y}$. Together, (13) and (14) imply

$$p^0 \cdot x^0 = M(p^0, u^0) = \inf_{x \in \mathscr{X}(u^0)} p^0 \cdot x, \tag{15}$$

i.e., that x^0 minimizes $p^0 \cdot x$ on $\mathscr{X}(u^0)$. Equivalently,

$$p^0 \cdot x \geq p^0 \cdot x^0 \qquad \text{for all} \quad x \in \mathscr{X}(u^0). \tag{16}$$

---

[6] McKenzie [25] defined them in the form $M(p,\bar{x}) = \inf p \cdot x$ for x preferred or indifferent to $\bar{x}$, carefully avoiding reference to a utility index. However, his work helped show that the postulated demand function *was* generable by a utility index! (Cf. Hurwicz and Uzawa [15].)

[7] Cf. Chipman [5, p. 213], where $\mathscr{Y}$ was also expressed explicitly as a function of factor endowments (the set $\mathscr{Y}$ depending on these endowments) and in this respect described (for fixed p) as a "production function for foreign exchange."

On the other hand, since y^0 maximizes $p^0 \cdot y$ on $\mathscr{Y}$, $x^0 = z^0 + y^0$ maximizes $p^0 \cdot x$ on $(z + \mathscr{Y}) \cap \mathscr{X}$; i.e.,

$$p^0 \cdot x \le p^0 \cdot x^0 \qquad \text{for all} \quad x \in (z^0 + \mathscr{Y}) \cap \mathscr{X}. \tag{17}$$

Together, (16) and (17) imply that x^0 maximizes $U(x)$ on $(z^0 + \mathscr{Y}) \cap \mathscr{X}$, and thus from (5) it follows that $U(x^0) = \hat{U}(x^0) = u^0$. ∎

It follows immediately from Proposition 9 that, analogously to the definition (5) of $\hat{U}$ in terms of U, we have the reverse or dual formula

$$U(x) = \min_{z \in x - \mathscr{Y}} \hat{U}(z) = \min_{x - z \in \mathscr{Y}} \hat{U}(z), \tag{18}$$

as long as U is assumed to be quasi-concave. This means that with knowledge of the (convex) production possibility set $\mathscr{Y}$, it is always possible to recover the original consumption utility function from the trade utility function.[8] This is a case of what Rader [28, p. 156] has called the principle of equivalence. We also have the result

PROPOSITION 10   If U is quasi-concave, then $\hat{U}(\mathscr{Z}) = U(\mathscr{X})$.

Proof   That $\hat{U}(\mathscr{Z}) \subseteq U(\mathscr{X})$ was shown in Proposition 7. To prove that $U(\mathscr{X}) \subseteq \hat{U}(\mathscr{Z})$, let $u^0 \in U(\mathscr{X})$, and let x^0 be such that $U(x^0) = u^0$. Define z^0 by the condition that z^0 minimizes $\hat{U}(z)$ on $x^0 - \mathscr{Y}$. Then from (18) we have

$$\hat{U}(z^0) = \min_{z \in x^0 - \mathscr{Y}} \hat{U}(z) = U(x^0) = u^0,$$

which proves that $u^0 \in \hat{U}(\mathscr{Z})$. ∎

4. THE TRADE DEMAND CORRESPONDENCE

Letting as before $\Omega(\mathscr{X})$ denote the set of pairs $(p, I) \in E^{n+1}$ for which the budget set (1) is nonempty, and taking $\mathscr{X} = E^n_+$, we define the (*consumption*) *demand correspondence* on $\Omega(\mathscr{X})$ by

$$h(p, I) = \{x \in B(p, I) : U(x) \ge U(x') \text{ for all } x' \in B(p, I)\}, \tag{19}$$

i.e., as the set of x that maximize $U(x)$ on $B(p, I)$. We shall denote by $\Omega'(\mathscr{X}) \subseteq \Omega(\mathscr{X})$ the set of (p, I) for which $h(p, I) \ne \varnothing$.

Likewise, we define for any $u \in U(\mathscr{X})$ and any p for which $\{x : p \cdot x \ge I\}$ is a supporting half-space for $\mathscr{X}(u)$ the *compensated* (*consumption*) *demand correspondence*

$$k(p, u) = \{x \in \mathscr{X}(u) : p \cdot x \le p \cdot x' \text{ for all } x' \in \mathscr{X}(u)\}, \tag{20}$$

---

[8] For an application of (18) to the theory of the "elasticity approach" to balance-of-payments adjustment theory, see Chipman [8, pp. 62–63].

i.e., as the set of bundles x that minimize expenditure on the upper contour set for u.

Assuming U to be continuous, locally nonsaturating, and quasi-concave on $\mathscr{X}$, Propositions 2 and 3 may now be restated in terms of the above notation, as follows: If $x^0 \in h(p^0, I^0)$, then $x^0 \in k(p^0, u^0)$, where $u^0 = U(x^0)$; and if $x^0 \in k(p^0, u^0)$ and $p^0 \cdot x^0 > \inf_{x \in \mathscr{X}} p^0 \cdot x$, then $x^0 \in h(p^0, I^0)$, where $I^0 = p^0 \cdot x^0$.

Defining the trade set $\mathscr{Z}$ by (3), where $\mathscr{X} = E^n_+$, we denote by $\hat{\Omega}(\mathscr{Z})$ the set of pairs $(p, D) \in E^{n+1}$ for which the *trade budget set*

$$\hat{B}(p, D) = \{z \in \mathscr{Z} : p \cdot z \leqq D\} \tag{21}$$

is nonempty. Just as I stands for "national income," D stands for "the deficit in the balance of payments on current account," or "payments deficit" for short. We define the *trade demand correspondence* on $\hat{\Omega}(\mathscr{Z})$ by

$$\hat{h}(p, D) = \{z \in \hat{B}(p, D) : \hat{U}(z) \geqq \hat{U}(z') \text{ for all } z' \in \hat{B}(p, D)\}, \tag{22}$$

i.e., as the set of trades z that maximize $\hat{U}(z)$ on $\hat{B}(p, D)$. We shall denote by $\hat{\Omega}'(\mathscr{Z}) \subseteq \hat{\Omega}(\mathscr{Z})$ the set of (p, D) for which $\hat{h}(p, D) \neq \varnothing$. Analogously to (20), we also define the *compensated trade demand correspondence* by

$$\hat{k}(p, u) = \{z \in \mathscr{Z}(u) : p \cdot z \leqq p \cdot z' \text{ for all } z' \in \mathscr{Z}(u)\}. \tag{23}$$

From (10), (20), and (23) we may write

$$M(p, u) = p \cdot k(p, u), \qquad \hat{M}(p, u) = p \cdot \hat{k}(p, u). \tag{24}$$

The *national supply correspondence* is defined for any p by

$$\hat{y}(p) = \{y \in \mathscr{Y} : p \cdot y \geqq p \cdot y' \text{ for all } y' \in \mathscr{Y}\}, \tag{25}$$

i.e., as the set of supplies y that maximize the value of the national product over the production possibility set. In view of (11) we may write

$$\Pi(p) = p \cdot \hat{y}(p). \tag{26}$$

PROPOSITION 11   Let U be continuous, locally nonsaturating, and quasi-concave on $\mathscr{X} = E^n_+$. Then for all $u \in U(\mathscr{X})$ and all $p \in E^n$ such that $\{x \in E^n : p \cdot x \geqq I\}$ is a supporting half-space for $\mathscr{X}(u)$, for some I, we have

$$\hat{k}(p, u) = k(p, u) - \hat{y}(p). \tag{27}$$

Proof By Propositions 7 and 10, (8) holds for all $u \in U(\mathscr{X})$. Let $u^0 \in \mathscr{X}(u)$ and p^0 of the required kind be given, and choose $z^0 \in \hat{k}(p^0, u^0)$. Then $p^0 \cdot z^0$ minimizes $p^0 \cdot z$ subject to $z \in \mathscr{Z}(u^0) = \mathscr{X}(u^0) - \mathscr{Y}$. By the properties of minima of linear functions on sums of sets (cf. Koopmans [20, p. 12]), it follows that $z^0 = x^0 - y^0$, where x^0 minimizes $p^0 \cdot x$ on $x \in \mathscr{X}(u^0)$ and y^0 maximizes $p^0 \cdot y$ on $\mathscr{Y}$; i.e.,

$$x^0 \in k(p^0, u^0), \qquad y^0 \in \hat{y}(p^0),$$

so that

$$z^0 \in k(p^0, u^0) - \hat{y}(p^0). \tag{28}$$

Conversely let (28) hold; then $z^0 = x^0 - y^0$, where x^0 minimizes x^0 on $\mathscr{X}(u^0)$ and y^0 maximizes $p^0 \cdot y$ on $\mathscr{Y}$; so z^0 minimizes $p^0 \cdot z$ on $\mathscr{X}(u^0) - \mathscr{Y} = \mathscr{Z}(u^0)$; i.e., $z^0 \in \hat{k}(p^0, u^0)$. ∎

We may now derive the basic relationship between the trade demand correspondence (22) and the national demand and supply correspondences (19) and (25). Before proceeding to the proof of Proposition 12 we may make a technical observation. Suppose U is quasi-concave (as well as continuous and locally nonsaturating); then from (12) and Proposition 10,

$$\min_{u \in \hat{U}(\mathscr{X})} \hat{M}(p, u) = \min_{u \in U(\mathscr{X})} M(p, u) - \Pi(p).$$

Consequently, if z^0 satisfies $p^0 \cdot z^0 = \inf_{z \in \mathscr{Z}} p^0 \cdot z$, where $z^0 = x^0 - y^0$, then x^0 satisfies $p^0 \cdot x^0 = \inf_{x \in \mathscr{X}} p^0 \cdot x^0$, and conversely. Proposition 12 then follows readily from Propositions 2 and 3 provided $D > \inf_{z \in \mathscr{Z}} p \cdot z$ (which holds if and only if $I > \inf_{x \in \mathscr{X}} p \cdot x$). However, a special argument would then be needed for the case in which $D = \inf_{z \in \mathscr{Z}} p \cdot x$. The argument of the proof of Proposition 12 covers both cases. The result was stated in Chipman [6, p. 34n] without proof.

PROPOSITION 12   Let U be continuous, locally nonsaturating, and quasi-concave. Then for all $(p, D) \in \hat{\Omega}(\mathscr{X})$,

$$\hat{h}(p, D) = h(p, D + \Pi(p)) - \hat{y}(p). \tag{29}$$

Proof   Let $(p^0, D^0) \in \hat{\Omega}(\mathscr{X})$. First we show that

$$\hat{h}(p^0, D^0) \subseteq h(p^0, D^0 + \Pi(p^0)) - \hat{y}(p^0). \tag{30}$$

Let $z^0 \in \hat{h}(p^0, D^0)$ and define

$$u^0 = \hat{U}(z^0). \tag{31}$$

Then by Propositions 2 and 11,

$$z^0 \in \hat{k}(p^0, u^0) = k(p^0, u^0) - \hat{y}(p^0);$$

i.e., $z^0 = x^0 - y^0$ where $x^0 \in k(p^0, u^0)$, hence

$$U(x^0) \geqq u^0, \tag{32}$$

and $y^0 \in \hat{y}(p^0)$. By Propositions 1 and 6,

$$p^0 \cdot x^0 = p^0 \cdot z^0 + p^0 \cdot y^0 = D^0 + \Pi(p^0).$$

To establish (30), it remains then to show that

$$x^0 \in h(p^0, D^0 + \Pi(p^0)),$$

i.e., that

$$U(x^0) \geq U(x) \qquad \text{for all} \quad x \in B(p^0, D^0 + \Pi(p^0)). \tag{33}$$

Let $x^1 \in B(p^0, D^0 + \Pi(p^0))$, and define $z^1 = x^1 - y^0$. Then

$$p^0 \cdot z^1 = p^0 \cdot x^1 - p^0 \cdot y^0 \leq D^0 + \Pi(p^0) - \Pi(p^0) = D^0;$$

hence $z^1 \in \hat{B}(p^0, D^0)$. Since $z^0 \in \hat{h}(p^0, D^0)$, it follows that

$$\hat{U}(z^0) \geq \hat{U}(z^1). \tag{34}$$

From (32), (31), (34), (5), (4), and the definition of z^1, we have

$$U(x^0) \geq u^0 \geq \hat{U}(z^0) \geq \hat{U}(z^1) = \max_{x \in (z^1 + \mathcal{Y}) \cap \mathcal{X}} U(x)$$

$$\geq U(z^1 + y^0) = U(x^1),$$

whence (33) follows, since x^1 was arbitrary. This establishes (30).

We now establish

$$h(p^0, D^0 + \Pi(p^0)) - \hat{y}(p^0) \subseteq \hat{h}(p^0, D^0). \tag{35}$$

The result certainly holds if $(p^0, D^0 + \Pi(p^0)) \notin \hat{\Omega}(\mathcal{X})$, for then the left-hand side is empty. Suppose then that $z^0 = x^0 - y^0$ where $x^0 \in h(p^0, D^0 + \Pi(p^0))$ and $y^0 \in \mathcal{Y}$, and define

$$u^0 = U(x^0). \tag{36}$$

From Propositions 2 and 11 it then follows that

$$z^0 \in k(p^0, u^0) - \hat{y}(p^0) = \hat{k}(p^0, u^0),$$

and thus

$$\hat{U}(z^0) \geq u^0. \tag{37}$$

We are to show that $z^0 \in \hat{h}(p^0, D^0)$, i.e., that

$$\hat{U}(z^0) \geq \hat{U}(z) \qquad \text{for all} \quad z \in \hat{B}(p^0, D^0). \tag{38}$$

Let $z^1 \in \hat{B}(p^0, D^0)$; then for all $y \in \mathcal{Y}$,

$$p^0 \cdot (z^1 + y) = p^0 \cdot z^1 + p^0 \cdot y \leq D^0 + \Pi(p^0);$$

i.e.,

$$z^1 + \mathcal{Y} \subseteq B(p^0, D^0 + \Pi(p^0)). \tag{39}$$

From (5), (4), (39), the definition of x^0, (36), and (37), it follows that

$$\hat{U}(z^1) = \max_{x \in (z^1 + \mathcal{Y}) \cap \mathcal{X}} U(x) \leq \max_{x \in B(p^0, D^0 + \Pi(p^0))} U(x) = U(x^0) = u^0 \leq \hat{U}(z^0).$$

This establishes (38) and hence (35). ∎

5. THE CASE OF A DIFFERENTIABLE TRADE DEMAND FUNCTION

Even if the consumption demand correspondence (19) is single valued and differentiable, this will not be the case with respect to the trade demand correspondence (22) unless the supply correspondence (25) is single valued and differentiable, in view of Proposition 12. The supply correspondence, in turn, is single valued if and only if (by definition) the production possibility set $\mathcal{Y}$ is strictly concave to the origin. Within the context of the Heckscher–Ohlin–Lerner–Samuelson model (cf. Samuelson [31]), in which $\mathcal{Y}$ depends uniquely on the vector l of m factor endowments, if this number m exceeds or equals the number of products n, then the supply function $\hat{y}$ (which will depend on l as well as on p) will be single valued for almost all values of the vector l.[9] Even then, the supply function will not be differentiable everywhere, since it will have kinks at points where the country switches from positive to zero production of any commodity. The most we can expect, therefore, is that $\hat{y}$ will be piecewise differentiable.[10] It is well known that the consumption demand function may fail to be differentiable even if it is single valued (cf. Katzner [16, p. 54], Chipman [6, p. 29n]), but with the usual convexity assumptions it can be shown to be differentiable almost everywhere.

Assuming (29) to be single valued and differentiable on a subset $\mathcal{O}$ of $\hat{\Omega}(\mathcal{Z})$, we obtain

$$\frac{\partial \hat{h}_i}{\partial p_j} = \frac{\partial h_i}{\partial p_j} + \frac{\partial h_i}{\partial I}\,\hat{y}_j - \frac{\partial \hat{y}_i}{\partial p_j}, \tag{40}$$

where use is made of Samuelson's result $\partial \Pi/\partial p_j = \hat{y}_j$ (cf. Samuelson [31, p. 10], Chipman [5, p. 221]). Defining the *consumption Slutsky terms* and the *transformation terms* by

$$s_{ij}(p, I) = \frac{\partial h_i(p, I)}{\partial p_j} + \frac{\partial h_i(p, I)}{\partial I} h_j(p, I) \tag{41}$$

and

$$t_{ij}(p) = \frac{\partial \hat{y}_i(p)}{\partial p_j}, \tag{42}$$

---

[9] The exceptional cases occur when there is factor-intensity reversal at the point where the production isoquants have a common tangent and when the country's endowment ray happens to pass through this point of tangency and the diversification cone becomes degenerate—with an empty interior (cf. Chipman [4, Part 3], McKenzie [24]). This can occur if and only if the matrix of factor-output ratios (which is the same as the Jacobian matrix of the mapping from factor rentals to commodity prices defined by the minimum-unit-cost functions—cf. Chipman [4, Part 3]) has rank less than n; cf. Chipman [5, p. 218], Khang [18], Khang and Uekawa [19].

[10] Even at points where all commodities are being produced in positive amounts, if the curvature of the production possibility frontier at a particular point is sufficiently small, derivatives of $\hat{y}$ may fail to exist there. For an example see Chipman [6, p. 31n].

respectively, and the "trade Slutsky term" by

$$\hat{s}_{ij}(p, D) = \frac{\partial \hat{h}_i(p, D)}{\partial p_j} + \frac{\partial \hat{h}_i(p, D)}{\partial D} \hat{h}_j(p, D), \tag{43}$$

we obtain immediately from (40)–(43) and (29) the result

PROPOSITION 13   Let (29) be differentiable on an open subset $\mathcal{O}$ of $\hat{\Omega}(\mathcal{L})$. Then everywhere on $\mathcal{O}$ we have

$$\hat{s}_{ij}(p, D) = s_{ij}(p, D + \Pi(p)) - t_{ij}(p). \tag{44}$$

This result turns out to be extremely useful in many applications of international trade theory.

It may be remarked that given the well-known fact that the Slutsky terms are the second derivatives of the corresponding compensated demand functions, the result (44) also follows immediately from (27) on setting $u = U[h(p, D + \Pi(p))]$.

6. TREATMENT IN TERMS OF INVERSE DEMAND FUNCTIONS

As remarked in the preceding section, one cannot in general expect trade demand correspondences to be single valued. This is unfortunate from the point of view of obtaining local comparative-statistics results, since conventional calculus methods cannot be used and the result (44) can no longer be applied.[11] As an example, if we assume a country has two factors of production (labor and capital) and is capable of producing three commodities, one export good, one import-competing good, and one nontradable domestic good, then (29) will in general be single valued as long as the country specializes in the production of the export and domestic goods, but will be multiple valued whenever all three commodities are produced. In order to avail oneself of calculus methods in such a situation, it is necessary to deal with inverse demand functions (cf. Chipman [8]).

Taking one commodity (say commodity n) as numéraire, the inverse consumption demand functions express the demand price of any other commodity relative to that of the numéraire as a function of the amounts consumed. Inverse trade demand functions express the same price ratios as functions of the amounts traded. Such functions can, of course, be defined only if the original utility function and the production possibility surface are differentiable; this rules out kinks in indifference surfaces and on production

---

[11] Unless generalized so that the expressions in (44) are interpreted as subdifferentials; cf. Rockafellar [29].

possibility surfaces, ruling out of consideration, for example, Leontief or other linear technologies. But this can be considered to be merely a technical assumption, whereas requiring supply functions to be single valued does violence to the basic structure of the model, since it forces one to assume that there are at least as many factors as products.

Taking commodity n to be the numéraire and U to be strictly quasi-concave, and assuming $\partial U/\partial x_n > 0$, the *inverse (consumption) demand functions* P_i for the first $n - 1$ commodities are defined by (cf. Samuelson [30], Katzner [16, p. 44])

$$\frac{p_i}{p_n} = P_i(x) = \frac{U_i(x)}{U_n(x)} \qquad (i = 1, 2, \ldots, n - 1) \qquad (45)$$

where $U_i(x) = \partial U(x)/\partial x_i$. Defining the function $\tilde{x}_n$ by the identity

$$U(x_{)n(}, \tilde{x}_n(x_{)n(}, u)) = u, \qquad (46)$$

where $x_{)n(} = (x_1, x_2, \ldots, x_{n-1})$, this gives the analytic expression of a consumption indifference surface at utility level u. The *compensated inverse consumption demand functions* Q_i are defined by

$$Q_i(x_{)n(}, u) = P_i(x_{)n(}, \tilde{x}_n(x_{)n(}, u)) \qquad (i = 1, 2, \ldots, n - 1) \qquad (47)$$

and satisfy

$$Q_i(x_{)n(}, U(x)) = P_i(x) \qquad (i = 1, 2, \ldots, n - 1). \qquad (48)$$

Differentiating (46), we obtain, with (45) and (47),

$$\tilde{x}_{ni}(x_{)n(}, u) = -Q_i(x_{)n(}, u) \qquad (i = 1, 2, \ldots, n - 1) \qquad (49)$$

(where $\tilde{x}_{ni} = \partial \tilde{x}_n/\partial x_i$), whence $\tilde{x}_{ni}(x_{)n(}, U(x)) = -P_i(x)$. Differentiating (47) with respect to x_j and evaluating the result at $u = U(x)$, we obtain upon observing that $\tilde{x}_n(x_{)n(}, U(x)) = x_n$ the consumption *Antonelli functions*

$$a_{ij}(x) = -\tilde{x}_{nij}(x_{)n(}, U(x)) = P_{ij}(x) - P_{in}(x)P_j(x) \qquad (i, j = 1, 2, \ldots, n - 1),$$

$$(50)$$

where $P_{ij} = \partial P_i/\partial x_j$ and $\tilde{x}_{nij} = \partial^2 \tilde{x}_n/\partial x_i \partial x_i$ (cf. Antonelli [1], Katzner [16, p. 45]). Under the assumed conditions $\tilde{x}_n$ may be shown to be a strictly convex function, whence its Hessian matrix $[\tilde{x}_{nij}(x_{)n(}, u)]$, and thus the Antonelli matrix $[a_{ij}(x)]$, $i, j = 1, 2, \ldots, n - 1$, is negative definite almost everywhere (cf. Katzner [16, p. 46]).

An exactly similar treatment holds for the *inverse trade demand functions* $\hat{P}_i$ defined by

$$\frac{p_i}{p_n} = \hat{P}_i(z) = \frac{\hat{U}_i(z)}{\hat{U}_n(z)} \qquad (i = 1, 2, \ldots, n - 1), \qquad (51)$$

except that U is not strictly quasi-concave unless $\mathscr{Y}$ is strictly concave to the origin. Analogously to (47) and (50) we define the *compensated inverse trade demand functions* $\hat{Q}_i(z)_{n(}, u)$ and the *trade Antonelli functions*

$$\hat{a}_{ij}(z) = \hat{P}_{ij}(z) - \hat{P}_{in}(z)\hat{P}_j(z) \qquad (i, j = 1, 2, \ldots, n - 1), \tag{52}$$

where $\hat{P}_{ij} = \partial \hat{P}_i / \partial z_j$. Unlike the situation depicted by Proposition 13, no simple decomposition exists of the trade Antonelli terms into consumption Antonelli terms and analogous inverse supply terms.

With a fair degree of generality we may assume that the production possibility set $\mathscr{Y}$ is a subset of a convex polyhedral cone $K = \{y : Cy \geq 0\}$. In the special case in which there are no imports of intermediate goods, C is the identity matrix I and K is the nonnegative orthant. The production possibility surface may be described by a differentiable function $T(y) = 0$, where $y \in K$. To obtain $\hat{U}(z)$ from $U(x)$, one then maximizes $U(x)$ subject to $T(x - z) = 0$ and $C(x - z) \geq 0$ to obtain $x = \xi(z)$ and $\hat{U}(z) = U(\xi(z))$. This is a straightforward problem in nonlinear programming. In the region where $\xi(z) > z$ (the country produces positive amounts of all commodities), the derivatives of ξ are given by solving

$$
\begin{bmatrix}
U_{11} - \dfrac{U_n}{T_n}T_{11} & U_{12} - \dfrac{U_n}{T_n}T_{12} & \cdots & U_{1n} - \dfrac{U_n}{T_n}T_{1n} & T_1 \\[2ex]
U_{21} - \dfrac{U_n}{T_n}T_{21} & U_{22} - \dfrac{U_n}{T_n}T_{22} & \cdots & U_{2n} - \dfrac{U_n}{T_n}T_{2n} & T_2 \\
\vdots & \vdots & & \vdots & \vdots \\
U_{n1} - \dfrac{U_n}{T_n}T_{n1} & U_{n2} - \dfrac{U_n}{T_n}T_{n2} & \cdots & U_{nn} - \dfrac{U_n}{T_n}T_{nn} & T_n \\[2ex]
T_1 & T_2 & \cdots & T_n & 0
\end{bmatrix}
\begin{bmatrix}
\dfrac{\partial \xi_1}{\partial z_j} \\[2ex]
\dfrac{\partial \xi_2}{\partial z_j} \\
\vdots \\
\dfrac{\partial \xi_n}{\partial z_j} \\[2ex]
\dfrac{\partial(U_n/T_n)}{\partial z_j}
\end{bmatrix}
$$

$$
=
\begin{bmatrix}
-\dfrac{U_n}{T_n}T_{1j} \\[2ex]
-\dfrac{U_n}{T_n}T_{2j} \\
\vdots \\
-\dfrac{U_n}{T_n}T_{nj} \\[2ex]
T_j
\end{bmatrix}.
$$

As a simple illustration we may take the Mill–Graham model with $n = 2$, $C = I$, and

$$U(x_1, x_2) = x_1^{\theta_1} x_2^{\theta_2} \quad (\theta_1 + \theta_2 = 1), \qquad T(y_1, y_2) = b_1 y_1 + b_2 y_2 - l, \quad (53)$$

where b_i is the labor-output coefficient in industry i, and l is the country's endowment of labor. Then we find that

$$\xi(z_1, z_2) = \begin{cases} \left(z_1, z_2 + \dfrac{l}{b_2}\right) & \text{if} \quad \xi_1(z) = z_1 \\[2mm] (l + b_1 z_1 + b_2 z_2)\left(\dfrac{\theta_1}{b_1}, \dfrac{\theta_2}{b_2}\right) & \text{if} \quad \xi(z) > z \\[2mm] \left(z_1 + \dfrac{l}{b_1}, z_2\right) & \text{if} \quad \xi_2(z) = z_2. \end{cases}$$

Clearly, ξ is not differentiable at switching points. The trade utility function is given by

$$\hat{U}(z_1, z_2) = \begin{cases} z_1^{\theta_1}\left(z_2 + \dfrac{l}{b_2}\right)^{\theta_2} & \text{if} \quad \xi_1(z) = z_1, \quad \xi_2(z) > z_2 \\[2mm] \left(\dfrac{\theta_1}{b_1}\right)^{\theta_1}\left(\dfrac{\theta_2}{b_2}\right)^{\theta_2}(l + b_1 z_1 + b_2 z_2) & \text{if} \quad \xi_1(z) > z_1, \quad \xi_2(z) > z_2 \\[2mm] \left(z_1 + \dfrac{l}{b_1}\right)^{\theta_1} z_2^{\theta_2} & \text{if} \quad \xi_1(z) > z_1, \quad \xi_2(z) = z_2. \end{cases}$$

This function is continuous (as may be verified), but not differentiable at switching points. In the intermediate linear stretch, the trade Antonelli coefficient vanishes. The example is illustrated in Fig. 4. We have $\xi_i(z_1, z_2) = (\theta_i/b_i)(l + b_1 z_1 + b_2 z_2)$; hence the above three cases correspond to those in which $z_2 - (\theta_2 b_1/\theta_1 b_2)z_1$ is $\leq -l/b_2$, greater than $-l/b_2$ but less than $\theta_2 l/\theta_1 b_2$, or $\geq \theta_2 l/\theta_1 b_2$, respectively.

A somewhat more interesting example is given by $n = 3$, $C = I$, and

$$U(x_1, x_2, x_3) = \prod_{i=1}^{3} x_i^{\theta_i} \quad \left(\sum_{i=1}^{3} \theta_i = 1\right), \qquad T(y_1, y_2, y_3) = b_1 y_1 + b_3 y_3 - l,$$

in which commodity 1 is exported, commodity 2 is imported and not produced at home, and commodity 3 is not traded (hence $z_3 = 0$ in equilibrium). For $y_1 > 0$, $y_3 > 0$ we verify that

$$\hat{U}(z_1, z_2, z_3) = \frac{(\theta_1/b_1)^{\theta_1}(\theta_3/b_3)^{\theta_3}}{(\theta_1 + \theta_3)^{\theta_1 + \theta_3}}(l + b_1 z_1 + b_3 z_3)^{\theta_1 + \theta_3} z_2^{\theta_2};$$

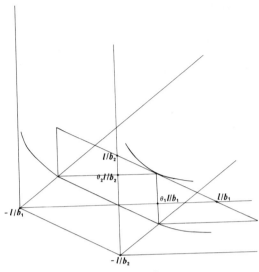

FIGURE 4

hence

$$\hat{P}_1(z) = \frac{b_1}{b_3}, \qquad \hat{P}_2(z) = \frac{\theta_2}{\theta_1 + \theta_3} \frac{l + b_1 z_1 + b_3 z_3}{b_3 z_2}. \tag{54}$$

Thus, the Antonelli coefficients $\hat{a}_{11}$, $\hat{a}_{12}$, $\hat{a}_{21}$ all vanish, but $\hat{a}_{22} < 0$. It was argued in Chipman [8] that the "elasticity models" of balance-of-payments adjustment may be given an interpretation such that the "elasticities of supply and demand for imports and exports" are interpreted as *reciprocals* of the elasticities (logarithmic derivatives) of the inverse trade demand functions (54)—provided the "cross elasticities" vanish. However, while the cross Antonelli terms vanish in the above case, the term $\hat{P}_{21} = \partial \hat{P}_2 / \partial z_1$ does not. This appears to be the basic flaw in the "elasticity approach." Nevertheless, a more general approach without this artificial restriction—such as that of Graaff [13]—is quite feasible, and it is hoped that with the foundations developed here, such an approach may find room for useful development in the theory of international trade.

REFERENCES

1. Antonelli, G. B., "Sulla teoria matematica della Economia politica," nella Tipografia del Folchetto, Pisa, 1886. English translation in J. S. Chipman, L. Hurwicz, M. K. Richter, and H. F. Sonnenschein (eds.), "Preferences, Utility, and Demand," pp. 333–364. Harcourt Brace, New York, 1971.

2. Arrow, K. J., An extention of the basic theorems of classical welfare economics, *Proc. Berkeley Symp. Math. Statistics and Probability*, *2nd* pp. 507–532. Univ. of California Press, Berkeley, California, 1951.
3. Berge, C., "Topological Spaces." Macmillan, New York, 1963.
4. Chipman, J. S., A survey of the theory of international trade: Part 1, The classical theory; Part 2, The neo-classical theory; Part 3, The modern theory, *Econometrica* **33**, 477–519 (1965); **33**, 685–760 (1965); **34**, 18–76 (1966).
5. Chipman, J. S., The theory of exploitative trade and investment policies: A reformulation and synthesis, *in* "International Economics and Development: Essays in Honor of Raúl Prebisch" (L. E. DiMarco, ed.), pp. 881–916. Academic Press, New York, 1972.
6. Chipman, J. S., The transfer problem once again, *in* "Trade, Stability, and Macro-economics: Essays in Honor of Lloyd A. Metzler" (G. Horwich and P. A. Samuelson, eds.), pp. 19–78. Academic Press, New York, 1974.
7. Chipman, J. S., Homothetic preferences and aggregation, *J. Econ. Theory* **8**, 26–38 (1974).
8. Chipman, J. S., A reconsideration of the "elasticity approach" to balance-of-payments adjustment problems, *in* "Breadth and Depth in Economics: Fritz Machlup—The Man and His Ideas" (J. S. Dreyer, ed.), pp. 49–85. Lexington, Mass.: Heath, Lexington, Massachusetts, 1978.
9. Chipman, J. S., and Moore, J. C. Social utility and the gains from trade, *J. Internat. Econ.* **2**, 157–172 (1972).
10. Debreu, G., "Theory of Value." Wiley, New York, 1959.
11. Edgeworth, F. Y., "Mathematical Psychics." C. Kegan Paul and Co., London, 1881.
12. Edgeworth, F. Y., "Papers Relating to Political Economy," Vol. 2. Macmillan, New York, 1925.
13. Graaff, J. de V., On optimum tariff structures, *Rev. Econ. Stud.* **17**, 47–59 (1949–50).
14. Haberler, G., Some problems in the pure theory of international trade, *Econ. J.* **60**, 223–240. (1950).
15. Hurwicz, L., and Uzawa, H., On the integrability of demand functions, "Preferences, Utility, and Demand" (J. S. Chipman *et al.* eds.), Chapter 6, pp. 114–148. Harcourt Brace, New York, 1971.
16. Katzner, D. W., "Static Demand Theory." Macmillan, New York, 1970.
17. Kenen, P. B., On the geometry of welfare economics, *Quart. J. Econ.* **71**, 426–447 (1957).
18. Khang, C., On the strict convexity of the transformation surface in case of linear homogeneous production functions: A general case, *Econometrica* **39**, 587–589 (1971).
19. Khang, C., and Uekawa, Y., The production possibility set in a model allowing inter-industry flows: The necessary and sufficient conditions for its strict convexity *J. Internat. Econ.* **3**, 283–290 (1973).
20. Koopmans, T. C., "Three Essays on the State of Economic Science." McGraw-Hill, New York, 1957.
21. Leontief, W. W., The use of indifference curves in the analysis of foreign trade, *Quart. J. Econ.* **47**, 493–503 (1933).
22. McKenzie, L. W., On equilibrium in Graham's model of world trade and other competitive systems, *Econometrica* **22**, 147–161 (1954).
23. McKenzie, L. W., Specialization and efficiency in world production, *Rev. Econ. Stud.* **21**, 165–180 (1954).
24. McKenzie, L. W., Equality of factor prices in world trade, *Econometrica* **23**, 239–257 (1955).
25. McKenzie, L. W., Demand theory without a utility index, *Rev. Econ. Stud.* **24**, 185–189 (1957).
26. Meade, J. E., "A Geometry of International Trade." Allen and Unwin, London, 1952.

27. Nikaido, H., On the classical multilateral exchange problem, *Metroeconomica* **8**, 135–145 (1956).

28. Rader, J. T. III, Edgeworth exchange and general economic equilibrium, *Yale Econ. Essays*, **4**, 133–180 (1964).

29. Rockafellar, R. T., "Convex Analysis." Princeton Univ. Press, Princeton, New Jersey, 1970.

30. Samuelson, P. A., The problem of integrability in utility theory, *Economica*, N.S. **17**, 355–385 (1950).

31. Samuelson, P. A., Prices of factors and goods in general equilibrium, *Rev. Econ. Stud.* **21**, 1–20 (1953).

32. Samuelson, P. A., Social indifference curves, *Quart. J. Econ.* **70**, 820–829 (1956).

Research supported by National Science Foundation Grant SOC77-27561.

DEPARTMENT OF ECONOMICS
UNIVERSITY OF MINNESOTA
MINNEAPOLIS, MINNESOTA

A Model of Trade and Unemployment

KAMRAN NOMAN

RONALD W. JONES

I. INTRODUCTION

Much of the literature on trade and the balance of payments describes a world in which perfectly flexible prices and wages serve to maintain full employment or some "natural" rate of unemployment. The key concern in the monetary approach to the balance of payments is the relationship between aggregate expenditures and the national income and the manner in which this relationship is affected by money and asset market considerations. But the real level of the national income is assumed not to be influenced by monetary factors, other than through possible variations in the terms of trade. This literature stands in sharp contrast to the Keynesian approach characterized by rigid prices and wages and sensitivity of real output and employment to changes in aggregate demand.

The purpose of this article is to present a model of trade and the balance of payments in which wage rates are considered to respond only sluggishly to the degree of unemployment in the labor market. Thus the short run describes adjustments in commodity markets to given money wages, while in the long run the wage rate settles at a rate appropriate to the "natural" rate of unemployment.

Ours is a small-country model in which a sharp distinction is made between all traded commodities, whose foreign currency prices are exogenously given to the small country, and nontraded commodities, whose

297

markets are assumed to clear instantaneously. Local prices of all traded commodities rise or fall together as the exchange rate changes. We assume a fixed exchange rate model in which currency devaluation may be undertaken, although expectations of such a possibility are not introduced. Thus all traded goods can be lumped together in a single traded commodity, and a two-commodity framework imposed by assuming the existence of only one nontraded commodity.[1] Further structure on the production side is provided by the specific-factor assumption that in each sector labor is combined with a factor of production used only in that sector to produce output at constant returns to scale. Although this model has typically been identified with the short-run immobility of certain productive factors, we neglect here the possibility of long-run intersectoral mobility of nonlabor factors or, indeed, the possibility of real capital accumulation. The crucial monetary assumption that we require is that starting from equilibrium any increase in the nominal value of national income produced causes the nominal value of aggregate expenditure to rise on impact, but by less than the increase in income. For example, the quantity of money demanded may depend directly on the nominal value of income and inversely on the interest rate paid on securities that have only a local market.[2] If the interest rate rises above some crucial rate, individuals are encouraged to spend less than their incomes (and similarly to dishoard if the rate falls below that crucial level). With the quantity of money fixed in the short run, any increase in nominal income would drive up the rate of interest and thus lead to a reduction in the expenditure/income ratio. This finds its reflection in the balance of payments, which goes into surplus. Money flows in, serving gradually to lower interest rates until expenditures once again match the level of national income.

An alternative version specifies a desired stock of assets (or money in a one-asset economy) linked to current (or expected) flows of income or expenditure.[3] From a position of equilibrium an increase in nominal income causes the demand for assets (money) to rise. Assuming no domestic credit creation, this greater asset demand can only be met by refraining from consuming the entire value of income. Further behavior specification would be required to determine the *rate* at which hoarding takes place. Here we only assume that the desire to build up money balances is not so intense

---

[1] The traded versus nontraded commodity distinction for small-country models was made popular by Salter [17], Meade [13], and Swan [18] and can be found in textbook treatments like Caves and Jones [3, Chap. 18].

[2] The concept of nontraded bonds is useful here, for it allows local interest rates to be determined in the local market despite the country being "small" in the market for traded commodities. The concept is further developed in Noman [15].

[3] For an example of this approach, in which desired money holdings are related to aggregate expenditures rather than income, see Caves and Jones [2, 1st ed., pp. 340–343] or Jones [8].

that the current value of money expenditures actually falls while money income rises.

The model we describe is one in which both real and monetary variables have key roles to play. There is one relative commodity price, the ratio of the nontraded goods price p_N to the local currency price of tradables p_T. A currency devaluation or changes in monetary or real conditions abroad can alter p_T, but the price of tradables is never determined endogenously in the model. The price of nontradables, by contrast, is always determined by local market-clearing conditions, so that the price ratio p_N/p_T is also always an endogenous variable. The money wage is considered constant in the short run, although we shall be concerned with the consequences of an exogenous change in money wages. This analysis, in turn, is a pre-requisite for the long-run treatment, in which money wages are endogenously determined by conditions in the labor market. Employment is endogenous, even in the short run. For example, a devaluation (with money wages held fixed) may increase aggregate employment in each sector both before and after the subsequent monetary disturbances have worked themselves out.

Aside from relative prices and real wages, several aggregate variables are explicitly analyzed: (i) Y, the money value of national income produced, is the key variable in determining the state of the balance of payments. If, from an initial full equilibrium, Y should rise, our asset market assumptions require that a balance of payments surplus be created as expenditures fall below income. This surplus will be moderated as money balances change and, as well, will be affected by long-run pressures for the wage rate to change. (ii) P refers to the price level and weights the exogenous price of tradables and that of nontradables. In the neighborhood of full equilibrium, these weights represent the shares of each commodity (α_T and α_N) in the production of national income.[4] (iii) Finally, we denote by y an index of real output uniquely related to the level of employment. The terms of trade remain constant so that y increases only if the community's transformation schedule shifts out (in the event more labor is called into production).

Section II of the paper discusses briefly several standard models containing some, but not all, of the features of this model. Following that we highlight some of the relationships characterizing the production side of the model that are crucial in the subsequent analysis. Section IV discusses the role of relative prices and real expenditures in allowing a positively sloped demand curve for nontradables when employment effects are considered. Sections V

---

[4] The subsequent algebraic development is restricted to the neighborhood of full equilibrium in which (a) the nontraded goods market clears, and (b) the current account is in balance. If either (a) or (b) is not satisfied, consumer weights for a consumer price index would differ from the price index P using production weights. For simplicity we choose to avoid this problem.

and VI, respectively, consider the short-run impact of an exogenous lowering of the money wage and an increase in the local price of tradables (via devaluation). In particular we stress those structural features of the model that might surprisingly allow a wage reduction to create a payments deficit (despite real growth) or a devaluation to reduce the level of employment. In the long run both the community's stock of money and the level of money wages are endogenously determined, and Section VII describes the adjustment process. Section VIII provides some concluding remarks.

The emphasis throughout the paper is on theoretical structure instead of policy analysis.[5] The model must be considered simple when compared with a larger n-sector model of general equilibrium. However, it is precisely the compression of the number of commodities to two that allows this model explicitly to consider certain features hinted at but usually only tangentially considered in more general models: (i) Different speeds of adjustment are integral to the model. Equilibrium in the market for traded goods is never considered in that this small country is always a price taker for these commodities. Nontradables are, by contrast, assumed to clear immediately. The wage rate responds, but only slowly, to market pressures. Thus states of underemployment and/or overemployment are possible (except in the long run). (ii) The classical form of the budget constraint, wherein all produced income is spent, is modified by allowing the nation to run balance of payments deficits or surpluses as monetary stock disequilibria get equilibrated via discrepancies between current expenditure and income flows.

II. PRELIMINARY MODELS

Probably the most simple model based on the two-sector framework of traded and nontraded commodities assumes full wage and price flexibility (and thus full employment) and a budget constraint that freezes out any monetary considerations in that expenditures and income always balance. A devaluation of the currency raises the price of tradables by the same relative amount. At the initial price of nontradables, excess demand for nontradables is created, as substitution effects in production (toward tradables) and in consumption (toward nontradables) serve to raise p_N until its original relationship with p_T is reestablished. Devaluation has not altered any real magnitude (such as relative commodity prices).

The monetary approach to the balance of payments provides a simple explanation of why, for a period of time, such a devaluation of the currency

---

[5] The applicability of this model for an analysis of monetary and fiscal policy is provided by Noman [15, Chap. 1].

creates balance of trade surpluses and increases in reserves. A rise in p_T entails a rise in the price level and the monetary value of produced incomes. This creates an increased demand for money, shifting the demand curve for all commodities leftward. In particular, the relative price of nontradables is driven down (but not so much that the price level falls), which encourages resources to shift toward tradables. The balance-of-payments surplus both causes nontradables to fall relatively (and perhaps absolutely) in price during the transition and provides the extramonetary reserves that eventually restore spending to the level of income and wipe out the surplus.

The models of trade and payments that introduce wage or price inflexibility typically have replaced the monetary approach view of aggregate demand with a fiscal policy mix whereby total spending is shaped both in volume and composition to accommodate full-employment production of nontradables at the prices dictated by the original constraints.[6] Occasionally both wage and price (of nontradables) rigidity is assumed,[7] in which case it would be accidental for production to be maintained at full-employment levels. (Each production point along the full-employment transformation locus is associated with a unique set of relative commodity prices and wage rate.) The prototype of this case is the Keynesian model for a small open economy with unemployed resources and fixed prices and wages. However, the volume of exports is typically assumed fixed in small-country Keynesian models. In our model we adhere to the more standard assumption in trade theory that it is export price that is determined for the small country by a larger world market.

III. PRODUCTION RELATIONSHIPS

The key property of the production side of the model is that output in each sector depends only on the real wage rate in that sector. With labor the only mobile productive factor, the intensity of its use (and therefore total output) is determined by the value of its marginal product. Let x_N and x_T denote outputs in each sector, e_N and e_T the output elasticities (both positive),

---

[6] For example, see the approach adopted by Dornbusch [5] or Jones and Corden [10]. Models of wage rigidity (or minimum wage constraints) have been developed by Brecher [1] and Helpman [6], but in the context of Heckscher–Ohlin models. The piece by Helpman [7] comes closest to our model in that the specific-factors production model is assumed and unemployed labor is a key feature of the model. The emphasis in Helpman [7], however, is on a wage function whereby money wages are indexed to the price level.

[7] For example, see Dornbusch [4, pp. 75–79]. In the preceding sections of this paper Dornbusch examines a full-employment version of the specific-factors model for such questions as currency devaluation.

and a circumflex ($\hat{\ }$) over a variable the relative change in that variable. Changes in outputs are then shown in Eq. (1) and (2):

$$\hat{x}_N = e_N(\hat{p}_N - \hat{w}), \tag{1}$$

$$\hat{x}_T = e_T(\hat{p}_T - \hat{w}). \tag{2}$$

The money wage rate is denoted by w, and the two local currency commodity prices by p_N and p_T.[8]

In a full-employment model, or equivalently a model with fixed labor force participation, the wage rate depends on the commodity prices and, indeed, $\hat{w}$ is a positive weighted average of the $\hat{p}_j$. This makes the output of each commodity, in turn, a function only of the relative output price ratio p_N/p_T. This link is broken if the quantity of labor employed can vary. For example, suppose the wage rate is fixed but the price of nontradables should rise. Output of nontradables would then expand, with absolutely no change in the output of tradables (since both p_T and w are fixed).

The output supply elasticities e_N and e_T show in the first instance how sensitive each output in turn is to a change solely in that output price. But they also indicate how much real national income can be expanded by a reduction in the wage rate at constant prices. In general, the change in real output $\hat{y}$ is the weighted average of each output change:

$$\hat{y} = \alpha_N \hat{x}_N + \alpha_T \hat{x}_T, \tag{3}$$

the weights α_N and α_T, representing output shares. At constant commodity prices an expansion of real output can be brought about by a wage reduction:

$$\hat{y} = \{\alpha_N e_N + \alpha_T e_T\}(-\hat{w}). \tag{4}$$

Let e be defined as this weighted average of output elasticities:

$$e \equiv \{\alpha_N e_N + \alpha_T e_T\}.$$

Then e reveals the percentage increase in real output associated with a 1% fall in wages (as of fixed commodity prices).[9] Note the source of the increased labor supply. This is not a model in which more labor is attracted into the labor force by better wages. Instead, employment in this model is completely

---

[8] Details of the production side of this model are provided in Jones [9], Mussa [14], or Mayer [12]. Also see the Supplement to Chapter 6 in Caves and Jones [3]. The output elasticities can be expressed in terms of underlying parameters of the technology. For example, e_T equals $\theta_{LT} \cdot (\sigma_T/\theta_{KT})$, where σ_T is the elasticity of substitution, and θ_{LT} and θ_{KT} represent, respectively, labor and capital distributive shares in each industry.

[9] The wage reduction could alternatively be related to the change in employment $\hat{L}$. With labor the only factor not fixed in overall supply, $\alpha^L \hat{L}$ must equal $\hat{y}$, where α^L denotes labor's share of the national income. (See, for example, Jones and Scheinkman [11].) Therefore a 1% drop in wages raises overall employment by e/α^L%.

demand determined. A lowering of the real wage increases the demand for labor in each sector, and such labor is assumed always to be available for hire. Whereas the term e indicates how responsive aggregate output is to a wage reduction, it is the relationship between each sector's output elasticity and e that reveals the composition of the output response. Define $\tilde{e}_N$ as e_N/e and $\tilde{e}_T$ as e_T/e. Then the value, say, of $\tilde{e}_T$ is the percentage expansion in the tradable sector that could correspond to a 1% increase in aggregate real output (triggered by a reduction in the wage rate). If a wage reduction at constant prices were to lead to a balanced expansion of both outputs (i.e., the transformation schedule shifting uniformly out from the origin), the values of $\tilde{e}_N$ and $\tilde{e}_T$ would each be unity. If, instead, $\tilde{e}_N$ were to exceed unity, we could describe nontradables as biased toward labor.[10] In any case, the output share weighted average of the relative output elasticities is unity:

$$\alpha_N \tilde{e}_N + \alpha_T \tilde{e}_T = 1. \tag{5}$$

The direction of bias will prove to be an important ingredient in our analysis of devaluation and wage rate changes.

IV. REAL EXPENDITURE AND THE DEMAND FOR NONTRADABLES

The market for nontradables is assumed to clear continuously. Supply behavior is straightforward and is summarized by Eq. (1): output rises if and only if price rises relatively more than the wage rate. Demand behavior is more complex. Out of any given level of aggregate real expenditure z, consumers demand more nontradables if and only if the relative price of nontradables, p_N/p_T, falls. Thus the price of tradable goods enters directly into the substitution term in demand even though it is absent on the supply side. Let E_N denote the (negative) value of the substitution elasticity of demand and ζ_N the expenditure elasticity—a 1% increase in real expenditures at constant prices leads to a ζ_N% increase in demand for nontradables. The demand function itself, written as

$$D_N = D_N(p_N/p_T, z) \tag{6}$$

can thus be differentiated to yield

$$\hat{D}_N = E_N(\hat{p}_N - \hat{p}_T) + \zeta_N \hat{z}. \tag{7}$$

---

[10] This was the terminology used in Ruffin and Jones [16] to describe the dual phenomenon in a full-employment model: the impact on the wage rate of a rise in the price of nontradables. Lack of bias in this case would have the wage rate rise in percentage terms by exactly the average of all factor prices.

It is in the breakdown of the real expenditure term that the particular features of our model become evident. First, real expenditure is defined as the money value of expenditure Z deflated by the price index $P,$[11] just as real income or output y is defined as the money value of current output Y divided by the price index P.

The relationship between money income Y and money expenditure Z reflects the monetary and asset market assumptions of this model. For given asset levels (and hereafter we assume that money represents the only asset) an increase in Y spills over only partly into an increase in expenditures Z. The remainder is saved in an attempt to increase money holdings to the higher level appropriate to the higher monetary value of income. Thus the *impact* effect of the increase in Y on Z is shown by

$$\hat{Z} = \beta \hat{Y}, \qquad 0 < \beta < 1. \tag{8}$$

Any increase in Y at a constant supply of money thus leads to a surplus in the balance of payments, which by building up reserves and the money supply M eventually allows expenditure to restore its equality to income. Put explicitly, if the money value of income and the money stock (the only asset) should both increase proportionally from a position of initial equilibrium, so would the money value of expenditures. That is, expenditures would remain equal to income. Therefore, allowing time for the money supply to change,

$$\hat{Z} = \beta \hat{Y} + (1 - \beta)\hat{M}. \tag{8'}$$

This relationship proves useful later when we analyze the adjustment process through time. In developing demand expressions, however, we limit attention to the impact effect of price changes as of a given money supply, in which case Eq. (8) provides the appropriate expression for the relationship between Z and Y.

As the demand function (6) makes clear, it is real expenditure z that influences demand, and this could be falling even if the money value of expenditures (or income) is rising. Since $\hat{Y} = \hat{y} + \hat{P}$, Eq. (8) can be used to yield two equivalent expressions for the change in real expenditures:

$$\hat{z} = \hat{y} - (1 - \beta)\hat{Y}, \tag{9}$$

$$\hat{z} = \beta \hat{y} - (1 - \beta)\hat{P}. \tag{10}$$

The first of these emphasizes that unless the money value of produced income changes, real expenditures will keep pace with real output. Any increase

---

[11] We are considering the price index P to reflect producer weights α_N and α_T. This procedure is literally accurate only in the neighborhood of full equilibrium. See footnote 4.

in Y out of a fixed monetary base causes real expenditure to fall relative to real output. The second of these expressions isolates the separate impact on real expenditures of increases in real output (causing a dampened rise in real expenditures) and of increases in the price level (causing real expenditures to fall). In the full-employment version of the model, with no terms-of-trade effects, $\hat{y}$ always equals zero, so that the monetary approach to the balance of payments can concentrate on price level effects. But the main feature of the present model is that changes in prices and/or wages will induce changes in employment and real output y.

The significance of these remarks for the demand curve can be observed by considering the impact on demand for nontradables in Eq. (7) of a rise in p_N, assuming that the price of tradables and the wage rate are kept fixed. From (3) and (1) the relative increase in real output is $\hat{y} = \alpha_N e_N \hat{p}_N$. The price rise encourages expansion and employment in nontradables while leaving the tradable sector unchanged. The monetary value of produced income Y rises relatively even more because the price level P has risen. ($\hat{P} = \alpha_N \hat{p}_N$ in this case). Combining into (9) yields

$$\hat{z} = \alpha_N e_N \hat{p}_N - (1 - \beta)\alpha_N(e_N + 1)\hat{p}_N. \tag{11}$$

This reveals the conflicting forces affecting real expenditures as the price of nontradables rises: On the one hand, output of nontradables, and therefore aggregate employment and real output, must rise. On the other hand, the rising *value* of the national income puts a brake on the expenditure–income relationship. The term $(1 - \beta)$ can range from zero to unity, with large values in this range reflecting an urgency to accumulate when money stocks become inadequate. Depending on the size of $(1 - \beta)$, the impact effect of a rise in p_N may be to raise or lower real expenditure. Of course as money supplies rise to match desired levels, the rise in real output will be matched by a rise in real expenditures.

Perhaps a surprising feature of this model is that the demand curve for nontradables can be positively sloped. In (7) the substitution term E_N must be negative so that the compensated demand curve is negatively sloped. But if real expenditures rise sufficiently, the rise in p_N could encourage an increase in the net quantity of nontradables demanded. The expenditure effects at work in this model differ from those in the model of full employment. The traditional real income effect of a change in the terms of trade is absent. But the expansion in real output triggered by the rise in p_N serves to raise the demand for nontradables, even if in the short run this is at least somewhat dampened by the monetary constraints on real expenditure.

Although the D_N curve may be positively sloped, stability is not threatened because the supply curve must be even more elastic if, as we assume, both classes of commodities are normal. The reasoning is basic: The only source for increased real expenditure, only part of which will fall on nontradables, is the expansion in the supply of nontradables. Therefore excess supply would be created as p_N rises, ensuring stability. This is embodied formally in the expression for Δ in the next section as we consider the impact on the market for nontradables of a wage reduction.

V. A FALL IN THE WAGE RATE

A fall in the money wage would, at constant commodity prices, cause both sectors to expand employment and output. Such an expansion may disturb the market for nontradables, but the required direction of change in p_N can be revealed by comparing the changes in demand and supply at the initial commodity prices.

The relative rise in D_N at constant prices is $\hat{D}_N = \zeta_N \hat{z}$ from (7). But the rise in real expenditures is, from (10), given by $\hat{z} = \beta \hat{y}$, and from (4) the expansion in aggregate output equals $e(-\hat{w})$. Therefore, at initial prices

$$\hat{D}_N = \beta \zeta_N e(-\hat{w}).$$

The production change $\hat{x}_N$ is by (1) shown by $e_N(-\hat{w})$ or by the definition of the *relative* output elasticity $\tilde{e}_N$:

$$\hat{x}_N = \tilde{e}_N e(-\hat{w})$$

at initial commodity prices. Thus the price of nontradables can either rise or fall. The formal expression for $\hat{p}_N$ is shown in Eq. (12):[12]

$$\hat{p}_N = (1/\Delta)e\{\beta\zeta_N - \tilde{e}_N\}(-\hat{w}) \tag{12}$$

where $\Delta \equiv -E_N + e_N(1 - m_N\beta) + (1 - \beta)m_N > 0$.

The "neutral" case provides an example. If, as wages fall, the transformation curve shifts out radially from the origin, $\tilde{e}_N$ will equal unity. If all demands are unit elastic (the homothetic case), ζ_N will also equal unity. In such a balanced case p_N will nonetheless fall, since aggregate expenditure expands by less than does production because of the monetary constraint. However, with the passage of time p_N will gradually rise to its initial value. In general, a wage reduction and consequent expansion of real output will more likely lower the price of nontradables if they are "biased" toward labor in the sense that $\tilde{e}_N$ exceeds unity.

---

[12] The expression Δ captures the impact of a rise in p_N on excess supply. It has been simplified by observing that the marginal propensity to consume nontradables out of an increase in expenditures m_N is equal to $\alpha_N\zeta_N$ in the neighborhood of the initial equilibrium (where α_N would thus represent the average propensity to consume nontradables out of a given level of expenditure).

Focus, now, on the effects of the wage reduction on the aggregate level of employment (or real output) and on the balance of payments. A surplus in the balance of payments will represent the impact effect of a wage reduction only if Y is forced to expand. But must the money value of income rise? Y is affected by the price level, as well as by real output, and, as we have seen, p_N may fall.

In pursuing this question it is convenient to establish limits on the possible fall in the price of nontradables. For this purpose consider Fig. 1. Demand and supply initially intersect at point A. The D_N curve shown is the compensated demand curve through the initial equilibrium. This compensated curve does not shift with a wage reduction, although the full D_N curve will. The supply curve x_N shifts downward to x'_N, the relative downward shift being given by the amount of the wage reduction $(-\hat{w})$, since by Eq. (1), a price reduction of the same relative amount would leave output unaltered. Now ask what would happen to real (aggregate) expenditure if p_N dropped to OC. Output of tradables has risen since p_T/w has risen. At OC the price

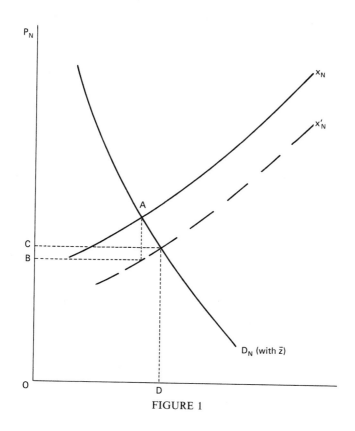

FIGURE 1

of nontradables has fallen, but by less than the wage rate. Therefore aggregate real output must be greater. At OC the price level P has fallen. Therefore by (10) the level of real expenditure z unambiguously has increased. Part of this spills over to nontradables. The upshot is that at price OC the demand for nontradables must be greater than the amount OD, which is accounted for by the pure substitution terms. Therefore equilibrium p_N must be higher than OC, which finally implies that $\hat{p}_N$ must exceed $\hat{w}$.

This result is important, for it immediately establishes that a wage cut must raise employment and output in each sector. But what about the monetary value of output Y, which is the key to balance of payments behavior? Figure 2 helps to distinguish the issues. Suppose p_N and $(1/w)$ are initially at A. The dotted rectangular hyperbola through A, together with our preceding result, establishes that as w falls the new $(p_N, 1/w)$ point must lie to the right of the hyperbola. The vertical line through A shows that the price level P would remain constant only if p_N does not change. The $\hat{y} = 0$ curve through point A is flatter there than a rectangular hyperbola. This result follows since a wage reduction coupled with a fall in p_N of the same relative amount would prevent employment in nontradables from rising, but not overall employment since the wage cut stimulates output in the traded goods sector. Therefore an even greater cut in p_N would be required to keep employment and aggregate output constant. Since

$$\hat{Y} = \hat{y} + \hat{P},$$

the curve showing a zero change in the monetary value of national production must lie between the $\hat{y} = 0$ locus and the $\hat{P} = 0$ locus. If above A the $\hat{Y} = 0$ locus were to lie to the left of the rectangular hyperbola, a wage reduction would have to cause Y to rise, and thus have an impact effect such that the balance of payments goes into surplus. If the $\hat{Y} = 0$ locus lies to the right of the rectangular hyperbola above A (as illustrated), further restrictions on the possible fall in the price of nontradables would have to be imposed to ensure a payments surplus.

To pursue this matter, ask what the sign of $\hat{Y}$ is when p_N falls exactly by the same relative amount as w. This would leave output x_N unaltered. With the price of tradables constant in any case,

$$\hat{Y} = \alpha_N \hat{p}_N + \alpha_T \hat{x}_T$$

By assumption $\hat{p}_N$ equals $\hat{w}$ and from the supply function given by (2), $\hat{x}_T$ equals $e_T(-\hat{w})$. Therefore

$$\hat{Y} = \{\alpha_T e_T - \alpha_N\}(-\hat{w})$$

when the price of nontradables falls by as much as the wage rate. Thus if the supply elasticity in tradables e_T is sufficiently high (exceeding α_N/α_T),

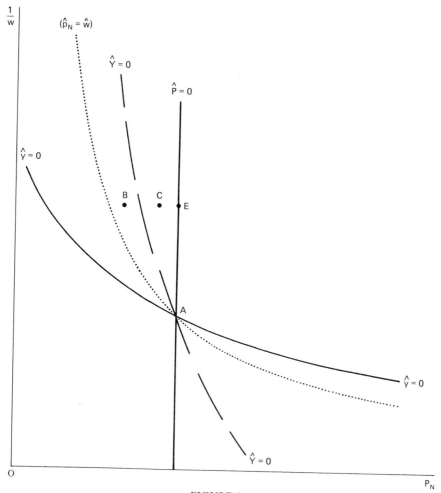

FIGURE 2

the $\hat{Y} = 0$ locus must be trapped between the rectangular hyperbola and the $\hat{y} = 0$ locus in Fig. 2 and the balance of payments must go into surplus. If e_T is smaller than this critical value, the wage reduction causes tradables output to expand only slightly. Thus if p_N falls enough (but still not as much as w), the monetary value of income could fall. Figure 2 illustrates a $\hat{Y} = 0$ curve appropriate for a small value of e_T (lower than α_N/α_T).

Demand behavior provides a condition sufficient to ensure that in Fig. 2 the new $(p_N, 1/w)$ point lies at a point C, where a surplus is created, as opposed to a point such as B, which would imply a balance of payments deficit. Let α_T be very small; so little help from this quarter is received.

Nonetheless, if the "ordinary" elasticity of demand for nontradables exceeds unity, a fall in p_N would, if Y were kept constant, raise total expenditure on nontradables $p_N x_N$. But that would imply that Y must rise (even though $p_T x_T$ is constant). Therefore a sufficient condition for a wage reduction to lead to surplus is a high enough demand elasticity.

These various sufficient conditions can explicitly be derived from a formal statement of the effect of a wage reduction on the monetary value of output. With an explicit solution for the market-clearing change in the price of nontradables provided by (12), and output responses given by (1) and (2), all the ingredients are available to solve for $\hat{Y}$ [equal to $\alpha_N(\hat{p}_N + \hat{x}_N)$ plus $\alpha_T \hat{x}_T$]. Thus[13]

$$\hat{Y} = (e/\Delta)\{[-E_N + m_N] + \tilde{e}_N[\alpha_T e_T - \alpha_N]\}(-\hat{w}). \tag{13}$$

We have already alluded to the "neutral" case in which both $\tilde{e}_N$ and the expenditure elasticity ζ_N are unity. A wage reduction has been seen to cause p_N to fall on impact (because of the monetary effect). But in this case the fall in p_N cannot lead to a payments deficit, even though the locus of $(p_N, 1/w)$ for which $\hat{Y} = 0$ can lie as pictured in Fig. 2. With unit expenditure elasticity, the marginal propensity to consume nontradables m_N will equal the average propensity α_N, which must equal $\alpha_N \tilde{e}_N$ in expression (13). In Fig. 2 the wage reduction on impact moves the economy from A to C, and as the monetary reserves are built up, from C to E.

VI. CURRENCY DEVALUATION

Just as a wage reduction has clear effects on employment and real output, though ambiguous results on the balance of payments, so a currency devaluation with fixed money wages must of necessity lead to a payments surplus on impact, although the effect on output and employment is left in doubt.

If expenditures were always kept equal to incomes, a devaluation would have to raise both the real and monetary values of aggregate output, assuming wages are kept constant: A rise in p_T would clearly cause expansion in the tradable sector. At initial p_N both substitution and expenditure effects would conspire to create excess demand for nontradables, thus forcing p_N, as well as p_T, to rise. However, as opposed to the fixed employment case, the *relative* price of nontradables could rise as well. The criterion depends precisely on the comparison of $\tilde{e}_N$ with the expenditure elasticity ζ_N, just as in the case of a wage rate change. At unaltered p_N/p_T there is no substitution effect in demand. Output expansion in the nontradables sector would equal $e_N \cdot \hat{p}_N$,

---

[13] The sufficient condition involving the "ordinary" elasticity of demand, $(-E_N + m_N)$ follows since the term $\alpha_N \tilde{e}_N$ is a positive fraction [see Eq. (5)].

while demand would expand by $\zeta_N e \cdot \hat{p}_N$ if monetary effects are ignored. Therefore if ζ_N exceeds $\tilde{e}_N$, the relative price of nontradables could actually rise on impact as a consequence of devaluation.

It is the monetary wealth effect, serving as a drag on the expenditure increase, that alters this story and opens up the possibility that the price of nontradables actually falls (thus reducing employment in that sector) and, indeed, that aggregate real output and employment could fall. But note that the monetary value of Y cannot fall with devaluation. For if it did, spending would rise relative to income. If spending only keeps pace with income, we have just argued that p_N must rise. Therefore a devaluation must on impact improve the balance of payments.

In pursuit of the impact of devaluation on the aggregate levels of employment and the price level, consider how these two aggregates are related with the aid of Figs. 3 and 4. A devaluation would have to cause a reduction in the price of nontradables if the price level is to be constant. Similarly, the devaluation encourages employment in tradables. Therefore p_N would have

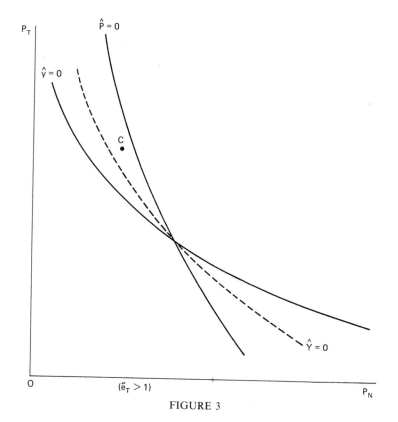

FIGURE 3

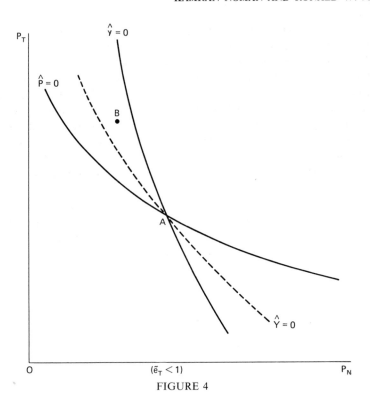

FIGURE 4

to fall if overall employment is held constant. In both diagrams the negatively sloped curves for $\hat{P} = 0$ and $\hat{y} = 0$ must between them trap the locus along which $\hat{Y}$ is zero. The diagrams differ in the relative position of the zero $\hat{p}$ and $\hat{y}$ loci. Along the $\hat{P} = 0$ curve,

$$\alpha_N \hat{p}_N + \alpha_T \hat{p}_T = 0,$$

while for constant y, it is required that

$$\alpha_N \tilde{e}_N \hat{p}_N + \alpha_T \tilde{e}_T \hat{p}_T = 0.$$

Thus if $\tilde{e}_T$ exceeds unity (or $\alpha_T \tilde{e}_T$ exceeds α_T), a devaluation at unchanged p_N has relatively higher impact on real output than on the price level, and consequently a greater reduction in p_N would be required to keep employment constant than to keep the price level from rising. This is Fig. 3. In such a case since an increase in p_T cannot cause p_N to fall so much as to lower Y, of necessity p_N cannot fall so much that aggregate employment falls. But in the context of Fig. 4, in which $\tilde{e}_T$ is smaller than unity, this argument suggests that p_N might fall so much (e.g., to point B) that aggregate output and employment declines (and the transformation schedule shifts toward the origin).

Note the asymmetry in the two sectors: A devaluation must raise p_T; so at a fixed wage rate high values of e_T encourage great employment gains. For severe enough monetary drag the price of nontradables could fall, and it would take a large value of e_N to bring overall employment levels down—thus the crucial role of the comparison between $\tilde{e}_T$ and $\tilde{e}_N$ or, what amounts to the same thing, $\tilde{e}_T$ and unity.[14] Of course, if the wealth effect that causes expenditures to fall relative to income is absent, employment and the price of nontradables must rise. That is, a devaluation (with money wages fixed) may *temporarily* cause employment levels to fall, but as reserves are accumulated, employment levels must rise, and the price of nontradables could rise even by a greater percentage than the devaluation.[15]

Figures 3 and 4 reveal the way in which the $\hat{P} = 0$ and $\hat{y} = 0$ loci are reversed, depending upon the relative ranking of $\tilde{e}_N$ and $\tilde{e}_T$. Under conditions shown in Fig. 4 it was possible that devaluation could lower employment. By analogy, is it possible for devaluation to lower the price level if $\tilde{e}_T > 1$ (as at point C in Fig. 3)? This possibility is ruled out for the following reason: At point C real output rises and the price level falls. But by eq. (10) this implies that real expenditures must rise, which contradicts the possibility that the price of nontradables will fall, since the substitution term as well works in favor of higher p_N.

To conclude: A devaluation must have an unambiguously favorable effect on the two aggregates to which it is most closely related, viz., the balance of payments and the price level. But a relatively weak response to new employment opportunities in the tradables sector opens up the possibility that if real expenditures fall (assuming the desire to accumulate new reserves is strong enough), the price of nontradables (and therefore employment in that sector) drops so much as to reduce real output. On impact this possible effect of a devaluation cannot be ruled out. But as reserves accumulate, employment in both sectors must ultimately rise.

VII. LONG-RUN ADJUSTMENTS

In the long run both the wage rate and the level of reserves adjust to the pressures encountered at the exchange rate and fixed price of tradables the small country has established. In previous sections no wage adjustment has

---

[14] A necessary condition on the monetary drag for p_N possibly to fall is that β fall short of $1/(1 + e_T)$, as can be seen from the formal solution for $\hat{p}_N$:

$$\hat{p}_N = (1/\Delta)\{-E_N + \zeta_N\alpha_T[\beta e_T - (1 - \beta)]\}\hat{p}_T. \tag{14}$$

[15] As we discuss in Section VII, a full adjustment would entail the wage rate's rising (by the same rate as the devaluation), and such a wage increase would drive the p_N/p_T ratio back down to its initial level.

been considered (although Section V analyzed the effects of exogenous wage changes). Now let the money wage rate change over time in response to the degree of unemployment. In general, the relationship between wage rate changes and the unemployment rate would depend on the expected rate of inflation. We disregard this complication here by assuming the expected rate of inflation is always zero. There is some natural level of unemployment, and if the quantity of labor seeking but not finding work exceeds this level, the wage rate is assumed to fall. If unemployment is lower than the natural level, market pressures exist for the wage rate to rise.

At any moment of time three key variables determine the price of nontradables, the level of employment and output in each sector and the balance of payments. These variables are the price of tradables established by the exchange rate p_T, the wage rate w, and the supply of money M. Of these three, the wage rate and money supply are, in the long run, endogenous. Their rates of change depend on the rate of unemployment and the state of the balance of payments, which in turn depend on the current values of w and M (and p_T). For a given exchange rate the relationships between w and M that would lead to the natural level of unemployment (so that no further pressure exists for the wage rate to change) and a zero balance of payments

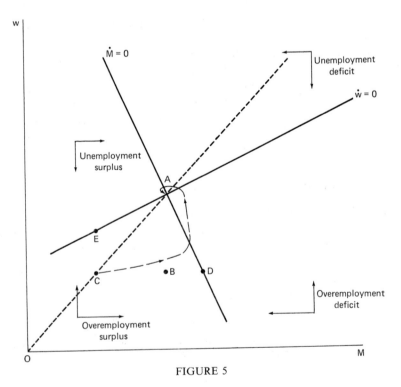

FIGURE 5

(so that reserves neither rise nor fall) are shown in Fig. 5 and 6 by the $\dot{w} = 0$ and $\dot{M} = 0$ loci, respectively.

Consider an initial long-run equilibrium at point A in Fig. 5 and ask about the impact of a reduction of the wage rate to point B. Such a change has a clear effect on the level of employment—it must rise. At that new, lower, wage rate the only way (at the fixed exchange rate) to prevent employment from rising is via a monetary contraction (which would lower demand and price for nontradables). Therefore the locus along which $\dot{w} = 0$ (or unemployment remains at the natural level) must be positively sloped. We consider below more details as to its shape. But first ask about the impact of the move from A to B on the balance of payments. As Section V has revealed, the wage reduction might normally be thought to create an initial surplus. However, if the price of nontradables should fall sufficiently that at B the money value of national income is also reduced, a deficit would ensue. In the former case (of surplus at B) two remarks are in order: First, the money supply will expand as reserves accumulate. Second, it is precisely such an increase in reserves that would be required (at the wage rate shown by B) to restore equilibrium in the balance of payments. Thus the $\dot{M} = 0$ locus would be negatively sloped (as drawn in Fig. 5). However, if the move from

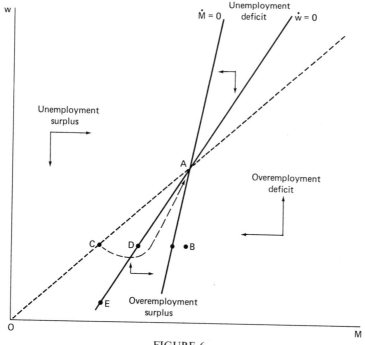

FIGURE 6

A to B resulted in a deficit, the money supply would fall, and such a fall would eventually choke back spending and wipe out the deficit. The $\dot{M} = 0$ locus would have positive slope, such as in Fig. 6.

Figure 6 shows the $\dot{M} = 0$ curve as steeper than a ray through the origin through initial equilibrium point A. That this must be the case can be seen by considering a potential move not from A to B, but from A to C, i.e., a move that reduces both the wage rate and the money supply in proportion. The effect of this move on the balance of payments is like the effect of a devaluation at fixed w and M.[16] Since such a devaluation must reduce spending below the level of income (the monetary wealth effect), an increase in M would be required to wipe out the surplus. Thus the $\dot{M} = 0$ curve, if positively sloped, must be steeper than a ray through the origin.

Two issues remain concerning the position of the positively sloped $\dot{w} = 0$ curve. Can it be steeper than a ray from the origin? And can it be steeper than the $\dot{M} = 0$ curve if the latter were positively sloped? The former question, not surprisingly, depends on the impact effect of a devaluation on the level of employment. If a devaluation would raise employment on impact, a uniform reduction in the wage rate and the money supply from A to C at constant p_T would have the same effect. Therefore a contraction in M (and therefore in p_N) would have to be made to keep employment constant. The $\dot{w} = 0$ curve would be flatter than a ray from the origin, which is the case shown in Fig. 5. But as Section VI revealed, a devaluation could lead to unemployment, in which case M would have to rise from its position at point C in Fig. 6 in order to restore employment to its initial level at A. That is, the $\dot{w} = 0$ would be steeper than a ray from the origin.

Movements upward along any $\dot{M} = 0$ curve depict the economy settling down to higher and higher wage rates and must thus correspond to lower levels of employment. Therefore, in Fig. 6 the $\dot{M} = 0$ curve must be steeper then the $\dot{w} = 0$ curve.

Although the cases shown in Fig. 5 and 6 do not exhaust all possibilities,[17] they do correspond to the two prototypes that we might call the "normal"

---

[16] Both the aggregate level of spending Z and the monetary value of income produced Y can be considered linear homogeneous functions of the three key variables, p_T, w, and M (just as real expenditures and real output and employment are zero homogeneous functions of these three variables). With obvious notation this means that $\hat{Z} = Z_T\hat{p}_T + Z_w\hat{w} + Z_M\hat{M}$ and $\hat{Y} = Y_T\hat{p}_T + Y_w\hat{w} + Y_M\hat{M}$. The movement from A to C in Fig. 6 has $\hat{w} = \hat{M} < 0$. Therefore $\hat{Z} = (Z_w + Z_M)(\hat{w})$ and $\hat{Y} = (Y_w + Y_M)(\hat{w})$. But by linear homogeneity $Z_w + Z_M$ equals $1 - Z_T$ and $Y_w + Y_M = 1 - Y_T$. Therefore $\hat{Y} - \hat{Z} = (Y_T - Z_T)(-\hat{w})$. If, instead, the exchange rate is devalued at constant w and M, $\hat{Y} - \hat{Z} = (Y_T - Z_T)\hat{p}_T$, the same expression. Of course Y_T is positive and $Z_T = \beta Y_T$ where $0 < \beta < 1$.

[17] The other two combinations show the $\dot{w} = 0$ curve steeper than a ray from the origin, although the $\dot{M} = 0$ locus is negatively sloped, on the one hand, and a positively sloped $\dot{M} = 0$ curve and a $\dot{w} = 0$ locus flatter than a ray from the origin on the other.

economy and the "abnormal" economy. In the "normal" economy, pictured in Fig. 5, the impact effect of a devaluation raises employment, and an exogenous cut in money wages would stimulate the monetary value of income produced and thus improve the balance of payments. Figure 6 shows the case, here called "abnormal" for contrast, in which a devaluation immediately lowers employment *and* a wage cut would lead to a payments deficit. Although each condition has been discussed previously, it is useful here explicitly to rewrite the conditions in a manner that highlights two paramount features leading to "normality." The effect of a cut in wages on Y, and therefore on the balance of payments on impact, has been given in Eq. (13). Rewrite this now as

$$\hat{Y} = (e/\Delta)\{[-E_N + (\alpha_T\tilde{e}_T)e_N] - \alpha_N(\tilde{e}_N - \zeta_N)\}(-\hat{w}). \tag{15}$$

Since $\hat{y}$ equals the weighted average $\alpha_N\hat{x}_N + \alpha_T\hat{x}_T$ and $\hat{p}_N$ is given by (14), the equation for the impact effect on real output of a devaluation can be developed:

$$\hat{Y} = (e/\Delta)\{[-E_N + (\alpha_T\tilde{e}_T)e_N] - m_N(1 - \beta)(\tilde{e}_N - 1)\}\hat{p}_T. \tag{16}$$

The large brackets in these expressions are positive in the "normal" case. "Abnormality" requires both (i) the productive *structure* strongly biased toward having the nontraded commodity as the labor good in the sense that output expansion due to higher employment would spill over primarily to increase output in the nontradable sector, and (ii) a *low price sensitivity* of both demand and supply in the nontradable sector (in the sense of low values for $-E_N$ and e_N). As an example, the "neutral" case in which $\tilde{e}_N$ and ζ_N are both unity (a condition only on taste and production structure) is obviously "normal." Even if the structure of the economy is biased toward "abnormal" results, high enough price sensitivity always suffices to establish "normality."

For each of the cases shown in Fig. 5 and 6, consider the possible effects of a currency devaluation by supposing that the initial long-run equilibrium is shown by point C (where the two loci, not drawn, initially intersected). The curves drawn through A correspond to a devaluation that roughly doubles the price of all tradables. Point A itself shows the new long-run full equilibrium in which all monetary magnitudes have doubled and all relative prices, employment, and real output are the same as at C before the devaluation. It is useful to consider two alternative extreme specifications of the adjustment process from C to A:

(i) If wages are very sluggish to respond relative to adjustments in the balance of payments, the economy moves horizontally from point C towards the $\dot{M} = 0$ curve. This corresponds to an initial surplus in the balance of payments as the higher monetary value of national income (which must result on impact from the devaluation) forces a reduction in expenditures relative to that higher income level in order that the economy can accumulate higher monetary stocks (by running payments surpluses). In the "normal" case shown in Fig. 5, the increase in Y finds support both in an increase in the price level P and in increases in employment and real output. But in Fig. 6 the impact effect of the devaluation has been to lower employment and real output (although P and Y expand). However, as reserves accumulate, employment starts rising again. Indeed, at point D employment and real output have in the aggregate reattained their initial levels (although at D tradable output is higher and nontradable output lower than in full equilibrium). As reserves pile up beyond the level shown by D, employment exceeds the "natural" long-run rate. In both cases an eventual response of the wage rate shows w rising roughly along the $\dot{M} = 0$ curves. This must entail a reduction of employment toward its old long-run level.

(ii) If wages respond rapidly so that "full employment" is maintained, a devaluation shifts the wage rate on impact and subsequent adjustment takes place along the $\dot{w} = 0$ locus. In the "normal" case illustrated by Fig. 5, the devaluation would cause the wage rate to rise to point E, but by an amount that is relatively less than the devaluation. Thus labor is released from the nontradable sector to tradables (at E), and during the adjustment process (the move from E to A along the $\dot{w} = 0$ locus) labor gradually returns (and the wage rate rises with the price of nontradables rising by a greater relative amount) until at the new long-run equilibrium at A, the same production pattern as originally at C is reestablished. By contrast, the situation illustrated in Fig. 6 calls for an immediate *reduction* in the wage rate (from C to E). The price of nontradables falls relatively more (and labor is released to the expanding tradable sector). As reserves accumulate, spending rises, the wage rate rises (and the price of nontradables rises relatively faster to attract labor from the tradables sector). The adjustment path in Fig. 6 would be $CEDA$.

The model of this paper suggests a path of adjustment between these extremes to allow wages to adjust sluggishly but partially to labor market pressures even while the balance of payments is still in surplus or deficit. The dashed paths in Figs. 5 and 6 follow a route bounded by the polar extreme cases discussed earlier, except that in the "normal" case shown in Fig. 5, cycles of deficits and surplus and over and under full employment may be observed, as the path can oscillate around equilibrium point A. Employment paths are shown explicitly in Fig. 7. In the "normal" case a devaluation has the immediate effect of raising employment, as the tradables sector expands with wages lagging behind the new higher price of tradables. However, as the wage rate begins to adjust upward, employment levels can fall and,

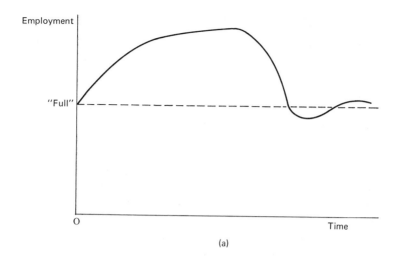

(a)

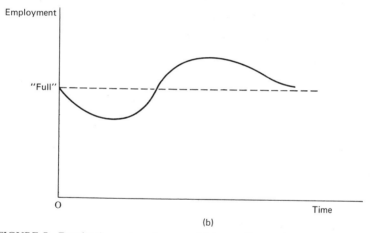

(b)

FIGURE 7   Devaluation and employment: (a) "normal" case; (b) "abnormal" case.

indeed to fall below the initial level of employment. However, most of the adjustment path is characterized by a buoyant labor market. By contrast, Fig. 7b illustrates that if demand and supply are price insensitive and labor is heavily biased toward nontradables, employment falls on impact following the devaluation, but a subsequent recovery must overshoot. As wages eventually rise, this period of over full employment gradually comes to an end. The balance of payments is in surplus throughout the process.

VIII. CONCLUDING REMARKS

Our primary task in this paper has been to set out a model in which aggregate levels of output are not predetermined by assumptions of full employment. Although full long-run equilibrium is characterized by full employment (or some natural rate of unemployment), the focus of the model is on the process of adjustment for a small open economy operating under a system of fixed exchange rates. The traditional monetary approach to balance of payments adjustments is thus extended to include the effect of labor market adjustments.

Two types of markets take time to equilibrate: Asset (or money) markets are eventually brought into line by the country's running balance of payments surpluses or deficits. And labor markets take time to adjust as wages respond sluggishly to states of unemployment or overemployment.

The nontraded goods market is assumed always to clear. This entails changes in the price of nontradables (either absolutely or relative to the price of tradables) when an initial full equilibrium is disturbed by either of two types of exogenous changes considered in this paper, viz., a wage reduction or a devaluation. Both such changes are expansionary in tone, but a wage reduction may not succeed in raising the monetary *value* of income produced (although employment will rise), and a devaluation may fail to raise employment (although the *value* of produced income must rise). Both of these "abnormal" possibilities depend on a sufficient fall in the price of nontradables. As the paper describes, the extent and direction of changes in absolute and relative commodity prices depends on both the *absolute* sensitivity of quantities demanded and supplied to price changes and to the *relative* adjustment of nontraded and traded goods output to employment variations.

The model tolerates a wide menu of asset market specifications. The basic requirement is that from a position of full equilibrium a rise in the monetary value of income produced induces the monetary value of expenditures to rise, but not by as much (since an attempt is made to raise asset levels to accommodate the higher income flows). Thus unlike many standard general equilibrium models, a distinction here is required between the monetary value of expenditures and incomes and, as well, between real expenditures and real incomes. The balance of payments is intimately related to Y, the monetary value of income produced; the level of employment depends on y, the real level of aggregate output; and the demand for nontradables depends on z, the real level of expenditures. As the literature on the monetary approach to the balance of payments has made clear in other contexts, these three aggregate variables need not rise or fall together.

This paper has ultimately considered only the long-run adjustment to a change in the exchange rate, since the analysis of the reaction to an exogenous wage reduction served only as a prelude to Section VII's treatment of wages as endogenously determined. Of course the local price of tradables could also be treated as endogenous if exchange rates are completely flexible, with the money supply in most models then ceasing to be endogenous. But even in the fixed exchange rate setting scope is possible for an analysis of monetary and fiscal policy.[18] Alternatively, changes abroad that affect the terms of trade could be accommodated rather simply. Finally, the model could be expanded to encompass explicit one- world determination of the prices of traded goods, as well as mutually consistent behavior of all countries' balance-of-payments and asset markets. The basic features of this paper's more simple setting would survive—the interrelated adjustments in relative prices, price levels, relative outputs, and aggregate employment levels that characterize movements from one long- run general equilibrium to another.

REFERENCES

1. Brecher, R., Minimum wage rates and the pure theory of international trade, *Quart. J. Econ.* 98–116 (1974).
2. Caves, R. E., and Jones, R. W., "World Trade and Payments." Little, Brown, Boston, Massachusetts, 1973.
3. Caves, R. E., and Jones, R. W., "World Trade and Payments," 2nd ed. Little, Brown, Boston, Massachusetts. 1977.
4. Dornbusch, R., Real and monetary aspects of the effects of exchange rate changes, *in* "National Monetary Policies and the International Financial System" (Aliber, Univ. of Chicago Press, ed.), pp. 64–81. Chicago, Illinois, 1974.
5. Dornbusch, R., Exchange rates and fiscal policy in a popular model of international trade, *Am. Econ. Rev.* 859–871 (1975).
6. Helpman, E., Macroeconomic policy in a model of international trade with a wage restriction, *Int. Econ. Rev.* 262–277 (1976).
7. Helpman, E., Nontraded goods and macroeconomic policy under a fixed exchange rate, *Quart. J. Econ.* 469–480 (1977).
8. Jones, R. W., Monetary and fiscal policy for an economy with fixed exchange rates, Supplement to *J. Political Econ.* (August 1968).
9. Jones, R. W., A three-factor model in theory, trade, and history, *in* "Trade, Balance of Payments and Growth" (J. Bhagwati *et al.*, eds.), Chapter 1. North-Holland Publ., Amsterdam, 1971.
10. Jones, R. W., and Corden, W. M., Devaluation, non-flexible prices, and the trade Balance for a small country, *Can. J. Econ.* (February 1976).
11. Jones, R. W., and Scheinkman, J., The relevance of the two-sector production model in trade theory, *J. Political Econ.* 909–35 (1977).
12. Mayer, W., Short-run and long-run equilibrium for a small open economy, *J. Political Econ.* 955–968 (1974).
13. Meade, J. A., The price adjustment and the Australian balance of payments, *Econ. Record* 32, 239–256 (1956).

---

[18] For example, see the details in Noman [15].

14. Mussa, M., Tariffs and the distribution of income: The importance of factor specificity, substitutability, and intensity in the short and long run, *J. Political Econ.* 1191–1204 (1974).
15. Noman, K., Output, Employment and the Balance of Payments: Related Essays on the Process of Adjustment in a Small Open Economy. Ph.D. Dissertation, Univ. of Rochester, 1976.
16. Ruffin, R., and Jones, R. W., Protection and real wages: The neoclassical ambiguity, *J. Econ. Theory* **14**, 337–348 (1977).
17. Salter, W. E. G., Internal and external balance: The role of price and expenditure effects, *Econ. Record* **35**, 226–238 (1959).
18. Swan, T., Longer-run problems of the balance of payments, *in* "The Australian Economy: A Volume of Readings" (H. Arndt and W. M. Corden, eds.). Univ. of Melbourne Press, 1963.

This article is based on a model presented in Chapter 1 of Noman's Ph. D. dissertation [15]. Support for Jones' research has been provided by the National Science Foundation.

Kamran Noman   Ronald W. Jones
DEPARTMENT OF ECONOMICS
UNIVERSITY OF ROCHESTER
ROCHESTER, NEW YORK

Two Propositions on the Global Univalence of Systems of Cost Function

ANDREU MAS-COLELL

I. INTRODUCTION AND STATEMENT OF RESULTS

1. Preliminaries and Definitions

Consider a C^1 function $F: Q \to R^l_+$ where Q is either R^l_{++} or $R^l_+ \backslash \{0\}$. We interpret F as a system of unit cost functions, the arguments being input prices. We assume that F is *linear homogeneous* [i.e., $F(\lambda w) = \lambda F(w)$ for all $\lambda \geq 0$] and call the Jacobian matrix of F at w, denoted $JF(w)$, the *input demand matrix*. If defined, the elasticity matrix $SF(w)$, i.e., the matrix with generic entry

$$s_{ij} = \frac{w}{F^i(w)} \frac{\partial F^i(w)}{\partial w^j},$$

is called the *input share matrix*.

We note that the interpretation of F as a system of cost functions demands that every component function be concave, but formally we will not impose this requirement.

2. The Problem

The factor price equalization problem in the pure theory of international trade (see Samuelson [11, 12], McKenzie [7], and Chipman [2]) prompted in an incidental way the following mathematical question: *Under which hypothesis has the equation $F(w) = v$ at most one solution for all $v \in R^l_+$, i.e., under which hypothesis is F globally univalent?*

With some disrespect for chronology and completeness, the rather complicated history of the analytical treatments of the univalence problem in the economic literature can be summarized thus. Samuelson [11] posed the question and showed that for $l = 2$ the everywhere nonsingularity of the input demand matrix (i.e., the Jacobian matrix) of F was a sufficient condition for univalence. Any hope that nonsingularity could suffice in the general case (Pierce [10]) was quickly dashed by an example of McKenzie [8]). One suggestion of Samuelson [12] involving the positive signedness of principal minors of the Jacobian of F was amended and finally led to the Gale–Nikaido theorem [4] of relevance for general, not just cost, functions. Sticking to cost functions, Samuelson [13, p. 908] suggested that if there existed a nested sequence of principal minor matrices of the input share matrices $SF(w)$ with determinants bounded away from zero uniformly on R^l_{++}, then F would be globally univalent on R^l_{++}. This was later established by Nikaido [9].

In this chapter we reexamine the global univalence problem for cost functions and provide improvements in the following two directions:

(1)   In the Samuelson–Nikaido theorem the restrictions on the principal minors of the input share matrix are irrelevant; all that matters is that the determinant of $SF(w)$ be uniformly bounded away from zero (Proposition 1). This provides a global univalence theorem for systems of cost functions with domain R^l_{++}.

(2)   In the context of cost functions with domain R^l_+, the Gale–Nikaido conditions can be substantially weakened (Proposition 2). The weakened conditions are of the same nature that the ones obtained in Mas-Colell [8] for general C^1 functions defined on compact polyhedra.

3.   *Conditions on the Input Share Determinant*

PROPOSITION 1   *Let* $F : R^l_{++} \to R^l_{++}$ *be* C^1. *If for some* $\varepsilon > 0$ *the absolute value of* $|SF(w)|$ *is larger than* ε *for all* $w \in R^l_{++}$, *then* F *is a homeomorphism onto.*

That is, for all $v \in R^l_{++}$ the equation $F(w) = v$ has a unique solution which in addition depends continuously on v.

Remark 1   Of course, $|SF(w)| \neq 0$ if and only if $|JF(w)| \neq 0$. Therefore McKenzie's example [7] proves that we cannot take $\varepsilon = 0$ in Proposition 1.

Remark 2   Proposition 1 generalizes the Samuelson–Nikaido theorem [9, 13] by dropping all the conditions on minors.

The strong conclusion of Proposition 2 is also its weakness. It yields not only that F is globally univalent but also that $F(R^l_{++}) = R^l_{++}$. This means that the ε restriction on the input share matrix determinant imposes stringent restrictions on the form of the isocost surfaces near the boundary of R^l_{++}.

For example, for no $1 \leq i \leq l$ can an isocost surface be bounded. See Fig. 1, where $(2, 3) \notin F(R^2_{++})$. Essentially, isocost surfaces must be as in Fig. 2.

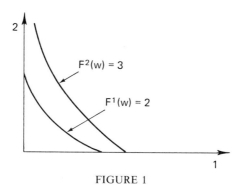

FIGURE 1

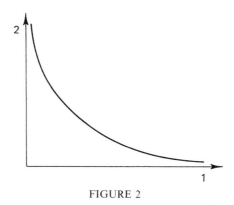

FIGURE 2

Summing up: Proposition 1 can be applied only if isocost surfaces are unbounded. This is an unduly strong requirement.

If isocost surfaces are bounded, then it is natural to assume that F is defined in R^l_+, (see Fig. 3). We can then appeal to the global univalence theorems based on weakened Gale–Nikaido conditions to be discussed in the next section.

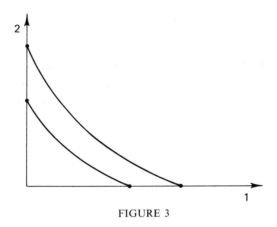

FIGURE 3

4. Generalized Gale–Nikaido Conditions

Let the system of cost functions be defined on R_+^l, i.e., $F: R_+^l \to R_+^l$.

For every subset $N \subset \{1, \ldots, l\}$ of variables, we can define a reduced system of cost functions $F_N: R_+^{l-n} \to R_+^{l-n}$, where $n = |N|$, by indentifying R_+^{l-n} with the inputs with index not in N, letting the inputs with index in N be free, i.e., $w_i = 0$ for $i \in N$, and disregarding the cost of variables with index in N. For example, if $l = 3$ and $N = \{3\}$, then $F_N: R_+^2 \to R_+^2$ is defined by $F_N^i(w^1, w^2) = F^i(w^1, w^2, 0)$ for $i = 1, 2$.

Note that for any $w \in R_+^{l-n} \backslash \{0\}$, if we let $\hat{w}^i = 0$ for $i \in N$ and $\hat{w}^i = w^i$ otherwise, then $|JF_N(w)|$ is nothing but the principal minor determinant of $JF(\hat{w})$ obtained by deleting the rows and columns with indices in N.

PROPOSITION 2   *Let $F: R_+^l \to R_+^l$ be C^1 on $R_+^l \backslash \{0\}$. Suppose that for all $N \subset \{1, \ldots, l\}$, $|JF_N(w)|$ is positive for every $w \in R_+^{l-n} \backslash \{0\}$. Then F is a homeomorphism.*

Remark 3   It is clear that Proposition 2 generalizes the Gale–Nikaido (GN) theorem as applied to systems of homogeneous functions on R_+^l. In particular we may note: (i) only infinitesimal conditions are imposed (as in the GN theorem); (ii) for $w \gg 0$ the only condition on $JF(w)$ is that $|JF(w)| > 0$. For an analogous generalization of the GN theorem for the case of arbitary C^1 functions on a compact convex polyhedron, see Mas-Colell [6].

Remark 4   One could perhaps wonder if Proposition 2 remains valid with the word "positive" replaced by "negative." It does, but in a vacuous manner. No system of homogenous cost functions $F: R_+^l \to R_+^l$ can satisfy the negative version of the condition of the theorem.

II. PROOFS

1. Proof of Proposition 1

The euclidean norm in R^l is $\| \ \|$. Given a linear map $T: R^l \to R^l$, its norm is $\|T\| = \max_{\|x\|=1} \|Tx\|$.

Proposition 1 is a consequence of the following theorem, which goes back to Hadamard [5]. It is taken from Berger [1, p. 222], where it is proved for maps on general Banach spaces.

THEOREM 1   Let $G: R^l \to R^l$ be C^1. Suppose there is a number k such that, for all $x \in R^l$, $JG(x)$ is nonsingular and $\|[JG(x)]^{-1}\| \le k$. Then G is a homeomorphism onto.

It follows from Cramer's rule that sufficient conditions for the uniform boundedness above of the norm of the inverse of $JG(x)$ are (i) $|JG(x)|$ is bounded away from zero uniformly; (ii) all the entries of the matrix $JG(x)$ are uniformly bounded in absolute value.

Let $F: R^l_{++} \to R^l_{++}$ satisfy the hypothesis of Proposition 1. Define then $G: R^l \to R^l$ by letting $G^i(x) = \ln F^i(e^{x^1}, \ldots, e^{x^l})$. At any $x \in R^l_{++}$ we have $JG(x) = SF(w(x))$ where $w(x) = (e^{x^1}, \ldots, e^{x^l})$. Because of the homogeneity of F, all the entries of $S(w(x))$ are less than or equal to one. Also, by hypothesis, the absolute value of $|S(w(x))| > \varepsilon > 0$. Therefore, by the Theorem, $G: R^l \to R^l$ is a homeomorphism onto and consequently so is $F: R^l_{++} \to R^l_{++}$.

Remark 5   Let $G: R^l \to R^l$ satisfy the hypothesis of the Theorem. Take any $y \in R^l$; then we know that $G(x) = y$ has a unique solution $\bar{x}$. In fact, $\bar{x} = x(1)$ where for some arbitrary x_0, $x(t)$ is the solution to the differential equation $\dot{x} = [JG(x)]^{-1} (y - G(x_0))$ with initial condition $x(0) = x_0$.

2. Proof of Proposition 2

Although the content of Proposition 2 is analogous to the one in Mas-Colell [6], we will take a different line of proof. While the demonstration in [6] was based on index-theoretic arguments, we will rely here on the following well-known topological fact (see, for example, Berger [1, p. 221]):

THEOREM 2   Let U be homeomorphic to R^l and $G: U \to U$ be given. Then G is a homeomorphism onto if and only if

(i) G is proper (i.e., if $K \in U$ is compact, then $G^{-1}(K)$ is compact).

(ii) G is a local homeomorphism (i.e., for every $x \in U$, G is a homeomorphism on some neighborhood of x).

Let us assume we have given a system of cost functions $F: R^l_+ \to R^l_+$ satisfying the hypothesis of Proposition 2.

Because of the homogeneity hypothesis, F is a homeomorphism of R^l_+ if and only if it is a homeomorphism of the unit simplex. Hence F is a homeomorphism if and only if it is one to one.

Note that if F is a homeomorphism of $R^l_+ \backslash \{0\}$, then it is a homeomorphism of R_+ because if $F(w) = 0$ and $w \neq 0$, then $F(\frac{1}{2}w) = 0$ by homogeneity; hence F would not be one to one on $R^l_+ \backslash \{0\}$.

For any $x \in R^l$ let $\Pi(x)$ be the point of R^l_+ closest to x in the euclidean norm. More explicitly, $\Pi^i(x) = \max\{x^i, 0\}$.

Define a map $G: R^l \backslash R^l_- \to R^l$ by $G(x) = F(\Pi(x)) + x - \Pi(x)$. Of course $G|R^l_+ \backslash \{0\} = F$. So it suffices to show that G is a homeomorphism. The region $R^l \backslash R^l_-$ is homeomorphic to R^l. Hence by Theorem 2, our task will be accomplished if we show (i) $G(R^l \backslash R^l_-) \subset R^l \backslash R^l_-$, (ii) $G: R^l \backslash R^l_- \to R^l \backslash R^l_-$ is proper, and (iii) G is a local homeomorphism.

(i) $G(R^l \backslash R^l_-) \subset R^l \backslash R^l_-$.

LEMMA 1   Let $F: R^m_+ \to R^m_+$ be a system of homogeneous functions. Suppose that for all $x \in R^m_+ \backslash \{0\}$, $JF(x)$ is nonsingular. Then $\|x_n\| \to \infty$ implies $\|F(x_n)\| \to \infty$.

Proof   Suppose there is $\|x_n\| \to \infty$ such that $\|F(x_n)\| \leq k$ for some k. Then $\|F((1/\|x_n\|)x_n)\|$ $(k/\|x_n\|)$. Without loss of generality we can assume $(1/\|x_n\|)x_n \to x$. By continuity $\|x\| = 1$ and also $\|F(x)\| = 0$, which implies $F(x) = 0$. By hypothesis $JF(x)$ is nonsingular. By the homogeneity of F we have (using Euler's rule) that $JF(x)x = 0$. So $x = 0$, which contradicts $\|x\| = 1$. Therefore no such sequence x_n can exist, and the lemma is proved. ■

Given $\bar{x} \in R^l \backslash R^l_-$ by relabeling variables if necessary, we can assume that $\bar{x}^i > 0$ for $i \leq k$ and $\bar{x}^i \leq 0$ for $i > k$. Let $N = \{k + 1, \ldots, l\}$ and Π^* be the linear operator $\Pi^*(x) = (x^1, \ldots, x^k, 0, \ldots, 0)$. Note that $\Pi(\bar{x}) = \Pi^*(\bar{x})$ and that $\Pi^* \circ F(\Pi^*(x))$, if defined, is naturally identified with $F_N(x^1, \ldots, x^k)$. Henceforth, since $\bar{x}^1 > 0$, it follows from Lemma 1 and the homogeneity of F_N that $F_N(\bar{x}^1, \ldots, \bar{x}^k) \neq 0$. On the other hand, suppose that $G(\bar{x}) \leq 0$. Then $\Pi^* \circ G(\bar{x}) \leq 0$. However, $\Pi^* \circ G(\bar{x}) = \Pi^* \circ F(\Pi^*(\bar{x}))$. So $\Pi^* \circ F(\Pi^*(\bar{x})) \leq 0$. But $F(\Pi^*(\bar{x})) \geq 0$ by hypothesis (this is the only point in the proof where the assumption $F(R^l_+) \subset R^l_+$ is appealed to). So $\Pi^* \circ F(\Pi^*(\bar{x})) = 0$. Contradiction.

(ii) $G: R^l \backslash R^l_- \to R^l \backslash R^l_-$ *is proper.*   To verify that $G: R^l \backslash R^l_- \to R^l \backslash R^l_-$ is proper, it suffices to check that given a sequence $x_n \in R^l \backslash R^l_-$, one has

(a)   if $\|x_n\| \to \infty$, then $\|G(x_n)\| \to \infty$;
(b)   if $\max_i x^i_n \to 0$, then $\max_i G^i(x_n) \to 0$.

That (b) holds is obvious; if $\max_i x_n^i \to 0$, then $\Pi(x_n) \to 0$, and by continuity, $F(\Pi(x_n)) \to 0$. So $\max_i G^i(x) = \max_i (F^i(\Pi(x_n)) + x_n^i - \Pi^i(x_n)) \to 0$.

Since there are only a finite number of orthants in R^l, it suffices to prove (a) for a sequence x_n all of which terms belongs to the same orthant. [Indeed, if (a) is not true, then $G(x_n)$ has a bounded subsequence. But any subsequence of x_n has a subsequence all of which terms are in the same orthant. Contradiction.] So, by relabeling variables if necessary, we can assume that for a, $1 \le k \le l$ and all n, $x_n^i \ge 0$ if $i \le k$, and $x_n^i \le 0$ for $i > k$.

Let $N = \{k + 1, \ldots, l\}$ and Π^* be the linear operator

$$\Pi^*(x) = (x^1, \ldots, x^k, 0, \ldots, 0).$$

For any x_n, $\Pi(x_n) = \Pi^*(x_n)$. Note, also, that $\Pi^* \circ F(\Pi^*(x_n))$ is naturally identified with $F_N(x_n^1, \ldots, x_n^k)$. In particular, by Lemma 1, if $\{\Pi^*(x_n)\}$ is unbounded, $\{\Pi^* \circ F(\Pi^*(x_n))\}$ must be unbounded.

Letting I be the identity map, we have $G(x_n) = \Pi^* \circ F(\Pi^*(x_n)) + (I - \Pi^*)(F(\Pi^*(x_n)) + x_n)$. So

$$\|G(x_n)\| = \|\Pi^* \circ F(\Pi^*(x_n))\| + \|(I - \Pi^*)(F(\Pi^*(x_n)) + x_n)\|.$$

Either $\{\|\Pi^*(x_n)\|\}$ or $\{\|(I - \Pi^*)(x_n)\|\}$ must be unbounded. If $\{\|\Pi^*(x_n)\|\}$ is bounded, then $\{\|(I - \Pi^*)(x_n)\|\}$ is unbounded, and therefore so is the second term of the previous sum. If $\{\|\Pi^*(x_n)\|\}$ is unbounded, then so is the first term of the sum by the observation of the preceding paragraph. In either case $\{\|G(x_n)\|\}$ is unbounded. Since x_n is arbitrary, this yields (b).

(iii) *G is a local homeomorphism.* To establish that G is a local homeomorphism, we will make use of the following theorem due to Clarke [3]:

Suppose that $G: Q \to Q$, $Q \subset R^l$ open, is a Lipschitzian function. Denote by $U \subset Q$ the region of differentiability of G, i.e., $U = \{x \in Q : JG(x) \text{ exists}\}$. For any $x \in Q$ define $\hat{J}G(x) = \{A : JG(x_n) \to A \text{ for some } x_n \to x, \ x_n \in U\}$. If every $A \in$ closed convex hull $\hat{J}G(x)$ is nonsingular, then G is a local homeomorphism at x.

Our function $G: R^l \backslash R_-^l \to R^l \backslash R_-^l$ is piecewise continuously differentiable, hence Lipschitzian. Also, G is C^1 at any $x \in R^l \backslash R_-^l$ such that $x^i \ne 0$ for all i. Henceforth, by Clarke's theorem, we must verify that, given $A \in$ convex hull $\hat{J}G(x) =$ convex hull $\{A : JG(x_n) \to A,$ for some $x_n \to x, x_n^i \ne 0$ for all $i, n\}$ is nonsingular. Note that $\hat{J}G(x)$ is a finite set.

So let $x \in R^l \backslash R_-^l$. By relabeling variables if necessary, we can assume that $x^i > 0$ for $i \le k$, $x^i = 0$ for $k < i \le h$, and $x^i < 0$ for $h < i \le l$. Note that $k \ge 1$. In order to compute $\hat{J}G(x)$, it suffices to consider sequences $x_n \to x$ with all x_n belonging to the same orthant; i.e., we can assume $x_n^i > 0$ for $i \le f \le h$ and $x_n^i < 0$ for $i > f \ge k$. Then $JG(x_n)$ exists. In fact, if we denote by $J_f F(\Pi(x))$ the first f columns of $JF(\Pi(x))$, we have

$$\lim JG(x_n) = \begin{bmatrix} J_f F(\Pi(x)) & 0 \\ & I \\ & {\scriptstyle (l-f)\times(l-f)} \end{bmatrix}.$$

Therefore, denoting by $\sigma_i F(\Pi(x))$ the ith column of $JF(\Pi(x))$, by e_i the ith column unit vector, and by a_i the ith column of a generic matrix A, we have

$$\hat{J}G(x) = \{A : \text{for } i \leq k,\ a_i = \sigma_i F(\Pi(x))$$
$$\text{for } i > h,\ a_i = e_i$$
$$\text{for } k < i \leq h,\ a_i = e_i \text{ or } a_i = \sigma_i F(\Pi(x))\}.$$

A set of matrices defined as $\hat{J}G(x)$ has an interesting property. The multilinearity of the determinant function implies that if $A \in$ convex hull $\hat{J}G(x)$, then $|A|$ is a positive linear combination of determinants of matrices belonging to $\hat{J}G(x)$. Therefore, if the determinant of the matrices in $\hat{J}G(x)$ have a uniform sign, A must be nonsingular.

As we have just seen, if $A \in \hat{J}F(\Pi(x))$, then

$$A = \begin{bmatrix} J_f F(\Pi(x)) & 0 \\ & I \\ & {\scriptstyle (l-f)\times(l-f)} \end{bmatrix}, \quad \text{for some } f \geq k.$$

Therefore $|A| = |J_{ff} F(\Pi(x))|$, where $J_{ff} F(\Pi(x))$ is the leading $f \times f$ principal minor of $JF(\Pi(x))$. But $J_{ff}F(\Pi(x)) = JF_{\{f+1,\ldots,l\}}(x^1,\ldots,x^f)$. So by hypothesis, all the $|A|$, $A \in JG(x)$ have the same sign and this concludes our proof.

REFERENCES

1. Berger, M., "Nonlinearity and Functional Analysis." Academic Press, New York, 1977.
2. Chipman, J., A survey of the theory of international trade: Part 3, The Modern Theory, *Econometrica* **34**, 18–76 (1966).
3. Clarke, F. H., On the inverse function theorem, *Pacific J. Math.* **64**, 97–102 (1976).
4. Gale, D., and Nikaido, H., The Jacobian Matrix and the global univalence of mappings, *Math. Ann.* **159**, 81–93. (1965).
5. Hadamard, J., Sur les equations fonctionelles, *C. R. Acad. Sci. Paris Ser. A–B* **136**, 351 (1904).
6. Mas-Colell, A., Homeomorphism of compact, convex sets and the Jacobian Matrix, *SIAM J. Math. Anal*, (1979).
7. McKenzie, L., Equality of factor prices in world trade, *Econometrica* **23**, 239–257 (1955).
8. McKenzie, L., The inversion of cost functions: A counterexample, *Internat. Econ. Rev.* **8**, 271–278 (1967).
9. Nikaido, H., Relative shares and factor Price equalization, *J. Internat. Econ.* **2**, 257–264 (1972).
10. Pierce, I., A further note on factor commodity price relationships, *Econ. J.* **69**, 725–732 (1959).

11. Samuelson, P., International factor-price equalization once again, *Econ. J.* **59**, 181–197 (1949).
12. Samuelson, P., Prices of factors and goods in general equilibrium, *Rev. Econ. Stud.* **21**, 1–20 (1953).
13. Samuelson, P., "Collected Scientific Papers," Vol. 2, p. 908. MIT Press, Cambridge, Massachusetts, 1966.

DEPARTMENT OF ECONOMICS
UNIVERSITY OF CALIFORNIA
BERKELEY, CALIFORNIA

On the Concepts of Factor Intensities and the Relation between Commodity Prices and Factor Rewards

YASUO UEKAWA

1. INTRODUCTION

Consider a competitive economy of the two-commodity and two-factor model. According to the Stolper–Samuelson theorem (1941), a rise in the price of a commodity will bring about a more than proportionate increase in the price of the corresponding intensive factor, while the other (less intensive) factor price must fall.

Recently, many economists have tried to generalize the Stolper–Samuelson theorem from the 2 × 2 case to the many-commodity and many-factor case.

In the $n \times n$ case, Chipman (1969) defined the Stolper–Samuelson criteria as follows:

(i) The weak Stolper–Samuelson criterion: There exists an association of goods and factors such that a rise in the price of a good will bring about a more than proportionate increase in the price of the corresponding intensive factor.

(ii) The strong Stolper–Samuelson criterion: There exists an association of goods and factors such that a rise in the price of a good will bring about a more than proportionate increase in the price of the corresponding intensive factor and no increase in any of the remaining factor prices.

Furthermore, Inada (1971) defined the other type of strong Stolper–Samuelson criterion as follows: There exists an association of goods and factors such that a rise in the price of a good will bring about a fall in the (money and real) reward of the corresponding less intensive factor and an increase in the money rewards of the remaining factors.

Kemp and Wegge (1969), Wegge and Kemp (1969), Uekawa (1971), and Uekawa et al., (1973) have investigated the following problems: Under what conditions would the validity of each type of Stolper–Samuelson theorem defined by Chipman be guaranteed? Any condition that they have investigated was to guarantee the full factor price equalization, that is, a global univalence between factor prices and goods prices. A sufficient condition for the global univalence of a mapping due to Gale and Nikaido (1965) is that its Jacobian matrix be a P matrix. However, the original Stolper–Samuelson theorem does not necessarily require the full factor price equalization. Hence, in the local version of the Stolper–Samuelson theorem, it may not be possible to reduce any diagonal element of the inverse of the share matrix larger than 1, by simply renumbering factors or products.

Ethier (1974) and Jones and Scheinkman (1977) have established that the following Stolper–Samuelson theorem holds in the general case of m goods and n factors ($n \geqq m$): An increase in one commodity price, with all other commodity prices frozen, is associated with a more than proportionate increase in the reward of at least one factor of production (and therefore with an unambiguous increase in the real reward of at least one factor) and with a decline in the money and real reward of at least one other factor. It is worth noting that they have established the above theorem, assuming only that the rank of the share matrix is m. However, they did not indicate unambiguously which factor rewards would rise and which would decline.

It will be shown by the counterexamples of Section 2 that this problem in the uneven case ($n > m$) will not be generally resolved from conditions on only the share matrix (or the input coefficients matrix).

This problem in the $n \times n$ case has been investigated by Egawa (1978). He has established some interesting theorems on the generalization of the Stolper–Samuelson theorem. However, it seems to this author that it is somewhat hard for us to understand the economic interpretation of his conditions on the share matrix.

The present paper is designed to complement Egawa (1978). We shall classify primary factors in the $n \times n$ case as follows: The i^0th good is said to be the j^0th factor intensive (or less intensive) in the weak sense if a rise in the i^0th good price is associated with an increase (or decrease) in the j^0th factor money reward. The i^0th good is said to be the j^0th factor intensive (or less intensive) in the strong sense if a rise in the i^0th good price is associated with an increase (or decrease) in the j^0th factor real reward. The i^0th good is said to be the j^0th factor properly intensive (or properly less intensive) if the j^0th factor has the highest increase rate (or decrease rate) among the strong intensive (or less intensive) factors of the i^0th good. The following principal results will be established in the paper:

(1) necessary and sufficient conditions for a primary factor to be intensive (or less intensive) in the weak sense for any given good;

(2) necessary and sufficient conditions for a primary factor to be intensive (or less intensive) in the strong sense for any given good;

(3) necessary and sufficient conditions for a primary factor to be properly intensive (or properly less intensive) for any given good.

2. GENERAL FORMULATION

Consider a competitive economy of the m-good and n-factor neoclassical model ($n \geq m$). The production function in each sector is assumed to be strictly concave, homogeneous of the first degree, and twice continuously differentiable. Let $p = (p_1, \ldots, p_m)'$ be a vector of goods prices, let $w = (w_1, \ldots, w_n)'$ be a vector of factor prices, and let $a_{ij}(w)$ be the amount of the ith factor needed in the production of one unit of the jth good at w. Then the functions $a_{ij}(w)$ are homogeneous of degree zero in the factor prices. It is assumed that the rank of the input coefficients matrix $A = (a_{ij})$ is m.

We have from the zero profit conditions and the full-employment conditions of the primary factors of production that

$$A'w = p \tag{1}$$

$$Ax = v \tag{2}$$

where $x = (x_1, \ldots, x_m)'$ and $v = (v_1, \ldots, v_n)'$ are the vectors of outputs and of factor endowments, respectively.

Differentiating totally Eq. (1), we obtain

$$A' \, dw = dp \tag{3}$$

since cost minimization ensures

$$(dA)'w = 0 \tag{4}$$

Differentiating totally Eq. (2), we get

$$D \, dw + A \, dx = dv \tag{5}$$

where

$$D \equiv \sum_{j=1}^{j=m} x_j D^j \tag{6}$$

and

$$D^j \equiv \begin{bmatrix} \dfrac{\partial a_{1j}}{\partial w_1} & \cdots & \dfrac{\partial a_{1j}}{\partial w_n} \\ \vdots & & \vdots \\ \dfrac{\partial a_{nj}}{\partial w_1} & \cdots & \dfrac{\partial a_{nj}}{\partial w_n} \end{bmatrix} \tag{7}$$

By the assumption of the strict concavity of the production function, D^j and therefore D are negative semidefinite and have rank $n - 1$. We see from (4) that

$$Dw = 0 \tag{8}$$

Combining (3) and (5), we get

$$\begin{bmatrix} D & A \\ A' & 0 \end{bmatrix} \begin{bmatrix} dw \\ dx \end{bmatrix} = \begin{bmatrix} dv \\ dp \end{bmatrix} \tag{9}$$

or

$$\begin{bmatrix} \sigma & \lambda \\ \theta' & 0 \end{bmatrix} \begin{bmatrix} \hat{w} \\ \hat{x} \end{bmatrix} = \begin{bmatrix} \hat{v} \\ \hat{p} \end{bmatrix} \tag{10}$$

where $\hat{z} \equiv dz/z$ for any variable z,

$$\sigma \equiv [\bar{v}]^{-1} D[\bar{w}], \qquad \lambda \equiv [\bar{v}]^{-1} A[\bar{x}], \qquad \theta' \equiv [\bar{p}]^{-1} A'[\bar{w}]$$

and $[\bar{q}]$ for any vector q is the diagonal matrix whose (i, i)th element is q_i.
The matrix

$$\begin{bmatrix} D & A \\ A' & 0 \end{bmatrix} \equiv G$$

is nonsingular. This results from the fact that the rank of the negative semidefinite matrix D is $n - 1$ and that of A is m.

Let

$$\begin{bmatrix} D & A \\ A' & 0 \end{bmatrix}^{-1} = \begin{bmatrix} H & B \\ B' & Q \end{bmatrix} \tag{11}$$

Then we have from (11) that

$$DH + AB' = I_n \tag{12}$$

$$DB + AQ = 0 \tag{13}$$

$$A'H = 0 \tag{14}$$

$$A'B = I_m \tag{15}$$

where I_n is the identity matrix of order n. If $n > m$, we see from (12) that $H \neq 0$, since $R(AB') \leq m$ and $R(I_n) = n > m$, where $R(A)$ denotes the rank of A for the matrix A.[1]

Consider the following two counterexamples.

[I]

$$
\begin{bmatrix}
-5 & 1 & 1 & \vdots & 2 & 3 \\
1 & -2 & 1 & \vdots & 1 & 2 \\
1 & 1 & -1 & \vdots & 3 & 1 \\
\cdots & \cdots & \cdots & & \cdots & \cdots \\
2 & 1 & 3 & \vdots & 0 & 0 \\
3 & 2 & 1 & \vdots & 0 & 0
\end{bmatrix}^{-1}
= \frac{1}{290}
\begin{bmatrix}
-25 & 35 & 5 & \vdots & -20 & 55 \\
35 & -49 & -7 & \vdots & -30 & 97 \\
5 & -7 & -1 & \vdots & 120 & -69 \\
\cdots & \cdots & \cdots & & \cdots & \cdots \\
-20 & -30 & 120 & \vdots & 100 & -130 \\
55 & 97 & -69 & \vdots & -130 & 169
\end{bmatrix}
$$

[II]

$$
\begin{bmatrix}
-7 & 2 & 1 & \vdots & 2 & 3 \\
2 & -7 & 4 & \vdots & 1 & 2 \\
1 & 4 & -3 & \vdots & 3 & 1 \\
\cdots & \cdots & \cdots & & \cdots & \cdots \\
2 & 1 & 3 & \vdots & 0 & 0 \\
3 & 2 & 1 & \vdots & 0 & 0
\end{bmatrix}^{-1}
= \frac{1}{615}
\begin{bmatrix}
-25 & 35 & 5 & \vdots & -95 & 185 \\
35 & -49 & -7 & \vdots & 10 & 110 \\
5 & -7 & -1 & \vdots & 265 & -160 \\
\cdots & \cdots & \cdots & & \cdots & \cdots \\
-95 & 10 & 265 & \vdots & 500 & -650 \\
185 & 110 & -160 & \vdots & -650 & 845
\end{bmatrix}
$$

The input coefficients matrix A, the goods prices vector p, and the factor prices vector w in [I], that is,

$$
A' = \begin{bmatrix} 2 & 1 & 3 \\ 3 & 2 & 1 \end{bmatrix}, \qquad w' = (1 \quad 2 \quad 3), \qquad p' = (13 \quad 10)
$$

are the same as those in [II], while D in [I] is different from that in [II]. Now we have[2]

$$
\frac{1}{290}
\begin{bmatrix} 1 & 0 & 0 \\ 0 & 2 & 0 \\ 0 & 0 & 3 \end{bmatrix}^{-1}
\begin{bmatrix} -20 & 55 \\ -30 & 97 \\ 120 & -69 \end{bmatrix}
\begin{bmatrix} 13 & 0 \\ 0 & 10 \end{bmatrix}
= \frac{1}{290}
\begin{bmatrix} -260 & 550 \\ -195 & 485 \\ 520 & -230 \end{bmatrix}
$$

$$
\frac{1}{615}
\begin{bmatrix} 1 & 0 & 0 \\ 0 & 2 & 0 \\ 0 & 0 & 3 \end{bmatrix}^{-1}
\begin{bmatrix} -95 & 185 \\ 10 & 110 \\ 265 & -160 \end{bmatrix}
\begin{bmatrix} 13 & 0 \\ 0 & 10 \end{bmatrix}
= \frac{1}{615}
\begin{bmatrix} -1235 & 1850 \\ 65 & 550 \\ 3445/3 & -1600/3 \end{bmatrix}
$$

Therefore,

$$
\partial \log w_2 / \partial \log p_1 = -195/290 < 0 \quad \text{and} \quad \partial \log w_2 / \partial \log p_2 = 485/290 > 1
$$

---

[1] H is negative semidefinite and Q is positive semidefinite. See Chang (1976) on the proof.
[2] Note that $[\partial \log w / \partial \log p] = [\bar{w}]^{-1} B [\bar{p}]$.

in example [I], while in example [II] we have $\partial \log w_2/\partial \log p_1 = 65/615 > 0$ and $\partial \log w_2/\partial \log p_2 = 550/615 < 1$. This implies that the Stolper–Samuelson theorem in the uneven case ($n > m$) will not necessarily hold.

Suppose $n = m$. Then we see from (14) that $H = 0$, since A' is nonsingular. Hence $B' = A^{-1}$. In the subsequent section, we shall assume $m = n$. And we shall consider the following problem: What conditions would guarantee the validity of the Stolper–Samuelson theorem for the $n \times n$ case?

3. THE CONCEPTS OF FACTOR INTENSITIES

In the case of two goods and two factors, if

$$a_{11}/a_{12} > a_{21}/a_{22} \tag{16}$$

then the first good is said to be relatively the first factor intensive and the second factor less intensive.

When extended to the $n \times n$ case, the concepts of factor intensities will perhaps best be described by using the following two approaches, which are equivalent to condition (16).

(i) The inequality

$$\begin{bmatrix} a_{11} & -a_{12} \\ -a_{21} & a_{22} \end{bmatrix} \begin{bmatrix} x_1 \\ x_2 \end{bmatrix} > 0 \tag{17}$$

has a positive solution $x = (x_1\ x_2)'$.

(ii) The inequality

$$\begin{bmatrix} \theta_{11} & -\theta_{12} \\ -\theta_{21} & \theta_{22} \end{bmatrix} \begin{bmatrix} x_1 \\ x_2 \end{bmatrix} > 0 \tag{18}$$

has a positive solution $x = (x_1\ x_2)'$.

However, when extended to the $n \times n$ case, these two approaches are no longer equivalent to each other. The inverse of a matrix A is denoted by $A^{-1} \equiv (a^{ij})$. The following additional notation is needed:

a^i the ith row vector of a matrix A;

a_j the jth column vector of a matrix A;

$v(i)$ the vector obtained from a vector v by deleting the ith component, for example, $\theta_k(i^0) = (\theta_{1k}, \ldots, \theta_{i^0-1,k}, \theta_{i^0+1,k}, \ldots, \theta_{nk})'$;

e_j the jth column vector of the $n \times n$ identity matrix;

N the set $\{1, \ldots, n\}$;

J a subset of N;

$\bar{J}$ the complement of J relative to N;

I_J the diagonal matrix obtained from the identity matrix by replacing each jth row e^j by $-e^j, j \in J$;

e the sum vector $(1, 1, \ldots, 1)$;

$\varnothing$ the null set;

$\subset$ proper inclusion.

By $x > 0$ we mean $x_i > 0$ for all i. By $x \geq 0$ we mean $x_i \geq 0$ for all i and $x_i > 0$ for at least one i. By $x \geqq 0$ we mean $x_i \geqq 0$ for all i.

In what follows, we shall assume

ASSUMPTION 1   The input coefficients matrix A is nonsingular.

ASSUMPTION 2   Each column of A has at least two positive elements.

CONDITION [1]   For any nonempty proper subset J ($j^0 \in J$) of N, the inequalities

$$\sum_{k=1}^{k=n} x_k a_{jk} \geqq 0 \quad \text{for} \quad j \in J \quad \text{and} \quad \sum_{k=1}^{k=n} x_k a_{jk} \leqq 0 \quad \text{for} \quad j \in \bar{J}$$

have a solution $x = (x_1, \ldots, x_n)'$ such that $x_{j0} > 0$.

The following theorem shows that Condition [1] is equivalent to that the i^0th good is the j^0th factor intensive in the weak sense.

THEOREM 1 $a^{i^0 j^0} > 0$ if and only if Condition [1] holds.

Proof   Necessity   Suppose $a^{i^0 j^0} > 0$. Let $J = \{ j \,|\, a^{i^0 j} > 0 \}$ and $y_j = a^{i^0 j} > 0$ for $j \in J$ and $y_j = -a^{i^0 j} \geqq 0$ for $j \in \bar{J}$. Then we have

$$\sum_{j \in J} y_j a_{ji^0} - \sum_{j \in \bar{J}} y_j a_{ji^0} = 1$$

$$\sum_{j \in J} y_j a_{jk} - \sum_{j \in \bar{J}} y_j a_{jk} = 0 \quad \text{for} \quad k = 1, \ldots, n \quad (k \neq i^0) \tag{1}$$

Since n vectors of order $(n-1)$, $a_1(j^0), \ldots, a_n(j^0)$ are linearly dependent, there exists a nonzero vector $x = (x_1, \ldots, x_n)'$ such that

$$\sum_{k=1}^{k=n} a_k(j^0) x_k = 0 \tag{2}$$

or

$$\sum_{k=1}^{k=n} a_{ik} x_k = 0 \quad \text{for} \quad i = 1, \ldots, n \quad (i \neq j^0) \tag{2'}$$

Since A is nonsingular by Assumption 1, we see from (2) that

$$\sum_{k=1}^{k=n} a_{j^0 k} x_k \neq 0 \tag{3}$$

We can assume without loss of generality that

$$x_{j0} \geqq 0 \tag{4}$$

Multiply each kth equality of (1) by x_k in (2) and sum it over $k \in N$. Then we get

$$\sum_{j \in J} y_j \left(\sum_{k=1}^{k=n} x_k a_{jk} \right) - \sum_{j \in \bar{J}} y_j \left(\sum_{k=1}^{k=n} x_k a_{jk} \right) = x_{i^0} \tag{5}$$

But since $j^0 \in J$, we see from (2), (3), and (5) that

$$y_{j^0} \left(\sum_{k=1}^{k=n} x_k a_{j^0 k} \right) = x_{i^0} \tag{6}$$

Since $y_{j^0} > 0$, we see from (3) and (4) that

$$\sum_{k=1}^{k=n} x_k a_{j^0 k} > 0 \quad \text{and} \quad x_{i^0} > 0 \tag{7}$$

Expressions (2) and (7) imply that Condition [1] holds.

Sufficiency   Suppose that Condition [1] holds but $a^{i^0 j^0} \leqq 0$. Then we have that $j^0 \in \bar{J}$ in Eq. (5). Therefore, we see from Condition [1] that

$$\sum_{k=1}^{k=n} x_k a_{jk} \leqq 0 \quad \text{for} \quad j \in J, \qquad \sum_{k=1}^{k=n} x_k a_{jk} \geqq 0 \quad \text{for} \quad j \in \bar{J},$$

and $x_{i^0} > 0$. Hence, the left-hand side of (5) is nonpositive, but the right-hand side is positive, a contradiction. We must have $a^{i^0 j^0} > 0$.   Q.E.D.

CONDITION [2]   For any nonempty proper subset J $(j^0 \in J)$ of N, the inequalities

$$\sum_{k=1}^{k=n} x_k a_{jk} \geqq 0 \quad \text{for} \quad j \in J \quad \text{and} \quad \sum_{k=1}^{k=n} x_k a_{jk} \leqq 0 \quad \text{for} \quad j \in \bar{J}$$

have a solution $x = (x_1, \ldots, x_n)'$ such that $x_{i^0} < 0$.

The following theorem shows that Condition [2] is equivalent to that the i^0th good is the j^0th factor less intensive in the weak sense.

THEOREM 2 $a^{i^0 j^0} < 0$ if and only if Condition [2] holds.

The proof is made similar to that of Theorem 1.
Thus we see from Theorems 1 and 2 that $a^{i^0 j^0} = 0$ if and only if there exists a factor, say the j^0th one, that belongs to neither Conditions [1] nor [2].

CONDITION [3]   For any nonempty proper subset J $(j^0 \in J)$ of N, the inequalities

$$\sum_{k=1}^{k=n} x_k \theta_{jk} \geqq 0 \quad \text{for} \quad j \in J \quad \text{and} \quad \sum_{k=1}^{k=n} x_k \theta_{jk} \leqq 0 \quad \text{for} \quad j \in \bar{J}$$

have a solution $x = (x_1, \ldots, x_n)'$ such that $\sum_{k=1 \neq i^0}^{n} x_k < 0 < x_{i^0}$.

THEOREM 3 $\theta^{i^0 j^0} > 1$ if and only if Conditions [3] holds.

Proof Necessity. Suppose $\theta^{i^0 j^0} > 1$. Consider the i^0th row of $\theta^{-1}\theta = I$. Then we have that

$$\sum_{h=1}^{h=n} \theta^{i^0 h}\theta_{hi^0} = 1, \quad \sum_{h=1}^{h=n} \theta^{i^0 h}\theta_{hk} = 0 \quad \text{for} \quad k = 1, \ldots, n \quad (k \neq i^0) \quad (1)$$

On the other hand, we have

$$e'\theta = e' \tag{2}$$

Subtract Eq. (2) from (1). Then we have

$$\sum_{h=1}^{h=n} y_h\theta_{hi^0} = 0, \quad \sum_{h=1}^{h=n} y_h\theta_{hk} = -1 \quad \text{for} \quad k = 1, \ldots, n \quad (k \neq i^0) \quad (3)$$

where $y_h = \theta^{i^0 h} - 1$ $(h = 1, \ldots, n)$.

Since n vectors of order $(n - 1)$, $\theta_1(j^0), \ldots, \theta_n(j^0)$ are linearly dependent, there exists a nonzero vector $x = (x_1, \ldots, x_n)$ such that

$$\sum_{k=1}^{k=n} \theta_{hk}x_k = 0 \quad \text{for} \quad h = 1, \ldots, n \quad (h \neq j^0) \tag{4}$$

Since the share matrix θ is nonsingular by Assumption 1, we have

$$\sum_{k=1}^{k=n} \theta_{j^0 k}x_k \neq 0 \tag{5}$$

We can assume without loss of generality that

$$\sum_{k=1 \neq i^0}^{n} x_k \leq 0 \tag{6}$$

Multiply each kth equation of (3) by x_k in (4) and sum it over $k \in N$. Then we get from Eq. (4) that

$$y_{j^0}\left(\sum_{k=1}^{k=n} \theta_{j^0 k}x_k\right) = -\sum_{k=1 \neq i^0}^{n} x_k \tag{7}$$

Since $y_{j^0} = \theta^{i^0 j^0} - 1 > 0$, we see from (5)–(7) that

$$\sum_{k=1}^{k=n} \theta_{j^0 k}x_k > 0 \quad \text{and} \quad \sum_{k=1 \neq i^0}^{n} x_k < 0 \tag{8}$$

On the other hand, we see from (4) and (5) that

$$\sum_{k=1}^{k=n} x_k = \sum_{k=1}^{k=n} \theta_{j^0 k}x_k,$$

since $e'\theta = e'$. Hence $\sum_{k=1}^{k=n} x_k > 0$ and therefore $x_{i^0} > 0$ from (8). Thus, Condition [3] holds.

Sufficiency   Suppose that Condition [3] holds but $\theta^{i^0 j^0} \leq 1$. Let $J = \{j \mid y_j = \theta^{i^0 j} - 1 \leq 0\}$. Therefore $j^0 \in J$. Multiply each kth question of (3) by x_k in Condition [3] and sum it over $k \in N$. Then we get

$$\sum_{h \in J} y_h \left(\sum_{k=1}^{k=n} \theta_{hk} x_k \right) + \sum_{h \in \bar{J}} y_h \left(\sum_{k=1}^{k=n} \theta_{hk} x_k \right) = - \sum_{k=1 \neq i^0}^{n} x_k \qquad (9)$$

The left-hand side of (9) is nonpositive by Condition [3], since $y_h \leq 0$ for $h \in J$ and $y_h \geq 0$ for $h \in \bar{J}$. On the other hand, the right-hand side of (9) is positive by Condition [3], a contradiction. Hence we must have $\theta^{i^0 j^0} > 1$.
$$\text{Q.E.D.}$$

CONDITION [4]   For any nonempty proper subset J ($j^0 \in J$) of N, the inequalities

$$\sum_{k=1}^{k=n} x_k \theta_{jk} \geq 0 \quad \text{for} \quad j \in J \quad \text{and} \quad \sum_{k=1}^{k=n} x_k \theta_{jk} \leq 0 \quad \text{for} \quad j \in \bar{J}$$

have a solution $x = (x_1, \ldots, s_n)'$ such that $\sum_{k=1 \neq i^0}^{n} x_k > 0$.

THEOREM 4 $\theta^{i^0 j^0} < 1$ if and only if Condition [4] holds.

Remark   In Condition [4] we see from Theorems 1 and 2 that $0 < \theta^{i^0 j^0} < 1$ if $x_{i^0} > 0$ and $\theta^{i^0 j^0} < 0$ if $x_{i^0} < 0$.

The proof is made similar to that of Theorem 3.

The i^0th good is said to be the j^0th factor intensive (or less intensive) in the strong sense if and only if Condition [3] (or [4]) holds. Thus we can state the Stolper–Samuelson theorem as follows: A rise in the price of a good will bring about an increase in the real reward of the corresponding intensive factor and a decrease in the real reward of the corresponding less intensive factor.

CONDITION [5]   For any nonempty proper subset J of N such that $j^0 \in J$, the inequalities

$$\sum_{k=1}^{k=n} x_k \theta_{jk} \geq 0 \quad \text{for} \quad j \in J \quad \text{and} \quad \sum_{k=1}^{k=n} x_k \theta_{jk} \leq 0 \quad \text{for} \quad j \in \bar{J}$$

have a solution $x = (x_1, \ldots, x_n)'$ such that $\sum_{k=1 \neq i^0}^{n} x_k \leq -x_{i^0} < 0$.

THEOREM 5 $\theta^{i^0 j^0} \geq \theta^{i^0 j}$ for any $j = 1, \ldots, n$ if and only if Condition [5] holds.

Proof   Necessity.   Suppose that $\theta^{i^0 j^0} \geq \theta^{i^0 j}$ for $j = 1, \ldots, n$. Let $y_h = \theta^{i^0 h}$ and $z_h = y_{j^0} - y_h$ for $h = 1, \ldots, n$. Then we have that

$$\sum_{h=1}^{h=n} z_h \theta_{hi^0} - y_j^0 \cdot 1 = -1 \tag{1}$$

$$\sum_{h=1}^{h=n} z_h \theta_{hk} - y_{j^0} \cdot 1 = 0 \qquad \text{for} \quad k = 1, \ldots, n \quad (k \neq i^0)$$

since $e'\theta = e'$ and $z_{j^0} = 0$. Furthermore, we see by the definition of z_h that $z_h \geq 0$ for $h = 1, \ldots, n$.

Since Eq. (1), that is,

$$(z' \ u)\begin{bmatrix} \theta \\ e' \end{bmatrix} = -e_{i^0} \tag{2}$$

has a nonnegative solution $(z' \ u)$ and θ is nonsingular, we see that the equation

$$(z' \ u)\begin{bmatrix} I_J \theta \\ -e' \end{bmatrix} = -e_{i^0}$$

for any $\bar{J}$ such that $i^0 \in J$, has no nonnegative solution $(z' \ u)$. Hence, we have by the duality[3] that the inequalities

$$\begin{bmatrix} I_J \theta \\ -e' \end{bmatrix} x \geq 0 \qquad \text{and} \qquad -e'_{i^0} \cdot x < 0 \tag{3}$$

that is,

$$\sum_{k=1}^{k=n} x_k \theta_{jk} \geq 0 \qquad \text{for} \quad j \in J, \qquad \sum_{k=1}^{k=n} x_k \theta_{jk} \leq 0 \qquad \text{for} \quad j \in \bar{J} \tag{4}$$

and

$$\sum_{i=1}^{n} x_i \leq 0 \qquad \text{and} \quad x_{i^0} > 0 \tag{5}$$

have a solution $x = (x_1, \ldots, x_n)'$. Equation (5) implies that $\sum_{k=1 \neq i^0}^{n} x_k \leq -x_{i^0} < 0$. Thus we see that Condition [5] holds.

Sufficiency   Suppose that Condition [5] holds but there exists at least one j such that $\theta^{i^0 j} > \theta^{i^0 j^0}$. Let $\bar{J} = \{j \mid \theta^{i^0 j} > \theta^{i^0 j^0}\}$. Then we see from Condition [5] that the inequalities

$$\sum_{k=1}^{k=n} x_k \theta_{jk} \geq 0 \qquad \text{for} \quad j \in J \qquad \text{and} \qquad \sum_{k=1}^{k=n} x_k \theta_{jk} \leq 0 \qquad \text{for} \quad j \in \bar{J} \tag{6}$$

---

[3] Exactly one of the following alternatives holds: Either the equation $x'A = b'$ has a nonnegative solution, or the inequalities $Ay \geq 0$ and $b'y < 0$ have a solution.

have a solution $x = (x_1, \ldots, x_n)'$ such that $\sum_{k=1 \neq i^0}^n x_k \leq -x_{i^0} < 0$. Multiply each kth equation of (1) by x_k in (6) and sum it over $k \in N$. Then we get that

$$\sum_{h \in J} z_h \left(\sum_{k=1}^{k=n} \theta_{hk} x_k \right) + \sum_{h \in \bar{J}} z_h \left(\sum_{k=1}^{k=n} \theta_{hk} x_k \right)$$

$$= x_{i^0}(y_{j^0} - 1) + y_{j^0} \left(\sum_{k=1 \neq i^0}^n x_k \right) \tag{7}$$

We see from (6) and (7) that the left-hand side of (7) is nonnegative, since $z_h \geq 0$ for $h \in J$ and $z_h < 0$ for $h \in \bar{J}$, where $y_{j^0} > 1$ by Theorem 3, since Condition [5] implies that Condition [3] holds. On the other hand, since

$$\sum_{k=1 \neq i^0}^n x_k \leq -x_{i^0} < -x_{i^0}(y_{j^0} - 1)/y_{j^0} < 0$$

the right-hand side of (7) is negative, a contradiction. We must have that $\theta^{i^0 j^0} \geq \theta^{i^0 j}$ for $j = 1, \ldots, n$.   Q.E.D.

CONDITION [6]   For any nonempty proper subset J of N such that $j^0 \in J$, the inequalities

$$\sum_{k=1}^{k=n} x_k \theta_{jk} \geq 0 \quad \text{for} \quad j \in J \qquad \text{and} \qquad \sum_{k=1}^{k=n} x_k \theta_{jk} \leq 0 \quad \text{for} \quad j \in \bar{J}$$

have a solution $x = (x_1, \ldots, x_n)'$ such that $\sum_{k=1 \neq i^0}^n x_k \geq -x_{i^0} > 0$.

THEOREM 6 $\theta^{i^0 j^0} \leq \theta^{i^0 j}$ for any $j = 1, \ldots, n$, if and only if Condition [6] holds.

The proof is made similar to that of Theorem 5.

The i^0th good is said to be the j^0th factor properly intensive (or properly less intensive) if and only if Condition [5] (or [6]) holds. Thus we can state the Stolper–Samuelson theorem as follows: A rise in the price of a good will bring about an increase (or a decrease) in the real reward of the corresponding properly intensive (or properly less intensive) factor; while real rewards of some other factors may increase (or decrease) too, their increase (or decrease) rates must be less (or larger) than that of the properly intensive (or properly less intensive) factor.

4.   ECONOMIC INTERPRETATION OF FACTOR INTENSITY CONDITIONS

In this section we try to interpret Conditions [1]–[6] economically.

Condition [1] will be presumed as a factor intensity condition in the following sense: Group the n separate factors into two composite factors,

J and $\bar{J}$ in any manner such that $j^0 \in J$. Regard the x_k, $k = 1, \ldots, n$, simply as a hypothetical amount of the kth commodity produced. Then $x_k a_{jk}$ is the amount of the jth factor used in the kth industry. Condition [1] will be interpreted as saying that the n separate industries are partitioned into two groups, J^* ($i^0 \in J^*$) and $\bar{J}^*$, as the following statements hold. There exists a set of semipositive output levels x_k, $k = 1, \ldots, n$ ($x_{i0} > 0$) depending on J, such that for any jth factor $j \in J$ (or $j \in \bar{J}$), no less (or no more) of this factor is used in the composite industry J^* than in the other composite industry $\bar{J}^*$. Condition [2] will be interpreted similarly as the above.

Conditions [3]–[6] are to replace the input coefficients matrix A in Conditions [1] and [2] by the share matrix θ.

Condition [3] is to be more strengthened than Condition [1], as having a solution x such that $\sum_{k=1 \neq i^0}^{n} x_k < 0$ as well as $x_{i0} > 0$.

Condition [3] will be presumed as a factor intensity condition in the following sense. Group the n separate factors into two composite factors, J and $\bar{J}$, in any manner such that $j^0 \in J$. Regard the x_k, $k = 1, \ldots, n$, simply as a hypothetical output value of the kth commodity produced. Then $x_k \theta_{jk}$ is the receipt of the jth factor payed by the kth industry. Condition [3] will be interpreted as saying that the n separate industries are partitioned into two groups, J^* ($i^0 \in J^*$) and $\bar{J}^*$, as the following statements hold: There exists a set of semipositive output value levels x_k, $k = 1, \ldots, n$, depending on J, such that $x_{i0} > 0$ and $\sum_{k \in \bar{J}^*} x_k > \sum_{k \in J^*} x_k - x_{i0}$ and such that for any jth factor $j \in J$ (or $j \in \bar{J}$), no less (or no more) of this factor's receipts is payed in the composite industry J^* than in the other composite industry $\bar{J}^*$. Condition [4] will be interpreted similarly as the above.

Condition [5] will be interpreted as saying that the n separate industries are partitioned into two groups, J^* ($i^0 \in J^*$) and $\bar{J}^*$, as the same statements as Condition [3], except that there exists a set of semipositive output value levels such that $x_{i0} > 0$ and $\sum_{k \in J^*} x_k > \sum_{k \in \bar{J}^*} x_k$ hold. Condition [6] will be interpreted similarly as the above.

REFERENCES

Chang, W. W. (1976). Some theorems of trade and general equilibrium with many goods and factors, *Econometrica* (to appear).

Chipman, J. S. (1969). Factor price equalization and the Stolper–Samuelson theorem, *Internat. Econ. Rev.* **10**, 399–406.

Egawa, I. (1978). Some Remarks on the Stolper–Samuelson and Rybczynski Theorems, *J. Internat. Econ.* **8**, 525–536.

Ethier, W. (1974). Some of the theorems of international trade with many goods and factors, *J. Internat. Econ.* **4**, 199–206.

Gale, D., Nikaido, H. (1965). The Jacobian matrix and global univalence of mappings, *Math. Annal.* **159**, 81–93.

Inada, K. (1971). Production coefficient matrix and the Stolper–Samuelson condition, *Econometrica*. **39**, 219–239.

Jones, R. W., and Scheinkman, J. (1977). The relevance of the two-sector production model in trade theory, *J. Political Econ.* **85**, 909–935.

Kemp, M. C., and Wegge, L. L. F. (1969). On the relation between commodity prices and factor rewards, *Internat. Econ. Rev.* **10**, 407–413.

Stolper, W. F., and Samuelson, P. A. (1941). Protection and real wages, *Rev. Econ. Stud.* **9**, 58–73.

Uekawa, Y. (1971). Generalization of Stolper–Samuelson Theorem, *Econometrica.* **39**, 197–217.

Uekawa, Y. (1979). The theory of effective protection, resource allocation and the Stolper–Samuelson theorem: The many-industry case, *J. Internat. Econ.* (to appear).

Uekawa, Y., Kemp, M. C., and Wegge, L. L. F. (1973). P- and PN-matrices, Minkowski- and Metzler-matrices, and generalizations of the Stolper–Samuelson and Samuelson–Rybczynski theorems, *J. Internat. Econ.* **3**, 53–76.

Wegge, L. L. F., and Kemp, M. C. (1969). Generalization of the Stolper–Samuelson and Samuelson–Rybczynski theorems in terms of conditional input-output coefficients, *Internat. Econ. Rev.* **10**, 414–425.

The work on this paper was partially supported by the National Science Foundation.

DEPARTMENT OF ECONOMICS
UNIVERSITY OF CHICAGO
CHICAGO, ILLINOIS

Factor Price Equalization with More Industries Than Factors

TROUT RADER

1. INTRODUCTION

The local version of factor price equalization is that small changes in factor endowments leave factor prices unchanged (given that goods prices are fixed). That is, factor prices are locally constant as functions of factor endowments. A global version is that two countries whose factor prices are locally constant and who face the same international prices and have the same technology also have exactly the same factor prices.

In the case of equal numbers of industries and factors, both local and global factor price equalization have been the subject of intense study. For global results see Samuelson [14], Lerner [6], Pearce [9, 10], McKenzie [8], and Rader [13]. For the local theory see McKenzie [7], Kuhn [5], Chipman [1], Rader [11, 12], Diewert and Woodland [2], and Jones and Scheinkman [4].

Factor price equalization, both local and global, depends critically on the comparison of the number of industries and the number of factors. For example, on the negative side, if the number of factors exceeds the number of goods, small changes in factor endowments will change factor prices and local factor price equalization does not hold (Samuelson [15], Diewert and Woodland [2], and Jones and Scheinkman [4]).

On the positive side, both local and global factor price equalization results have been shown for the cases where there are exactly as many factors as industries. However, in the modern industrial world with many

347

countries producing the many goods from relatively homogeneous factors, the more realistic case would seem to be that where there are more industries than factors.

The case of an excess number of industries is our present concern. The only known result seems to be as follows. If the number of industries exceeds the number of factors and there are only two factors, then local factor price equalization holds for some factor endowment (Rader [11, Theorem 15], [12, Chap. 5, Theorem 28]). Our purpose is to extend this to the case of more than two factors.

We show local, but not generally global, factor price equalization. In particular, as a country's capital stock grows per capita, it may move from one factor endowment to another, both of which have locally constant factor prices, but the factor prices are different. Equivalently, two countries in different stages of development but facing the same international prices may have unequal factor prices that are nevertheless fixed in their respective places even after modest changes in factor endowments. It is only when all industries operate in one country that local factor price equalization by another implies that its factor prices are necessarily equal to that of the one.

2. DEFINITIONS

The assumptions to be used are derived from [13]. We define *unit cost* (by industry) to be the values of function $c: \Omega^n \to R^m,$[1] $c(w)$, where w is the vector of *factor wages*. Ordinarily, c is derived from cost minimization by each industry, given a unit value of the industry production function. In that case c is convex, but convexity will play but a minor role in what follows.

Conditions will be put directly on c:

(B1)　$X(w) \equiv [\partial c / \partial w]' \geq 0.$

(B1) holds if industries have independent production functions and they minimize costs wx^i, given a production function f, output $f(x^i)$, and factor inputs $x^i \in \Omega^n$.

Let $\#I$ be the *cardinal number* of set I. Define c_I to be the vector $(c_i, i \in I)$.

(B2)　Let $\#I = n$. Then $\det X^I(w) \neq 0.$

For CES production functions, defined by

$$f(x^i) = \xi_i = [\sum \beta_j^i (X_j^i \xi_i)^{1/b_i + 1}]^{b_i + 1}, \qquad x_j^i = X_j^i = X_j^i \xi^i,$$

it is shown in [13] that $\det X^I(w) \neq 0$ if and only if $\det (\beta_j^i, i \in I) \neq 0$. Therefore, (B2) is an *independence assumption applied to production functions of industries in I.*

---

[1] R is the real line, Ω the positive half of the real line, and Ω^n the Cartesian product of Ω and hence the strictly positive vectors with n components, R^m euclidean m space.

For $n = 2$, (B2) is the condition that there is no reversal in the rank of factor intensities among industries.

(B3) If $\#I = n$, then for any j, $w_j^r \to 0$ or $w_j^r \to \infty$, $r \to \infty$, implies that, for some $i \in I$, either $c_i(w^r) \to 0$ or $c_i(w^r) \to \infty$.

(B3) amalgamates two conditions in [13]. In the first place, (B3) implies that as one wage tends to zero, the others bounded, costs tend to zero for at least one industry. In the second place, (B3) implies that as one wage tends to infinity, costs tend to either zero or infinity for at least one industry. In [13], (B3) is shown to hold in the CES case provided the elasticity of substitution is not greater than 1, $b_i \leq 1$, and the production functions are independent.

Since the standard application is to constant returns to scale, we exclude positive unit profits. This restricts attention to the *admissible wages*:

$$W = \{w \in \Omega^n \,|\, p \leq c(w)\}.$$

Since p is the common values added by all countries, it is assumed that there are no transport costs. (For the derivation of values added, see [13, Appendix].)

An industry is said to be *profitable* at w if $c_i(w) = p_i$. Given values added, we define $I(w) = \{i \,|\, c_i(w) = p_i\}$ to be the set of *profitable industries* at w.

A wage vector w is said to be an *equilibrium wage*, given factor endowments $x \in \Omega^n$, if $x = X^{I(w)}(w)\,\xi$ for some $\xi \in \Omega^{\#I(w)}$. The definition is relevant to production functions linear homogeneous and independent between industries. Perfect mobility of factors between different industries but in the same country is implicitly assumed.

A *cone of factor price equalization* is an open cone of factor endowments such that a small change in endowments does not lead to any change in the equilibrium wage. The definition divides into two parts. First, if w is an equilibrium wage, given x and factor endowments $\bar{x}$ near x, then w is an equilibrium wage given x. Second, w is the only equilibrium wage, given either x or $\bar{x}$.

3. THREE THEOREMS

We begin with the basic result that if there are enough profitable industries, then local factor price equalization holds.

THEOREM 1   (McKenzie [7])   If (B1) and rank $X^{I(w)}(w) = m$, then $C(w) \equiv \{X^{I(w)}(w)\xi \,|\, \xi \gg 0\}$ defines a cone of factor price equalization.[2]

---

[2] $\xi \gg 0$ if $\xi_i > 0$ for all i.

COROLLARY   IF $\#I(w) \geq n$ and (B1) and (B2), then $C(w)$ is a cone of factor price equalization.

By the corollary to McKenzie's theorem, the question of the existence of a cone of factor price equalization reduces to showing $\#I(w) = n$. With our assumptions, we show that such a cone exists, which is to say that whatever world prices are, there is some factor endowment for which at least n industries are profitable.

THEOREM 2   Given (B1)–(B3) and $p \gg 0$, there exists at least one $w \gg 0$ such that n industries are profitable, $\#I(w) \geq n$, and $C(w)$ is a cone of factor price equalization.

Proof   Suppose $\#I(\tilde{w}) < n$ and let $I(\tilde{w}) \subset J$ such that $\#J = n$. Then perturb $\tilde{w}$ by the differential equation system

$$\frac{dw}{dt} = y\left(\frac{\partial c_J}{\partial w}\right)^{-1} = y[X^J(w)']^{-1} \tag{1}$$

where

$$y_i = \begin{cases} 0, & i \in I(w) \\ -1, & i \in J - I(w) \end{cases}$$

Evidently,

$$\frac{dc_J}{dt} = \frac{dw}{dt}\left(\frac{\partial c_J}{\partial w}\right) = y\left(\frac{\partial c_J}{\partial w}\right)^{-1}\left(\frac{\partial c_J}{\partial w}\right) = y$$

and

$$\frac{dc_i}{dt} = \begin{cases} 0, & i \in I(w) \\ -1, & i \in J - I(w) \end{cases} \tag{2}$$

By *Peano's theorem*, (1) can be solved and the solution $w(t)$ continued over all $t > 0$ so long as $w(t)$ remains bounded from the boundary of the domain of the function $f(w) = y[X^J(w)']^{-1}$. In our case, the domain is Ω^n so that (1) can be solved and the solution $w(t)$ continued over all $t > 0$ so long as $w(t)$ is bounded from infinity and bounded from zero.

Given (B3), we prove that $w(t)$ is appropriately bounded until an additional industry becomes profitable. If, for example, $w_i(t) \to 0$, then by (B3) either $c_k(w(t))$ falls in a finite time to the level of p_k, contrary to hypothesis, or else $c_k(w(t)) \to \infty$, for some $k \in J$, contrary to (2). Alternatively, if $w_i(t) \to \infty$, then again by (B3), either $c_k(w(t)) \to 0$ or $c_k(w(t)) \to \infty$ for some $k \in J$, neither of which are possible so long as $c_k(w) > p_k$ for all $k \notin I(w)$.

Next we show that an additional industry becomes profitable in finite time. So long as $\#I(w(t)) < n$, some industry cost c_i is decreasing exponentially and c_i must reach p_i in finite time t (possibly not $i \in J$). It follows that solving (1), $w(t)$ may be continued until such time as $p_i = c_i(w(t))$ for some $i \notin I$, since at worse $c_i(w(t))$ would decrease to p_i for some $i \notin J$. Consequently, there is some strictly positive $\bar{w}$ such that $I(\bar{w}) \subset I(\tilde{w})$ and $\#I(\bar{w})) > \#(I(\tilde{w}))$. Therefore, we can change w to increase the number of profitable industries until such time as $\#I(w) \geq n$.

Applying the corollary to Theorem 1, $C(w)$ is the associated cone of factor price equalization.   Q.E.D.

Our next result shows limits on the number of cones of factor price equalization. Although the cone is not unique, owing to the excess number of industries, the theorem following is essentially Theorem 2 in Rader [14]. However, we use Theorem 2 above to give a shorter version of an already easy proof.

THEOREM 3   If $c(w) \gg 0$ for all $w \gg 0$, (B1), (B2), and (B3), then for every I such that $\#I \geq n$, there is at most one wage $w \in W$ such that $I \subset I(w)$.

Proof   By (B2), if $J \subset I$, $\#J = n$, c_J is locally a *diffeomorphism* on Ω^m. From Theorem 2, for every value $p_J \in \Omega^n$, there exists at least one w such that $c_J(w) = p_J$. Therefore c_J is onto Ω^m.

Applying *Hadamard's theorem* [3], a local diffeomorphism from Ω^n onto itself, c_j, is $1 - 1$ and there is at most one w such that $c_J(w) = p_J$.

Let $I \subset I(w)$ and $I \subset I(\bar{w})$, $\#I \geq n$, and $J \subset I$, $\#J = n$. Then $c_J(w) = P_J$, $c_J(\bar{w}) = p_J$, and, therefore, $w = \bar{w}$.   Q.E.D.

Let $W_0 = \{w \in W \,|\, \#I(w) \geq n\}$ be those wages at which industries are profitable.

COROLLARY

$$1 \leq \#W \leq m!/(m - n)!n! \equiv \binom{m}{n}.$$

Proof   By the theorem, $c_I^{-1}(p)$ is a single point when $\#I = n$. Therefore W_0 at most contains as many points as there are combinations of n points out of m, namely, $m!/(m - n)!n!$ Q.E.D.

Define $W_i = \{w \in W_0 \,|\, i \in I(w)\}$ to be those wages at which industry i and $n - 1$ other industries are profitable.

Remark   If the cost function c is strictly quasi-convex,[3] the points in W_i are convexly independent, $i = 1, 2, \ldots, m$. Given the hypothesis of Theorem 3 and $n \leq m \leq n + 1$, W_0 is the finite union at most $n + 1$ of convexly independent vectors.

---

[3] Cost functions are strictly quasi-convex if production functions are strictly quasi-concave.

Proof Suppose to the contrary, that $w \in W_i$, $\sum_{r=1}^{R} t^r w^r = w$, $w^r \in W_i$, $\sum t^r = 1$, $1 \geq t^r > 0$, $R > 1$. Then $c_i(w) < \min c_i(w^r) = p_i$ contrary to $w \in W$.

If there are but n or $n + 1$ industries, then the corollary to Theorem 3 is that there are at most $n + 1 = (n + 1)!/(1!n!)$ wages $w \in W$ at which n industries are profitable. If one such w is a convex combination of the others, then it is a convex combination of n w^r in W such that $\#I(w^r) = n$. The n sets $\#I(w^r) \subset \{1, \ldots, n + 1\}$ must have in common at least one i. Again, $c_i(w) < \min c_i(w^r) = p_i$ contrary to $w \in W$.   Q.E.D.

4. EXAMPLES AND CONCLUSIONS

When the number of industries exceeds the number of factors, uniqueness of the cone of factor price equalization cannot be expected. We show this in Fig. 1 for two factors and three industries. Isoquants that produce one dollar's worth of outputs for each of industries I, II, III are drawn. The usual line tangent to isoquants I and II gives, by its normal, factor wages. Cone 1, bounded by the expansion paths for I and II at wages (w_K, w_L), is a cone of factor price equalization; so is cone 2. The ranking of factor intensities by industries is unchanged throughout and therefore (B2) holds [as does (B3) if the isoquants are appropriately extended toward the K–L axes].

In Fig. 2 we elaborate Fig. 1 to show three cones of factor price equalization with each pair of industries being profitable at one cone. Therefore,

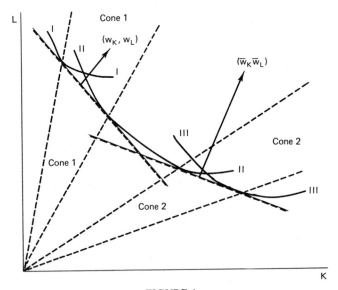

FIGURE 1

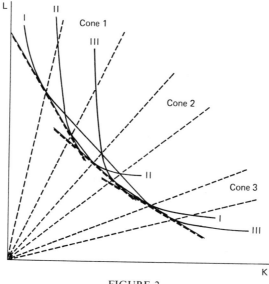

FIGURE 2

the remark following Theorem 3 is all that can be expected in specifying the number of cones of factor price equalization. [Here, $m!/(m - n)!n! = 3!/1!2! = 3.$]

Consequently, a big difference between the cases of equal and unequal numbers of industries and factors is that in the former case, the cone of factor price equalization is unique, whereas it need not be in the latter, more realistic, case. In the most realistic case, positive production in n industries by each of two countries is not, by itself, evidence for equal factor prices. However, it is still true that a country's factor prices are equalized with factor prices of any other countries that have n profitable industries and whose profitable industries are a subset of the one country. Consequently, if one country produces all goods, then any other country that produces n goods has the same factor prices.

REFERENCES

1. Chipman, J., A survey of the theory of international trade III, *Econometrica* **34**, 18–76 (1966).
2. Diewert, E., and Woodland, A., Frank Knight's theorem in linear programming revisited, *Econometrica* **45**, 375–398 (1977).
3. Gordon, W. B., On the diffeomorphism of euclidean space, *Am. Math. Mon.* **79**, 755–759 (1972).
4. Jones, R., and Scheinkman, J., The relevance of the two sector production model in trade theory, *J. Political Econ.* **85**, 909–935 (1977).

5. Kuhn, H., Factor endowments and factor prices, mathematical appendix, *Economica* **26**, 142–144 (1959).
6. Lerner, A., Factor prices and international trade, *Economica* **21** (1952).
7. McKenzie, L. W., Equality of factor prices in world trade, *Econometrica* **23**, 239–257 (1955).
8. McKenzie, L. W., The inversion of cost functions: A counter-example, *and* Theorem and counter-example, *Internat. Econ. Rev.* **8**, 271–285 (1967).
9. Pearce, I., More about factor price equalization, *Internat. Econ. Rev.* **8**, 255–270 (1967).
10. Pearce, I., Rejoinder to Professor Samuelson's Summary, *Internat. Econ. Rev.* **8**, 300–306 (1967).
11. Rader, T., "International Trade and Development In a Small Country" (J. Quirk and A. Zarley, eds.), Papers in Quantitative Economics 1, pp. 399–431. Univ. of Kansas Press, Lawrence, Kansas, 1968.
12. Rader, T., "Theory of General Economic Equilibrium." Academic Press, New York, 1972.
13. Rader, T., On factor price equalization, *J. Math. Econ.* **5** (1978), 71–82.
14. Samuelson, P., International trade and the equalization of factor prices, *Econ. J.* **43**, 163–184 (1948).
15. Samuelson, P., Prices of factors and goods in general equilibrium, *Rev. Econ. Stud.* **21**, 21, 1–20 (1953–1954).

The author is indebted to Wilhelm Neuefeind of Washington University for many useful comments.

DEPARTMENT OF ECONOMICS
WASHINGTON UNIVERSITY
ST. LOUIS, MISSOURI

The General Equilibrium Framework of Economic Analysis: Stocks and Flows—With Special Application to Macroeconomic Models

JOHN Z. DRABICKI

AKIRA TAKAYAMA

One of the most conspicuous features of Professor McKenzie's work is its emphasis on general equilibrium. In fact Lionel never ceases to insist on its importance, and his works, each of which shows a huge concentration of the human intellect, have contributed greatly to the advancement of economic science. Although the importance of general equilibrium analysis has, as is well known, been well acknowledged in the profession, the attempt to apply it by various other writers to macromodels in the context of stocks and flows has generated unbelievable confusions during the last forty years. The purpose of this chapter is to attempt to disentangle the threads of such confusions. Therefore, this paper addresses the basic principle (i.e., general equilibrium) that is prevalent throughout Lionel's work.

The most well-known and celebrated static general equilibrium macroeconomic model is probably the so-called IS–LM framework, which was introduced by Hicks (1937) as an exposition of Keynes (1936). Equilibrium in this model is given by a flow equilibrium condition for the goods market and a stock equilibrium condition for the money market. Under the full-employment assumption these two equations determine the price of the output and the interest rate, while under the assumption of a constant price level they determine the level of output and the interest rate. Hence in both cases the equilibrium system is complete and looks rather simple.

However a moment of reflection forces us to consider the following questions, which suggest that this model may not be as simple as it initially appears:

(i) The classical theory of interest rate determination (the "loanable funds theory") singles out the importance of equilibrium of the *flow* of loanable funds (securities). How do we know that such a flow equilibrium of securities is guaranteed by the equilibrium specified by the IS–LM model?

(ii) What about the *stock* equilibrium of securities? That is, how do we know that the total stock of securities that various economic agents wish to hold at the IS–LM equilibrium is equal to the total stock of securities that other economic agents wish to supply for the current period?

(iii) By a similar token, since the money market equilibrium is described by only a stock condition, it is not clear whether flow equilibrium in this market is achieved.

(iv) Since only one type of output is produced in the IS–LM economy, this good is used both for consumption and accumulation purposes. Hence, since the goods equilibrium is described by only a flow condition, it is not clear whether or not stock equilibrium in the goods market is achieved.

(v) Stock quantities and flow quantities obviously have different time dimensions. Are we, therefore, certain that the mixture of the flow and the stock relations in the IS–LM model does not contain any confusion in this respect?

Of course conventional wisdom has it that the equilibrium conditions for all the markets of any economy are not required to guarantee equilibrium in all the markets. This is due to a "Walras law" which points to a redundancy in the equilibrium relations. This was true in the Walrasian (1926) system, and hence it is natural that economists have attempted to solve some, if not all, of the above questions by appealing to some sort of "Walras law." However this task is not as simple as it seems. It appears that for the IS–LM economy we have to guarantee six equilibrium conditions, two (one stock and one flow) for each of the three markets (goods, money, and securities). Yet the IS and the LM relations only describe two out of the six equilibrium conditions. Then, to guarantee the equilibrium of the remaining four do we need four identifies (i.e., four "Walras laws")? If not, how many and what are they? And, how can they be obtained?

Obviously these questions are not particularly inherent only to the IS–LM model or even to more general macromodels. Similar questions can arise in any economic problem that deals with equilibrium. It is the purpose of this paper to answer such questions.

In Section I we attempt to answer these questions in the context of a general framework where the economy under consideration can have any number of goods or assets. Here we point out that there are two "Walras laws," one for stocks and one for flows, and that the distinction between "statics" and "dynamics" plays a crucial role in answering the above questions. In Section II we illustrate our discussion of Section I by using a simple macromodel. We explicitly obtain the two Walras laws in connection with the macromodel used in this section, and clarify the framework of analysis for macroequilibrium. The specific questions raised in connection with the IS–LM model are answered here in the context of both statics and dynamics.

Finally, in Section III we sketch the history of the debate on this topic in light of our discussion in Sections I and II (especially in connection with macroeconomic models), and thereby hope to straighten out some confusions on this topic that prevail in the literature. Our discussion includes the prolonged debate on the loanable funds theory versus the liquidity preference theory, e.g., Fellner and Somers (1941), the Patinkin (1965) model, more recent dynamic models such as Enthoven (1960) and Foley and Sidrauski (1971), and discussions on the Patinkin model (e.g., May 1970). The paper ends with a critical summary of the recent discussion concerning the end-of-period equilibrium and the beginning-of-period equilibrium by Foley (1975) and others (e.g., Buiter and Woglom, 1977, and Turnovsky and Burmeister, 1977). In reading through the literature on macroequilibrium, we are struck with the impression that the market structure by which equilibrium can be brought about is not explicitly specified in some of the literature. We believe that this is unfortunate for theoretical works, as such works ought to clarify the logical consistency of various ingredients in the model. In this chapter we therefore make the underlying market structure used in the chapter explicit at the outset of Section I.

I. STOCKS AND FLOWS

Our approach here is concerned with the economy that Hicks (1965) calls the "flexprice economy," as opposed to the "fixprice economy." Namely, our interpretation of economic models, including macromodels, is confined to an aspect that is strictly in the tradition of neoclassical equilibrium analysis (in which the well-known Hicksian "week" plays a crucial role in dynamics).

The real world is no doubt characterized by a mixture of the features of the flexprice and the fixprice economies. Furthermore, we realize that the classics in macroanalysis, e.g., Keynes' *General Theory*, may more properly be interpreted in the context of a fixprice economy. On the other hand, the neoclassical flexprice economy has attracted considerable interest in the literature, and it is therefore worthwhile to focus our attention on this aspect. As Morishima (1976, p. 169) puts it, "there is no way of discovering the whole ecology of the system except by such artificial cultivation." Furthermore, as Foley (1975, p. 303) remarked, "Although current research focuses on 'disequilibrium' models, most writers have an 'equilibrium' notion that lies behind their disequilibrium formulation." As Hicks (1973) recently reported, Keynes himself accepted the Hicksian (1937) IS–LM interpretation of the *General Theory* in terms of equilibrium analysis.[1]

In this connection we should briefly summarize some of the difficult problems that arise as soon as we depart from equilibrium analysis, i.e., problems that are, unfortunately, somewhat arbitrarily ignored frequently in the literature. One of the crucial problems that emerges in a disequilibrium economy is the one that Malinvaud (1977) aptly calls "rationing." In disequilibrium the desires of some economic agents are bound to be frustrated as "rationing" takes place. This suggests a number of questions: (a) What is the market structure that handles the rationing? (b) What is the mechanism under which rationing takes place (in a manner that is compatible with rational behavior of each economic agent)? (c) What would be the rational behavior of each individual concerning the holding of stocks of assets or "inventories" as buffers to cope with the situation when his desires are frustrated? In much of the literature, point (b) is usually simply avoided by imposing a somewhat arbitrary mechanism called the "short-side principle," and not much progress has been made on (a) and (c).[2] These points, however, obviously do not negate the importance of disequilibrium analysis.

Confining ourselves to the flexprice economy the key adjustment parameters are, of course, prices instead of quantities. In terms of the usual IS–LM macroframework, for example, we are thus concerned with the adjustment via output price and the interest rate instead of via output and the interest rate.[3] Given such adjustments via prices it will be most convenient to develop

---

[1] Hicks (1973, pp. 9–10) reproduces Keynes' letter to him (dated March 31, 1937) in which Keynes, responding to the IS–LM interpretation, wrote "I found it very interesting and really have next to nothing to say by way of criticism." Hicks concludes from this letter that "Keynes accepted the SILL diagram as a fair statement of his position" (1973, p. 10). On the other hand, Hicks goes on to say that this is "not a statement which I believe myself." Hicks' uneasiness here is based on the fact that his IS–LM model "reduces the *General Theory* to equilibrium economics" (1976, p. 141). In his paper (1976), Hicks summarizes the history of his intellectual *Wanderjahre* stemming from his uneasiness with equilibrium analysis à la his "week." He then states "I am afraid that for many years I got no further, or very little further." (p. 147).

[2] The following additional questions may be asked regarding the fixprice economy: (a) What is the mechanism that changes prices? (b) In the adjustment process via quantities, is intermediate trading allowed or not allowed before "equilibrium" is reached? The reader may ask these questions in connection with some of the well-known recent works on disequilibrium analysis.

[3] The neoclassical macromodel with full employment obviously provides such an example. On the other hand, as is well known, it is not necessary to assume full employment in this connection (cf. any standard textbook exposition of macromodels in terms of aggregate demand and aggregate supply following Marschak, 1951). See also Patinkin (1965) and Modigliani (1963).

our discussion in the framework of the standard neoclassical notion of a trading (or market) period or the Hicksian "week," which Hicks discussed in his *Value and Capital* (1946, especially Parts III and IV).[4] A notable application of this concept to macroeconomic analysis is found in Patinkin (1965).

Here it may be worthwhile, given its importance, to recall briefly the gist of dynamics à la the Hicksian "week." The market opens only on "Monday," at which time "competitive trading" (cf. Morishima, 1976) or "tâtonnement" takes place.[5] The rest of the week is used to carry out the contracts, so that "Monday's prices will rule during the week, and they will govern the disposition of resources during the week" (Hicks, 1946, p. 123). Each economic agent (household or firm) makes a definite plan for *all* its relevant futures during the tâtonnement process on Monday, for which optimization behavior over time is the crucial element. Concerning expectations for future periods (weeks), it is assumed that "people expect particular definite prices, and they have *certain* price expectations" (Hicks, 1946, p. 126) when they come to the market on Monday. Thus expectations are constant during the week, or conversely, the length of a week is defined as the period in which expectations are constant. When the next Monday comes, people may revise their expectations, so that their plans may be revised accordingly. It is possible that economic conditions or data such as tastes, technology, resources, and the distribution of resources among individuals change during the week, which would certainly affect people's expectations or plans for the *next* Monday. However these changes do not affect the equilibrium prices that are contracted on *this* Monday. Under the tâtonnement assumption the expected price for the current week is actually realized, so that "myopic perfect foresight" prevails during the week. The equilibrium within the week is called "temporary equilibrium," and dynamics is the study of the succession of temporary equilibria.[6] It is certainly possible that the prices that prevail in the next week will be different from those that prevail in this period. When

---

[4] For extensions and an elaboration of this concept, see Morishima (1950), for example. See also Morishima (1976).

[5] The concept of tâtonnement is explicitly applied to macroanalysis by Patinkin (1965), for example. Note also that comparative statics, a standard analytical procedure in economic analysis, virtually presupposes the tâtonnementlike mechanism for establishing equilibrium. This point is explicitly and quite frankly admitted even in textbook expositions. See, for example, Crouch (1972, pp. 154–156). Whether or not Hicks (1946) is clearly aware of the need for the tâtonnement assumption in his discussion of dynamics à la "weeks" is debatable (cf. Morishima, 1950, p. 9, footnote 1). Morishima (1950) emphasizes the crucial importance of the tâtonnement assumption in the Hicksian apparatus.

[6] Apparent discontent with the "unrealistic" nature of the Hicksian apparatus has generated many attempts to free the analysis from the mold of such an "equilibrium" analysis. Unfortunately, these attempts often seem to contain logical inconsistencies, primarily because they do not properly account for the problems that arise in the course of "rationing" under disequilibrium.

the price system that prevails this Monday stays the same in future weeks, the economy is said to be in "full equilibrium" or to have reached "equilibrium over time" (Hicks, 1946, p. 132).[7]

This much of the analysis is well known, and it is used (implicitly or explicitly) widely as a general framework of general equilibrium analysis for dynamics. On the other hand, when it is applied to macroanalysis, the discussion often becomes quite confusing. This is primarily due to the fact that the IS and the LM conditions are, respectively, concerned with "flow equilibrium" and "stock equilibrium" conditions, and the relationship between these conditions is not clear. The confusion here is apparent in the debate that has prevailed over the last forty years on this topic. As mentioned earlier, the present paper attempts to disentangle the threads of these confusions, and as such this paper is not really concerned only with macromodels, but rather it addresses the problem of stocks and flows in the context of equilibrium analysis.

Now that the scope of the paper has been clarified, we are ready to proceed with the main discussion. It is probably best to begin our discussion with a classification of goods (and assets) in terms of their stock and flow characteristics [as was done by Bushaw and Clower (1957), for example]. Goods can be classified on this basis as follows: *pure flow goods*, *pure stock goods*, and *stock-flow goods*. A pure flow good is one that is produced and consumed in one market period but is never held as an "asset" (i.e., carried into the future). A classic example is "fish" in the days when there was no effective means of refrigeration. Another example may be electricity or services such as haircuts. Hicks (1965) argued that Marshall (1920) was predominantly concerned with such pure flow goods ("fish").[8] A pure stock good, on the

---

[7] An excellent example of the application of the distinction between temporary equilibrium and full equilibrium is seen in Archibald and Lipsey (1958). There is little doubt that many followers of equilibrium analysis have been aware of the artificial nature of the Hicksian (1946) apparatus of dynamics à la "week." Neither do we wish to insist that such an apparatus is "realistic." The trouble with this device is, as Hicks (1976, p. 142) aptly remarks, "Much too much had to happen on that 'Monday'!" On the other hand, this apparatus perhaps provides the most important (if not the only) theoretical device that validates a countless number of theoretical and empirical studies in the literature via equilibrium analysis. Abandoning this apparatus and seeking a new one, though it is obviously an extremely important task, is almost like opening Pandora's box, generating many difficult questions. In the present paper we follow this apparatus in order to avoid these questions and to focus attention on some other important issues. It is well known that such a practice has produced numerous very useful results.

[8] For example, Hicks (1965, pp. 78–79) states: "The standard case of Marshallian microtheory assumes that the traded commodity is non-storable ('fish') so that there can be no carryover from one period to another" (See also his pp. 53–54). Needless to say, Marshall (1920) also realized the importance of stock–flow goods, as is clear from his famous trichotomy of market equilibrium into temporary, short-run, and long-run periods.

other hand, is one that is held but not currently produced or "used up." Examples may be the paintings of Rembrandt, Munch, or Picasso.[9] Finally a stock–flow good is one that is currently produced and/or consumed, as well as held for the future. Even fish under refrigeration becomes such a good. The usual macroanalysis is concerned with these types of goods. Notice that while certain stock–flow goods, such as refrigerated fish, may be consumed (or used up—eaten), some stock–flow goods are not consumable in the same sense as fish. An example is "money."

In describing the static and dynamic equilibrium of a given market, the above distinction of goods (or assets) is very important. To consider this problem, it is crucial to define certain key concepts. Paraphrasing Clower (1968, p. 243) slightly, we define the *stock demand* $D(t + 1, t)$ as "the gross quantity of a particular commodity (or asset) that individuals plan during the tth trading period (Monday) to hold for future disposal at the end of the current (or the tth) period," i.e., at the beginning of the next period $t + 1$.[10] By $D(t, t)$, we denote the gross quantity of a particular commodity (or asset) that individuals plan to hold at the end of this (i.e., the tth) Monday. Namely, $D(t + 1, t)$ is the *stock demand* planned during this Monday for the next Monday, whereas $D(t, t)$ is the stock demand planned this Monday for the end of this Monday. The distinction between these two concepts follows the spirit of the discussion that follows Foley (1975) (cf. Turnovsky and Burmeister, 1977, and Buiter and Woglom, 1977). Similarly, we denote by $S(t + 1, t)$ the gross quantity of a particular commodity (or asset) that individuals plan during the tth trading period to supply at the end of the current (or the tth) period, i.e., at the beginning of the next period (the $(t + 1)$th period). Namely, $S(t + 1, t)$ is the *stock supply* planned during this Monday for the next Monday. By $S(t)$ we denote the stock of a particular

---

[9] In the usual static macromodel, in which the supply of "money" is treated as an exogenous variable, money is often treated as though it were a pure stock good. Although this is a convenient assumption in that we are able to ignore the flow equilibrium condition for money, it ignores the basic difference between money and, say, Rembrandt's paintings: Money can be produced in the current period, and the important function of money as a means of payments creates a *flow* demand for money (as contrasted to the *stock* demand for money, or the "speculative demand" for money). Of course the question may arise whether or not pure stock goods can exist in any significant way, although they may have played an important role in theoretical exercises.

[10] Namely, the decision regarding $D(t + 1, t)$ is made during the tth market period (Monday). For those seeking to understand the application of this concept of stock demand in macroanalysis, the following passage from Patinkin (1965, p. 24) may be useful: "By the term 'amount of money demanded' we mean the amount of money the individual plans during the market period this Monday afternoon to hold in his possession next Monday morning—after he has, in the course of the week, made and received all the payments on the contracts into which he plans to enter this afternoon." Let "this Monday" be the tth Monday. Then Patinkin's (stock) demand for money (denoted by L) referred to in the above passage may be denoted by $L(t + 1, t)$.

commodity (or asset) that *exists* at the beginning of the tth Monday, whereas by $S(t, t)$ we denote the stock supply of a particular commodity (or asset) that *is made available* for the end of the tth Monday. The *flow supply* $s(t)$ is the gross quantity of a particular commodity (or asset) that individuals plan to produce (create or destroy) during the current (i.e., the tth) period. The difference between $S(t + 1, t)$ and $S(t)$ is equal to the flow supply of a particular commodity (or asset) *minus* the gross quantity of that commodity (or asset) that individuals plan to consume or use up during the tth period [which we denote by $d_1(t)$]; i.e.,

$$S(t + 1, t) - S(t) \, [\equiv \Delta S(t)] \equiv s(t) - d_1(t). \tag{1}$$

Namely, $S(t + 1, t) - S(t)$ is equal to the net additional quantity of a particular commodity (or asset) that is planned to be made available for the beginning of the next period. Note that the concept $\Delta S(t)$ involves the decision of "demanders" as well *as* "suppliers" since it includes the term $d_1(t)$. In contrast to this concept, we denote by $d_2(t)$ the *additional* amount of a particular commodity (or asset) that individuals plan to carry over into the next period; i.e.,

$$D(t + 1, t) - D(t, t) \, [\equiv \Delta D(t)] \equiv d_2(t). \tag{2}$$

Namely, $d_2(t)$ corresponds to "investment" or "hoarding" demand. Needless to say, $d_2(t)$ can be negative, signifying disinvestment or dishoarding. We call the quantity $d(t) \equiv d_1(t) + d_2(t)$ the *flow demand* for period t. Note that while it is meaningful to define the concept of $S(t)$ as opposed to $S(t, t)$, it is not possible to define the concept that would have to be denoted by $D(t)$. This is because the decisions concerning $D(t + 1, t)$, $D(t, t)$, $S(t + 1, t)$, and $S(t, t)$ are formulated during a particular trading period (the tth Monday), whereas no such decision making is involved in $S(t)$. $S(t)$ is independent of the concept of market.

It is important to be aware of the convention that the "individuals" referred to in the above include the government, the central bank, etc., as well as the households and the firms. The term "commodity" or "good" includes such assets as money and securities.

To illustrate some of the these concepts, we may use fish under refrigeration as an example of a stock–flow good. In this case $d_2(t)$ signifies the net additional quantity of fish that individuals plan to put in refrigerators by the end of the tth period, whereas $d_1(t)$ signifies the amount of fish that is "eaten" or consumed during the tth period. Note that the amount $d_1(t)$ disappears permanently after the tth period. For certain stock–flow goods, such as money and securities, it would be more reasonable to suppose that this portion is negligible, or more specifically $d_1(t) \equiv 0$, so that $d(t) \equiv d_2(t)$. Namely, the flow demand for money is equal to its hoarding (or dishoarding) demand, in which both demands, money to hold and money to spend (or any other demand), are incorporated into the decision involved in $D(t + 1, t)$ or $d(t)$ (e.g., recall the quotation from Patinkin in footnote 10). Hence for these stock–flow goods such as money and securities (1) and (2) are, respectively, simplified as

$$S(t + 1, t) - S(t) \; [\equiv \Delta S(t)] \equiv s(t), \tag{1'}$$

$$D(t + 1, t) - D(t, t) \; [\equiv \Delta D(t)] \equiv d(t). \tag{2'}$$

The flow supply of fish is simply the amount of fish caught in the water (which is offered to the market), whereas the flow supply of money is the net additional money created during the period. It is therefore useful to distinguish further between physical goods and financial assets (such as money and securities). Namely, the production of a physical good takes time, whereas we may assume that the creation of financial assets takes virtually no time. Consequently, we may suppose that the flow supply or the delivery of physical goods is made during the week, whereas the flow supply of financial assets is made during the *trading* period, i.e., on Monday. Namely, for physical stock–flow goods we have $S(t, t) \equiv S(t)$, whereas for financial assets we have $S(t + 1, t) \equiv S(t, t) \equiv S(t) + \Delta S(t)$. In *both* cases Eq. (1) holds as it is, except that $d_1(t) \equiv 0$ in the case of financial assets (as mentioned earlier).

Define $x(t)$, $X(t, t)$ [which is abbreviated as $X(t)$], and $X(t + 1, t)$ by

$$x(t) \equiv d(t) - s(t), \qquad X(t) \equiv D(t, t) - S(t),$$

$$X(t + 1, t) \equiv D(t + 1, t) - S(t + 1, t). \tag{3}$$

Then, subtracting (1) from (2), we obtain the following fundamental identity:

$$X(t + 1, t) - X(t) \equiv x(t). \tag{4}$$

In the case of a pure flow good we have no stocks carried over to the present period from the past. If fish cannot be refrigerated, then any fish that was not consumed during the previous period is spoiled and disposed of. Hence for a pure flow good the identity (4) reduces to

$$X(t + 1, t) \equiv x(t). \tag{4'}$$

Market equilibrium of this good at time t is completely described by the *flow equilibrium* condition

$$x(t) = 0. \tag{5}$$

That is, current output must be equal to current consumption, which then determines the equilibrium price of the good, $p(t)$.[11] By virtue of (4'), (5) is

---

[11] Needless to say one cannot talk about price without referring to the numéraire, say, money. Here money is used only as a means of payment and as the accounting unit and is assumed to play no role in equilibrium, as is the case in the usual microeconomics textbook exposition of an isolated market.

equivalent to $X(t + 1, t) = 0$, which should not be surprising. Since the pure flow good cannot be stored, we must have $D(t + 1, t) = S(t + 1, t) = 0$ [so that $X(t + 1, t) = 0$]; i.e., these planned quantities to be carried over into the next period are zero. This, of course, means that individuals plan to achieve $x(t) = 0$, which is, in turn, realized via the fluctuation of $p(t)$. Dynamic equilibrium can be described by requiring (5) *for all* t, which in turn determines the sequence of equilibrium prices, $p(t)$, $p(t + 1)$, $p(t + 2)$, ...

Next consider an isolated market for a *pure stock good*. In this case, by definition, we have

$$x(t) \equiv d(t) \equiv s(t) \equiv 0, \tag{6}$$

so that (4) is reduced to

$$X(t) \equiv X(t + 1, t). \tag{4''}$$

Hence the equilibrium for this good is described by the stock equilibrium condition

$$X(t + 1, t) = 0 \quad \text{or} \quad X(t) = 0, \tag{7}$$

which then determines the equilibrium price of the good, $p(t)$. Notice that when the next [the $(t + 1)$th] Monday comes, the stock demand can be different from that of this Monday, reflecting changes in expectations, etc., so that the stock equilibrium condition may have to be revised, generating a new equilibrium price $p(t + 1)$. Dynamics can be described by the succession of such equilibrium prices, i.e., by $p(t)$, $p(t + 1)$, $p(t + 2)$, ...

In the case of a *stock–flow good* the analysis is not so simple, which has caused a great amount of confusion in the literature. On the other hand, in the real world, many important goods or assets are of this type. One way of describing the case of a stock–flow good may be simply to recognize that equilibrium for such a good requires that both a flow equilibrium condition and a stock equilibrium condition be satisfied. That is,

$$x(t) = 0 \quad \text{and} \quad X(t + 1, t) = 0. \tag{8}$$

Considering the isolated market of such a good and confining ourselves to period t, what then do the two equations in (8) determine? Given only one price of the good, $p(t)$, many economists are puzzled by this. One answer to this question is provided by saying that we only require one condition,[12]

$$X(t) + x(t) = 0, \tag{9}$$

---

[12] Since $x(t)$ is a flow and $X(t)$ is a stock, the unit of measurement of the period must be chosen somewhat carefully. Condition (9) was once offered as a reconciliation of the loanable funds theory and the liquidity preference theory. Lloyd (1960, p. 207) correctly realized that we need the two conditions in (8) for each stock–flow good.

instead of the two conditions of (8). But then the price $p(t)$ determined by (9) may not guarantee either $x(t) = 0$ or $X(t) = 0$. It may be natural to expect that such a disequilibrium will change $p(t)$.

Another answer to this problem is to simply assume away stock–flow goods from the model, i.e., assume that the economy contains only pure flow goods and pure stock goods, but no stock–flow goods.[13] However, such an economy may be too artificial.

Still another popular solution to the above question is to assume that the flow excess demand is proportional to the stock excess demand; that is,

$$x(t) \equiv \alpha X(t + 1, t), \tag{10}$$

where α is a positive constant. Furthermore, it is sometimes assumed that $\alpha = 1$. With (10) there is only one independent equation in (8), which then determines the equilibrium value of the price for t, $p(t)$. However, assumption (10) looks rather arbitrary.

Thus the problem remains: what then do the two equations of (8) determine? When an individual plans to carry over a good or asset to the next period, his plan, among other things, would depend on the rate of return of doing so. Then it should be natural to think that the two equations of (8) determine the equilibrium values of the good's rate of return $r(t)$ and its price $p(t)$. Needless to say, both $p(t)$ and $r(t)$ are, in general, affected by the flow condition $x(t) = 0$, as well as by the stock condition $X(t + 1, t) = 0$.

To ease our conceptual experiment, let us suppose that the return in carrying over a particular stock–flow good consists only of a capital gain (or loss) due to a higher (or lower) price in the next period. Then the rate of return $r(t)$ can be computed as

$$r(t) = \frac{p(t + 1) - p(t)}{p(t)} \left[\equiv \pi(t) \right]. \tag{11}$$

Then it is easy to see that the two conditions of (8) determine the equilibrium values of the following two variables:

$$p(t) \quad \text{and} \quad \pi(t),$$

where $\pi(t)$ is the rate of capital gain (or the rate of "inflation"), *or*

$$p(t) \quad \text{and} \quad p(t + 1),$$

since $p(t)$ and $\pi(t)$ are determined *if and only if* $p(t)$ and $p(t + 1)$ are determined. Although it may appear somewhat strange that two equilibrium

---

[13] Clower (1968, p. 274) seems to believe that the model of the "contemporary monetary theory" is such an example, in which money and bonds are pure stock goods and the (physical) goods are pure flow goods.

prices are determined on a single Monday, this may not be too surprising. After all, the decision to carry over a certain good or asset into the next period should be based on the rate of return $r(t)$ for doing so, which must involve the determination of $p(t + 1)$ as we remarked above.

Note that given identity (4), any one of the following conditions in (12), (13), and (14) equivalently determine the equilibrium values of $p(t)$ and $\pi(t)$, or $p(t)$ and $p(t + 1)$:

$$x(t) = 0 \quad \text{and} \quad X(t + 1, t) = 0, \tag{12}$$

$$X(t) = 0 \quad \text{and} \quad X(t + 1, t) = 0, \tag{13}$$

$$x(t) = 0 \quad \text{and} \quad X(t) = 0. \tag{14}$$

For example, if (12) is satisfied, then $X(t) = 0$ is automatically satisfied. On the other hand, any one of (12)–(14) requires two conditions to define equilibrium. It is elementary to see from (4) that

$$X(t + 1, t) = 0 \quad \text{alone does } not \text{ necessarily imply} \quad x(t) = 0, \tag{15a}$$

$$x(t) = 0 \quad \text{alone does } not \text{ necessarily imply} \quad X(t + 1, t) = 0. \tag{15b}$$

That is, in such a static analysis, stock equilibrium neither implies nor is implied by flow equilibrium. Therefore, as they are independent, both equilibrium conditions of (8) are necessary for stock–flow goods, while for pure flow goods and pure stock goods only one condition is necessary (as argued above.)

The above conceptual experiment assumes a somewhat peculiar stock–flow good. However the argument can be easily extended so as to include those stock–flow goods that yield some additional return (e.g., interest) other than a capital gain or loss. We shall observe this in the next section in terms of the usual macromodel.

In many analyses in the literature that involve stock–flow goods, we do not, however, usually worry about the determination of two prices $p(t)$ and $p(t + 1)$. The question that then arises is how to justify such discussions. One popular solution seems to be simply to *assume* (often implicitly) that the stock equilibrium condition holds *a priori* at the beginning of the current period. That is, we assume $X(t) = 0$, which may be called the *initial stock equilibrium condition*. Then from (4) it is clear that only $x(t) = 0$ is required to achieve $X(t + 1, t) = 0$, which then determines $p(t + 1)$ [or $p(t)$].[14] In the usual static analysis the time variable t is missing, and it becomes immaterial, at least in appearance, whether $p(t + 1)$ or $p(t)$ is determined by condition $x(t) = 0$. We may simply assert that $x(t) = 0$ determines p.

---

[14] It may be more natural to say that $x(t) = 0$ determines $p(t)$ rather than $p(t + 1)$.

The crux of the initial stock equilibrium condition is that stock *equilibrium* at the beginning of the current period is regarded as a historically given fact. This is of course valid, as we shall argue later, if we consider equilibrium in the current period as just one of those in a dynamic chain consisting of the succession of the equilibria of each period and if we assume what we shall later call the "consistency condition." However, if we confine ourselves to the "static" equilibrium of one period alone, this assumption should be explicitly recognized. The failure to do so seems to be a source of some confusions in the literature, as such a failure leads to an error if the initial stock equilibrium condition is violated.

In spite of such a danger the initial stock equilibrium condition is a very convenient assumption because it validates most of the static analysis that uses only the flow equilibrium condition $x(t) = 0$ as the complete equilibrium condition. Furthermore notice that *given* the assumption $X(t) = 0$, the flow equilibrium condition $x(t) = 0$ is equivalent to the stock equilibrium condition; that is, *given* $X(t) = 0$,

$$x(t) = 0 \quad \text{if and only if} \quad X(t+1, t) = 0. \tag{16}$$

Namely, the flow equilibrium condition for period t is equivalent to the stock equilibrium condition at the beginning of $t + 1$. Although it is simple, this is a very useful result. It, among other things, gives at least a partial answer toward reconciling the obvious inconsistency in the usual IS–LM framework of macroanalysis: Equilibrium in this model is given by a *flow* equilibrium condition for the (physical) goods market and a *stock* equilibrium condition for the money market. It is not particularly clear what guarantees stock equilibrium for the goods market and flow equilibrium for the money market. Relation (16) gives an answer to this problem in a static framework. That is, given initial stock equilibrium in the goods market, the flow equilibrium condition, as represented by the IS curve, guarantees the stock equilibrium for the (physical) goods market by (16). Similarly the stock equilibrium condition, as represented by the LM curve, guarantees the flow equilibrium for money. That is, with (16), it becomes immaterial whether we describe the static equilibrium by the flow condition or by the stock condition. In using (16) however, to avoid possible confusion, it may be important to bear in mind the following two points:

(i)   It is assumed that $X(t) = 0$ holds *a priori*.
(ii)   Condition (16) does *not* say that $x(t) = 0$ if and only if $X(t) = 0$.

We may also note that a relation such as (16) is actually recognized in the literature, although there is a lack of clear understanding of the key condition, $X(t) = 0$. More specifically, *given* $X(t) = 0$, we may rewrite (4) as

$$x(t) = X(t+1, t) \tag{16'}$$

from which (16) follows immediately. Equation (16′) says that the *excess* flow demand $x(t)$ is equal to the *excess* stock demand $X(t + 1, t)$, and there is no confusion here with regard to the dimensional integrity. Note that (16′) validates the "proportionality" condition (10) that we earlier criticized. A relation such as (16′) was recognized by Patinkin (1958, see especially p. 303) and has been used by other economists. Unfortunately, few of these writers seems to be aware of the key role played by the initial stock equilibrium condition $X(t) = 0$ in obtaining (16′).

So much for the "static" or "one-period" analysis.[15] Let us now turn to "dynamics," in which we are concerned with the time path of the equilibrium price $p(t)$, which is determined by the succession of period equilibria. This does not present much of a problem in the case of a pure flow good or a pure stock good, for only one price is determined for each t. On the other hand, in the case of a stock–flow good two prices are determined for each t. During the current (the tth) market period (i.e., this Monday) both the current price $p^t(t)$ and the price of the next period (the next Monday) $p^t(t + 1)$ are determined. Here we add superscript t to signify that these equilibrium prices are determined on this Monday. When the next Monday comes, another set of equilibrium prices, $p^{t+1}(t + 1)$ and $p^{t+1}(t + 2)$, is determined. The distinction between $p^t(t + 1)$ and $p^{t+1}(t + 1)$ corresponds to that between $X(t + 1, t) = 0$ and $X(t + 1) = 0$. Note that $p^{t+1}(t + 1)$ can be different from $p^t(t + 1)$. This is because when the next Monday comes, economic conditions can be different from those that prevail on this Monday, and also because expectations may be revised.[16] Hence the sequence of equilibrium prices may be described as

$$p^t(t), \quad p^t(t + 1)$$
$$p^{t+1}(t + 1), \quad p^{t+1}(t + 2)$$
$$p^{t+2}(t + 2), \quad p^{t+2}(t + 3).$$

[15] The phrase "one-period" analysis or even "static" analysis, although often used in the literature, may be confusing, as (8) is in essence concerned with two periods. However from the initial stock equilibrium condition $X(t) = 0$, we can focus our attention on one period [i.e., either $x(t) = 0$ or $X(t + 1, t) = 0$].

[16] Also the planned supply $s(t)$ (of, say, fish) may not be realized because of hazardous weather, etc., in which case $S(t + 1) \neq S(t + 1, t)$. Hence in such a case, even if $D(t + 1, t + 1) = D(t + 1, t), p^{t+1}(t + 1)$ will be different from $p^t(t + 1)$. On the other hand, if there is any such genuine uncertainty regarding the planned quantities for any of $s(t)$, $d(t)$, $S(t + 1, t)$, and $D(t + 1, t)$, it is likely that the contract of the tth Monday will be written in such a way as to accommodate it (with the help of other assets such as securities). We may then suppose that these planned quantities are always realized by the equilibrium prices $p^t(t)$ and $p^t(t + 1)$, which are contracted at the end of the tth Monday. In fact, this is probably the assumption implicit in most of equilibrium analysis. In this case, if $D(t + 1, t + 1) = D(t + 1, t)$ and $S(t + 1, t + 1) = S(t + 1, t)$, we will have $p^t(t + 1) = p^{t+1}(t + 1)$.

Needless to say, the difference between $p^{t+1}(t + 1)$ and $p^t(t + 1)$ generates unexpected capital gains or losses that should be incorporated into the behavioral functions. On the other hand, if the economic conditions are unchanged and if expectations are not revised, it would be reasonable to suppose $p^t(t + 1) = p^{t+1}(t + 1), \ldots$, and so on, in which case we have a succession of prices

$$p^t(t), p^{t+1}(t + 1), \ldots, \tag{17}$$

given that the equilibrium conditions are satisfied for all t. More specifically, we require

$$D(t, t - 1) = D(t, t) \quad \text{and} \quad S(t, t - 1) = S(t) \quad \text{for all} \quad t, \tag{17'}$$

so that $X(t, t - 1) = X(t)$ for all t.[17] In fact this seems to be the implicit assumption that is often used in the usual dynamic analysis in the literature. We may call condition (17′) the *consistency condition* in the sense that the present decision is "consistent" with the decision made in the previous period. In fact this condition has an important implication in the static analysis. Namely, given the consistency condition, the initial stock equilibrium condition $X(t) = 0$, which play a vital role in the static analysis, is nothing but the market equilibrium condition $X(t, t - 1) = 0$ for the previous period. Thus one may wish to emphasize the consistency condition instead of the initial stock equilibrium condition as the condition that validates the static analysis. In this case, as mentioned earlier, the static analysis is viewed as a part of the chain of the succession of temporary equilibria that constitutes dynamics.

Given (17′) for a stock-flow good (or asset), the equilibrium conditions for dynamics are described by the stock and flow equilibrium conditions, which can, respectively, be written as

$$X(t) = 0 \quad \textit{for all} \quad t \quad [\textit{or } X(t + 1) = X(t + 1, t) = 0 \quad \textit{for all } t], \tag{18}$$

---

[17] It may be useful to recall that $X(t)$ is really the shorthand notation for $X(t, t) \, [\equiv D(t, t) - S(t)]$. Hence the reader may prefer to write $X(t, t - 1) = X(t)$ as $X(t, t - 1) = X(t, t)$. Note also that by requiring (17) or (17′), we do not preclude the possibility of $p^t(t + 1) \neq p^{t+1}(t + 1)$ altogether. As mentioned earlier, such a divergence certainly occurs when there are changes in economic conditions. Another subtle question that is involved in the possible gap between $p^t(t + 1)$ and $p^{t+1}(t + 1)$ is the question of a wealth change from this Monday to the next Monday. For example, if the government increases the (outside) money supply by printing it and transferring it to the public on this Monday, the public's wealth position increases. The question that arises is whether such a governmental action increases the public's wealth position as of this Monday or as of the next Monday. Many economists interpret it to be this Monday, whereas some recent writers seem to insist that it is next Monday. Although we shall interpret it to be an increase on this Monday, such an interpretation may involve a subtle and difficult problem (cf. Turnovsky, 1977).

and as

$$x(t) = 0 \quad \text{for all} \quad t. \tag{19}$$

In the *static* analysis both $X(t + 1, t) = 0$ and $x(t) = 0$ in (8) are required only for *some* t (say the "current" period), while in the *dynamic* analysis $X(t) = 0$ and $x(t) = 0$ are required for *all* t. On the other hand, since (4) holds for all t, it is evident that (18) implies (19). That is, stock equilibrium over time *automatically* implies flow equilibrium over time. Moreover, assuming $X(0) = 0$, Eq. (19) for all $t = 0, 1, 2, \ldots$ implies (18) for all $t = 1, 2, \ldots$. In other words stock and flow equilibria are *not* independent in dynamic analysis.[18] This is the central result in dynamics, which may be summarized as

$$x(t) = 0, \quad t = 0, 1, 2, \ldots, \quad \text{if and only if} \quad X(t) = 0, \quad t = 1, 2, \ldots, \tag{20}$$

given $X(0) = 0$ and the consistency condition $X(t + 1) = X(t + 1, t)$ for all t. Note that (20) can thus also be rewritten as

$$x(t) = 0, \quad t = 0, 1, 2, \ldots, \quad \text{if and only if} \quad X(t + 1, t) = 0, \quad t = 0, 1, 2, \ldots . \tag{21}$$

Allowing time to vary, either *one* of the two conditions, (18) or (19), can be used to determine the time path of $p(t)$ or $\pi(t)$. Notice that the time path of $\pi(t)$, $t = 0, 1, 2, \ldots$ is determined once the time path of $p(t)$, $t = 0, 1, 2, \ldots$ is determined. Conversely, the time path of $p(t)$, $t = 1, 2, \ldots$, is determined once the time path of $\pi(t)$, $t = 0, 1, 2, \ldots$, is determined, where $p(0)$ is properly chosen so as to satisfy $X(0) = 0$. Hence it is rather immaterial whether we say that the time path of $p(t)$ or that of $\pi(t)$ is determined by the system.

We may briefly remark here on the distinction between the discrete time model and the continuous time analog. The most natural interpretation of the latter may be to view it as the case in which the Hicksian "week" is shrunk to a point in time. In such a case there should be no crucial distinction between the two types of models, contrary to the writings of some economists. We believe that if the models are to describe the same economy, basically the same results should be obtained regardless of whether we use the discrete time formulation or the continuous time analog. Analytically, the continuous time analog can be obtained by choosing the unit of period to be h (instead of unity) and letting $h \to 0$. Thus we first rewrite (4) as

$$X(t + h) - X(t) = \int_t^{t+h} x(\tau)d\tau, \tag{4*}$$

---

[18] The IS–LM model of the usual macroanalysis may be considered as one piece of the dynamic chain of equilibria. Then, by the interdependence of (18) and (19), the flow IS condition and the stock LM condition, respectively, also guarantee, under the *dynamic* context, the stock equilibrium for goods and the flow equilibrium for money.

by using the consistency condition $X(t + h) = X(t + h, t)$, where $x(\tau)$ here signifies the *rate* of the flow excess demand at time τ. Then dividing (4*) by h and letting $h \to 0$, we obtain $\dot{X}(t) = x(t)$, where the dot signifies the time derivative. From this the continuous time analog of (20) follows trivially; i.e.,

$$x(t) = 0 \quad \text{for all} \quad t \quad \text{if and only if} \quad \dot{X}(t) = 0 \quad \text{for all} \quad t. \quad (20^*)$$

Either of $x(t) = 0$ or $\dot{X}(t) = 0$ determines the time path of $p(t)$ or $\pi(t)$. Aside from the integration constant, $p(t)$ is determined if and only if $\pi(t)$ is determined. With this remark we now return to the original discrete time formulation.

So far we have confined our attention to the determination of the static and dynamic equilibrium of an isolated market for *one* good or asset. We now turn our attention to the general equilibrium of *multi*good or asset economies. That is, when there are n goods or assets, how are the prices of these n goods determined? Given that one good (say, money) is used as the numéraire, how can the prices of $(n - 1)$ goods be determined? Using the usual IS–LM framework of macroanalysis, we may pose the same question in a slightly different manner. Given the stock and the flow equilibrium of the goods and money markets in the IS–LM relations, what guarantees the flow equilibrium and the stock equilibrium of the securities (or bonds) market?

The answer to the above question obviously lies in the "Walras law." Given the Walras law, one of the n equations becomes superfluous and can thus be deleted from the system that defines the equilibrium. However the literature often recognizes only one "Walras law," and fails to realize that there are *two* Walras laws. In the IS–LM framework, for example, the literature often fails to answer (or is ambiguous regarding) how the two equilibrium conditions (stock and flow) for securities can be guaranteed by one Walras law. Thus Lloyd (1960), for example, ends up with a solution to the problem by constructing a highly fictitious economy in which the excess flow demand function for money is equivalent to the excess flow demand function for bonds. However, if we realize that there are two Walras laws, it is easy to see that such an artificial solution is unnecessary as well as implausible.

To ease our exposition, let us suppose that there are no pure flow goods and no pure stock goods; i.e., the only goods or assets in the economy are of the stock–flow variety.[19] Let $x_i(t)$ be the (market) flow excess demand for the ith good or asset $(i = 1, 2, \ldots, n)$, and let $X_i(t)$ and $X_i(t + 1, t)$ be the

---

[19] The introduction of pure flow goods and pure stock goods does not alter our discussion in any essential way.

corresponding stock excess demand for i. Let $p_i(t)$ be the price associated with $x_i(t) = 0$. We can then obtain the following two identities:

$$\sum_{i=1}^{n} p_i(t)x_i(t) \equiv 0 \qquad \text{for all} \quad t, \tag{22}$$

$$\sum_{i=1}^{n} p_i(t)X_i(t+1,t) \equiv 0 \qquad \text{for all} \quad t. \tag{23}$$

We may call condition (22) the *flow Walras law* and (23) the *stock Walras law*. Note that given (22), (23) holds if and only if $\sum_{i=1}^{n} p_i(t)X_i(t) \equiv 0$ by virtue of (4). Furthermore, if we assume the initial stock equilibrium condition $X_i(t) = 0$ (for all i) *a priori* in the case of statics, the two Walras laws become identical; i.e., they are not independent under such an assumption. The flow Walras law is obtained by aggregating the *budget identities* of all the agents (the consumers, producers, commercial banks, central government, etc.) in the economy, while the stock Walras law is obtained by aggregating the *balance sheet identities* of these agents.

With the two Walras identities two equations become superfluous. More precisely, we have to again consider the two cases, statics and dynamics. In the static case we require, for a given t, the following two sets of equilibrium conditions:

$$x_i(t) = 0, \qquad i = 1, 2, \ldots, n; \qquad X_i(t+1,t) = 0, \qquad i = 1, 2, \ldots, n, \tag{24}$$

which then determine

$$p_i(t), \qquad i = 1, 2, \ldots, n \qquad \text{and} \qquad \pi_i(t), \qquad i = 1, 2, \ldots, n.$$

By the two Walras laws (22) and (23), only $(2n - 2)$ conditions of (24) are independent. That is, one flow and one stock equilibrium condition is redundant. Let the nth good or asset be chosen as the numéraire, so that $p_n(t) = 1$ for all t.[20] Then $\pi_n(t) = 0$. Therefore these $(2n - 2)$ independent conditions determine the equilibrium values of the $(2n - 2)$ variables[21]:

$$p_i(t), \qquad i = 1, 2, \ldots, n - 1 \qquad \text{and} \qquad \pi_i(t), \qquad i = 1, 2, \ldots, n - 1.$$

In the case of dynamics the situation is different due to the dependence of stock and flow equilibria. Since for each i we have (20) [or (21)], it becomes

---

[20] Usually, "money" is chosen to be the numéraire; i.e., the p_i's in (22) and (23) refer to prices expressed in terms of the monetary unit. However, in stating (22) and (23) and deriving the subsequent conclusions, the choice of the numéraire can clearly be arbitrary. In the discussion of the macroframework, we choose the current ("aggregate") output as the numéraire, so that, for example, (22) and (23) are obtained in terms of "real" units, i.e., in terms of current output.

[21] Under the initial stock equilibrium assumption, $X_i(t) = 0$ for all i is assumed *a priori*. Then $x_i(t) = 0, i = 1, 2, \ldots, n - 1$, determine the equilibrium values of $p_1, \ldots, p_{n-1}$.

immaterial in dynamics whether we use $x_i(t) = 0$ or $X_i(t) = 0$ [or $X_i(t + 1, t) = 0$]. Hence in this case, given $X(0) = 0$, the $(n - 1)$ independent conditions in

$$x_i(t) = 0, \qquad i = 1, 2, \ldots, n \quad \text{for all } t, \tag{25}$$

or in

$$X_i(t) = 0, \qquad i = 1, 2, \ldots, n \quad \text{for all } t, \tag{26}$$

then determine the equilibrium values of

$$p_i(t), \qquad i = 1, 2, \ldots, n - 1 \quad \text{for all } t,$$

where the nth good is taken to be the numéraire and the consistency condition (17') is assumed.

II. THE FRAMEWORK OF MACROEQUILIBRIUM

In this section we illustrate the general framework discussed in the previous section in terms of a specific macromodel. To ease our exposition, we consider a simple macromodel consisting of the public (households and firms) and the government with three assets in the economy: (outside) money, securities (bonds), and physical assets ("equities"). International transactions are assumed away. Although this model is very simple, it is more or less a standard one. The banking sector (commercial banks and the central bank) and the endogenous aspect of the money supply can be introduced easily.[22] But the approach would be analogous and the essence of our discussion would not be altered, and hence we omit these features.

We assume that all three assets are stock–flow goods. The securities consist of both private and government bonds, which are assumed to be indistinguishable in all respects, such as the rate of return, risk, etc. The price of current output is assumed to be equal to the price of the existing physical assets; i.e., "Tobin's q" (cf. Tobin, 1969) is assumed to be unity. This is again done to ease the exposition, and the introduction of Tobin's q as a variable would not alter the essence of our discussion.

Following Tobin (1969), we summarize the symbols used and the balance sheets of the public and the government in Table 1, where the entries are measured in real units, that is, in terms of the current output. A negative entry represents a liability. The balance sheet of each sector recorded in Table 1 describes the *desired* portfolio of each sector at the end of the current

---

[22.] For a discussion of the endogenous supply of money with an explicit treatment of the banking sector, see Takayama and Drabicki (1976). Modigliani (1963) considers the banking sector explicitly but ignores the endogenous aspect of the money supply.

TABLE 1   *The Summary of the Balance Sheets*

Assets ╲ Sector	Public	Government	Exogenous supply
Money	L	$-M$	0
Bonds	B	$-B^g$	0
Equities	V	0	K
Net worth	A	$-(M + B^g)$	K

(or the tth) period. The government is a net debtor, where its debt is equal to $M + B^g$.

In order to make the meaning of the desired portfolio at the end of the tth period clear, it will be convenient to add the time subscript. Thus the public's balance sheet identity is written as

$$L_{t+1} + B_{t+1} + V_{t+1} \equiv A_{t+1}, \qquad (27)$$

where $L_{t+1} \equiv L(t + 1, t)$, for example, in terms of the notation of the previous section. When lending and borrowing among households and firms cancels out, B_{t+1} signifies the *net* excess demand for government bonds (the stock of government bonds that the public desires to carry over to the $(t + 1)$th period). Also, M, B^g, and K in Table 1 can be written, respectively, as M_{t+1}, B^g_{t+1}, and K_{t+1}, which signify the stock supplies of these variables to be achieved by the end of the tth period; i.e., these correspond to $S(t + 1, t)$ in the previous section. Note that $K_{t+1} \equiv \bar{K}_t + \Delta K_t$ and $\bar{K}_t [\equiv K(t, t) \equiv K(t)]$ is equal to the physical stock of capital inherited from the previous period ("exogenous supply"), where ΔK_t is the planned increase in K (netting out depreciation). Namely, the K in Table 1 is, strictly speaking, *not* totally "exogenous."

The stock equilibrium condition, $X(t + 1, t) = 0$, of each asset is obtained by setting the sum of the respective rows, i.e., the sum over the two sectors, equal to the item in the last column; i.e.,

$$L_{t+1} = M_{t+1}, \qquad B_{t+1} = B^g_{t+1}, \qquad V_{t+1} = K_{t+1}. \qquad (28)$$

The sum of the column for a particular sector represents the net worth of the sector. Since the sum of the final column must be equal to the sum of the net worth of the two sectors, for the sake of consistency in the economic system, we have (cf. Modigliani, 1963, p. 80, Eq. (iv), and also Tobin, 1969):

$$A_{t+1} \equiv M_{t+1} + B^g_{t+1} + K_{t+1}. \qquad (29)$$

Combining (27) and (29), we obtain the following fundamental identity

$$(L_{t+1} - M_{t+1}) + (B_{t+1} - B^g_{t+1}) + (V_{t+1} - K_{t+1}) \equiv 0. \qquad (30)$$

I.e., the sum of the stock excess demands is identically equal to zero. (30) is the *stock Walras law*. By virtue of this, one of the three stock equilibrium conditions in (28) is superfluous; i.e., there are two independent stock equilibrium conditions in (28).

We now turn to the *flow* conditions. Here the budget condition of each sector plays the central role. Assume that the government makes expenditures G, pays interest on the national debt, collects taxes net of transfer payments in the amount of T, and pays wages to its employees α, where G, T, and α are all measured in real units. Then the budget condition of the government for period t can be written as

$$G_t + r_t B^g_{t+1} + r^M_t M_{t+1} + \alpha_t \equiv T_t + \Delta M_t + \Delta B^g_t \qquad (31)$$

where r and r^M, respectively, denote the *real* rates of return on securities and money. The terms ΔM and ΔB^g, respectively, denote the planned changes (i.e., the *flow supplies*) in money and government securities. These correspond to $s(t)$ in the previous section. The right-hand side of (31) signifies three ways to "finance" the total government spending. To finance spending, the government sells new bonds and issues new money during the trading period ("Monday"), as well as levies taxes. Thus in terms of the notation of the previous section, we have, for example, $B^g_{t+1} \equiv B^g(t+1, t) \equiv B^g(t, t)$ and $B^g(t, t) \equiv \bar{B}^g_t + \Delta B^g_t$, where $\bar{B}^g_t$ signifies the total amount of government bonds outstanding at the beginning of the period (i.e., on the Monday morning of the tth week). Here it is assumed that all financial transaction are carried out on Monday, so that, for example, the government's interest payment on securities are made with respect to B^g_{t+1} and not to $\bar{B}^g_t$.[23] Note also that $\Delta B^g_t \equiv B^g_{t+1} - \bar{B}^g_t$, and similarly $\Delta M_t \equiv M_{t+1} - \bar{M}_t$ where $M_{t+1} \equiv M(t+1, t)$ and $\bar{M}_t$ is the money stock at the beginning of the tth period.

The public produces real output that is equal to Y and makes expenditures on consumption C and investment I. The quantities C and I are measured in real units. Then the public's budget condition for period t can be written as

$$C_t + T_t + \Delta L_t + \Delta B_t + I_t \equiv Y_t + \alpha_t + r_t B^g_{t+1} + r^M_t M_{t+1}, \qquad (32)$$

where ΔL_t and ΔB_t, respectively, denote the (public's) flow demand for money and government bonds.

[23.] It is often argued that the interest payment should be specified by $r_t \bar{B}^g_t$ (cf. footnote 17). In this case we will have a rather peculiar situation in that the current interest rate r_t, which is to be determined by the current market equilibrium conditions, applies to the debt outstanding at the beginning of the period (i.e., the one inherited from the previous period) $\bar{B}^g_t$ and not to the debt to be floated for the current period (which presumably determines r_t).

Consolidating the two budget conditions (31) and (32), we obtain

$$(\Delta L_t - \Delta M_t) + (\Delta B_t - \Delta B_t^g) + (C_t + I_t + G_t - Y_t) \equiv 0. \qquad (33)$$

Namely, the sum of the flow excess demands is identically equal to zero. (33) is the *flow Walras law* of the present system.[24] The flow equilibrium conditions of the three assets are now written as

$$\Delta M_t = \Delta L_t, \qquad \Delta B_t^g = \Delta B_t, \qquad Y_t = C_t + I_t + G_t. \qquad (34)$$

In view of the flow Walras law one of the three conditions in (34) is superfluous: i.e., there are only two independent flow equilibrium conditions. Note that in terms of the continuous time version (33) can be written as

$$(\dot{L}_t - \dot{M}_t) + (\dot{B}_t - \dot{B}_t^g) + (C_t + I_t + G_t - Y_t) \equiv 0, \qquad (33^*)$$

using the procedure outlined in connection with (4*).

As we argued in the previous section, the full description of a complete model crucially depends on whether we are interested in 'statics" or "dynamics." In the static case, where we are concerned with the single period t, two conditions for equilibrium are required, one for flows and the other for stocks [i.e., (8)] for each good or asset. In this case all of the equilibrium conditions in (28) and (34) become relevant. By the flow Walras law only two conditions in (34) are independent, and by the stock Walras law only two conditions in (28) are relevant. Therefore there are altogether four relevant equilibrium conditions. To answer what these conditions determine, let p and q, respectively, signify the money prices of the current output and bonds. Then, under full employment, the four independent equilibrium conditions in (28) and (34) determine the equilibrium values of the four variables,

$$p(t), \qquad q(t), \qquad p(t + 1), \qquad \text{and} \qquad q(t + 1).$$

[24.] The procedure of obtaining the flow identity by consolidating the budget conditions of various economic agents is due to Walras (1926), of course. Hicks (1946) utilized such a procedure to obtain his reconciliation between the loanable funds theory and the liquidity preference theory (cf. Section III below). Recently, various writers have aptly emphasized the importance of the explicit recognition of the government budget condition to obtain the flow identity (e.g., Turnovsky, 1977). Enthoven, in his work of 1960, obtained the flow identity with the explicit recognition of the government budget condition. Incidentally, we should emphasize that the flow identity is obtained by *consolidating* or aggregating (rather than by summing) the budget conditions of each economic agent. This is the reason, for example, why interest income and payments are canceled out in the aggregate. One may prefer the use of $r_t B_{t+1}$ instead of $r_t B_t^g{}_{+1}$ in the right-hand side of (32). However, since these cancel out in aggregation, it is immaterial which notation we use. On the other hand, one should realize this does not imply $B_{t+1} \equiv B_{t+1}^g$. Cancellation of interest income and payments occurs as a result of preserving the consistency of the system in the aggregate and is *not* the consequence of $B_{t+1} \equiv B_{t+1}^g$.

If the bonds are all in the form of consols, one unit of which pays a dollars every period, then the interest rate $i(t)$ is determined by $q(t) = a/i(t)$ and the nominal rate of return on consols is equal to $[a + \{q(t+1) - q(t)\}]/q(t) = [i(t) + \{q(t+1) - q(t)\}/q(t)]$. Hence, we may also say that the above four equilibrium conditions determine the equilibrium values of the four variables[25]

$$p(t), \qquad i(t), \qquad p(t+1), \qquad \text{and} \qquad i(t+1).$$

There is, however, another important static case. This is the case in which the initial stock equilibrium assumption is imposed. To see this, we first observe[26]

$$\{L_{t+1} - L(t,t)\} - (M_{t+1} - \bar{M}_t) \equiv \Delta L_t - \Delta M_t,$$
$$\{B_{t+1} - B(t)\} - (B^g_{t+1} - \bar{B}^g_t) \equiv \Delta B_t - \Delta B^g_t, \qquad (35)$$
$$\{V_{t+1} - V(t,t)\} - (K_{t+1} - \bar{K}_t) \equiv (C_t + I_t + G_t) - Y_t,$$

by virtue of (1′), (2′), and (4). In the present context, we may write the *initial stock equilibrium condition* as

$$L(t,t) = \bar{M}_t, B(t) = \bar{B}^g_t, V(t,t) = \bar{K}_t, \qquad (36)$$

where $\bar{M}_t \equiv M(t)$, $\bar{B}^g_t \equiv B^g(t)$, and $\bar{K}_t \equiv K(t) [\equiv K(t,t)]$, respectively, signify the initial stocks of money, government bonds, and physical assets. Imposing (36) on (35) we at once obtain

$$L_{t+1} = M_{t+1} \qquad \text{if and only if} \quad \Delta L_t = \Delta M_t, \qquad (37a)$$

$$B_{t+1} = B^g_{t+1} \qquad \text{if and only if} \quad \Delta B_t = \Delta B^g_t, \qquad (37b)$$

$$V_{t+1} = K_{t+1} \qquad \text{if and only if} \quad Y_t = C_t + I_t + G_t. \qquad (37c)$$

Note also that under condition (36), the two Walras laws (30) and (33) are not independent: They become identical. More importantly, given (36), we

---

[25] It is possible that the securities are all in the form of bonds with a fixed nominal value (such as one dollar per unit of securities) and with a variable interest rate [e.g., Modigliani (1963) and Foley and Sidrauski (1971)]. Then $q(t) \equiv q(t+1) \equiv 1$. However, our system still determines the equilibrium values of $p(t)$, $i(t)$, $p(t+1)$, and $i(t+1)$.

[26] Here $B(t)$ corresponds to $X(t) \equiv D(t,t) - S(t)$ in the previous section [cf. (3)]. Since the demand and supply of private bonds cancel out in aggregation, $B(t)$ signifies the *excess* demand for government bonds by the public (households and firms). [Hence if government bonds are assumed away, as in some works in the literature, $B(t) = 0$ signifies the initial stock equilibrium condition for bonds.] To obtain the third identity of (35), simply note that $[V_{t+1} - V(t,t)] - (K_{t+1} - \bar{K}_t) \equiv (V_{t+1} - K_{t+1}) - [V(t,t) - \bar{K}_t]$, which in turn is equal to $(C_t + I_t + G_t - Y_t)$ by virtue of (4); i.e., $X(t+1,t) - X(t) \equiv x(t)$. Alternatively, simply observe $K_{t+1} - K_t \equiv Y_t - C_t - G_t$ and $V_{t+1} - V(t,t) \equiv I_t$ [cf. Eqs. (1) and (2)].

may choose either (28) or (34) as the equilibrium conditions. Thus for example, if we choose (28), (34) is automatically guaranteed [given (36)]. Furthermore, since only two of the three equations in (28) are independent, the equilibrium can be described in one of the following conditions:

$$Y_t = C_t + I_t + G_t \quad \text{and} \quad \Delta L_t = \Delta M_t, \tag{38a}$$

$$Y_t = C_t + I_t + G_t \quad \text{and} \quad \Delta B_t = \Delta B_t^g, \tag{38b}$$

$$\Delta L_t = \Delta M_t \quad \text{and} \quad \Delta B_t = \Delta B_t^g. \tag{38c}$$

The two equations in any one of (38a)–(38c) determine the equilibrium value of price (p) and interest rate (i) [or p and q]. The determination of equilibrium (38b) is the familiar *loanable funds theory*, as $\Delta B_t = \Delta B_t^g$ states the demand equals supply condition for the flow of loanable funds. Also by virtue of (37a), we may rewrite (38a) as

$$Y_t = C_t + I_t + G_t, L_{t+1} = M_{t+1}. \tag{39}$$

The determination of equilibrium by (39) is the Keyneisan *liquidity preference theory*. Condition (39) obviously corresponds to the familiar IS–LM relations.

We now turn to the case of dynamics, which considers the chain of "static" equilibria. As argued in the previous section, the flow equilibrium condition for each asset can be replaced by its stock equilibrium condition, and vice versa. Namely,

$$L_{t+1} = M_{t+1}, t = 0, 1, 2, \ldots, \Leftrightarrow \Delta L_t = \Delta M_t, \qquad t = 0, 1, 2, \ldots, \tag{40a}$$

$$B_{t+1} = B_{t+1}^g, \ t = 0, 1, 2, \ldots, \Leftrightarrow \Delta B_t = \Delta B_t^g, \qquad t = 0, 1, 2, \ldots, \tag{40b}$$

$$V_{t+1} = K_{t+1}, \ t = 0, 1, 2, \ldots, \Leftrightarrow Y_t = C_t + I_t + G_t, \quad t = 0, 1, 2, \ldots. \tag{40c}$$

The left-hand side of (40) gives the three stock equilibrium conditions and the right-hand side of (40) gives the three flow equilibrium conditions. By the stock Walras law (30) one of the three stock equilibrium conditions is superfluous, while by the flow Walras law (33) one of the three flow equilibrium conditions is superfluous. We may then delete the flow and the stock equilibrium conditions for securities. This, in turn, enables us to concentrate on money and (physical) goods. By (40) it is immaterial for each asset whether we choose the stock equilibrium condition or the flow equilibrium condition. Hence we may choose the stock equilibrium condition for money and the flow equilibrium condition for goods [as we did in obtaining (39)]. That is, the following set of equations guarantees the dynamic equilibrium of the macroeconomy:

$$Y_t = C_t + I_t + G_t \quad \text{and} \quad L_{t+1} = M_{t+1}, \quad t = 0, 1, 2, \ldots, \tag{41}$$

which then determines the time path of the prices of goods and securities; that is,

$$p(t), \qquad q(t), \qquad t = 0, 1, 2, \ldots,$$

or the time path of the price of goods and the rate of interest

$$p(t), \qquad i(t), \qquad t = 0, 1, 2, \ldots.$$

Throughout the above discussion the households and the firms have been integrated into one sector, the public. However it is sometimes useful and important to decompose the public into the two sectors and explicitly consider the repercussions between the households and the firms. Without going into detail the merit of such decomposition is clear.[27] Since the household sector is the source of labor supply and the firms are the primary source of the demand for labor, disaggregation of the public will more adequately illuminate the equilibrium of the labor market. Another important consequence of this disaggregation is that it clarifies the link between saving and investment through securities, as the household sector, by its saving, supplies the investment funds to the firms through purchase of securities. On the other hand, the case in which the public is disaggregated into the households and the firms is discussed in a manner strictly analogous to the above. Hence such a discussion is left to the interested reader.

III. A HISTORICAL NOTE

Historically, the problem of stocks and flows came into prominence in the midst of the well-known controversy between the liquidity preference and loanable funds theories of interest. The controversy arose when the classical doctrine of the rate of interest being determined by the supply and demand of loanable funds (a *flow* theory) was challenged by the Keynesian belief that the rate of interest was determined by liquidity preference (a *stock* theory). Using the (flow) Walras law, Hicks, in his *Value and Capital* (Chap. XII), demonstrated that these two theories are equivalent in the sense that regardless of whether the bond market or the money market equilibrium condition is deleted, the equilibrium rate of interest is the same. In this demonstration, the theory that eliminated the bond market equation was called a "liquidity preference theory" and the theory that chose to eliminate

---

[27] Macroeconomic analysis is based on highly aggregated models. The level of aggregation, however, although it is very similar, differs between authors. It is possible that more disaggregated models provide more information and that the conclusion of a particular model depends on the level of aggregation.

the money market equation was termed a "loanable funds theory."[28] It has
been pointed out, however, that this demonstration used the concepts of
the demand and supply of money in the flow sense (e.g., Tsiang, 1956, see
especially p. 542), whereas in the Keynesian theory of liquidity preference,
the demand and supply of money are used in the sense of stocks. In other
words, the crux of the Hicks reconciliation is based on the Walras law in
flow form; i.e., it is based on

$$\sum_{i=1}^{n} p_i x_i(t) \equiv 0. \tag{22}$$

Then letting the $(n-1)$th and the nth good (asset) be "securities" and
"money," respectively, the Hicks reconciliation amounts to saying that if we
delete $x_n(t) = 0$, in view of (22) we have the loanable funds theory in which
the equilibrium condition for securities $x_{n-1}(t) = 0$ is used as one of the
independent conditions to define the equilibrium system. On the other
hand, if we delete $x_{n-1}(t) = 0$, then we have the liquidity preference theory
in which the monetary equilibrium condition $x_n(t) = 0$ is used as one of the
independent equilibrium conditions. Although this attempt by Hicks rightly
directs the debate to the general equilibrium framework, it has invited the
above-mentioned criticism that the Keynesian liquidity preference theory
is a stock theory. That is, the liquidity preference theory should be represented by the stock equilibrium condition.

In 1949, not long after Hicks' reconciliation, there was an interesting
debate that had its origins in the Fellner and Somers article in 1941. The
gist of the Fellner–Somers argument was based on the observation (which
may have been influenced by Hicks) that the "demand for money during
the period" is facilitated from the "sale of goods, sale of securities, and
keeping money already held," while "the supply of money during a period
derives partly from the demand for goods, partly from the demand for
securities, and partly from the willingness to keep money already held"
(Fellner–Somers, 1949, p. 145). To interpret Fellner–Somers, write $\Delta B_t \equiv$
$\Delta B_t^d - \Delta B_t^s$, where ΔB_t^d and ΔB_t^s, respectively, denote the flow demand for
and the flow supply of securities (bonds), so that ΔB_t denotes the (net) excess
flow demand for securities. Then, ignoring government bonds as well as
government expenditures, taxes, and transfer payments, we may roughly

---

[28] In fact the classification of theories of interest on the basis of which equilibrium condition
is ignored is, strictly speaking, rather meaningless, for the interest rate like any other price
variable is determined by not only one but by the full set of equilibrium conditions. This seems
to be the source of the "peanuts theory," often attributed to Lerner, which more or less ridicules
this point by asking what theory of interest we obtain if the equilibrium condition of peanuts
is deleted. Obviously Hicks would have been the last person who would have confused such
points.

interpret the above remarks by Fellner and Somers to mean

$$L_{t+1} \equiv Y_t + \Delta B_t^s + \bar{M}_t, \tag{42a}$$

$$M_{t+1} \equiv E_t + \Delta B_t^d + \bar{M}_t, \tag{42b}$$

where E_t denotes the public's demand for the current output, and $\bar{M}_t$ denotes the actual stock of money at the beginning of the period. Then from (42) we can obtain[29]

$$L_{t+1} - M_{t+1} \equiv (Y_t - E_t) - \Delta B_t. \tag{43}$$

Thus if (flow) equilibrium in the goods market, $Y_t = E_t$, is assumed, we obtain

$$L_{t+1} = M_{t+1} \quad \text{if and only if} \quad \Delta B_t = 0. \tag{44}$$

That is, stock equilibrium for money holds (liquidity preference theory) if and only if flow equilibrium for securities holds (loanable funds theory), which constitutes the Fellner–Somers reconciliation of the two theories of the rate of interest.

The Fellner–Somers reconciliation led to a well-known debate[30] when Klein (1950a) argued that they had incorrectly formulated the loanable funds theory as a stock (as opposed to a flow) equilibrium of securities. Much of this misunderstanding may be attributed to the failure of Fellner and Somers to explicitly formalize their argument. However, in responding to Klein's charges, Fellner and Somers (1950a) explicitly state that "in considering stocks at the end of any period t, we assumed ... that equilibrium was established at the beginning of period t, i.e., the end of period $t - 1$" (p. 242). Thus, they argue, "the relation between the demand and supply of the stock of securities in period t is equivalent to the relation between the respective flows during the period" (p. 243). In essence, Fellner and Somers clearly realize that their entire analysis presupposes the initial stock equilibrium condition

$$L(t, t) = \bar{M}_t \quad \text{and} \quad B(t) = 0, \tag{45}$$

in view of which they argue

$$L_{t+1} = M_{t+1} \quad \text{if and only if} \quad \Delta L_t = \Delta M_t, \tag{46a}$$

$$B_{t+1} = 0 \quad \text{if and only if} \quad \Delta B_t = 0, \tag{46b}$$

---

[29] Here we ignore government bonds. The discussion follows, with suitable modifications of (42), when government bonds are introduced. The reader should easily be able to modify our exposition of the Fellner–Somers argument accordingly for such a case. In this case simply replace ΔB_t^s in (42a) by ($\Delta B_t^s + \Delta B_t^g$), and ΔB_t in the relevant subsequent equations, such as (43), by ($\Delta B_t - \Delta B^g$).

[30] See, for example, Fellner and Somers (1941, 1949, 1950a,b), Klein (1950a,b), Brunner (1950), and Patinkin (1958).

which is certainly correct as we observed earlier in (37). Thus it appears that Fellner and Somers had a clear understanding of the dependence between stock and flow equilibrium given the initial stock equilibrium condition, which is in turn based on what we called the "consistency condition" in Section I.

Note that given (45), condition (43) may be rewritten as

$$\Delta L_t - \Delta M_t = (Y_t - E_t) - \Delta B_t. \tag{43'}$$

This is a special case of our flow Walras law (33) for the case in which government bonds are assumed away. From this we may interpret the Fellner–Somers method, in obtaining the reconciliation (44), is to derive the flow Walras law, impose the initial stock equilibrium condition (45), and then obtain (43), from which (44) follows. We believe that there is nothing wrong in this. In fact, it was indeed ingenious to obtain this reconciliation at such an early date. However, it is unfortunate that they did not emphasize the importance of the initial stock equilibrium condition and that they obtained the flow Walras law in a somewhat *ad hoc* manner from (42) (instead of in the more transparent and systematic way of aggregating the budget conditions). On the other hand, their derivation of (43) from (42) is useful as it offers an insightful economic interpretation of the flow Walras law for the simplified economy.

It is clear that in the discussion above that the flow Walras law plays a key role. In fact this is the case in many discussions concerning the loanable funds theory and the liquidity preference theory. For example, letting $E_t \equiv C_t + I_t$ (consumption plus investment) and assuming away government bonds as well as government expenditures, taxes, and transfer payments, we may rewrite (33) as

$$\Delta B_t \equiv [(Y_t - C_t) + \Delta M_t] - [I_t + \Delta L_t]. \tag{33'}$$

Hence flow equilibrium for securities $\Delta B_t = 0$ holds if and only if

$$I_t + \Delta L_t = (Y_t - C_t) + \Delta M_t, \tag{47}$$

Equation (47) is, for example, used by Ohlin (1937) and Lerner (1938) as the key equation of the loanable funds theory, signifying the demand equal to supply equilibrium of loanable funds where government expenditures and taxes are assumed away.[31]

More recently Akerlof (1973) obtained a condition similar to (47), except that he explicitly introduced government expenditures, taxes, and govern-

---

[31] Incidentally, Lerner's theory (1938) seems to be muddled by his apparent belief that saving is identically equal to investment.

ment bonds. To this end, he first explicitly assumes that the public's savings are used solely for increasing its holdings of securities and that the excess supply of money $M_{t+1} - L_{t+1}$ is immediately channeled into demand for securities (so that none of it goes to the purchase of physical goods). Then the total flow demand for securities is equal to saving ($= Y_t - C_t - T_t$) plus the "portfolio shift," $M_{t+1} - L_{t+1}$.

Second, Akerlof assumes that the firms' investment is financed exclusively through the issue of securities, and that the entire government budget deficit is financed by printing securities. Thus the flow supply of securities consists of the firms' supply of securities I_t and the government's supply of securities $G_t - T_t$. Akerlof thus states the flow equilibrium condition for securities as (1973, p. 117)

$$(Y_t - C_t - T_t) + (M_{t+1} - L_{t+1}) = I_t + (G_t - T_t). \tag{48}$$

This is the same as (47) except for the inclusion of government expenditures and taxes.

We may relate Akerlof's (48) to our flow Walras law (33). For this, simply note that given Akerlof's assumptions, (33) holds for the Akerlof economy. Rewrite (33) as

$$[(Y_t - C_t - T_t) + (\Delta M_t - \Delta L_t)] - [I_t + (G_t - T_t)] \equiv \Delta B_t - \Delta B_t^g. \tag{33''}$$

Assuming the initial stock equilibrium condition for money $[L(t, t) = \bar{M}_t]$, we may conclude that flow equilibrium for securities ($\Delta B_t = \Delta B_t^g$) holds if and only if (48) holds. Thus Akerlof's discussion may, in a sense, be viewed as providing an insightful economic interpretation of the flow Walras law (33). On the other hand, we should point out that some of his detailed assumptions are unnecessary and that he also missed some key assumptions.

No discussion of stocks and flows and the macro framework can be complete without referring to the important discussion by Patinkin. Although Patinkin's argument on this topic is quite diversified, here we shall mainly consider his discussion that appears in his monumental book (1965), which is probably the more or less definitive message that he wishes to convey. In a nutshell, Patinkin assumes (like us) that all money is outside money that is constant *and* that bonds are issued only by firms and demanded by households (i.e., no government bonds).[32]

Given these assumptions, Patinkin states his "Walras law" as (1965, p. 227)

$$M - L \equiv [(C + I + G) - Y] + B. \tag{49}$$

---

[32] In (1965) he later introduces government bonds (p. 288) and the banking sector (p. 295). The change in the money supply is also discussed. These complications do not change the essence of the present discussion.

Although he does not clearly specify how this is obtained, the source of (49) seems to be his "budget restraint for the economy as a whole" specified as (1965, footnote 17, p. 224)[33]:

$$L_{t+1} \equiv M_t + (Y_t - E_t) - \Delta B_t, \tag{50}$$

where $E_t \equiv C_t + I_t + G_t$. Here it is assumed that there is no change in the money supply. We may also note that ΔB_t here refers to the flow excess demand for bonds by the public, which is equal to the net flow demand by the households minus the flow excess supply by the firms. Since the government does not issue any bonds, the flow equilibrium condition requires $\Delta B_t = 0$.

Although (50) appears to be intuitively obvious, the procedure used to obtain (50) is not entirely clear in Patinkin (1965). On the other hand, the basic idea of this procedure is briefly sketched elsewhere [cf., e.g., Patinkin (1958, p. 303), where he calls the budget condition the "accounting identity"]. Basically he obtains (50) by aggregating the individual's budget conditions, as we obtained our flow Walras law (33) (although his discussion is not as explicit as ours).

To relate Patinkin's Walras law to our (33), simply recall (37), which holds under the initial stock equilibrium condition (36). Then using Patinkin's assumption of no government bonds, we can at once obtain (49) from (33). Namely, Patinkin's Walras law (49) follows from our flow Walras law (33) if we assume the initial stock equilibrium condition

$$L(t, t) = \bar{M}_t \quad \text{and} \quad B(t) = 0. \tag{51}$$

With time subscripts, (49) should be written as

$$M_{t+1} - L_{t+1} \equiv (C_t + I_t + G_t) - Y_t + B_{t+1}. \tag{52}$$

Equation (50) follows immediately from (52) under the assumptions of a constant money supply and the initial stock equilibrium condition for bonds $B(t) = 0$.

In summary, we may conclude that Patinkin's contribution is that he obtains his "Walras law" by the transparent procedure of aggregating or consolidating the individual's budget conditions, as opposed to the rather ad hoc method used by Fellner–Somers and others. On the other hand, his description of the derivation of his Walras law is rather sketchy, and, above all, he has not precisely specified the role of the initial stock equilibrium

---

[33] As Patinkin explains (1965, footnote 17, p. 224), (50) states that the demand for money at the end of period t is identically equal to the sum of the amount of money at the beginning of the period and the (planned) net inflow of money from the sale of goods and securities during the period.

condition (51). While there may be other condition(s) that validate Patinkin's analysis without the initial stock equilibrium condition, we cannot find any discussions of such condition(s) in Patinkin's work.

Given the identity (52), it is clear that one of the following three equations is superfluous:

$$M_{t+1} = L_{t+1}, \quad Y_t = C_t + I_t + G_t, \quad \text{and} \quad B_{t+1} = 0. \quad (53)$$

Hence, for example, the following two equations,

$$M_{t+1} = L_{t+1} \quad \text{and} \quad Y_t = C_t + I_t + G_t, \quad (39')$$

define the complete system of equilibrium in which the price of goods and the interest rate are determined under the assumption of complete flexibility of the wage rate or of full employment. The reader should have realized that we have now interpreted Patinkin's system in terms of our earlier discussion of the static equilibrium condition under the *initial stock equilibrium assumption*, where the above (39') is nothing but our Eq. (39).

In his 1958 article Patinkin also obtained (p. 302)

$$\Delta L_t - \Delta M_t \equiv (Y_t - E_t) - \Delta B_t, \quad (54)$$

in a manner somewhat similar to that employed by Fellner and Somers (1949) to obtain (43), except that he made interest income and payments explicit, and he did not assume $L(t, t) = \bar{M}_t$. Comparing (50) and (54), and substituting M_{t+1} for M_t in (50), he then obtained

$$\Delta L_t - \Delta M_t \equiv L_{t+1} - M_{t+1}. \quad (55)$$

Namely, "the *excess* demand for money as a flow is identical with the *excess* demand for money as a stock" (Patinkin, 1958, p. 303). Patinkin claims that this answers Tsiang's criticism (1956) that Hicks' reconcilation, which we discussed earlier, confuses the Keynesian liquidity preference theory (which defines the monetary equilibrium in terms of a stock equilibrium condition) as a flow theory; i.e., given (55), the stock equilibrium for money holds if and only if the flow equilibrium for money holds (cf. Patinkin, 1958, p. 303).

Although Patinkin is basically correct here, he seems to have failed to realize that condition (50), which is used to obtain (55), presupposes the initial stock equilibrium condition for money $L(t, t) = \bar{M}_t$. In fact, given such a condition, (55) is rather obvious from (4), as it in essence states $x(t) = X(t + 1, t)$ *given* $X(t) = 0.$[34] More importantly, Patinkin does not seem to be aware of the fact that (50) and (54) are not really independent: Both (50) and (54) follows from the flow Walras law (33).

---

[34] Although Patinkin claims that in obtaining a condition like (55) he does not require the initial equilibrium condition (1965, footnote 1, p. 305), we fail to see any other way to obtain this identity.

In connection with Patinkin's model, May (1970) argues that discrete time analysis is misleading when compared to continuous time analysis. Although his discussion of the Patinkin system seems to be well regarded in some of the literature, his argument seems to contain some flaws.

Following Patinkin (1965) in essence, May assumed away government bonds and the banking sector. May exercised special care in distinguishing between flow variables and stock variables. Let the length of period be h (instead of unity), and let the volumes of consumption and output for the period $[t, t + h)$ be denoted by $\bar{C}_t$ and $\bar{Y}_t$ respectively, both of which are stock variables. Then define their flow counterparts c_t and y_t by $c_t \equiv \bar{C}_t/h$ and $y_t \equiv \bar{Y}_t/h$.[35] Following Patinkin (1965), May also exercised special care in distinguishing two dates: "one refers to the date when the plan is made, the other refers to the date (or period) when the plan should be executed" (p. 2). This statement seems to correspond to our distinction in the present paper. May's basic equation is the budget equation of an individual (cf. his Eq. (8), p. 3), which may be written as (in terms of our notation)[36]

$$[y_t^* + rB^*(t + h, t) - c_t^*]h \equiv [L^*(t + h, t) - \bar{M}_t^*] + [B^*(t + h, t) - \bar{B}_t^*], \quad (56)$$

where the asterisk signifies that these variables are for an *individual* rather than for the aggregate. $\bar{B}_t^*$ and $\bar{M}_t^*$, respectively, signify the individual's actual net holdings of bonds and money at the beginning of the period (Monday). Thus $\bar{B}_t^*$, for example, is different from $B^*(t, t)$, the individual's *desired* net holding of bonds at the end of this Monday. Note that May assumed that all physical goods are nondurable, so that $I_t \equiv 0$. Namely, (56) conforms with the Patinkin-type budget constraint. Letting $h \to 0$, (56) becomes

$$[L^*(t, t) - \bar{M}_t^*] + [B^*(t, t) - \bar{B}_t^*] \equiv 0, \quad (57)$$

which is May's stock constraint for an individual. May claims that an individual faces the additional "constraint" (p. 3),

$$s_t^* \equiv y_t^* + rB^*(t + h, t) - c_t^*, \quad (58)$$

where s_t^* is the individual's *desired* rate of savings at time t.

---

[35] Alternatively, letting c_t and y_t, respectively, be the rate of consumption and output at time t, we may define $\bar{C}_t$ and $\bar{Y}_t$ from c_t and y_t as

$$\bar{C}_t \equiv \int_t^{t+h} c_\tau \, d\tau \quad \text{and} \quad \bar{Y}_t \equiv \int_t^{t+h} y_\tau \, d\tau.$$

Our C_t and Y_t correspond to the case when $h = 1$.

[36] Here r signifies the rate of interest. It appears that May implicitly assumed that financial transactions are carried out during the trading period ("Monday") (like us), so that $rB^*(t + h, t)$ signifies interest income for the tth period.

Aggregating over all individuals (and thus deleting the asterisks), (57) and (58), respectively, become[37]:

$$[L(t, t) - \bar{M}_t] + [B(t, t) - \bar{B}_t] = 0 \tag{57'}$$

$$(c_t - y_t) + r[\bar{B}_t - B(t + h, t)] + [s_t - r\bar{B}_t] \equiv 0. \tag{58'}$$

May calls (57') and (58') the "Walras' Law for stocks" and the "Walras' Law for flows," respectively (p. 4). From (58') May asserts, "among the three terms—excess demand for commodities, excess supply of interest income, and excess of desired wealth accumulation—any two determine the third, and in particular if any two are zero, then the third, too, is zero" (1970, p. 4). But, as pointed out by Chand (1973), since May assumed that all bonds are issued by households (and hence there are no government bonds), interest income will cancel out in aggregation so that $rB(t + h, t) = 0$ (cf. our footnote 24). Hence the correct form of (58') ought to be

$$s_t \equiv y_t - c_t. \tag{59}$$

In view of this, the above-quoted remark by May makes little sense. Furthermore, note that May's "aggregate Walras' Law for flows" (58') now reduces to the well-known simple identity (59), which is often used as the *definitional* relation for saving (rather than as a "constraint") in the literature.

In addition, we may point out a minor flaw of May's work. Since there are no government bonds in the economy, we must have $\bar{B}_t \equiv 0$; i.e., the actual borrowing of some individuals is canceled out by the actual lending of others. On the other hand, given May's assumption of no durable physical assets, his (57') with $\bar{B}_t = 0$ is a correct specification of the stock Walras law. To see this, simply impose May's assumptions of no government bonds and $\Delta M_t = 0$ on our stock Walras law (30), in which we replace $(t + 1)$ by $(t + h)$ and let $h \to 0$. On the other hand, if commodities are durable, (57') is no longer correct, which can easily be seen from (30).

Although (58) does not lead to the flow Walras law, it is possible to obtain such a law from May's formulation. To this end, we first aggregate the budget condition (56) over all individuals (hence deleting the asterisk—but not taking the limit of $h \to 0$) and then combine the resulting expression with (57') to obtain

$$(y_t - c_t)h = [L(t + h, t) - L(t, t)] + [B(t + h, t) - B(t, t)], \tag{60}$$

---

[37] Recall that $B(t, t)$ corresponds to $X(t) [\equiv D(t, t) - S(t)]$ of Section I (cf. footnote 26). Here we find it less confusing if we do not abbreviate $B(t, t)$ as $B(t)$. Corresponding to this, we did not abbreviate $B^*(t, t)$ as $B^*(t)$.

where interest income cancels out in the aggregate. Dividing (67) by h and letting $h \rightarrow 0$, we obtain

$$y_t - c_t = L_1(t, t) + B_1(t, t) \tag{61}$$

where $L_1(t, t)$ is the partial derivative of the function L with respect to the first argument evaluated at (t, t). $B_1(t, t)$ is defined similarly. These concepts of L_1 and B_1 are due to Turnovsky and Burmeister (1977). In the spirit of the present apparatus à la Hicksian week with tâtonnement, it would be reasonable to assume that the "unanticipated rates of change"[38] are zero (myopic perfect foresight); i.e., $L_2(t, t) \equiv 0 \equiv B_2(t, t)$, where the subscript 2 refers to the derivative with respect to the second argument. Furthermore, under the consistency condition (17′), such will hold anyway. Hence from (61) we obtain

$$y_t - c_t \equiv \dot{L}_t + \dot{B}_t \tag{62}$$

where $\dot{L}_t \equiv dL(t, t)/dt$ and $\dot{B}_t \equiv dB(t, t)/dt$, i.e., the total derivatives of the functions L and B. Note that (62) is only a special case of our flow Walras law (33*) under May's specification of the model and his assumption of no change in the money supply, where we may recall that (33*) is obtained by aggregating the budget conditions. In the discrete time analog (62) can be written as

$$Y_t - C_t \equiv \Delta L_t + \Delta B_t, \tag{62′}$$

which is obviously a special case of (33).

Conversely, we may also obtain (62′) from May's formulation. To this end, we return to the budget equation (56), from which (62) is derived. Namely, from (60) we at once obtain

$$\bar{Y}_t - \bar{C}_t \equiv [L(t + h, t) - L(t, t)] + [B(t + h, t) - B(t, t)], \tag{60′}$$

where we recall $y_t \equiv \bar{Y}_t/h$, $c_t \equiv \bar{C}_t/h$. When $h = 1$ (a "week"), $\bar{Y}_t$ and $\bar{C}_t$ are, respectively, replaced by our familiar Y_t and C_t, and thus we obtain (62′). We may therefore conclude that contrary to May's claim, there is nothing "misleading" in the discrete form (62′) or in the discrete time analysis. The two relations (62′) and (62) are therefore, in essence, identical.

Finally, we may note that the desired rate of saving is identically equal to the desired rate of accumulation of financial assets; i.e.,

$$s_t \equiv \dot{L}_t + \dot{B}_t. \tag{63}$$

Given (63), it is easy to obtain May's identity (in its correct form) (59) from the flow Walras law (62). Conversely, given (63), (59) implies (62). Namely,

---

[38] See Turnovsky and Burmeister (1977, p. 382).

given (63), the identity (59) holds if and only if (62) holds. Thus, contrary to May's claim, (59) is not an additional "constraint," but rather it is equivalent to our flow Walras law (in its continuous time version) (62). Furthermore, the savings defined in (59), as is usual in the literature, is a well-defined concept in the sense that it is consistent with the flow Walras law.

So far, we have confined our discussion to static equilibrium. We now turn to dynamics, in which we briefly review Enthoven (1960) and Foley and Sidrauski (1971). Enthoven (1960) is concerned with an economy that consists of the government, the households, and the firms, but no banking sector. By consolidating the budget identities of these three sectors, he correctly obtained the flow Walras law (1960, p. 324), which may be written (by omitting the time subscript) as

$$(\dot{L} - \dot{M}) + (\dot{B} - \dot{B}^g) + (C + I + G - Y) \equiv 0. \tag{64}$$

This is identical to our flow Walras law (33*), except that we now omit the t subscript. Enthoven's equilibrium system may be written as

$$\dot{L} = \dot{M}, \qquad \dot{B} = \dot{B}^g, \qquad \text{and} \qquad C + I + G = Y, \tag{65}$$

where in view of (64), one of the three equations in (65) is redundant. Since Enthoven's analysis is dynamic, in view of our discussions in Sections II and III, his formulation is totally adequate to guarantee the full stock and flow equilibria of all markets over time, although he nowhere states that this can be the case. Rather, Enthoven seems to choose a pure flow formulation only for its "simplicity and compatibility with dynamic analysis" (1960, p. 318), showing little concern about whether or not the stock equilibrium for money can be guaranteed.

Dynamic macromodels that include money have attracted much attention since the publication of Tobin's paper (1965), which led to a considerable number of follow-up works. One of the most important works in this connection is probably Foley and Sidrauski (1971) (henceforth F–S). They considered a dynamic economy consisting of four goods or assets, i.e., two physical goods (a consumption good and a capital good), (outside) money, and government bonds. The consumption good is used solely for consumption in each period and cannot be accumulated (i.e., a pure flow good), while the capital good is used solely for accumulation. Although F–S, in essence, offered the correct analysis, they may not have fully realized it. Henceforth, we shall spell out their equilibrium system and clarify the key steps that make their analysis correct.

Foley and Sidrauski begin by specifying the stock equilibrium in the assets markets, which satisfies three conditions:

$$L = M, \qquad B = B^g, \qquad \text{and} \qquad V = K, \tag{66}$$

and the stock Walras law

$$(L - M) + (B - B^g) + (V - K) \equiv 0, \tag{67}$$

in view of which, one of the three stock equilibrium conditions is superfluous (1971, pp. 30–39). As we have seen earlier, this procedure is correct with their correct specification of the stock Walras law. However, F–S did not derive the stock Walras law; instead, they merely asserted it. As we discussed earlier, (67) can be obtained by aggregating all of the sectoral balance sheets.

In turning to the flow side, F–S begin by describing the budget identities of the two agents (the government and the public) of their economy and then consolidating the two balance sheets. They, like Enthoven (1960), correctly obtained the flow Walras law, which is stated in the continuous time form as

$$(\dot{L} - \dot{M}) + (\dot{B} - \dot{B}^g) + (I - Y_I) + (C + G - Y_C) \equiv 0, \tag{68}$$

where Y_C and Y_I, respectively, denote the planned production of the consumption good and the capital good.

In describing flow equilibrium, they only require

$$C + G = Y_C, \tag{69}$$

whereas we know that for complete flow equilibrium the conditions,

$$\dot{L} = \dot{M}, \qquad \dot{B} = \dot{B}^g, \qquad \text{and} \qquad I = Y_I, \tag{70}$$

must also hold. Of course, in view of the flow Walras law (68), if any three of the four flow conditions hold, then the fourth holds automatically.

In determining the dynamic path of their economy, F–S required three conditions, two stock conditions $L = M$ and $B = B^g$, and one flow condition (69) (1971, pp. 89–90). As mentioned above, F–S duly realized that these two stock conditions guarantee the complete stock equilibrium.

What about the complete flow equilibrium? We know that the stock equilibrium over time implies flow equilibrium over time for each asset, as we discussed in Sections I and II. Hence, together with the required flow condition (69), the complete flow equilibrium condition for the economy is guaranteed under dynamics.

F–S may not have realized this. Indeed, they claimed that the three conditions $L = M$, $B = B^g$, and (69) do *not* guarantee the complete flow equilibrium. For example, they claimed that the flow conditions (70) may not hold. Thus they asserted that

> it is possible for individuals to be content to hold existing stocks of capital and debt, to purchase the quantities of consumption goods desired, and therefore to be accumulating in total the value of assets they wish to accumulate and at the same time at the current equilibrium

prices to desire to add to their holdings of assets in proportions that are different from the rates at which the stocks of assets are increasing (Foley–Sidrauski, 1971, p. 96).

In mathematical form, this quotation may be interpreted as

It is possible to have $L = M$, $B = B^g$, $V = K$, and $C + G = Y$, so that, from (69), we also have $\dot{L} + \dot{B} + I = \dot{M} + \dot{B}^g + Y_1$, and yet at the same time $\dot{L} \neq \dot{M}, \dot{B} \neq \dot{B}^g, I \neq Y_1$.

As interpreted, this is wrong or at least misleading in the context of dynamics, especially in its assertion of the possibility of $\dot{L} \neq \dot{M}$, $\dot{B} \neq \dot{B}^g$, and $I \neq Y_1$, while it is correct in the context of statics.

Questions concerning stocks and flows in the context of macroequilibrium have recently been revived to prominence by Foley's interesting work (1975), which is followed by Buiter and Woglom (1977), Turnovsky and Burmeister (1977), and Karni (1978), for example Foley (1975), as in Foley and Sidrauski (1971), considers the usual two-sector economy that produces a consumption good (Y_C) and an investment good (Y_1). In Foley (1975), both private and government bonds are assumed away, and government money is the only asset other than physical capital (K). Government spending and taxes are also assumed away, except that the government creates money in each period and transfers it to households.

Under such a framework Foley (1975) examines two specifications of asset market equilibrium conditions, i.e., "beginning-of-period (B.) and "end-of-period" (E.) formulations. He develops a number of interesting discussions in comparing them.

One of his key conclusions is that these two formulations may not necessarily be equivalent. In particular he concludes that, at least under the continuous time model, the (E.) formulation is "ill-formed" (Foley, 1975, p. 312) and "perfect foresight" is necessary for the equivalence of the two specifications.

On the other hand, this conclusion has recently been criticized by Buiter and Woglom (1977) and others. The gist of Foley's discussion and the criteria that it follows can be illustrated by using the stock equilibrium condition of one asset (say, physical capital), without developing the entire general equilibrium model. Following the writers in the debate, we define the periods by $[t - h, t), [t, t + h)$, etc. Interpreting their discussions in terms of our notation, the (B.) equilibrium condition requires

$$V(t, t) = K(t), \tag{71}$$

where $K(t)$ is the actual stock of physical capital at the beginning of the tth period. It is assumed that

$$K(t) \equiv K(t - h) + Y_1(t - h)h, \tag{72}$$

where the rate of output Y_I is assumed to be constant during the period. On the other hand, the (E.) equilibrium requires

$$V(t + h, t) = K(t + h), \tag{73}$$

where it is assumed that

$$K(t + h) \equiv K(t) + Y_I(t)h. \tag{74}$$

Using (74), Foley rewrites (73) as

$$\frac{V(t + h, t) - V(t, t)}{h} + \frac{V(t, t) - K(t)}{h} = Y_I(t), \tag{75}$$

and argues that the second term of the left-hand side has no finite limit when $h \to 0$, from which he concludes that "the equilibrium condition is revealed to be ill-formed" (p. 312). Foley's suggested solution to this problem is to introduce an adjustment parameter for the "current portfolio imbalance" $V(t, t) - K(t)$, and to then carry out a rather tedious computation to obtain his "perfect foresight" assumption for reconciliation.

Buiter and Woglom (1977), (henceforth B–W) object to Foley's conclusion (in which they call Foley's adjustment parameter "arbitrary") and offer a reconciliation of the (B.) and (E.) formulations under a much more satisfactory assumption. The key assumption in this context is (1977, p. 397, Eq. (5),)

$$V(t, t - h) = K(t). \tag{76}$$

In order to understand the B–W reconciliation, it will be useful to modify our notation slightly, following the spirit of B–W, as

$$V(t, t - h) \equiv \tilde{V}(h, t - h), \; V(t, t) \equiv \tilde{V}(0, t), \; V(t + h, t) \equiv \tilde{V}(h, t). \tag{77}$$

Namely, the first argument of the $\tilde{V}$ signifies the length of the time period h. Then, using (74) and (76), (73) can be rewritten as

$$[\tilde{V}(h, t) - \tilde{V}(h, t - h)]/h = Y_I(t), \tag{78}$$

In the limit, as $h \to 0$, (78) becomes[39]

$$\tilde{V}_2(0, t) = Y_I(t), \tag{78'}$$

where the subscript 2 refers to the partial derivative with respect to the second argument. Notice that $\tilde{V}_2$ should be distinguished from the second partial derivative of the function V. From (78') B–W can conclude, contrary

---

[39] As B–W remark (p. 400), $\tilde{V}_2(0, t)$ "measures the rate at which the demand for capital changes when time passes." In contrast to this, B–W interpret the first partial derivative of $\tilde{V}$ as "the rate at which demand at time t for capital to hold at some future point in time changes when that future point in time varies" (p. 400).

to Foley's claim, that the stock equilibrium condition for the (E.) formulation has a clear limit when $h \to 0$. B–W (1977, p. 399, especially footnote 8) then show how even the second term of the left-hand side of (75) can have a clear limit when $h \to 0$ under the assumption (76).

For the stock equilibrium condition in the (B.) formulation, i.e., for (71), B–W simply assume

$$V(t - h, t - h) = K(t - h) \left[\text{or } \tilde{V}(0, t - h) = K(t - h) \right]. \tag{79}$$

Then, using this and (72), (71) can be written as

$$[\tilde{V}(0, t) - \tilde{V}(0, t - h)]/h = Y_I(t - h). \tag{80}$$

Hence in the limit, as $h \to 0$, (80) reduces to (78′). From this, B–W conclude that the (E.) and (B.) formulations are equivalent for the continuous time model.

It is our belief that this reconciliation is indeed ingenious. It only remains to interpret their key assumptions, (76) and (79), and to relate these to our formulation in Section I. Since $K(t - h) = K(t - h, t - h)$, it is easy to see that condition (79) is nothing but the initial stock equilibrium condition for the period $[t - h, t)$. Namely, in terms of our notation in Section I, (79) may be written as $X(t - h) = 0$. Condition (76) corresponds to our consistency condition (17′), as it says that the decision made at time $(t - h)$ for time t is consistent with the decision made at time t for time t.[40] To see this more formally, observe that $D(t, t - 1) = D(t, t)$ in (17′) precisely corresponds to $V(t, t - h) = V(t, t)$ here (except that the unit of period now becomes h instead of unity). Then, given this consistency condition, the B–W assumption (76) is nothing but the initial stock equilibrium condition $X(t) = 0$.[41] Conversely, given the initial stock equilibrium condition $V(t, t) = K(t) [\equiv K(t, t)]$, (76) is equivalent to the consistency condition. In other words, the B–W reconciliation amounts to highlighting the importance of the initial stock equilibrium condition or the consistency condition.

It may be worthwhile to consider these discussions by Foley and B–W in terms of our apparatus. Foley's (B.) equilibrium condition can be expressed as $X(t) = 0$, while his (E.) equilibrium condition (73) can be expressed as

[40] B–W (pp. 395–396) describe this as "each period production, consumption and trading plans are realized given the values assumed by the parameters of the temporary equilibrium" More specifically, B–W interpret condition (76) as follows: "If the capital market cleared during the $(T - 1)$th period, the stock of capital actually held at the end of that period $K(T)$ equals the stock of capital economic agents were planning, at the beginning of the period, to hold at the end of the period" (p. 397). Here their $(T - 1)$th period refers to the period, $[T - h, T)$.

[41] Condition $S(t, t - 1) = S(t)$ in (17′) is implicitly assumed by B–W. Their conditions (72) and (74) require that $S(t) = S(t, t - h)$ for all t. It is also assumed that delivery of the investment good does not take place during the trading period (our "Monday"). Thus we have $S(t, t - h) \equiv S(t, t) [\equiv S(t)]$.

$X(t + h, t) = 0$. These two conditions are independent and do not necessarily provide the same equilibrium value. On the other hand, the (B.) condition for the period $[t + h, t + 2h)$ and (E.) condition for the period $[t, t + h)$ are the same; i.e., $X(t + h) = 0$ under the consistency condition $X(t + h) = X(t + h, t)$. Namely, these two will yield the same equilibrium value. Also, under the consistency condition (17′), we have by virtue of $(4*)$[42]

$$X(t + h) - X(t) = \bar{x}(t), \qquad X(t) - X(t - h) = \bar{x}(t - h), \qquad (81)$$

where

$$\bar{x}(t) \equiv \int_t^{t+h} x(\tau) d\tau.$$

Dividing both sides of these equations and letting $h \to 0$, we can easily observe that *both* equations of (81) reduce to the same equation:

$$\dot{X}(t) = x(t), \qquad (82)$$

which corresponds to the B–W (78′). Equation (82) is identical to our (20*).

In his recent article Karni (1978) applies Foley's formulation to May's discussion (1970) that continuous time analysis leads to conclusions that are different from period analysis. Using Foley's two specifications, the (B.) and the (E.) equilibria, Karni (1978, p. 134) concludes that "in transforming Patinkin's model from discrete into continuous time, May actually transformed the nature of the asset equilibrium specification from an 'end-of-period' into a 'beginning-of-period,' thus changing an essential feature of Patinkin's original formulation." Although Karni's discussion is interesting and also conforms in spirit with our earlier criticism of May, it unfortunately critically depends on Foley's procedure of introducing the adjustment parameter for the second term of (75) [since May's model has no durable goods, this procedure is applied to money and bonds (cf. Karni, 1978, p. 137)]. On the other hand, since this procedure is more or less convincingly discredited by Buiter–Woglom (1977) and since we have already discussed May's model in detail, we shall leave it to the interested reader to more thoroughly examine Karni's discussion.

Another interesting discussion of Foley's 1975 article is developed in Turnovsky–Burmeister (1977), (henceforth T–B). They aptly observe (like others) that in many macromodels two dates play an important role, i.e., (a) the time when plans are formed (t), and (b) the time for which they are made ($t + h$). One of their central concerns is that this should introduce the question of expectations concerning the future date $t + h$. Thus, letting z be any

---

[42] The two equations in (81), when divided by h, correspond to the B–W equations (78) and (80).

economic variable (say a price), they distinguish between two concepts, $z(t)$ and $z^e(t + h, t)$, where $z(t)$ = actual value of z at time t and $z^e(t + h, t)$ = expectations formed at time t for time $t + h$ (cf. T–B, p. 380). Then they distinguish between three concepts: "weak consistency" (W), "strong consistency" (S), and "perfect foresight" (P). These are defined by

$$(\text{W}): z^e(t, t) = z(t); \qquad (\text{S}): z^e_1(t, t) = z(t);$$

$$(\text{P}): z^e(t + h, t) = z(t + h) \qquad \text{for all} \quad h \geq 0, \tag{83}$$

where z^e_1 is the partial derivative of the function z^e with respect the first argument. It is clear that $(\text{P}) \Rightarrow (\text{S}) \Rightarrow (\text{W})$, but not vice versa (cf. T–B, pp. 381–382), and that (P) is a very strong condition, as it is required to hold for all h.

Using these concepts T–B critically examine Foley (1975), in which there are two specifications of asset market equilibrium, the (B.) and the (E.) formulations. Their conclusions can be summarized as follows (p. 388): (a) given (W), (B.) and (E.) specifications give the same set of equilibrium values in a *continuous time model* (i.e., for the case $h \to 0$), and (b) in order for the (E.) conditions for the period $[t, t + h)$ and the (B.) conditions for the period $[t + h, t + 2h)$ in a *discrete time* model to provide the same set of equilibrium values, T–B can provide only much stronger sufficient conditions, i.e., perfect foresight in predicting all quantities *and* no accumulation of physical capital. While conclusion (a) in the above constitutes a sharp criticism of Foley (1975), conclusion (b) seems to have a strong implication in that it apparently implies that discrete time models may not be appropriate for the analysis of economic growth, which involves capital accumulation. Hence, the validity of many works on economic growth in the literature that use discrete time models becomes questionable.

Although the T–B analysis is quite interesting, we believe that their conclusions are rather disheartening because of the suggestion of a strong asymmetry between the continuous time model and the discrete time model. On the other hand, we are not persuaded by this result, since we are not ready to accept the implication that two formulations of the same economy can give different results. However we do not feel, nearing the end of this already prolonged paper, that it is appropriate to ask the reader to go through our critical examination of the T–B analysis. Instead, we simply record here some fundamental questions that are left somewhat unresolved in reading T–B.[43]

(i) What is the market structure that will bring about "equilibrium?" How is the market cleared? They are concerned with the "equilibrium"

---

[43] The same criticisms may apply to Turnovsky (1977).

economy, and yet it seems that they do not particularly wish to follow the Hicksian apparatus. On the other hand, nowhere have they specified the mechanism for the equilibrium economy.

(ii)   If expected quantities are different from the actual quantities, some "rationing" à la Malinvaud (1977) seems to be inevitable. If this is the case, how will such "rationing" take place and how will the "frustration" of various economic agents be allocated? Furthermore, what are the effects of such "rationing" on the determination of "equilibrium"? Do they allow intermediate trading during the period? If so, how is the equilibrium at the "end-of-period" (E.) affected by expectations within the week and how do the capital gains or losses (due to trading) affect the (E.) equilibrium? On the other hand, if intermediate trading is not allowed (like the usual tâtonnement process), why do we not always have myopic perfect foresight for the period? Among others, how is the "period" defined in T–B anyway?

If we interpret T–B in terms of our apparatus, the gist of their analysis may not be too difficult to understand and it is similar to the one we provided earlier in this context of B–W. The (B.) equilibrium condition for $[t + h, t + 2h]$ and the (E.) equilibrium condition for $[t, t + h)$ are identical; i.e., $X(t + h) = 0$ under the consistency condition. On the other hand, the (B.) and the (E.) equilibrium conditions for $[t, t + h)$ are, respectively, $X(t) = 0$ and $X(t + h, t) = 0$, which are *not* identical for $h > 0$. However, these two yield the same equilibrium value when $h \to 0$, since both reduce to $X(t) = 0$ [where we may recall that $X(t)$ is the shorthand notation for $X(t, t)$].

Foley's 1975 article also contains a discussion of the stock and the flow identities, which is elaborated on considerably by Turnovsky (1977). On the other hand, our formulation of the two Walras laws is somewhat different from those of these writers. Instead of going through a detailed evaluation of their identities, it may be more useful to give further consideration to our two Walras laws and to leave any detailed comparison to the interested reader.[44]

In particular, we wish to examine here the relationship between the stock Walras law (30) and the flow Walras law (33). Since the former is obtained from the balance sheet identities and the latter is obtained from the budget identities, and since the balance sheet identities of a particular agent at the two points of time are closely related to the budget identity of that agent

---

[44] Foley (1975) considers the two-output economy (in contrast to the conventional one-output economy that we have discussed). Turnovsky (1977) exercised a special care by distinguishing "equities" from the existing stock of physical assets. This may be interesting in view of the recent concern with "Tobin's q" in the profession. Turnovsky (1977) obtained his identities by aggregating the budget conditions.

for the period between these two dates, it might be natural to expect that there is a close connection between the two identities (30) and (33). From (30) we can at once observe

$$(L_{t+1} - M_{t+1}) + (B_{t+1} - B_{t+1}^g) + (V_{t+1} - K_{t+1}) \equiv 0, \qquad (30a)$$

$$(L_t - M_t) + (B_t - B_t^g) + (V_t - K_t) \equiv 0, \qquad (30b)$$

where (30a) is identical to (30), and (30b) is obtained from (30a) by lagging one period. It is important to recall that $L_{t+1}, M_{t+1}, L_t, M_t, \ldots$ denote $L(t+1, t), M(t+1, t), L(t, t-1), M(t, t-1), \ldots$, respectively. Our *consistency condition* (17′) is written, in terms of the present context, as

$$L(t, t) = L(t, t-1), \qquad M(t) = M(t, t-1),$$
$$B(t) [\equiv B(t, t)] = B(t, t-1), \qquad B^g(t) = B^g(t, t-1), \qquad (84)$$
$$V(t, t) = V(t, t-1), \qquad K(t) = K(t, t-1).$$

Needless to say, $M(t)$, $B^g(t)$, and $K(t)$, respectively, correspond to $\bar{M}_t$, $\bar{B}_t^g$ and $\bar{K}_t$. Subtracting (30b) from (30a) *and* using (84), we obtain

$$[\{L(t+1, t) - L(t, t)\} - \{M(t+1, t) - M(t)\}]$$
$$+ [\{B(t+1, t) - B(t)\} - \{B^g(t+1, t) - B^g(t)\}]$$
$$+ [\{V(t+1, t) - V(t, t)\} - \{K(t+1, t) - K(t)\}] \equiv 0. \qquad (85)$$

Then recalling the identities in (35), we can at once obtain the flow Walras law (33) from (85). Namely, the flow Walras law follows from the stock Walras law for the two dates, provided that the consistency condition (84) holds. Furthermore, under the consistency condition, we can also show the converse; i.e., we can obtain the stock Walras law from the flow Walras law.[45]

Note that if we impose the *initial stock equilibrium condition*,

$$L(t, t) = M(t) (\equiv \bar{M}_t), \qquad B(t) = B^g(t) (\equiv \bar{B}_t^g), \qquad V(t, t) = K(t) (\equiv \bar{K}_t),$$
$$(36)$$

on (85), then using the third identity of (35), we at once obtain

$$(L_{t+1} - M_{t+1}) + (B_{t+1} - B_{t+1}^g) + (C_t + I_t + G_t - Y_t) \equiv 0. \qquad (86)$$

---

[45] Subtracting (33) for $t - 1$ from (33) for t, and imposing the consistency condition, we can obtain (30) by assuming

$$[L(t-1, t-1) - M(t-1)] + [B(t-1) - B^g(t-1)] + [V(t-1, t-1) - K(t-1)] \equiv 0,$$

which follows from the balance sheet identity of the public on the $(t - 1)$th Monday. This should be distinguished from (30), which follows from the *desired* portfolio allocation for the end of the period.

As a matter of fact, (86) can also be obtained from (30) directly by recalling the third identity of (35) and imposing the initial stock equilibrium condition $V(t, t) = \bar{K}_t$. Needless to say, condition (86) reduces to the "Patinkin Walras law" (52) if we assume away government bonds. Furthermore, we may recall our observation in Sections I and II that given the initial stock equilibrium condition (36), the stock and the flow Walras laws, (30) and (33), are in fact equivalent. Namely, under the initial equilibrium condition, one of the two Walras laws (stock and flow) follows from the other. Hence under such an assumption we can obtain the desired identities either from the balance sheet identities or from the budget conditions. Earlier, we obtained the "Patinkin Walras law" (52) from the flow Walras law, which is obtained from aggregating budget conditions, whereas in the above (52) is obtained from the stock Walras law.

In any case, the stock Walras law and the flow Walras law are closely connected. On the other hand, such a relationship between the two identities *and* the role of either the consistency condition or the initial stock equilibrium condition in such a context are not well recognized in the literature, which is rather unfortunate.

REFERENCES

Akerlof, G. A. (1973). The demand for money: A general equilibrium inventory-theoretic approach, *Rev. Econ. Stud.* **40**, (January), 115–130.

Archibald, G. C., and R. G. Lipsey, (1958). Monetary and value theory: A critique of Lange and Patinkin, *Rev. Econ. Studies* **26**, (October), 1–22.

Baumol, W. J. (1962). Stocks, flows and monetary theory, *Quart. J. Econ.* **76**, (February), 46–56.

Brainard, W. C., and Tobin, J. (1968). Pitfalls in financial model building, *Amer. Econ. Rev.* **58** (May), 99–122.

Brunner, K. (1950). Stock and flow analysis: Discussion, *Econometrica* **18** (July), 247–251.

Buiter, W. H., and Woglom, G. (1977). On two specifications of asset equilibrium in macroeconomic models: A note, *J. Political Econ.* **85** (April), 395–400.

Burstein, M. L. (1963). "Money" Schenkman, Cambridge, Massachusetts.

Bushaw, D. W., and Clower, R. W. (1957). "Introduction to Mathematical Economics," Irwin, Homewood, Illinois.

Cass, D., and McKenzie, L. W. (eds.) (1974). "Selected Readings in Macroeconomics and Capital Theory from Econometrica." MIT Press, Cambridge, Massachusetts.

Chand, S. (1973). Period analysis and continuous analysis in patinkin's macroeconomic model—A critical note, *J. Econ. Theory* **6** (October), 520–524.

Clower, R. A. (1954). An Investigation into the dynamics of investment, *Amer. Econ. Rev.* **44** (March), 64–81.

Clower, R. A. (1959). Stock and flow quantities: A common fallacy, *Economica* **26** (August), 251.

Clower, R. A. (1968). Stocks and flows, *In* "International Encyclopedia of the Social Sciences" (D. L. Sills, ed.), Vol. 15. Macmillan and Free Press, New York.

Clower, R. A., and Bushaw, D. W. (1954). Price determination in a stock-flow economy, *Econometrica* **22** (July), 328–343.

Crouch, R. L. (1972). "Macroeconomics." Harcourt Brace, New York.

Drabicki, J. Z., and Takayama, A. (1974). On the Interpretation of Patinkin's Model, unpublished manuscript.

Enthoven, A. (1960). A neo-classical model of money, debt, and economic growth, "Money in a Theory of Finance" (J. D. Gurley and E. S. Shaw, eds.), Brookings Institution, Washington, D.C.

Fellner, W., and Somers, H. M. (1941). Alternative monetary approaches to interest theory, *Rev. Econ. Statist.* **23** (February), 43–48.

Fellner, W., and Somers, H. M. (1949). Note on 'Stocks' and 'Flows' in monetary interest theory, *Rev. Econ. Statist.* **21** (May), 145–146.

Fellner, W., and Somers, H. M. (1950a). Stock and flow analysis: Comment, *Econometrica* **18** (July), 242–245.

Fellner, W., and Somers, H. M. (1950b). Stock and flow analysis: Note on the discussion, *Econometrica* **18** (July), 252.

Foley, D. K. (1975). On two specifications of asset equilibrium in macroeconomic models, *J. Political Econ.* **83** (April), 303–324.

Foley, D. K., and Sidrauski, M. (1971). "Monetary and Fiscal Policy in a Growing Economy." Macmillan, New York.

Hahn, F. H. (1955). The rate of interest and general equilibrium analysis, *Econ. J.* **65** (March), 52–66.

Hicks, J. R. (1937). Mr. Keynes and the 'Classics'; A suggested interpretation, *Econometrica* **5** (April), 147–159.

Hicks, J. R. (1946). "Value and Capital." Oxford Univ. Press (Clarendon), London and New York, 1st ed., 1937. 2nd ed., 1946.

Hicks, J. R. (1956). Methods of dynamic analysis, *In* "25 Economic Essays in Honour of Erik Lindahl." Ekonomisk Tidskrift, Stockholm.

Hicks, J. R. (1965). "Capital and Growth." Oxford Univ. Press (Clarendon), London and New York.

Hicks, J. R. (1973). Recollections and documents, *Economica* **40** (February), 2–11.

Hicks, J. R. (1976). Some questions of time in economics, *In* "Evolution, Welfare, and Time in Economics: Essays in Honor of Nicholas Georgescu-Roegen" (A. M. Tang *et al.*, eds.). Heath, Lexington, Massachusetts.

Horwich, G., and Samuelson, P. A. (eds.) (1974). Trade, Stability, and Macroeconomics: Essays in Honor of Lloyd A. Metzler." Academic Press, New York, especially articles by P. H. Hendershott–G. Horwich (pp. 375–395), W. E. Perg (pp. 401–425), and G. Bilkes–E. Ames (pp. 455–484).

Johnson, H. G. (1962). Monetary theory and policy, *Amer. Econ. Rev.* **52** (June), 335–384.

Karni, E. (1978). Period analysis and continuous analysis in Patinkin's macroeconomic model, *J. Econ. Theory*, **17** (February), 134–140.

Keynes, J. M. (1936). "General Theory of Employment, Interest and Money." Macmillan, London.

Keynes, J. M. (1937). Alternative theories of the rate of interest, *Econ. J.* **47** (June), 241–252.

Klein, L. R. (1950a). Stock and flow analysis in economics. *Econometrica* **18** (July), 236–241.

Klein, L. R. (1950b). Stock and flow analysis: Further comment, *Econometrica* **18** (July), 246.

Kuenne, R. E. (1964). Say's Law and Walras' Law once more: Comment, *Quart. J. Econ.* **77** (August), 478–483.

Lange, O. (1942). Say's Law: A restatement and criticism, *In* "Studies in Mathematical Economics and Econometrics" (O. Lange, ed.) Univ. of Chicago, Chicago, Illinois.

Lerner, A. P. (1938). Alternative formulations of the theory of interest, *Econ. J.* **48** (June), 211–230.

Lerner, A. P. (1944). Interest theory—Supply and demand for loans or demand and supply for cash, *Rev. Econ. Statist.* **26** (February), 88–91.

Lerner, A. P. (1953). "Essays in Economic Analysis." Macmillan, London.

Lloyd, C. L. (1960). The equivalence of the liquidity preference and loanable funds theories and the new stock-flow analysis, *Rev. Econ. Stud.* **27** (June), 206–209.

Lutz, F. A. (1968). "The Theory of Interest" (transl. by C. Wittich). Reidel, Holland.

Malinvaud, E. (1977). "The Theory of Unemployment Reconsidered." Oxford Univ. Press (Blackwell), London and New York.

Marschak, J. (1965). "Income, Employment and the Price Level." Augustus M. Kelley, New York. (Originally published by Cowles commission, 1951.)

Marshall, A. (1920). "Principles of Economics," 8th ed. Macmillan, New York.

May, J. (1970). Period analysis and continuous analysis in Patinkin's macroeconomic model, *J. Econ. Theory* **2** (March), 1–9.

Mishan, E. J. (1964). Say's Law and Walras' Law Once More, *Quart. J. Econ.* **77** (November). Reply, **77** (August), 617–625.

Modigliani, F. (1963). The monetary mechanism and its interaction with real phenomena, *Rev. Econ. Statist.* **45** (February), 79–110.

Morishima, M. (1950). "The Theory of Dynamic Economics" (Dogakuteki-Keizai-Riron), Kobundo Tokyo (in Japanese).

Morishima, M. (1976). "The Economic Theory of Modern Society," Cambridge Univ. Press, London and New York (translated by D. W. Anthony from the Japanese edition, 1973).

Negishi, T. (1972). "General Equilibrium Theory and International Trade." North Holland Publ., Amsterdam.

Ohlin, B. (1937). Some notes on the Stockholm theory of saving and investment, II, *Econ. J.* **47** (June), 221–240.

Ohlin, B., Robertson, D. H., and Hawtrey, R. G. (1937). Alternative theories of the rate of interest: Three rejoinders, I, II, III, *Econ. J.* **47** (September), 423–443.

Patinkin, D. (1949). The indeterminacy of absolute prices in classical economic theory, *Econometrica* **17**, 1–17.

Patinkin, D. (1958). Liquidity preference and loanable funds: Stock and flow analysis, *Economica*, **25**, 300–318.

Patinkin, D. (1959). Reply to R. W. Clower and H. Rose, *Economica*, **26**, 253–255.

Patinkin, D. (1961). Financial intermediaries and the logical structure of monetary theory, *Amer. Econ. Rev.* **2** (March), 95–116.

Patinkin, D. (1965). "Money, Interest, and Prices," 2nd ed. Harper, New York.

Robertson, D. H. (1940). Keynes and the rate of interest, in "Essays in Monetary Theory." King & Sons, London.

Rose, H. (1957). Liquidity preference and loanable funds, *Rev. Econ. Stud.* **24** (February), 111–119.

Rose, H. (1959). The rate of interest and Walras' Law. **26** (August), 252.

Shackle, G. L. S. (1961). Recent theories concerning the nature and the role of interest, *Econ. J.* **71** (June), 209–254.

Takayama, A., and Drabicki, J. Z. (1976). On the endogenous supply of money, *Keizai Kenkyu (Econ. Rev.)* **27** (October), 336–348.

Tobin, J. (1965). Money and economic growth, *Econometrica* **33** (October), 671–684.

Tobin, J. (1969). A general equilibrium approach to monetary theory, *J. Money Credit and Banking.* **1** (February), 15–29.

Tsiang, S. C. (1956). Liquidity preference and loanable funds theories, multiplier and velocity analysis: A synthesis, *Amer. Econ. Rev.* **46** (September), 539–564.

Tsiang, S. C. (1966). Walras' Law, Say's Law and liquidity preference in general equilibrium analysis, *Internat. Econ. Rev.* **7** (September), 329–345.

Turnovsky, S. J. (1977). On the formulation of continuous time macroeconomic models with asset accumulation, *Internat. Econ. Rev.* **18** (February), 1–28, also, "Macroeconomic Analysis and Stabilization Policy." Chapter 3. Cambridge Univ. Press, London and New York, 1977.

Turnovsky, S. J., and Burmeister, E. (1977). Perfect foresight, expectational consistency and macroeconomic equilibrium, *J. Political Econ.* **85** (April), 379–394.

Valvanis, S. (1955). A denial of Patinkin's contradiction, *Kyklos* **8**, 351–368.

Walras, L. (1954). "The Elements of Pure Economics" (transl. by W. Jaffe), Irwin, Homewood Illinois [translated from the Edition Definitive (1926) of the Elements of d'Economie Politique Pure, annotated and collated with previous editions].

We are grateful to Michihiro Ohyama and Ngo Van Long for useful comments. An earlier version of this paper was presented at the Las Vegas Meeting of the Western Economic Association in June 1974.

John Z. Drabicki
DEPARTMENT OF ECONOMICS
UNIVERSITY OF ARIZONA
TUCSON, ARIZONA

Akira Takayama
DEPARTMENT OF ECONOMICS
KRANNERT SCHOOL OF MANAGEMENT
PURDUE UNIVERSITY
WEST LAFAYETTE, INDIANA

DEPARTMENT OF ECONOMICS
COLLEGE OF LIBERAL ARTS
TEXAS A & M UNIVERSITY
COLLEGE STATIONS, TEXAS

ECONOMIC THEORY, ECONOMETRICS, AND MATHEMATICAL ECONOMICS

Consulting Editor: Karl Shell

UNIVERSITY OF PENNSYLVANIA
PHILADELPHIA, PENNSYLVANIA

Edmund S. Phelps. Studies in Macroeconomic Theory, Volume 1: *Employment and Inflation.*

Marc Nerlove, David M. Grether, and José L. Carvalho. Analysis of Economic Time Series: *A Synthesis*

Thomas J. Sargent. Macroeconomic Theory

Jerry Green and José Alexander Scheinkman (Eds.). General Equilibrium, Growth, and Trade: *Essays in honor of Lionel McKenzie*

In preparation

Michael J. Boskin (Ed.). Economics and Human Welfare: *Essays in Honor of Tibor Scitovsky*

Carlos Daganzo. Multinomial Probit: *The Theory and Its Application to Demand Forecasting*